of the World by Membership
of International Settlement

FOREIGN EXCHANGE IN THE POSTWAR WORLD

THE TWENTIETH CENTURY FUND

FOREIGN EXCHANGE
IN THE
POSTWAR WORLD

By

RAYMOND F. MIKESELL

New York
THE TWENTIETH CENTURY FUND
1954

COPYRIGHT 1954 BY THE TWENTIETH CENTURY FUND, INC.

Library of Congress Catalog Card Number: 54-7606

First published May 1954
Reprinted February 1955

PRINTED IN THE UNITED STATES OF AMERICA BY
THE LORD BALTIMORE PRESS, BALTIMORE, MARYLAND

FOREWORD

NOT SINCE THE DAYS before World War I have we lived in the kind of world described by John Maynard Keynes as one in which a British citizen would feel "greatly aggrieved and much surprised" if he could not "despatch his servant to the neighboring office of a bank for such supply of the precious metals as might seem convenient and could then proceed abroad" by "cheap and comfortable means of transit to any country or climate without passport or other formality."

Among the nations of that world, with few exceptions, there was freedom of travel for foreigners as well as for their own citizens. Goods could move without hindrance across national boundaries, subject only to straightforward and generally modest import duties. With the gold standard functioning efficiently and the pound sterling available as a sort of international currency, it was as easy to pay for foreign travel and foreign goods as for domestic purchases. In that distant world foreign exchange practices were of concern only to the technicians, and "foreign exchange policies," except for the well-nigh universal acceptance of the gold standard, were almost nonexistent.

Today the movement of both people and goods from one country to another is hedged about with a multitude of obstacles and restrictions, and the complexities and difficulties of making payments across national boundaries constitute one of the most perplexing of economic problems. This book represents an attempt to bring together in one volume information on the exchange control systems and international payments arrangements of the countries of the world, heretofore available only in hundreds of articles and public documents. It is not intended as a handbook of foreign exchange practices, however, but rather as an attempt to describe the policies underlying exchange arrangements and to evaluate these policies in terms of economic analysis.

In the discussion of the world's currency problems, this volume makes tentative suggestions for dealing with such questions as disequilibrium and dollar shortage, development of a code of fair exchange practices, sterling convertibility, and the roles of the International Monetary Fund and the European Payments Union. The book makes suggestions as to possible policies of our government in dealing with these problems. It should be understood that the tentative proposals advanced regarding these and other timely and important issues are solely the responsibility of the author. The Twentieth Century Fund itself takes no position on these or on other policy matters discussed in the reports of its research staffs or committees.

The author is well qualified for his task. For many years a member of the economics faculty of the University of Virginia, he participated in the Bretton Woods Monetary and Financial Conference in 1944 and in the World Fund and Bank Conference at Savannah in 1946. During the past several years he has served as consultant on foreign exchange matters to the Department of State and has been a staff member of several official commissions and a number of financial missions sent abroad by the United States government.

The Fund is grateful to the author for the knowledge and the diligence and skill he has brought to the difficult task of presenting highly technical subject matter in a manner understandable to the layman, without sacrifice of accuracy and detail. The Fund also joins the author in expressing appreciation for the generous aid he has received from many scholars in this field and especially from the members of the staff of the International Monetary Fund.

J. FREDERIC DEWHURST, *Executive Director*
The Twentieth Century Fund

330 WEST 42D STREET
NEW YORK 36, NEW YORK
JANUARY 27, 1954

AUTHOR'S PREFACE

THE PURPOSE OF THIS BOOK is to provide a better understanding of foreign exchange practices and policies since World War II. It is not intended to be either a handbook of current usage or a documentary record of foreign exchange practices in existence at the time of writing. The large amount of descriptive material dealing with foreign exchange systems as they were in 1952 and early 1953 is to be regarded as illustrative of types of exchange practices which have characterized the postwar period, or as case studies in foreign exchange policy. In the area chapters contained in Part III, emphasis is given to the international financial problems which countries have had to face as a basis for understanding the particular foreign exchange and trade policies which were adopted. No attempt is made to provide a comprehensive description and analysis of the exchange systems of the more than seventy-five countries which are dealt with in this book. For current and detailed descriptions of the exchange control systems of individual countries readers may consult the *Annual Report on Exchange Restrictions* which is published each year by the International Monetary Fund.

The author has not cited a reference for every one of the several thousand factual statements made in this book. Literally hundreds of published sources in the form of newspaper and current news journal articles were employed. Moreover, much of the information has been gathered from unpublished sources including interviews with scores of specialists in public and private agencies. While an effort has been made to check unpublished sources wherever possible, there are undoubtedly many errors of fact and of interpretation in this book.

Where the present tense is employed in describing exchange practices or economic conditions, an effort has been made to reflect the situation as it existed on June 1, 1953, unless a later date is mentioned. Owing to a lack of information in certain fields, however, there are undoubtedly cases in which developments before June 1953 have not been taken into account. Major developments between June 1953 and November 1953, which are significant for the analysis and broad conclusions of this book, are summarized in a short Addendum following Chapter 23.

While the author accepts full responsibility for all errors of fact and for all conclusions based upon the analysis and interpretation of factual material, this book was made possible in large measure by the cooperation of dozens of specialists in the field of international finance.

Primary recognition for this assistance must go to the members of the staff of the International Monetary Fund. The author wishes to acknowledge the valuable assistance provided by the following members of the Monetary Fund staff: Roger V. Anderson, R. J. Cunnell, Johan H. C. de Looper, Julio G. del Solar, Barend A. de Vries, Irving S. Friedman, Joergen H. Gelting, Edgar Jones, Roland Kalivoda, F. A. G. Keesing, Jorge Marshall, Albert Mattera, Subimal Mookergee, J. S. Raj, Ugo Sacchetti, Josef Swidrowski, Cornelis van Wijk, Yuan Chao Wang, Ernest A. Wichin and John B. Wright, all of the Exchange Restrictions Department; Edward M. Bernstein, Stanley Christovich, Walter R. Gardner, Earl Hicks, Gertrud Lovasy and J. J. Polak, of the Research Department; Andreas Abadjis, Arthur Billings, Ettore Bompard, Jocelyn Clark, Christophe F. Dupont, Evangelos Eliades, Erik Elmholt, Rolf Evensen, Charles L. Merwin, Jr., Albin Pfeifer, Huibert Ponsen, Brian Rose, H. Austin Shannon, Emil Spitzer, Ernest Sturc, Violette Thouvenin, Marcin R. Wyczalkowski and Herbert K. Zassenhaus, of the European Department; Paul J. Brand, Jorge Del Canto, Howard K. Carlson, Frederick C. Dirks, Richard Radford and Edward W. Robichek, all of the Western Hemisphere Department; Ching Gwan Chang, Hirendra L. Dey, Ching Chun Liang, Henry C. Murphy, Prabhakar R. Narvekar, S. A. Pandit and Roger H. Star, of the Asian Department; John W. Gunter, M. M. Hassanein, Paul J. Klat and William H. Taylor, of the Middle Eastern Department; and Ervin P. Hexner of the Legal Department. Special mention should also be made of the assistance provided by the Acting Secretary of the Fund, Dr. Roman L. Horne, in arranging interviews and in making valuable suggestions for the conduct of the author's research.

The author would also like to make special mention of the assistance provided by Hal Lary of the Economic Commission for Europe (Geneva); Robert L. Sammons, George Wythe, Hill Houston,

George Sarames, Paul Flores and John E. Walsh, all of the U. S. Department of Commerce; Raymond Jones and Edward J. O'Connor of the Export-Import Bank of Washington; Francis B. Appelbee, William Salant and Alex Lochman of the Foreign Operations Administration; Gordon Street and William Bennett of the International Bank for Reconstruction and Development; Edward Ames of the Federal Reserve Board; Arthur Bloomfield, H. J. Dernburg, Fred Klopstock and Thomas Roche, all of the Federal Reserve Bank of New York; Raymond Vernon of the U. S. Department of State; Henry J. Bittermann, John S. Debeers, George Eddy, William L. Hebbard, Frederick L. Springborn and Frank L. Widman, all of the U. S. Treasury Department.

The author benefited greatly from the suggestions of James W. Angell of Columbia University, Gardner Patterson of Princeton University and Robert Triffin of Yale University.

Merlyn Nelson Trued of the University of Virginia has not only assisted in the preparation of the text but is mainly responsible for the basic research and preparation of the appendix material. The end-paper maps were prepared by Norman J. W. Thrower of the University of Virginia Geographical Institute. Most of the typing services were provided by the University of Virginia Institute for Research in the Social Sciences. Typing and administrative assistance was provided also by the Bureau of Population and Economic Research of the University of Virginia.

The staff of the Twentieth Century Fund deserve a great deal of credit for their patient and competent guidance in the preparation of this book. J. Frederic Dewhurst and S. N. Whitney offered valuable criticism and suggestions for the improvement of the manuscript. The difficult task of editing the manuscript fell to Miss Beulah Amidon whose skill and patience in bringing a semblance of order and coherence out of a manuscript of great complexity warrants the highest praise.

RAYMOND F. MIKESELL

POSTSCRIPT ON BRITISH EXCHANGE REGULATIONS

On March 19, 1954, after this book had gone to press, the British Treasury announced the unification of all nonresident sterling accounts with the exception of American, Canadian and blocked accounts, and, for the time being, accounts held by residents of Iran, Hungary and Turkey. This means in effect that all bilateral accounts, with few exceptions, became transferable accounts, and sterling became transferable without restriction for both current and capital transactions, among residents of the expanded transferable account group. While the unification of most British nonresident accounts held outside the dollar area does not bring Britain any closer to dollar convertibility, it greatly expands the area within which sterling is automatically transferable.

R. F. M.

CONTENTS

Part III: THE COUNTRIES AND MONETARY AREAS

FIGURES

TABLES

PART I

THE EMERGING PATTERN OF POSTWAR
PAYMENTS PRACTICES

Chapter 1

THE DEVELOPMENT OF POSTWAR
PAYMENTS SYSTEMS

THE INTERWAR PERIOD

THE BASIC ROOTS of the systems of foreign exchange payments following World War II are not to be found in the postwar period itself or in the period of hostilities. The economic and political conditions of the recent past have certainly influenced the development of current systems of regional multilateral settlements, but we must look for their antecedents in the interwar years and it is by no means clear that in the absence of World War II something similar to the present system would not have emerged.

World War I brought about the destruction of a world payments system based upon sterling as the principal international medium and gold as the common regulator of national monetary systems. For a brief time after 1925 the world's currencies were largely interchangeable with one another and with gold at more or less fixed ratios of exchange, but there were two important differences between this system and that prevailing prior to 1914. First, the U.S. dollar emerged as a rival of sterling as an international payments medium; second, gold no longer provided a common regulator of the quantity of money in national currency systems. The growing practice of managing currencies independently of gold movements became incompatible with the maintenance of the international gold standard during the economic and financial disturbances after 1929.

Foreign Exchange Shortages of the 1930s

The world economy had experienced many depressions and financial crises before the 1930s, but until then foreign exchange shortages and balance of payments difficulties had not become important terms in the financial jargon. So long as nations did not adopt independent national monetary policies, domestic monetary stringency and foreign exchange stringency were one and the same phenomenon. If the exports of a Latin American country fell there may have been a money shortage in that country but not a foreign exchange shortage as such.

By the end of the 1920s most countries had established central banking, and currency and credit systems permitting changes in the quantity of circulating media quite independent of their balance of external payments. It was inevitable, therefore, that with a sharp reduction in the supply of international means of payment such as occurred after 1929, many countries would be faced with the problem of an excess of demand over the supply of foreign exchange. Moreover, the supply of international means of payment had become far less stable than before World War I as a result of two important developments. One was the appearance of the dollar as a rival key currency,[1] partially taking over the function of sterling. The sterling-gold-exchange standard of the pre-1914 era provided a much more stable and dependable supply of international payments media than the two-key currency system of the late 1920s. A second factor was the large short-term foreign balances held in the banks of European capitals. Movements of these funds from weaker centers to stronger ones—largely in response to political and financial events—tended to produce erratic changes in the supply of international means of payment available for current trade.

International trade, like domestic trade, requires an adequate and stable means of payment. The supply of international payments media is determined by the imports and foreign investments of countries whose currencies are financing international transactions, supplemented by the production of gold outside the key currency countries. The demand for such media is determined by the requirements of international traders and by the desire for international liquidity.

In the early 1930s the supply of payments media was reduced principally by the fall in U.S. imports and foreign investments,[2] while demand was affected by an increase in liquidity preference due to economic depression and political disturbance. This situation was ag-

1. A "key currency" is one which is widely used as a means of international payments.
2. The dollars supplied by the United States to the rest of the world through imports of goods and services and new investment declined by $5 billion between 1929 and 1932 or by 68 per cent. (*The United States in the World Economy*, U.S. Department of Commerce, 1943, p. 6.)

gravated by the withdrawal of short-term sterling balances from London in the form of gold which not only reduced the total volume of international means of payment but immobilized an additional amount in gold hoards.

The process was analogous to the drawing down of bank deposits in currency notes during the banking crisis in the United States. The gold drain from London was brought to an end with Britain's departure from the gold standard in September 1931. However, international liquidity was also reduced by the withdrawal of balances from other European countries, since these short-term balances payable in gold were part of the total supply of international funds even though they were not held in the key currency countries.[3]

Three Ways Used to Conserve Foreign Exchange

The adjustments to the sharp change in the supply of international means of payment relative to the demand in terms of national currencies differed from country to country. Assuming that a nation has limited foreign exchange reserves and that it is not prepared to apply deflationary measures to the point of equating the demand for, and the supply of, foreign exchange, three general types of measures are possible:

1. It can devalue, either by an amount believed to be sufficient to equate the demand and supply or by letting its currency find its own level in terms of gold and international currencies.

2. It can ration its supply of international means of payment.

3. It can circumvent the international payments mechanism by arrangements with other countries whereby transactions are financed without the use of international currencies. This third type of adjustment, adopted by a number of countries in the 1930s and expanded to include nearly the entire world outside of the United States during and after World War II, has constituted the most fundamental change in the world's system of payments. Just as the world departed

---

3. Some international trade, perhaps no more than 20 per cent, was financed with currencies other than sterling and the dollar. In addition, balances held in Paris, Vienna and other financial centers performed the function of an international store of value even though such balances may not have been widely used as an international exchange medium. It will also be remembered that gold itself rarely was used as a means of financing current transactions, but was employed principally as a store of value and a settler of net international balances.

from the pre-1914 gold standard in the interwar period, so also has the world departed in considerable measure from a system in which one or two key currencies provided the principal supply of international liquidity. We should keep this development—which began in the early 1930s—clearly in mind when we seek to characterize the present system of international payments and to speculate regarding its future.

Balance-of-payments difficulties first appeared in the raw-material-producing countries, where the prices of exports were sharply reduced at the outset of the depression in 1929–1930. Beginning late in 1929 there occurred a wave of currency depreciations among the primary-producing countries, including Australia, New Zealand, Argentina, Uruguay and Brazil, followed by a number of others after the depreciation of sterling in 1931. Depreciation among primary-producing countries was a frequent phenomenon in periods of falling raw materials prices, even before 1914. What was new was the adoption by many of these countries of exchange controls and bilateral arrangements. Thus in 1931 exchange controls of one form or another were established by Brazil, Chile, Uruguay, Colombia, Bolivia, Argentina and Nicaragua, followed by Costa Rica and Paraguay in 1932.[4]

Primary-producing countries of the Eastern Hemisphere devalued with, or even before, the devaluation of sterling [5] but few imposed exchange controls. The reason is to be found in the strong economic and financial ties between the economies and the currencies of the primary-producing countries of the Eastern Hemisphere and the sterling and other Western European monetary areas. For example, the currencies of many countries having close ties with Britain were backed by sterling up to as high as 100 per cent, while, except for the Central American and Caribbean countries, Latin American currencies were not in general supported by a high percentage of gold or foreign exchange reserves.

The Sterling Bloc

Perhaps there were, however, more fundamental reasons why countries with close economic and financial ties to Britain did not adopt

4. Ecuador also established exchange controls in May 1932 but they were abandoned in October of the same year.
5. Australia devalued at the end of 1929.

exchange controls during the 1930s. British imports and foreign investments provided a stable and for the most part adequate supply of international currency for conducting the transactions of the group of countries that came to be known as the "sterling bloc." [6]

While the sterling bloc included a number of countries that pegged their currencies to sterling, the inner circle of countries which became members of the more formalized "sterling area" during and following World War II was largely limited to those which were a part of the British Empire or had close political ties to it. Within this group, which included the Dominions (except Canada and Newfoundland), the British colonies and mandates, and Egypt and Iraq, capital moved freely and trade among the Empire countries enjoyed preferential tariff privileges. Capital movements were facilitated by the several large British banks with headquarters in London, which maintained branches in the other members of the group. [7]

Britain's Bilateral Agreements

Except for mild restrictions on capital movements for a few months after the devaluation of sterling in September 1931, Britain herself did not restrict exchange payments of residents until the outbreak of war in 1939. Nevertheless she entered into a number of bilateral exchange arrangements of a restrictive nature. For example, under the

6. During the 1930s the sterling bloc had no formal or legal structure except in the case of British dependencies which were required to maintain a currency reserve (usually 100 per cent) in the form of sterling balances or securities. Some of the independent members of the British Commonwealth also maintained their currency reserves in the form of sterling. The distinguishing characteristic of the members of the sterling bloc, however, was that they pegged their national currencies to sterling which in turn fluctuated in terms of gold and the dollar between 1931 and 1939. Although membership in the sterling bloc changed from time to time, at its greatest extent before the war it included the following in order of degree of attachment: (1) the United Kingdom, the British colonies and mandates excepting Hong Kong and British Honduras; (2) the British Dominions, including Eire and India, but excluding Canada and Newfoundland; (3) Egypt, Iraq, Portugal, parts of the Portuguese empire and Thailand; (4) Scandinavia and Iceland; (5) Finland, Estonia, and Latvia; (6) Greece and Iran. (Donald F. Heatherington, "The Sterling Area," *International Reference Service,* November 1945, Vol. II, No. 32, U.S. Department of Commerce, p. 6.)

7. British banks with numerous branches in the sterling bloc included Barclays Bank (Dominion, Colonial and Overseas) with branches throughout the Middle East, Africa and the British possessions in the Caribbean area; the Ottoman Bank with branches in the Middle East, and the Imperial Bank of Iran, with branches in Iran and Iraq. In addition many of the locally incorporated banks such as for example, the National Bank of Egypt, were British owned and managed.

terms of the Roca-Runciman Pact with Argentina in 1933,[8] Argentina agreed to make available for payments to the United Kingdom the full amount of sterling exchange arising from Argentine exports to the United Kingdom, except for an amount required to service Argentina's public debt to other countries. Britain also entered into a payments agreement with Germany which provided that a certain portion of the sterling proceeds of German exports to Britain were earmarked to pay for British exports to Germany.

There were two principal reasons why Britain and other free-exchange countries—including Belgium, Switzerland, France and the Netherlands—entered into bilateral payments agreements with exchange control countries. First, such agreements frequently provided a means of collecting debts owed by countries unable or unwilling to pay in convertible currencies.[9] But equally important, they enabled the free-exchange countries to secure a larger proportion of the trade of exchange-control countries. By participating in these arrangements Britain weakened the system of international payments based on freely transferable international currencies, and limited the transferability of sterling itself. The bilateral payments agreements, which Britain initiated with the Roca-Runciman Pact, became the principal mechanism of financial settlements among nondollar countries in the war and early postwar periods.

Latin American Exchange Controls

The heavy pressures on the balance of payments of the Latin American countries caused by the sharp reduction in the demand for their exports and the deterioration in their terms-of-trade after 1929 led first to a depreciation of their exchange rates and then to the adoption of exchange controls in 1931 and 1932. This second step was taken only when depreciation failed to relieve the exchange difficulties of most of these countries. Depreciation did not increase their foreign exchange earnings since the demand for their exports was inelastic. Continual devaluation also led to capital flight and direct

8. Virgil Salera, *Exchange Control and the Argentine Market,* Columbia University Press, New York, 1941, Chapter 5.

9. For a discussion of British bilateral agreements during the 1930s see Henry J. Tasca, *World Trading Systems,* Institute of International Cooperation, League of Nations, Paris, 1939. Britain concluded payments agreements with Argentina, Uruguay, Germany, Hungary, Romania, Yugoslavia, Latvia and Italy during this period.

controls were imposed in order to prevent this drain on their foreign exchange resources.

Considering the Latin American countries as a group, the most important use of exchange controls occurred in South America where nine out of the ten countries adopted controls during the 1930s.[10] The trade of these nations was oriented largely toward Europe, while that of the Central American and Caribbean countries was more closely linked with the United States. Moreover, the currencies of the latter group were for the most part gold or dollar currencies, some of them backed 100 per cent by dollars. Hence it is not surprising that only one out of the ten Central American and Caribbean countries adopted exchange controls in the 1930s.

The fact that the countries of South America were so dependent upon European markets was an important factor in their adoption of discriminatory trade and exchange practices. Many European countries were experiencing balance of payments difficulties during the 1930s and nearly all of them were seeking to utilize their bargaining power as consumers of raw materials to promote their markets for manufactures. Further, the Latin American countries were in competition with primary-producing countries in the Eastern Hemisphere, many with close economic and financial ties to Western Europe.[11]

Under these conditions several Latin American countries, notably Argentina, Brazil, Chile, Colombia, Ecuador and Uruguay, entered into bilateral arrangements with Britain, Germany, Italy and other European countries during the 1930s. The arrangements took the form of clearing agreements, compensation arrangements and bilateral payments arrangements such as that provided under the Roca-Runciman Pact.[12] In addition to the motive of expanding trade, the existence of blocked currency balances in South American banks representing amounts owed to European creditors was also a factor in the introduction of bilateral arrangements. Thus under the Roca-Runci-

10. Peru alone was free of exchange controls during the period while Venezuela employed only mild restrictions.

11. Under the Ottawa Agreement of 1931 the British Commonwealth countries established a system of preferential tariffs which undoubtedly placed certain Latin American countries in a disadvantageous position.

12. Several Central and South American countries, which did not have clearing agreements with Germany, accepted payment for exports to Germany in the form of deposits in special mark accounts known as "aski-marks." The aski-marks were generally not transferable between countries or even between banks within countries, and could be used only for the purchase of certain designated German exports.

man Pact, Argentina agreed to reserve a certain amount of her sterling receipts for paying off frozen peso balances owned by British citizens.[13]

While the Latin American exchange control countries employed exchange permits and import quotas for limiting the demand for foreign exchange, during the 1930s they relied in large measure on "cost" restrictions. These included the more orthodox measures such as customs duties and export taxes, but there also was heavy reliance on multiple exchange rates and exchange surtaxes. These reduced the need for import licensing machinery and other administrative devices for rationing foreign exchange and controlling foreign transactions. They also made it possible to turn over the administration of the exchange control to the central banks the staffs of which are in most cases less subject to political pressures and, in general, more competent than those of other government bureaus.

Exchange Controls in Europe

From the standpoint of foreign exchange developments in the 1930s, we may divide the countries of continental Europe (excluding the USSR) into three groups. First, there were the so-called gold-bloc countries which included France, Italy, Switzerland, Poland, Belgium, Luxembourg and the Netherlands. These remained on the gold standard and avoided depreciation until the second half of the 1930s. Although the gold-bloc countries employed import quotas over a wide range of commodities and entered into bilateral payments agreements with exchange-control countries, all of them except Italy and Poland retained freedom of exchange dealings until 1939.[14]

A second group of European countries pegged their currencies to the pound sterling after Britain left the gold standard in 1931. This continental group, which included Portugal, Finland, Denmark, Norway and Sweden, tended to maintain free exchange markets or adopted only mild restrictions.

In contrast with the sterling bloc countries, the third group of European countries, which included most of Central and Eastern Eu-

13. See Margaret S. Gordon, *Barriers to World Trade*, Macmillan, New York, 1941, p. 190.
14. Belgium left the gold standard in November 1935; France, the Netherlands, Switzerland and Italy devalued in September 1936. Italy and Poland adopted exchange controls in 1934 and 1936, respectively.

rope, sought to avoid depreciation by the adoption of rigid exchange controls. As was the case with the gold-bloc countries, devaluation in Central and Eastern Europe was politically and psychologically difficult. Their wartime experience had led the peoples of continental Europe to associate devaluation with inflation. But while the gold-bloc countries were able to maintain their gold parities under free exchange conditions at least for a time after the United States and British devaluations, the Central and Eastern European countries were forced to adopt exchange controls in order to retain their old gold parities.

At first, exchange controls in Central and Eastern Europe were emergency measures adopted to stop the foreign exchange drain which threatened their parities. These measures frequently took the form of blocking local currency accounts held by nonresidents. In many instances imports were not controlled through quantitative restrictions but restrictions were imposed either on the making of payments to foreign sellers or upon the use of local currency proceeds by foreign recipients. Consequently, blocked balances owned by foreigners began to accumulate in Austria, Hungary, Yugoslavia, Greece, Bulgaria, Romania and Germany.[15] Under these circumstances some countries began to refuse to permit their own citizens to make payments in free foreign exchange to debtor countries which had blocked the accounts belonging to residents of other countries. This situation led to the adoption of bilateral clearing agreements between exchange-control and free-exchange countries and between exchange-control countries themselves.[16]

The advantage of such arrangements to the creditor country was twofold. First, it provided a means of liquidating the indebtedness by a provision in the clearing agreement whereby a portion of the proceeds from the exports of the debtor country must be applied against the blocked accounts. Second, it made it possible for the creditor country to maintain a market for its exports to the exchange-control country, since the latter would not be required to pay in free exchange. This gave the creditor country an advantage over a country like the

15. See A. Basch, *The Danube Basin and the German Economic Sphere,* Columbia University Press, New York, 1943. Dr. Basch points out (pp. 74–75) that while Czechoslovakia adopted exchange controls in October 1931, she refrained from interfering with the settlement of legitimate foreign claims.

16. For a good discussion of the operation of clearing agreements during the 1930s see Gordon, *op. cit.,* Chapters 6 and 7.

United States which demands free foreign exchange in payment for its exports. There was a further advantage to the creditor country in the fact that it could encourage imports from the exchange-control country by any means at its disposal without the loss of free or convertible exchange.

From Clearing Agreements to Payments Agreements

A more flexible type of bilateral arrangement and one perhaps better suited for financing trade between free-exchange and exchange-control countries was the bilateral payments agreement.[17] These permitted exporters in the free-exchange country to be paid in their own currency; but when payments were made by importers to the exchange-control country, such balances were placed in a special account which could only be used to make payments to the free-exchange country.

This type of agreement, which tended to supplant the clearing agreement between free-exchange and controlled countries after 1934, differed from the bilateral clearing agreement in three important respects. First, it permitted actual transfers of balances between traders in the two countries; second, it eliminated the waiting period which characterized the clearing agreements since exporters could be paid immediately by selling their foreign exchange to the banks rather than having to wait until importers had paid local currency into the clearing account; third, it made it unnecessary for the free-exchange country to exercise control over the foreign exchange dealings of its own residents with the residents of the exchange-control country. While residents of the free-exchange country could make payments to the exchange-control country without restriction, residents of the exchange-control country were not free to dispose of the currency of the free-exchange country except in accordance with the terms of the bilateral agreement. For example the Anglo-German Agreement of 1934 determined precisely how the sterling exchange accruing to Germany from exports to the United Kingdom was to be allocated.

Multiple Exchange and Discriminatory Cross-Rates

The widespread use of multiple exchange rates and discriminatory cross-rates in the postwar period also had its roots in the exchange

17. See Gordon, *op. cit.,* pp. 191–93.

practices of the 1930s.[18] Latin American countries with exchange control systems tended to influence both the character and the direction of their trade by means of devices which involved differential values for foreign exchange in terms of the domestic currency. Thus instead of reducing imports of luxury commodities by means of import quotas, Latin American countries required importers to pay a higher price for the foreign exchange used to buy luxury imports than they paid for exchange to buy more essential commodities. Differential conversion rates were also employed as a means of encouraging certain exports.

Exchange rates which discriminated between currencies were also used to influence the direction of trade. Thus Argentina placed a 20 per cent exchange surcharge on about half the imports from the United States, while practically all imports from Britain could be purchased at the official rate.[19] Special rates were also employed in connection with the clearing agreements entered into by Central and Eastern European countries during the 1930s. By shifting the rates it was often possible to achieve a better balance of trade between two countries whose trade was conducted under a clearing agreement. The famous German aski-mark system involved special rates which applied to different types of commodities and to different countries.

The System of International Payments in 1939

Immediately before World War II there were two major systems of multilateral settlements comprising roughly (1) those countries of North America, the Caribbean area and northern South America which pegged their currencies to the dollar and tended to make and receive payments in dollars; and (2) the sterling bloc countries which pegged their currencies to sterling and tended to finance their trade with one another and with other nondollar countries in sterling. Except for the former gold-bloc countries—France, Belgium-Luxembourg, Switzerland and the Netherlands, whose currencies were used to some extent in financing their own trade and that of their

18. By multiple exchange rates we mean the use of different rates for different categories of merchandise and service transactions. By discriminatory cross-rates we mean a system in which the exchange rates applicable to different foreign currencies do not conform to the effective rates between the foreign currencies themselves. Thus if the dollar-sterling rate were $5 = £1, a discriminatory cross-rate would exist if the number of pesos per pound were appreciably greater or less than five times the number of pesos per dollar.

19. Salera, *op. cit.*. p. 150.

dependencies—most of the rest of the world employed exchange controls and financed trade by a variety of devices such as clearing, payments and compensation agreements among themselves and with certain free-exchange countries.

Since the bulk of the world's trade was financed either with dollars or sterling, its multilateral character depended upon the convertibility of these two currencies. But the link between the dollar bloc and the sterling bloc was weak and imperfect. The defects of the system arose in part from the fact that most of the countries outside the dollar and the sterling blocs employed exchange controls, and also from the clearing and payments agreements entered into by many of the free-exchange countries of the world with the exchange-control countries. For example, in January 1939 Britain was a party to nine bilateral payments or clearing agreements, Switzerland to twelve, Belgium-Luxembourg to thirteen, the Netherlands to seven, and France to twelve.[20]

The motive of these agreements was a desire to collect financial obligations and to preserve commercial markets in the exchange-control countries. Their operation placed certain limitations upon the convertibility of the currencies of the free-exchange countries involved. Had all free-exchange countries followed the practice of making or receiving international payments only in freely convertible currencies, the area of bilateral trade would have been limited to that arising from special bilateral arrangements between exchange-control countries. But as we have seen, the free-exchange countries, including Britain and the gold-bloc nations of western Europe played an important role in undermining the world-wide system of multilateral payments by signing bilateral arrangements with exchange-control countries. Thus, while the bulk of the world's trade during the 1930s was financed with convertible currencies there was a growing tendency, even among countries not faced with exchange difficulties, to by-pass the multilateral payments mechanism several years before the term "dollar shortage" became a part of the standard jargon of international finance.

DEVELOPMENTS DURING WORLD WAR II

During World War II, foreign exchange systems functioned largely as an intergovernmental accounting device and foreign ex-

20. Gordon, *op. cit.*, pp. 130–31.

change values lost much of their significance for determining the character and direction of international trade. Trade among the allies was directed not by competitive advantage and ability to pay but by international shipping and commodity allocation arrangements. Any shortage of finance for carrying out the allocation decisions was met by such intergovernmental grants as U.S. Lend-Lease and Canadian Mutual Aid, or in the case of British expenditures in the sterling area, by the accumulation of sterling balances. On the continent, Germany assumed fairly complete control of intra-European trade and financed her own large trade deficits by credits granted by her involuntary partners in clearing agreements.

Because of transportation and commodity shortages, the neutrals tended to have export surpluses in exchange for which they were willing to accept gold and foreign exchange, i.e., dollar balances and sterling. Relative prices and exchange rates played only a minor role in determining the trade of either belligerents or neutrals. Nevertheless, the wartime payments mechanisms are of considerable interest for this study since certain of the techniques have become important features of the postwar payments arrangements.

The Sterling Area Controls

Exchange controls were introduced in Britain immediately after the outbreak of war in September 1939, and by March 1940 only four of the principal currencies of the world remained relatively free from official regulation: the dollar, the belga, the florin and the Swiss franc.[21] The British exchange control regulations provided for centralization of exchange dealings in authorized banks and the issuance of regulations under which foreign exchange could be bought and sold by British residents. At first, however, Britain did not control transfers of sterling between nonresidents, nor was there a complete control of payments of "free sterling" from residents to nonresidents.[22] This situation resulted in a dual rate for sterling in terms of dollars. There were official buying and selling rates in London initially fixed at $4.06 and $4.02 respectively;[23] and a free-market

21. Britain placed restrictions on foreign security dealings on August 24, 1939 and on September 3 introduced controls on current international transactions.

22. This discussion is based in large part upon material to be found in the *Tenth Annual Report*, Bank for International Settlements, Basel, 1940, pp. 18–21.

23. The official buying and selling rates were changed to $4.035 and $4.025, respectively, in January 1940.

rate in other countries which fluctuated daily in response to the demand for and supply of sterling held by nonresidents. The London market for foreign exchange was a controlled market, limited to transactions with authorized banks and exchange dealers. Thus the official London market was insulated from the free markets for sterling in New York and other financial centers.

The supply of "free sterling" balances available in foreign markets was derived from two sources: (1) sterling balances previously accumulated by nonresidents; (2) balances accruing to nonresidents as a result of payments for imports into the United Kingdom. At first free sterling was valid for use in making payments for British exports except in the case of countries with which Britain had special clearing and payments arrangements. The demand for free sterling was, however, sharply reduced in March 1940 by a new exchange regulation. This required exporters of certain commodities—among them whisky, furs, tin, rubber and jute—from the controlled sterling area, to a number of nonsterling countries including Belgium, the Netherlands, Switzerland, North and South America (except Canada, Argentina and Uruguay) to receive payment either in acceptable foreign currencies or in sterling which had been purchased at the official rate.

The result was a sharp fall in the price of free sterling from a level only slightly below the official London dollar price to $3.50 in April 1940 and in May to a low of $3.10. A regulation of June 8, 1940 further reduced the fungibility of free sterling by requiring that all exports from Britain and the controlled sterling area to the United States and Switzerland must be paid for in sterling obtained at the official rate or in dollars or Swiss francs. On this same date a regulation blocked the sale of British securities by nonresidents. This tended to dry up the supply of free sterling so that what remained soon rose to parity with the official London price.[24]

In 1940 an arrangement was concluded with American banks (with the approval of the U.S. Treasury and the Federal Reserve authorities) which blocked American investments in the United Kingdom, thereby envisaging a gradual extinction of the New York market for "free sterling." [25] There also developed a system of "registered

24. *Eleventh Annual Report*, Bank for International Settlements, Basel, June 1941, p. 40.
25. *Ibid.*, p. 41. Free markets for other types of sterling will be discussed in a later chapter.

accounts" for residents of the United States and Switzerland, which could at any time be converted into dollars or Swiss francs at the official rate. United States and Swiss banks could purchase registered sterling with dollars or Swiss francs at the official rate under conditions determined by the British authorities.

Member Countries of the Sterling Area

The establishment of exchange controls after September 1939 converted the highly informal and voluntary system known as the "sterling bloc" into a set of formal and legal arrangements which we now call the "sterling area." A British Defense Order of July 17, 1940 defined the sterling area as including the following territories in addition to the United Kingdom itself: any Dominion, except Canada and Newfoundland; British colonies, self-governing territories, etc.; mandated territories and protectorates; Egypt, the Anglo-Egyptian Sudan and Iraq.[26] Exchange control regulations similar to those imposed by the United Kingdom were adopted by other members of the sterling area. Thus there was created an area of free currency transfers, surrounded by a more or less uniform wall of exchange control regulations imposed by the authorities in each dependent territory or independent country.[27]

Trade between the sterling area and the United States, Canada and Newfoundland and Switzerland was conducted in terms of either dollars or Swiss francs (in the case of Switzerland), or in terms of the registered accounts of the residents of these countries which carried conversion privileges. Trade with a group of Latin American countries was financed with either dollars or Central American account sterling. British trade with most of the rest of the world was conducted under special bilateral agreements, and sterling accumulated in these accounts was not freely usable for payments outside the sterling area itself. The development of the so-called transferable account area came after the war.

The London Dollar Pool

Members of the sterling area obtained their dollars and other hard currencies from the Bank of England and in turn sold their hard-cur-

---

26. For complete text of the British orders defining the sterling area that were issued from 1940 to 1945, see Heatherington, "The Sterling Area," *loc. cit.*, p. 20.

27. Contrary to popular opinion there was no central exchange control authority but each self-governing country modeled its regulations on the British control system.

rency earnings to the Bank of England for sterling. Thus there developed what has come to be known as the London dollar pool, which served as a centralized reserve for the hard-currency earnings of the sterling area.[28] Except for South Africa, however, the principal members of the sterling area tended toward hard-currency deficits rather than surpluses. Drawings on the London dollar pool were limited by exchange restrictions on capital movements, foreign travel and other invisible transactions and by import licensing systems which conserved foreign exchange for essential imports.[29] During the war the shortage of commodities and shipping together with Anglo-American allocation controls provided an automatic limit to the demands of the sterling area members for dollars and other hard currencies.[30] (After V-E day certain sterling area countries, including Egypt and Iraq, were set limits within which they were required to confine their net dollar drawings from the London pool.) Since nearly all the sterling area countries outside Britain and most of the nonsterling area countries having bilateral payments agreements with Britain had current account surpluses with Britain during the war, a large volume of sterling balances owned by non-British governments, banks and individuals accumulated.[31]

The sterling area emerged from the war as a rather large region of multilateral settlements and unrestricted currency transfers in a world of almost universal currency restrictions. The German mark and Japanese yen systems represented other attempts during the war to create limited areas of full multilateral settlements between countries with separate currency systems, but they were not very successful.

The German Clearing System

Before the war Germany developed a network of bilateral clearing and payments agreements covering practically every country in Eu-

28. Some of the sterling area countries maintain sizable independent gold and dollar reserves.

29. Sterling area countries generally followed the practice of automatically granting foreign exchange to holders of import licenses. Exporters to nonsterling countries were required to receive payment in foreign exchange acceptable to the exchange authorities and to sell their foreign exchange earnings to the monetary authorities.

30. Hard currencies were those which could not be acquired in unlimited amounts with the payment of sterling. They included the United States and Canadian dollars, the Swiss franc, the Portuguese escudo and the Swedish krona.

31. British liabilities rose from about £400 million at the beginning of the war to £3,350 million on June 30, 1945. During the same period there was net liquidation of

rope and a large number of non-European countries as well. After the German occupation of most of Europe, trade among all European countries was conducted by means of clearing arrangements. Germany sought to make Berlin the clearing center of the continent and required that most of the clearings between the occupied countries as well as with Germany be made through accounts kept at the German Clearing Institute in Berlin.[32]

By the beginning of 1942, seventeen of the twenty countries of continental Europe were linked in one way or another to the German Clearing Institute. Yet Germany's goal to create a system of multilateral clearing for the continent was not realized. The reason is to be found in the fact that Germany was in debt to every other member of the system.[33] A successful multilateral clearing arrangement must involve a settlement among a group of countries each of which is both a bilateral creditor and a bilateral debtor in relation to other individual members. Of course each creditor might have received payment equal to his net creditor position in the form of a balance in reichsmarks, and indeed RM credits were occasionally transferred from one country to another in the settlement of bilateral clearing balances. But unlike the pound sterling (which was accumulated in large volume by British creditors but still provided a means of making international payments) the reichsmark was not an international currency and reichsmark clearing credits were not acceptable in trade between third countries.

The Yen Area

For the sake of completeness it is necessary to mention the yen area created by Japan in her occupied territories during the war. However, the yen area was little more than a network of fixed exchange rates for local currencies in terms of yen. Trade was largely of the barter variety and, as in the German case, there is little evidence of multilateral settlements with yen.

British long-term assets abroad amounting to about £1,000 million and net sales of gold and dollars of £1,050 million.

32. For a discussion of German clearing practices during the war see the *Twelfth, Thirteenth* and *Fourteenth Annual Reports,* Bank for International Settlements. See also P. N. Anderson, *Exchange Clearing Policy,* Oxford University Press, London, 1946, pp. 34–35.

33. Germany's clearing debts amounted to RM 14.5 billion at the end of 1942, half of which was accumulated during that year. By September 1943 Germany's clearing debt had increased to over RM 18 billion. *Thirteenth Annual Report,* Bank for International Settlements, Basel, 1943, p. 153.

PAYMENTS AGREEMENTS NEGOTIATED DURING THE WAR

Shortly after the outbreak of war, in December 1939, Britain and France concluded a comprehensive financial agreement which in certain respects provided the pattern for the European payments system which emerged at the close of the war. The principal foreign exchange features were: [34]

1. The two governments agreed that it was to the interest of both countries to avoid alterations in their official exchange rates.

2. Britain agreed to provide sterling required by France (including that required for the purchase of raw materials in the British Empire) against payment in francs, and France agreed to provide francs required by the United Kingdom (including those needed by the British army) against sterling.

3. Sterling held by the French monetary authorities was to be available for use throughout the sterling area, and francs held by the United Kingdom were to be available for use throughout the French Empire.

4. The French and British Treasuries were to hold frequent meetings to review the position of the allied governments as regards their gold and foreign exchange reserves.

While this agreement lost most of its practical significance with the occupation of France in 1940 and special arrangements were subsequently made with the Free French which brought their territories temporarily into the sterling area, it established certain precedents for a series of European payments agreements. These began with the agreement concluded between the exiled governments of the Belgo-Luxembourg Union and the Netherlands in October 1943 and continued throughout the remainder of the war and into the early postwar period.[35] We shall examine the operations of the European bilateral payments agreements in a later chapter.

34. *Fifteenth Annual Report,* Bank for International Settlements, Basel, 1945, pp. 99–100.

35. In 1944 payments agreements were concluded between the United Kingdom and Belgium and between France and Belgium; in 1945 payments agreements were concluded between Britain and Sweden; France and Switzerland; Britain and France; Britain and Turkey; Sweden and the Belgo-Luxembourg Union; Sweden and Norway; France and Sweden; Switzerland and the Belgo-Luxembourg Union; Switzerland and Italy; Britain and Denmark; Britain and Finland; Britain and the Netherlands; Switzerland and Turkey; Switzerland and the Netherlands; Britain and Czechoslovakia; Britain and Norway; and France and Switzerland. *Ibid.,* p. 100.

Although these agreements were designed to provide a payments mechanism for the immediate postwar period, they were a product of the war and an attempt to deal with the economic problems brought about by the war. They must be thought of as a compromise between two basic systems of trade and payments. On the one hand these countries could have permitted free exchange dealings and allowed their currencies to find their own levels in terms of gold and hard currencies. In view of the swollen currencies left over from the German occupation and of the great shortages of goods and productive capacities, this probably would have meant hyperinflation on a scale equal to the German experience of 1923.[36] On the other hand the governments could have placed all trade on a completely controlled basis and conducted trade with other soft-currency countries in terms of government-to-government barter. The alternative provided by the bilateral payments agreements permitted private trade to be conducted with a measure of freedom.

Most students of international finance looked upon both the wartime sterling area and the network of bilateral payments agreements which encompassed most of the nondollar countries of the world as postwar transitional arrangements, to be followed by a return to some mechanism which would permit multilateral settlements on a worldwide basis. In fact, intergovernmental discussions of postwar possibilities to this end were taking place in 1944 and 1945, at the time that the new payments agreements were being negotiated. Although the expectations of the Bretton Woods Conference of 1944 were not to be fulfilled in the decade which followed, the postwar multilateral financial and trade conventions had an important influence on the development of trade and foreign exchange policies in the postwar period.

36. During that inflation the external value of the mark decreased more rapidly than did its internal purchasing power. A rapid decrease in external value tends to feed internal inflation and, if unchecked, may lead to hyperinflation.

Chapter 2

THE EARLY POSTWAR AGREEMENTS

AT THE END of World War II most of the free nations entertained high hopes that international monetary and trade problems would henceforth be dealt with by international cooperation through special United Nations organizations established for this purpose. The Bretton Woods Conference of 1944, in which the United States played a leading role, presented a sharp contrast to the Brussels and Genoa international financial conferences of 1920 and 1922, to which the United States refused to send representatives for fear of being drawn into a discussion of war debts; and to the London Monetary and Economic Conference of 1933 where the delegates were hopelessly divided over basic policies for dealing with world economic stability.[1]

United States interest in actively promoting international cooperation in foreign exchange and trade dates from 1934 with the passage of the Reciprocal Trade Agreements Act and the establishment of the U.S. Exchange Stabilization Fund under the Gold Reserve Act of 1934. While the approach to these problems during the late 1930s was largely bilateral,[2] the fundamental elements in the earlier bilateral trade and exchange agreements were carried over into the International Monetary Fund and the General Agreement on Tariffs and Trade (GATT) established in the early postwar period. No attempt will be made to present a systematic description of these postwar organizations.[3] Rather, the purpose here will be to review the interna-

1. See R. F. Mikesell, *United States Economic Policy and International Relations*, McGraw-Hill, New York, 1952, pp. 51–55.
2. An important exception was the Tripartite Monetary Agreement of 1936 with Britain and France, subsequently expanded to include Belgium, the Netherlands and Switzerland.
3. See William Adams Brown, Jr., *The United States and the Restoration of World Trade*, The Brookings Institution, Washington, 1950; see also Mikesell, *op. cit.;* and Brian Tew, *International Monetary Cooperation, 1945–1952*, Hutchinson's University Library, London, 1952.

tional monetary and trade policies which most of the governments of the free world agreed to follow as members of these institutions, and to discuss these policies in the light of the actual course of world events.

The Basic Agreements

The basic agreements with which we shall be concerned in this chapter are the International Monetary Fund Agreement formulated at the Bretton Woods Conference, the Anglo-American Financial Agreement of 1946,[4] and the General Agreement on Tariffs and Trade [5] adopted in 1947. The Anglo-American Financial Agreement was in fact a supplement to the Monetary Fund Agreement since it was designed to make possible an early restoration of sterling convertibility.

Under this agreement the United States loaned Britain $3.75 billion on condition that she would make sterling convertible within one year. Sterling convertibility was rightly believed to be basic to the restoration of a world system of multilateral trade and payments. Once the world's payments difficulties were dealt with, the rapid removal of trade restrictions—including discriminatory trade practices—was to be achieved through the operation of a proposed International Trade Organization, the Charter of which was formulated at the UN Conference on Trade and Employment in Havana in March 1948.[6] While the Havana Charter was never ratified by the governments represented at the conference, many of its provisions dealing with trade restrictions were embodied in the General Agreement on Tariffs and Trade. The contracting parties to the GATT have met from time to time to bargain for tariff reductions and to implement the provisions relating to trade restrictions.

THE PROMOTION OF EXCHANGE STABILITY

The promotion of exchange stability was undoubtedly the most important objective of the American postwar international planners.

4. *Articles of Agreement, The International Monetary Fund,* Washington, 1946; and *Anglo-American Financial and Commercial Agreements,* U.S. Department of State, December 1945.
5. *The General Agreement on Tariffs and Trade* (Amended Text), U.S. Department of State, February 1950.
6. *Havana Charter for an International Trade Organization,* March 1948, U.S. Department of State, 1948.

They remembered the exchange instability of the early 1920s and the competitive devaluation of the 1930s and were determined to avoid these deterrents to trade and foreign investment. The method proposed and adopted in the Bretton Woods Agreements was that the members of the International Monetary Fund would agree on an initial set of par values for their currencies and that they would not change these parities by more than 10 per cent except by majority vote or by less than 10 per cent without consultations.[7] Members were obligated to maintain their exchange rates within one per cent above or below the agreed par values, with provision for assistance to countries which experienced difficulty in stabilizing their exchange rates.

Certainly the idea of international cooperation and consultation in adjusting exchange rates is sound since by definition these rates are of concern to all countries. Without some understanding of exchange rates and the conditions under which they may be altered, the development of fair trading standards and orderly commercial and financial practices becomes impossible. Yet the Fund has not succeeded in the important objective of making exchange rate changes a matter of international deliberation and judgment. Even the general realignment of exchange rates in September 1949 which accompanied the devaluation of sterling was undertaken with little more than token consultations with the Monetary Fund.[8] This is not to say, of course, that significant discussions of exchange rate policies have not influenced the policies of Fund members. But by and large the decisions themselves have been unilateral, with the Fund concurring in the formal proposals submitted a day or two before the event.

Failure to Stabilize Exchange Rates

One of the reasons for this situation lies in the reluctance of members to discuss with the representatives of other member countries im-

7. The prescribed method for changing par values is given in Article IV of the *Articles of Agreement.*

8. In his radio speech on September 18, 1949, announcing the devaluation of sterling Sir Stafford Cripps said that the decision taken "had to do with matters that were entirely our own concern and upon which there was no question of consulting others, even our best friends." (*The New York Times,* September 19, 1949.) For a discussion of Britain's consultation with the Monetary Fund on the sterling rate see Gardner Patterson, *Survey of United States International Finance, 1949,* International Finance Section, Princeton University, Princeton, 1950, pp. 115–16.

pending decisions regarding their exchange rates. This stems in part from the fear that information will leak out and precipitate a flight of capital. Perhaps even more significant is the fact that nations are as yet unwilling to submit to an international tribunal certain matters which they regard as vital to their own welfare, even though the decisions may be equally vital to other countries. The Fund may, however, be able to achieve greater success in this field as time goes on. The postwar atmosphere of crisis has not been conducive to the evolution of orderly procedures. But the failure of the Fund to achieve exchange stability is not to be found simply in the manner in which countries have changed their official par values. Rather, it is to be found in the relationship of those par values to the pattern of exchange rates themselves.

The system of declaring par values with the Fund has not achieved exchange rate stability in the postwar period for several reasons. First, the Fund Agreement as interpreted by the Fund's Executive Board, permits the members to employ multiple exchange practices involving two or more exchange rates for an indefinite period of time after the beginning of the Fund's operations.[9] While the Fund's Articles of Agreement and the policy statements of the Executive Directors look toward a gradual removal of such practices, the fact remains that multiple exchange rates were employed by more countries in 1953 than was the case in 1946. Some of the exchange rates used by multiple currency countries are free or floating rates while in other cases the rate structure is changed from time to time by governmental decree. The Executive Board of the Fund has taken the position that changes in multiple rate structures must be submitted in advance for its approval[10] but all too often the Fund has not been informed until after the action has been taken. Even during periods when the structure of a multiple rate system remains constant, countries continually shift commodities and services from one category to another for reasons of their own. In many cases the exchange rate corresponding to the agreed par value applies to only a few governmental transactions —or to none at all. About 40 per cent of the Fund's members employ

9. Multiple exchange rates, broken cross-rates and other so-called "disorderly exchange arrangements" may be regarded as a form of exchange rate instability.
10. For a statement of the position of the Executive Board on multiple exchange rates see *Annual Report of the Executive Directors for the Fiscal Year Ending April 30, 1948*, International Monetary Fund, Washington, 1948, Appendix II.

explicit multiple exchange rate systems and even though most of them have agreed par values with the Fund, genuine exchange rate stability does not exist for these countries. However, the Fund has been successful in persuading several of its members to simplify their multiple rate systems.

Evasions of the Official Exchange Rate

A controlled exchange rate is valid only to the extent that the monetary authorities succeed in achieving a complete consummation of international transactions at the official rate. In a free exchange market there can be only one exchange rate, but in a controlled market any number of effective rates may exist. Even in the most efficiently operated exchange control system there is a persistent tendency for market forces, legal and illegal, to undermine an overvalued exchange rate. This process is especially evident in the case of an international currency such as sterling, which is widely used in third country transactions.

Sales of sterling and other currencies at prices which do not conform to official exchange rates are widespread. But of even wider significance is the implicit depreciation or appreciation of currencies in a world of artificial parities and controlled official exchange rates. When a country finds itself with a surplus of sterling or other soft-currencies and a scarcity of dollars, it will generally ration its supplies of various currencies according to their relative scarcity, and it may seek by various measures to increase the supply of the scarcer currencies at the expense of the weaker ones. While to some extent these objectives can be achieved by direct controls, to a considerable degree the actual process may involve the existence of implicit rates of exchange which differ substantially from the official parities. For example, an implicit exchange rate is involved in the practice of permitting exporters to retain a portion of the dollar proceeds of their exports for their own use. Under these arrangements, which are called "retention quotas," the exporter is usually given the right to employ the dollar proceeds for importing relatively scarce commodities which can be sold at a substantial profit, thus giving him in effect an exchange premium over the official rate. The widespread use of such devices which give rise to implicit exchange rates other than those officially in force have much the same economic effects as exchange rate instability arising from explicit rate changes and explicit multiple rates.

Finally, it may be observed that certain Fund members, including Canada and Mexico, have from time to time employed freely fluctuating exchange rate systems, favored by most official and private thinking in the United States and in many other countries as an alternative to a fixed controlled rate. As compared with exchange control systems which involve explicit or implicit multiple exchange rates, freely fluctuating unitary rate systems are perhaps less damaging to trade and are less likely to involve competitive exchange depreciation. In fact the system of fixed exchange parities combined with a complex of neo-Schachtian devices has provided far less exchange stability in the postwar period than did the fluctuating free exchange rates of the 1930s.

THE PROBLEM OF EXCHANGE CONTROLS AND CURRENCY CONVERTIBILITY

The Monetary Fund Agreement did not commit the members of the Fund to a policy of complete freedom in foreign exchange dealings such as existed in the United States and in most Western European countries before 1939. First, it recognized the desirability of controls over capital movements, and the obligations of members with respect to freedom of exchange transactions were limited to the avoidance of restrictions on payments and transfers on *current* international transactions.[11] Second, the Fund Agreement provides for the retention of wartime restrictions for a transition period of indefinite duration, although five years after the beginning of the Fund's operations (March 1952) members are required to justify the further retention of restrictions on current transactions. It was expected, however, that the postwar transition period would be greatly shortened by the restoration of sterling convertibility in 1947, as provided by the Anglo-American Financial Agreement. Finally, the monetary agreements permitted the use of discriminatory controls against any

11. Payments for current international transactions include: (1) payments due in connection with trade in goods and services; (2) payments due as interest on loans and net income from investments; (3) moderate amounts for amortization and depreciation of direct investments; and (4) moderate remittances for family living expenses. (Article XIX.)

currency or currencies declared by the Fund to be "scarce." While the "scarce" currency exception was not intended to be invoked during the transition period, it nevertheless recognized an important principle which has pervaded postwar exchange policies.[12]

The scarce currency principle as developed in the Monetary Fund Agreement was carried over into both the Anglo-American Loan Agreement and the General Agreement on Tariffs and Trade. Thus, once the Monetary Fund has declared a currency to be "scarce," both discriminatory exchange and trade controls may be invoked against the scarce currency country.

Since the obligations of the Fund Agreement as to exchange restrictions relate to restrictions on current international transactions, there is obviously a close relationship between trade restrictions including import quotas and licensing, and exchange restrictions as such. In most countries the possession of an import license permits the holder to purchase the required foreign exchange from his bank. The question naturally arises, therefore, whether a particular restriction is an import or trade restriction or whether it is an exchange restriction. While the legal distinction may be clear, the existence of either type of restriction will interfere with or limit current transactions, and the jurisdiction of the Fund is confined to restrictions on payments. Fortunately, the regulations adopted under the General Agreement on Tariffs and Trade are in part parallel with those of the Monetary Fund. Thus, for example, the exceptions to the rules regarding discriminatory import restrictions during the transition period in GATT are similar to those of the Fund. The GATT also permits nondiscriminatory import restrictions in situations where members are experiencing a serious decline in their monetary reserves.[13] While the Monetary Fund Agreement does not provide for the automatic imposition of exchange restrictions by members experiencing a sharp fall in their monetary reserves, the Fund is authorized to permit its members to employ such restrictions.

12. Article VII, Sec. 3 of the Fund Agreement provides that before the Fund can declare a currency to be "scarce," the demand for that currency must be such as to threaten the ability of the Fund to supply it. The Fund has been following a cautious lending policy since it began exchange operations in 1946, and hence it has had ample gold and dollars to meet the "legitimate" demands made upon it. It is obvious, of course, that should the Fund liberalize its lending policy, the demand for dollars would soon be great enough to threaten its ability to meet it.

13. Article XII, the General Agreement on Tariffs and Trade.

Transition Period Still Continues

With the exception of the United States, Canada and a few Central American republics all members of the Monetary Fund have availed themselves of the right to continue their exchange and trade restrictions under the escape clause covering the transitional period.[14] While Britain waived her right to invoke the transitional period escape clause (Article XIV) when she signed the Anglo-American Financial Agreement, American recognition of Britain's inability to maintain sterling convertibility in 1947 and the concessions made to Britain at the time of the Anglo-American-Canadian financial discussions in September 1949 [15] largely freed Britain from this obligation of the 1946 loan agreement. Thus until March 1952 the Monetary Fund was not in a position to question seriously the exchange restrictions of its members.

In accordance with the requirements of Article XIV of the Fund Agreement, the Monetary Fund began in the spring of 1952 a series of consultations with its members regarding their exchange restrictions. While the Fund has had some influence on particular restrictive practices here and there, no fundamental change has resulted from these consultations. Before the Fund could require a country to abandon all or a substantial portion of its exchange restrictions it would be necessary to show that its balance of payments position was such that no serious drain of foreign exchange reserves would take place. But most countries would be quite willing to abandon controls under these circumstances. Even where a country might be willing to adopt the policies necessary for the achievement of over-all balance, it may

14. Article XIV of the Fund Agreement provides that "In the postwar transitional period members may, notwithstanding the provisions of any other Articles of this Agreement, maintain and adapt to changing circumstances (and in the case of members whose territories have been occupied by the enemy, introduce where necessary) restrictions on payments and transfers for current international transactions." Article XIV also provides that five years after the Fund begins operations, i.e., March 1952, and each year thereafter, members retaining exchange restrictions inconsistent with other Articles "shall consult the Fund as to their further retention." It is also provided that "The Fund may, if it deems such action necessary in exceptional circumstances, make representations to any member that conditions are favorable for the withdrawal of any particular restrictions, or for the general abandonment of restrictions, inconsistent with the provisions of any other article of the Agreement." The failure to heed such representations would subject the member to forced withdrawal proceedings.

15. See "The British Crisis," *Federal Reserve Bulletin,* September 1947, pp. 1071–82; see also "Text of Three-Power Talks Communique," *Washington Post,* September 13, 1949, p. 9. See also Mikesell, *op. cit.,* pp. 174–77.

be difficult or hazardous to eliminate exchange restrictions unless a number of that country's trading partners do likewise. Thus, for example, a restoration of sterling convertibility is undoubtedly the *sine qua non* for the reduction or removal of exchange and trade restrictions on the part of a large number of the Fund's members.

For the time being the forces which determine whether the free world will move toward or away from a system of multilateral trade and payments and currency convertibility lie outside the Fund and GATT. Power in this field resides largely in three cities: (1) in London where decisions are taken with respect to the sterling area; (2) in Paris where decisions are made regarding the European Payments Union or any possible successor organization; (3) in Washington where financial and political support must be obtained for any major effort in the direction of freeing the world's trade and payments from its shackles. The Fund and GATT have a role to play in any broad program of this type, but because of their limited resources and because they have been largely by-passed by the great powers in the determination of major financial policies, their role can only be an auxiliary one. Meanwhile there is an important job for the Fund and GATT within the context of a world of restrictions and of bilateral and limited multilateral trade. This is the development of fair trading practices and the elimination of certain objectionable and unnecessary features of the present system of trade and payments.

Financial Assistance for Exchange Stability

Both the Monetary Fund and the British Loan Agreement of 1946 provided for financial assistance for exchange stability and convertibility. Such assistance from the Fund was designed to supplement members' monetary reserves to meet foreign exchange drains of a temporary and reversible nature and to enable countries to avoid changes in exchange rates or the imposition of controls in dealing with short-term balance of payments deficits.

From the beginning, however, the Fund has had difficulty in developing a lending policy which would be both consistent with its Charter and realistic in meeting the financial needs of its members. Except for a few cases such as the aid to Mexico in 1949, financial assistance for genuine currency stabilization was out of the question because most members of the Fund were experiencing deep-seated disequilibriums in their balance of payments, unlikely to be corrected over a short period. Since the mechanism for repayment of foreign exchange drawn from the Fund depended largely upon an increase in the members' exchange reserves, large-scale assistance from the Fund under these circumstances would have meant a freezing of its gold and dollar assets in long-term loans to its members.[16] The Fund has therefore followed a fairly cautious lending policy [17] since its inauguration, but the basic dilemma remains: whether to use its resources liberally or husband them for a day when true stabilization assistance will be possible.

In the face of the vast needs of Western Europe and other areas for assistance in reconstructing and reorganizing their economies in order to realize certain economic and political objectives, the Fund's resources were meager. Moreover, the transition period did not turn out to be a shift from the economic disruption caused by war to an era in which the basic conditions for world equilibrium were restored. In spite of tremendous gains in production and trade the world has not made satisfactory progress toward international equilibrium.

The financial provisions of the Anglo-American Loan Agreement designed to restore sterling convertibility were more generous than those of the Fund.[18] The $3.75 billion loan to Britain, repayable over a fifty-year period at 2 per cent interest, was designed to enable that country to meet a major share of her reconstruction needs, to deal with her large short-term sterling indebtedness, and to supplement her dollar reserves by an amount sufficient to restore sterling convertibility. Events have proved that the loan was far from sufficient to enable Britain to deal even with her reconstruction problem. Thus at the end of the Recovery Program in June 1952, after receiving

16. Under the automatic repurchase provisions a member whose currency is held by the Fund in an amount in excess of 75 per cent of its quota, must use 50 per cent of any increase in its monetary reserves for the repurchase of such excess currency holdings from the Fund. (See Article V.)

17. During the period of the European Recovery Program 1948–1952, the Fund adopted a rule which stated in effect that no assistance would be given to ERP members except in extraordinary circumstances. As a consequence very little assistance was made available to Western European countries by the Fund during this period. During the first five years of its operation the Fund maintained a more or less unwritten rule for limiting assistance to any country to 25 per cent of that member's quota. Recent developments in the Fund's lending policies are discussed in Part IV.

18. The United States subscription to the Monetary Fund is only $2.8 billion and the total gold and dollar subscriptions to the Fund, by all countries, was less than $3.6 billion as of June 30, 1952.

several billions of dollars of ERP aid, Britain experienced a serious financial crisis, and had only a slender margin of foreign exchange reserves.

INTERNATIONAL TRADE POLICY AND ECONOMIC NATIONALISM

Perhaps the basic reason for the failure of the international monetary and trade agreements to achieve their postwar objectives lies in the conflict between the philosophy of economic liberalism and free trade embodied in the trade and financial agreements, and the economic policies of the majority of the signatories. Some attempts were made in the proposed ITO Charter and in GATT to reconcile this conflict. For example GATT provides for exceptions to the fundamental rules with regard to the use of quantitative import restrictions, which would permit a continued subsidization of domestic agriculture.[19]

The Basic Causes of Failure

Many causes have been assigned for the inability of the postwar agreements to achieve their basic objectives. It is true that the postwar planners grossly underestimated the difficulties of economic reconstruction, nor were they able to foresee the political events which split the world into two armed camps and the economic repercussions of that division. On the other hand, the international economic climate has been in many ways far better than the planners anticipated. The widely heralded postwar depression in the United States did not occur and the country's levels of imports and foreign investment have been high and reasonably stable. The volume of foreign aid for postwar reconstruction has been generous and economic recovery in most countries is virtually complete.

The most significant cause of the failure of the postwar monetary and trade agreements is the fact that the nations whose representatives formulated the liberal trading policies underlying them were unable to accept the disciplines necessary to permit these policies to work. Nevertheless the agreements have been continually on the conscience of the United States, whose own international economic poli-

19. See GATT, Article XI; see also *The Havana Charter for an International Trade Organization,* Chapter 3.

cies they in large measure reflect, as well as on the conscience of those nations which for one reason or another could not live up to their solemn undertakings.

The failure to realize their fundamental objectives does not mean that the Monetary Fund and the GATT have not achieved significant results in a limited sphere or that they will not have important roles in the future. These organizations have more than justified their existence by deterring harmful trade restrictions by their members, by giving technical advice, and by providing a forum for reducing tensions among members. Their possible roles in the development of a more orderly trading community in the future will be discussed in later chapters.

Chapter 3

THE EMERGING PATTERN OF TRADE
AND PAYMENTS

THE ACTUAL COURSE of history has rarely followed the paths indicated by the broad statements of good intentions by the world's leaders. Governmental actions are determined more by events and by short-run expediency than by adherence to long-run policy pronouncements. This has been particularly true in the field of international economics in the postwar period. We must therefore seek an explanation as to how and why the present system of international payments developed, not through an examination of long-run policy statements and international agreements, but rather from an analysis of basic economic and political conditions.

At the close of World War II nearly all the countries of the world except the United States and a few Central American republics maintained exchange controls.[1] Even before the war most of the South American countries had employed controls of one degree or another, but in the case of Britain and the sterling area, the countries of Western Europe, and Canada, the exchange controls were generally regarded as temporary wartime measures.[2] The belief that trade and exchange restrictions could be removed gradually after the close of hostilities was based on the expectation of a rather speedy return to prewar economic conditions. These expectations were doomed for three basic reasons: (1) the resources required for reconstruction were grossly underestimated; (2) the war had more or less perma-

1. Even the United States had a form of exchange control designed to immobilize the assets of enemy and enemy-occupied territories and of certain individuals in neutral countries who were known to carry on trade with the enemy.

2. It should be pointed out that there were influential people in England who believed that the sterling area controls should be maintained indefinitely as a means of providing a protected market that would be free from the influence of American depressions. These forces were temporarily defeated when the British Parliament ratified the Anglo-American Financial Agreement and accepted membership in the Monetary Fund and International Bank in December 1945.

nently altered the postwar pattern of trade and payments; (3) no one anticipated the economic impact of the new social and political forces both in Western Europe and in other areas.

The immediate problem of Britain and Western Europe was to restore trade. The German-based clearing network was swept away by the liberation, and the restored governments of Western Europe were not interested in pooling their dollar resources with Britain to form an expanded sterling area. The goods most desperately needed by all the belligerent countries could only be purchased with dollars in the Western Hemisphere. These countries were therefore unwilling to use their precious gold and dollars to buy from one another, except for a few commodities regarded as "dollar goods." Even before the liberation, plans were laid by the governments in exile (largely in London) for a restoration of trade under bilateral payments agreements.

The Network of Bilateral Payments Agreements

The first postwar bilateral payments agreement to come into operation was the Anglo-Belgian Agreement of October 5, 1944.[3] This, which became something of a model for many other payments agreements, was followed by the rapid development of a vast network of bilateral agreements linking together the countries of Western Europe, not only among themselves but with most of the other nondollar countries of the world.

Governments were drawn into this web of payments agreements for one of two reasons: they may have been short of gold and dollars and hence unwilling to buy from nondollar countries with convertible currencies; or alternatively, they may have had plenty of gold and dollars but sought to maintain markets for their exports in nondollar countries. The latter was clearly the case with Switzerland and with certain Latin American countries.[4]

The bilateral agreements varied considerably in detail, but certain basic features were common to most of them. First of all they estab-

---

3. *Monetary Agreement between the United Kingdom of Great Britain and Northern Ireland and the Government of Belgium,* October 1944, Cmd. 6557, H.M.S.O., London, 1944.

4. It is estimated that about 200 bilateral monetary agreements were in effect by March 1947. See *Seventeenth Annual Report,* Bank for International Settlements, Basel, 1947, p. 75.

lished an exchange rate for transactions between the partner countries and provided for some form of consultation or accord before a
rate change could be made by either party. The rates defined in the
bilateral agreements were generally consistent with one another, thus
making for a uniform pattern of cross-rates. However, some countries
including Greece, Italy and France at one time or another had legal
free rates for the dollar which violated the cross-rates in the bilateral
agreements. With the inauguration of operations by the Monetary
Fund in March 1947 most member countries established gold parities
with the Fund and multilateral arrangements largely replaced the
bilateral ones for consultation and accord on exchange rates.

Anglo-Belgian Agreement: Settlement of Net Deficits

The most significant feature of the postwar bilateral monetary
agreements was the machinery for making payments for current transactions.[5] The typical bilateral payments agreement provided that each
country would sell its own currency in exchange for the currency of
the other country up to a certain limit or in some cases without limit.
For example, under the Anglo-Belgian agreement Belgian importers
would obtain from their own banks drafts on London banks to pay
for imports from the sterling area. The Central Bank of Belgium
could replenish its sterling holdings by purchasing sterling from the
Bank of England, up to £5 million on credit. Further net purchases
had to be made with gold.

Conversely, British importers could obtain drafts on Belgian banks
from the British banking system or they could remit in sterling. The
Bank of England could obtain Belgian francs from the Central Bank
of Belgium up to £5 million (or BF 883,125,000) or the Central
Bank of Belgium would buy sterling acquired by Belgian exporters
from sales to the sterling area. Net holdings of sterling by the
Central Bank of Belgium (beyond minimum balances of £100,000)
would be added to Belgium's net credit to Britain or subtracted
from Britain's net credit to Belgium. Again, credits extended by
Belgium to Britain could not exceed £5 million. These credit limits
were sometimes spoken of as the "gold points" since when a country's

---

5. In most cases countries prohibit capital movements not related to the financing of
current transactions. However, since exchange controls are never perfect, substantial
amounts of capital transactions are undoubtedly financed under the agreements.

net deficit to a partner exceeded the limits of credit extension it was required to cover any additional deficit in gold.

Some bilateral agreements did not provide for any formal limits to the mutual sales of currency over the life of the arrangement. This was true of the British bilateral agreements with Denmark, Norway and Sweden early in the postwar period.[6] It is significant that these three countries later became members of the transferable account group, an important prerequisite for membership being a willingness to accept sterling payments without limit and without demanding liquidation of sterling holdings in gold.

Where one of the pairs of currencies involved was considered too unstable or otherwise unsuitable for international payments, the bilateral agreement provided for maintaining accounts in one currency only. Thus in the case of the Anglo-Finnish agreement (August 1945) transactions were conducted in sterling.

Trade-Quota Agreements: Restrictive Effects

Another significant feature of these agreements was the fact that currency balances acquired by one country through trade or through an extension of credits by the partner could only be used for financing current trade with the currency area of the other country. It was this circumstance that gave the agreements their bilateral character since it was ordinarily not possible to use a currency surplus with one bilateral partner to discharge a deficit with another. This meant that in order to avoid gold payments when the credit limits were reached, or to avoid an indefinite extension of credits or large indebtedness to any one country—which would eventually lead to a breakdown of the agreement—countries had to achieve an approximate bilateral balance in their current trade.

This was accomplished by a bilateral commodity or trade-quota agreement usually drawn up on an annual basis. A typical trade-quota agreement provided for the issuance of import licenses by each country for lists of commodities to be purchased in the partner country and for purchases by state trading organizations of each country in

6. For a summary of the bilateral payments and financial agreements in the early postwar period see Judd Polk and Gardner Patterson, "The Emerging Pattern of Bilateralism," *Quarterly Journal of Economics*, November 1947, pp. 118–42; see also the annual *Reports* of the Bank for International Settlements.

the other, so negotiated as to achieve an approximate balance in trade. Frequently the agreements included the amounts which each country would allow its citizens to spend in the other for tourism and other services.

Not only did these bilateral trade-quota agreements rule out a certain amount of economical trade which could only take place on a multilateral basis, but some of the actual trade was uneconomical. Thus, in order to find markets for certain of its exports, a country might be required to issue import licenses for goods which it could ill afford to buy or which, perhaps, could be obtained more cheaply elsewhere. Frequently nations would be required to purchase luxuries in order to obtain essential commodities from another country. This practice of tied-sales arose from the existence of severe shortages of certain essential commodities in the nondollar countries after the war.

Multilateral Aspects

It should not be thought that the bilateral payments and trade arrangements completely excluded multilateral trade and settlements in the early postwar period. Countries frequently developed bilateral deficits above the credit margins provided for in the bilateral payments agreements and were consequently required to pay gold or dollars. Thus gold and dollar settlements between European governments amounted to $550 million in 1947 and $437 million in 1948.[7] There were also multilateral dollar settlements by European countries with non-European countries other than the United States. Thus it is estimated that the European Recovery Program (ERP) countries made net gold and dollar payments to countries other than the United States totaling $327 million in 1946, $2,740 million in 1947 and $1,947 million in 1948.[8]

The fact that the bilateral payments agreements covered trade between two monetary areas each of which frequently included several countries and territories tended to widen the trading area beyond the two countries directly negotiating the agreement. Thus, the British bilateral agreements covered all the independent nations and depend-

7. *Balance of Payments Yearbook, 1948,* International Monetary Fund, Washington, 1950, pp. 36–37.

8. *The Balance of International Payments of the United States, 1946–48,* U.S. Department of Commerce, 1950, p. 174.

ent territories which constitute the sterling area; the Belgian agreements covered Luxembourg and the territories of the Belgian empire;
and the French and Dutch agreements covered the overseas possessions of these countries. The possibilities of multilateral settlement
were expanded further by the establishment by Britain of the transferable account system in 1947. Still another avenue for multilateral
trade within the bilateral payments network was the possibility of one
country making purchases in another country for export to a third.[9]
While some of the agreements specifically excluded the financing of
re-exports, most of the bilateral agreements permitted the financing
of entrepôt trade.

Why Bilateral Agreements Were Necessary

Considering the economic and financial conditions in most European countries immediately after the war the bilateral agreements
must be looked upon as instruments for facilitating trade rather than
as restrictive devices. The restoration of currency convertibility with
freely fluctuating rates in the face of swollen currencies and extreme
shortages would probably have led to hyperinflation in all European
countries except the few wartime neutrals. Such a result could have
been avoided only by internal monetary and fiscal measures so stringent that no government would be willing to undertake them. Alternatively, each nation might have controlled its trade with its European neighbors and other soft-currency countries as rigidly as it did
with hard-currency countries. Such a policy, however, would have
kept intra-European trade and trade among all nondollar countries
at a low level.

Two conditions were necessary to restore trade among nondollar
countries. First, a means had to be found whereby countries could
make payments for imports in their own currencies without being
required to pay gold or dollars urgently required for imports from
hard-currency areas. Second, there was a need for sufficient liquidity
in the payments system to permit temporary swings in the bilateral
balances between countries. By meeting these two requirements, the
bilateral payments agreements served to introduce a measure of
freedom in trade between pairs of countries. Since most of the parties

9. See Polk and Patterson, *loc. cit.*, p. 131.

to these agreements were represented at the Bretton Woods Conference and subsequently joined the Monetary Fund, the majority of the bilateral agreements contained clauses providing for renegotiation in the event that they were inconsistent with the obligations of either party to the Monetary Fund.

Trade Not Bilaterally Balanced

In spite of the efforts to keep trade in bilateral balance through agreements governing the issuance of import and export licenses and purchases by state trading organizations, trade continually ran into difficulty through the exhaustion of credit margins. By the end of 1946 European countries had extended a total of more than $500 million in credits to one another [10] and by the end of 1947 the total credits outstanding had increased to $1,500 million.[11] While a considerable part of the gross credits could have been eliminated by offsetting bilateral debits against bilateral credits, certain countries such as Belgium and Switzerland tended to have large net credit positions. Some relief was granted by a consolidation and funding of current debts and the granting of new credits so that trade could go on. However, the growing severity of the dollar shortage—particularly acute after the suspensions of sterling convertibility in August 1947 —tended to reduce the willingness of European debtors to pay gold or dollars after the credit limits had been reached. This fact, combined with the reluctance of creditors to provide further credits under the payments agreements, threatened a substantial reduction in trade before the advent of the European Recovery Program.

THE POSTWAR CURRENCY AREAS

When the European powers were developing their empires during the 18th and 19th centuries they introduced into the colonial territories currency systems based on the currencies of the metropolitan countries. They also established trading banks which were owned and controlled by the mother country and which financed trade between the dependent territory and the rest of the empire with the currency of the mother country. When these colonial empires began

10. *Seventeenth Annual Report,* Bank for International Settlements, p. 128.
11. *Eighteenth Annual Report,* Bank for International Settlements, p. 145.

to break up the currency ties usually remained, although in a sub-stantially modified form. Thus when the Western European powers adopted exchange controls during and following World War II, trade and payments tended to remain free between the metropolitan countries and certain other territories or countries, some of which had become politically independent. Since trade within these groups is financed with the currency of the metropolitan country they have come to be called currency areas.

The principal currency areas in existence immediately following the war were the sterling area which included the British Dominions (except Canada and Newfoundland), certain formerly dependent territories such as Burma, Egypt and Iraq and a few other independent countries; the French franc area which included Lebanon, Syria and Indochina; the Dutch monetary area which included Indonesia; and the Belgium-Luxembourg monetary union which included Belgium's overseas possessions. These currency areas do not have unitary exchange control systems since each politically independent member and many a dependent member has its own exchange control authority. The relationship between independent members of the group is usually loose and informal and it may differ substantially as between individual members of the group.

Common Features of These Areas

While these currency areas are by no means uniform, they have certain features in common. First, there are fewer restrictions on payments for current trade and capital between members of the currency area than on the trade of individual members and the outside world. The basic reason is that all members are willing to accept from one another the currency of the metropolitan country without limit and most individual members possessed an abundant supply of that currency at the end of the war. Second, bilateral payments agreements entered into by the metropolitan country with other nations provide for the financing of mutual trade between their currency areas. A third characteristic of these currency areas is that they usually involve some pooling of their foreign exchange reserves.[12] The pooling of

12. This is not true in the case of Indonesia which, although a member of the Dutch monetary area, does not pool dollar resources with the Netherlands. Neither can it be said to be true of South Africa, a member of the sterling area.

gold and dollar reserves presents the most serious problem for the maintenance of the currency areas since this requires a degree of cooperation difficult to achieve among politically independent countries. The failure to discover an adequate formula for distributing gold and dollar earnings presents the chief threat to the continued existence of the sterling area as it is presently constituted.

The Sterling Area

Of the several currency areas existing at the close of World War II, the sterling area is by far the largest and the most important. Britain was obligated under the Anglo-American Financial Agreement of 1946 to remove restrictions on the use of sterling for making payments arising out of current transactions with any other country or currency area.[13] Britain, however, had no intention of destroying the sterling area as such. Britain expected that controls over capital movements out of the sterling area would continue to be restricted by individual sterling area members but that capital might continue its fairly free flow within the sterling area itself. Britain also expected that individual sterling area members would continue to turn over to London banks their surplus earnings of gold, dollars and other convertible currencies and to control their hard-currency purchases with a view to maintaining the solvency of the area.[14]

Another factor that tended to hold the sterling area together was the large sterling balances owned by members of the area. One of the provisions of the loan agreement [15] stated Britain's intention to fund

13. The availability of sterling balances for making payments arising out of current transactions meant that holders of sterling could use it to make payments for goods and services, interest and dividends, amortization payments and other current transactions as defined by the Articles of Agreement of the Monetary Fund (Article XIX) but that they could not employ sterling to acquire foreign securities, capital assets, gold or currency balances (not required for the making of current payments).

14. Britain herself was prohibited from discriminating against the United States in her trade restrictions but this prohibition did not extend to other members of the sterling area. Moreover, the nondiscrimination clause (Section 9 of the Agreement) was so vague as to permit a considerable latitude in Britain's trade policy with respect to the United States. For example, the Agreement said nothing specifically regarding the practice of making long-term bulk purchase contracts by the British government, which at the time constituted about 60 per cent of British imports.

15. Section 10 of "The Financial Agreement Between the Governments of the United States and the United Kingdom" stated Britain's intention to reach settlements with the sterling area countries "on the basis of dividing these accumulated balances into three categories: (a) balances to be released at once and convertible into any currency for cur-

a portion of these balances and to release them over a period of years, beginning in 1951. But the holders of these balances considered them to be demand obligations and opposed formal funding. Britain did, however, "block" a portion of the sterling balances and other sterling assets of some members of the area and of certain nonsterling countries as well.[16] The sterling holdings of Australia, New Zealand, Ireland and South Africa were not blocked, since these countries were expected to cooperate with Britain in limiting purchases from the dollar area and from other nonsterling countries. In summary, Britain expected that sterling convertibility as required by the Loan Agreement would modify the sterling area but that it would not destroy it or even reduce it to the status of the loose and informal sterling bloc of the 1930s.

The Transferable Account Countries

In accordance with the provisions of the Loan Agreement, Britain was also required to renegotiate her bilateral payments agreements with countries outside the sterling area. Just as Britain wanted to avoid destroying the sterling area in the process of making sterling convertible for current transactions, so also did she want to retain her bilateral payments agreements on a modified basis. Most of the countries with which Britain had negotiated bilateral payments agreements held substantial sterling balances. In some cases a portion was blocked under the new agreements, but a substantial share was permitted to be held in No. 1 (free) accounts which were available for making payments in current transactions with any other country, including countries in the dollar area.

The new agreements negotiated following the signing of the Anglo-American Financial Agreement on July 15, 1946, gave rise to a new category of sterling balances known as "transferable accounts."

---

rent transactions; (b) balances to be similarly released by installments over a period of years beginning in 1951; and (c) balances to be adjusted as a contribution to the settlement of war and postwar indebtedness and in recognition of the benefits which the countries concerned might be expected to gain from such a settlement."

Except for £10 million which was written off by Australia, Britain was not successful in achieving adjustments indicated in (c) above.

16. "Blocked" balances cannot be used for current transactions except as they are released from so-called No. 2 (blocked) accounts to No. 1 (free) accounts by action of the British Treasury. At the end of 1947, out of a total of £3,573 million in sterling holdings owned outside of Britain, £1,860 million were blocked or restricted. "The Sterling Balances," *The Economist*, May 13, 1950, p. 1075.

These agreements with nonsterling area countries included the following provisions: (1) Britain agreed to permit transfers from the transferable account of one country to that of another transferable account country or from a transferable account to an American account,[17] provided the transfers were to finance current transactions (noncapital) and provided the country would report such transactions to the Bank of England; (2) the transferable account country agreed to accept without limit or restriction sterling from the sterling area or from other transferable account countries in payment for current transactions; (3) the transferable account country agreed to adopt controls necessary to prevent transfers to nonresident accounts of a capital nature.[18]

Most of the new agreements were with countries with whom Britain had negotiated bilateral payments agreements prior to 1946. By mid-July 1947 the transferable account system included Argentina, the Belgian monetary area, Brazil, Canada and Newfoundland, Czechoslovakia, Egypt and the Sudan,[19] Ethiopia, Finland, Iran, Italy and Vatican City, the Netherlands monetary area, Norway, the Portuguese monetary area, Spain, Sweden and Uruguay.

So far as Britain was concerned, the primary purpose of these agreements was to limit the convertibility of balances currently held or subsequently acquired by the transferable account country to payments arising out of current trade. Thus while Argentina could, under the terms of her agreement, transfer sterling to an American account in payment for imports from the United States, transfers for the purpose of acquiring dollars or gold were prohibited. The agreements also assured Britain that sterling would be acceptable by other countries in payment for their exports, whether the sterling came from the sterling area, the American account countries or other transferable account countries.

17. As was pointed out in Chapter 1, American account sterling was freely marketable in New York and other free markets against dollars and other convertible currencies and the British Treasury maintained its market value within a narrow range of parity—$4.03 from September 1939 to September 1949.

18. *Seventeenth Annual Report,* Bank for International Settlements, pp. 78–80; see also J. Burke Knapp and F. M. Tamagna, "Sterling in Multilateral Trade," *Federal Reserve Bulletin,* September 1947, pp. 1088–98.

19. Egypt and the Sudan had left the sterling area in July 1947. Egyptian currency (National Bank of Egypt notes) circulates in the Sudan.

Why Sterling Convertibility Failed

Had Britain been able to maintain the convertibility of sterling the transferable account system would have gone far toward solving the problem of the acute shortage of international liquidity in the early postwar period. Many countries in both Hemispheres tended to be long on sterling, but they might have been willing to maintain a substantial portion of their foreign exchange reserves in sterling (as they did before the war) provided they were assured of its stability and convertibility into dollars. On the other hand, Britain would have been able to meet short-term deficits with countries outside the dollar area through an extension of her sterling liabilities, so long as the sterling balances acquired by the nondollar countries were not immediately converted into dollars. Unfortunately the attempt to restore convertibility failed.

There were many reasons for this failure. The basic factors were (1) the inability of Britain to maintain an over-all balance in her current international accounts; (2) the urgent need on the part of the sterling area and transferable account countries for imports which were only available in the United States and Canada; (3) the inability of Britain to compete with dollar countries in the sale of such goods as Britain had for sale in world markets; (4) the rapid drawing down of sterling balances for purchases in dollar markets by members of the sterling area and the transferable account group; (5) the lack of confidence in sterling, coupled with the failure of many countries, including Argentina, to abide by or enforce their agreements with Britain with respect to the use of sterling for capital transactions.

The suspension of sterling convertibility on August 20, 1947, meant that the sterling balances of the transferable account countries were no longer valid for making payments to the United States and to other American account countries. This resulted in the withdrawal from the transferable account system of countries unwilling to accept sterling unconditionally without the right of using it to make purchases in the dollar area. Canada and Newfoundland withdrew immediately on August 20, 1947 and a number of other countries including Belgium, Italy,[20] Portugal, Argentina, Brazil, and Uruguay soon left the transferable group. The remaining transferable account

20. Italy subsequently rejoined the transferable account system.

countries, including (as of June 1948) Czechoslovakia, the Dutch monetary area, Egypt, Ethiopia, Finland, Iran, Norway, Poland, Siam, Spain, the Sudan, Sweden and the USSR, continued to accept sterling from the sterling area and from one another without limit in payment for current transactions. The countries that left the transferable account system did so for the most part because they were unwilling to accept sterling without limit from the sterling area and from other members of the transferable group.[21]

Most of these countries, plus a number of countries which never were transferable account members, have bilateral payments agreements with Britain but these do not provide for automatic transferability privileges. They are known as bilateral agreement countries. The bilateral agreement (November 1947) with Belgium provided for a ceiling on inconvertible sterling of £27 million to be held by Belgium; any amounts accumulated beyond this sum had to be converted into gold by the British Treasury.[22] Canada also accepted sterling in payment for exports to the sterling area but required conversion into dollars of accumulations above normal working balances.[23]

EARLY POSTWAR ARRANGEMENTS IN LATIN AMERICA

The countries of Central and northern South America usually fall in the dollar group and hence remit and receive payments in dollars or in American account sterling; while the southern Latin American republics tend to fall in the soft-currency group and conduct their trade with Europe and with one another through bilateral payments arrangements. The latter group of countries has therefore become an integral part of the network of bilateral payments agreements which emanated from Western Europe in the early postwar period.

During World War II, the trade of all Latin American countries shifted substantially from Europe to the United States. But owing to the shortage of shipping and of commodities these countries had substantial export surpluses during the war with a consequent increase

---

21. In some cases countries are not members of the transferable group because Britain cannot rely on their maintaining exchange controls which will assure adherence to the conditions of the agreement.

22. *Eighteenth Annual Report,* Bank for International Settlements, p. 97.

23. Sterling held by Canadian Exchange Fund Account at the end of 1948 amounted to $7.9 million. *Annual Report of the Foreign Exchange Control Board, 1948,* Canadian Finance Ministry, Ottawa, March 1949.

in their gold and dollar holdings.[24] Throughout the war the Latin American republics also had active trade balances with Britain and the sterling area. Transactions of the sterling area with the Central American states and Colombia, Venezuela and Ecuador were financed through the Central American account system which in 1945 was merged with the American account system and these accounts became convertible into dollars.

The wartime sterling surpluses of Argentina, Brazil and Uruguay, however, resulted in the accumulation of inconvertible sterling balances which amounted to £137 million in June 1945.[25] Although these sterling balances continued to rise after the war, they were reduced by the repayment of long-term sterling debts owed to British citizens and the purchase of British-owned public utilities operating in these countries. By December 1949 the sterling holdings of these three countries had been reduced to £88 million.

Latin American Agreements with Europe

During 1946-1949 Latin American countries entered into over forty bilateral agreements with European countries, most of them of the payments agreement type.[26] Three fourths of these agreements were negotiated by the southern Latin American countries, and of these fifteen were negotiated by Argentina.[27] Nearly all the Latin American countries outside the American account system had payments agreements with Britain. After a short period of membership in the transferable account system in 1947, Argentina and Brazil became bilateral countries in May 1948. Chile is now the only Latin American country in the transferable account system.

The agreements negotiated by Argentina, Brazil and certain other Latin American countries with the nations of Europe are frequently

24. Gold and short-term dollar holdings of Latin American countries rose from $963 million at the close of 1938 to $3,652 million on June 30, 1945. *First Semiannual Report,* Export-Import Bank of Washington, 1946, p. 41.

25. "The Sterling Balances," *The Economist,* May 13, 1950, p. 1076.

26. Some of the agreements covered lists of products to be traded in an effort to achieve equilibrium; others were compensation or outright barter agreements. See "Multilateral Compensation of International Payments in Latin America" (mimeograph), Economic Commission for Latin America, UN Economic and Social Council, New York, May 1949, Appendix II, for summaries of Latin American postwar trade and payments agreements.

27. The Latin American countries negotiating agreements with European countries included Argentina (15), Brazil (11), Chile (3), Colombia (3), Mexico (2), Peru (1), Paraguay (1) and Uruguay (7).

detailed, covering a number of items of trade and finance. For example, the Anglo-Argentine agreement of September 1946 provided for the sale to Argentina of British-owned railroads, and for the sale of Argentine meat to Britain. The Franco-Argentine agreement of December 1946 also provided for the sale of French railroad holdings in Argentina as a means of liquidating French commercial debts. The Franco-Argentine payments agreement of July 1947 provided for a unilateral credit of 600 million pesos to be granted by Argentina with accounts kept in francs. A commercial agreement between the two countries concluded on the same date set forth the import quotas for lists of commodities to be traded. It was designed to balance trade between the two countries.

Bilateral Agreements within Latin America

In addition to bilateral trade and payments agreements with European countries a number of Latin American countries are linked by similar arrangements among themselves. Intra-Latin American trade —only 6 per cent of total Latin American trade in 1938—increased substantially during the war, principally because of the lack of goods from other sources. Before 1946 this trade was for the most part financed in dollars.

When gold and dollar reserves accumulated during the war began to decline, some Latin American countries became reluctant to use their dollars for purchases within Latin America and resorted to bilateral agreements as a means of maintaining trade. This was particularly true of the southern countries since, unlike those of the north, they were unable to obtain dollars for their exports to Europe. During 1946-1948 Argentina concluded payments agreements with Brazil, Chile, Bolivia, Paraguay and Uruguay. The agreement with Paraguay provided for payments in sterling under a special arrangement with Britain. Brazil also negotiated payments agreements with Bolivia, Chile, Uruguay and Paraguay. In addition a payments agreement was negotiated between Colombia and Ecuador although both these countries conducted most of their international trade in dollars.

While most Latin American countries retained exchange controls throughout the war there was little need for severe restrictions on imports until after the war when industrial goods again became available in substantial quantities on world markets. Many of the Central

American countries have either maintained no controls or only mild ones in the postwar period.

The southern Latin American countries have tended to keep tight controls over trade through both exchange restrictions and import licensing. The need for such controls is due partly to inflationary conditions in these countries and partly to export surpluses with Europe financed by inconvertible currencies. Although Latin American countries have employed various trade controls—import and export licensing, limitations on access to foreign exchange, tariffs, and exchange taxes—they have resorted to multiple exchange rates rather more than most other countries. Frequently it has been easier for administrative reasons to control their trade by varying the cost of foreign exchange than through more direct measures.

The postwar Latin American exchange systems represent in large measure a continuation of prewar practices. They are not, as in the case of the exchange systems of Western Europe, a heritage of the war. The world conflict did not impair the productive capacities of the Latin American republics and the demand for their products has been far higher and more stable than before the war. To some extent it may be said that the unwillingness or inability of the European countries to pay dollars or convertible currencies for the exports of the South American countries forced them into the web of European bilateralism. On the other hand, considering the seller's market which has characterized most Latin American exports during the postwar period, Latin America probably could have demanded dollars for her products. Certainly the basic factor in Latin American exchange and trade policies has been the inflationary forces generated by the monetary, fiscal and investment policies of these countries.

THE FAR EAST

Most of the countries of the Far East outside of China and Japan have until recently been colonial areas with close political and financial ties with Western Europe. While the war greatly hastened the process of independence from Europe, most of the Far Eastern countries emerged from the war with their currencies closely tied to Western Europe. For example, the newly independent countries of Burma, Ceylon, India and Pakistan are in the sterling area; Indonesia, which became independent in 1949, remained in the Netherlands monetary area; and the Associated States of Cambodia, Laos and Vietnam (formerly French Indochina) are in the franc area. Thailand is a transferable account country while Taiwan, China and Japan have bilateral agreements with Britain.

Local currencies are not generally used in international trade but the monetary ties with Western currencies have tended to simplify the problem of payments transfers between the Far Eastern countries themselves and the outside world. Thus, Far Eastern members of the sterling area are not only able to use sterling as a means of financing trade among themselves but they can finance their trade with neighboring members of the Dutch or French monetary areas under the mechanisms provided by the Anglo-Dutch and Anglo-French payments agreements.

The end of the war found the Japanese-occupied areas of the Far East, as well as Japan herself, devastated by war and in great need of consumers' goods and capital for reconstruction. Even in the non-occupied countries, as for example India, there was a heavy demand for foreign goods owing to the widespread currency inflation and the low volume of imports during the war. Moreover, the far-reaching social and political changes in these countries during the war and early postwar period increased the demands for imports, including capital goods for economic development. This created wide disparities between the demand for and the supply of foreign exchange. While some of these countries, including India and Ceylon, had sizable sterling reserves, these were only partially available for purchases in the dollar area. Hence, both because of the lack of balance in their own international accounts and because of their membership in European currency areas, the countries of the Far East found it necessary to maintain exchange and trade controls after the war.

As was the case with many Latin American countries, the countries of the Far East became a part of the network of payments emanating from Western Europe. The Far Eastern members of European currency areas did not as a rule negotiate payments agreements of their own but financed their trade through accounts established under the agreements entered into by the Western European powers. However, the Far Eastern countries have tended to negotiate their own bilateral commodity agreements. These follow the Western European pattern of providing for the issuing of import and export licenses for lists of commodities with the objective of balancing trade between the partner countries.

China, Japan and the Philippines

Three important Far Eastern countries—China, Japan [28] and the Philippines—had no close currency ties with Western Europe. China's early postwar trade and payments arrangements were so greatly affected by the civil war and by her generally disorganized system of monetary controls as to defy any attempts to classify them.[29] With the overthrow of the Nationalist government on the mainland, Communist China became identified with the trade and payments system of Eastern Europe under the leadership of the USSR.

For a time after the Allied occupation in September 1945, Japan was in effect a monetary extension of the dollar area. Although the Supreme Commander for the Allied Powers (SCAP) negotiated agreements with the sterling area and with other monetary areas, the Japanese monetary authorities held only small working balances of nondollar currencies and demanded conversion into dollars of balances above a minimum level. More recently, however, Japan's payments agreements with the sterling area and other currency areas have afforded more liberal credit terms.

Before the war the Philippine peso was backed 100 per cent by dollars and was freely convertible into the dollar. Although these currency reserves were rapidly drained away after the war, the Philippines remained in the "dollar area" [30] and did not institute exchange controls until December 1949.

THE SOVIET SATELLITE COUNTRIES

Before the war the Central and Eastern European countries, unlike most countries of Western Europe, maintained exchange controls and conducted most of their nondollar trade through clearing and payments agreements. During the war such trade as took place was

28. For a short period during the 1930s the Japanese yen was linked to sterling and some writers have regarded Japan as a member of the sterling bloc.

29. China negotiated a bilateral payments agreement with Britain and with certain other countries before the Nationalist government was forced to flee from the mainland.

30. The "dollar area" includes the countries of North America, Bolivia, Colombia, Ecuador, Venezuela, Cuba, Dominican Republic, Haiti and the Philippine Republic. With few exceptions these countries pay for their imports in dollars or convertible currencies and require dollars or convertible currencies in payment for their exports.

financed through the German-controlled clearing system. After the Russian occupation the trade of these countries [31] came under more or less complete Soviet domination and trade with the West was discouraged in favor of trade with the USSR. Trade within the Soviet orbit has been influenced to a large degree by reparations and the transfer of profits of Soviet-owned enterprises which were taken over on the alleged grounds that they were owned by Germans. Large amounts of capital equipment were also taken from Germany after the war.[32] Trade within the Soviet satellite group, which after 1949 has included Communist China, has been conducted largely by state trading organizations and financed under barter arrangements with accounts kept in dollars or in rubles.

Most of the satellite countries have negotiated payments agreements with the countries of Western Europe. But because the trade of the Eastern European countries is conducted by state enterprises and rigidly tied to bilaterally balanced commodity trade agreements, the financial arrangements lack the flexible character of the payments agreements between Western European countries.

Nearly all the Soviet-orbit countries have payments agreements with Britain, and Czechoslovakia and the USSR are members of the transferable account group. For reasons which will be explained in Chapter 15 the currencies of the USSR and its satellites are not international currencies and are not used in international trade except as artificial units of account. The Soviet authorities apparently intend to form a kind of ruble bloc as a counterpart of the Economic Mutual Assistance Program announced in January 1949.[33] There is, however, little evidence that Russia has established a system of multilateral settlements for the Soviet orbit based on transfers of ruble credits in Moscow.

OTHER COUNTRIES

Certain countries of the world do not fit readily into a particular payments category. Good examples are Switzerland and Canada,

31. Czechoslovakian trade did not come under complete Soviet domination until 1949. Until that time Czechoslovakia carried on more or less normal trade relations with Western Europe and participated in the network of payments agreements.

32. Reparations collected by the USSR have been estimated at from $4 to $5 billion, up to the end of 1950. See Harry Schwartz, *Russia's Soviet Economy*, Prentice-Hall, New York, 1950, p. 517.

33. *The New York Times*, January 26, 1949.

before Canada abolished her exchange controls in 1951.[34] Both countries emerged from the war with strong currencies enjoying a substantial degree of convertibility with the U.S. dollar. Both, however, maintained bilateral payments and trade agreements with nondollar nations. Following the war Canada entered into a bilateral payments agreement with Britain which provided for payments from the sterling area to be made in Canadian account sterling, in Canadian dollars held in special accounts,[35] or in U.S. dollars. Canada also entered into bilateral arrangements with certain other countries whereby Canada's exports and imports could be financed through Canadian dollar accounts.[36] Exports to all countries other than to the sterling area or to the special arrangement countries were paid for in dollars. While Canadian sterling holdings in excess of a mimimum working level were convertible into U.S. dollars, Canada made substantial postwar loans to Britain for financing her exports to that country.

The system of special Canadian accounts which were not convertible into U.S. dollars introduced an element of bilateralism into Canada's international transactions. The degree of bilateralism depended upon the extent to which Canada and her trading partners discriminated in favor of one another in their trade negotiations. Canadian exchange restrictions affecting trade with the dollar area were relatively mild. Capital exports were controlled but foreign exchange was automatically granted for authorized imports. Some imports required licenses but after 1950 most of them could be imported freely from the dollar area or any other country.

Strength of the Swiss Franc

From the standpoint of her gold and dollar reserves and general balance of payments position Switzerland has one of the strongest currencies in the world. During the postwar period Switzerland has discouraged capital imports as an anti-inflation measure while capital

34. Canada removed nearly all of her import restrictions in January 1951 and abolished all exchange controls in December 1951.

35. These special accounts were of two types: (a) those of sterling area residents and (b) those of residents of special arrangement countries. See *Second Annual Report on Exchange Restrictions*, International Monetary Fund, 1951, p. 59.

36. Countries with which Canada negotiated special payments arrangements included Austria, Belgian monetary area, Czechoslovakia, Denmark, Egypt, French franc area, Israel, Italy, Netherlands monetary area, Norway, Sweden and the Sudan. *Ibid.*

exports to the dollar area can be freely effected. Any exchange restrictions imposed by Switzerland for limiting imports have been undertaken for purely commercial reasons, not to safeguard her balance of payments.

Switzerland began negotiating bilateral trade and payments agreements with other countries as early as 1931 and in 1951 there were twenty-four such agreements in force.[37] Swiss exchange controls therefore exist primarily for the purpose of implementing the nation's bilateral trade and payments agreements. Exchange proceeds of exports to bilateral agreement countries are received through the appropriate accounts and the exchange must be surrendered. The receiver is free to dispose of exchange proceeds from dollar area countries or from other countries with which Switzerland has no bilateral agreements. Exchange for authorized imports from bilateral agreement countries is granted readily but payments must be made through the appropriate bilateral accounts in accordance with the terms of the agreements and such imports frequently require licenses. Payments for imports from countries with which Switzerland has no bilateral agreement can be freely effected.

Finally, mention should be made of a few countries in the Latin American group which are in the dollar area and hence do not have bilateral payments agreements with foreign countries, but which nevertheless maintain exchange restrictions.[38] Venezuela, Costa Rica and Ecuador are good examples of dollar area countries with mild exchange restrictions, the controls being exercised principally as a means of implementing their system of multiple exchange rates. In these countries control over imports, exports and invisible transactions is achieved principally through varying the price of foreign exchange. These systems will be dealt with in a later chapter.

37. *Ibid.*, Part II, pp. 22–23. As of April 1951 Switzerland had payments or clearing agreements or compensation arrangements with the following countries or monetary areas: Austria, Argentina, Belgium, Bulgaria, Czechoslovakia, Denmark, Eastern Germany, Egypt, Finland, French franc area, Greece, Hungary, Iran, Italy, Netherlands, Norway, Poland, Portugal, Romania, Spain, sterling area, Sweden, Turkey, Western Germany and Yugoslavia.

38. Countries having virtually no exchange restrictions on current transactions are the United States, Mexico, Haiti, Honduras, Panama, Cuba, El Salvador, Dominican Republic and Guatemala. Cuba maintains a two per cent tax on all exchange remittances, which is scarcely a significant restriction. The Dominican Republic has a formal exchange control system but it is virtually inoperative. Honduras also has a formal system with no restrictions other than a 2 per cent spread between the buying and selling rates for foreign exchange.

SUMMARY

Prior to the setting up of the arrangements for financing intra-European trade after the inauguration of the European Recovery Program, most of the world's trade was financed as follows:

(1) Trade between dollar account countries and between the dollar account countries and all others was financed largely with U.S. dollars and to a limited extent with American account sterling.

(2) Trade within the sterling area and between the sterling area and most other nondollar countries was financed in large part with sterling and to a limited extent with the currencies of the countries with which Britain maintained bilateral payments agreements.

(3) A portion of the trade among the transferable account countries and between certain other nonsterling area countries (under close supervision of the British exchange control authorities) was also financed in sterling.

(4) Trade between the rest of the countries of the world was financed largely through bilateral payments agreements or barter arrangements.

Most of the payments agreements were accompanied by commercial agreements aimed at balancing trade. Where the commercial agreements dealt with export and import licenses and general understandings with respect to invisibles, no exact balance was likely to be struck in practice. In fact most Western European, Latin American and Far Eastern trade agreements were permissive rather than contractual. In some cases, however, chiefly in Eastern Europe, agreed quantities of goods at agreed prices were traded with no underlying foreign exchange payments.

Multilateral Aspects of the System

The payments system which emerged after the war was by no means wholly bilateral, even as regards the financing of trade among nondollar countries. There were large areas of multilateral settlements such as those represented by the sterling area and the transferable account group, the Dutch and Belgian monetary areas and the French franc area. Sterling area countries were able to convert their sterling into dollars, although discriminatory trade restrictions adopted by common consent among the sterling area countries limited the demands for dollars from the London pool.

The bilateral trade agreements which generally accompanied the bilateral payments agreements failed to secure an exact balancing of trade and substantial settlements in gold and dollars were made between parties to bilateral agreements. Current trade imbalances were also financed with credits, by the transfer of capital assets, through postwar U.S. financial aid, and through the purchase of goods from one country for re-export to another.

PART II

THE FUNDAMENTAL PAYMENTS MECHANISMS

Chapter 4

EXCHANGE CONTROL SYSTEMS

THIS STUDY WILL DEFINE an exchange control or exchange restriction as any interference on the part of the government with the freedom of the market for the exchange of one country's money for that of another.[1] Such limitations on the freedom of the market include interferences with transactions between persons owning currencies or bank balances at home or abroad, regardless of whether the transaction takes place in the home market or in a foreign market. For example the fact that the British Treasury will not permit the transfer of a sterling balance owned by a Frenchman to an American to whom the Frenchman desires to sell his balance, is an exchange restriction even though the attempt to sell the foreign exchange may take place in New York.

Exchange controls cannot be considered apart from the whole complex of governmental regulations which characterize modern economies. Not only do exchange controls represent only one among many tools in the bureaucratic kit for accomplishing a given purpose, but they are usually combined with other devices for achieving the desired ends. It is frequently difficult to decide therefore, whether a particular objective is being realized through the use of an exchange restriction or through some other type of restriction. For example, is an importer in an exchange control country unable to import a commodity because he cannot obtain an import license or because he is denied the foreign exchange with which to purchase it?

Strictly speaking, exchange restrictions are governmental measures which limit the ability of a resident to agree on and to perform an international financial transaction, but an import licensing system may be an indirect means of limiting international financial pay-

1. Sometimes restrictions on the exportation or importation of gold or of securities and other claims to foreign or domestic assets are regarded as exchange restrictions but I prefer to limit exchange restrictions to interferences with transactions involving the exchange of one country's money for that of another.

59

ments.[2] Therefore, we shall be concerned not only with exchange restrictions in the narrow sense of the term, but also with direct import and export restrictions which are employed in conjunction with exchange controls and which have as their purpose the control of international payments or receipts.[3]

Purposes of Exchange Controls

Modern exchange restrictions are used for a variety of purposes and it is frequently difficult to discern the primary aim of any particular device or arrangement. With relatively few exceptions, the basic reason for the establishment and maintenance of modern exchange control systems has been the protection of the balance of payments.[4] A notable exception is Switzerland's use of exchange restrictions to implement bilateral agreements which serve a commercial purpose, while at the same time permitting unrestricted current and capital payments with the United States and other countries with which Switzerland has no bilateral payments agreements. A few Latin American countries have no restrictions with respect to financial transactions with the United States and with most other countries and yet prescribe the method of payment in trade with a few countries with which they have payments agreements. Still another exception is Venezuela which has a multiple exchange rate system for the purpose of taxing foreign-owned oil companies, but imposes no other restrictions on international payments and transfers.

2. The question frequently arises as to whether a country maintains exchange restrictions on current international transactions if it places no restrictions on the purchase of foreign exchange for payments authorized by the licensing authorities. This question is significant in determining the obligations of members of the Monetary Fund not to impose "restrictions on the making of payments and transfers for current international transactions" (Article VIII, Section 2 (a)). The Fund has not given an official interpretation of this requirement. However, for our purposes, this obligation refers to limitations on the ability of residents to agree on and to perform in a specified way a financial settlement in connection with international current transactions. Thus the requirement that a resident must have an import license would not constitute an exchange restriction on current transactions but a requirement to pay for an import in a specified way would constitute such a restriction unless the requirement were for the purpose of preventing capital movements.

3. There are, of course, a number of quantitative import and export controls which are employed for protectionist, security or other purposes not related to the control of the means of payment.

4. By protecting the balance of payments we mean limiting the drain on foreign exchange reserves which would take place at the existing rate of exchange in the absence of exchange restrictions.

Few countries, probably, would maintain exchange control systems, except perhaps to limit capital exports, in the absence of the need to equalize the demand for foreign exchange for current international payments against the supply of the means of payment. The manner in which most exchange control systems are administered, however, reveals a variety of secondary purposes.

Thus if a country finds it necessary to limit imports it may decide to place the heaviest restrictions on goods which compete with domestic products. If it adopts a multiple exchange rate system, which necessarily involves an interference with international payments, it may decide to establish a more favorable rate of exchange for certain industrial products over other commodity exports. It may also use its exchange restriction system as a means of improving its commercial position through bilateral agreements, or it may establish a pattern of multiple exchange rates which taxes certain transactions or subsidizes other transactions. Exchange control systems, in fact, serve a variety of purposes and are closely related to the whole complex of national economic and political policies and the various measures employed by governments to realize them.

Both Current and Capital Transactions Controlled

Most exchange control systems today provide for controls over both current and capital transactions. Even in the absence of need to control current transactions, most countries would undoubtedly exercise some control over outward capital movements. Disturbed political and economic conditions both at home and abroad render all but the financially strongest countries subject to hot money flights which can do serious damage to their stock of international reserves and to their domestic monetary structure. Apart from this, most countries are anxious to mobilize their domestic savings for productive investments at home and do not feel themselves in a position to make investments abroad except on terms which would provide special advantages to their foreign commerce. There are a few exceptions, to be noted later, in which countries control current transactions but leave capital movements relatively free.

This chapter will describe the fundamental characteristics of current exchange control systems mainly from the standpoint of the techniques employed. Certain of these techniques will be considered in more detail in separate chapters, while other techniques and arrangements can best be understood in the context of particular exchange control territories or currency areas.[5]

COST VS. QUANTITATIVE EXCHANGE RESTRICTIONS

There are two general means by which the demand for or the supply of foreign exchange can be controlled through restrictions on the operation of free exchange markets. One is to place quantitative limits or prohibitions on certain types of transactions; the second is to control the volume of particular types of transactions by establishing differential rates for the foreign exchange which is purchased or sold. Quantitative restrictions involve complex administrative problems of allocation of foreign exchange, and frequently they are ineffective in stimulating exports in particular directions. For this reason many exchange control systems rely partly or mainly upon cost restrictions involving artificial price or cost differentials in the foreign exchange market.[6]

By making the foreign exchange required for certain imports cost more than that demanded for other imports it is possible to control the allocation of exchange for different purposes. Also, by varying the local currency price for the sale of foreign exchange to the banks,

5. Most countries and their dependent territories constitute a single *exchange control territory* within which no controls over payments and transfers exist with respect to transactions within the exchange control territory and common regulations exist with respect to transactions with residents outside the territory. There are exceptions to this rule, however, since some dependent territories have semiautonomous exchange control systems and in some cases restrictions on payments and transfers exist between the metropolitan country and the dependent overseas territories. *Currency areas* may include two or more independent countries as well as dependent territories. In general there are two distinguishing characteristics of a currency area: (1) all international transactions between members of the currency area are conducted in terms of a single currency; and (2) the country whose currency is employed as the means of payment for the area places no restrictions on transfers of its own currency between any other members of the area (although it may impose restrictions on its own residents). A currency area may include one or more exchange control territories. Thus the sterling currency area contains a number of independent exchange control territories and most members impose certain restrictions on payments and transfers with other members of the sterling area. The United Kingdom on the other hand imposes no restrictions on the transfer of sterling among residents of the sterling area. The Belgian monetary area, which includes two independent countries (Belgium and Luxembourg), constitutes a single exchange control territory by reason of the existence of the Belgium-Luxembourg Economic Union (B.L.E.U.).

6. Cost differentials can also be achieved by means of exchange taxes which vary as between different types of transactions.

it is possible to subsidize certain exports which may require special encouragement. The use of differential foreign exchange prices can also influence the source of imports and destination of exports.

Multiple exchange rate systems—that is, those involving more than one legal exchange rate other than the normal spread between buying and selling rates—exist in nearly 50 per cent of the sixty countries whose exchange control systems are described in this book and their popularity seems to have increased in the postwar period. In addition, a number of countries which maintain unitary rate systems employ exchange arrangements which give rise to "implicit" multiple exchange rates in the sense that they have the same economic effects as multiple rates.

Thus many countries permit exporters of certain commodities or those who export for certain currencies such as the dollar or the Swiss franc, to retain a portion of their export proceeds which they may use to purchase imports they might not otherwise be able to buy. Since such imported commodities as exporters are able to buy under these arrangements usually sell in the home market substantially above cost, the exporters obtain a special monetary inducement which is said to involve an implicit multiple exchange rate.[7] These arrangements are called "export retention quotas."

THE CONTROL OF FOREIGN EXCHANGE PAYMENTS

The control of foreign exchange payments is concerned not only with the purposes for which payments to residents of other countries may be made but also the form those payments may take. There are some exchange control systems that place virtually no restrictions on the purposes for which payments are made but nevertheless supervise the form in which they are made.[8]

The Meaning of Foreign Exchange Payments

Payments for goods and services from other countries may be made in several different ways and it is a matter of definition as to which of these constitute a foreign exchange payment. Clearly the transfer

---

7. Frequently exporters can sell their rights to use the retained foreign exchange although in most cases the actual transfer of the exchange proceeds at other than the official rate is illegal.

8. For example, this is largely true in the case of Peru and Switzerland.

of a convertible currency by a resident of one country to a resident of another is a foreign exchange payment; it is equally clear that a pure barter deal in which so many tons of wheat are traded for so many tons of steel without a time lag in deliveries does not constitute a foreign exchange payment. However, much of the world's trade is conducted in neither of these two ways, but under conditions which have elements of both barter and free foreign exchange transactions. For example, trade between some countries is financed through clearing accounts maintained by their central banks. Although these accounts are usually denominated in dollars, dollars are not paid into them in the course of trade. When an exporter in one country draws a draft on the importer or on the importer's bank the draft is not paid by transferring currency but simply by crediting the account of the exporter's central bank in the clearing account. The exporter is paid in his own currency when he discounts the draft with his bank, while the importer pays his own bank in domestic currency when the draft is presented for payment. The debiting or crediting of the clearing accounts held by the central banks provide the means of settlement between the two countries.

Under some definitions this would not be a foreign exchange transaction because neither the exporter nor his bank received payment in a foreign currency, or, conversely, neither the importer nor his bank made payment in the currency of the exporter. But this would not only exclude from the category of foreign exchange transactions the means employed for financing a substantial proportion of the world's trade, but it would set up an artificial distinction between this type of transaction and other transactions, which it would be difficult to justify in practice. Some payments arrangements between countries afford a greater degree of flexibility and transferability of foreign currency balances than is the case with others. But this is largely a matter of degree since all involve certain limitations as compared with financing with free foreign exchange. Realistically considered, all current international transactions, with the exception of gifts, reparations in kind, and barter,[9] involve some form of foreign exchange payment.

9. Barter is a transaction involving the direct exchange of goods against goods.

Payments for Merchandise Imports

In most countries today the control of payments for imports is exercised by the import licensing authorities. Possession of a valid license, or the existence of an Open General License (OGL) for the importation of a commodity from all countries or from a group of countries, usually enables the importer to purchase the appropriate means of payment from his bank without delay. There are exceptions to this rule particularly in certain Latin American countries where licenses are sometimes granted in excess of available exchange. But in Western Europe and the sterling area the appropriate foreign exchange is automatically granted upon the presentation of a valid import license.

Import control regulations differ in detail from country to country but they follow a more or less common pattern. Imports are usually divided into several categories, the most typical being: (1) imports generally licensed from all countries without limit; (2) imports generally licensed without limit from a group of soft-currency countries; (3) imports requiring individual licenses but which are freely licensed up to certain quota limits either from all countries or, more likely, on a country or country-group basis; and (4) imports subject to specific *ad hoc* licensing.

For most countries the first category will be very limited, confined to a few commodities which the country is anxious to obtain from any available source because of their world scarcity. The second category may be very wide, depending upon the over-all balance of payments position of the individual country. For example during 1950 and 1951 Australia and certain other sterling area countries placed most of their imports under OGL from all soft-currency countries, but as a result of the growing deficits on the part of both Australia and the sterling area as a whole with other soft-currency countries, including the EPU countries, Australia severely tightened up on her imports.

Category 3 usually applies to most hard-currency imports and to imports from countries with which trade agreements calling for specific import quotas have been negotiated. Quotas are frequently announced in advance by the import control authorities. Category 4 may involve machinery and other capital goods for which specific applications for licenses must be made and for which quotas are not announced in advance of licensing.

Where import quotas are established, several methods may be used to allocate licenses among the importers. In some European countries allocation is handled by the trade associations working in conjunction with the licensing authorities. An attempt is usually made to preserve commercial ties so that the Danish dealer in British automobiles will obtain a certain amount of the British automobile quota and the dealer in French cars a certain amount of the French quota, etc. Allocations are frequently based on a certain percentage of imports during the base period, usually a prewar period when imports were free. While provision is usually made for the establishment of new firms, nevertheless import restriction schemes generally tend to freeze the pattern of trade and to discourage competition. Other means of allocating import licenses include the first-come-first-served basis, and the method of *ad hoc* decisions based on judgments as to the public importance of the industry. In this connection producers of essentials and of commodities for export are generally given favored treatment by import authorities. In fact, exporters in many countries are permitted to retain a certain percentage of their export proceeds for their own use in obtaining imports required by their business.

Resemblance to Normal Foreign Exchange Practice

Even though imports are controlled through the licensing machinery, it is the function of the exchange control authorities to see that the appropriate amount and type of foreign exchange is paid. Payment for imports is generally arranged by the importer with a bank authorized to deal in foreign exchange.[10] Except for the fact that some commodities require import licenses, the actual importing procedure differs little from what it was before exchange controls were established. Probably the bulk of the world's trade is financed by means of a letter of credit drawn on a bank in the country of either the importer or the exporter. However, most exchange control systems permit other means of financing such as D/P or D/A bills,[11]

10. As a rule, all banks which formerly engaged in foreign exchange business have been authorized to deal in foreign exchange under regulations prescribed by the government.

11. D/P bills require payment by the importer before the documents giving title to

depending upon the practice of the trade. In some cases importers are permitted to use their own foreign exchange in making payments. But even where this is true, the exchange control systems frequently require that actual payment be made through an authorized bank.

A fairly common practice among exchange control countries is to require importers to deposit all or a portion of the value of their imports with an authorized bank as a condition either for obtaining an import license or for opening up a letter of credit. This arrangement serves to reduce the demand for imports by tying up the importer's funds well in advance of the receipt of the goods. Certain Western European countries have also blocked a portion of the exporter's receipts for a period of time in order to reduce an excessive creditor position.

One of the important functions of the exchange control administration is to prevent illegal capital flight through an overvaluation of imports. This may be prevented by requiring importers to submit evidence of the actual importation of the commodity including the valuation made by the customs authorities. If prepayment is requested, the importer must promise to submit evidence of the actual importation of the commodity and its value. In other cases copies of applications for foreign exchange may be sent to the customs authorities for checking against the goods themselves.

Payments through Authorized Banks

To insure that the appropriate type of payment is made, importers in exchange control countries cannot pay foreign exporters in their own or another currency except through an authorized bank. Local currency payments must be made into an appropriate nonresident account of the exporter or his bank. Although a British resident is permitted to hold Swedish kronor, he must transfer his kronor to a Swedish exporter in making payment for an import from Sweden through an authorized bank.

This requirement serves two purposes. First, it determines whether the foreign exchange is used in accordance with the exchange control regulations. Second, it provides a statistical check on the acquisition and disposition of foreign exchange holdings. This is particularly

the goods are surrendered. D/A bills require only the "acceptance" of the bill by the importer, thereby fixing the time of payment.

significant in determining a country's bilateral payments position vis-à-vis another country. It may also serve to prevent or mitigate undesirable capital imports into a country. For example, Belgian residents may purchase the currencies of other EPU countries in the free market but they cannot be used to pay for commodity imports. Payments for imports must be made with exchange purchased through authorized banks. This regulation tends to keep Belgium's EPU surplus from being increased through capital imports from other EPU countries.

While the allocation of foreign exchange as between different commodity imports and their sources is determined by the import licensing authorities, they must operate within a foreign exchange budget which takes into account all the foreign exchange requirements in relation to existing and accruing supply. Practices differ from country to country but as a rule budget estimates are drawn up for a year or six months in advance by representatives of the ministries of finance, foreign trade, industry and perhaps other governmental bodies. Where the central bank is very strong, the foreign exchange budget may be prepared by a department of the central bank in consultation with other governmental officials. In still other cases, there seems to be very little attempt to budget foreign exchange expenditures, and requests for exchange are handled on an *ad hoc* basis.

Payments for Invisibles [12]

Both the degree of restrictions on invisibles and the administration of controls in this field differ substantially from country to coun-

---

12. The Monetary Fund includes the following categories of items as invisible transactions:

1. International transportation of goods, including warehousing while in transit and other transit expenses.

2. Travel for reasons of business, education, health, international conventions or pleasure.

3. Insurance premiums and payment of claims.

4. Investment income, including interest, rents, dividends and profits.

5. Miscellaneous service items such as advertising, commissions, film rentals, pensions, patent fees, royalties, subscriptions to periodicals and membership fees.

6. Donations, migrants' remittances, legacies.

7. Repayment of commercial credit.

8. Contractual amortization and depreciation of direct investment. (Other capital payments are included in a separate category apart from invisible items.)

The above is a summary of the list of invisible items given in the Annex to the *Third*

try. However, certain uniform tendencies may be noted. Payments for invisibles to residents of other countries generally require a license. In the case of certain types of payments, such as transportation and other payments in connection with the shipment of goods, authorized banks are usually permitted to sell the foreign exchange upon the receipt of a proper declaration, a copy of which is forwarded to the exchange control authorities. Where specific regulations covering the conditions under which authorized banks may sell foreign exchange for invisibles do not exist, applications for payments must be made to the exchange control authorities.

In most Western European countries and in the sterling area invisible payments in connection with the authorized importation or exportation of merchandise may be made more or less automatically through an authorized bank. Premium payments on insurance and annuity policies can usually be made automatically, although there may be restrictions on taking out new policies with companies located abroad. Exchange-control countries establish annual foreign travel allowances for business or pleasure; these differ from country to country, depending upon the hardness of the currency. For example, most Western European countries permit their citizens to spend up to a certain limit in travel to other Western European countries or their currency areas, but have no tourist allowance for travel in the United States. Application to the exchange control authorities can usually be made for travel allowances not covered by the exchange regulations.

The treatment of earnings on foreign investment and contractual amortization and depreciation varies widely from country to country. In most Western European countries and the countries of the sterling area payments of interest, dividends and profits to foreigners are automatically approved. The treatment of foreign investment in underdeveloped areas is dealt with in Chapter 19.

The Form of Payment

Control over the form of payment as contrasted with the control of the amount and purpose of foreign exchange payments is signifi-

Annual Report on Exchange Restrictions, International Monetary Fund, Washington, 1952. It corresponds to the definition of current international transactions (except for the exclusion of merchandise trade) which is given in Article XIX of the Fund's Articles of Agreement.

cant when countries discriminate between other countries and currency areas. In the absence of discrimination the particular form of payment would not be of interest to the control authorities. Thus a country which financed its trade entirely with convertible currencies might seek to control its total foreign payments, but it would not ordinarily be concerned with the form of payment.

For a country whose own currency is not employed (or is not permitted to be employed) as a medium of international payments, control over the form of payment is achieved by requiring all foreign payments to be made through authorized banks whose business it is to see that payments against documents are made in the proper currency. For example an Argentine importer would not be permitted to obtain dollars to pay for something purchased in the sterling area or even to use his own dollars for that purpose. The correct form of payment between two exchange-control countries is usually set forth by the terms of the payments agreement to which they are parties. When a country finances a part of its international trade with its own currency, special arrangements are necessary for the control of nonresident accounts.

Nonresident Accounts

When countries have no foreign exchange controls, residents are free to transfer to nonresidents [13] balances in their own currency either in payment for imports or for any other purpose. But while a citizen of the United States is free to send a check drawn on his local bank account to a relative in England, his British cousin cannot send him a check drawn on Barclay's Bank since the British bank is not permitted to transfer sterling from a resident account to a nonresident account. Such transfers can only be consummated through authorized banks and under conditions established by the exchange control authorities. On the other hand a British resident could send his personal check to his cousin in Australia since British exchange con-

13. Exchange control laws are not uniform in the definition of a resident for exchange control purposes. Normally all nationals residing in their own country are residents and foreign nationals residing abroad are nonresidents. Under certain circumstances nationals residing abroad and doing business abroad may be treated as nonresidents for exchange control purposes, while foreign nationals residing in the exchange control country may be treated either as residents or nonresidents, depending upon the purpose for which their accounts may be employed.

trols regard all residents of the sterling area as residents for exchange control purposes.[14]

Nearly all exchange control countries have adopted regulations governing the transfer of bank accounts of residents to the accounts of nonresidents. In some countries, international payments are rarely if ever made in the national currency. Even so there must be some provision for the use of local accounts by foreign businessmen operating in the country, embassy staffs, travelers, and others. In the case of countries like Britain, France, Belgium and the Netherlands, whose currencies are widely used in international transactions, the control of payments to and from nonresident accounts is one of the most, if not the most, important elements in their exchange control system. Whether the national currency or a foreign currency is used in making a particular foreign payment depends upon the provisions of the bilateral payments agreement which may exist between the two countries and upon the practices of the business and financial community.[15]

Regardless of the method employed, all transfers to nonresident accounts must take place through authorized banks, and in most exchange control countries all payments from nonresident accounts to resident accounts for exports and other transactions must also be supervised by an authorized bank. In most cases this does not represent a substantial departure from commercial practices in operation before the imposition of exchange controls since most foreign traders do not carry foreign currency accounts or have financial dealings with foreigners except through their own banks.

Categories of Nonresident Accounts

Most exchange control countries have a number of categories of nonresident accounts designated by countries, by the purpose for which they may be used, and sometimes by the status of the holder, e.g., private person, bank, insurance company, etc. Though nonresident accounts available for making payments in current international

14. An Australian could not freely transfer his account to a resident of another sterling area country, however, since this would contravene Australian regulations.

15. Frequently dealers in certain commodities will tend to invoice in one currency rather than another. In other cases the exporter may prefer to invoice in his own currency.

transactions are usually held by foreign banks, in some cases they may be held by individuals or firms. Some countries permit only authorized banks to hold such accounts. Most countries have a category of nonresident accounts which may be used for payments within the country but not for international payments. These are used by foreign business firms in connection with local business transactions. A third type of nonresident account, known as the blocked account, is usually limited to the purchase of government securities or other securities with a low yield and a long maturity.

Nonresident accounts almost always are classified according to the country or currency area of the nonresident holder. Such accounts are usually transferable between residents of the designated country or currency area, but not between residents of different currency areas. The reason for these restrictions is related to the operation of the bilateral payments agreements, discussed in Chapter 5. Exceptions to this rule are the nonresident "American" accounts which certain countries have established for use in trade with the dollar area. American account sterling or American account guilders or Swedish kronor are freely transferable to residents of any currency area since they are readily convertible into dollars. Except for American account sterling, however, nonresident foreign accounts are not widely used in financing trade with the United States and other countries of the dollar area.

THE CONTROL OF FOREIGN EXCHANGE RECEIPTS

The control over foreign exchange receipts is basic to most foreign exchange systems since without control over the supply of the means of international payments, the allocation of exchange and the control of market price become quite difficult to administer.[16] Hence most countries require exporters and other recipients of foreign exchange to surrender their proceeds to a bank or a dealer authorized to handle foreign exchange.

16. Control over the use of foreign exchange for imports and other purposes is of course possible without surrender requirements. However, if exporters are not required to surrender their foreign exchange proceeds they might be content simply to hold their proceeds in the form of foreign balances, thereby denying its use to their fellow residents. Nevertheless, there are a few foreign exchange systems which seek to control the use of foreign exchange for imports and other purposes while not requiring its surrender by foreign exchange earners.

In some cases the authorized bank or dealer acts as an agent for the government in the purchase of foreign exchange; in others, the dealer buys the exchange on his own account.[17] In still other cases the authorized dealer operates simply as a broker for transactions between sellers and buyers of foreign exchange holding valid exchange or import licenses. This arrangement is sometimes employed when governments establish so-called "free" markets for foreign exchange or for foreign exchange arising from a particular source. Whatever the device, the purpose is to compel the exporter to make his foreign exchange earnings available to the community so they can be allocated among the various claimants.

In general, two methods of control are used to enforce the surrender requirements. First, all exports may be licensed by the trade control authorities—usually by the ministry of commerce or of foreign trade. Before the commodity to be exported is passed through customs the exporter must have his license validated by an authorized bank. This procedure requires the exporter to fill out forms indicating the destination of the export and the amount and form of the payment, together with an agreement to turn over to the bank the export proceeds within a certain time, usually three to six months. If payment is to be made under a letter of credit or by a draft drawn on the importer, the draft on the importer or on the bank issuing the letter of credit is either discounted or taken for collection by the authorized bank. In such cases the means of financing automatically provide the authorized bank with the foreign exchange proceeds from the transaction.

Second, in countries where export licenses are not generally required [18] the exchange control authorities usually require all exporters to obtain a "sworn declaration" from an authorized bank before the goods will be passed by the customs. Such declarations are issued

17. Since December 1951 British authorized banks have been permitted to purchase dollars and certain other currencies on their own account rather than as agents for the Bank of England, as was previously the case.

18. Even where export licenses are not employed to compel surrender of the exchange proceeds they may be required (1) for exports of relatively scarce goods as a means of obtaining other scarce goods under bilateral bargaining arrangements; (2) in the case of goods which the exchange control authorities are anxious to export for hard currencies; (3) as a means of limiting exports of goods of strategic importance to potential enemies; (4) for the purpose of conserving scarce goods for domestic use; (5) for implementing international allocation agreements.

upon submission of full information as to the amount and form of payment and of an agreement by the exporter to surrender the exchange proceeds. The customs authorities check the sworn declaration against the goods themselves and the shipping documents, before the goods are permitted to leave the country.[19] The authorized bank in turn is responsible for seeing that the payment is made in the amount and form indicated by the exporter's declaration, within the permitted time period. Failure on the part of the exporter to tender the exchange proceeds may result in a fine or a denial of the right to export.

Some countries permit their exporters to retain all or a portion of their export proceeds from the sale of certain commodities either for their own use or for sale in a legal free market. Frequently, however, retained foreign exchange proceeds must be kept in special accounts with an authorized bank rather than in accounts held by the exporter in a foreign bank. In such cases the exporter can dispose of his proceeds only by the purchase of permitted imports through an authorized bank or sell the retained foreign exchange at the free market rate to an authorized bank. Where free markets are provided for by the exchange regulations, transactions are frequently limited to those with authorized banks or dealers.

Prescribing the Form of Payment for Exports

The purpose of these control procedures is not only to make sure that the exporter surrenders the foreign exchange proceeds but to enforce the regulations regarding the form of payment. Nearly all exchange control countries prescribe the type of payment for their exports according to the destination of the export and sometimes according to the type of commodity. The form of payment between two exchange control countries is usually determined by the terms of the payments agreement to which they are parties or sometimes by an informal understanding or agreement that they will accept a third currency in payment for exports to one another.[20] (See Chapter 5.)

19. Customs officials seek to prevent undervaluation of exports as a means of achieving illegal capital exports by comparing their estimate of the market value of the export with the export license or declaration. It is also important to check on the destination of the export in order to prevent the direct or indirect sale of commodities to hard-currency areas against soft currencies.

20. When the agreed third currency is not a free currency it is usually necessary to

When two countries have no agreement with one another as to the form in which payments are to be made, trade will generally be financed with dollars, or if the authorities in both countries permit, by means of barter or compensation deals. Trade with nonexchange control countries will almost always be on a dollar or other free currency basis.[21] Barter or compensation trade is most prevalent today between exchange control countries which lack any formal agreement regarding a regular means of making payment. Such transactions are closely supervised by the trade authorities and the commodities which can be bartered are frequently limited to marginal exports which are hard to sell for foreign exchange.

If all countries demanded gold, dollars or other convertible currencies for their exports, we might still have exchange controls but they would be nondiscriminatory, and we would have a world-wide system of multilateral payments. Except for a few Latin American countries, however, most exchange-control countries conduct the bulk of their trade with other exchange-control countries in inconvertible currencies or special clearing account arrangements. The operation of these arrangements requires either bilateral balancing of trade or, in some cases, limited multilateral balancing. Gold or free currencies may still be used, however, in settling final balances either between countries or for the settlement of intraregional balances as in the case of the European Payments Union. Thus, while much of the world's trade is now conducted under bilateral payments arrangements, a considerable degree of multilateralism is still achieved both through the periodic settlement of final balances in gold or free currencies and through limited or regional multilateral payments systems such as the sterling currency area and the EPU. Nevertheless, the prevailing systems of payments require countries to adopt bilateral trade policies which shift the matrix of world trade from its normal multilateral pattern.

---

have an agreement or at least an informal understanding with the country whose currency is being used. Thus for example, Belgium accepts sterling from both Egypt and Thailand in payment for exports. Since Belgium is not a member of the sterling transferable account group, such transfers require the permission of the British authorities. On the other hand transferability of sterling between Egypt and Thailand is automatically provided for in the bilateral agreements which these countries have with Britain.

21. The most important free currencies are the U.S. and Canadian dollars and the free Swiss franc. (The free Swiss franc must be distinguished from bilateral account Swiss francs.)

Why Are "Soft" Currencies Accepted?

The reason why countries are willing to export for inconvertible currencies is twofold. First, they seek markets in other exchange-control countries that would not be available to them if they were unwilling to accept inconvertible currencies. Of course, if a country requires all other countries to pay in convertible currencies it may be able to sell at least some of its exportable commodities to "soft-currency" countries.[22] How much it will sell depends upon the nature of the markets for its principal exports. Countries selling raw materials in short supply and for which there are accessible dollar markets have little to gain from accepting inconvertible currencies for their exports. Thus Chile demands dollars for her copper and Bolivia for her tin, regardless of the country to which these materials are exported.[23] On the other hand, countries seeking to export textiles or tobacco to soft-currency markets may find it desirable to trade on a bilateral or inconvertible basis, since normally there are adequate nondollar sources of these commodities, and soft-currency countries are unlikely to pay dollars for them if they can obtain them by other means.

The second reason why countries are willing to accept inconvertible currencies for the exports is because by so doing they can obtain imports from other soft-currency countries without having to pay dollars or convertible currencies for them. Thus Britain may be willing to sell steel and machinery to Argentina against inconvertible sterling because she expects to be able to buy meat from Argentina without having to pay dollars. Sweden sells Britain iron ore for inconvertible sterling in order to buy coal with sterling rather than dollars.

There are, of course, other reasons why nations are willing to accept inconvertible currencies for their exports. Countries with strong

22. In general "soft-currency" countries are countries which accept inconvertible currencies for their exports. However, some countries like Belgium, Switzerland and Portugal are sometimes considered to be "hard-currency" countries even though they make bilateral payments agreements providing for the acceptance of inconvertible balances. The designation of hard currency is determined by the tendency of other countries to run deficits with these countries, which must frequently be settled in gold or dollars.

23. Chile demands dollars for her copper but is willing to sell her nitrates and her wines for soft currencies. Uruguay sells her wool exclusively for dollars when wool is scarce but is willing to sell for soft currencies at other times. Even European countries have been known to demand dollars for so-called "dollar goods" from other soft-currency countries.

commercial, financial and political ties with soft-currency countries are reluctant to break these ties by becoming "dollar" countries even if there were an immediate trade advantage in doing so. South Africa remains at least partially in the sterling area since to leave would mean that capital imports from other sterling area countries would probably cease. Ceylon remained a sterling area member even while that country had a large dollar surplus. Switzerland trades with Europe and elsewhere through bilateral agreements, not because of any necessity to restrict her dollar payments, but because she wants to preserve the market for her products in soft-currency countries.

Prices in Hard- and Soft-Currency Markets

The fact that countries sell the same commodities for dollars to the United States, which they sell to other countries for inconvertible currencies, frequently leads to dual pricing and special bilateral trading deals. Prices for the same commodities are sometimes lower in dollar markets than in soft-currency markets.[24] Where such price differentials do not exist, countries will sometimes limit their exports to other soft-currency countries of commodities which are readily marketable in the dollar area, or will demand certain other "dollar" goods in return. In some cases countries have tied the sale of these dollar goods to a certain amount of other goods not readily marketable for dollars.

Where prices in both soft-currency and hard-currency markets are approximately the same, arbitrage is likely to take place as a consequence of the difference between the "real" and the official values of hard and soft currencies. The re-exportation of commodities imported for soft currencies to hard-currency countries is fairly widespread and tends to reduce the hard-currency sales of the country in which the commodity originated. Thus Australian wool and Brazilian coffee are sometimes consigned to European ports and paid for in sterling or other European currencies but somehow end up in the United States. In order to limit such transactions, countries some-

24. For a comparison of prices of basic commodities between dollar markets and sterling markets, see "Two Basic Conditions," The Economist, June 7, 1952, p. 639; see also Barend de Vries, "Immediate Effects of Devaluation on Prices of Raw Materials," Staff Papers, September 1950, pp. 238–53. (Staff Papers is an academic journal published three times a year by the International Monetary Fund.)

times require exporters to obtain a sworn statement from the customs officials of the country to which the export was originally consigned to the effect that the commodity actually passed through the customs of that country and was not transshipped. Commodity arbitrage is likely to continue, however, so long as there are inconvertible currencies.

Receipts from Invisibles

Most countries require the surrender of receipts from invisibles. As in the case of receipts from merchandise transactions, all foreign exchange dealings in most exchange control countries must be handled through authorized banks whose duty it is to see that the payment is received in the appropriate form. It is more difficult to enforce surrender requirements in the case of invisibles than in merchandise exports which must go through customs, and exchange control authorities frequently take special measures to enforce compliance. For example, owners of foreign securities must register them with authorized banks; in some cases they must be held by the authorized bank under a trustee arrangement. When the bank receives dividend payments in foreign currency it pays the owner of the security in local currency at the official rate.

Tourist receipts also present a special problem for the exchange control authorities. Tourists frequently buy local currency in the exchange control country below the official rate from residents who evade the exchange regulations by not surrendering the travelers checks, banknotes, or other foreign exchange instruments. To prevent this practice some countries require tourists to declare the amount of foreign exchange they have when they enter the country and to show how they have disposed of it before they leave.

CONTROLS OVER CAPITAL MOVEMENTS

With few exceptions, exchange control systems regulate both the inflow and outflow of capital funds. Nations that find it necessary to ration their supply of foreign exchange for current imports naturally want to prevent any reduction in their foreign exchange reserves through capital exports, unless the exports are likely to be highly productive of foreign exchange.[25] The control mechanisms governing the making of payments for imports and the surrender of export proceeds are in large part designed to prevent unauthorized capital exports. To the extent that these mechanisms operate efficiently, most illegal capital movements can be prevented. The regulations regarding the transfer of resident accounts to nonresident accounts and the uses to which various categories of nonresident accounts may be put are especially important in preventing unauthorized capital movements. But where these controls are not effective, a resident of an exchange control country can purchase foreign currencies with his own currency, thereby exporting his capital. These transactions are ordinarily prevented not by censoring outgoing letters and cablegrams, but by requiring banks not to transfer the bank balances of residents to the accounts of nonresidents except under official license or regulation.[26] Exchange control systems are never fully effective. The fascinating subject of illegal currency markets and capital movements is discussed in Chapter 9.

Exchange control countries usually require licenses for the export of capital. In addition to permitting certain types of productive foreign investments—usually related to the development of foreign sources of supply or of foreign markets for exports—most exchange control systems provide for limited exports of capital by emigrants and modest payments of inheritances to foreign beneficiaries. If countries want to attract foreign capital, they must make provision for the repayment of loans, which is a form of capital export, and for the repatriation of capital in the form of direct foreign investments.

Controlling Inflow of Capital

Countries also control inward movements of capital for a variety of reasons. They may want to avoid the inflationary effects of such movements. This was the reason for measures adopted by Switzerland in the early postwar period. Countries may want to control inward capital flow so that they will not be required to remit earnings

25. For example, the British government may permit new dollar investments in Venezuelan oil fields but is not likely to permit its citizens to export capital from Britain to purchase U.S. government bonds or shares of stock in U.S. firms.

26. Exchange control countries usually attempt to prevent travelers from bringing appreciable amounts of banknotes in or out of the country or from smuggling securities out of the country.

on unproductive or undesirable investments to the foreign owners. Controls on inward movements of capital are also imposed for reasons of national political and social policy, and finally, in order that the monetary authorities receive the foreign exchange which is being transferred.

Control over inward capital movements is generally achieved by requiring the foreign exchange representing the capital import to be turned over to the exchange control authorities. Normally this is handled by requiring the individual importing the capital to sell his foreign exchange to an authorized bank. As a rule foreign exchange regulations forbid sales of foreign currencies to anyone other than an authorized bank. Where the authorities desire to limit or otherwise control the use of the funds derived from the sale of the foreign exchange by the capital importer, the local currency account might be blocked or available for use only under license from the monetary authorities.

The regulations regarding capital movements differ substantially from country to country, depending in large degree upon the economic circumstances and the national policies of each country. Such regulations are of particular significance for private foreign investment in the less developed countries. This subject is discussed in Chapter 19.

Chapter 5

POSTWAR TRADE AND PAYMENTS AGREEMENTS

THE VAST BULK of the trade between the nondollar countries of the world is conducted in accordance with agreements between the governments of the trading countries, which affect either the method of payment, or the commodities and services which may be traded, or both. While the principal focus of this study is on arrangements related to the financing of international transactions, the payments mechanism is often so closely tied to the arrangements for determining what goods and services are to be exchanged, that the two processes must be considered together.

In some cases the commercial arrangements and the financing of trade are provided for in a single bilateral agreement; in other cases the agreements are separate. For purposes of analysis we shall divide agreements affecting the flow of goods, services and capital between nations into three broad categories: (1) those concerned with the movement of goods and services; (2) those concerned with the financing of current transactions; (3) those concerned with long-term credits and capital movements.

Agreements may be bilateral, multinational or international in character. (By international we mean broad agreements open to all or most nations as opposed to multinational agreements which are limited to a few nations or to nations within a given region.) Since we have considered multinational and international agreements elsewhere, in this chapter we shall deal for the most part with bilateral agreements.

AGREEMENTS AS TO GOODS AND SERVICES

Trade agreements or arrangements cover broadly the conditions affecting trade in goods and services, except the means of financing. These conditions include tariffs, customs formalities, quotas, licensing of imports and exports, and purchases and sales of state trading organizations. Trade agreements take several forms; among the more important are the following:

Treaties of Friendship, Commerce and Navigation (FCN). These agreements typically deal with such matters as tariffs, customs formalities, the rights of consular representatives, the treatment of foreign business representatives and foreign property, the protection of patents, trade-marks and copyrights, the treatment of foreign shipping, etc. They tend to establish broad principles of commercial relations such as the granting of *national* and *most-favored nation* treatment rather than to deal with specific commodity and service transactions. Many of this country's FCN treaties include provisions governing the use of exchange controls and the treatment of foreign investments.

Bilateral or multilateral agreements for the reduction of tariffs, import quotas, and other barriers to trade. The reciprocal tariff agreements entered into by the United States with a number of other countries since 1934 under the Reciprocal Trade Agreements Act and the multilateral General Agreement on Tariffs and Trade are representative of this type of agreement. The Code of Trade Liberalization adopted by the Council of the Organisation for European Economic Co-operation (OEEC) is an example of a regional agreement of this general type. In recent years bilateral and multilateral tariff agreements have usually provided for most-favored-nation treatment, and have not sought to achieve bilateral balancing of trade. As a rule, the agreements include statements of principles relating to fair trade practices and the use of trade and exchange controls.

Bilateral trade-quota agreements. Perhaps the most important agreements from the standpoint of determining the character of postwar trade are the bilateral trade-quota agreements. These usually provide for two lists of commodities with corresponding quantities or values for which the partner countries agree to grant import and export licenses. As a rule these agreements do not exclude trade in other commodities for which the partner countries may wish to grant import licenses. Nor does either country guarantee that the trade indicated by the agreed quotas will take place, since the undertaking relates only to the issuance of licenses up to the amount of the quotas. The agreements may cover services such as tourism as well as commodities. Where the list includes relatively scarce commodities which the countries are anxious to obtain from each other, export quotas may be written into the agreement. Export quotas may represent more binding undertakings since scarce goods are frequently subject to government allocation and their exportation to certain countries may require government action.

Trade-quota agreements have been the chief means by which countries have sought to achieve a bilateral balance in their current account in the postwar years. Exact balancing has seldom been achieved but the commodity lists are frequently drawn up with a view to establishing target amounts for trade in either direction.

However, bilateral balancing of trade is by no means the only purpose for which trade quota agreements have been employed. For example, members of the sterling area negotiate such agreements between themselves, as do members of the European Payments Union. In neither case is bilateral balancing of trade necessary on balance of payments grounds. Trade-quota agreements are frequently used to expand trade between two countries. Each may be willing to grant import licenses for certain commodities provided the partner country grants import licenses for commodities which it is anxious to export. The net result of these bilateral arrangements is likely to be a lower level of total trade and a loss of economic advantages from trade, as compared with a condition of unrestricted trade. But so long as other countries engage in the practice, each feels it must play the game or lose trade. Trade-quota arrangements are also motivated by a desire to bargain certain relatively scarce export goods against other scarce goods which are urgently needed. Thus Sweden agrees to ship iron ore to Germany on condition that Germany supply coal to Sweden.

Trade-quota agreements between state-trading countries tend to be much more rigid than those between free enterprise economies. Instead of agreements to issue import licenses, such agreements provide for the exchange of specific quantities of goods. When the lists of goods to be exchanged provide for balanced trade without foreign exchange payments, the agreement becomes a *barter* arrangement.

Bulk purchase contracts. These agreements are generally negotiated between governments or government controlled enterprises, and specify quantities and prices of commodities (usually raw materials) to be purchased over a period of one or more years. Their usual purpose is to achieve such commercial objectives as the assurance of markets, sources of supply or the stability of prices, rather than to balance trade as a means of conserving foreign exchange. For example, Britain has contracts with Denmark and the Netherlands for the purchase of butter, eggs and bacon, and a contract with Belgium for copper from the Belgian Congo.

AGREEMENTS AS TO FINANCING CURRENT TRADE

Agreements which have as their purpose the financing of trade without the use of convertible currencies are both numerous and varied. Moreover the official nomenclature employed by governments and financial writers to identify these arrangements is not standardized so that the same type may be given many names.[1] In the prewar literature on this subject the principal types of agreements for financing current trade without the use of freely convertible currencies were generally identified as (1) bilateral clearing agreements; (2) bilateral payments agreements; (3) compensation agreements; and (4) barter agreements. In order to clear up a certain amount of confusion, we shall avoid using the term "bilateral clearing agreement" in connection with postwar agreements and redefine "bilateral payments agreement" to conform to present usage. The typical prewar payments agreement and clearing agreement no longer exist in current practice and so the usual prewar definitions of these terms are irrelevant.[2]

Under the typical prewar clearing agreement the importer in each country paid his own currency into a special account in the central bank or clearing office in that country, and exporters in each country were paid out of these national accounts. When trade was not balanced, exporters in the creditor country had to wait until importers paid a sufficient amount of local currency into the account. Sometimes the central bank or the clearing office made loans to the exporters to enable them to go on exporting more than the country was importing from the partner country.

1. For a description and classification of prewar payments and clearing arrangements see M. S. Gordon, *Barriers to World Trade,* Macmillan, New York, 1941; and H. S. Ellis, *Exchange Control in Central Europe,* Harvard University Press, Cambridge, 1941.
2. For a comparison of prewar and postwar agreements see *17ᵐᵉ Rapport de Gestion 1949,* Swiss Clearing Office, Zurich, July 1950, pp. 16–18.

The typical prewar payments agreement, on the other hand, was negotiated between an exchange control country (A) and a free exchange country (B). The exchange control country (A) agreed to allocate a certain percentage of B's currency which A received as a result of exports to B, for the payment of imports from B; and to reserve another portion of the receipts of B's currency for the payment of certain debts.[3]

Change from Prewar Practice

The author is not aware of any current agreement that provides for financing trade through local currency accounts operated in accordance with the "waiting" principle. Under modern systems, either definite "swing" credits [4] or periodic settlement dates within which trade can be unbalanced, are substituted for the waiting period. While countries may establish accounts through which debits and credits arising out of current international transactions are recorded and cleared, the credit balances in these accounts are usually available for the purchase of goods and services by the creditor country.

Nor are prewar payments agreements typical of postwar arrangements since nearly all agreements are now between exchange control countries. Some agreements, principally between Western European countries, permit rather wide freedom for traders and banks in foreign exchange dealings involving the two currencies. In other cases, the exchange control regulations and payments arrangements limit the holdings of foreign currencies to central banks, so that trade between two countries under the bilateral agreement is financed through one or two central bank accounts. In most Japanese bilateral agreements, a clearing account is established with the dollar as the unit of account.[5] Yet most bilateral agreements, whether they allow transfers of currency balances or employ a clearing account, are referred to as "payments agreements" in the official documents of the governments employing them.

To avoid confusion with the prewar type of clearing agreement, we shall adhere to present usage and include both the "currency-

---

3. See Gordon, *op. cit.,* pp. 131–32.
4. "Swing" credits are reciprocal credits which permit trade to be unbalanced in either direction up to certain limits without settlement during the life of the agreement.
5. In practice, there is virtually no difference between the operation of a centralized currency-balance arrangement and of one which provides for a clearing account.

balance" and the "clearing account" arrangements in our definition of a "bilateral payments agreement."

Definition of a Bilateral Payments Agreement

A "bilateral payments agreement," as here used provides a general method of financing current trade between two countries, giving rise to credits which are freely available for use by one country in making payments for goods and services imported from the other. We may define more precisely what is meant by a bilateral payments agreement by listing its five basic elements: (1) It must provide for a general method of financing trade (or certain categories of trade) between two countries or currency areas and not simply for the financing of a specific commodity or service transaction; (2) it must establish a unit of account or two or more units of account with agreed ratios of exchange between them; (3) each transaction must result in a credit or a debit (or both) in the accounts of the two countries, however the accounts may be kept; (4) net credits arising out of transactions under the agreement must be freely available for use in making payments for a wide range of imports; (5) the use of credits arising out of the operation of the agreement to make purchases in third countries must be limited.

Bilateral payments agreements, as here defined, lead to foreign exchange payments, since each commodity or service transaction involves a payment in the form of a deposit balance or clearing account credit, which can be used either to buy goods or services in the country making the payment or to discharge or offset a debt to that country. Barter and compensation agreements [6] do not involve foreign exchange payments since the trade and its financing are one and the same transaction. Barter agreements for the exchange of a number of items with varying delivery dates usually have some form of accounting mechanism but unlike payments agreements, the accounting credits are not freely available to purchase additional goods and services.

Some of the bilateral arrangements between countries in the Soviet orbit establish clearing accounts similar to those under payments

6. A compensation agreement is a special form of barter agreement in which an exporter and an importer in one country arrange the exchange of specific quantities of goods or services with an importer and an exporter in another country.

agreements. Yet they differ from payments agreements in that the credits arising from their operation are not automatically available for additional purchases. While trade between non-Soviet countries may be conducted in accordance with trade-quota agreements which provide for the issuance of import and export licenses for specific quantities of goods, the resulting trade is by no means completely planned in advance and its movement is responsive to changes in the bilateral debit or credit position of each country.

BILATERAL PAYMENTS AGREEMENTS

Bilateral payments agreements may be classified in various ways depending upon the particular interest of the investigator. However, the differences among the several hundred current agreements are so great as to defy any attempt at general classification. We may consider postwar payments agreements from the standpoint of (1) the currency or currencies of account; (2) the nature of the accounting arrangements; (3) the provision for credits; (4) the means of settling excess credits during the life of the agreement; (5) the means of settlement at the termination of the agreement; (6) the types of transactions which are permitted to be financed under the agreement; (7) the measures employed for preventing the emergence of excessive credit or debit positions during the life of the agreement; (8) the extent to which it is permitted to transfer to third countries balances arising under the operation of the agreement.

The Currency of Account

In payments agreements which provide for the use of two currencies, it is necessary to establish a fixed exchange rate between them, at least for a given accounting period. If the exchange rates were to change from day to day the value of each country's holdings of the other's currency would fluctuate, thereby exposing their central banks to the danger of loss. Some agreements provide for an exchange guarantee on balances held in the event of a change in the official rates.

Where the currency of one partner is not ordinarily used to finance international trade or where one of the currencies is permitted to fluctuate from day to day, the usual practice is to use the currency of the other country as the unit of account and medium of payments. Thus most British bilateral agreements provide for the use of sterling and all trade between the two countries is so invoiced. Although it is not necessary to maintain a fixed exchange ratio between the currencies of the two countries when only one of them is employed in trade, the country whose currency is used is frequently asked for an exchange guarantee against depreciation in terms of gold or the dollar.

Where neither currency is used appreciably in international trade or where neither country is willing to accept the other's currency as the unit of account, a third currency, usually the dollar, is adopted. Under these circumstances the dollar is not the actual means of payment, even though exports may be invoiced in dollars or in "special account dollars." The dollar is simply the unit in which the accounts are carried.

The Nature of the Accounting Arrangements

The most flexible type of arrangement, and the one which most nearly approximates financial practices before the introduction of exchange controls and payments agreements, provides for invoicing exports and drawing drafts in either currency according to normal trade practice, with no restrictions on the transfer of balances of either currency between residents of the currency areas of the two countries. If the exchange control authorities do not require the surrender of the currency of the partner country the central bank of each country must stand ready to purchase the partner's currency from its own residents—including the banks—in order to prevent depreciation of the market rate for the foreign currency.[7]

On the other hand the central bank of each country must be able to supply the banking system with the currency of the partner country in amounts required for authorized payments. Thus, except for normal working balances held by banks and individual traders, the foreign currency balances of each country will be held by its central bank and any change in the bilateral trading position of the two will be

7. It is almost universal among exchange control countries to limit foreign exchange transactions to those in which a bank or authorized dealer is a partner. Hence even where surrender of exchange receipts is not required the holder of a foreign currency balance can dispose of it only through a bank.

reflected in each central bank's holdings of the currency of the other country. It should also be pointed out that when a bank in one country sells a balance in a private foreign bank to its own central bank, the latter will normally exchange the balance in the foreign private bank for an equivalent credit in the central bank of that country. Hence the net position between the two countries is determined by offsetting the deposit balances of the two central banks.

This payments mechanism may be modified in certain respects and still remain decentralized. For example the payments agreement may provide for the use of only one of the currencies, say sterling, in which case all the trade between the two countries or currency areas is invoiced in sterling and paid for by drafts on deposits in British banks. While banks and possibly individuals in the partner country may hold working balances in sterling, they will sell any excess holdings to their own central bank and look to their central bank for additional supplies of sterling. Thus the net position between Britain and the partner country will be determined by the latter's holdings of sterling deposits with the Bank of England. If the other currency is not normally used in international trade, the use of sterling as the sole unit of account may not involve a significant departure from commercial practice before the institution of the agreement. The only real difference created by the bilateral payments agreement may be the inability to use the sterling balances in making payments to certain countries outside the sterling area.

The more centralized types of agreements involve a greater departure from prewar practices. First, most exchange control countries require private individuals to surrender all foreign exchange earnings to authorized banks. This is not a serious departure from normal commercial practice, however, since ordinarily foreign traders sell their drafts on foreign countries to their bank, or turn them over to their bank for collection. Most payments agreements between Western European countries permit normal correspondent relations between the banks in each country, including the maintenance of working balances with foreign correspondents. But in the centralized or clearing type of payments arrangement trade between the two countries is financed solely through accounts maintained by the central banks. Thus drafts drawn by an exporter in one country on a bank or a firm in the partner country are not collected by the transfer of a currency balance in a private bank but by crediting the account of the central bank in the exporter's country or, alternatively, by debiting the account of the central bank in the importer's country.[8]

In some cases there is a single account in the central bank of one of the partner countries, while in others, accounts are kept in the central bank of each country. There is a third variant, under which the accounts may be kept in a private bank operating in one of the countries, but owned or incorporated in a third country. The unit of account may be the currency of one of the partners or the currency of a third country, or, where dual accounts are maintained, the currency of each of the partner countries is employed.

The Credit Provisions

Essential to all bilateral payments agreements is the provision for credits, without which trade between the two countries would either have to be bilaterally balanced at all times or any deficits covered by payment in gold or a convertible currency as soon as they appeared. The basic purpose of a payments agreement is to assure a margin in the current account balance of the two countries or currency areas without the necessity for gold or convertible currency settlements within this margin.

Swing credits are handled in various ways. The typical two-currency payments agreement provides that the central bank of each country will hold currency balances in the central bank of the other country up to a certain level and that each central bank will sell its own currency in exchange for the currency of the other country up to a stated amount. When the net debit position of either country exceeds the agreed limit, further debits arising out of current trade must ordinarily be settled in gold or agreed third currencies. There have been a number of two-currency agreements which did not provide for gold payments but simply for discussion between the two countries when the credit balance of either became excessive.[9]

8. This procedure is sometimes modified by the provision of a subaccount for each authorized bank in the centralized account.

9. The Anglo-French financial agreement of December 12, 1940, provided that the central bank of each country would sell its own currency against the currency of the other country in whatever amounts might be needed to finance trade between the sterling area and the French franc area. Such an agreement—tantamount to a currency union—was superseded by the more usual type of agreement in 1945, after the liberation of France.

In the one-currency type of agreement the credit element is sometimes unilateral. It arises from the willingness of one of the countries to hold the currency of the other country either up to a maximum amount fixed by the agreement, or without limit. This is true of most of the sterling one-currency agreements, although if the partner country began to accumulate large amounts of sterling it would probably seek means of reducing its exports for sterling or request a modification in the agreement.

In agreements which provide for a system of centralized accounts the swing credit is usually established by permitting either country to run a limited deficit in the clearing account. As a rule, the effective swing margins are narrower in clearing-account agreements than in the more decentralized type. For example, a country may be willing to hold fairly substantial amounts of sterling, which, though not convertible into gold or dollars, is nevertheless usable for payments over a wide area. The relative strength and stability of a currency is also a determining factor in the willingness of countries to hold it. Thus, for example, countries ordinarily are unwilling to run up large credits in a centralized account with Argentina, or to hold big balances in Argentine pesos.

There are some clearing-type payments agreements which do not make specific provision for swing credits, but simply for regular settlement dates. Between settlement dates the balances could presumably reach any level, but as a rule settlement periods under such agreements are rather short.

The Settlement of Excess Credits

Where specific provision is made for definite swing margins, the settlement of excessive credit balances accruing during the life of the agreement may be made in gold or convertible currencies, inconvertible currencies of third countries, clearing credits in international organizations, securities, or goods and services. Some agreements such as the Anglo-Belgian one of 1944 provide for a rigid and automatic settlement in gold. Others are less rigid and provide for consultation, with the creditor having the right to demand gold payment if a mutually acceptable settlement cannot be reached within a reasonable time.[10]

10. Credit limits under such agreements are sometimes spoken of as "talking points" as opposed to the "gold points" of the Anglo-Belgian type of agreement.

Under a few agreements transfers of sterling instead of gold or dollars are regularly used as a means of settling excess credits. Monthly settlements of bilateral positions between members of the European Payments Union are made through that agency's mechanism and the net position of each member with the EPU as a whole is settled by a credit or a debit on that country's EPU account.

Where large credit balances have accumulated under the operation of bilateral payments agreements they are sometimes settled by a long-term or intermediate-term loan or funding credit. Thus Belgium has funded the credits of some of her payments agreements partners during the postwar period. Settlement may also be made by using accumulated balances to purchase securities or other capital assets owned by the debtor country. Thus Argentina and Brazil utilized a portion of their excessive sterling and French franc balances to buy utilities owned by foreign investors in Britain and France. Finally, settlement is sometimes made by the export of commodities from the debtor country. Unless this can be arranged through a special contract for the delivery of a quantity of goods which would not ordinarily be made in the regular course of trade, settlement in goods must be achieved by a total or partial stoppage of exports from the creditor country. Such interference with the flow of trade would represent a temporary breakdown of the payments agreement the purpose of which is to finance normal trade without resort to barter.

Settlement at Termination of Agreement

Payments agreements may be negotiated for definite periods, usually from one to three years, or they may run indefinitely, with each party reserving the right to withdraw upon reasonable notice. The typical provision for final settlement of credits outstanding at the termination of the agreement is that these must be paid in gold within a given period unless other arrangements are mutually adopted. Most postwar agreements are renewed or revised from time to time and the usual practice is to wipe the slate clean by funding the balance left over from the previous arrangement. Many of the Western European agreements with Latin American countries have provided for the liquidation of balances arising out of the operation of the wartime agreements by the purchase of European investments in Latin America.

Transactions Permitted under the Agreements

Some payments agreements provide for the financing of all current international transactions, while others severely limit the trade which may be financed under the bilateral payments mechanism. Where payments agreements are separate from commodity-exchange agreements, the payments agreement is usually drawn quite broadly to permit the financing of all merchandise transactions together with expenses incurred in connection with the movement of the goods, interest and dividend payments, tourist expenditures, emigrant remittances and other services. Sometimes specific commodity or service items are excluded from the agreement. For example, Chile will not ordinarily accept inconvertible currencies for her copper and her agreements usually state that such exports must be financed with dollars outside the regular payments agreement mechanism.

Private capital movements, other than service payments on amortized debt, are usually excluded from bilateral payments agreements, except in cases where the agreement specifically provides that a portion of the accumulated balance is to be set aside for the repayment of a debt or the repatriation of equity capital. Thus if a resident of one country sells a security in the market of the partner country the balance so acquired will ordinarily be "blocked" and therefore unavailable for current transactions between the two countries. When the payments arrangements are of the more decentralized type, the volume of capital transactions, other than those related to the movement of goods and services, depend upon the organization and efficiency of the exchange controls of the two countries.

As a rule, payments agreements merely provide for the financing of trade between two countries; they do not indicate what trade will take place although they sometimes specifically exclude the financing of certain transactions. The actual movement of the goods and services depends upon the character of the trade and exchange controls in the two countries and upon the operation of any agreements governing the movement of goods and services between them.

Preventing Excessive Debit or Credit Positions

The successful functioning of a payments agreement depends upon the avoidance of continuing bilateral deficits in current trade between the two countries or currency areas.[11] In some instances, payments agreements are not accompanied by bilateral trade-quota agreements designed to achieve a bilateral balance of current trade between the two countries. These are unlikely to prove successful unless the agreements permit the transfer of balances acquired by one of the partners to a number of other countries. Thus, for example, Britain's bilateral payments agreement with Chile provides that sterling acquired by Chile in trade with Britain or any other sterling area country may be used in making payments for goods from any sterling area or transferable account country.

The establishment of the EPU has made it possible for Western Europe to abandon the earlier type of trade-quota agreements which sought to achieve a bilaterally balanced trade. Before the EPU, for example, the bilateral payments agreement between France and Italy had to be accompanied by a trade-quota agreement which set forth a program of trade between the two countries to achieve a bilateral balance. Since the EPU came into operation in July 1950, either country can run a more or less continuous surplus with the other, and this can be used to discharge deficits with other EPU members. While trade-quota agreements have been negotiated between EPU countries since that agency was established, they have been less comprehensive than the earlier arrangements, and have not aimed to balance trade bilaterally.

Trade agreements designed to achieve a bilateral balance between two countries may take a variety of forms. Sometimes they are little more than an exchange of notes in which each government agrees to encourage trade in certain categories of goods. As a rule, however, they consist of lists of commodities and corresponding quantities or values for which the governments agree to issue the appropriate import and export licenses necessary for the exchange. Where most of the trade is in private hands there is no assurance that this will in fact take place or that trade will even be approximately balanced.

11. If one of the countries had an interest in making long-term investments in the deficit country it would be possible to have a continual deficit on current account without interference with trade. Unfortunately, this is rarely the case.

Agreements covering the exchange of commodities and services frequently contain provisions for tourism, shipping and other services. For example, Swiss trade agreements usually include the amount of Swiss francs which the partner country will permit its citizens to spend in Switzerland should they choose to visit there.

When one or both of the parties to a payments agreement maintains a high degree of state control over trade, the underlying arrangements are likely to be very rigid. Trade under the payments agreement may be limited strictly to the quantities or values of particular goods and services set forth in the trade agreement. In some cases the trade agreement is less rigid and is subject to frequent revision.

Transferability of Balances

One of the most important differences in payments agreements lies in the extent to which balances or credits can be transferred to third countries. It will be recalled that during the period between July 15, 1946 and July 15, 1947, Britain negotiated a number of payments agreements in which sterling balances acquired under the agreements were transferable over a wide area, including the dollar countries. While the failure to maintain convertibility into dollars reduced the area of sterling transferability, sterling agreements nevertheless permit transferability among a large number of countries. Britain has tried to increase the transferability of sterling by including provisions in all her payments agreements permitting the transferability of sterling between nonsterling countries either automatically or by special permission of the Bank of England. Other countries have been less willing to permit such transferability of their own currencies.[12]

BARTER AND COMPENSATION ARRANGEMENTS

Barter and private compensation arrangements, unlike trade under bilateral payments agreements, do not involve a foreign exchange transaction. When countries engage in barter they frequently negotiate agreements covering the exchange of a number of commodities

12. An example of administrative transferability is the permission given to Italy by Sweden to transfer up to 25 million kronor which the former had accumulated in trade with Sweden to Brazil, in payment for coffee. Sweden also permitted Germany to use kronor balances for the purchase of Argentine grain. See *International Trade News Bulletin*, No. 22, November 1951, GATT, Geneva.

in stated quantities and at specified prices. It is usually necessary to maintain accounts which reveal leads and lags in deliveries.

These accounts, which may be kept in the currency of one of the partners or in a third currency, may resemble centralized clearing accounts in bilateral payments agreements. Owing to their underlying rigidity, however, credits to these accounts cannot be considered as foreign exchange payments—they simply measure the progress of the barter exchange. Thus, the trade agreements between the USSR and her satellites provide for balanced deliveries for each six-months period. If one party fails to make good on its deliveries, it is given a limited extension of time in which to do so. This arrangement does not give rise to credits which are freely available for use by the partner country.

Clearly, the distinction here suggested between a barter agreement and a payments agreement depends upon the rigidity of the underlying trade agreement. At times this distinction is difficult to draw. But the usual trade-quota agreement between free enterprise economies, involving the agreement to issue permissive import and export licenses to private traders up to certain limits, is far more flexible in trade relations than is the customary arrangement between two state trading countries. Changes in import licensing and credit policies may occur in response to shifts in the creditor-debtor position of the two countries. Moreover, payments are made by importers in one country to exporters in the other through the respective banking systems. Even though these payments, in the more centralized type of bilateral payments agreements, are recorded as debits or credits in a single clearing account, they may be regarded as actual foreign exchange payments. On the other hand, debiting and crediting accounts maintained to record the progress of a rigidly balanced trade agreement covering specific quantities at specific prices hardly represent foreign exchange payments.

Private Barter and Compensation

Barter transactions sometimes take place between private residents of two countries, one or both of which may maintain exchange controls. United States firms sometimes engage in barter deals with exchange control countries to preserve a market for their exports. If one party is a resident of an exchange control country, he must usually have both an import and an export license. A somewhat more complicated type of transaction is the private compensation transaction involving an importer and an exporter in both countries. A balanced trade is arranged by the four parties and the importer in each country pays the exporter in the same country in his own currency, there being no exchange of currency balances between residents of different countries. As in the case of barter deals, compensation arrangements must be authorized by the import and export control authorities when one or both countries maintains exchange controls. In barter and compensation transactions the parties are frequently brought together by dealers who act as brokers in this type of trade.

While private barter and compensation transactions probably do not constitute a large proportion of world trade, certain countries, including Austria and Greece, permit such dealings under government supervision on a fairly substantial scale. Usually such transactions are confined to luxury or nonessential commodities which may be difficult to sell in world markets. However, some barter deals have involved the exchange of scarce raw materials against essential manufactures.

Agreements and Multilateralism

Mention has already been made of the fact that while most countries trade with one another in accordance with the terms of bilateral trade and payments agreements, trade among the nondollar countries is by no means entirely bilateral. Examination of the bilateral trade accounts of the world reveals large and frequently continual imbalances between nearly all pairs of countries which cannot be accounted for by invisible items and movements of long-term capital.[13] This is partly due to the fact that the swing credits permit a substantial volume of current account surpluses and deficits. Further, when the swing credits are exhausted continual deficits are often settled by gold, funding loans or by convertible currencies such as dollars and Swiss francs. Much more important, however, are the settlements which take place through the transfer of credits or currency balances arising out of the operation of bilateral payments agreements to third countries.

13. See *Direction of World Trade,* published quarterly by the Statistical Office of the United Nations, New York.

We noted earlier the opportunities offered by the system of sterling payments arrangements for such settlements, not only within the sterling areas but among countries with bilateral payments agreements with Britain. (These arrangements will be described in greater detail in Chapter 11.) Since July 1950, however, the most important vehicle for multilateral transfers among nondollar countries has been the European Payments Union. The EPU is a multinational payments agreement created not as a substitute for the existing bilateral network of payments agreements, but to give the existing system greater flexibility and efficiency.

Other Financial Agreements

Our discussion of agreements concerned with the movement and financing of goods and services in international trade would be incomplete without some mention of the role of grants, governmental credits and special financial arrangements such as releases of blocked balances. If intergovernmental credit and grant arrangements simply provided for the delivery of free foreign exchange by the lender or grantor no special financing mechanism would be involved. However, this is not the case today.[14] Both loans and grants tend to be tied to specific items of procurement agreed to by the two governments involved. While procurement in countries other than that of the lender or grantor is sometimes permitted, such procurement is a matter of administrative decision by the lender.[15]

A number of postwar financial agreements have dealt with the release of blocked balances or other assets owned by one or both of the partner countries. For example, British agreements with Egypt, India, Iraq and Pakistan have provided for the release of blocked balances to accounts available for making payments for goods and services. In some cases these agreements also stipulate the amount of the country's sterling balances which can be converted into dollars or

14. An important exception was the American loan of $3.75 billion to Britain in 1946, made available in free dollars with no strings attached to their use. There were, of course, conditions in the loan agreement but they did not relate to the actual employment of the funds. Drawings from the Monetary Fund are likewise free from restrictions but loans from the International Bank must be employed under Bank supervision for the project or projects for which the loan is made.

15. Portions of the grant assistance made available by the Economic Cooperation Administration (ECA) and by the Mutual Security Administration (MSA) have been spent for goods and services outside of the United States.

other hard currencies over the period of the agreement. Several of the postwar financial agreements between Latin American and European countries provide for the release of blocked balances accumulated in the past.

Finally, a number of postwar agreements have involved the settlement of long-term indebtedness or the repatriation of equity capital. These agreements have affected current trade since they provided foreign exchange which could be used by the European countries for increased purchases in Latin America. They have influenced the direction of trade since as a rule balances arising out of debt settlements or from the sale of equities can be used only in the country whose balances are held. Financial agreements of this type are usually accompanied by, or are an integral part of, commodity-exchange and payments agreements.

Chapter 6

THE EUROPEAN PAYMENTS UNION

THE EUROPEAN PAYMENTS UNION is an important part of the postwar payments mechanism, and an understanding of this complex institution is a prerequisite to the consideration of the foreign exchange practices and policies of the world's trading countries. Evaluation of the EPU and its prospects for the future will be found in Part IV of this book.

The origin of the European Payments Union goes back to the beginning of the European Recovery Program in the summer of 1947.[1] To free intra-European trade from the restrictions and artificial channels imposed by the existing payments mechanism was recognized as one of the most important steps toward the economic recovery of Europe. The bilateral trade and payments arrangements of the early postwar period made possible a more rapid restoration of European trade than would have been possible if all trade had been conducted with dollars or gold, but they were at best temporary and imperfect solutions. There were, of course, some multilateral settlements through gold and dollars and through transfers of sterling. But by and large countries sought to balance their trade with one another to avoid payments in gold or hard currencies or to prevent an indefinite accumulation of bilateral credits. In 1947 the volume of trade among Western European countries was only 59 per cent of the 1938 level while trade between Eastern and Western Europe was only 32 per cent.[2] This sluggish movement of intra-European trade could not be accounted for solely by a relatively lower volume of production since

1. For a more comprehensive discussion of the development of the EPU see William Diebold, Jr., *Trade and Payments in Western Europe* (Council on Foreign Relations, Publications), Harper and Brothers, New York, 1952. Diebold's excellent study was published after this chapter was written.
2. *Economic Survey of Europe in 1948,* Economic Commission for Europe, Geneva, 1949, p. 134.

by 1947 industrial output had recovered to 83 per cent of the 1938 level and agricultural production to 76 per cent.[3]

Surplus and Deficit Countries

Aside from the political shadows on the economic relations between Eastern and Western Europe there were two problems which had to be solved in order to expand intra-European trade. The first was the creation of a mechanism by which European countries having bilateral surpluses with certain European countries could use those surpluses to discharge bilateral deficits with other European countries. Not only were gross deficits substantially larger than net deficits, but the ability to transfer bilateral credit positions would help substantially to free trade among European nations.

Closely related to this problem, was the question of how to deal with continuing over-all deficits or surpluses in intra-European trade. Prewar intra-European trade was by no means multilaterally balanced. For example, in 1938 Britain had a trade deficit of $478 million with the rest of Europe. This was settled largely by Britain's invisible surplus with the rest of the world.[4] Belgium and Germany on the other hand tended to have prewar surpluses with the rest of Europe; these were balanced by transfers of gold and convertible currencies available for making payments outside Europe.

While the war brought major shifts in the structure of production and trade within Europe, there was no reason to believe that the normal pattern of trade was to have each country in balance with Europe as a whole or with any particular group of European countries. Thus in the absence of controls certain European countries might be expected to run deficits and others to have surpluses with their European trading partners as a group, even though each country was in balance with the world as a whole. However, under such a system the countries with European deficits would need surpluses with countries outside of Europe, compensated in gold or in acceptable—and freely transferable—foreign exchange.

But in the postwar years countries with intra-European deficits lacked the external foreign exchange earnings with which to settle

3. *Ibid.,* p. 14.
4. *A Survey of the Economic Situation and Prospects of Europe,* Economic Commission for Europe, Geneva, 1948, pp. 95–97.

them. This was a problem of over-all balance which made more difficult and intractable the question of achieving a mechanism for multilateral settlements within Europe. Britain, for example, would not permit Italy to use her sterling surplus to discharge a deficit with Belgium since Britain was not in a position after August 1947 to make substantial gold payments to cover Belgium's excess sterling holdings.

In the early postwar period some European countries, as, for instance, France and the Netherlands, tended to have deficits with nearly all their European trading partners, while Belgium tended to have surpluses. This situation made it extremely difficult to establish a payments system through which even the bilateral positions which in theory could be offset against one another could actually be cleared. Thus it became clear that there was no solution for the problem of multilateral settlements within Europe until the problem of over-all deficits of the European countries was met. This was the fundamental contribution of American aid under the European Recovery Program.

REGIONAL MULTILATERAL SETTLEMENTS [5]

Before considering the measures employed to solve the problem of intra-European trade, it is necessary to deal briefly with the theoretical aspects of regional multilateral settlements. First, why are special payments mechanisms ever necessary? Why wasn't the restoration of gold or dollar convertibility of Western European currencies the best solution for Europe's trade problem immediately after the war?

The answer is that this would have kept intra-European trade, as well as trade between all soft-currency countries, at a very low level. Given the great need for goods available only in the dollar area, European countries and their associates in the same monetary areas would have sought to limit drastically their imports from one another in order either to earn dollars or to avoid making dollar payments. This

5. For a more complete discussion of this subject, see R. F. Mikesell, "Regional Multilateral Payments Arrangements," *Quarterly Journal of Economics,* August 1948, pp. 500–18; see also Robert W. Bean, "European Multilateral Clearing," *Journal of Political Economy,* October 1948, pp. 403–15; Ragnar Frisch, "On the Need for Forecasting a Multilateral Balance of Payments," *American Economic Review,* September 1947, pp. 535–51; M. H. Ekker, *Equilibrium of International Trade and International Monetary Compensation,* Central Planning Bureau, The Hague, 1950.

circumstance led most countries to negotiate bilateral trade and payments agreements with one another immediately after the war. Therefore, so long as most countries preferred dollars to other currencies, trade between them conducted on the basis of dollars or currencies convertible into dollars could not reach a satisfactory level. The causes and remedies for this situation—frequently referred to as the "dollar shortage"—will be discussed in a later chapter. The question here is, given a situation which has led a large group of countries to adopt bilateral payments arrangements, how can a system of multilateral settlements within the group be established?

Several mechanisms are possible. One is represented by the sterling transferable account system. Trade among transferable account and sterling area countries is financed by sterling transfers, with each accepting sterling without limit. The success of such a system, however, depends upon a fair degree of balance among the members as well as the existence of a relatively strong currency which all members are willing to hold. Sterling proved impractical as a universal exchange medium for Western Europe because of Britain's persistent deficit with certain countries, notably Belgium. Thus when, after August 1947, sterling was no longer convertible, Belgium withdrew from the transferable account group.

How Circuit Clearing Works

Another approach to group multilateral settlements is the multilateral offset or circuit clearing system. Under this, bilateral positions resulting from the operations of the existing bilateral payments agreements could be cleared periodically by a process of canceling individual bilateral surpluses against individual bilateral deficits. Assume the following pattern of bilateral relationships at the end of a given period:

Country A has a surplus of $11 million with country B
Country A has a surplus of $6 million with country C
Country B has a surplus of $4 million with country C
Country B has a surplus of $7 million with country D
Country C has a surplus of $8 million with country D
Country D has a surplus of $5 million with country A

We may show these relationships by means of the following diagram in which the arrow represents the direction of the surplus:

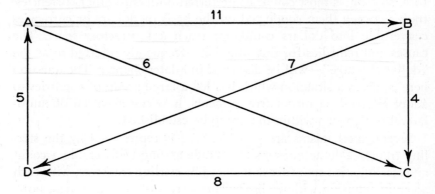

Several types of circuits could be arranged from the same data. If the objective is to clear the maximum volume of balances, a simple rule is as follows: construct the longest circuit possible and if there is more than one of equal length, select the one in which the largest volume of bilateral balances can be cleared. After clearing this circuit construct another with the remaining uncleared balances, again choosing the longest circuit with the largest common denominator. Repeat this until further clearings are impossible.[6] Thus in the example above, after clearing the circuit ABCD the bilateral relations are as follows:

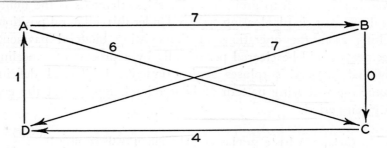

Just two circuits are now possible: ABDA and ACDA. They are of equal length and have the same least common denominator. Unless

---

6. This method becomes exceedingly cumbersome when a large number of countries are involved. Dr. M. H. Ekker has developed a mathematical formula for clearing balances by means of the offset method. See Ekker, *op. cit.*

there is some special reason for reducing B's surplus with D rather than, say, C's surplus with D, there is no choice between them.[7] Either choice will eliminate $19 million of debit balances after clearing the two circuits. It will be observed, however, that this method of clearing, which is called "first category compensation," involves only the mutual cancellation of balances and not a transfer of balances from one country to another. If transfers of balances between countries were possible, a larger volume of total debit balances could be eliminated. Thus if A were willing to accept D's currency in settlement of A's surplus with B and C, $10 million in additional deficits could be eliminated and all that remained would be A's creditor position with D and C of $10 million and $2 million, respectively.

"Second Category" Compensations

The results obtained in the last operation—the reduction of each country's gross debit and credit positions to a single net position with all other members—cannot generally be achieved without actual transfers of debit balances or currency holdings, or some form of pooling of bilateral positions in a single clearing account. In a system where actual transfers of balances are permitted, the clearings are called "second category compensations."

Second category compensations, of course, raise serious questions as to which currencies a country will end up holding. If D's currency were particularly weak, A might not agree to exchange its credits with the other countries for a credit position with D which it did not have in the beginning. It was this reluctance on the part of creditor countries to become the involuntary creditors of certain others that made it difficult for the Bank for International Settlements to secure acceptance of second category compensations.

The limited clearing possibilities of first category compensation and the obstacles to second category compensation can be overcome by the adoption of a system in which all bilateral positions are pooled and net credits or debits recorded in a clearing account in terms of a common unit. This is essentially the procedure employed by an association of domestic banks for clearing checks. Banks exchange their

---

7. Sometimes it is more desirable to clear one bilateral balance rather than another because a continued flow of trade may depend upon the clearing of certain balances while this may not be true in the case of others.

bilateral claims on others in the system for a credit with the clearing house. Their net credit or debit with the clearing house for a particular period is determined by subtracting their gross bilateral debits from their gross bilateral credits. In this way net creditors have a claim against the clearing house rather than against any individual debtor, while the obligation of the debtors is to the clearing house and not to individual creditors. This is the principle of the European Payments Union.

Over-all Credits and Deficits

The establishment of a satisfactory clearing mechanism by no means solves everything involved in settling trade balances among a group of countries. There remains the problem of over-all credits and deficits. If the net positions of the members of the group are the result of temporary fluctuations in balances of payments due to seasonal or other short-term causes, they could be handled by asking each country to accept credit balances in the clearing account up to a stated limit. But if the net deficits and credits are large and persistent, some means must be found to finance them or the system will break down. A second alternative, of course, would be for the member countries to achieve an over-all balance through export or import controls, but this would weaken the system's effectiveness in expanding trade.

A regional clearing system which permits its members no continuing surpluses or deficits is likely to bring about an uneconomical trade pattern and to perpetuate a level of prices and costs which are out of relation to the rest of the world. It becomes a permanently isolated trading bloc and thereby perpetuates the very conditions which made its creation necessary and desirable.

On the other hand, if all net positions in the clearing account had to be settled fully in gold or hard currencies, it would defeat the purpose for which the arrangement was made since members would restrict their trade with one another in order either to earn gold or outside currencies or to keep from paying them. It is necessary, therefore, to adopt some form of compromise between full settlements in gold or dollars on the one hand, and a completely closed system on the other. This has been, perhaps, the most serious problem the EPU has had to face.

Possible Solutions

There are three ways to cover net deficits and credits in a clearing system. First, the creditor countries can extend credits to the clearing union. But credits eventually have to be repaid and there is a limit to the willingness or capacity of creditor countries to lend. A second method is to make grants or loans to the clearing system from the outside. This permits countries running continual surpluses to be compensated in gold or dollars. A third method is to require debtors to cover at least a portion of their deficits in gold or dollars. All three methods have been employed in the EPU.

Mention should be made of still another method of dealing with over-all surpluses and deficits: the pooling of all external foreign exchange and gold earnings by several members of a multilateral payments system for their joint use in settling external deficits. This is essentially the method of the sterling area. There is no attempt to force a balance between each sterling area member and the area as a whole. It is recognized that some members, by virtue of the nature of their production and trade, will have surpluses with the dollar area and other nonsterling countries, while others will have deficits. With more or less common policies as to import controls and discrimination against hard-currency areas, each member obtains the hard currencies it needs from the Bank of England. Such an arrangement seems possible only among countries with close political and economic ties. It also requires a strong "center" country whose currency is generally acceptable to members of the group. It would probably not be feasible to attempt such a system for Western Europe without a greater degree of political and economic integration than is now in sight.

One of the important objectives of a clearing arrangement should be to eliminate the conditions which brought it into existence.[8] While the ultimate objective is to reach a condition in which net positions are compensated fully in gold or dollars, this can only be approached gradually if intraregional trade is not to be seriously reduced. If the system encourages creditor countries to earn dollars easily by exporting high-priced goods to members of the clearing system, they will

8. For a discussion of this problem see R. F. Mikesell, "Discrimination and International Trade Policy," *Review of Economics and Statistics*, August 1950, pp. 227-34.

have little incentive to export to the dollar area. If debtor countries are able to obtain large credits from the clearing organization they will have little incentive to get into balance. We shall see how these problems have been met in the arrangements for facilitating intra-European trade.

PAYMENTS SCHEMES PRIOR TO THE EPU [9]

From the beginning of the European Recovery Program both American and European economists realized that the restoration of a high level of intra-European trade on a multilateral basis was essential to European recovery. The *General Report* of the Committee of European Economic Cooperation recommended the establishment of a mechanism to permit automatic clearing of the bilateral positions arising out of the operation of the payments agreements between European countries.[10] The *Report* also recommended that a portion of the American assistance be set aside as a fund for the conversion of excess credits arising out of the operations of the payments system. But progress toward implementing these recommendations was slow and the objectives were not fully achieved until the establishment of the European Payments Union in July 1950.

The development of a multilateral payments arrangement ran into difficulties from the beginning because of conflicting national interests among the ERP countries. Some—including Benelux, France and Italy—favored the adoption of a completely multilateral payments system for Western Europe, with excess credit positions covered by an arrangement of American aid.[11] This was rejected by Brit-

9. For a more complete discussion of the development of the intra-European payments arrangements prior to the establishment of the EPU see Diebold, *op. cit.,* Chapters 3 and 4; see also R. F. Mikesell, *United States Economic Policy and International Relations,* McGraw-Hill, New York, 1952, pp. 179–86.

10. See *General Report,* Committee of European Economic Cooperation, Paris, Vol. I, September 1947, pp. 133–34; see also "Report of the Committee on Payments Agreements," *General Report,* Vol. II, pp. 525–37. The Benelux proposal (given in Appendix C of Vol. II) provided for the establishment of a pooling type clearing mechanism based on the existing bilateral payments agreements. At the end of every clearing period each creditor country would be allotted a share of each of the debtor countries' currencies equal to its net creditor position.

11. Since the total amount of aid appropriated by Congress for ECA assistance was geared to Western Europe's dollar deficit, the scheme suggested by the Benelux countries would have permitted intra-European creditors to earn a larger share of ECA dollar aid.

ain and other members of the Organisation for European Economic Co-operation (OEEC) on the grounds that it would introduce too much dollar competition into intra-European trade.

Essentially, these countries feared that too large a proportion of dollar aid would be captured by Belgium, with her strong creditor position. Britain was reluctant to enter into any kind of European payments scheme since she was the center country in the sterling area. Finally, the United States, while favoring a multilateral payments arrangement for Western Europe, was unwilling in the initial stages of the ERP to allocate aid to a special clearing fund to be used automatically. The Economic Cooperation Administration Act of April 1948 did not authorize such an allocation. Further, it was the intent of Congress that ECA aid should cover specific dollar deficits of Western European countries for programs to achieve specific recovery goals. To permit Belgium to earn more ECA dollars than she needed for her recovery program through her surpluses with other Western European countries was considered by some U.S. officials an improper use of dollar aid.[12] Belgium, on the other hand, did not favor a multilateral payments arrangement for Western Europe which did not permit the conversion of credit positions into gold or dollars.

The First Agreement on Multilateral Monetary Compensation

The operations under the "First Agreement on Multilateral Monetary Compensation of November 18, 1947" represented the first concrete effort of the ERP countries to achieve a degree of multilateral clearing of their bilateral payments positions.[13] The five signatory countries—Belgium-Luxembourg, the Netherlands, France and Italy —agreed to automatic first category compensations with respect to their bilateral payments positions, and to second category compensations (involving a transfer of balances) upon recommendation of the clearing agent, provided the consent of the countries whose balances were affected could be obtained.

Each member reported its bilateral position to the clearing agent— the Bank for International Settlement (BIS)—at the end of each

12. It should be said that some U.S. government economists favored an arrangement of U.S. aid similar to ECA's contribution to the EPU from the beginning of the ERP.

13. The text of this Agreement is reprinted in the *Eighteenth Annual Report*, Bank for International Settlements, Basel, 1948, pp. 167–70.

month. The BIS then reported the compensations to be effected automatically and made recommendations for second category compensations. In addition to the regular members (Bizonal Germany later joined as a regular member) eight countries became "occasional" members: Austria, Denmark, Greece, Norway, Portugal, Sweden, the United Kingdom and the French Zone of Germany. Occasional members reported their bilateral positions to the BIS each month but they could elect to accept or reject even the first category compensations suggested by the clearing agent.

The results were extremely meager. The accounts of the countries reporting to the BIS showed total bilateral debits of over $700 million at the end of 1947, of which about $400 million represented net debits (or credits). This meant that $300 million of the gross indebtedness could have been compensated, given a mechanism for complete multilateral offsetting. The maximum possibilities for first category compensations alone, however, were about $40 or $50 million, and those depended upon the willingness of all occasional members to agree to the compensations recommended by the BIS.[14] Actual compensations amounted to less than $2 million for the first clearing operation in December 1947 and by the end of March 1948 compensations totaled only $39 million.

Without the full cooperation of the occasional members the possibilities for first category compensation among the regular members were exceedingly narrow since Italy, France and the Netherlands were in debt to the Belgium-Luxembourg Economic Union (B.L.E.U.).[15] To construct closed circuits for multilateral offsetting, all members must have both creditor and debtor positions. Frequently a successful operation depended upon the willingness of Denmark, an occasional member, to agree to a compensation since that country was the only member which tended to have a credit balance with the B.L.E.U. Denmark, however, was reluctant to agree to relinquish a credit with a strong-currency country in order to discharge a deficit with a weak-currency country.

It was obvious that two conditions had to be met if the clearing system was to succeed. First, all the OEEC countries had to be brought

14. *Eighteenth Annual Report,* Bank for International Settlements, Basel, 1948, pp. 148 and 159.

15. Belgium and Luxembourg have an economic and currency union and hence their accounts in the postwar payments agreements are pooled.

into the system. Second, some means had to be found to keep certain countries from getting into the position of creditor or of debtor to all or nearly all the other members. Both these conditions were dealt with in the Agreement for Intra-European Payments and Compensations, signed by all the OEEC members on October 14, 1948.

Offshore Purchases and Conditional Aid

The ECA Act of 1948 authorized the ECA to make purchases with dollars in one country for delivery to another country entitled to receive assistance. In addition to the so-called offshore purchases in Latin America and elsewhere, ECA made available a limited amount of dollars to finance the imports of some ERP countries from others. These dollars did "double duty" in the sense that they financed intra-European deficits while at the same time they provided some of the dollars required by the creditor countries to finance Western Hemisphere deficits.[16]

This arrangement had definite disadvantages. Congress had placed limitations on the making of offshore purchases [17] so that this technique had to be confined to certain commodity transfers. More serious, however, was the fact that it was difficult to develop a system of multilateral payments within Europe alongside a special system of dollar trade. It was therefore decided to merge the arrangement for meeting intra-European deficits with the system of multilateral payments.

Beginning with October 1948, the ECA adopted a new arrangement for the settlement of intra-European deficits. Under this, part of the assistance to ERP countries was granted in the form of "conditional aid," based upon the amount of each country's planned bilateral surplus with each of the other members. Recipients of conditional aid would, in turn, be required to provide drawing rights to each bilateral partner with whom they expected to have a surplus over the quarter. Thus each ERP country would receive drawing rights upon the member countries with whom they were expected to

16. During the quarter ended September 30, 1948, ECA supplied about $140 million to finance purchases in one ERP country for delivery to another. (*Second Report to Congress of the Economic Cooperation Administration,* Washington, 1949, p. 12.)

17. For example, offshore procurement of agricultural commodities declared to be in surplus by the United States was prohibited. There were also some price limitations.

have bilateral deficits, entitling them to incur a given amount of deficit without being required to pay gold or to accumulate an indebtedness. By this device, nearly every country entitled to ECA aid both extended drawing rights to other members (equal to the amount of conditional aid received) and received drawing rights from others. Even Belgium, a large net creditor on intra-European account, received drawing rights of $11 million from Italy, but extended drawing rights to nearly every other country, to a total of $218.5 million.[18]

Countries receiving conditional aid from ECA obtained no more dollar assistance than they would have received in the absence of this arrangement, except possibly to the extent that their intra-European export surpluses may have affected the level of their planned dollar deficits. That is, the larger their exports, the more dollars they would need for raw materials, etc. The device was simply a means of requiring countries to finance their planned intra-European surpluses by making grants to other ERP members, in exchange for grants from ECA.

There was considerable justification for this system. If European creditor countries like Belgium had been able to sell their exports for dollars, they would have needed fewer dollars from ECA to cover their Western Hemisphere deficits. In fact, most of the ECA aid to Belgium was conditional. The creditor countries were willing to go along with this scheme because it enabled them to keep their industries operating at a high level by selling goods in the European and sterling area markets.

The Agreement for Intra-European Payments and Compensations

This agreement was signed by the representatives of the OEEC countries including the military governors of the Bizone and French Zone of Germany and the Territory of Trieste. It established the conditions for the use of the drawing rights under ECA's conditional aid program and established a new system of multilateral compensations, superseding the "First Agreement on Multilateral Monetary Com-

18. For a discussion of the conditional aid system see *A Report on Recovery Progress and United States Aid,* Economic Cooperation Administration, Washington, February 1949, pp. 204–18. See also *Nineteenth Annual Report,* Bank for International Settlements, Basel, 1949, pp. 200–13.

pensation of November 1947." [19] Under the new agreement all participating countries, except Portugal and Switzerland, accepted "first category compensations" as determined by the BIS. As under the earlier agreement, however, "second category compensations" remained optional. First category operations involving the balances of Switzerland and Portugal were also optional.

In spite of improvements in the system of monthly compensations, the volume of clearings continued small. There were no second category compensations in the first quarter of the plan's operation and only $3.2 million in the second quarter, although a number of such operations were recommended by the clearing agent. In the first quarter of operations $31 million was cleared by first category compensations and $198 million of bilateral deficits were financed through the use of drawing rights.[20] Total first category compensations during the nine months ending June 30, 1949, amounted to $104 million.[21] As in the case of the earlier system, the reasons for the small volume of compensations were the limited possibilities of first category compensations and the general imbalance of Europe's trade due to the persistent deficits of certain countries, e.g., France, and the persistent surpluses of others, e.g., the B.L.E.U.

Another difficulty with the Intra-European Payments Scheme (IEPS) was the disparity between the established drawing rights and their rate of utilization. Some countries quickly exhausted some bilateral drawing rights but failed to utilize others. At the end of the operations for 1948–1949, only $677 million had been utilized out of $805 million established.[22] If the members had been able to transfer drawing rights from one country to another, they could have been utilized more fully.

Not only were the trading programs unfulfilled, but the fact that trade had to be conducted on the basis of the underlying trade-quota

19. The text of "The Agreement for Intra-European Payments and Compensations of October 1948" together with supplementary agreements is printed in the *Nineteenth Annual Report*, Bank for International Settlements, Basel, 1949.

20. *Third Report to Congress of the Economic Cooperation Administration*, Washington, May 1949, p. 25. After conducting clearing operations, the BIS was authorized to utilize the drawing rights for a further reduction of bilateral balances. Total drawing rights established by ECA for the first year of the Intra-European Payments Scheme (IEPS) amounted to $805.5 million.

21. *Twentieth Annual Report*, Bank for International Settlements, Basel, 1950, p. 226.

22. *Ibid.*, p. 225.

agreements served to inhibit trade and stifle competition within Europe. Moreover, countries which granted drawing rights had no incentive to meet their export goals since they received the conditional aid from the United States whether or not the rights were utilized. On the other hand, debtor nations had little to gain by getting into a more balanced position since drawing rights were extended to them in accordance with a program fixed nine months in advance, and there was no reward for not utilizing their rights.

ECA's Proposal

The ECA and a number of the OEEC governments were acutely conscious of the shortcomings of the IEPS and anxious to introduce reforms. In particular, ECA wanted to stimulate substantial competition in intra-European trade, both as among European producers and with those of other areas, including the dollar area. In April 1949, ECA proposed that a new agreement be concluded which would provide for the transferability of drawing rights from one ERP country to another, so that a country having a drawing right could use it against any member country with which it had a deficit. Thus if France had drawing rights from Britain over and above the amount needed to settle her deficit there, the sterling could be transferred to Belgium in settlement of a deficit with that country. In addition, ECA proposed that holders of unused drawing rights should be able to convert them into ECA dollars for expenditure anywhere in the world.[23]

Belgium and certain other OEEC countries favored the ECA proposal, but it was vigorously opposed by Britain. Throughout the spring of 1949 Britain's payments position was steadily deteriorating and her representatives argued that she could not afford to risk a loss of conditional aid either to Belgium or some other ERP creditor country or to the recipient of the drawing right if that creditor should decide to convert the right into ECA dollars.[24] In the course of the negotiations, ECA finally withdrew the proposal for making the drawing rights convertible into dollars. In place of automatic transferability, Britain proposed "administrative" transferability

23. See Gardner Patterson, *Survey of United States International Finance, 1949*, International Finance Section, Princeton University, Princeton, 1950, pp. 137–38.
24. See *The Economist*, June 11, 1949, p. 1099.

within the OEEC countries. Administrative transferability would take place whenever a transfer of drawing rights would not involve a loss of gold for the country which had extended the rights. Thus, if Italy had $10 million in sterling rights it could transfer the sterling to the Netherlands (a transferable account country) but not to Belgium or Switzerland, if Britain's payments position with these countries was such as to require a gold payment.

Revised Agreement: 1949

After long debate, on September 7, 1949, a compromise was reached in a new Agreement for Intra-European Payments and Compensations for 1949–1950.[25] It followed the lines of the 1948 agreement except for the provision that 25 per cent of the drawing rights were made multilateral, the other 75 per cent being bilateral. Thus each country received multilateral drawing rights equal to one fourth of its total bilateral drawing rights, as originally established. The conditional aid corresponding to the multilateral drawing rights was allotted to the country on which the drawing rights were actually exercised. If a country had exhausted its bilateral drawing rights in covering a deficit with another country, the BIS clearing agent was authorized to utilize automatically the multilateral drawing rights to cover the amount of the deficit up to one third of the drawing rights. At the request of the debtor country, the multilateral drawing rights could be used to cover a deficit amounting to more than one third of the original drawing rights, or to cover a deficit with a country which had not established a drawing right in favor of the debtor country.

A special feature of the 1949 intra-European payments agreement was the arrangement for covering Belgium's surplus with the rest of the OEEC countries. Belgium's intra-European surplus was estimated to be at least $400 million for 1949–1950, double its planned Western Hemisphere deficit of $200 million. It was feared that if Belgium were granted $150 million as conditional aid to cover her bilateral drawing rights, she would earn far more than her share— $50 million—of the multilateral drawing rights.

25. For the text of this agreement see *Twentieth Annual Report,* Bank for International Settlements, Basel, 1950, pp. 263–93.

It was decided to cover the first $200 million of Belgium's intra-European surplus by bilateral and multilateral drawing rights similar to those of other countries; the second $200 million, by special multilateral drawing rights covered by a special allocation of ECA aid equal to $112.5 million, and the remaining $87.5 million by credits granted by Belgium. Both the special multilateral drawing rights and the Belgian credits were made available to France, the Netherlands and Britain, the countries with the greatest estimated deficits with Belgium.

System Still Basically Bilateral

Except for the addition of the multilateral drawing rights, the compensation arrangements under the 1949 agreement were essentially the same as under that of 1948. First category compensations were automatic, while second category compensations remained subject to the approval of the countries concerned in the transfers of balances. During the life of the agreement, which ended on June 30, 1950, $63 million in first category compensations and $86.3 million in second category compensations were effected. Total balances settled by utilized drawing rights amounted to $702.8 million, with an additional $39.1 million settled by the special Belgian loan.[26] While an element of multilateralism was introduced by the use of multilateral drawing rights totaling about $285 million, the system remained basically bilateral.

Some progress was made by the OEEC toward liberalizing intra-European trade from quota and licensing restrictions during the operation of the 1949 payments agreement. In November 1949 the participating members agreed to abolish quantitative restrictions on at least 50 per cent of their private imports from one another. Some countries also substituted global quotas for bilateral quotas for certain imports, thereby eliminating discrimination among the participating members.[27] However, further progress toward freeing trade

26. *Ninth Report to Congress of the Economic Cooperation Administration,* November 1950, pp. 24–25. Total drawing rights finally established for the period amounted to $784.3 million which, with the $87.5 million Belgian credit, provided resources for meeting deficits of $871.8 million.

27. *Second Report of the Organisation for European Economic Co-operation,* Paris, 1950, pp. 220–21.

in Western Europe had to await the establishment of a fully multi-lateral intra-European payments scheme.

The 1949 IEPS was a compromise arrangement which improved on the 1948 version only in degree. The scheme perpetuated the basic system of bilateral trade and payments arrangements. Further, it gave the receiver of drawing rights little incentive to get into balance. The fact that drawing rights had to be established in advance and related to conditional aid required considerable planning of intra-European trade, a circumstance at odds with the objective of the ECA and a majority of the OEEC countries for the liberalization of trade. Finally, the United States was anxious to see a payments system for Western Europe which eventually could be merged into a world-wide multilateral system, including convertibility into dollars. The first step in this direction was a fully multilateral system within Western Europe coupled with an arrangement for at least partial conversion of net intra-European credit balances into gold or dollars. This was in essence the ECA proposal of December 1949 which, in the fall of 1950, became the European Payments Union.

The Organization of the EPU [28]

The signing of the Agreement for the Establishment of a European Payments Union in Paris, on September 19, 1950,[29] was the culmination of three years of negotiations and experimentation for achieving a completely multilateral system of current payments for Western European countries and the currency areas with which they were associated. The EPU differs radically from earlier compensation arrangements—it provides for a complete netting of all bilateral payments positions at the end of each accounting period.

Each member country reports its position with every other member to the BIS at the end of each month. The BIS then determines for each country its "accounting surplus or deficit" for that month. This is calculated from the sum of its bilateral surpluses and deficits (that

28. Unless otherwise noted the material in this section is based on *The First Annual Report of the Managing Board of the European Payments Union* OEEC, Paris, August 1951; and *The Twenty-First Annual Report,* Bank for International Settlements, Basel, 1951.

29. *Agreement for the Establishment of a European Payments Union,* OEEC, Paris, September 1950. The Agreement was signed by all OEEC countries (except Switzerland) including the Free Territory of Trieste. Switzerland became a member in November, 1950.

is, its net position vis-à-vis all other members), adjusted for any use of "existing resources" and "initial balances."

The bilateral positions with other members are thus eliminated in exchange for a position with the EPU. The complicated nature of the EPU derives from the method of net settlement and not from the clearing operation, which is similar to that of a clearing house in offsetting the bilateral positions among banks. As with previous payments arrangements, the BIS is responsible for maintaining the accounts of the Union and acts as the clearing agent. Policy decisions are made by the Managing Board, appointed by the Council of the OEEC.

It is important to note that the EPU does not introduce a new currency nor are actual transactions involving goods and services financed through the EPU. Payments relations between countries are conducted in accordance with existing bilateral payments arrangements. Thus Frenchmen buy goods in Britain with francs or with sterling received from sterling area importers, and the foreign balances acquired by private traders are sold to the banks for national currencies. In both cases the currency balances owned by foreign banks are held in special bilateral accounts, not ordinarily transferable to third currency areas.

Periodically the commercial banks in each country turn over excess foreign balances to their own central bank in exchange for balances in national currency. The Bank of France reports to the EPU its holdings of sterling acquired during the accounting period and the francs held for the account of the Bank of England. When these bilateral positions are reported to the EPU at the end of each month the currency holdings arising from commercial transactions are canceled out. Only the foreign currency holdings of the central banks and not those of other banks and individuals are reported to the EPU.

Initial Balances and Special Resources

Before a member's "accounting surplus or deficit" with the EPU can be determined, its net surplus or deficit with other members over the accounting period is subject to certain adjustments. These adjustments include (1) the use of initial credit or debit balances; (2) the use of special resources; (3) the use of existing resources.

The system of initial balances used during 1950–1951 corresponded to the drawing rights and conditional aid under the old IEPS system, except that under the EPU they were fully multilateral, not bilateral. Thus Austria was allotted an initial balance of $80 million for 1950–1951, which meant that Austria could run a cumulative net deficit with other EPU members of that amount before being charged with an accounting deficit with the EPU.

These initial credit balances were matched by initial debit balances allotted to the creditor countries. For example, Britain was allotted an initial debit balance of $150 million for 1950–1951, which meant that Britain was required to run a cumulative net surplus with the other members before she could be credited with an accounting surplus with the EPU. For the first year of operations, beginning with July 1950, total initial credit balances were $314 million, of which $279 million were grants and $35 million were loans. The effective total debit balances allotted to creditors was $201 million.

At the end of the first year of the EPU, ECA announced that instead of allotting initial balances to debtor countries during the second year it would make dollars available to the Union to finance the creation of "special resources" in favor of certain countries which had incurred deficits with other EPU members. Under this arrangement, ECA dollars amounting to over $200 million were paid to the EPU which in turn were used to reduce the accounting deficits of Austria, Greece, Iceland and Turkey. This form of assistance not only made possible larger imports by these countries from the EPU countries and their associated monetary areas, but it also increased the liquidity of the Union by providing it with additional dollars.

Existing Resources

The adjustments due to the use of existing resources arose out of the unfunded debts in the bilateral payments agreements between the OEEC countries at the time EPU came into existence. The participating countries agreed to enter into negotiations for the funding of these balances so that so far as possible the EPU could begin operations without overhanging indebtedness. In some cases, the balances were funded and subject to regular amortization payments. In other cases, it was agreed that holders of balances could use them with the

EPU as "existing resources" for the settlement of net deficits. For example, members of the sterling transferable account group are permitted to use their sterling holdings in settling net deficits with the Union.

Britain was anxious to maintain the transferable account system. At the same time, she was fearful lest by giving transferable countries the right to use past accumulations of sterling for settling EPU deficits, she might be required to pay gold to the Union on account of large transfers of sterling to the EPU by members of the transferable account group.[30] Under a separate agreement ECA agreed to reimburse the United Kingdom for any net payment of dollars to the EPU which might result from the use of accumulated sterling holdings by participating countries to cover their EPU deficits.[31]

The Settlement of Accounting Surpluses and Deficits

Within certain limits, the settlement of accounting surpluses and deficits consists simply of the crediting or debiting of each member's account on the books of the Union.[32] EPU credits are available for use in covering a deficit with other EPU members since each member agrees to accept EPU credits in settlement of a credit against any other member. When a member's accounting credit or debit reaches a certain level (a percentage of its quota) additional accounting surpluses or deficits must be settled partly in gold. Each member of the EPU has a quota—normally 15 per cent of its total visible and invisible trade with the other members for 1949.[33] The quotas determined the normal limit of the cumulative accounting surplus or deficit of each member with the EPU. Certain debtors and creditors have been permitted to exceed these limits by special arrangements negotiated

30. OEEC countries which are members of the transferable account group are Austria, Denmark, Greece, Italy, the Netherlands monetary area, Norway, Sweden and Western Germany.

31. *Ninth Report to Congress of the Economic Cooperation Administration*, 1950, p. 30. The ECA paid Britain $39.9 million in December 1951 for losses of reserves sustained as a result of the use of accumulated sterling balances by EPU members. See *The New York Times*, January 2, 1952, p. 1.

32. The unit of account of the EPU is fixed at .8887 grams of fine gold and has a gold value equivalent to that of the present U.S. dollar.

33. There were several exceptions to the 15 per cent rule: Belgium's quota was somewhat smaller than the calculated amount and Switzerland's was larger. During the first year the quotas of Germany and the Netherlands were increased. No individual quotas were allotted to Ireland or Trieste, since these were members of the sterling and lira monetary areas, respectively.

with the Managing Board of the EPU. Accounting surpluses and deficits are settled by a combination of credits given or received and gold received or paid in accordance with the schedules established by the EPU agreement. When the EPU was extended for an additional year after July 30, 1952, the schedule of gold payments and credits was revised in favor of larger gold payments by the debtors.

Under the original EPU Agreement, an accounting deficit equal to 20 per cent of a country's quota could be settled entirely by a credit from the EPU. Thereafter, debtors had to pay an increasing proportion of their deficits in gold as their accounting deficit increased, the rest being covered by a credit from the Union. The proportion of gold payments increased with the accounting deficit measured as a percentage of the quota so that when a country's deficit reached 80 per cent of its quota the next 20 per cent had to be settled by gold payments equal to 16 per cent of the quota and a credit from the EPU equal to 4 per cent of the quota.

In the case of creditor countries an accounting surplus equal to 20 per cent of their quota was settled in the form of a credit to the Union. Thereafter additional accounting surpluses were settled by partial settlements in gold, the remainder in credits to the Union. Thus the next 20 per cent of the quota was settled 10 per cent in gold and 10 per cent in the form of a credit to the Union. (See Table 1.) In July 1952 the percentages of gold payments by debtors were increased for the earlier stages of the utilization of their quotas so that 20 per cent of the second 10 per cent of their quota had to be settled in gold.

When a country which has been a creditor becomes a debtor, it will begin to repay gold immediately in the same proportion as it was received in the process of reaching its creditor position. Likewise, a debtor nation which shifts to a current creditor condition will receive gold until its net cumulative debtor position has reached 10 per cent of its quota. Thus the process is completely reversible for both creditors and debtors. Once a debtor has reached a cumulative deficit equal to its quota it must cover further deficits 100 per cent in gold, unless, of course, its quota is increased by the OEEC. The Agreement leaves to the OEEC Council the decision as to how accounting surpluses in excess of the quota are to be settled.

TABLE 1

GOLD PAYMENTS AND CREDITS BY EPU MEMBERS

(Per Cent)

Percentages of Quotas	Creditors		Debtors (Old Scale)		Debtors (after July 1952)	
	Receive Gold from EPU	Grant Credit to EPU	Pay Gold to EPU	Receive Credit from EPU	Pay Gold to EPU	Receive Credit from EPU
Over-all percentages of total quotas	40	60	40	60	40	60
Above 0 and up to 10 ...	—	10	—	10	—	10
" 10 " " " 20 ...	—	10	—	10	2	8
" 20 " " " 40 ... 10	10	10	4	16	6	14
" 40 " " " 60 ... 10	10	10	8	12	8	12
" 60 " " " 80 ... 10	10	10	12	8	10	10
" 80 " " " 100 ... 10	10	10	16	4	14	6

Sources: First Annual Report of the Managing Board of the European Payments Union, OEEC, Paris, 1951; and Second Annual Report of the Managing Board of the European Payments Union, OEEC, Paris, 1952.

ECA Supplies Working Capital

While most of the liquidity of the payments system is provided by the members themselves through the extension of credits, the initial balances and the existing resources, some working capital has been provided by the ECA. At the beginning of the Union's operations in the summer of 1950, ECA made available $350 million in working capital to the EPU to be used in the event that gold payments to creditor countries exceeded gold receipts from debtors.[34] This fund was necessary for four principal reasons:

1. The schedule of gold payments and receipts permitted debtor countries in utilizing the first 60 per cent of their quotas to pay less gold to the Union than creditor countries with surpluses up to the first 60 per cent of their quota would receive. However, debtor countries using their entire quota would pay in gold a proportion equal to what creditor countries received when they ran cumulative surpluses equal to 100 per cent of their quota.

2. If accounting surpluses were concentrated in a few countries and deficits in many, the EPU would need to pay relatively large

34. Public Law 535 of June 5, 1950 (Sec. 111(d)) authorized the ECA "to transfer funds directly to any central institution . . . to facilitate the development of transferability of European currencies, or to promote the liberalization of trade by participating countries with one another and with other countries." Public Law 759 of September 6, 1950, provided that up to $500 million of the ECA appropriation could be used for this purpose.

amounts of gold while receiving only small amounts of gold or perhaps none at all, since no gold payments were required for the first 20 per cent of the quotas utilized.

3. The initial credit balances granted to the debtors exceeded the initial debit balances granted by the creditors.

4. The fact that the remainder of the ECA fund is available for distribution among the creditors at the time of its liquidation was a factor in making potential creditor countries more willing to join the Union.

In addition to the $350 million granted by ECA to the Union during the first two years ECA made available $206.8 million to the EPU for financing special resources granted to Austria, Greece, Iceland and Turkey to cover part of the EPU deficits of these countries.

The EPU, July 1, 1950 to June 30, 1952

During its first year EPU reported total monthly bilateral surpluses (or deficits) to the BIS of $3,173 million. Of this sum, $1,450 million was compensated multilaterally and $619 million by reversals of net positions, through the operation of the cumulative principle. ("Reversals of net positions" means that some countries which initially ran surpluses subsequently ran deficits so that their initial credits were canceled out.) This record may be compared with total first and second category compensations of $149 million under the IEPS during 1949–1950 and $305 million for the period beginning with the operations under the First Agreement on Multilateral Monetary Compensation in December 1947 to June 1950.[35]

During the second year of the Union's operations, the total bilateral surpluses were $4,290 million. During the first two years of operations 42.6 per cent of the bilateral deficits and surpluses were settled by multilateral compensations and 31.3 per cent by reversals of net positions. Thus, nearly 75 per cent of the monthly bilateral surpluses or deficits for the two-year period were settled on a multilateral basis without the use of special or existing resources, gold or net grants of credits by the creditor countries. (See Table 2.)

Persistent deficits on the part of some countries and persistent

35. *Twenty-First Annual Report,* Bank for International Settlements, Basel, 1951, p. 219.

TABLE 2

PERCENTAGES OF TOTAL MONTHLY BILATERAL SURPLUSES OR DEFICITS REPORTED TO
EPU, JULY 1, 1950 TO JUNE 30, 1952, BY TYPE OF SETTLEMENT

Type of Settlement	Surplus	Deficit
Total monthly bilateral surpluses or deficits............	100.0	100.0
Monthly multilateral compensation...................	42.6	42.6
Reversals of net positions through the operation of the cumulative principle	31.3	31.3
Special resources	—	2.7
Settlements within and beyond the quotas in the form of:		
Grants of credit.............................	16.2	13.2
Gold payments	11.0	9.6
Cumulative impact of the use of existing resources and initial balances	−1.1	0.5

Source: Second Annual Report of the Managing Board of the European Payments Union, OEEC, Paris, 1952.

creditor positions on the part of others have threatened the continued operations of the EPU. When deficit countries reach a cumulative net debit balance equal to their quota, they must pay to the Union 100 per cent of any additional deficit in gold, unless, of course, the Union grants postquota credits. When members reach an extreme debtor position, they usually increase their import quota restrictions against other members, which tends to weaken the trade liberalization program, especially if other members retaliate. A more desirable solution is to be found in efforts of the deficit countries to increase exports and reduce imports by lowering internal inflationary pressures.

Persistent creditor countries also create problems for the EPU. Even without extreme debtor positions, there could still be extreme creditor positions if all or a large part of the bilateral deficits were concentrated in one or two countries. Once a creditor country has a cumulative accounting surplus equal to its quota, it can refuse to extend further EPU credits against its bilateral credits with other members and demand 100 per cent gold payments. Since the gold and dollar resources of the Union are limited, the solvency of the Union can be threatened by excessive creditor positions even when there are no extreme deficit positions. During the first two years Belgium, Portugal and Italy exceeded their credit quotas (see Figure 1). The Managing Board was able to reach agreements with these countries for the settlement of these excessive credit positions on the basis of

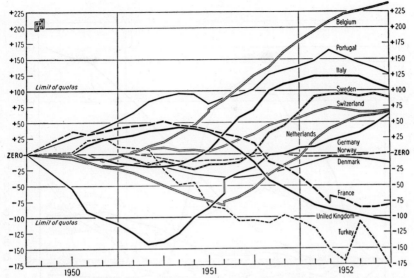

FIGURE 1. CUMULATIVE ACCOUNTING SURPLUS OR DEFICIT OF EACH EPU MEMBER
COUNTRY, EXPRESSED AS A PERCENTAGE OF ITS QUOTA, JULY 1950 TO JUNE 1952

Austria, Greece and Iceland are not shown. While Austria and Iceland have cumulative accounting deficits, their quotas are deemed to be zero; Greece's deficits have been
fully covered by antequota settlements.

Adjustments have been made in the curves for Belgium, France, Germany and the
Netherlands in those months when their quotas were modified.

Source: *Second Annual Report of the Managing Board of the European Payments
Union.*

a partial payment in gold (usually 50 per cent) and the remainder in
additional credits to the EPU.

Persistent Deficits

The problem of the persistent debtor countries was more tractable
over the first two years of operation, to June 1952. Western Germany
and the Netherlands had extreme debtor positions in the first year,
followed by substantial creditor positions in the second. On the
other hand, two of the largest creditor countries in the first year—
Britain and France—became extreme debtors in the second year.
(See Figure 1.) The utilization of the credit and deficit quotas shown
in Figure 1 is a reflection of the cumulative net surpluses and deficits
of each member, which are shown in Figure 2. These variations in
the utilization of the quotas are not surprising since the sum of the

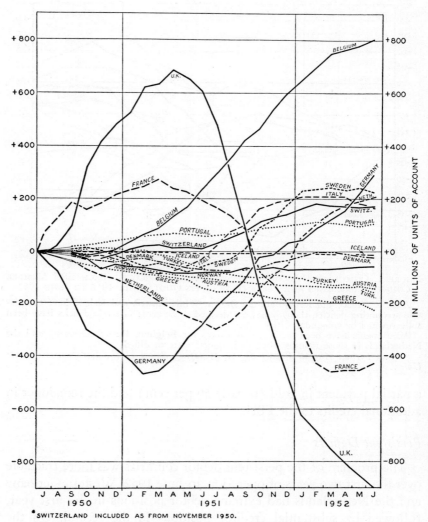

Source: *Second Annual Report of the Managing Board of the European Payments Union.*

FIGURE 2. NET SURPLUSES AND DEFICITS OF EACH EPU MEMBER COUNTRY VIS-À-VIS ALL OTHER MEMBERS, JULY 1, 1950 TO JUNE 30, 1952. (On a Cumulative Basis)

quotas of all members was only $4,155 million, while the gross monthly bilateral surpluses amounted to $7,513 million for the two-year period. Moreover, the total trade in goods flowing between EPU members and their associated monetary areas in 1951 was about 7 times the aggregate EPU quotas.

One of the important functions of the Managing Board of the EPU is to make recommendations to both deficit and surplus countries as to measures for readjusting their positions. The Board naturally prefers adjustments which do not call for a tightening of trade restrictions. This course is not only contrary to the purposes of the EPU but is likely to worsen the position of other deficit countries. The Board has also recommended tighter central bank credit controls, the elimination of fiscal deficits by deficit countries, and broader trade liberalization by creditor countries. The Board has been more successful than the Monetary Fund in influencing balance-of-payments policies of EPU members. This is partly because the Board is dealing with a smaller group of countries with common interests; also, its decisions have been backed up by the influence and resources of the ECA.[36] In addition, of course, the problems of intra-European balance are much more tractable than those involving balance with the dollar area.

The EPU after June 30, 1952 [37]

In June 1952 the OEEC Council agreed to extend the EPU Agreement for an additional year to June 30, 1953. Few changes were made in its underlying structure but before an extension could be agreed upon certain basic problems had to be met. First, there was the fact that the gold and dollar resources of the EPU were insufficient to cover the maximum drain that might occur when surpluses were concentrated in a few creditor countries.[38] Since the U.S. government de-

---

36. For a discussion of the influence of the EPU Board on internal policies see Robert Triffin, "Monetary Reconstruction in Europe," *International Conciliation,* June 1952, pp. 288–97.

37. The material in this section is based largely on the *Second Annual Report of the Managing Board of the European Payments Union,* Chapter 3.

38. At the end of June 1952 the gold and dollar capital fund of the EPU was $271.6 million. The original capital contribution by the U.S. government was $350 million, to which $11.4 million was added in 1951.

cided against any further direct contribution to the capital of the EPU, other measures had to be adopted to insure the continued solvency of the Union. These were (1) an increase in the proportion of gold payments by debtor countries in the lower segments of the quota and a reduction in the higher segments (see Table 1); and (2) a commitment by each member to make gold loans to the EPU whenever such loans became necessary to prevent the gold and dollar assets from falling below $100 million.

The aggregate commitment of members is for $100 million distributed in proportion to the size of their quotas, but in calling for the loan, the clearing agent will turn first to the creditor countries. The first measure will not only encourage debtor members to reverse their positions at an early stage but will substantially increase the gold payments to the Union.[39] This meant that several countries were required to make gold payments after June 1952 on the basis of their net accounting deficit at the beginning of the third year of EPU operations.

Funding the Belgian Credit

The second problem had to do with the fact that certain members —Belgium, Italy, Portugal and Switzerland—had either exceeded their credit quotas or (in the case of Switzerland) had developed an accounting surplus which threatened to exceed the quota. The largest creditor was Belgium which had extended credits to the EPU to the amount of $223 million in excess of its original quota. It was not only necessary to reach an agreement on the settlement of the postquota surplus but to provide for additional credit facilities for use in 1952–1953. The final settlement with Belgium included a dollar payment by the EPU of $80 million; the funding of $50 million to be paid in five annual installments; deliveries of $50 million in defense equipment from Britain and France; an additional credit of $43 million to be extended by Belgium to the EPU; and an agreement that Belgium would run up to $250 million in new surpluses, half to be covered by gold payment to Belgium and the remainder in credits to the EPU.

Two related agreements were also arranged as a part of this pack-

39. Denmark was excluded from the new gold payment scale because of the low level of her reserves in relation to her quota.

age deal. First, the International Monetary Fund agreed to extend to Belgium a line of credit of $50 million; second, the U.S. government agreed to spend $50 million for "offshore" military purchases in Belgium during 1952–1953.[40]

Arrangements were also made for settling the postquota surpluses of Italy and Portugal, and for the future settlement of any surpluses of Italy, Portugal and Switzerland during 1952–1953, up to $100 million, $55 million and $125 million, respectively. Settlements are to be made half in gold and half in credits to be extended to the EPU.

During the second half of 1952, a better balance was achieved within the EPU area. Belgium, the outstanding creditor of the first two years, was in approximate equilibrium from June 30, 1952 to January 31, 1953. Switzerland was also in virtual equilibrium during the first half of 1952, and Italy, Sweden and Portugal, which had been large creditor countries, had deficits during the second half of 1952. After exhausting her quota in the summer of 1952, Britain's EPU position was reversed so that during the last few months of 1952 she ran a net surplus of over $300 million. A portion of this surplus was attributed to the temporary practice of permitting British traders to acquire raw materials with dollars and sell them against sterling and other EPU currencies during August, 1952.[41] More significant, however, was the reimposition of quotas by Britain and the other sterling area countries on a number of commodity imports from the EPU area.

The principal deficit countries during the second half of 1952 were France and Turkey. By November 1952, France had exhausted her quota and was required to settle her EPU deficit by 100 per cent payments in gold.

THE TRADE LIBERALIZATION PROGRAM

Before 1949, the OEEC countries conducted their trade with one another largely under bilateral trade-quota and bulk purchase agreements. The creation of a multilateral payments system by no means

40. See "The European Payments Union after Two Years," *Monthly Review*, Federal Reserve Bank of New York, August 1952, p. 116.

41. After Britain had exhausted her quota all deficits with the EPU had to be settled 100 per cent in gold. Hence Britain had nothing to lose by selling dollar materials to reduce her EPU deficit, and could permit her traders to reap the profits from the sale.

guaranteed an expansion of multilateral trade. It merely removed the currency or balance of payments barrier to nondiscriminatory trade within the OEEC countries and the other territories in the same monetary area. While some progress had been made in liberalizing intra-European trade before the establishment of the EPU,[42] so long as members had to consider their bilateral payments position with every other member, there had to be planning of trade through discriminatory arrangements in order to balance payments. But, with the establishment of the EPU, no member country had to worry about its bilateral position with any other member, but only its over-all position with the EPU.

On August 18, 1950, the Council of the OEEC adopted a "Code of the Liberalisation of Trade"[43] which went into force on September 19, 1950, the date of the signing of the EPU Agreement. This provided that each member was to eliminate import restrictions covering private trade amounting to 60 per cent of the 1948 value of its imports on private account from other members and their overseas territories by October 4, 1950, and to increase the percentage of liberalization to 75 by February 1, 1951. With certain exceptions, all discrimination against other member countries was to be removed for both liberalized and nonliberalized imports. Liberalization was also to be extended to certain invisible imports.[44]

Because of the possibility that some countries would extend liberalization to some groups of commodities but not to others, commodity imports were divided into three groups: food and feedstuffs; raw materials; manufactures. Each member was required to extend liberalization to at least 60 per cent of the value of the 1948 imports to each group, in addition to the over-all liberalization requirement of 75 per cent.[45] In addition, the Council drew up a list of commodities—principally textiles and certain agricultural and chemi-

42. OEEC members had agreed to eliminate trade restrictions on 50 per cent of their imports from one another on private account by December 15, 1949. Although several members were unable to extend liberalization measures to Switzerland and the Belgium-Luxembourg Economic Union, most members did reach the 50 per cent target.

43. See *Code of Liberalisation*, OEEC, Paris, July 1951. This text includes amendments to the original Code to July 1951.

44. See *Code of Liberalisation*, Annex B.

45. See *Code of Liberalisation*, Annex A, Sec. II.

cal products—which were to be subject to liberalization before August 15, 1951.[46]

Owing to the inflationary pressures which developed after the Korean war and to the accelerated defense program, the 75 per cent liberalization goal was not realized by February 1951 and certain deficit countries, including Germany and Greece, were temporarily exempted from compliance with even the 60 per cent goal. The rapid improvement in Germany's balance of payments position during 1952 made it possible for that country to increase its percentage of trade liberalization to 81 per cent by the end of 1952, while Italy liberalized imports from the EPU area to 99 per cent. The large EPU deficits incurred by Britain and France during 1951 and 1952 necessitated the reimposition of quotas by these countries after they had achieved the 75 per cent liberalization stage early in 1951.[47] Thus France suspended liberalization of her EPU trade entirely and Britain reduced the liberalization of her private trade to 46 per cent. (See Table 3.)

TABLE 3

PERCENTAGE OF PRIVATE IMPORTS UNDER OPEN GENERAL LICENSE FROM OEEC COUNTRIES, FOR SELECTED OEEC COUNTRIES, MARCH 1953

Country	Per Cent [a]
Italy	99
Switzerland	92
Sweden	91
Belgium-Luxembourg	90
Portugal	85
Germany	84
Denmark	75
Ireland	75
Netherlands	75
Norway	75
Turkey	63
United Kingdom	58 [b]
France	Liberalization suspended

Source: International Financial News Survey (IFNS), January 30, 1953, p. 229.
a. Reference period for all countries is 1948, except for Germany, for which the reference period is 1949.
b. Britain increased her percentage of liberalization to 58 in March 1953.

Even a complete realization of the 75 per cent goal would leave a large proportion of intra-European trade under bilateral control. A substantial amount of trade is conducted by state trading organiza-

46. Code of Liberalisation, Annex A, Sec. III.
47. The United Kingdom reached 90 per cent liberalization before deliberalizing in November 1951.

tions, and so is outside the liberalization agreement. In addition, bilateral agreements continue to govern the nonliberalized portion of private trade, and the provisions of the Code with regard to nondiscriminatory treatment of nonliberalized trade have not been fully implemented. It should also be mentioned that in 1950 a number of countries increased their tariffs on commodities which later became subject to trade liberalization.[48]

Sterling in the EPU

As originally proposed, the EPU represented a threat to sterling as an international currency. First, many influential people in Britain wanted to enlarge the transferable account group to include most—perhaps all—of the countries of Western Europe and possibly the rest of the nondollar world. Thus sterling would have afforded a medium of multilateral settlements for all or most of the nondollar countries of the world. The EPU provided for a multilateral system based on the clearing of bilateral balances rather than transfers of sterling balances held in London.

The EPU, therefore, represented a threat to the existing transferable account system as it operated in Europe, since under the original proposal sterling held by EPU members would have been blocked and funded along with other balances, and settlements between EPU members of the transferable account system would no longer have been made with sterling. Finally, Britain's relationship with the sterling area was such that sterling payments between sterling area countries and EPU members had to be treated as payments between the EPU and Britain. In other words, if the sterling area were to continue to exist, the EPU had to operate with respect to the sterling area as a whole and not simply Britain alone. This meant, of course, that Britain would have to cover with gold payments EPU deficits of the rest of the sterling area as well as her own.[49]

An agreement was reached whereby Britain's position with the EPU would be established on the basis of the transactions of the other OEEC countries with the sterling area as a whole. In addition, EPU members holding sterling balances could use these to discharge a

---

48. For an excellent discussion of the OEEC trade liberalization program see Diebold, *op. cit.,* Chapters 10 and 11.

49. See "Britain's EPU Proposals," *The Economist,* June 3, 1950, pp. 1231–32.

deficit with the EPU, whether or not they had a deficit with the sterling area. This meant that Britain was liable for gold payments which might arise from sterling payments to the EPU by other members but, as was mentioned earlier, ECA agreed to make up any gold loss which Britain might incur as a result of such transfers. Finally, EPU creditors were permitted to hold the portion of their EPU surplus which corresponded to their surplus in sterling in the form of sterling balances rather than EPU credits.[50] These provisions preserved the transferable account system in Western Europe and Britain sought to broaden it by offering to extend transferable account status to all EPU countries.[51] While the sections applying to sterling balances are also applicable to other balances under the same conditions, they were obviously designed to fit the needs of Britain.

AREAS OF MULTILATERAL SETTLEMENTS

The EPU countries and their possessions together with the non-EPU members of the sterling area represent a large trading area within which, through the EPU machinery, full multilateral settlements take place with respect to balances arising from transactions between members of this group. In 1951, trade within this area accounted for 39 per cent of world commodity trade, and the trade of the area with the nondollar world accounted for 58 per cent of the world's total. (See Nos. 4 and 7 of Table 4.) The EPU multilateral trading area is by no means a closed system. The link with the dollar area is threefold: the gold payments to the EPU by the deficit countries and from the EPU to the creditors, the gold payments from the EPU's fund of working capital provided by ECA, and the financing of special resources through dollar grants to the EPU by the United States government.

There are also links between the EPU system and the sterling transferable account and bilateral account countries outside of the EPU orbit. Eight of the EPU countries are members of the transferable

50. For a good discussion of the position of sterling in the EPU see A. O. Hirschman and R. Hinshaw, "The European Payments Union," *The Review of Economics and Statistics,* February 1951, pp. 51–52.

51. To date (June 1953) Austria, Denmark, Greece and Western Germany have accepted the invitation. Other EPU transferable account countries are the Netherlands, Norway, Sweden and Italy.

TABLE 4

MERCHANDISE EXPORTS BY CURRENCY GROUPING BY VALUE AND PER CENT OF
WORLD EXPORTS IN 1951

Currency Group	F.O.B. Value (Millions of Dollars)	Percentage of World Exports
Total World [a]	74,789.9	100.0
A. Nondollar countries, between:		
1. Sterling area countries....	9,314.9	12.4
2. Sterling area and continental EPU countries, including dependencies...	8,437.9	11.3
3. Continental EPU countries and dependencies	11,795.2	15.8
4. Countries clearing through EPU, or total of 1, 2 and 3	29,548.0	39.5
5. Sterling area countries and rest of nondollar world..	6,754.6	9.0
6. Continental EPU including dependencies and rest of nondollar world	6,940.2	9.3
7. Total 4, 5 and 6.........	43,242.8	57.8
8. Nondollar countries [b] (other than continental EPU and dependencies, and sterling area)	2,455.5	3.3
9. Sterling area countries and total nondollar world (including sterling area) or total of 1, 2 and 5..	24,507.4	32.8
B. Dollar countries, between:		
10. Dollar countries [c]	9,438.3	12.6
C. Dollar, nondollar countries, between:		
11. Dollar countries and sterling area	6,224.0	8.3
12. Dollar countries and continental EPU countries and dependencies	6,800.5	9.1
13. Dollar countries and rest of world except continental EPU and dependencies, and sterling area.	6,628.8	8.9
14. Total 11, 12 and 13.....	19,653.3	26.3

Source: Monthly Bulletin of Statistics, August 1952, pp. x–xiii.

a. Excluding intra-Eastern Europe and China mainland trade and excluding U.S. exports of $1,552.1 million in special category items not reported as to destination.

b. Albania, Bulgaria, Czechoslovakia, Eastern Germany, Hungary, Poland, Romania, USSR, Egypt, Sudan, Ethiopia, Iran, Israel, Lebanon, Saudi Arabia, Syria, Argentina, Brazil, Chile, Paraguay, Peru, Uruguay, Japan, Taiwan, Indonesia, the Philippines, South Korea, Thailand, Finland, Spain and Yugoslavia.

c. United States, Canada, Central American republics (including Caribbean republics), Bolivia, Colombia, Ecuador, Mexico and Venezuela.

account system and two are members of the sterling area.[52] This means that ten of the EPU countries and the countries associated with them in the same monetary area may conduct current trade in terms of sterling with a number of transferable account countries in Latin America, Eastern Europe and the Middle and Far East. There is, of course, free transferability of sterling between sterling area countries and all bilateral account countries and to a considerable degree between bilateral account countries themselves under a procedure known as administrative transfers.

Exports between sterling area countries and between sterling area countries and the rest of the nondollar world constitutes about 33 per cent of total exports. The bulk of this trade is financed with sterling. In addition, sterling transferability affords a means of multilateral settlement for a considerable proportion of the trade between nondollar countries outside the sterling area. Thus if to trade directly related to the EPU system we add that which is financed with sterling—but outside of the countries encompassed by the EPU and associated monetary areas—we have a soft-currency area accounting for about 60 per cent of the world's commodity trade. While within this larger area there is not a completely multilateral system of current payments, the opportunities for multilateral settlements are certainly substantial.

The remaining 40 per cent of the world's trade is largely on a dollar or convertible currency basis (including American account sterling). In 1951 intradollar area trade accounted for 12.6 per cent of the world's total while dollar area trade with the nondollar countries of the world accounted for the remaining 26.3 per cent of the world commodity trade. (See Table 4.)

52. The United Kingdom and Ireland have a joint quota in the EPU while Iceland has an independent status in the EPU.

Chapter 7

POSTWAR EXCHANGE RATE POLICIES

FEW IMPORTANT QUESTIONS of national policy have given rise to so much theoretical discussion and such variation in views among economists as has the exchange rate. From the days of David Ricardo, exchange rates have provided economists with interesting problems for the application of their theoretical tools; but the exchange rate has taken on new significance since World War II.

After World War I the major issue for countries that had left the gold standard was the level at which the new gold parity should be established. Conservative opinion tended to favor a return to the pre-1914 gold parity, where its restoration was at all possible, while most economists who had studied the question favored a more scientific determination in terms of a reestablishment of prewar relationships between price levels at home and abroad.[1] When, after 1929, pressures on their balance of payments forced a number of countries off the gold standard, the principal issue for debate among economists interested in foreign exchange was whether rates should be fixed (with currencies tied to gold) or floating (with short-term stability maintained by stabilization operations). Some countries avoided depreciation of their currencies for a time by adopting exchange controls, but such practices were generally frowned upon by economists. Exchange controls were regarded either as short-term expedients to meet emergency conditions or as "Schachtian" weapons in "economic warfare." The techniques of stabilization funds aroused considerable interest. Here the problem was how to distinguish short-term forces from fundamental changes in the demand for, and

1. See Gustav Cassel, *Money and Foreign Exchange after 1914,* Macmillan Company, New York, 1922, p. 157; see also Morris E. Garnsey, "Postwar Exchange Rate Parities," *Quarterly Journal of Economics,* November 1945, pp. 113–35; and R. F. Mikesell, "The Determination of Postwar Exchange Rates," *Southern Economic Journal,* January 1947, pp. 263–75.

the supply of, foreign exchange so that the market rate could be supported at an "equilibrium" level.

By the end of the 1930s majority opinion among economists seemed to favor a flexible rate policy as opposed to a rigid link with gold; short-term stability was to be maintained by stabilization fund operations. International cooperation along the lines of the Tripartite Agreement was to be used to avoid competitive exchange depreciation. Economists in both the Western Hemisphere and in Europe developed these ideas further during World War II in the direction of some kind of an international stabilization fund coupled with an agreement for cooperation in exchange rate policies. The product of the deliberations of economists and statesmen was the establishment of the International Monetary Fund, discussed in Chapter 2.

Criterion of Equilibrium Rate

So long as economists, bankers and statesmen postulated a world free of exchange restrictions—at least, on current payments—the problem of what a country's rate ought to be was—in concept, at any rate—fairly simple. It was a rate which could be maintained without a net loss of foreign exchange reserves over a period of time sufficient to allow for seasonal and short-term cyclical variations in the balance of payments and which would not adversely affect employment and income levels. However, once the ability or even the desirability of international equilibrium without balance of payments controls came to be doubted, either as a short-run goal or even for the long run, entirely new problems arose. The question was no longer, "What is the equilibrium rate?" but, "What rate will best help to realize certain national economic objectives?"

These national economic objectives vary somewhat from country to country but the principal ones are (1) internal economic stability; (2) the maintenance of a certain living standard either for the country as a whole or for particular economic classes; (3) the maximization of terms of trade or more broadly, of real gains from trade; (4) the promotion of economic development. Thus exchange rates take on a new significance in a world of controlled economies and controlled balances of payments.

POLICIES BEFORE SEPTEMBER 1949

Of the thirty-two gold parities certified by the International Monetary Fund prior to the beginning of its operations in March 1947, about half were approximately the same or higher than they were in September 1939, and only one gold parity (the French franc) was less than 50 per cent of its September 1939 figure.[2] The parities established were based on official exchange rates prevailing in the fall of 1946. Except for the few countries with free exchange markets there is little evidence that the official rates were based on a determination of what rate might be required for the maintenance of balance of payments equilibrium. Prices in many countries had risen from 300 to as much as 1,000 per cent above prewar levels; some countries had incurred large international debts or were forced to liquidate their foreign assets; in the case of most belligerent countries the capacity to produce and to export was seriously impaired.

Between December 1946—when the initial parities of most Fund members were announced—and September 1949, only two countries, Colombia and Mexico, changed their official parities with the Fund. It is true, of course, that France devalued the franc but she established no official parity with the Fund. Not only were most exchange rates out of line with equilibrium levels during this period, but before 1949 there was little disposition on the part of the Fund or of the United States government to recommend adjustments.[3] The IMF position that reflected the views of most member governments was as follows:

1. There could be no equilibrium for most countries during the postwar reconstruction period except with sharp decreases in currency values. In many cases this would have been accompanied by a drastic deterioration in the terms of trade, not compensated for by an increase in foreign exchange revenues. It would have led to severe internal inflationary pressures as a result of labor's demands for higher wages to compensate for increases in the cost-of-living index.

2. Brazil, China, the Dominican Republic, Greece, Poland, Uruguay, Yugoslavia, France in respect of French Indochina and the Netherlands in respect of the Netherlands Indies, did not establish parities with the Fund before March 1947. Brazil established a par value for the cruzeiro in July 1948 approximately equal to the free rate in September 1939. Australia joined the Fund in 1947 with an initial par value approximately equal to the official rate for the Australian pound in September 1939.

3. See R. F. Mikesell, *United States Economic Policy and International Relations*, McGraw-Hill, New York, 1952, pp. 134–38.

2. Until countries had achieved a reasonable amount of internal stability, any improvement in the trade balance through devaluation would be quickly dissipated by price rises.

3. The principal limitation on exports by war-ravaged countries was their inability to produce.

4. Devaluation would not reduce imports since they were largely limited by direct controls. To limit imports by exchange depreciation would work a severe hardship on low-income groups, increase luxury imports at the expense of essential commodities, and disrupt recovery through inflation.[4]

It is perhaps worth noting that in the discussions of Britain's obligation to restore sterling convertibility in July 1947 and during the preparations to establish convertibility, almost no questions were raised regarding the appropriateness of the sterling-dollar rate for the maintenance of equilibrium. Devaluation was not seriously suggested after the failure of convertibility in August 1947. In fact, it was not until the latter part of 1948 and early 1949 that IMF and United States government officials began to suggest that economic conditions were ripe for a revision of exchange rates.

Most countries were reluctant even to consider devaluation until sterling was devalued. While some may have recognized an advantage in reducing the dollar value of their currencies, they saw only disadvantage in reducing their terms of trade vis-à-vis the sterling area. Since devaluing against the dollar but not against sterling would have involved broken cross-rates, a practice severely criticized by the Fund, a readjustment of currency values had to await action by Britain.

Changed Conditions in 1949

Several factors helped change the climate of opinion regarding exchange parities in 1949. First, production was recovering rapidly in Europe and a fair degree of internal stability had been achieved by most Western European countries. Exports to the United States and to other dollar countries, however, were hampered by the high prices of European goods. The seller's market in most commodities

4. For a statement of the IMF's policy on exchange rates in 1946, see *Annual Report of the Executive Directors for the Year Ending June 30, 1947*, International Monetary Fund, Washington, Appendix 10.

was at an end and exporters had to compete for markets. High prices in soft currency markets were attracting exports which ought to have been shifted to hard currency areas. A recession in the United States sharply reduced its imports, and gold and hard currency drains on Britain and certain other countries were reaching alarming proportions.

Finally, there was a growing loss of confidence in sterling and other European currencies which could not be restored without a revision of official values. This resulted in a gold and dollar drain brought about by the withdrawal of short-term capital from London and a tendency on the part of purchasers of sterling commodities to delay payment, because they believed that sterling would be devalued.

The debate over the exchange rate question, which was carried on in most deficit countries prior to September 1949, was concerned less with the rate required to establish equilibrium, than with the effects of devaluation on real incomes and living standards. In general, equilibrium in the sense of the elimination of the dollar shortage was not considered attainable through the price mechanism, at least not until after 1952. In fact, equilibrium in the minds of most Europeans was not a market phenomenon but rather the achievement of an accounting balance between foreign exchange receipts (in the absence of foreign aid) and foreign exchange expenditures required for the maintenance of a satisfactory level of real consumption and investment. Thus devaluation would be desirable only if the advantage of the larger volume of imports purchased with the proceeds of increased exports was greater than the disadvantage of offering greater exports on less favorable terms.[5]

Approached in this way, most British economists and government officials opposed devaluation.[6] This was due in part to the widely held belief that the United States demand for imports was fairly inelastic as to relative price changes of imports and domestic com-

---

5. For a theoretical discussion of the effects of devaluation on domestic welfare, see Sidney S. Alexander, "Devaluation versus Import Restrictions as an Instrument for Improving Foreign Trade Balance," *Staff Papers,* International Monetary Fund, Washington, April 1951, pp. 379–96.

6. See *The Economist,* April 30, 1949, pp. 778–79. From conversations with British officials and economists during the spring and summer of 1949, the author concluded that most of them were against devaluation. For a statement of the case against devaluation see R. F. Harrod, *The Pound Sterling,* International Finance Section, Princeton University, Princeton, 1952, pp. 23–33.

modities.[7] Unless the elasticity of demand for dollar goods was substantially above unity, it could be argued that the additional dollar
exchange earned through devaluation was not worth the price paid in
reduced terms of trade.[8]

Political and Social Factors

In view of the skepticism as to the effects of devaluation on exports
to hard currency areas, political and social objections carried great
weight in Britain. The Labor party was fearful lest devaluation, by
raising the prices of essentials, would lower the real incomes of the
workers. To offset such increases by higher subsidies would put an
additional strain on the budget and increase inflationary pressures.
On the other hand, it was feared that a rise in the cost of living
would destroy the policy of voluntary wage restraint then pursued by
the trade unions, and lead to a wage-price spiral which would offset
any possible gains from devaluation. In addition, left-wing spokesmen usually suspect any action which seeks to achieve economic ends
through market or competitive devices as opposed to controls. For
example, Dr. T. Balogh and other left-wing British economists consider devaluation an instrument of capitalistic competition, the successful operation of which leads to deflation, unemployment and
lower real wages.[9]

The Conservatives and Devaluation

Nor was support to be found for devaluation among the majority
of the members of the Conservative party in Britain. While a few

7. Several statistical studies of the elasticity of demand for imports during the interwar period indicated import elasticities of less than unity. See, for example, J. H.
Adler, "United States Import Demand during the Interwar Period," *American Economic
Review,* June 1945, pp. 418–30; and T. C. Chang, "International Comparisons of Demand for Imports," *Review of Economic Studies,* 1945–46, pp. 53–67. For a critical
discussion of the methods and the implications of these studies, see Guy H. Orcutt,
"Measurement of Price Elasticities in International Trade," *The Review of Economics
and Statistics,* May 1950.

8. Since the purpose of this book is to discuss policies and how they are determined,
it is impossible to debate at length the theoretical issues involved. It is probably true
that short-term elasticities of demand are low and that devaluation by itself has definite
limitations for restoring equilibrium, unless it is carried to the point where the economic repercussions would be intolerable for a modern state. Other conditions such as
the degree of internal inflationary pressures, price and cost rigidities, trade and payments agreements, and internal controls and rigidities of all kinds are just as important
as exchange rates for expanding foreign exchange proceeds from exports.

9. See T. Balogh, *The Dollar Crisis,* Blackwell, Oxford, 1949; see also review of

right-wing economists and businessmen favored an immediate return to convertibility through the adoption of a freely fluctuating pound, most right-wing leaders were not only convinced that devaluation would not increase export receipts but they feared the possible effects of devaluation on internal stability.

Few British capitalists had any desire to leave the protected marketing preserve of the sterling area abroad and trade association regulations at home, for the harsh wilderness of dollar competition. Nor was devaluation popular among the sterling-using Dominions, since this would mean a cut in the dollar value of the large sterling balances held by Britain's creditors. It was feared, therefore, that devaluation might weaken the sterling area and with it the solidarity of the Commonwealth. As an alternative to devaluation and competition with the dollar area this group favored a shift by Britain away from dependence on dollar goods by means of intensified discrimination and a strengthening and perhaps widening of a protected trading area based on sterling.

The Liberal View

An important body of liberal opinion, of course, was prepared to consider devaluation as a step toward the eventual restoration of sterling and the re-entry of British exports into world markets on a competitive basis.[10] British liberals in the postwar period [11] have taken

Balogh's book, by R. F. Mikesell, "The Dollar Crisis," *The Journal of Political Economy,* December 1950, pp. 542–45.

10. Economic liberalism in Britain is represented by such journals as *The Economist* and the *Manchester Guardian* as well as by outstanding academic economists, among them, D. H. Robertson and Lionel Robbins. The liberals were not in agreement, however, as to the timing of sterling convertibility nor the desirability of devaluation. For example, *The Economist* has been critical of liberals who wanted to move too fast in dispensing with discriminatory trade and exchange controls. For a discussion of the differing British schools of thought on devaluation see *The Economist,* July 19, 1949, pp. 113–14 and September 24, 1949, p. 650.

11. Britain's outstanding liberal in the postwar period was J. M. Keynes. Lord Keynes' faith in a free, nondiscriminatory trading system is revealed in his participation in the development of the Bretton Woods institutions, the early proposals for an international trade organization and the Anglo-American Financial Agreement. In his speeches and articles Keynes advocated that Britain should join with the United States in the restoration of currency convertibility and multilateral trade. In his last article, published posthumously, Keynes called for a dose of "classical medicine" in international trade policy and less reliance on controls. ("The Balance of Payments of the United States," *Economic Journal,* June 1946, pp. 172–78.) See also R. F. Harrod, *The Life of John Maynard Keynes,* Macmillan, London, 1951, Chapter 14.

the position that Britain and the sterling area could not become independent of the dollar area without some sacrifices in living standards. They also have doubted the ability of Britain to hold the sterling area together indefinitely on the basis of sterling inconvertibility. Finally, the liberals believed that if Britain were to compete in world markets on a nondiscriminatory basis she would need not only to adjust the pound to a realistic level, but to get rid of suppressed inflation and of the controls and rigidities which dull the zeal of her exporters to develop markets in the dollar area.

But the sterling devaluation of September 1949 is not to be interpreted as a victory for economic liberalism. In fact, the liberals argued with considerable justification that devaluation alone was no panacea for Britain's dollar problem, and still less would it assure equilibrium and the conditions for convertibility. Actually, devaluation was forced upon Britain by a general loss of confidence in sterling at home and abroad, and a universal expectation—in spite of vigorous official denials—that devaluation was inevitable.

Following the formulation of a plan for sterling convertibility at the Commonwealth Conference in December 1952, there has been increasing sentiment in Britain for a flexible exchange rate. This development will be discussed in Part IV of this book.

The Eve of Devaluation

From the end of the first quarter of 1949 to the eve of devaluation, British gold and official dollar reserves declined by $568 million to a low of $1,330 million. Only a part of this drain could be attributed to the decline in British exports to the dollar area. Some of it was due to the increased dollar deficits of the rest of the sterling area and some to speculative action against sterling.[12]

In time, some of the short-term speculative drain on British reserves would have been reversed, even without devaluation, and losses through violations of sterling area exchange regulations could have been lessened by a tightening of controls. But only a dictatorial power with the most rigid controls over currency and trade can ignore a loss of confidence in a currency. Considering the position of sterling as a freely transferable currency over a wide area which included a number of independent governments, the world's judgment regard-

12. This problem will be taken up in Chapter 9.

ing its present and future value could not be ignored. There was only one way to prevent a further loss of confidence in sterling in the midst of Britain's balance of payments crisis—to devalue.[13]

While this analysis has emphasized the British attitude toward devaluation and the function of exchange rates, the British position was to a considerable degree echoed on the continent. On the other hand, Western European countries generally favored greater exchange flexibility in the form of a combination of exchange controls and floating exchange rates, to be discussed in Chapter 8.

THE SEPTEMBER 1949 DEVALUATIONS

The devaluation of sterling by 30.5 per cent announced on September 18, 1949, initiated a readjustment of the values of most of the world's principal currencies, including the Canadian dollar, nearly all the Western European currencies, all the sterling area currencies except the Pakistani rupee, and certain other currencies tied to sterling or to other European currencies.[14] While the nondollar Latin American countries did not formally devalue, most of them so adjusted their multiple exchange rate systems as to take into account the European devaluations. Most of the changes were approximately equal to the percentage devaluation of the pound sterling. However, many of the devaluing countries were shocked and annoyed by the extent of the British devaluation.[15] Except for countries with strong currencies, failure to follow the pound would have meant a substantial disadvantage in trade with the soft-currency countries.

13. An important psychological factor was the attitude of many American congressmen and administrative officials who were convinced that Britain's failure to devalue was holding up British recovery and prolonging the need for aid. Had Britain not devalued there would undoubtedly have been strong pressure for a reduction in dollar aid to Britain.

14. Switzerland and Spain did not devalue in 1949. Belgium–Luxembourg devalued by only 12.3 per cent in 1949, and Portugal by 13 per cent. Italy and France had previously devalued against the dollar and had adopted floating rate systems, but they permitted their exchange rates in terms of dollars to fall by 9.1 per cent and 22.3 per cent, respectively. For a discussion of the 1949 currency adjustments see "Readjustment of Foreign Currency Values," *Federal Reserve Bulletin,* October 1949; see also *Second Special Report,* National Advisory Council on International Monetary and Financial Problems, May 1950, pp. 14–18.

15. The French Finance Minister, Maurice Petsche, called the new sterling parity Britain's "trade war rate." (See *The Economist,* September 24, 1949, p. 651.) Many countries were not only critical of the sharpness of the sterling devaluation but of the failure of Sir Stafford Cripps to consult other governments before announcing the change to the Monetary Fund just two days before the new rate went into effect.

Two countries whose international payments position was fairly close to equilibrium—Belgium and Canada—revalued their rates to a point midway between the old parity and a 30.5 per cent devaluation. This step was clearly taken to establish a rate most nearly compatible with international equilibrium.

Such countries as Belgium and Canada, which have tended to be in over-all equilibrium or even to have surpluses in the postwar period, but deficits with the dollar area not readily offset by surpluses with soft-currency countries, have faced a difficult problem. A parity low enough to achieve a balance with the dollar area, encouraged a surplus with soft-currency countries. The devaluation of sterling gave these countries an opportunity to depreciate vis-à-vis the dollar and appreciate vis-à-vis sterling and other soft currencies.

In summary, the September 1949 devaluations took place initially because Britain saw this step as the only way to check the loss of confidence in sterling and to reverse a drain on her reserves which had reached crisis proportions.[16] It was decidedly not a popular act in Britain. Many saw it as a step forced upon Britain by the instability of American capitalism and by unpatriotic capital movements.[17] Some countries welcomed the opportunity to devalue their currencies vis-à-vis the dollar without having to devalue against sterling. Others resented the British action but felt compelled to follow the pound. Sterling area countries and countries holding large sterling balances would have suffered a reduction in the local currency value of their reserves had they failed to devalue. In addition, they would have been at a trade disadvantage with the devaluing countries. Only one sterling area country, Pakistan, refused to devalue.[18]

16. A substantial part of the improvement in Britain's reserve position was the result of a reversal of the earlier capital outflow. This took the form of a rebuilding of sterling balances by dollar countries and a repayment of short-term funds borrowed in the sterling area. Foreign concerns had also delayed purchases in the sterling area and sterling area firms had stepped up their purchases and made prepayments in dollars, in anticipation of sterling devaluation.

17. See Margaret Hall, "The United Kingdom After Devaluation," *American Economic Review*, December 1950, p. 867.

18. Pakistan's action was partly motivated by political considerations but there was also some economic justification in that Pakistan had an export surplus with both the dollar area and the sterling area at the time. The consequent disparity between the Indian and the Pakistani rupees caused severe trade dislocation between the two countries.

Results of the Devaluations

The effects of the 1949 devaluations on the world's payments positions are obscured by several international economic developments. First, the gold and dollar positions of the sterling area and of the other Western European countries improved rapidly. The U.S. current account surplus with the OEEC countries alone was reduced from $3.7 billion in the first half of 1949 to $1.9 billion (annual rate) in the first half of 1950. During the same period the U.S. current account surplus with the entire world declined from $7.6 billion to $3 billion annually.

In spite of the sharp drop in U.S. aid, foreign countries increased their gold and dollar holdings from $14.7 billion on September 30, 1949, to $18.2 billion at the end of September 1950.[19] However, to determine the contribution of the devaluations to this improvement in the world's dollar position is both complex and controversial. There were, of course, short-term speculative influences which simply reflected a reversal of the gold and dollar drain from Britain and other countries that had occurred in anticipation of the currency adjustments.

Among the more significant factors in the improved balance of payments of the devaluing countries were the business revival in the United States which began in the latter part of 1949, and the sharp rise in the prices of raw materials produced in Latin America, Africa and the Far East. Most of the raw materials producing countries outside Latin America were members of the sterling area or other European currency areas, and the metropolitan countries benefited from their increased dollar earnings. The tightening of import controls against dollar imports by sterling-area countries was certainly important in improving the British dollar position and accounting for the rapid rise in British reserves from $1.3 billion in September 1949 to $3.3 billion by the end of 1950. Finally, a major share of this gain must be attributed to the recovery of the OEEC countries whose production both for home use and for export continued to expand at an impressive rate. The increase in production plus the rise in intra-European trade tended to reduce the dependence of Western Europe on dollar imports.

19. *Semiannual Report to the President and to the Congress for the Period April 1– September 30, 1950,* National Advisory Council on International Monetary and Financial Problems, 1951, p. 12.

Studies of the Data

In a recent article Dr. J. J. Polak has sought to distill from these complex ingredients an estimate of the contribution of the September 1949 devaluations to the improvement of Europe's balance of payments with the dollar area.[20] Without attempting to analyze Polak's study, a summary of his principal conclusions may clarify the basic issues involved in the determination of exchange rate policies. Polak finds that between the first half of 1949 and the first half of 1950 "the devaluations increased the volume of exports to the United States by an amount little more than enough to offset the fall of about 15 per cent in dollar export prices." [21] He also estimates that "the devaluations were responsible for a 10 per cent increase in the dollar value of Western Europe's exports to other markets in the Western Hemisphere, in Canada and in Latin America." Because of the existence of import controls the effects of devaluations on imports cannot be determined from the statistical data.[22]

A study made by the Economic Commission for Europe (ECE) shows that the European countries which devalued 20 per cent or more increased their share of the world market by 10 to 15 per cent, while the Western European countries which did not devalue— Belgium-Luxembourg, Italy and Switzerland—lost ground, relatively speaking, in nearly every commodity group.[23] The expansion of exports by the European devaluing countries was at least as great as the relative decline in export prices measured in dollars. Import prices measured in dollars (but not in local currencies) also declined for these countries so that according to the ECE report, "it must be con-

20. J. J. Polak, "Contributions of the September 1949 Devaluations to the Solution of Europe's Dollar Problem," *Staff Papers*, International Monetary Fund, September 1951, pp. 1–32.

21. United States imports (by value) from the OEEC countries in the first half of 1950 were 3 per cent above 1948, 15 per cent above the first half of 1949, and 25 per cent above the third quarter of 1949 (values seasonally adjusted). However, in the first half of 1950, GNP was 3.5 per cent above the level of the corresponding period in 1949. Taking into account the movements in U.S. business activity, and the high short-term income elasticity of demand for U.S. imports, Polak estimates that the devaluation was responsible for an increase of about 5 per cent in the value of U.S. imports from the OEEC countries between the first half of 1949 and the first half of 1950.

22. Two further possible effects of devaluation were the stimulation given to the production of dollar-type commodities and to the production of gold in the countries which had devalued their currencies.

23. *Economic Survey of Europe in 1950*, Economic Commission for Europe, Geneva, 1951, Table 49, pp. 104–05.

cluded that devaluation contributed to the improvement in the balance of payments on current account of the devaluing countries, even allowing for the import content of the increased export volume." [24] In other words, for the countries resorting to it, devaluation provided a larger amount of real purchasing power with which they could buy imports.

Limited Effects of Devaluation

Under present conditions of controlled economies and imperfect markets, devaluation is unlikely to produce spectacular results over short periods. Market imperfections make for comparatively low short-run demand elasticities for manufactured goods. Low supply elasticities, on the other hand, prevent the realization of increased foreign exchange proceeds from the sale of raw materials.[25] Export prices in terms of foreign currencies, as a rule, fall much less than does the foreign exchange value of the currency. The dollar prices of some British exports—for example, whisky—did not drop at all after devaluation, while the average decline between the time of the devaluation and the first half of 1950 was about 15 per cent, or half the devaluation.

Dollar prices of exports of France, Germany, the Netherlands, Norway and Denmark also declined less than the currency devaluations. This meant, of course, that local currency prices of exports rose immediately in relation to other prices in the devaluing country. There was a consequent increase in the profits of exports except, of course, as exporters' costs reflected higher prices for dollar imports. Given time, this increase in profits should lead exporters to enlarge their markets in the dollar area and either increase the production of export goods or shift the direction of their sales from soft currency to dollar markets.

On the other hand these tendencies may be offset by continued inflation in the devaluing country, and by rigidities which inhibit the transfer of resources to export industries. Producers may prefer to continue to sell in a stable though somewhat less profitable domestic or soft-currency export market than to spend money to exploit a more

24. *Ibid.*, p. 106. Comparison was made between the first nine months of 1949 and the corresponding period in 1950.
25. Demand elasticities for raw materials also tend to be quite low in the short run.

profitable but less secure dollar market. It may take a certain amount of domestic deflation to spark a real dollar export drive.

Effects on Raw Materials Prices

Since short-run demand elasticities of raw materials are notoriously small, it is generally argued that dollar receipts from raw materials exports of soft-currency countries will be adversely affected by devaluation. The influence on dollar prices of exports sold in world markets (both dollar and soft-currency areas) which can be expected from devaluation of soft currencies is difficult to determine.[26]

Unless both the elasticity of total supply and of demand in soft-currency markets are zero, the dollar price of the raw material will probably fall and the soft-currency price rise by something less than the amount necessary to maintain the original dollar price after devaluation.[27] As a matter of fact, the effects of the devaluation on the dollar and sterling prices of basic raw materials varied substantially between commodities. Thus dollar prices of wool and tea declined by 27 per cent and 20 per cent respectively between August and October 1949, while dollar prices of rubber and tin declined by 2 per cent and 8 per cent during the same period. Sterling prices of tea and tin rose by 44 and 32 per cent respectively, while cocoa rose only 2 per cent, and wool only 9 per cent. (See Table 5.)

It might be argued that the immediate effect of devaluation was to reduce both dollar prices and dollar receipts of sterling area exports —as a result of the inelasticity of dollar demand—and to reduce Britain's terms of trade with the raw materials producing areas, since British export prices rose less than those of raw materials imports. While in the months that followed, dollar prices of most raw materials imports rose to the August 1949 levels and beyond, the causes are obscured by the increase in world demand brought about by the business upturn in the United States and by the rearmament program.

26. The change in the dollar price will depend upon the demand elasticities in both the dollar and the soft-currency markets and upon the supply elasticities if the commodity is produced in both areas. For an interesting theoretical formulation of the problem see B. A. de Vries, "Immediate Effects of Devaluation on Prices of Raw Materials," *Staff Papers,* International Monetary Fund, September 1950, pp. 238–53.

27. A 30.5 per cent devaluation of the pound ($4.03 to $2.80) implies a 44 per cent rise in the sterling price of a commodity whose dollar price has remained constant. On the other hand, if the sterling price remains constant after devaluation, the dollar price of the commodity will decrease by 30.5 per cent.

TABLE 5

PERCENTAGE CHANGE IN DOLLAR AND STERLING PRICES OF FIVE PRIMARY
COMMODITIES—AUGUST 1949 TO OCTOBER 1949

Commodity	Percentage Decrease in Dollar Price in U.S. Market	Percentage Increase in Sterling Prices in Nondollar Area [a]
Wool	27	9
Tin	8	32
Rubber	2	27
Cocoa	10	2
Tea	20	44

Source: B. A. de Vries, "Immediate Effects of Devaluation on Prices of Raw Materials, *Staff Papers*, IMF, September 1950, p. 245.
a. Owing to isolation of dollar and nondollar markets, percentage increases in sterling prices do not correspond to percentage decreases in dollar prices except (approximately) in the case of tin.

It is difficult to determine, therefore, how much (if any) of the increase in dollar prices of raw materials to predevaluation levels would have occurred in the absence of shifts in demand. Considering the low intermediate-run supply elasticities (short-run elasticities being higher because of the existence of stocks) there is reason to believe that prices of sterling area raw materials exports would have risen anyway. This view is enforced by the fact that the demand for raw materials in Europe was not only inelastic but was growing with the increase in production.

British and other Western European economists have argued that the devaluation was responsible for the rapid deterioration in British terms of trade after August 1949. British terms of trade [28] changed from 87 in August 1949 (1950=100) to 99 in June 1950, before the impact of the Korean war on commodity markets.[29] This represents a deterioration of about 13 per cent, as compared with a deterioration of U.S. terms of trade of about 11 per cent.[30]

With most of the nondollar currencies of the world devaluing against the dollar, U.S. import prices might have been expected to fall. Actually, however, the U.S. index of unit values of imports in October 1949 was the same as in August 1949, and after December 1949 it began a sharp rise. By June 1951, the ratio of British import prices to export prices had risen to 119 (1950=100), or a deterio-

28. The ratio of the import price index to the export price index. A rise in the index indicates an adverse movement in terms of trade.
29. See *The Economist*, August 11, 1951, p. 355.
30. Based on Department of Commerce unit value indexes for imports and exports. See monthly issues of *Survey of Current Business*.

ration from August 1949 of about 33 per cent. Over the same period the U.S. terms of trade had deteriorated by about 26 per cent. While the U.S. and British indexes may not be wholly comparable, it seems clear that the deterioration of Britain's terms of trade between August 1949 and June 1951 is mainly attributable to the increases in world demand for raw materials both before and after the outbreak of war in Korea.[31]

APPRECIATION OF CONTROLLED CURRENCIES

Following the onset of war in Korea in June 1950 there was a rapid improvement in the gold and dollar positions of the sterling area and of certain Western European countries, and a sharp rise in world commodity prices and the generation of new inflationary pressures. These conditions precipitated fresh debate on the exchange rate issue. This debate reveals some of the objectives of postwar exchange rate policy. The research staff of the Economic Commission for Europe, together with several prominent British and continental economists, argued for an appreciation of European currencies to help combat internal inflation and to improve Europe's terms of trade.[32] Exchange rate depreciation was frequently advocated during the 1930s as a means of raising prices, even though the devaluing country was running an export surplus.[33]

Exchange rate appreciation might quite properly be justified for a country with an export surplus caused by an undervalued currency. For example, Canada appreciated its dollar in July 1946 to parity with the U.S. dollar to offset inflationary pressures originating in the United States.[34] Again, in September 1950, Canada permitted her currency to appreciate by suspending her fixed parity and permitting the Canadian dollar to find its own level in the market. The purpose of

31. See also Randall Hinshaw, "Currency Appreciation as an Anti-Inflationary Device," *Quarterly Journal of Economics,* November 1951, pp. 447–62.

32. See *Economic Survey of Europe in 1950,* Economic Commission for Europe, Geneva, 1951, pp. 157–64; see also R. F. Harrod, "Revaluation of Sterling," *Financial Times* (London), April 25, 1951; and R. F. Harrod, "Currency Appreciation as an Anti-Inflationary Device: a Comment," *Quarterly Journal of Economics,* February 1952, pp. 102–16.

33. To increase domestic prices was the principal motive for the devaluation of the dollar in 1933, at a time when the United States had a favorable trade balance.

34. Following the 1946 appreciation the Canadian balance of payments deteriorated and Canada was forced to impose import controls. In September 1949 Canada depreciated by 10 per cent.

this action was to reduce inflationary pressures arising from heavy capital movements into Canada from the United States. In both instances, however, Canada's balance of payments position was favorable and she was not maintaining severe import restrictions.

But in 1950 and 1951 Britain and the countries of Western Europe were still in a condition of serious disequilibrium and such temporary surpluses as did exist resulted from fairly rigid exchange and trade controls. In fact, most of these countries were currently receiving U.S. aid under the Marshall Program.[35] Thus the argument for an appreciation of European currencies seemed to have rejected completely the balance of payments criterion in favor of other objectives.[36]

Reduction of Inflationary Pressures

It was argued that appreciation of European currencies would help insulate the economies of these countries from a post-Korean rise in world prices. Since most European countries maintain restrictions against dollar goods, the question arises: Will the lower prices for imports be passed on to the consumer? But if prices come down, consumers will either seek to purchase more of the lower-priced imports, or, if the quantity of imports is not increased, they will bid up the prices of domestic goods. Consequently, for countries which do not have external surpluses, currency appreciation probably will not have a deflationary effect unless there is an increase in the quantity of goods imported. But most countries with import controls cannot afford increased imports unless, of course, currency appreciation brings an improvement of the terms of trade; that is, unless the country can buy more imports with the same or fewer exports.[37]

Whether or not European currency appreciation would benefit Europe's terms of trade without reducing the volume of imports is difficult to foresee. There was a strong tendency for dollar prices of international raw materials to remain high after devaluation. An appreciation of European currencies may leave the dollar prices of many international raw commodities unaffected. Dollar prices would rise only in the event that (1) exports available for dollar markets de-

---

35. ERP aid to Britain was suspended in December 1950.
36. Some British economists have argued that devaluation was unnecessary even in 1949.
37. This analysis is based on that given by Dr. Hinshaw in his article "Currency Appreciation as an Anti-Inflationary Device," loc. cit.

cline; or (2) world demand for raw materials increased as a result of appreciation. Since short-run supplies of exports are not likely to be adversely affected, dollar prices would increase only if Europe bought larger supplies of raw materials in world markets. But Europe would buy more raw materials if (1) she could afford them; and (2) raw materials were not subject to allocation controls and agreements.

If dollar prices remained fairly constant, sterling prices would fall so that Europe could afford to buy more, at least in nondollar areas. Under these conditions, Europe would improve its terms of trade with other nondollar areas. To the extent that Europe sought to bid nondollar exports away from dollar area countries, however, dollar prices would rise, thus tending to wipe out the original advantage of lower nondollar prices. While dollar earnings from raw materials might be expanded by a rise in dollar prices of raw materials exports to the dollar area, to the extent that dollar earnings were increased in this way Europe would lose the advantage of lower nondollar prices for imports from the nondollar area. So far as commodity imports from the dollar area are concerned, appreciation would not reduce dollar outlays.

Thus far we have considered the world markets for raw materials as if they were unified. Actually, this is not the fact. In the case of a number of raw materials produced in nondollar areas and sold largely in such markets, it is most unlikely that nondollar prices would fall as a result of an appreciation of these currencies.[38] The only way that prices of commodities sold largely in those markets could decline would be as a result of sharp competition from producers of the same commodities in dollar markets.

The Monetary Fund and U.S. Policies

While the exchange rate policies discussed above have had substantial support among economists and statesmen in Europe and elsewhere, they do not represent the thinking of countries like the United States and Canada nor do they conform to official statements of the International Monetary Fund. For reasons already pointed out, both

38. It is worth noting that nondollar area prices (in terms of sterling) of Indian cotton, sugar, bacon, butter, pig iron, nitrate and cocoa were scarcely affected by the 1949 devaluation, while the prices in U.S. markets (in terms of dollars) also remained fairly close to predevaluation levels. See B. A. de Vries, *loc. cit.*, p. 248.

the United States and the IMF condoned exchange rates which preserved wide disparities between domestic price levels during the early postwar reconstruction, but urged a realignment of rates well before the general readjustment of September 1949. Under its charter the Monetary Fund is committed to promoting equilibrium rates. It is therefore critical of exchange rate policies which seek to establish other rates in order to improve terms of trade or to reduce inflationary pressures.

In their *Annual Report* for 1951, the Executive Directors of the IMF were highly critical of proposals to appreciate the currencies of countries with weak balance of payments positions. The Fund argued that to increase their currency values would not only weaken the competitive position of these countries in world markets, but would lead the public to expect that an upward revaluation soon would be reversed, and thus "invite the kind of speculation against currencies which was a major trouble before the 1949 devaluation." [39] The *Report* also stated that the proper way to deal with inflation was by internal monetary and fiscal measures, not by seeking to export inflation through unwarranted appreciation. The *Report* compared proposals for appreciation under present conditions with the "beggar my neighbor" depreciation proposals of the 1930s, stating:

> The creation of the International Monetary Fund was due in no small measure to the realization that the world had been ill served by the exchange policies of the thirties, whose effect was to unload on other countries the curse of deflation. The pressing world problem today is inflation. Widespread appreciation would be as ineffective for solving this problem as depreciation was for solving the problem of deflation in the thirties. [40]

On the question of appreciation of foreign currencies with weak balance of payments positions, U.S. exchange rate policy is in line with that of the Fund. At a press conference on June 5, 1951, Secretary of the Treasury Snyder rejected the suggestion of the ECE report that European currencies be appreciated as an anti-inflationary measure for reasons similar to those given by the Monetary Fund in its September 1951 *Report*. [41]

As to the U.S. position regarding the par value of the dollar, the

39. *Annual Report*, 1951, IMF, Washington, September 1951, p. 35.
40. *Ibid.*, p. 36.
41. See *The New York Times*, June 6, 1951, p. 1.

government has rejected all suggestions for either an appreciation or a depreciation during the postwar period.[42] While an appreciation of the dollar might be justified on the basis of a persistent favorable balance on current account,[43] the position of the United States appears to be that the initiative for exchange rate adjustments should come from countries with balance of payments deficits. Although to appreciate the dollar might eventually improve the current position of other countries, it would immediately impair their position in two ways: first, the dollar value of their accumulated gold reserves would decrease with a downward revaluation of gold in terms of dollars; second, the dollar income of foreign gold-exporting countries would fall. A depreciation of nondollar currencies would avoid these disadvantages.

Position on Fluctuating Rates

While the Monetary Fund and the U.S. government firmly favor the maintenance of equilibrium exchange rates, their attitude toward fluctuating exchange rates has been more flexible. Officially, the Fund is committed to support the system of fixed par values, which may be changed only after consultation with the Fund, and a concurrence of the Fund if the cumulative change exceeds 10 per cent. On the other hand, the Fund has on several occasions sanctioned the temporary adoption of a fluctuating exchange rate.[44]

In recent years many economists and governmental officials have been increasingly dissatisfied with the system of fixed parities. They argue that in the case of many of the Fund's members the par value is little more than a fiction. Many countries employ multiple exchange rate systems in which few, if any, transactions take place at the official parity rate for the currency. There has also developed a complex of

42. On October 5, 1949, Secretary Synder issued a formal denial of any intention to devalue the dollar, and in response to persistent rumors President Truman gave "positive" assurance that there would be no alteration in the price of gold so long as he was in the White House. *Survey of United States International Finance, 1949,* Princeton University Press, Princeton, 1950, p. 125.

43. The United States was in approximate balance on current account in the latter half of 1950. Strictly speaking, however, the country was not in equilibrium because of the widespread restrictions against dollar imports imposed by other countries.

44. The official position of the Fund on fluctuating exchange rates and the conditions under which they will be sanctioned are given in the *Annual Report,* 1951, pp. 36–41.

trading practices, and from this come implicit exchange rates very different from the nominal rates at which the transactions take place. Moreover, it is argued that for many countries the easiest and most direct path to exchange freedom is through a flexible exchange rate system.

THE CASE FOR A FLUCTUATING EXCHANGE RATE

The favorable experience of Canada following the complete removal of all exchange controls and the adoption of a fluctuating exchange rate in December 1951 has stimulated much discussion as to the desirability of this step for other countries.[45] While there have been numerous examples of controlled rates which have been permitted to fluctuate or to float, there have been only two cases of freely fluctuating rates in the postwar period, namely the Mexican peso (July 1948—June 1949) and the Canadian dollar.[46] In this section we shall confine our discussion to genuinely free rates, the movements of which are not controlled by exchange restrictions on current transactions.[47] The following chapter will discuss "floating rates" or controlled rates permitted to fluctuate under conditions established by the exchange control authorities.

The current debate over fluctuating rates turns on three principal questions: (1) Can balance of payments equilibrium be restored and maintained by the substitution of a free and fluctuating exchange rate for a completely controlled exchange rate? (2) How will a fluctuating rate affect trade relations with other countries? (3) How will a fluctuating rate affect confidence in a currency, which will in turn be reflected in capital movements?

Balogh's Position

In discussing the first question, it is necessary to distinguish between the argument which rejects the desirability of achieving equi-

45. See "Set Sterling Free?" *The Economist,* July 26, 1952, pp. 205–08; see also a symposium by several British writers expressing different points of view on the question of adopting a free and flexible rate for sterling in *The Banker,* July 1952, pp. 18–31.

46. Canada suspended its fixed official rate of exchange in September 1950 and gradually removed her remaining exchange restrictions until December 1951 when all exchange controls were removed.

47. Most students would admit the necessity of maintaining controls on capital movements in advocating a removal of restrictions on current transactions. Tariff and quota restrictions can also be used to protect the balance of payments, but a complete system

librium through the price mechanism and that which questions the efficacy of exchange rate changes for achieving equilibrium. This latter position, best represented by the left-wing British economist, Dr. T. Balogh,[48] rests on a broad social and economic philosophy which rejects the market mechanism and chooses economic planning as the best means of achieving certain goals for the production and distribution of social income. Since a discussion of the relative merits of socialism vs. free enterprise would take this study far afield, we shall simply note the basic elements of Balogh's approach.

Briefly stated, Balogh's argument is that any attempt on the part of Britain and Western Europe to achieve balance of payments equilibrium through the market mechanism would subject these nations to unemployment and social injustice. Unemployment and depression are inevitable for countries dependent on unprotected world markets in competition with the United States because of the unreliability of the American market and the ability of U.S. exporters to capture European markets through their superior competitive position. Social injustice would result from the necessity of British and European producers to keep down real wages, through devaluation, deflation, or both in order to adjust to the rapid increases in the productivity of American industry. In other words, the continual lowering of costs of U.S. exports made possible by rapid technological advance would have to be matched by a continual reduction of real wages in British industry.[49] According to Balogh the imbalance between the dollar area and Western Europe can only be removed through large U.S. investments in Europe which will restore "equality of opportunity" between the two continents.[50]

That equilibrium with the dollar area cannot be restored through the market mechanism without grave internal economic consequences is widely believed in Britain and Western Europe. This position has had an important bearing on policy decisions as to exchange rates and currency convertibility.

---

of trade (as opposed to exchange) controls would simply involve *de facto* exchange controls by another name.

48. See Balogh, *op. cit.;* see also review of Balogh's book by J. N. Behrmann, "Dollar Crisis: Cured by World Socialism?" *Kyklos,* Vol. V. (1952), pp. 17–40.

49. In advancing this argument, Balogh overlooks the tendency of American money wages to rise with increased productivity.

50. Balogh, *op. cit.,* p. 87.

But there is also the argument that international equilibrium is feasible, though it should not be maintained through exchange rate adjustments.[51] According to this, world markets today are subject to private and governmental controls and, in general, imperfect and rather unresponsive to changes in prices. This makes for an inelastic demand for exports. If exporters lower prices in terms of foreign exchange the earnings of the depreciating country will decline. If, on the other hand, exporters maintain prices in terms of foreign exchange, they reap large and potentially inflationary profits. In any case, rate changes should be infrequent, with no attempt to maintain equilibrium by means of a freely fluctuating rate. Both Harrod and Hawtrey stress the control of the volume of domestic investment as perhaps the most efficient way to combat inflation and adjust the balance of payments. The volume of investment is affected by the rate of interest and by government spending for public works, for housing projects, and so on.

Main Burden on Internal Measures

There is certainly much to be said for the position that fiscal, monetary and other internal economic measures should be chiefly responsible for adjustments to maintain balance of payments equilibrium. A British manufacturer, producing at full capacity for domestic and sterling area markets, may not be attracted by higher profits in the dollar area resulting from a depreciation of the pound. He may prefer to continue to supply his customers in the protected sterling market rather than make the marketing outlays required to enter a highly competitive and uncertain dollar market. Further, in the face of full employment of men and resources at home, he may find it difficult to expand his output to get into other markets made profitable by devaluation. On the other hand, a deflation which reduces home demand may force him to seek foreign markets in order to continue in business. The stick may prove more effective than the carrot! And deflation will also release men and resources for production for

51. This position is represented by Professor R. G. Hawtrey in his *Balance of Payments and the Standard of Living*, Royal Institute of International Affairs, London, 1950, pp. 60–64; and by R. F. Harrod, *Are These Hardships Necessary?* Hart-Davis, London, 1947; see also R. F. Harrod, "Currency Appreciation as an Anti-Inflationary Device," *loc. cit.*

more attractive markets and facilitate the transfer of resources to production for export.

Those who favor adjustment through the fluctuating rate mechanism will be ready to admit that a fluctuating rate will not only prove ineffective, but perhaps quite dangerous, in the absence of anti-inflationary measures. Uncontrolled inflation and a free exchange rate may quickly lead to hyperinflation, with disastrous consequences to the economy. Indeed, one of the arguments advanced for fluctuating rates is that a fall in the external value of the currency would make both governmental officials and the public aware that something is wrong. Officially fixed rates shored up by controls create a sense of false security. When the crisis arises it may be too late to prevent a heavy loss of reserves and an eventual devaluation of 20 or 30 per cent. Under a fluctuating rate system, however, the public might become aware of the danger in time to demand appropriate countermeasures before serious harm befell the economy.[52] It is readily admitted that short-term market forces will frequently cause a rate to depart from its long-term equilibrium level. But a genuinely free rate will never be wholly out of line with economic realities over long periods of time, and short-term speculative and seasonal movements can be offset by the stabilization operations.

Increased Confidence

A final argument for the freeing of exchange rates is that this would benefit the exchange position of the country by strengthening the currency. This argument has special weight for a currency which, like sterling, is widely used in international transactions.[53] If confidence in sterling were restored by making it convertible, other countries would be more willing to hold it, and Britain's former position as the world's banker and the center of international commodity markets could be restored. Further, much of the protection to British reserves sought by restricting the convertibility of foreign-held sterling into dollars is lost through cheap sterling deals.[54]

52. For a good discussion of the arguments for and against fluctuating exchange rates, see *Twenty-Second Annual Report*, Bank for International Settlements, Basel, June 1952, pp. 142–49.
53. See David Keswick, "Unshackle Sterling!" *The Banker*, July 1952, pp. 18–21.
54. Those who oppose freeing sterling have argued that by making it convertible Britain would legalize the sale of sterling against dollars and the loss of dollars to

It may be argued, of course, that confidence in sterling requires not simply that it be convertible but that it be stable in value. However, it is undoubtedly true that there was greater confidence in sterling during the 1930s when it fluctuated widely in terms of the dollar than during the postwar period when it was inconvertible. One may also point to the enormous strength of the Canadian dollar. After it was set free in September 1950, the Canadian dollar rose from U.S. $.91 to a high of U.S. $1.04 in the summer of 1952. While it is true that a fluctuating currency is liable to depreciate at any moment, sharp declines of 20 or 25 per cent do not take place over a week-end, as in the case of currencies with "fixed" rates. The holder can sell a free currency whenever he is convinced that market conditions indicate a fall in its value. He can also have confidence that the value of the currency at any given moment represents a market judgment fairly close to economic realities rather than an arbitrary level fixed by governmental fiat.

The Other Side

A major argument against fluctuating exchange rates has always been that they create uncertainties in trade relations, and increase the risks of business conducted across international borders. Certainly no one would argue that fluctuating rates per se are superior to stable exchange rates. The alternative however may lie between fixed rates maintained by exchange controls and the organization of trade on the basis of bilateral agreements on the one hand, and free exchange dealings on the other. It seems all too clear that the risks and barriers to trade caused by postwar exchange restrictions and multiple rate systems have been far greater than those occasioned by fluctuating rates before the war.

Another argument brought against fluctuating rates is that they may lead to competitive exchange depreciation. One of the principal functions of the IMF is to prevent this by providing for orderly adjustment of rates through consultation among the members affected by changes in currency parities. As has been pointed out, however, the par value system of the Fund has been substantially weakened by the development of multiple exchange rates and unofficial rates

the British Treasury would be far higher than it is at present under partially effective controls.

of various kinds. These nonparity rates have not been stable, and for the most part they have not been subject to control by the Fund, nor has the Fund's par value system avoided a type of implicit competitive exchange rate depreciation.

For example, during 1952 there developed among European countries a kind of competition in the use of export retention quotas which some have regarded as just as harmful and vicious as exchange depreciation. Since official parities have been undermined or bypassed by a complex of multiple exchange rates and special dealings which involve nonofficial rates, why not clear away the whole disorderly structure and substitute unitary fluctuating rates? This study will return to this question in a later chapter after examining more fully the nature and function of multiple rate systems.

Interim Stability

Before leaving the subject of fluctuating *vs.* fixed exchange rates, it is necessary to deal briefly with the relative advantages of a freely fluctuating rate over one which may be reviewed and changed at frequent intervals but in the interim is kept stable. From a purely economic standpoint there is little advantage in permitting day-to-day fluctuations in an exchange rate. Over a short period, it is impossible to tell whether certain market forces are temporary, or whether they represent a fundamental shift in demand and supply. To stabilize exchange rates for a brief time may be advantageous, assuming, of course, that the monetary authorities are able to distinguish between the temporary and the more basic market forces. Reviewing exchange rates at intervals would also make it possible to observe the Monetary Fund's rules and better to preserve international relations by consultations with other members of the Fund before adjusting rates.[55]

On the other hand, important political and psychological considerations favor fluctuating rates over flexible rates stabilized for short periods. A change in a country's official gold parity is a highly publicized act with many political overtones. Governments are reluctant

---

55. Some government officials believe that serious consultations on exchange rate matters are impossible because of the danger of information leaks. For example, if it became generally known in the financial community that a key currency country contemplated a rate change, short operations against its currency could cause a loss of millions of dollars in reserves.

to take such a step and usually avoid it until long after it has become economically desirable. Once a new parity is established, governments feel they must defend and maintain it even though events soon prove the new rate's unsoundness.

For example, the Canadian Finance Minister in announcing the freeing of the Canadian rate on September 30, 1950 rejected an appreciation of the Canadian dollar to a fixed official parity with the American dollar on the grounds that such revaluation "would not necessarily be justified by fundamental conditions and might be found to require reversal or further adjustment within the not too distant future. To move the Canadian exchange rate to any other fixed point than parity with the United States dollar would be open to the same objections." [56] While the Monetary Fund gave recognition to the Canadian action, the Fund has made it clear that it does not favor the establishment of a fluctuating rate except "under special circumstances and for temporary periods."

Probably some members of the Fund would favor the adoption of a fluctuating exchange rate so that they need not consult with the Fund regarding possible future adjustments. It is an impressive fact that in every case of a change in the par value of a major currency the Fund has had virtually no opportunity for serious consultation. For these and other reasons—political and psychological—it is quite possible that other nations contemplating the restoration of currency convertibility will choose to adopt a fluctuating rate as an initial step in that direction.

FORWARD EXCHANGE TRANSACTIONS

Where free currency markets exist, the volume of transactions in contracts for the delivery of a currency at some future date is usually quite important. Sometimes it amounts to as much as half the spot transactions in that currency. The bulk of the business in forward exchange arises from the desire of importers, exporters and other firms which have contracts to make or receive payment in a foreign currency, to hedge against a change in the exchange rate. Banks and other foreign exchange dealers normally seek to supply the demand for forward exchange from their customers and to "cover" their own

56. Quoted by the *Monthly Review,* Federal Reserve Bank of New York, November 1950, p. 135.

position, hedging against loss from a movement of the rates in either direction.

For example, if a British bank sells a million Canadian dollars three months forward to certain of its customers and buys a million Canadian dollars for three months delivery from other customers, it is adequately protected against loss and is satisfied to earn a small commission as profit. But if it agrees to deliver a million Canadian dollars and has only brought a half-million forward, it must cover the other half if it is to avoid a speculative position. This it can do by purchasing Canadian dollars to hold until its forward sales contracts mature, or by making a contract with another bank at home or abroad for the delivery of sterling against Canadian dollars three months hence.

In a free market, the price of forward Canadian dollars in sterling will vary with the requirements of trade and the speculative outlook for the two currencies. With rumors that sterling is to be devalued, the price of U.S. and Canadian dollars might rise very rapidly in the London market unless the Bank of England intervened.[57] On the other hand, if there were rumors that the Canadian dollar would be stabilized at par with the U.S. dollar (thus eliminating the premium over U.S. dollars which exists at the time of writing) the price of forward Canadian dollars might drop below the spot price in London.

Varying Policies

The policies with regard to forward exchange transactions differ markedly from country to country. Some exchange control countries provide no facilities whatever for such dealings. However, nearly all major trading countries permit foreign exchange banks to make forward exchange contracts with business firms having a *bona fide* need for protection against exchange rate changes. In many cases the purchases and sales of foreign exchange must be made at a fixed rate above or below the spot selling or buying rate. In these instances the authorized banks or dealers are permitted to cover by making contracts with the central bank. This was the situation in Britain before December 1951, and is still true in the case of certain other European

---

57. During the summer of 1949, before the September devaluation, the price of forward sterling in the New York market fell from around $4.00 to a low of about $3.77.

countries. Prior to December 1951, there was a free and fluctuating forward market in American account sterling in New York and other free markets, but the sterling-dollar forward rate in New York varied substantially from the rates fixed by the Bank of England for forward dollars in London.

With the establishment of Britain's controlled free market on December 17, 1951, British banks were permitted to operate freely in the forward markets in New York, Canada and London for U.S. and Canadian dollars, as well as in the forward markets of certain other countries for sterling against their currencies. Since December 1951, therefore, the forward rates on sterling-dollar exchange in the New York and London markets have fluctuated together because arbitrage transactions would eliminate any substantial difference between the two markets. Although British banks are limited in their forward dealings with customers to meeting needs arising out of *bona fide* commercial transactions, they are permitted to cover their forward contracts by spot purchases of dollars and by operations in other forward markets.[58]

58. See Chapter 17 for a discussion of the New York forward market.

Chapter 8

MULTIPLE EXCHANGE RATES AND CONTROLLED "FREE" RATES

THE POSTWAR PERIOD has witnessed a number of developments in exchange rate practices. Although they are an integral part of the exchange control systems, they warrant separate consideration. The usual procedure of countries adopting postwar exchange controls was to require that all foreign transactions take place through authorized banks at fixed buying and selling rates established within narrow margins above and below parity. In the case of currencies such as American account sterling, which are traded in free markets abroad, the central bank undertook to maintain the rates within a narrow range of parity. The principal exceptions to the practice of maintaining fixed unitary rates were in the Latin American countries, many of which had adopted multiple rates before the war.

During the postwar period this standard practice of exchange control countries has been modified in two important respects. First, there has been a tendency toward greater use of multiple exchange rates and of practices giving rise to implicit rates which depart from the official exchange parities. Second, a number of countries have established markets for foreign currencies in which the rates are allowed to fluctuate within limits determined by a system of controls over the demand for, and the supply of, exchange.

MULTIPLE EXCHANGE RATES

As used here, a multiple exchange rate system is an arrangement having more than one legal buying rate or more than one legal selling rate, or having the spread between a unitary buying rate and a unitary selling rate more than the 2 per cent range provided in the Monetary Fund Agreement.

Of the sixty-six countries and territories whose exchange rates are quoted regularly by the monthly statistical publication of the Monetary Fund [1] over one third have more than one legal rate which is used in commercial transactions. Countries with multiple rates include the ten independent countries of South America; Cuba,[2] Costa Rica, and Nicaragua in Central America and the Caribbean; Iceland and Spain in Europe; Taiwan, Hong Kong, Indonesia, Iran, Israel, Jordan, Korea, Lebanon, Syria, the Philippines and Thailand in Asia; and Egypt.

Multiple rates cannot exist without exchange controls, since in a perfectly free market a currency can have only one price in terms of another free currency.[3] The minute exchange controls are imposed, even mild controls on capital exports, the possibility of a dual rate arises. Thus, if there are illegal dealings in foreign exchange, a black market price for foreign exchange will appear. If exchange control regulations differ as between dealings with different currency areas, the possibility of additional gray or black market rates increases. The next chapter will discuss rates arising out of illegal or unofficial dealings.[4] The present chapter is concerned with multiple rates specifically provided for by the monetary authorities.

The motives for establishing multiple exchange rate systems are similar to those for the deliberate setting and maintenance of other than equilibrium rates. (See Chapter 4.) Multiple exchange rates achieve their objectives by means of cost restrictions and price incentives as opposed to direct quantitative restrictions. Their advantage over a unitary rate system in carrying out the desired policies stems from the fact that an exchange rate which will realize a particular economic objective for one category of international transactions may be inappropriate for another.

For example, an appreciated rate for imports of wheat will keep down the domestic price of bread; that same rate applied to the export of Panama hats might put the hat makers out of business. Exchange rates may vary according to the type of commodity or service

1. *International Financial Statistics,* published monthly by the International Monetary Fund, Washington.
2. Cuba has a 2 per cent tax on all sales of exchange for payments abroad. According to the Monetary Fund this constitutes a multiple rate practice.
3. By a single rate for a foreign currency we mean that there can be only one value for demand bankers' bills drawn on that country at any particular moment of time.
4. Frequently, free markets for balances or currency notes of a particular country, which are restricted as to use, may develop in foreign markets. While foreign dealings in these balances or notes may not be illegal, they are nevertheless not provided for in the official exchange control regulations of the country in question.

imported or exported. They may also vary for the same type or category of transaction as between foreign currencies or currency areas. Here the term *multiple rates* will be used where a nation deliberately establishes different rates for different transactions, and the term *disparate cross-rates* where rates for the same type of transaction differ as between currency areas, in other words, where cross-rates are broken.[5] The motive for establishing disparate cross-rates is similar to that for using discriminatory trade or exchange controls, since in both cases the objective is to discriminate in trade as between two or more foreign countries or currency areas.

There are several ways to make multiple exchange rates effective: (1) fixed multiple rates; (2) taxes on purchases or sales of foreign exchange; (3) one or more fixed rates and a fluctuating rate or rates; (4) exchange certificate systems. Some countries combine two or more of these arrangements.

Fixed Multiple Rates

The most common method is to require all foreign exchange receipts to be surrendered to the exchange control authorities at rates which vary with the type of transaction. Thus exporters of oranges in Israel receive one Israeli pound for every dollar of foreign exchange earned, while exporters of diamonds receive one Israeli pound for every $2.80 in foreign exchange. Importers and others requiring foreign exchange must obtain it from the authorities at rates which differ according to the purpose for which it is to be used. For example, an Israeli firm which has a license to import lamps from the United States will pay twice as much in Israeli currency for each dollar of foreign exchange required, as will an importer of wheat.

A number of multiple rate systems apply a certain rate to one portion of the value of the transactions and a different rate to another. The effective rate resulting from such a combination of rates is known as a "mixing" rate. Thus exporters of wool in Argentina surrender 50 per cent of their proceeds at 5 pesos per dollar and the remainder at 7.5 pesos per dollar. "Mixing" rates may also be applied to imports. In this case, part of the foreign exchange is paid for at one rate and another portion at a higher rate.

5. For example, if the official value of the pound sterling is $4 and a country establishes a rate of 400 pesos to the pound and 125 pesos to the dollar, the cross-rate between the pound and the dollar is broken.

Exchange Taxes

Another method of effecting a multiple rate is a tax on purchases of foreign exchange. Brazil, for example, required all buyers of foreign exchange to pay a tax of 8 per cent, while in Colombia and Cuba the tax is 3 per cent and 2 per cent, respectively.[6] In March 1951 the Philippine government imposed a 17 per cent exchange tax on all sales of foreign exchange except those to be used in payment for designated essential imports and for certain nontrade payments.

Combination of Fixed and Fluctuating Rates

Several countries require exporters to surrender some portion of their exchange proceeds to the exchange control authorities at the official rate, but allow the remainder to be sold at more favorable free market rates. Thailand is one of these. She requires exporters of rubber and tin to surrender 20 per cent of their dollar or sterling proceeds at the official rate of 12.45 baht to the dollar and 80 per cent at the fluctuating free market rate. This system makes for different effective rates for different classes of exports.

Many multiple rate systems include a "free" rate which is controlled only indirectly by limiting the types of transactions to which it can apply. In such cases recipients of foreign exchange from certain kinds of transactions are free to sell the exchange to banks or to anyone authorized to make use of it at prices determined in the market. Thus, in Ecuador tourists may sell their dollars on the free market. There they may be bought by individuals needing foreign exchange for luxury imports, not permitted to come in under the more favorable rates for essentials, or by residents who want to travel or make investments abroad. A variant of the free market rate is the "auction" rate, the term used when the exchange control authorities sell a portion of their exchange receipts to importers of luxuries or less essential commodities at a price determined by competitive bidding.

Exchange Certificates

In recent years several countries have employed an exchange certificate system to establish multiple rates. While the details vary from

6. Brazil's system was changed in February 1953. In Colombia the tax is levied on import applications.

country to country, exporters are generally required to surrender all or some proportion of their foreign exchange proceeds to the exchange control in return for marketable exchange certificates. The exchange certificates may then be sold to importers either in free markets or in controlled markets at stabilized buying and selling rates. When exporters have to turn over less than 100 per cent of their exchange proceeds with the remainder to be sold in the free market, the effective rate at which they sell foreign exchange is likely to be higher than the rate paid for imports and other transactions permitted at the certificate rate.[7]

Categories of Transactions

The operation of a multiple rate system depends upon the ability of the exchange control authorities to limit the application of a particular exchange rate or exchange market—if a free market exists—to a designated category of transactions. Some countries have several categories of commodity transactions, each including a number of import or export items, to which specified exchange rates apply. Since exchange transactions are usually handled by the banks acting as agents for the exchange control authorities, exporters and importers, as a rule, are required to obtain export or import licenses and present them when they sell or buy foreign exchange.

Government authorities frequently shift items from one exchange rate category to another; they may even change the whole structure of rates and the categories of items to which the rates apply. Substantial changes in multiple rate systems amount to *de facto* appreciation or depreciation of the currency, even though the basic rate or par value remains unchanged. Thus, for example, in March 1951 Colombia changed the buying rate applicable to most of her exports, except coffee, from 1.95 to 2.50 pesos to the dollar and her basic selling rate for imports from 1.95 pesos to the dollar to 2.51 pesos, plus an exchange tax of 3 per cent. While this action was, in fact, a substantial depreciation of the peso, Colombia's par value of 1.95 pesos, which now applies only to a portion of the coffee exports, remained the same. Colombia was, however, required to obtain the ap-

7. For example, the free market rates for dollar and sterling drafts in Peru tend to be somewhat higher than the certificate rates.

proval of the Monetary Fund before making this change in her multiple rate system.[8]

The Structure of Multiple Rate Systems

Multiple rate systems range all the way from relatively simple schemes in which the spread between the export or buying rate and the import or selling rate is larger than the normal spread in free exchange countries, to systems having dozens of effective rates which vary with the type of transaction. Most multiple rate systems, as a rule, apply higher rates to imports than to exports. Frequently the maintenance of a spread between the price at which the exchange control authorities buy foreign exchange from exporters and the price at which they sell it to importers provides a convenient means of taxation. In some countries, this is the principal means of taxing foreign companies. In such cases a special export rate may be applied to the petroleum or copper or bananas exported by foreign concerns.

A spread between buying and selling rates may also be used to conserve foreign exchange. The preference for this device over straight devaluation arises from the fact that most of the multiple rate countries export raw materials, the supplies of which are not immediately responsive to price increases. Straight devaluation as a means of limiting imports would mean higher profits for exporters with little or no expansion in exports. With a less favorable rate for exports these profits can be captured and their inflationary impact avoided. Of course, in the longer run higher profits to exporters should result in an expansion of production. By maintaining less favorable rates for exporters, those countries may be discouraging additional investment in their export industries.

Multiple Import Rates

Most multiple exchange countries have more than one import rate. In many instances, the rate for luxury commodities is higher than for essentials. Two reasons have been advanced in favor of this method of conserving foreign exchange. First, the demand for essentials may be so inelastic that a rise in the domestic price would not appreciably affect imports; second, reasons of social welfare may demand that import cuts fall heaviest on the less essential goods.

8. *Annual Report, 1951,* International Monetary Fund, p. 51.

On the other hand, the use of a favorable—or subsidy—rate for essential imports may have undesirable results. Sometimes to bring in essential imports at a favorable rate tends to restrict domestic production of the commodities. For example, in 1950 Ecuador permitted the import of wheat at 15 sucres to the dollar. But if the rate of 20 sucres to the dollar (that for nonessentials) had been applied to wheat, domestic producers could have supplied wheat in competition with imports, and thereby reduced foreign exchange expenditures.[9]

The importation of essential items at favorable rates tends to feed inflationary forces by subsidizing their consumption. Frequently the favored category of imports represents substantially more than half of a country's imports.[10] Favorable rates for certain imports may also encourage commodity arbitrage in these commodities. It has been reported that the subsidized rate for imports of food from dollar countries into Peru in 1950 led to their re-export to other countries.[11] In this case, Peru was using dollar exchange to subsidize the imports of other countries from the dollar area.

Multiple import rates may also be used to protect domestic industries and foster industrialization, much as a protective tariff is used. While protection is usually secured through the use of such devices as tariffs and import quotas, multiple rate countries frequently put items which are produced at home in the less favored category. A study of Argentina's exchange system, for example, clearly indicates the influence of protectionism. Argentina usually favors exports of manufactures by putting them in a preferential export rate category and discourages imports of manufactures which compete with domestic production by putting them in unfavorable import rate categories.

Multiple Export Rates

Multiple export rates have two basic purposes. A high rate for foreign exchange in terms of local currency may be used to subsidize or encourage exports of certain commodities. For example, Venezuela pays exporters of unwashed coffee and cacao 4.25 bolivars per dol-

9. See E. M. Bernstein, "Some Economic Aspects of Multiple Exchange Rates," *Staff Papers,* September 1950, pp. 230–31.
10. Bernstein estimates that in Colombia 90 per cent of the aggregate imports in 1950 came in under the most favorable import rate. *Ibid.,* p. 229.
11. *Ibid.,* p. 280.

lar [12] as against a buying rate for most other exports of 3.32 bolivars. Some countries have one or more preferential rates covering categories of exports they want to favor.

A second purpose of multiple export rates is to tax certain classes of exporters. In many instances, an unfavorable rate for converting foreign exchange proceeds into local currency is applied to foreign companies. Thus Venezuela requires the petroleum companies to acquire bolivars at a rate of 3.09 to the dollar as against a basic buying rate of 3.32. The penalty rate or tax imposed by Chile on the mining companies is even higher—they are required to buy pesos at 19.37 to the dollar though most other exporters sell their dollars to the exchange control at 110 pesos to the dollar.

There may be short-run advantages to a special tax on the more profitable export industries and to a subsidy for the less profitable. But the long-run effects will be to discourage investment in the more productive industries and to encourage investment in the less productive. Perhaps there is some justification for affording temporary protection to infant enterprises and fostering industrialization by this method. However, the subsidy is frequently paid to certain agricultural exporters at the expense of more efficient and productive undertakings. For example, in many countries an unfavorable rate is imposed on the exports of foreign investors. Multiple exchange rate practices rank high among the obstacles to foreign investment cited by American companies.[13]

Multiple Rates for Invisibles

As a general rule, the exchange rates of multiple rate countries applying to invisible transactions such as capital movements, travel, dividend and interest remittances, and transportation, insurance and other services tend to be higher than most other rates. Frequently certain invisible transactions are permitted at a so-called "free" rate which fluctuates from day to day in response to demand and supply. In most cases, dividends and interest payments on approved capital

12. The subsidy rates apply only when export prices are below specified levels.
13. *Obstacles to Direct Foreign Investment*, Report Prepared for the President's Committee for Financing Foreign Trade, National Industrial Conference Board, New York, April 1951; see also E. R. Schlesinger, *Multiple Exchange Rates and Economic Development*, Princeton University Press, Princeton, 1952. This problem will be considered in a later chapter of this book.

imports are permitted at the same rate or rate category at which capital is imported. In some instances, however, there is a special tax on all exchange remittances and in a few cases there is a substantial spread between the rate applying to capital imports and that for transfers of earnings. Obviously, such practices tend to discourage foreign investment. If basic rates are substantially overvalued, favorable rates for tourist expenditures are sometimes employed to encourage this industry. Latin American countries frequently follow this practice.

Disparate Cross-Rates

Systems involving disparate or broken cross-rates are the result of a country's desire to maintain an exchange rate on one foreign currency different from that on another as determined by the official rate between the two foreign currencies. For example, when the dollar-sterling rate was approximately four to one, a country might set 20 units of its own currency to the pound sterling. But because of its balance of payments relationships to the dollar area it might consider that the proper rate for the dollar was six to one, rather than five to one. This, however, would not conform to the cross-rate between the dollar and the pound. Obviously, if the dollar and sterling were freely convertible there would be no reason, from a balance of payments standpoint, to break the cross-rate.[14]

Since World War II disparate cross-rates have usually occurred in countries which wanted to establish a free market for the dollar and other hard currencies while maintaining controlled rates with countries where they have payments agreements. Thus in January 1948 France adopted a new official rate equivalent to 214 francs to the dollar which applied to most transactions with the sterling area and other soft-currency countries. At the same time France established a free market for dollars and Portuguese escudos and, later, for Swiss francs. Except for certain essential imports which came in at the official rate, importers were required to obtain their dollars at the free market rate. This ranged from 305 to 314 francs to the dollar during

14. A rate which discriminated against the dollar might also be established for reasons of commercial policy. Thus before 1939 Argentina had a system which, in effect, meant discrimination against the dollar.

1948.[15] Exporters had to surrender half their hard-currency proceeds at the official rates and sell the other half on the free market. In October 1948 the French exchange system was altered and the disparate cross-rate feature abolished for most transactions.

Italy adopted a similar system in March 1946, giving rise to disparate cross-rates but this was abandoned in November 1948. In Lebanon there are no exchange controls, but the Lebanese maintain payments agreements with exchange control countries. Free market transactions in sterling, francs, dollars and other currencies take place at rates which do not reflect official cross-rates.

Exchange Certificate Systems

Disparate cross-rates may result from the operation of an exchange certificate system if the exchange certificates are denominated in particular currencies and if the market for the certificates is not so controlled as to maintain official cross-rates.

In October 1947 Greece established a system in which all exchange proceeds were sold to authorized banks at the official rate; sellers received exchange certificates denominated in dollars or pounds equal in amount to the particular currencies tendered. These were negotiable on the open market and buyers of foreign exchange were required to obtain the certificates in the desired foreign currency. Dollar exchange certificates usually sold at a premium above sterling certificates. Hence the effective buying and selling rates for dollars and pounds (the official rate plus the price of certificates) reflected cross-rates ranging from $2.72 to $3.22 between October 1947 and September 1949, as compared with the official cross-rate of $4.03. After September 1949 the certificate rates were controlled to yield effective rates of 15,000 drachmas per dollar and 42,000 drachmas per pound, representing the official dollar-sterling rate of $2.80.

The Peruvian exchange system provides another example of the development of disparate cross-rates under an exchange certificate scheme. All exchange transactions are conducted at fluctuating rates, with no import restrictions. Exporters are required to surrender part of their export receipts against exchange certificates, the proportion

15. In March 1948 the system was changed to permit importers to acquire half their hard-currency exchange at the official rate and the remainder at the free rate.

varying from 100 per cent to as low as 10.[16] The free markets for both certificates and for drafts in foreign currencies are supported at times by the central bank. Certificates are designated in dollars, sterling, Argentine pesos and other currencies with no effort to maintain official cross-rates in the markets for either drafts or certificates.[17] Since sterling, as a rule, is more plentiful than dollars, sterling and other soft currencies usually sell at a discount in relation to dollars. Even if cross-rates in the free market were maintained, the fact that exporters are required to turn over a higher percentage for their dollar than for sterling proceeds in exchange for certificates may produce a differential in the effective export rates for the two currencies.

British Position on Cross-Rates

Britain requires most countries with which she has payments agreements to maintain the cross-rate for the pound in their markets, at least for current trade. Thus in the Anglo-Italian agreement of November 24, 1948, the Italian government agreed that the sterling-lira rate would be based on the dollar-lira rate in order to maintain the official dollar-sterling cross-rate.[18] Before that time fluctuations in the two rates resulted in disparate cross-rates. However, British agreements are frequently violated by the partner countries. For example, France overstepped her agreement with Britain in January 1948 when she adopted a floating rate for the dollar. A number of other countries, including Peru, Lebanon and Thailand, are apparently violators of British agreements.

The authorities of many countries make no attempt to control the rates on their currencies in foreign markets. For example, in April 1950 the Egyptian government entered into a special agreement with Switzerland under which the Egyptian pound would be bought and sold freely on the Swiss market.[19] However, most countries which

16. Prior to April 1952 exporters had to surrender 100 per cent of their dollar proceeds and only 10 per cent of their sterling proceeds for certificates.

17. An orderly cross-rate is maintained between the dollar and the French franc in accordance with the terms of the Franco-Peruvian payments agreement.

18. Dr. C. Brescani-Turroni, Chairman of the Banca di Roma, stated in an article in the *Corriere Della Sera* of Milan (November 27, 1951) that British insistence on the maintenance of the cross-rate was harmful to Italy. (*The New York Times*, December 3, 1951.) Italy has tended to have a surplus with the sterling area and a deficit with the dollar area.

19. *The Economist*, April 29, 1950, p. 963.

have payments agreements with one another maintain official rates between their currencies for purposes of commercial transactions. Thus Switzerland maintains controlled rates for commercial transactions with most payments agreement countries by requiring exchange to be bought and sold through authorized banks at the official rates, though currencies of countries not linked to Switzerland by payments agreements are bought and sold in free markets. The same thing is largely true in Belgium which also has a free foreign exchange market. Both Switzerland and Belgium have free markets for sterling, but this sterling generally is available only for capital transactions, some of which may be illegal from the standpoint of British exchange regulations.

Discrimination by Commodity Classification

It is possible for a country to establish a system of multiple exchange rates in which the types of commodity transactions applying to each rate category are chosen in a way to involve rate discrimination between foreign currencies. Mention has already been made of Argentina's use in the 1930s of multiple exchange rates to discriminate against imports from the United States. Argentina has employed similar practices since World War II, again not by the explicit use of disparate cross-rates, but by so rigging her rate structure as to accomplish implicit rate discrimination.

After the 30.5 per cent devaluation of the pound sterling on September 19, 1949, Argentina devalued her preferential rate A by 18 per cent (with respect to the dollar) and her preferential B rate by 30.5 per cent, but maintained her basic export rate at the old dollar value. This applies to exports of meat, grain and oilseeds—products exported chiefly to the United Kingdom. Thus Argentine wool, hides and vegetable oils were exported to the United States at the preferential rate of 4.8 pesos to the dollar and quebracho extract and casein at the preferential B rate of 5.7 pesos to the dollar, while exports which went largely to nondollar countries were sold at the basic rate of 3.4 pesos to the dollar. According to the U.S. Tariff Commission, "The new scheme of exchange rates was designed to encourage dollar-paid exports in general with a greater inducement to move products for which the dollar demand has been falling off than was

offered on products for which the dollar demand has been steady." [20]
Another reason for Argentina's failure to devalue her basic export
rate was that as it stood it gave her a better claim to a higher sterling
price for her meat exports to Britain.

Effects of Disparate Cross-Rates

The economic effects of disparate cross-rates are complex and often
difficult to determine. For a country like Peru they provide a mechanism for balancing trade with both the dollar area and the sterling
area without the use of direct import restrictions and export controls.
If there is a surplus of sterling exchange and a shortage of dollar
exchange, an adjustment in the prices of the two currencies in terms
of Peruvian soles will establish an equilibrium of supply and demand.
But what will be the effect on Britain's trade?

To reduce the value of the pound relative to the dollar leads Peruvian exporters to divert their exports away from Britain and the sterling area to the dollar area. This means that British importers will
have to offer higher sterling prices for the same amount of goods,
which is to reduce Britain's terms of trade. On the other hand, British
goods will be somewhat more attractive to Peruvian importers as
compared with dollar goods, though it is doubtful whether this would
have much effect on British export prices as compared with the usual
arrangement under which purchases are diverted to the sterling area
by discriminatory trade and exchange controls. The net effect of the
use of broken cross-rates, then, is to make it more difficult for Britain
to buy in Peru. While this also makes it easier for Britain to sell to
Peru, the amount of her sales depends upon the amount of her
purchases, which the higher rate for dollar exports tends to reduce.

A broken cross-rate in Peru may also work to the disadvantage of
Britain through triangular transactions. If it were possible for residents of other countries, say Venezuelans, to purchase Peruvian soles
with dollars at the higher dollar rate and then use these to purchase
pounds at the reduced rate in terms of the dollar-sterling cross-rate,
then Britain might stand to suffer an additional loss: instead of using
dollars to buy British goods the Venezuelans would purchase sterling at a reduced rate through Peru. Even though the British exchange

20. *Recent Developments in the Foreign Trade of Argentina*, United States Tariff
Commission, Washington, 1950, p. 33.

controls prohibit shipment to Venezuela except for payment in dollars, Venezuela might buy goods in the sterling area consigned to Peru and then transshipped to Venezuela. In fact, Peruvian merchants might buy the sterling-area goods and then re-export them to Venezuela, Colombia or other dollar countries through a process called commodity arbitrage or commodity shunting.

From this hypothetical case it is clear why the British have opposed disparate cross-rates in the Monetary Fund and elsewhere. As to their over-all economic effects, such rates probably involve a less serious distortion of trade than do discriminatory trade controls. One can imagine a system in which a group of countries maintained no discriminatory trade controls but each pair of countries balanced its trade bilaterally by means of a fluctuating exchange rate, with multilateral exchange arbitrage barred.[21] Initially, of course, none of the bilateral cross-rates would be consonant: the value of A's currency in terms of B's currency would differ from the price of A's currency in terms of C's currency valued in terms of B's currency at the rate prevailing between B and C. If, however, it were possible for merchants in A to purchase goods in B for transshipment to C—given, that is, unrestricted commodity arbitrage among all countries—the pattern of rates would tend to become consonant in spite of the absence of exchange arbitrage among the three bilateral currency markets.[22]

Commodity Arbitrage

Commodity arbitrage is encouraged by disparate cross-rates but the vast bulk of this important trade does not depend upon the existence of legal multiple exchange rate systems which break the cross-rates. When there were no currency barriers to the movement of international trade, commodity arbitrage kept prices in all national markets the same except for tariffs and transportation costs. The development of soft-currency markets, partially isolated from dollar and other hard-currency markets, has resulted in substantial price disparities for the same commodities between countries and currency

21. A resident of one country could not buy the currency of another country in a third.
22. For a discussion of this problem see G. D'Ippolito, "On the Congruence of Cross-Rates," *Quarterly Review*, Banca Nazionale Del Lavoro, Rome, January–March 1950, pp. 31–41.

areas. While the absence of free commodity arbitrage is responsible for these disparities, the disparities themselves make such arbitrage as can take place quite profitable.

Commodity arbitrage involving exchange-control countries may assume several forms. In Belgium, for example, where restrictions against dollar imports have been less severe, traders have bought dollar goods for re-export to France or the Netherlands, countries in which dollar goods are less plentiful and hence higher in price. Such transactions have been partly responsible for Belgium's large surplus with other Western European countries.[23]

Another type of arbitrage takes place when traders in one soft-currency country purchase goods in another for re-export to a hard-currency country. The dollar proceeds from such sales can then be used to buy dollar goods to be sold at a substantial profit in soft-currency countries for their own currency.

Implicit Exchange Rates

Disequilibrium exchange rates maintained by exchange controls are continually undermined by market forces and even by governmental measures which legalize operations tending to bypass or undermine the official rate structure. Illegal or unofficial markets in foreign exchange are always likely to develop when exchange restrictions are imposed. But many transactions, while the official exchange parities are observed, nevertheless involve implicit rates of exchange differing from the nominal rates at which the actual currency transfers take place. Implicit rates are involved in "commercial switch" transactions and in "export retention quotas."

Commercial Switch Transactions

Commercial switch transactions may occur at official exchange rates and yet involve implicit rates in the sense indicated above.[24] An example of a switch transaction frequent in Western Europe is this: a continental firm buys manufactured goods in Britain for sterling. The goods are then sold for dollars, at a loss, in the United States or

23. Belgium has taken steps to prohibit re-exports of dollar goods.
24. For a discussion of commercial switch transactions see J. F. Haccou, "Structural Changes in Trade and Marketing Conditions," *Quarterly Review,* Amsterdamsche Bank, Amsterdam, Second Quarter, 1952, pp. 1–11.

Canada, and the continental firm surrenders the dollars to its own bank at the official exchange rate. However, the continental firm obtains a "switch right" against these dollars from the exchange control authorities which it can either sell to another firm or use itself—usually the former. The firm exercising the right buys with the dollars U.S. goods which it can then sell at a premium in, say, Germany, against Deutsche marks, and these, in turn, are sold to the bank at the official rate. Sometimes this arrangement is complicated by a requirement that a portion of the switch dollars must be sold to the exchange control authorities at the official rate before the second part of the transaction can take place.

Transactions of this type may or may not have the knowledge or consent of the country whose goods are being sold for dollars at a loss. In most cases it would seem to work against their advantage, since such sales undermine the dollar market for their exports. On the other hand, sellers in the country whose goods are involved may be unwilling to sell in the dollar market at a loss and therefore be glad to have the additional nondollar sales of their products.[25] The advantage to the country whose residents engage in switch transactions lies in the fact that their traders earn a profit in foreign exchange; in addition, the exchange control authorities, who make transactions of this kind possible, may earn some additional dollars.

Commercial switch transactions differ from the so-called "cheap sterling" deals discussed in the following chapter because they involve the use of official exchange rates. The "real" rates are seen in the price differentials for the same commodities and in the premium price paid for the switch dollars in terms of soft currencies.

Export Retention Quotas

In the past couple of years there has developed, particularly among Western European countries, extensive use of export retention quotas. These permit the exporter to retain part of his export proceeds to import whatever he chooses, or he is granted licenses to import a rather wide range of goods and services. As a rule, retention quotas

25. Argentine products have been sold to the United States by European firms with the full knowledge of the Argentine authorities. On the other hand switch sales involving Brazilian coffee have been officially opposed by the Brazilian government but they are known to take place nevertheless.

apply only to exports for dollars. In some cases, they may apply to other currencies but the percentage which may be retained is higher for dollars than for other currencies. The dollars retained are usually placed in a special dollar account in the exporter's bank. In most cases he cannot sell them outright except at the official rate, but he can sell the dollar goods and services which he is permitted to buy with them at a premium over cost.

For example, a Dutch exporter might use his export dollars (equal to 10 per cent of his dollar exports) to buy a Cadillac car, which he can then sell at a premium price in the Netherlands since ordinarily it is not possible to obtain a license to buy American automobiles. This device involves an export subsidy in the form of an implicit export rate more favorable to dollar exports than to exports to soft-currency countries, which do not involve the retention quota privilege.[26]

CONTROLLED "FREE" EXCHANGE RATES

Even though a country has exchange controls the rate at which its currency is legally exchanged against foreign currencies is not necessarily fixed by the monetary authorities and may be influenced by market forces. Exchange control countries frequently permit restricted trading in foreign currencies among authorized banks or dealers, between foreign traders and authorized dealers, or between authorized banks and foreign banks or dealers. While the exchange rates determined in these markets are referred to as "free" rates, they are nevertheless hedged by controls which limit the demand for and supply of the currencies traded. Such currency markets must therefore be distinguished from genuinely free markets like those in the United States, Canada and other countries which do not maintain exchange controls.[27]

Free markets may also exist for currencies subject to exchange controls in other countries which permit such markets. Transactions in these markets may be legal from the standpoint of the countries whose currencies are dealt in, or they may be illegal or unofficial.[28]

26. Even if there were the same retention quotas for exports to soft-currency countries they would have less value than the export dollars.

27. Switzerland is a special case since it permits free exchange markets in dollars and other free currencies but controls payments to and from countries with which it has payments agreements.

28. Unofficial transactions do not necessarily involve an illegal act within the juris-

Discussion here will be limited to legal transactions provided for by the exchange regulations of the countries whose currencies are involved.

Controlled "free" exchange rates include three categories of markets or arrangements: (1) markets for controlled currencies in foreign countries which do not maintain exchange controls; (2) markets in exchange control countries where exchange rates are maintained within a narrow range of the official parity; (3) controlled rates which are permitted to fluctuate rather widely, or "floating" exchange rates.

Markets in Free Exchange Countries

In the United States the market for all foreign exchange is completely free; the government does not give direct support to the exchange value of its own currency in U.S. markets or abroad.[29] Indirectly, the parity of the dollar is maintained by the willingness of the U.S. government to buy and sell gold at a fixed price in transactions with foreign central banks and monetary authorities. Most foreign currencies available for use by Americans to pay for imports from other countries are maintained at rates near their official parities in the American market because they are supported by the monetary authorities of the foreign country.[30] Thus Britain supports the price of American account sterling within a range of $2.78–$2.82. She does not need to support transferable account sterling, which, although bought and sold in the American market, cannot legally be used for commercial transactions by U.S. residents. The only way Britain can maintain a fixed parity in foreign markets for inconvertible sterling is to negotiate payments agreements under which other countries undertake not to permit sterling to be traded against dollars or other currencies in free markets.

diction of the country whose currency is dealt in but nevertheless they are not contemplated by the exchange regulations of that country.

29. The United States has no obligation to support the exchange value of its own currency or of any other currency. The *Articles of Agreement* of the Monetary Fund provide that a member which freely buys and sells gold within the limits prescribed by the Fund is deemed to be fulfilling its undertaking with respect to the maintenance of exchange stability. (Article IV, Section 4, b.)

30. The only controlled currency traded to any appreciable extent in the U.S. market is American account sterling. A few other countries maintain nonresident accounts which are freely convertible into dollars. They are analogous to American account sterling but there is little traffic in these accounts.

A few countries maintain no exchange controls and yet have payments agreements with other nations involving the use of inconvertible currencies. This is true, for example, in Lebanon and certain other Middle Eastern countries. In these markets inconvertible or bilateral sterling and other inconvertible currencies fluctuate freely in terms of Lebanese pounds and other currencies. These are relatively unimportant markets and they are ignored in the main by the exchange control authorities of Britain and other countries whose currencies are traded.

The Sterling Exchange Market

On December 17, 1951, the British authorities announced the resumption of private trading in dollar exchange for the first time since the introduction of exchange controls in 1939. Between 1939 and 1951 British authorized banks bought and sold dollars and other foreign exchange as agents for the Bank of England. Spot purchases and sales to customers holding import licenses or exchange permits, were made at $2.80 less one eighth of a cent for purchases and plus one eighth of a cent for sales. Forward transactions with customers for bona fide commercial purposes were also conducted at the $2.80 rate, plus a charge of one per cent per year.

Under the new regulations, the one hundred and eight authorized banks were permitted to deal in U.S. and Canadian dollar exchange—subsequently in French, Dutch, Belgian, Swiss, German, Portuguese and Scandinavian exchange—on their own account and at rates determined by the market. The British Exchange Equalization Account, which is under the control of the Bank of England, operates to prevent the market rate from falling below $2.78 or rising above $2.82.[31] Authorized banks can deal in foreign exchange with one another and with foreign banks, as well as with their customers. Individuals can deal in exchange only with authorized banks. They are subject to the same exchange regulations as before the new arrangements were introduced.[32]

31. The permitted range is roughly 0.75 per cent on either side of the $2.80 parity. The Monetary Fund permits a maximum range of one percent on either side of parity.
32. Dealings between authorized banks are frequently conducted through foreign exchange brokers who operate as agents for the banks for a brokerage fee. For a good dicussion of these dealings see "Exchange Control and the Foreign Exchange Market," *Midland Bank Review* (London), August 1952, pp. 1–4.

Authorized banks may also engage in forward transactions in dollars and in certain other currencies. No attempt is made to maintain forward rates within a fixed range.[33] British banks can cover forward contracts with their customers by contracts with other banks at home or abroad, or they can cover their forward commitments by the purchase of spot currencies. They are not supposed to have large speculative holdings for their own accounts and they are required to observe agreed quotas for spot currency holdings and open positions in each currency.

As with spot transactions, forward dealings with customers are limited by the fact that only those engaging in commercial transactions which require a hedge against exchange fluctuations are permitted to negotiate forward contracts with banks. Nevertheless, the opinion of the market regarding the relative strength of sterling vis-à-vis other currencies can have substantial influence on the forward rates.

It should be made clear that the so-called "free" exchange market in Britain has not altered the fundamentals of the British exchange control system. It is merely a technique which provides greater flexibility for the operations of the exchange banks and does not affect the fundamental controls over the demand for, and the supply of, exchange. Nor should the British system be confused with the so-called floating rate systems which permit significant changes in the exchange rates in response to demand and supply. The new British system merely widened the permissible range of fluctuations in the pound-dollar rate from less than one-half cent to four cents.

European Arbitrage Dealings

During 1952 and 1953 the British practice of permitting authorized banks to operate in controlled free exchange markets was adopted by a number of other EPU countries. Before May 1953, however, operations of authorized banks in foreign markets were, with a few minor exceptions, confined to bilateral exchange transactions. On May 18, the United Kingdom, France, Germany, Belgium, the Netherlands, Denmark, Sweden and Switzerland entered into an arrange-

33. Article IV, Section 3 of the Fund Agreement provides that forward rates cannot exceed the margin for spot transactions "by more than the Fund considers reasonable."

ment whereby their authorized banks were permitted to engage in arbitrage transactions involving any of the currencies of the members of the group. This means that if Belgian banks have a surplus of sterling, they can sell it in Amsterdam for Dutch guilders. Such transactions reduce the volume of multilateral clearing operations of the EPU since much of the work is done on a day-to-day basis by the authorized banks in each country. Buying and selling rates for the currencies traded are maintained within 0.75 per cent on either side of the official parities.[34]

"Floating" Exchange Rate Systems

Floating exchange rates are controlled rates which are permitted to fluctuate beyond a narrow range. They have several purposes.[35]

Where the floating rate is a unitary rate applying to all transactions, the purpose or purposes may be much the same as those leading to the use of a flexible rate by a country with no exchange controls. Thus a country may want to permit the value of its currency to find its own level within a given set of demand and supply controls. It may prefer for political or psychological reasons this method of devaluing its currency as against a change in its official gold parity.

Again, a nation may believe that conditions which dictate an appreciation or depreciation of its currency may be temporary; therefore it establishes a floating rate rather than a new fixed parity which may have to be altered soon. Thus Canada in September 1950 permitted the Canadian dollar to appreciate in response to a heavy inflow of long-term capital instead of fixing a new parity.

Most floating rates involve more than one free rate or a combination of floating and fixed rates. In such systems the purposes served by the floating rates are similar to those of the fixed multiple rate systems. In many multiple rate systems the free rate applies to invisible transactions and to certain luxury imports. Since the supply of foreign exchange for these purposes is limited, the higher free rate provides an automatic means of rationing the exchange for less essential uses. In many cases, however, demand is also controlled directly by licensing.

34. *International Financial News Survey,* May 22, 1953, pp. 357-58.
35. There are some cases in which floating rates are not legally established but are simply tolerated in unofficial markets. (See Chapter 9.)

When nations permit one or more foreign currencies to be traded freely in their own markets, disparate cross-rates will almost invariably exist unless special measures are taken to prevent them. In fact, most of the disparate cross-rate situations today are a product of floating rate systems under which one or more foreign currencies are permitted to be traded in free or partially free markets. In some instances, countries desire to maintain a free market for dollars for all dealings or for certain types of transactions, while maintaining fixed parities for transactions in other currencies. The fact that payments agreements with nondollar currencies have called for the maintenance of a particular rate has often motivated such systems. By permitting a free dollar rate it is possible to depreciate against the dollar without depreciating against countries with which there is a satisfactory trade balance.

Floating rates may also be used between two or more countries with inconvertible currencies while each country maintains a stable relationship between its currency and the dollar or gold. Although there have been relatively few examples of fixed dollar rates and floating soft-currency rates, such a system has found support in Western Europe during the postwar period. In the fall of 1949 the French Finance Minister, Maurice Petsche, sponsored a plan under which France, Italy, the Netherlands and Belgium-Luxembourg would adopt floating rates in respect to each other's currencies, with more or less complete interconvertibility of the currencies of the five countries.[36] Though it had many adherents, the plan was not adopted.

Finally, a few nations have adopted floating rates for all foreign currencies, with a separate market (without arbitrage) maintained for each by means of exchange controls. This makes it possible to equalize the demand and supply with respect to each currency without resorting to discriminatory import or export controls.

The Mechanism of Floating Rates

Floating rate systems are feasible under various exchange control arrangements. Where the government is a party to all legal exchange dealings within the country, the exchange control authorities may permit the rate to fluctuate in response to demand and supply.

36. "Fritalux," *The Economist,* November 5, 1949, pp. 1018–19.

Some floating rate systems make provision for private citizens and institutions to deal in foreign exchange at rates determined by market forces and under conditions governing the acquisition and disposition of foreign exchange laid down by the control authorities. In other cases trading in foreign exchange can only take place with or through an authorized bank acting as intermediary. Whatever the mechanism, they differ from free exchange systems in that either the demand for or the supply of the exchange in the floating market is limited by the authorities.

Because floating rate systems take their character from the type of exchange control system employed, they are rather difficult to classify. Roughly, they may be divided into three categories: (1) unitary rate systems; (2) multiple rate systems with consonant cross-rates; (3) systems with disparate cross-rates.

1. Unitary Rate Systems. Unitary floating rate systems characteristically involve a "free" market for one currency, usually the dollar, with the rates on others determined by the exchange authorities with reference to the dollar rate in order to maintain consonant cross-rates. If there are "free" markets for other currencies, the exchange authorities must preserve official cross-rates by stabilization operations. The markets are free only in the sense that those having a right to use foreign exchange under the control regulations may bid for the available foreign exchange. The exchange control regulations may be mild, perhaps applying only to capital movements, or they may require licenses for all transactions.

An example of a floating rate with mild exchange regulations is provided by the Canadian experience between September 1950 and December 1951, when a completely free flexible rate system was established. During this period, Canadian residents had to declare receipts of foreign exchange and either sell the exchange to an authorized dealer or deposit it in a special account, to be liquidated within ninety days. Foreign exchange could be purchased without a license for most imports but invisible payments required a license and exports of capital (except investments by nonresidents after September 1939) were strictly limited. Within these regulations there was a free market for U.S. dollars and sterling, but Canadian monetary authorities maintained official cross-rates. Banks were permitted to deal in sterling currencies against Canadian dollars or other sterling currencies, and in other currencies against U.S. or Canadian dollars. Thus there were no legal arbitrage transactions involving both sterling and the U.S. dollar. There was, however, a free market for Canadian dollars in New York, the rates on which were kept consonant with those in Canada by arbitrage transactions. The same was true of Canadian and London markets for sterling and Canadian dollars.[37]

2. Multiple Exchange Rates with Consonant Cross-Rates. Several Latin American countries including Argentina, Bolivia, Costa Rica, Ecuador, Paraguay and Uruguay maintain a so-called "free rate" in their multiple rate structures. Nevertheless, they control the market in such a way as to prevent the breaking of official cross-rates. Costa Rica and Ecuador also maintain free market rates, but since they are dollar-area countries these rates mainly affect dollar transactions. The free rates generally apply to capital transactions, and to certain invisible and luxury imports. Since rates on other currencies must conform to the dollar rate, only the dollar market is free, even within the context of the regulations which surround the operations of the market.[38]

3. Multiple Rate Systems with Disparate Cross-Rates. The maintenance of official cross-rates in any system which involves one or more floating rates requires day-to-day adjustment of the rate structure. Moreover, with official cross-rates it is not possible to equate demand and supply for foreign currencies which are not interconvertible in the market. This must be done by discriminatory import and export controls. A few countries including Peru, Lebanon, Syria and Thailand maintain fluctuating rates for different currencies. It is, of course, impossible to have a free market in two or more foreign currencies which are not interconvertible and still maintain official cross-rates between them.

Thailand is a good example of a country with floating rates for two or more different currencies.[39] Except for the surrender of the

---

37. In October 1950 Britain permitted the development of a controlled free market for Canadian dollars which was dealt in by authorized banks and others carrying on trade with Canada under license. This occurred more than a year before similar arrangements were extended to the U.S. dollar in December 1951.

38. In the case of such countries as Costa Rica which trade only in dollars and convertible currencies, there is no problem of maintaining cross-rates.

39. For a description of Thailand's exchange rate structure in 1950 see B. R. Shenoy, "The Currency Banking and Exchange System of Thailand," *Staff Papers,* September 1950, pp. 239–314. See also current issues of *International Financial Statistics.*

export proceeds from the sale of rubber, rice and tin at the official rate of 12.45 baht to the dollar [40] and for government payments, certain favored private imports, e. g., petroleum, and student remittances, all exchange transactions are conducted at the free market rates.

Since the war the market in foreign exchange for the principal currencies employed in Thailand's trade has been relatively free, including the U.S. dollar and sterling and currencies linked to sterling.[41] While the official baht-sterling and baht-dollar rates, which apply to only a limited number of transactions, conform to the official sterling-dollar cross-rates, the cross-rates vary considerably in the free markets for sterling and dollars. For example, the average rate on the dollar in 1950 was 21.13 baht and the average rate on the pound was 56.28 baht, representing a cross-rate of $2.66 to the pound as against the official rate of $2.80.

40. There is also a special rate for most trade transactions with Japan.

41. In March 1952 the government announced the imposition of controls on capital movements.

Chapter 9

UNOFFICIAL TRANSACTIONS

SYSTEMS OF CONTROLS which interfere with the freedom of the market have always been accompanied by transactions which are illegal, not covered by the law or are simply tolerated by lax administration. Markets for such transactions—called black, gray, curb or simply free or unofficial—are especially widespread in currencies and gold [1] Many persons otherwise law-abiding feel no moral compunction about breaking or evading currency laws or cooperating with others who do so. The fact that illegal foreign exchange transactions generally involve the residents of at least two countries though they usually contravene the laws of only one, encourages such deals and makes control more difficult.

This chapter will consider transactions in currencies and in gold, which take place outside the official channels provided by governmental exchange control and gold regulations. Many of the unofficial currency transactions and most of the private international transactions in gold contravene the laws of at least one of the countries involved. In other cases, the activity may not be illegal either because of loopholes in official regulations or, as with so-called "security sterling" transactions, the transfers may not be considered as exchange transactions from the standpoint of the country whose currency is concerned.

Unofficial dealings may also be conducted entirely by nonresidents of the country whose regulations are disregarded. Frequently this involves a breach of an international agreement or understanding between the country whose exchange laws are contravened and the country permitting its citizens to engage in the unofficial transaction. Some of the so-called cheap sterling deals are of this type since they

1. In this study, the term "unofficial foreign exchange transactions" will cover both illegal transactions and those not contemplated by the official regulations of one or both of the countries concerned.

arise from the failure of countries to require their own citizens to abide by their bilateral payments agreements with Britain.[2] Few bilateral payments agreements attempt to dictate the partners' exchange regulations for implementing the arrangement.

While the United States government has not undertaken to enforce the foreign exchange control laws of other countries, the Monetary Fund Agreement provides that "Exchange contracts which involve the currency of any other member and which are contrary to the exchange control regulations of that member maintained or imposed consistently with this Agreement shall be unenforceable in the territories of any member." [3]

UNOFFICIAL FOREIGN EXCHANGE TRANSACTIONS

Unofficial foreign exchange markets fall into two basic categories: (1) markets (usually illegal) for free currencies within exchange control countries; (2) markets for the currencies of exchange-control countries in countries which maintain free (legal) markets for them.

Markets for Free Currencies

There are unofficial markets—most of them illegal—for dollar drafts (sometimes called "payments New York") and for dollar travelers checks in virtually every country in the world. The principal sources of dollar funds are: (1) dollar assets held by residents before the imposition of exchange controls but not registered in accordance with regulations; (2) undervaluation of exports and overvaluation of imports, the difference being deposited to the dollar account of the foreign trader; (3) the sale of dollar travelers checks, banknotes, bank drafts and personal checks by American travelers for local currency to private persons in exchange control countries; (4) the conversion of third currencies into dollars through unofficial channels.

The demand for dollar funds is affected to a considerable degree by the ease with which they may be used. In some countries, notably in Latin America, importers are permitted to use their own exchange

2. In some cases, the central banks themselves participate in transactions which violate agreements with other countries.

3. For a legal interpretation of this provision see Joseph Gold, "The Fund Agreement in the Courts," *Staff Papers*, September 1950, pp. 315–33, and Joseph Gold, "The Fund Agreement in the Courts II," *Staff Papers*, November 1952, pp. 482–98.

to import goods not readily obtainable with exchange procured through official channels. In countries where this is not allowed, the demand is restricted to investment and speculative purposes or to use by individuals for travel abroad. In these markets, the premium on dollars or other convertible currencies over the official rate is determined, in part, by local conditions of demand and supply. Nevertheless, the market price of dollars is directly affected by events which influence public confidence in either the local currency or the dollar.

For example, in December 1952 the price of dollar drafts payable in New York was 51 Belgian francs in Belgium as against the official rate of 50 Belgian francs per dollar. Similarly, in Portugal, which, like Belgium, has a strong currency and relatively mild restrictions, the black market rate was only slightly higher than the official rate of 28.75 escudos to the dollar. On the other hand, the black market rate for dollar drafts in Brazil was double the official rate in December 1952 and nine times the official rate in Czechoslovakia. (See Table 6.)

TABLE 6

LOCAL CURRENCY RATES FOR DOLLAR DRAFTS PAYABLE NEW YORK, DECEMBER 1952

Currency	Unofficial Rate	Official Rate
Sterling	$2.65 per £	$2.80 per £
Belgian franc	51 B frs. = $1	50 B frs. = $1
French franc	410 F frs. = $1	350 F frs. = $1
Peseta	47.7 pesetas = $1	39.4 pesetas = $1
Lira	634 lire = $1	625 lire = $1
Guilder	3.94 guilder = $1	3.80 guilder = $1
Swedish krona	5.76 S kr. = $1	5.18 S kr. = $1
Cruzeiro	37.0 cr. = $1	18.75 cr. = $1
Deutsche Mark	4.65 D M = $1	4.20 D M = $1
Czech koruna	440 C K = $1	50 C K = $1
Escudo	29.0 escudo = $1	28.75 escudo = $1

Source: Pick's World Currency Report, January 8, 1953, p. 5.

Probably only a small proportion of U.S. current trade in goods and services is conducted at unofficial or black market rates for dollars, the chief function of which is to transfer speculative holdings of dollars between residents of foreign countries. Some of these dollars, however, are used to finance purchases of gold from gold-producing countries. While the premium over the official rate for dollars is a fair indication of public confidence in a currency, it provides little guide for the determination of an equilibrium rate.

For example, before the devaluation of sterling in September

1949, the black market rate for dollar payments was well above $2.80; after devaluation, the rate fell substantially below the new official parity of the pound. The black market being divorced from current trade transactions, does not reflect basic demand and supply forces in the exchange market. Black market prices for inconvertible currencies, therefore, do not give a reliable indication of their equilibrium value. In fact, black market prices may at times overvalue a currency in terms of its true equilibrium value.

The volume of private foreign holdings of dollars is rather difficult to determine because of the many ways such assets may be concealed when they are held or acquired illegally. At the end of November 1951 total dollar deposits and other short-term dollar assets owned by foreigners other than banks and official institutions were reported to be about $1.5 billion.[4] However, official U.S. Treasury estimates do not reveal balances owned by U.S. citizens for the account of foreigners or, in some cases, balances owned by Swiss banks for the account of private citizens. Hence the volume of private dollar balances in the hands of foreigners may be much larger than the official figure. Estimates of the foreign private holdings of U.S. dollar notes range all the way from $2 billion to $6 or $7 billion with $2.8 billion in U.S. currency notes held in France alone. These large figures are believed to be exaggerations, however, and the actual total for all countries may not be much over $2 billion.

The free Swiss franc is also widely traded in the world's unofficial markets.[5] The acquisition of free Swiss francs is one means of acquiring dollars or gold, since the free Swiss franc is convertible into either. Before Belgium restricted payments to Switzerland in the latter part of 1951, the acquisition of Belgian francs provided an easy channel for getting Swiss francs or dollars for European foreign exchange dealers. In the Far East, private individuals can acquire dollars by first obtaining Hong Kong dollars in trade with the Colony, and then converting them into dollars in the free market in Hong Kong.

4. *Treasury Bulletin,* U.S. Treasury Department, April 1952, p. 60. Of the $1.5 billion, $655 million was held by Europeans, and $509 million by Latin Americans.

5. A distinction must be made between free Swiss francs and bilateral account Swiss francs which are held in special nonresident accounts for countries maintaining bilateral payments agreements with Switzerland. The second are available only for making current payments for imports from Switzerland into the agreement country, whereas the free Swiss franc is convertible into gold or dollars.

Markets for Controlled Currencies

The chief purpose of unofficial transactions in dollars and other free currencies is to finance capital movements for hoarding and speculation. More significant in financing movements of goods and services are the markets for controlled currencies in free market countries, frequently referred to as "cheap currency markets." Most countries whose currencies are employed in international transactions establish special nonresident accounts, available to pay for exports only to certain countries outside the dollar area.

Thus, transferable account sterling may be used to pay for exports from the sterling area or the transferable account group to members of the transferable account group and, by special administrative approval, to certain bilateral account countries. Argentine account guilders are available only for financing transactions between the Netherlands monetary area and the Argentine. When special nonresident accounts arising out of payments agreements are used to finance exports to the United States, it is a violation of the exchange regulations of the country whose currency is involved.

New York is the most important market for this type of unofficial transaction and sterling, because of its general use in international trade, is the most widely traded currency in unofficial markets for inconvertible currencies.[6] The weekly turnover of inconvertible sterling in the New York market has been variously estimated at from £500,000 to £2,000,000 during 1951 and 1952.[7]

The actual volume of transactions varies with conditions of demand and supply. When certain countries have large amounts of inconvertible sterling which they are anxious to exchange for dollars, the dollar price, of course, will fall. As the spread between American account sterling and inconvertible or cheap sterling widens, it be-

6. The unofficial sterling markets should not be confused with the market for American account sterling in the United States which is supported by the Bank of England. Sterling acquired in the second market is legally valid for all payments by dollar account residents to the sterling area. In addition to New York, there are important unofficial markets for inconvertible currencies in Amsterdam, Beirut, Tangier, Switzerland, Hong Kong, Kuwait and Bangkok.

7. Franz Pick has estimated the daily turnover in New York during 1951 at £200,000–£400,000. See Franz Pick, *Black Market Yearbook, 1951* (pub. by the author), New York, 1952, p. 15. Another source suggested to the author a more conservative figure of £100,000 per day. However, at certain times the turnover has been substantially higher.

comes profitable for American importers to finance their imports from sterling and other soft-currency countries with cheap sterling. At times, 20–25 per cent of this country's private imports of wool, rubber, jute, cocoa, tin and other sterling area commodities have been financed in this way.[8] Because of the additional risks and expenses involved in this method of financing imports, the spread between official and cheap sterling must be fairly substantial in order to make it profitable for the importer to use it.

Cheap Sterling Transactions

Most of the commercial transactions financed with cheap sterling involve the use of sterling accounts of countries which have bilateral payments agreements with Britain. While both bilateral account and transferable account sterling are employed, the latter is usually preferred because its ownership can be shifted over a wider range of countries without requiring the permission of the Bank of England.

Inconvertible sterling cannot be held in the name of an American resident, so the actual transfers of the sterling accounts must always be between residents of foreign countries. American dealers, therefore, arrange for their agents in other countries to hold sterling for them and to transfer it upon instruction to someone in another country to whom they want to make a payment. An American wool importer, for example, may buy £10,000 sterling from a dealer in New York for $26,000, the pounds being held in the name of an agent in Amsterdam. The New York dealer may ask his Amsterdam agent to arrange for a letter of credit to be issued to an Australian wool exporter for £10,000, available upon presentation of documents for shipping a certain amount of wool to the agent in Amsterdam. When the wool reaches the Netherlands, it will be transshipped to an American port and consigned to the American wool importer. (In some cases, by special arrangement with the shipping firm, the wool may go directly to the United States without having to be transshipped. This may involve a falsification of the shipping documents.) The wool importer will save $2,000 on the shipment—the

8. This estimate is based on conversations both with commercial bankers, who ordinarily do not deal directly in cheap sterling, and with dealers in unofficial currency markets. Estimates of New York commercial bankers of the volume of cheap sterling financing are based, in part, upon how much business they lose when customers find it profitable to shift to cheap sterling payments.

196 FOREIGN EXCHANGE IN THE POSTWAR WORLD

difference between the official rate of $2.80 and $2.60 per pound, less certain additional costs for transshipment or the falsification of papers.

But where did the New York dealer obtain the £10,000 sterling held by his Dutch agent? He may have bought it from another Dutchman by paying into the Dutchman's New York account say, $25,800, or he may have obtained it from someone in Thailand, who, upon the payment of dollars into his New York account, transferred the sterling to the account of the Dutch agent. If the sterling were acquired from someone in Peru, a bilateral account country, it could not be transferred to a Dutch account without the permission of the Bank of England. If this were refused, the wool would probably have to be consigned to Peru and then transshipped to New York. This transaction might be so costly that Peruvian sterling would not be used. However, if the Peruvian bilateral account sterling were being employed to buy spices from India, the goods could be put on a ship which was stopping at an American west coast port before going to Peru, and the spice cargo taken off there. The risk involved in such transactions lies in the possibility that the British authorities might refuse to transfer the sterling to the account of the seller. The seller of the commodity could then demand American account sterling in settlement, but the price might be higher than the importer could pay and still make a profit on the transaction. Cheap sterling is also used extensively to pay for services including transportation, insurance and tourism. Such transactions may be financed with little risk, since the British exchange authorities are less able to check payments not related to commodity sales.

Other Inconvertible Currencies

Sterling is by no means the only currency used to finance deals of this type. For example, Argentine-account Swedish kronor sometimes finance the sale of Argentine wool to the United States and Brazilian account guilders have financed coffee going to American ports. French and Belgian francs in various nonresident accounts are also at hand in New York to pay for imports from Argentina, Brazil, Uruguay and other countries. Some fifteen to twenty kinds of nonresident sterling accounts are always available for sale in New York and are used for commercial transactions every day.

While much of the demand for cheap sterling and other inconvertible currencies is for financing of imports *of goods and services* from soft-currency countries by dollar countries, cheap currencies have additional uses. For example, a nondollar country which is short of sterling is more likely to acquire the sterling it needs by selling dollars, Swiss francs or gold against sterling in the unofficial markets of the world than to purchase it on the official London market at the $2.80 rate. If the country is a member of the transferable account group it can purchase transferable account sterling with little difficulty, since such sterling accounts are readily transferable.[9] If it is a bilateral account country it can buy bilateral or transferable account sterling from another country for dollars at a discount, but the transfer will require administrative approval by the British authorities. Such approval, however, is readily obtained, as a rule, unless the transaction is likely to result in a direct gold or dollar drain on Britain.

Exports from dollar countries to soft-currency countries are sometimes financed by cheap sterling and other inconvertible currencies.[10] Suppose a man in India desires to import typewriters from the United States but is unable to obtain the dollar exchange to pay for them. He may arrange to buy them with sterling from a Dutch agent who, in turn, acquires the typewriters from an American firm against payment in transferable account sterling. The American exporter arranges for the sale of the transferable account sterling for dollars through his dealer in New York. The typewriter exporter must charge enough for his wares to cover the discount on the sterling which he sells to the dealer.

9. The purchase of transferable account sterling against dollars by a resident of one transferable account country from a resident of another is in fact a violation of Britain's bilateral agreements. (See Chapter 11.) However, the British authorities do not check individual transactions between nonsterling countries. Rather, they depend upon the monetary authorities of the countries with whom they have payments agreements to police such transactions. When large-scale violations take place, such as the Egyptian sales of transferable account sterling to the USSR against gold, the British authorities may protest or refuse to make certain transfers except on the presentation of evidence of underlying commercial transactions.

10. New York dealers in unofficial currency markets state that the financing of exports from the United States through inconvertible currencies is less important by volume and more difficult to arrange than the financing of imports.

Rates for Cheap Sterling

Dollar rates for inconvertible sterling tend to fluctuate with the spot and forward rates for convertible or American account sterling. In January 1952 Britain was losing gold at an alarming rate and all types of sterling were under pressure. On January 8, the spot rate was 2.78¼, 6-months sterling sold at $2.76, and transferable account sterling was $2.45. By November 1952 the spot rate for American account sterling had risen to parity and forward rates were within one cent of parity. That month transferable account sterling ranged from $2.69 to $2.70 per pound. (See Table 7.) By January 1953 the spot rate for American account sterling was above parity at $2.81½ per

TABLE 7

SELECTED NEW YORK STERLING QUOTATIONS, 1952
(*U.S. Dollars per £. All Rates Approximate*)

Type of Sterling	Jan. 8, 1952	June 24, 1952	Nov. 18, 1952
American account:			
Spot	2.78¼	2.78⅜	2.80
1 month	2.77⅞	2.77⅝	2.79⅝
2 months	2.77½	2.76⅞	2.79⅜
3 months	2.77	2.76⅛	2.79⅛
6 months	2.76	2.74	2.78⅛
Securities switch sterling	2.35	2.48	2.64
Banknotes	2.37	2.57	2.58
Transferable accounts (unspecified as to origin)	2.45	2.62	2.69
Miscellaneous accounts:			
Argentine	2.43	2.56	2.65
Belgian	2.42	2.62	2.71
Brazilian	2.42	2.56	2.72
Chilean	2.44	2.62	2.69
Danish	2.42	2.54	2.69
Dutch	2.44	2.62	2.69
Egyptian	2.39	2.61	2.67
French	2.43	2.62	2.70
Greek	2.44	2.62	2.70
Israeli	2.47	2.65	2.73
Italian	2.43	2.61	2.70
Japanese	2.48	2.61	2.73
Lebanese	2.42	2.60	2.73
Norwegian	2.45	2.62	2.69
Paraguayan	2.35	2.53	2.65
Peruvian	2.39	2.77	2.71
Portuguese	2.58	2.64	2.75
Spanish	2.42	2.54	2.69
Turkish	2.42	2.56	2.66
Uruguayan	2.40	2.62	2.67
Yugoslav	2.35	2.49	2.65

Source: Quotations supplied by J. Henry Schroder Banking Corporation, New York City.

pound and transferable account sterling reached $2.76 in April 1953, indicating a discount of only 1½ per cent from parity.

Should the rate on transferable account sterling be regarded as the equilibrium rate for the pound sterling? Even though dollar prices for cheap sterling and other inconvertible currencies are free market prices, in the sense that the markets in New York, Switzerland and elsewhere are not subject to direct governmental regulation, the markets are, in fact, controlled indirectly by the exchange control systems of the countries whose currencies are involved. For example, the supply of cheap sterling is limited by exchange controls of sterling area countries over sterling transfers for all purposes and is further limited by the efforts of exchange control authorities to prevent its sale in unofficial markets. Relative to the demand for American account sterling, the demand for cheap sterling is limited by the risks and expense of employing it for purchases in sterling area countries. In addition, the market for inconvertible currencies is frequently narrow, and hence subject to wide price fluctuations over short periods of time; it is highly sensitive to rumors and to various speculative influences.

The sharp increase in dollar rates for bilateral account and transferable account sterling which occurred during 1952 and early 1953 were due in considerable measure to the reduction in sterling balances held by nonsterling countries, and to the development of a sterling shortage in a number of these countries. The present small margin between American account and transferable account sterling probably makes it unprofitable to use cheap sterling for financing most commodity transactions. However, it is still profitable to finance invisible transactions since they involve less risk of detection by the British authorities.

The effects of cheap currency dealings vary greatly with the circumstances. If Americans buy Australian wool with Dutch transferable account sterling, it is obvious that the Dutch seller of the sterling gets the dollars, not the Bank of England.[11] On the other hand, if American importers buy coffee with Brazilian account sterling or with Brazilian account guilders the Brazilians apparently lose the dollars which would otherwise have been paid directly to Brazil.

11. It has been estimated that during 1949 the Bank of England lost $100 million on wool sales financed by cheap sterling.

When Americans buy from nonsterling area countries with cheap sterling, the principal effect is to change the distribution of the sterling among nonresident holders. In some cases, the change in distribution may be important. For example, before the EPU was established, an increase in Belgian sterling holdings at the expense of Italian holdings might have caused a gold drain on Britain.[12] On the other hand, a movement of sterling from Japan to Peru or Brazil might prove beneficial, from Britain's standpoint, since Japan might require Britain to pay gold or to reduce imports of Japanese goods into the sterling area if Japan's sterling holdings continued to rise.

Economic Effects of Cheap Currency Deals

During 1952 Argentine wool was shipped to the United States against payment in Argentine-account kronor purchased from Swedish banks. Perhaps this transaction benefited both Argentina and Sweden. Sweden was able to sell for dollars excess payments-agreement credits accumulated in the course of her trade with Argentina. Argentina marketed some low-grade wool which she would not otherwise have been able to sell. There is considerable evidence that the exchange control authorities of both countries were well aware of the nature of these transactions.[13] There is also evidence that at times the Brazilians have sold coffee for inconvertible currencies knowing it was going to New York; and that South Africa has sold wool to the United States via Italy with the tacit consent of the authorities licensing the transactions.

There is little doubt that a fair proportion of the cheap currency financing goes on with the awareness and even the connivance of the authorities in the countries whose currencies are involved. Why do these authorities permit transactions which contravene their own regulations? Of course, there are bound to be leaks in any system of regulations, but the volume of business is too great to be explained in this way.

The British certainly could cut down the volume of exports from the sterling area to hard-currency countries financed with cheap ster-

12. Britain's bilateral agreement with Belgium required her to pay gold to Belgium when Belgium's sterling holdings exceeded a certain amount.
13. However, the Argentine authorities might not license high-grade wool which could readily be sold for dollars, for sale against soft currencies.

ling, by requiring exporters to produce declarations that their exports actually passed through the customs of the country to which they were consigned and that they were consumed in that country. Further, the British could tighten up on the transfers between nonresident accounts by requiring that each request for transfer be accompanied by evidence of an underlying commercial transaction. But such regultions would very sharply reduce the transferability of sterling and its use as an international currency. To this extent, British banks and commodity exchanges would lose business, and many countries would be less willing to hold sterling. Thus dealings in sterling in unofficial markets and at prices which depart from official rates may be said to be the price which must be paid for maintaining free transferability of sterling over a wide area. The British authorities, however, do act to prevent certain transfers which contravene their regulations, especially those which are harmful to British interests.

Cheap currency deals usually involve a form of competitive exchange depreciation since the importer buys the currency below the official rate. Like retention quotas, commercial switch deals and multiple exchange rates, the financing of trade through unofficial markets is a product of economic disequilibrium. All these devices and arrangements tend to undermine the official exchange rate structure.

Traffic in Resident Sterling Accounts

These cheap sterling deals do not all have features which violate the laws of the countries in which the transactions actually take place. The Australian wool exporter or the Malayan rubber exporter may not know that his wool or rubber is to end up in New York. He has received his sterling in a regular manner from a Dutch account or from the account of a resident of some other country with which Britain has a payments agreement. He has falsified no documents in connection with the shipment. With certain exceptions, however, every dealing which makes use of the accounts of residents of the sterling area to finance goods and service transactions with the United States is unlawful, and punishable by fine or imprisonment.

For example, it is possible to purchase resident account sterling in New York. Such sterling is frequently used to purchase gold or diamonds in a sterling area country, and these are then smuggled to another country.[14] American firms operating in the sterling area or even tourists may also buy their sterling in this way. Thus a dealer in New York may keep an account in London in the name of a fictitious resident of Britain, against which he draws checks payable to someone who wants to use sterling in the sterling area.[15] This is rather dangerous business, however, since the British authorities may uncover these illegal accounts.

An illegal sterling transaction which gets around the hazard of putting checks through banks is known as "handpayment" or "inland transfer" sterling. The purchaser of handpayment sterling pays dollars into the account of a British dealer who, in turn, arranges to pay sterling banknotes to the purchaser or his agent in Britain. The supply of this sterling may come from British residents who want to build up secret dollar accounts in the United States. This sterling is likely to be used by tourists, by business firms or by smugglers of diamonds and furs.

In every country in the world there are unofficial markets—frequently illegal—for foreign currency notes. Most countries limit the amount of their own currencies that travelers can bring in or take out and forbid the sending of currency notes through the mails.[16] Since the notes sell at a discount in countries with stronger currencies, there is a considerable traffic in smuggled banknotes.

Unofficial Markets in Blocked Accounts

When exchange controls were introduced by most countries in 1939, the bank balances and other capital assets of nonresidents could no longer be withdrawn by the foreign investor. These balances and the proceeds from the sale of assets owned by foreigners

14. It is reported that an important source of supply of resident sterling is Kuwait, a sterling area territory with no exchange control laws. Sterling is acquired by smuggling gold into Bombay and converting the rupee proceeds into sterling, selling this in New York for dollars, which are used to purchase more gold from South Africa or elsewhere.

15. One New York dealer informed the author that he has written checks on a London account and sent the checks through the mail to Britain. Sometimes such accounts are kept in the names of "British residents" who have been dead for years!

16. Persons in the United States with friends or relatives abroad frequently send foreign currency through the mails as gifts, since they can buy such currencies at a substantial discount below the official rates for drafts. I am told that the British authorities catch a large proportion of these transfers by an electric spotting device. The notes are then confiscated. Merchant seamen and airline personnel are also important channels for smuggled currency.

were placed in "blocked" accounts, which were available (if at all) for only limited uses within the country imposing the controls. Some of these blocked balances could not even be transferred between non-residents of the same country, so the owner was unable to dispose of them. However, a number of countries permitted unofficial markets either in the currency balances or in securities which could be bought with them. Markets have been developed in New York and in other financial centers, where holders of capital assets can dispose of them at a discount from their local currency value, calculated at the official rate of exchange.

Some countries allow blocked balances to be used only to purchase certain types of securities, the interest or dividends on which are transferable into the currency of the nonresident owner. Frequently the balances are transferable as between residents of the same country but not internationally. This is true, for example, of British and French blocked balances. Sometimes they can be used for tourist expenditures or to make remittances to friends and relatives in the country where the balances are held. This is the case, for example, with the Italian blocked balances.

The Unofficial Market in Canadian Dollars

After Canada inaugurated exchange controls at the beginning of World War II, there developed an unofficial market for inconvertible Canadian dollars in New York.[17] The supply of dollars in the un-official, but legal, market came from U.S. residents who wanted to withdraw their capital from Canada, but could not do so at the official rate because of Canadian exchange controls. Americans could sell the Canadian dollar proceeds from the liquidation of their assets to other Americans who wanted to make investments in Canada. Such balances could also be used for travel in Canada. However, they could not legally be used to pay for exports from Canada.

Since the unofficial market was used principally to transfer capital investments between nonresidents, it was not a major source of net capital withdrawal.[18] An important aspect of the market in 1947 and

17. This market was terminated in September 1950 when a single free market for the Canadian dollar was established.

18. To the extent that the inconvertible balances were used by American tourists in Canada, the unofficial market facilities did constitute capital withdrawal. For a description of this market see *Annual Report to Minister of Finance for the Year 1948*, Canadian Foreign Exchange Control Board, Ottawa, March 1949, pp. 18–21.

1948 was the sale of American-owned Canadian government securities, the proceeds of which were transferred to Americans for direct investment in Canada. These operations reduced Canada's bonded indebtedness and encouraged foreign investment in Canadian industry. In addition, the existence of the market sustained the confidence of the foreign investor since he was always able to liquidate his holdings at a discount which ranged from 5 to 10 per cent.

Security Sterling

Financial journals frequently quote rates in dollars for "security sterling" as though an actual exchange transaction were involved in the purchase of British securities by Americans. Such rates are only implied, however, since they result from a calculation of the value of sterling based on the ratio of the U.S. market price of a share of stock traded on the London stock exchange to the London (sterling) price of the same stock converted into dollars at the official rate. The funds of Americans holding capital assets in Britain before 1940 were blocked by the British exchange control. Such funds could not be repatriated, but they could be used to purchase British securities in the London market, and the interest and dividends were transferable into dollars.[19] British regulations permit the holders of securities to switch from one security to another, and Americans can sell such assets in the New York market.[20]

Since only the returns on these securities are convertible into dollars—and even these are subject to an exchange risk—they sell in the New York market at a substantial discount from the London price, converted at the official dollar-sterling rate. For example, if a share in London is selling at £100 sterling, while the same share can be purchased in New York with dollars at $140, the rate for security sterling is said to be $1.40, or half the official rate of $2.80. Arbitrage transactions tend to keep the discount on all British shares about the same. Unlike transactions in transferable and resident account sterling, these so-called security sterling deals are entirely legal.[21]

19. See Norman Crump, *The ABC of Foreign Exchanges,* 11th ed., Macmillan, New York, 1951, pp. 317–21.

20. Americans can sell their shares in any market, but they cannot buy British securities from residents outside the dollar area.

21. In March 1953 the British government announced that holders of blocked sterling could henceforth sell it to any other resident of the same monetary area. Thus it is no

If securities issued by firms incorporated in exchange control countries are bought and sold in U.S. markets, they are traded in the form of American depository certificates or American share certificates.[22] Depository receipts are issued by the trust department of an American bank against the deposit of the actual shares with a foreign branch or correspondent of that bank. The correspondent or branch collects the dividends and forwards them to the American owner through the bank issuing the certificate after conversion into dollars.[23] In 1951 there were twenty-one foreign stock issues of twenty foreign companies traded on the New York Stock Exchange, thirty-four issues on the Curb Exchange and several more over the counter.

The Market for Blocked D-Marks (Sperrmarks)

In 1951 there developed in London, New York and other financial centers a market for blocked German marks (Sperrmarks) which represented foreign-owned balances and the proceeds from the sale of foreign-owned assets immobilized by war and postwar regulations in Germany. These balances may now be used for a wide range of investments in Germany, including the acquisition of shares, but not to pay for exports from that country. Unlike most nations in which such balances are held, the German authorities permit their transfer between nonresidents of different currency areas.[24] In the fall of 1952 the blocked D-mark was selling at a discount of about 30 per cent below the official rate for the mark.

Unofficial Transactions in Gold

In a world of exchange controls there have come to be unofficial as well as official transactions in gold, just as there are in foreign

---

longer necessary for American holders of blocked sterling to acquire sterling securities in order to convert their sterling into dollars.

22. See Jacob O. Kamm, "American Trading in Foreign Securities," *Journal of Finance*, December 1951, pp. 406–18.

23. American share certificates are similar to depositor receipts except that they do not indicate the rights of the holder.

24. See "D-marks as International Currency," *The London Financial Times*, October 25, 1951, p. 4. British holders of D-marks have been permitted by the British government to sell their marks in New York for dollars for the purpose of acquiring American securities. Since the London prices of dollar securities are at a premium over American prices, the D-mark has been selling at a premium in London over the New York price. On September 19, 1952, the German Sperrmark was quoted in New York at 16.1 cents as against the official rate of 23.8 cents.

exchange. While most nations have established an official value of their currencies in terms of gold, no country has a free market for gold in which the government supports the gold value of its currency at the official gold parity.

Gold serves as a means of final settlement between the treasuries and central banks of individual countries and between a nation and such international institutions as the EPU and the International Monetary Fund. For the most part these transactions take place at the official gold prices of the currencies of the countries involved. The U.S. Treasury buys and sells gold at a fixed price of $35 an ounce (plus a quarter of 1 per cent commission); South Africa sells gold to Britain at the rate of 2.49 grams of fine gold per pound, the official gold value of both the British and the South African pounds; and members of the EPU make gold settlements with that institution at ratios corresponding to the official gold parities of their currencies.

But gold also moves as a commodity in international markets at prices divorced from the official gold values of the currencies in which it is traded. There are two reasons why these unofficial markets for gold exist: the restrictions placed by governments on dealings in the official market; and the fact that the world's currencies are not freely convertible into gold at their official gold values.

The regulation of private dealings in gold differs greatly from country to country. Since 1933 the United States government has prohibited private dealings in monetary gold, but the Treasury sells and buys gold at the official price of $35 per ounce to and from the central banks and monetary authorities of other countries. It will also sell gold for industrial purposes but the Treasury supervises the use of such gold in an effort to keep it out of unofficial markets. Many nations permit internal dealings in gold at free market prices while prohibiting or controlling private imports or exports of the metal. Completely free international markets in gold exist in only a few areas; hence most private dealings across national borders are illegal. In recent years the governments of most of the gold-producing countries outside the United States have licensed the sale of all or a portion of their gold output in the unofficial markets. This practice became a thorny issue among members of the International Monetary Fund.

The Controversy over Premium Gold Sales

The Monetary Fund Agreement requires members to buy and sell gold at prices based on their official par values (plus or minus a margin prescribed by the Fund).[25] The logic of this requirement is that only as countries observe their official parities in international gold dealings do they maintain their official exchange rates. Clearly this obligation applies to official gold movements between monetary authorities or central banks for the purpose of settling international balances.

If, for example, the United States were to raise the price at which it buys gold to $40 per ounce, this would represent a devaluation of the dollar. But does this obligation extend to a gold-producing country like South Africa, which permits its producers to sell a portion of their output on the unofficial gold markets of the world? It might be argued, of course, that unofficial gold movements are simply another form of commodity trade and that they do not involve the settlement of international currency balances as do transactions between monetary authorities.[26] On the other hand, most of the gold acquired in the unofficial gold markets is intended for monetary purposes (mainly as a store of value) rather than for industrial uses.

In its statement of June 18, 1947, the Executive Board of the Fund took the position that members should avoid all international transactions in gold at other than parity prices. The reasons: such transactions tend to undermine existing exchange parities; also, they involve a loss of monetary gold reserves into private hoards which most countries outside the United States can ill afford.[27] While the Fund did not object to purely domestic transactions, it did request members to refrain from paying subsidies to their gold mining industries tending to increase the domestic price of gold above parity.[28]

25. See Article IV, Sec. 2.
26. In the case of gold-producing countries, exports of current production should be viewed as commodity exports, but most gold imports cannot be regarded so simply. The Monetary Fund's *Balance of Payments Yearbook* considers the current exportable output of gold-producing countries and movements of gold into and out of industrial uses or private hoards as nonmonetary gold movements. Monetary gold movements are confined to changes in official reserves of governments and central banks.
27. *Annual Report of the Executive Directors for the Fiscal Year Ending June 30, 1947*, International Monetary Fund, Washington, Appendix XII.
28. See "Statement on Gold Subsidies," *Annual Report, April 30, 1948*, International Monetary Fund, Appendix VI. The Fund did consent to the payment of subsidies to

The Fund's strictures against gold sales at premium prices perhaps deterred, but certainly did not halt, the heavy traffic in private gold. During 1950 only about half the world's gold production outside the Soviet Union, some $420 million, was reflected in the rise in the gold reserves of monetary authorities, excluding the USSR.[29] The remainder went into private hoards and to industrial use.[30] New gold production is not the only source of free market gold, however, since in a number of countries the free market is fed by gold sales of the central banks.[31] In selling gold in the premium markets abroad, South Africa has maintained the formalities of selling for industrial purposes. Gold is sold in 22-carat sheets or bars or sometimes in the form of ashtrays or other simple objects which are easy to melt down into bars of standard weight and fineness for sale in the gold markets.[32] Australia, on the other hand, sells gold bars in the premium markets.

In September 1951, after a long controversy, mainly with South Africa, the Fund gave up trying to police international gold transactions. While reaffirming its position that "sound gold and exchange policy of members continues to require that, to the maximum extent practicable, gold should be held in official reserves rather than go into private hoards," the Fund left to individual countries the operating decisions for implementing the Articles of Agreement with respect to gold dealings.[33] Following this decision, many gold-producing countries began openly to sell a portion of their output directly or indirectly in the free gold markets.[34] Partly as a result of the in-

marginal producers, and, in fact, some gold-producing countries outside the United States have adopted subsidies which satisfy the conditions established by the Fund.

29. *Annual Report, 1951,* International Monetary Fund, p. 80. The *Annual Report* of the Union Corporation estimates the net absorption of gold for nonmonetary purposes (outside official reserves) at 18.3 million ounces for 1951 as compared with a total production of 25.7 million ounces. *Annual Report for 1951,* The Union Corporation, London, 1952, pp. 16–17.

30. In 1951 the U.S. Treasury sold about $100 million worth of gold for industrial purposes and for the arts, the bulk of it in the United States.

31. The Bank of France and the Bank of Greece have sold substantial amounts of gold in the free markets. This is done partly to obtain revenue, since the premium in terms of local currencies is quite high, and also to prevent sharp rises in gold prices which tend to weaken confidence in the local currency.

32. See "Searchlight on Gold," *The Banker,* March 1952, p. 146.

33. See "The Fund's Gold Statement," *International Financial News Survey,* October 5, 1951, p. 109.

34. South Africa is reported to be selling 40 per cent of her output in unofficial markets. South African sales on premium markets are deliberately limited to prevent

creased supply of gold on the free markets, the price fell in most markets from around $42 per ounce at the beginning of 1951 to less than $37 in mid-1953.

The Structure of the Premium Gold Markets

The principal international markets for premium gold are to be found in Switzerland and Tangier and in the countries of the Middle and Far East, especially Syria, Lebanon, Egypt, Kuwait, the Portuguese colonies of Goa and Macao, Thailand, Indochina and Hong Kong. Internal gold markets are legal in most of the Middle and Far Eastern countries and external transactions are either free or subject to only nominal restrictions in Syria, Lebanon, Goa, Macao, Uruguay, Tangier and Kuwait. Tangier issues a negotiable gold certificate known as the "Tangerine" which circulates throughout Europe. Imports into Egypt must have licenses, but these are freely granted if the gold is procured with nondollar currencies. There are also free internal markets in a number of European countries and substantial amounts of premium gold are absorbed in France, Italy and Greece. In December 1951 Switzerland largely abolished its restrictions on international transactions. Permits are still required for imports but these are readily given. There remains, however, a 4 per cent purchase tax which tends to restrict activity in the market.[35]

The chief gold consumers in the Middle and Far East are probably India, Pakistan and Egypt. Kuwait is an important entrepôt center for smuggling into India and Pakistan. Before 1949 China absorbed large amounts of premium gold largely through Hong Kong, but since that time the movement has been from Communist China to Hong Kong and thence to Saigon, Bangkok and other markets.[36]

Before the major gold-producing countries—South Africa, Australia and Canada—began to sell a large part of their output on the premium market, the principal sources of newly-mined gold for these markets were the Latin American countries, particularly Mexico,

a flooding of the market. Beginning in October 1951 Canada licensed the export of newly mined gold to premium markets provided the gold was in nonmonetary form of 22 carats or less. Australian gold producers are also free to sell their entire output in premium gold markets for dollars.

35. See "Free Gold-Trading in Switzerland Deadlocked," *The Statist*, January 5, 1952, pp. 9–10.

36. See H. R. Reinhardt, "Trailing Illicit Gold," *The Reporter*, July 22, 1952, pp. 17–21.

Colombia, Nicaragua, Chile, Brazil and Ecuador. A good portion of Ethiopia's output also finds its way into the premium markets of the East, and the USSR is known to sell gold in premium markets in annual amounts estimated at $30–$50 million. Before 1948 Switzerland sold gold from its reserves as a means of reducing inflationary pressure. Saudi Arabia has bought gold coins at official prices from the United States for internal circulation. Large amounts of gold sovereigns are believed to have been smuggled out of Arabia to Egypt and Kuwait.[37]

International dealings in gold are financed mainly with dollars, while sales to the ultimate consumer (hoarder) are generally made against local currency.[38] The price paid by the small hoarder involves a double premium: the difference between the official and the premium dollar price for gold plus the premium represented by the official rate over the black market rate for dollars. To finance these sales the gold dealers must find a way to convert the local proceeds of their gold sales into dollars in order to purchase more gold from the producing countries. This may be accomplished by buying goods which are sold for export against dollars. Frequently the local currency is exchanged for sterling which is then sold in the New York market at a discount; or goods may be bought with sterling— say, in Britain—for shipment to a Latin American country, and the proceeds used to purchase gold. There is, of course, a close relationship between unofficial or black market currency dealings and the gold traffic, since the gold dealers are an important source of supply of cheap currencies for the unofficial markets.

The Economics of Free Gold Markets

There are only a few places in the world, as was mentioned earlier, where international dealings in gold are completely free. On the other hand, internal trading and the private holding of gold are

37. Until 1950 the Arabian-American Oil Company paid its royalties to the Saudi Arabian government in gold sovereigns, which are used extensively as currency in that country.

38. The local demand for gold in the Middle and Far East is not simply a speculative demand based on a distrust of the local currency but is due to the fact that in those countries gold is a normal medium of saving. Frequently, gold coins are made into necklaces or trinkets and worn by members of the family as a traditional way of holding savings. There is a substantial premium, sometimes as high as 20 per cent, on gold coins over gold bars in the Middle East.

permitted in a number of countries including France, Belgium, Italy, Switzerland, Portugal, Turkey, most of the Middle and Far Eastern and many Latin American nations. In addition, many countries license the private importation of gold, if this does not mean a direct drain on the country's dollar reserves. Obviously, no country would pay more than $35 per ounce for gold which it had to buy with its official dollar holdings, since it can always buy gold from the U.S. Treasury at that price. But the U.S. Treasury will not issue licenses for the private export of fine bar gold except for industrial use.[39] This explains why gold can sell in the free markets of the world at a price above $35 per ounce, while the United States stands ready to sell gold against official dollar holdings of foreign governments in unlimited amounts at $35 plus 0.25 per cent. Since in nearly all countries it is not permitted either to hold private dollars or to export them for this purpose, most private international gold transactions financed with dollars are illegal.

But gold is also sold for other currencies. Indeed, most of the internal gold sales and a considerable portion of the external dealings are in terms of inconvertible currencies. Sometimes gold imports paid for in these currencies are licensed; the governments themselves may buy gold abroad in exchange for their own or for such other currencies as sterling.[40] The prices of gold in terms of local currencies fluctuate in response to the demand and supply peculiar to each national market. Prices are sensitive to internal and external economic and political developments, which may affect confidence in the local currency.[41] Prices also fluctuate with changes in supply, and in some countries the central banks deliberately intervene in the market to keep down the price of gold. Supply is also influenced by the ease of smuggling—where imports are illegal—and by the amounts producers are willing to sell on the free markets. The price of gold in terms of local currency may also change with the premium market dollar price of gold since the two markets will be linked together

39. *Annual Report of the Secretary of the Treasury 1948,* U.S. Department of the Treasury, p. 47.
40. Egypt is reported to have sold transferable account sterling to the USSR for gold. Most of Russia's gold exports are reported to be sold for nondollar currencies.
41. Between June 1950 and February 1952 the price of gold in Paris in terms of francs rose 48 per cent and the wholesale price index rose 43 per cent. The offtake on the Paris market ranged between 200,000 and 300,000 ounces per month. See *The Statist,* February 16, 1952, p. 230; see also *The Banker,* November 1951, pp. 247–48.

through the market—usually illegal—for dollars in terms of local currency. Such a change might occur quite apart from any shift in public confidence in the local currency.

Fluctuations in Gold Prices

Fluctuations in the price of gold in terms of dollar drafts are the result of complex forces. It is frequently said that the value of the dollar determines the value of gold—not vice versa—and that if the U.S. Treasury lowered the price of gold to $20 per ounce, the dollar price in premium gold markets would fall proportionately. While the drop in dollar price might not be at the same rate, it undoubtedly would fall, perhaps substantially below $35 per ounce. Moreover, if the United States were to permit its citizens to obtain gold freely for sale on the premium markets of the world the premium on gold, in the opinion of the author, would be reduced to $35 per ounce plus the cost of shipping and of smuggling, when imports are illegal.[42]

Apart from the cost of transportation and smuggling, the dollar premium on gold in unofficial markets is the result, mainly, of two factors. First, there is the view—more widely held abroad than in the United States—that the dollar sooner or later will be devalued and that devaluation is far more likely than appreciation. Perhaps more important, however, is the strong demand for gold to hoard. Only a few traders in a foreign country are in a position to carry dollar balances. Moreover, there are real risks in holding dollar funds since they may be subject to confiscation by the local government or to blocking by the U.S. government, as happened with foreign-owned dollar balances during the war. Dollar banknotes provide a better hoarding medium than do bank balances for the average citizen but these instruments have no intrinsic worth and their ultimate value depends on the ability to spend them in the United States. Nevertheless, they are reported to be widely held in Europe.[43]

The unofficial price of gold in U.S. dollars at any given time may vary widely from market to market. Prices quoted may represent local currency prices converted into dollars at the official exchange

42. The cost of smuggling gold into France is reported to be about $3 per ounce. *The Banker*, November 1951, pp. 267–68.
43. *The Statist*, February 14, 1952, p. 230.

rate or at free or black market rates. Prices in countries with free foreign exchange and gold markets—for example, Switzerland and Tangier—are generally lower than in countries where there are no legal free foreign exchange markets. Prices in individual markets tend to move together but arbitrage between them is limited by restrictions on exports and imports of gold.

Prices of gold have also varied widely since the war. Gold prices fell to $49 per ounce in December 1948 in the Paris and the Hong Kong markets, and to $43 in Zurich. Prices rose before the 1949 devaluations, indicating a loss in confidence in local currencies, but they fell after the September devaluations. Prices in Paris and Hong Kong rose again following the outbreak of the Korean war, to $43 in June 1951, but by June 1953 gold prices in the Paris, Zurich, Hong Kong and Tangier markets were under $40 per ounce. (See Table 8.)

TABLE 8

FREE MARKET GOLD PRICES, 1946–1952

(*U.S. Dollar Equivalents of Local Currencies per Fine Ounce of Bar Gold*)

End of Month	Paris	Zurich	Tangier	Hong Kong
1946, Dec.	$62	$47	$63	$51
1947, Dec.	53	42	53	50
1948, Dec.	49	43	57	49
1949, Sept.[a]	52	46	47	47
Dec.	46	41	40	39
1950, June [b]	39	37	37	38
Dec.	41	40	40	45
1951, June	43	40	40	43
Dec.	41	39	39	42
1952, June	38	37	38	40
Dec.	39	37	37	41
1953, June	38	36	36	39

Sources: *Monthly Letter on Economic Conditions,* National City Bank of New York, August 1952, p. 93; and *International Financial Statistics,* September 1953, p. 28.
a. Prior to the general currency devaluation.
b. Prior to the outbreak of the Korean war.

While complex forces were responsible for these movements, it is clear that the demand for gold *in terms of U.S. dollars* was closely related both to the confidence of the public in their own currencies and to the supply of gold on the premium markets. The rapid decline in gold prices since 1951 undoubtedly reflects, in part, increased supplies of gold available on the premium markets from the gold-producing countries.

Private trading in monetary gold is illegal in the United States because all such gold must be surrendered to the Treasury. However, dealings in gold concentrates are permitted, and there is a small market in gold coins and bar gold. In December 1951 double-eagles were quoted in the New York market at $44.50 a piece and bar gold at $40 per ounce.[44] Gold hoarding would probably not reach substantial proportions in the United States, even if gold were freely available from the Treasury. There are no U.S. restrictions on traffic in gold in its natural state. However, efforts to develop a market for high-grade gold ores for hoarding in this country have failed for lack of buyers willing to pay a premium price.

Private Gold Hoarding and International Reserves

One of the principal arguments against international gold dealings in unofficial markets at premium prices is that they divert gold from official reserves otherwise usable for the settlement of international balances and for currency stabilization. If the billions of dollars worth of privately held gold could be mobilized in official currency reserves [45] and if that portion (approximately 75 per cent in 1951) of the current gold production outside the United States now going into private hoards abroad could become available to national treasuries and central banks, there could be a substantial increase in the world's foreign exchange reserves. Before World War II, only a small fraction of the world's gold production disappeared in private hoards and during the 1930s official reserves frequently increased by more than the estimated gold production. In the 1920s even the Eastern gold sink absorbed less than 10 per cent of the annual gold production.[46]

Most of the loss of gold and dollar reserves resulting from the gold drain into private hoards is borne by the countries in which the hoards are accumulating. In the main, the gold-producing countries, including South Africa, Australia, other sterling area countries and Canada, require their producers to sell gold only against dollars and, except for Canada, where there are no exchange controls, most coun-

---

44. Private gold holdings, including gold concentrates, are estimated in Pick's *Black Market Yearbook* at $300–$500 million, certainly a small sum compared with foreign holdings.

45. Private gold hoards are estimated at over $11 billion by *Pick's World Currency Report;* see *The Banker,* March 1952, p. 143.

46. *The Banker,* March 1952, pp. 143–44.

tries require surrender to the monetary authorities of the dollar proceeds from exports. Thus gold sales at premium prices have increased the dollar reserves of most gold-producing countries, over what they would have been had the gold been sold at $35 per ounce.

When gold is sold by private dealers in one country to individuals in another for local currency, there is a foreign exchange loss for the gold-buying country, a loss which may show up sooner or later in the form of a gold or dollar drain.[47] If the government purchases the gold with a nondollar currency, the incidence of the loss of official reserves becomes more difficult to trace. It may simply mean a transfer from a private hoard in one country to an official reserve in another.

It may be argued, of course, that if private dealers were unable to buy gold from producers with dollars, they would hold dollar assets instead of gold as a store of value. This reasoning, however, assumes that the dollar holders would not have used these assets for other purposes, such as income-earning investments or imports which indirectly would have benefited the official gold and dollar position of the country. This assumption seems unrealistic. The conclusion is that private gold sales will reduce directly or indirectly the official exchange reserves of the buying countries.

Possible Solutions

Three possible remedies for this situation have been suggested. First, countries could ban all free markets in gold. The abolition of free internal markets would probably reduce imports now illegal in most countries. This would be unpopular, and might lead to a bidding up of other inflation hedges, such as commodities and real estate, with a consequent increase in inflationary pressures. Black markets would flourish and the price of gold might rise substantially, with a further loss of confidence in the local currency.

A second suggested remedy is to raise the official U.S. price of gold.[48] This would tend to reduce the private demand for gold since

47. For example, if a Frenchman buys gold from Belgium with French francs and the francs are transferred to Belgian banks, France's EPU deficit is increased and therefore her gold payments may increase.

48. For an excellent discussion of this problem see M. A. Kriz, *The Price of Gold*, (International Finance Section), Princeton University, Princeton, 1952; see also "The Price of Gold," *Monthly Letter on Economic Conditions*, National City Bank of New York, January 1953, pp. 3–8.

the purchase of an ounce of gold would take more dollars. It would also require more local currency to buy an ounce of gold if local currency prices rose proportionately. The extent to which a rise in the official price of gold above $35 per ounce would reduce demand in the premium gold markets would depend upon the elasticity of the demand and possible shifts in demand, determined by economic and psychological forces. A cut in the gold value of the dollar and of other currencies would certainly increase the volume of gold production throughout the world. While a case might be made for a rise in the price of gold as a means of expanding the world's supply of international reserves, such a step cannot be justified simply as a means of eliminating premium gold sales.

The third, and by far the most desirable solution, is to restore confidence in world currencies so that private gold and dollar hoarding would not prove attractive on today's scale. Until public confidence in currencies is restored individuals will try to acquire gold; or they may hoard other assets which tend to remain stable in value, the consequences of which may be more serious than a flight to gold.

It is frequently argued that the official price of gold ought to be raised, since its real value or purchasing power has fallen sharply since 1934, when the U.S. dollar was stabilized at $35 per ounce. While it is true that the purchasing power of gold has declined since the 1930s, in 1949 its purchasing power in terms of U.S. wholesale prices was 9 per cent above that in 1926; in terms of the cost of living, its purchasing power in 1949 was 27 per cent above 1926. U.S. prices have of course risen substantially since 1949. However, if the price of gold were raised or lowered with every fluctuation of the general price index, gold would lose what little influence it still may have as a stabilizing force.[49]

49. See Chapter 22.

PART III

THE COUNTRIES AND MONETARY AREAS

Chapter 10

EXCHANGE PRACTICES AND POLICIES OF THE UNITED KINGDOM

THE SPECIAL SIGNIFICANCE of sterling and of the British regulations relating to sterling held outside the United Kingdom is derived from the wide use of sterling as a means of international payments. How it may be employed for this purpose is determined by British exchange regulations, together with a number of formal and informal understandings between the British government and the governments and financial agencies of many countries throughout the world. But insight into British trade and payments relations with other countries derives from a knowledge of Britain's own exchange control regulations.

It should be clear that each independent member of the sterling area [1] has its own exchange control administration, independent of the British system. Each member, therefore, governs the foreign exchange activities of its own residents. The British government, however, establishes the rules according to which sterling accounts in British banks can be transferred or utilized for making payments or exchanged for other currencies. While these regulations may be subject to consultation with other sterling area members, they are basically the responsibility of the British authorities. Their acceptance by the exchange control authorities of the other members is the basis of the sterling area exchange system.

BRITISH EXCHANGE AND TRADE CONTROL POLICIES SINCE 1949

Exchange and trading policies of the United Kingdom have shifted from time to time in recent years in response to changing economic developments. Britain's most immediate concern has been to increase

---

1. There is considerable decentralization of exchange and trade controls even within the British colonies, trust territories, protectorates and self-governing territories. The degree of independence over external trade differs with the degree of self-government.

gold and dollar reserves from the dangerously low level of $1.3 billion at the time of the September 1949 devaluation. The sharp cuts in dollar imports by Britain and the other sterling area members in 1949 and 1950, coupled with the general rise in the demand for sterling products, increased Britain's gold and dollar reserves to $3.9 billion in June 1951. But by the spring of 1952 the decline in raw material prices and a subsequent expansion of sterling area imports from the dollar area and the EPU countries brought Britain's gold and dollar reserves down to $1.7 billion. This was reversed in the summer and fall of 1952 by a severe tightening of restrictions on imports by Britain and the other members of the sterling area, by improved terms of trade and by a change in internal policies, so that by March 1953 British reserves had climbed to $2.2 billion. Britain's gold and dollar deficits have been substantially greater than her losses of gold and dollar reserves. Except for the year 1950 Britain has had a gold and dollar deficit throughout the seven-year period 1946 to 1952. These deficits have been financed, in large part, by foreign loans and U.S. grants.

The aim of British exchange and trade control policies has been to keep down Britain's dollar expenditures by the use of discriminatory controls against dollar imports, in favor of imports from the sterling area and other soft-currency countries. During 1950 and 1951 Britain and the other members of the sterling area greatly liberalized their imports from soft-currency countries, including other members of the sterling area. This liberalization took the form of placing imports representing better than 75 per cent of her private trade with other soft-currency countries under open general license. In the last half of 1951 and in early 1952 a combination of factors, including falling raw material prices, British rearmament, inflationary pressures and the reduction of import restrictions, brought about a substantial sterling area deficit not only with the dollar area but with the EPU and other soft-currency countries. Both the United Kingdom and the independent sterling area countries were responsible for these deficits; only the colonial or dependent overseas territories maintained a surplus with the dollar area and on over-all account.

In order to check the sharp decline in British gold and dollar reserves, the United Kingdom and the other sterling area countries removed a number of commodities from the open general license list. Since Britain's cumulative EPU deficit had reached the point where Britain had to cover any additional deficits with 100 per cent gold payments, it became just as important for the sterling area to cut expenditures in the EPU countries as to reduce expenditures in the dollar area. It was equally important for sterling area countries to stop selling so much to one another and to divert these exports to nonsterling countries. Hence several of the independent sterling area countries, including Australia, South Africa and New Zealand, cut their 1952 imports from Britain and other sterling area countries in order to reduce or eliminate their over-all balance of payments deficits.[2] Britain, however, does not impose quantitative restrictions on imports from the sterling area.

Major Burden on Restrictions

The principal means of adjustment in Britain's several financial crises in the postwar period has been to increase her import restrictions. On only one occasion, in September 1949, did she resort to devaluation. Britain's full employment policy and the large volume of internal expenditures for social benefits have limited severely her ability to adjust her foreign trade balance by deflationary measures. The large volume of defense expenditures since 1950 has further strained her balance of payments. Britain has also maintained a high level of capital investment, within the United Kingdom and in the sterling area. Taxation has been heavy throughout the postwar period and savings out of income to finance capital investment have been extremely low compared with American standards.[3]

Until November 1951 Britain had followed a cheap money policy throughout the postwar period. This was altered by the Conservative government and the Bank of England rate was gradually raised from 2 per cent in the fall of 1951 to 4 per cent in March 1952. The Treasury bill rate was also raised from 0.5 per cent to over 2 per cent by the summer of 1952. These recent developments indicate a desire to use restrictive credit policies along with other domestic financial measures, including a reduction in food subsidies, to achieve balance of payments adjustments.

2. See "Cuts in Sterling Trade," *The Economist*, March 22, 1952, pp. 744–47.
3. See "Thriftless Britain," *The Economist*, September 13, 1952, pp. 601–02; see also *National Income and Expenditure, 1946–1951* (H.M.S.O.), September 1952.

British exchange control policies have been strongly influenced by the desire to preserve the sterling area and to maintain and expand the use of sterling as an international currency. Britain's reluctance to block more than a portion of the large sterling balances accumulated during the war and her rapid unblocking of the balances immobilized in 1947 have been motivated in large measure by her desire to preserve the sterling area. However, the existence of these heavy demand liabilities has undoubtedly weakened sterling and constituted a continual threat to Britain's external solvency. While the sterling balances have actually increased in value (in pounds) since the end of the war, their distribution has changed substantially.[4] Since 1945 the holdings of the nonsterling countries have tended to decline while those of the dependent overseas territories have risen very rapidly. The holdings of the independent sterling area countries have shifted from India and Pakistan to Australia and New Zealand.

Britain has also sought to support the sterling area by permitting British residents to export capital with few restrictions to the rest of the sterling area. Capital investment by the United Kingdom in the outer sterling area from January 1947 to the end of 1951 amounted to about one billion pounds sterling.[5] In order to stop this drain on her resources, Britain would have to place controls on capital movements to the sterling area. This, however, would eliminate one of the major advantages of membership in the area.

Mention should also be made of the willingness of Britain to finance the large gold and dollar deficits of the independent sterling area countries incurred during most of the postwar years. These payments covered not only the deficits with the dollar area but also the dollar drain due to deficits with other nondollar countries. While Britain has sought to reduce this dollar drain, she has relied mainly upon informal agreements rather than direct controls over their net drawings from the London dollar pool.

Before 1952 Britain's policy was to maintain relatively mild restrictions on imports from the OEEC countries and other soft-currency

4. On December 31, 1945 the sterling balances totaled £3,663 million; on December 31, 1951 they were £3,807 million. For an analysis of the changes in sterling balances during the postwar period see Roy F. Harrod, *The Pound Sterling,* International Finance Section, Princeton University, Princeton, 1952, pp. 17–22.

5. Harrod, *op. cit.,* p. 20 and *United Kingdom Balance of Payments 1948–1951,* Cmd. 8505, H.M.S.O.

nations, but to keep rather rigid control over expenditures in the dollar area.[6] Britain also encouraged the sterling area countries to follow similar policies with respect to their own import controls. Britain has made some effort to divert exports to the dollar area. But except for commodities in world short supply and those having strategic military importance, British exports have been relatively free from control. The net result of these policies has been to foster trade among soft-currency countries, a trade which has been, to some extent at least, at the expense of exports to the dollar area. The implications of these policies will be discussed in Part IV of this book.

UNITED KINGDOM EXCHANGE RESTRICTIONS

The legal basis for the British exchange regulations is the Exchange Control Act of 1947. This is a consolidation of earlier laws and regulations including the Defence (Finance) Regulations of 1939, which was the basis for Britain's wartime controls. Exchange control is the responsibility of the Treasury, but the practical administration is in the hands of the government-owned Bank of England. The Bank of England, in turn, delegates authority for most of the administrative operations to over one hundred "authorized" banks, a group which includes nearly all the commercial banks in the country.[7]

For most commercial transactions, a British resident need deal only with his own authorized bank which is empowered to approve applications for foreign exchange and arrangements for financing exports in accordance with general instructions transmitted by the Bank of England. There are also general regulations covering many noncommercial transactions. For other transactions it is generally necessary to have Bank of England approval.[8]

6. In 1952 Britain placed import restrictions upon a number of commodities from the EPU countries.

7. British banking is characterized by large branch banking systems so that the majority of bank offices are branches of five large British banks. Many of the banks operating in other parts of the sterling area have their head offices in London. This fact tends to simplify the problem of administration. In addition to the authorized banks, there are several exchange dealers who act as brokers for the banks in their dealings in foreign exchange markets.

8. According to reliable estimates, over 95 per cent of the applications for foreign exchange payments by British residents are approved by the authorized banks without reference to the Bank of England.

Exchange Transactions

All dealings in gold and foreign exchange in Britain must be with authorized banks. Residents acquiring certain specified currencies [9] must sell them to an authorized bank unless for special reasons the resident needs working balances. Other foreign currencies, including all those of the sterling area, may be retained by the recipient but they cannot be sold except to an authorized bank or used without a license for making foreign payments. Until December 17, 1951 authorized banks acted solely as agents for the Bank of England in the purchase and sale of specified currencies. All transactions were conducted at official rates established by the Bank of England and each authorized bank had to settle daily its net foreign exchange position in each of the specified currencies. Forward transactions were permitted if a foreign trader needed protection against exchange loss arising out of authorized commercial transactions. Buying and selling rates on forward exchange were fixed by the Bank of England without regard to demand and supply.

British exchange control regulations were changed in December 1951 to permit authorized banks to deal as principals in both spot and forward exchange in United States and Canadian dollars and certain other currencies. These modifications ease the administration of British exchange restrictions, but the basic regulations affecting the movement of goods, services and capital (except short-term working capital operations of banks) remain unchanged.

Normally, British trading firms hold no balances in foreign currencies but, just as do most American firms when they are importing goods, they make payments with drafts drawn on their own banks or with bankers' drafts drawn on foreign banks or they arrange for letter-of-credit facilities. They sell drafts to their banks when they receive payment for their exports. To the average British trader, the existence of exchange control makes little difference except for the paper work. The import licensing authorities determine what he may buy abroad and where he must make his purchases.

---

9. The specified currencies are Belgian and Belgian-Congolese francs, Canadian dollars, francs of the French franc area, Djibouti francs, Indochinese piasters, Luxembourg francs, Netherlands guilders, Panamanian dollars, Philippine pesos, Pondicherry rupees, Portuguese escudos, Swiss francs and U.S. dollars. Nonspecified foreign currencies need not be offered for sale, but approval for their use—other than by sale to an authorized bank—must be obtained.

Some business firms and individuals, however, would find it almost impossible to engage in foreign dealings if they had to make payments exclusively through banks. Among these are firms with branch offices or plants abroad, shipping and insurance firms, and dealers on the commodity markets who must execute transactions quickly. In such cases firms and individuals are permitted to maintain their own accounts in foreign currencies. These accounts are subject to periodic audits, and balances in specified currencies above normal working requirements must be surrendered.

Control over Imports

In Britain and generally throughout the sterling area, control over imports is exercised not by the exchange control but by the import licensing authorities in each country or territory. While an authorization to import does not carry with it a guarantee that the exchange control will provide the appropriate means of payment, in Britain and in most other sterling area countries, exchange will almost invariably be made available. For this reason, import policy, as implemented by the Board of Trade in granting import licenses, must be closely coordinated with exchange policy, which is the province of the Treasury and the Bank of England.

While all merchandise imported into Britain must be under a license issued by the Board of Trade,[10] not all imports require a license granted to the individual importer. For a limited list of items world open general licenses have been issued. These provide that the commodity can be freely imported from any country.[11] A much longer list of commodities may be imported under open general license from all except a specified list of countries, mainly hard-currency nations and Soviet satellites.[12] The reason for excluding state-

10. Except fresh fish landed by vessels registered in certain countries.
11. A partial list of world open general license items in 1950 included ivory; live animals; bauxite; books, newspapers and periodicals; rough diamonds; cobalt; fur skins; nickel ores; olives; shellac; wool.
12. Countries from which goods may not be imported under open general license (as of October 1951) include Albania, Argentina, Bolivia, Bulgaria, Canada, Colombia, Costa Rica, Cuba, Czechoslovakia, Dominican Republic, Ecuador, El Salvador, French Somaliland, Eastern Germany, Guatemala, Haiti, Honduras, Hungary, Iran, Japan, Korea, Liberia, Mexico, Nicaragua, Panama, the Philippines, Poland, Romania, Tangier, the United States, the USSR, Venezuela and Yugoslavia. (*The Use of Quantitative Import Restrictions to Safeguard Balances of Payments,* GATT, Geneva, November 1951, p. 72.)

controlled economies from the list is largely to facilitate the process of bilateral bargaining since trade with these countries is, in effect, on a barter basis. Since the OEEC trade liberalization program went into effect, all EPU countries are included in the list of those from which items under open general license are unrestricted.[13] For all other commodities importers must apply to the Board of Trade for individual licenses.[14] In some cases, however, open individual licenses may be granted to importers authorizing the purchase of unspecified amounts of a particular commodity. These are given to dealers in such commodity markets as coffee, tin and rubber where continual buying and selling operations require maximum freedom. There also are special licensing arrangements for token imports [15] and for imports for use in the export trade.[16]

In 1951 about half of all British imports could be imported only for government account. These imports consisted mainly of basic foodstuffs, fertilizers and raw materials. Any appraisal of British import and payments restrictions must take into account the large segment of state-monopolized trade.[17] While balance of payments con-

---

13. Prior to the imposition of new import restrictions announced in November 1951, approximately 90 per cent of private British imports (as of 1948) from other OEEC countries were under open general license. ("European Scapegoat," *The Economist,* November 17, 1951, p. 1169.) In November 1951 a number of commodities on the open general license list were made subject to individual license from all countries except members of the sterling area. In January 1953 only 46 per cent of Britain's private imports from EPU countries (1948 base) were free from quota restrictions.

14. The following information must be submitted: description of goods, value, weight and quantity, country of origin and address of overseas consigner, method of payment, purpose of acquiring goods and ultimate use intended. If rentals, fees or royalties are involved, additional authorization must be obtained from the Bank of England.

15. The token import plan was inaugurated in 1946 for about two hundred products imported from the following countries: Australia, B.L.E.U., Canada, Denmark, Finland, France, India, Italy, the Netherlands, Norway, Pakistan, Sweden, Switzerland and the United States. In 1950–1951 Britain issued import licenses to British dealers to the amount of 20 per cent of the value of each individual manufacturer's average trade with Britain in the period 1936–1939 for the item covered. Token imports were reduced during 1952 to 75 per cent of the 1951 rate and the operation of the scheme has been restricted to imports from the United States and Canada. In 1948 Britain issued licenses totaling £525,142 for imports from the United States under the token plan, which otherwise would not have been permitted. The purpose of the scheme is to keep trade channels open for foreign products during periods of import restrictions.

16. Special consideration is given to imports required by the export industries. Exporters to the dollar area are given more liberal treatment for their requirements of dollar imports.

17. A partial list of United Kingdom government imports in 1950 include the following:

Aluminum (virgin)	Butter	Cheese
Bacon	Carrots (nonfancy)	Chrome ore

siderations, including the achievement of a bilateral balance with countries like Argentina, undoubtedly have played a role in Britain's state trading policy, commercial policy and administrative factors have probably been more important. The government frequently enters into one-to-ten-year contracts with foreign suppliers or their governments. In the longer-term contracts, prices are subject to negotiation from year to year, except that in some cases prices cannot vary by more than a fixed percentage from one year to another. British government spokesmen have argued that bulk purchasing will secure more favorable prices and greater stability of supply from soft-currency sources. In addition, many of the food items imported by the government have been sold below cost in order to hold down the cost of living.

Since 1951 the British government has restored a number of commodities to private trading. Steps have also been taken to ease exchange restrictions on commodity traders to enable them to reestablish Britain's international commodity markets.

Payments for Imports

Once an import has been authorized (either by a specific license or under an open general license) the importer applies to his authorized bank for the foreign exchange. If the type of exchange requested is appropriate for the transaction, and the application is supported by copies of the invoice and the import license, the exchange is ordinarily granted.[18] If the goods have already arrived, the application for exchange must be supported by a copy of the customs entry form;

Cocoa	Glucose	Poultry
Coffee	Hemp	Pulses
Copper	Jute and jute goods	Rice
Copra	Lead metal	Soybeans
Eggs	Meat	Starch and starch products
Feedstuffs	Milk	Steel (finished)
Fertilizer	Molasses	Sugar
Fish (canned; fresh salmon; frozen whitefish)	Nuts	Tea
	Oils and fats	Timber (except hardwoods
Flour	Oilseed	and certain others)
Fruits (apples, bananas, canned fruit, dried fruit)	Orange juice	Wheat
	Potatoes	Zinc

Private trading has recently been restored (wholly or in part) for a number of commodities previously under government monopoly, including cocoa, coffee, cotton, grains, lead, rubber, shellac, sugar, tin, wool and zinc.

18. If payment is requested in, say, dollars for an import from a soft-currency country, the request would have to be referred to the Bank of England.

if not, the importer undertakes to supply the form in due course. Both the application for foreign exchange and the customs entry form are transmitted by the authorized bank through the Bank of England to the customs, so that the exchange application can be checked against a record of the goods actually imported.

Payments may be made in either foreign exchange or by transferring the sterling paid by the importer to an appropriate foreign account in the name of the exporter or his bank. If the importer purchases more foreign exchange than he uses for the purposes stated on the application, the remainder must be resold to the authorized bank.

Control over Exports

Except for a few items controlled for reasons of security or for allocating scarce supplies, British exports in general are not licensed. For exports to countries outside the sterling area, however, exporters must complete an exchange control form giving particulars regarding the nature and value of the goods and the form of payment. The proceeds from exports must normally be received within six months of the filing of the application and the means of payment must be in accordance with Treasury regulations. In order to check export proceeds against customs records of the goods actually exported, the exporter's bank forwards to the Bank of England the certified application form after it has received the proceeds from the exporter. The Bank of England checks the amount and form of the proceeds and then sends the documents to the customs for verification based on that agency's more specialized knowledge of commodities. The purpose of the checking is to make sure that the appropriate form of payment has been made, and that the exporter has not undervalued the merchandise in order to export capital illegally.[19]

Both exports and imports may be financed in accordance with the normal practice of the trade—by letter of credit, sight or time draft on the importer, open book account, or other recognized practice. Acceptance financing of exports has been limited to a maximum pe-

---

19. A common leak in exchange control systems occurs when exporters arrange for part of the proceeds of their exports to be placed in secret foreign accounts and not sold to the authorized banks. There is a similar leak when an importer overpays the exporter who in turn, places the excess receipts in a secret account in favor of the importer.

riod as a credit control measure and as a means of cutting the time between the export of the goods and the collection of foreign exchange. When the market believes that sterling may be devalued there is a tendency on the part of foreign importers to delay sterling payment as long as possible, while at the same time sterling area importers from other countries seek to make sterling payments in advance of the receipt of goods. These leads and lags have sometimes brought about a heavy drain of British gold and dollar reserves.

Nontrade Items

Residents of the United Kingdom may ordinarily transfer funds to any place in the sterling area without exchange formalities.[20] All payments and transfers to countries outside the sterling area or to a nonresident sterling account require an exchange control application. Many applications will be approved by the authorized banks from which the exchange is purchased; in other cases the application must be forwarded to the Bank of England for approval. The regulation of nontrade payments is complicated, and subject to change from time to time. The rules vary as between countries, depending in part upon the degree of hardness of the currency involved. The regulations (at the time of writing) may be summarized as follows: [21]

1. Profits, dividends, interest, rents and royalties may be remitted to any country. Depreciation of direct investments is not ordinarily allowed.

2. Expenses relating to the movement of goods including freight, storage charges, customs duties, etc., are approved for payment to the country to which they are due.

3. Limited expenditures for tourist travel and education are approved for certain countries.

4. Pensions and annuities from life insurance purchased by nonresidents are authorized, as are other contractual payments by British insurance companies to nonresidents. Normally, only insurance premiums of residents on policies taken out before September 3, 1939

20. There are certain restrictions on transfers to Hong Kong because of the free hard-currency markets there. Transfers to South Africa "which serve no useful economic purpose" also are restricted.

21. See *Digest of the United Kingdom Exchange Regulations*, 10th ed., District Bank Limited, London, April 1953.

are authorized if the payments must be made to insurance companies outside the sterling area.

5. Business travel and advertising expenses are permitted on an approved scale in all countries.

6. Transfers to the United States of film royalties and rentals are limited under a special agreement. Transfers to other countries are authorized.

7. Wages and salaries of nonresidents temporarily employed in the United Kingdom may be remitted to the country of which the employee is a permanent resident.

8. Repayment of commercial credits and contractual amortization on sterling securities are permitted freely. Contractual amortization on mortgages and other loans are allowed freely if the original borrowing occurred prior to September 1939 or was subsequently approved by the Exchange Control.

9. In general, transfers of capital outside the sterling area by residents are not authorized, with the exception of expenditures for direct investments which may benefit the British balance of payments, e.g., petroleum operations in the Middle East or Latin America.

10. Limited amounts of capital may be transferred by emigrants and recipients of legacies. Allowable transfers are more liberal in the case of emigrants to soft-currency countries than for those going to hard-currency countries.

11. The proceeds from the sale of securities and other capital assets owned by nonresidents of the sterling area may not ordinarily be transferred but must be placed in blocked accounts available only for investment in other sterling securities. There are special arrangements for the repatriation of new investments made after January 1, 1950.[22]

Most of the applications for foreign exchange payments in connection with nontrade items are approved by the authorized banks. For items which come under no general rules and for cases where an exception to a rule is requested, the matter must be submitted to the Bank of England. Profits transfers which necessitate an examination of the balance sheets of subsidiaries of nonresident concerns also require special approval. Applications involving substantial invest-

---

22. British regulations regarding dealings by nonresidents in sterling securities will be described in another section.

ments abroad and credit terms beyond the normal limits must be submitted to the Foreign Exchange Control Committee. Finally, certain transfers between nonresident accounts must be submitted to the Bank of England for approval.

All specified currencies received by British residents must be sold to authorized banks, unless special arrangements have been made for the maintenance of private accounts subject to periodic reporting and control. This includes receipts in the form of travelers checks, bank drafts and other claims on specified foreign currencies. Payments for services must be received in the currency appropriate to the resident of the country for whom the service is performed or from the appropriate nonresident sterling account. Travelers are not permitted to bring in more than £10 in banknotes or to take more than £5 with them when they leave.

STERLING ACCOUNTS

As this study frequently has mentioned, payments and receipts from transactions with nonresidents must be executed either by paying or receiving the appropriate foreign currency or by debiting or crediting the appropriate sterling account. Regulations as to the appropriate means of payments and receipts vary from country to country depending upon the nature of Britain's bilateral agreement or other arrangements. (Details of the British bilateral payments agreements will be discussed in Chapter 11.) However, certain categories of countries are recognized by British and other sterling area exchange control regulations with which the payments arrangements are more or less standardized. These categories and the countries in each are summarized in Figure 3.

Resident Accounts

The accounts of residents of areas listed in the amended Exchange Control Act of 1947 (the Scheduled Territories) are known as resident accounts. Transfers from one account to another may be made without formalities or restrictions throughout the Scheduled Territories (or the sterling area). Current transactions between residents of the sterling area are financed by transfers to and from resident accounts and, to a limited extent, by transfers of other sterling area currencies.

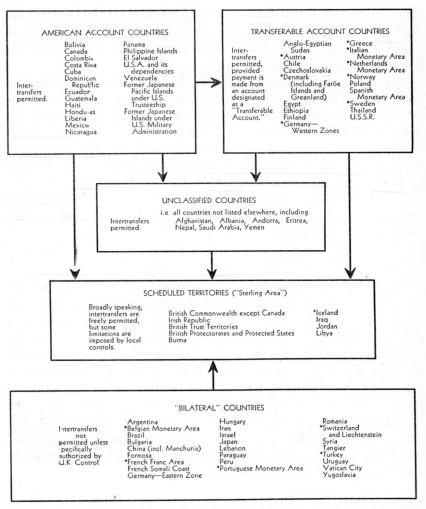

AMERICAN ACCOUNT COUNTRIES

Intertransfers permitted.

Bolivia	Panama
Canada	Philippine Islands
Colombia	El Salvador
Costa Rica	U.S.A. and its dependencies
Cuba	Venezuela
Dominican Republic	Former Japanese Pacific Islands under U.S. Trusteeship
Ecuador	
Guatemala	
Haiti	
Honduras	Former Japanese Islands under U.S. Military Administration
Liberia	
Mexico	
Nicaragua	

TRANSFERABLE ACCOUNT COUNTRIES

Inter-transfers permitted, provided payment is made from an account designated as a "Transferable Account."

Anglo-Egyptian Sudan	*Greece
*Austria	*Italian Monetary Area
Chile	*Netherlands Monetary Area
Czechoslovakia	*Norway
*Denmark (including Faröe Islands and Greenland)	Poland
	Spanish Monetary Area
Egypt	*Sweden
Ethiopia	Thailand
Finland	U.S.S.R.
*Germany— Western Zones	

UNCLASSIFIED COUNTRIES

i.e all countries not listed elsewhere, including Afghanistan, Albania, Andorra, Eritrea, Nepal, Saudi Arabia, Yemen

Intertransfers permitted.

SCHEDULED TERRITORIES ("Sterling Area")

Broadly speaking, intertransfers are freely permitted, but some limitations are imposed by local controls.

British Commonwealth except Canada	*Iceland
Irish Republic	Iraq
British Trust Territories	Jordan
British Protectorates and Protected States	Libya
Burma	

"BILATERAL" COUNTRIES

Intertransfers not permitted unless specifically authorized by U.K Control.

Argentina	Hungary	Romania
*Belgian Monetary Area	Iran	*Switzerland and Liechtenstein
Brazil	Israel	Syria
Bulgaria	Japan	Tangier
China (incl. Manchuria)	Lebanon	*Turkey
Formosa	Paraguay	Uruguay
*French Franc Area	Peru	Vatican City
French Somali Coast	*Portuguese Monetary Area	Yugoslavia
Germany—Eastern Zone		

FIGURE 3. UNITED KINGDOM EXCHANGE CONTROL REGULATIONS: OUTLINE OF PERMISSIBLE TRANSFERS, MAY 1953

The arrows indicate direction of transfers permitted without the necessity of individual approval by the U.K. control between different categories of sterling accounts. All other transfers require separate approval.

Countries marked with asterisk are members of the European Payments Union. Transfers between all EPU members are on an automatic basis. Iceland is a member in her own right though also included in the Scheduled Territories.

Source: *Twenty-second Annual Report,* Bank for International Settlements, Basel, 1952, p. 141. Figure has been amended to take account of recent revisions.

In practice, an Australian making a payment to someone in India would purchase a sterling draft from his bank and send it to the Indian resident who would then sell it to his bank for rupees. The London sterling account of the Australian bank would be debited in favor of the account of the Indian bank when that bank sent the draft to London for collection. British residents may make payments directly to residents of other sterling area countries simply by mailing a check drawn on a British bank. However, most sterling area countries require that all transfers of sterling be made through an authorized bank. Transfers between resident and nonresident accounts can only be made by application to and approval of authorized banks which act as agents of the exchange control authorities.

Some of the sterling balances held by other members of the sterling area are blocked in the sense that they may not be used to finance current trade transactions; they are limited to investment in approved sterling securities. These balances, which are held in No. 2 accounts,[23] were largely accumulated during the war and were immobilized in order to reduce the strain on Britain's balance of payments. The status of these accounts will be discussed in Chapter 11.

Nonresident Accounts

Nonresident accounts are balances held in British banks for natural or legal persons not residents of the sterling area.[24] With a few exceptions, these accounts are designated according to the country or monetary area in which the holders or owners reside. Holders of nonresident sterling accounts may transfer them by ordinary bank draft or cable to the accounts of other persons in their own country or monetary area or to residents of the sterling area. British regulations also provide for automatic transfers to accounts in other countries or monetary areas.

1. *American Accounts.* Payments between residents of the sterling area and the United States and certain other countries may be made either in U.S. dollars or in sterling held in an American account— sterling balances owned by residents of a group of countries which includes the United States and its territories, the Philippines and a

23. Balances in No. 1 accounts are freely available for current transactions.
24. There are also some nonresident accounts held by British firms on behalf of their foreign correspondents.

number of Latin American Republics.[25] These countries constitute what is known as the "dollar area." American account sterling is freely convertible into dollars and is bought and sold on the New York market. Its price in terms of dollars is maintained by the Bank of England within a narrow range of the dollar-sterling parity, as established with the International Monetary Fund. While American account sterling may be used to purchase any of the sterling currencies or transferred to any other nonresident sterling account, transfers from other sterling accounts—except Canadian accounts—to an American account, are strictly controlled and limited largely to payments for authorized imports of goods and services into the sterling area from the dollar area. In other words, sterling from other nonresident accounts (except Canadian accounts) cannot ordinarily be transferred to an American account.

2. *Canadian Accounts.* Transactions with Canada may be financed by payments to and from (a) Canadian sterling accounts, (b) Canadian dollar accounts in Canadian banks, (c) American sterling accounts, or (d) U. S. dollar accounts. The regulations with respect to Canadian sterling accounts are similar to those pertaining to American account sterling. Canadian and American dollars being freely interconvertible, Canadian and American account sterling are also interconvertible and both types of sterling accounts are freely convertible into U.S. or Canadian dollars. Since December 1951 British authorized banks have been permitted to conduct arbitrage operations in the markets of the three countries. In this way the sterling-Canadian dollar rate reflects changes in the Canadian dollar-U.S. dollar rate, which has been permitted to fluctuate since September 1950.

3. *Transferable Accounts.* Transferable account sterling is sterling held by residents of certain countries outside the sterling area, known as transferable account countries. Under the terms of payments agreements with Britain they are permitted to make and receive payments to and from these accounts in financing current transactions with the sterling area and with other members of the transferable account system. While transferability to and from these accounts is automatically effected within the area set forth by British regulations, actual transfers must be made by and through authorized British

25. Not all sterling balances owned by residents of American account countries are held in American accounts. Some of the sterling holdings of these countries are in blocked accounts, the use of which is strictly limited.

banks in which the accounts are held. Thus a Dutch importer of cotton may purchase a draft from his bank on its transferable account in London. This he remits to the Egyptian cotton exporter who in turn sells the draft to his own bank. The Egyptian bank may then send the draft to a London correspondent where its transferable account is credited and the transferable account of the Netherlands bank debited. Transfers from such accounts to other nonresident accounts outside the transferable account group require the approval of the British Exchange Control.

Most payments between residents of the sterling area and those of the transferable account countries are made in sterling. There are, however, certain transferable account countries from which British exporters are permitted to accept drafts on the importers' banks. Not all sterling held by residents of transferable account countries are transferable accounts. In general, such accounts are limited to foreign banks whose transactions are under the supervision of the exchange control of their country. A primary condition for the maintenance of a transferable account is that it will be so supervised that it can be used only for *direct current* transactions with the sterling area and other transferable account countries. The aim is to prevent the use of these accounts to pay for imports from the sterling area which are then sold to hard-currency countries. As was pointed out in Chapter 9, however, there have been many violations of these regulations.

Nontransferable accounts of residents of transferable account countries are subject to much the same limitations as to their use as are bilateral accounts except that they may be transferred to a transferable account of a resident of the same country. These accounts may be credited by transfers from any transferable account, from other accounts of residents of the same monetary area, or from American accounts.

4. *Bilateral Accounts.* Bilateral accounts are nonresident accounts which carry no automatic rights of transferability to the nonresident accounts of other countries, nor can sterling from nonresident accounts of other countries (except the United States or Canada) be credited to them without specific permission of the British Exchange Control. In other respects they operate like transferable accounts. In some bilateral account countries, British traders may make and receive

payments in the currency of the bilateral account country as well as by means of credits or debits to the appropriate nonresident account. Transfers of bilateral account sterling are freely permitted between residents of the same country.

5. *Accounts of Unclassified Countries.* There are some countries with which Britain has no formal bilateral agreements but which are permitted to maintain and use sterling balances to finance transactions with the sterling area and with certain other soft-currency nations. These "unclassified account countries" include virtually every country not in the sterling area, the dollar area or the bilateral or transferable account group. Their accounts may be used to make payments to the sterling area or to another "unclassified country." They may be automatically credited from sterling area, American and transferable accounts as well as from accounts of other members of the group.

The various types of sterling accounts and the countries included in each category are summarized in Figure 3. For an outline of methods of payment between residents of the sterling area and other countries, see Table 9.

TABLE 9

APPROPRIATE METHODS OF PAYMENT BETWEEN RESIDENTS OF THE STERLING AREA
AND OTHER COUNTRIES AND MONETARY AREAS, MAY 1953

Country	Payments to the Sterling Area				Payments from the Sterling Area		
Transferable account countries							
Austria	A	B	C		A¹	B¹	
Chile	A	B	C		A¹	B¹	
Czechoslovakia	A	B	C		A¹	B¹	
Denmark, Faeroes, Greenland......	A	B	C	F	A¹	B¹	F
Egypt	A	B	C		A¹	B¹	
	but not an Egyptian No. 2 a/c						
Ethiopia	A	B	C		A¹	B¹	
Finland	A	B	C		A¹	B¹	
Western Zones of Germany and the Western sectors of Berlin........	A	B	C	F	A¹	B¹	F
Greece	A	B	C		A¹	B¹	
Italian monetary area..............	A	B	C		A¹	B¹	
Netherlands monetary area........	A	B	C	F	A¹	B¹	F
Norway	A	B	C	F	A¹	B¹	F
Poland	A	B	C		A¹	B¹	
Spanish monetary area............	A	B	C		A¹	B¹	
Anglo-Egyptian Sudan	A	B	C		A¹	B¹	
Sweden	A	B	C	F	A¹	B¹	F
Thailand	A	B	C		A¹	B¹	
USSR	A	B	C				

TABLE 9—Continued

Country	Payments to the Sterling Area		Payments from the Sterling Area		
American account countries (including Canada)	C	E	C	E	
Bilateral countries					
Argentina	B		B¹		
Belgian monetary area............	B	F	B¹		F
Brazil	B		B¹		
Bulgaria	B		B¹		
China	B with prior consent of Bank of England		B¹		
Formosa	B with prior consent of Bank of England		B¹		
French franc area, including the Saar.	B	F	B¹		F
French Somaliland	B	F	B¹		F
Hungary	B		B¹		
Iran	B with prior consent of Bank of England		B¹		
Israel	B other than No. 2 a/c		B¹		
Japan	B		B¹		
Lebanon	B		B¹		
Paraguay	B		B¹		
Peru	B		B¹		
Portuguese monetary area.........	B	F	B¹		F
Romania	B		B¹		
Switzerland–Liechtenstein	B	F	B¹		F
Syria	B				
Tangier	B		B¹		
Turkey	B but *not* a Turkish private a/c		B¹		
Uruguay	B		B¹		
Vatican City	B		B¹		
Yugoslavia	B		B¹		
Unclassified countries (includes Afghanistan, Albania, Andorra, Nepal, Saudi Arabia and the Yemen)	A B C D		B¹		

NOTE: The symbols indicate the following types of accounts:

A. Sterling from a transferable account relating to *any* country or monetary area.
A¹. Sterling to a transferable account held by the country or monetary area.
B. Sterling from an account appropriate to the country to which the goods are consigned.
B¹. Sterling to an account appropriate to the country or monetary area.
C. Sterling from *any* American account or Canadian account.
D. Sterling from an account appropriate to *any* country included in "Unclassified countries."
E. U.S. dollars or Canadian dollars.
F. The local currency of the country.

6. *Blocked Nonresident Accounts.* Blocked sterling accounts may be held in the name of any nonresident of the sterling area. These accounts are not available for financing current trade with the sterling area. Their use is limited to investment in sterling securities with

a maturity of more than ten years. Most of these accounts have originated in the sale of securities and other capital assets by nonresidents or in the distribution of legacies. Income on investments made with blocked sterling funds may be remitted to the nonresident owner. Since March 1953 transfers of blocked balances between residents of the same monetary area have been permitted.

CAPITAL MOVEMENTS

Capital exports from Britain to residents of other sterling area countries are generally free from controls.[26] However, capital exports have been restricted in recent years by the regulations of independent sterling members outside Britain. But capital movements from Britain to countries outside the sterling area are closely regulated. These restrictions apply to the repatriation of capital owned by nonresidents as well as to capital exports by British citizens. However, capital invested in Britain after January 1, 1950 by persons outside the sterling area may be repatriated (including capital gains),[27] provided the investments are made with the approval of the British authorities. New investments are not approved unless they are likely to benefit the foreign exchange position of the United Kingdom. Thus Britain may permit an American oil company to build a refinery in Britain but it might not approve a dollar investment in a soft-drink bottling plant or in a night club.

Foreign investments by British citizens in countries outside the sterling area also require permission; they must meet the test of making a net contribution to Britain's foreign exchange position. A British firm, for example, might be allowed to make a dollar investment in Venezuelan petroleum production, since this would earn dollars for the sterling area. Of course dollar earnings on the foreign investments of British companies must be surrendered to the British exchange control authorities against sterling. Nonresidents may transfer their net earnings on investments in the sterling area into the currency of the country in which they are residing.

26. There are certain restrictions on capital payments to Hong Kong in order to prevent capital exports to the dollar area via the free dollar market in Hong Kong.

27. The application of the repatriation privilege to capital gains as well as to original capital invested after January 1, 1950 was announced in February 1953. *The New York Times,* February 21, 1953.

Securities

British regulations regarding transactions in securities are quite detailed and only their major features can be discussed here.[28] The purpose of these regulations is twofold: to prevent an exchange drain arising from a capital outflow which may accompany transactions in British securities; and to prevent a loss of exchange through interest and dividend payments which may result from a shift in the ownership of securities as between residents and nonresidents, or as between nonresidents in different currency areas. A change in the ownership of a sterling security from a resident of a bilateral or transferable account country to an American account country, for example, means that interest payments will have to be made in dollars or American account sterling rather than in inconvertible sterling.

With a few minor exceptions, all resident holders of bearer securities [29] and of securities issued by a registrar outside the sterling area must deposit them with an authorized bank; if the securities are outside the sterling area, they must be held to the order of an authorized bank. This enables the authorized banks to control both the sale and disposition of the proceeds of a resident's security and the income from it, in accordance with exchange control regulations. Foreign currency proceeds from interest and dividends or from the sale of a security must be sold for sterling to an authorized bank; if such proceeds are retained, their use is supervised in accordance with British exchange control regulations. Thus, if a British resident sells 100 shares of U.S. Steel on the New York Stock Exchange he may reinvest in General Motors or in some other U.S. security or he may sell the proceeds for sterling to his authorized bank. British residents may of course buy and sell for sterling both sterling and nonsterling securities on a stock exchange in the United Kingdom. Residents of other sterling area territories may purchase securities on a British stock exchange with the exception of prescribed securities.[30]

28. For a detailed description of these regulations see *Digest of the United Kingdom Exchange Regulations*, 10th ed., District Bank Limited, London, April 1953.

29. Control over securities registered in the sterling area is exercised by restrictions on the actions of registrars.

30. Prescribed securities are those payable in Belgian francs, Canadian dollars, Swiss francs or U.S. dollars.

Purchases by Nonresidents

While desiring to protect her reserves from a capital drain, Britain has also been anxious to preserve the international status of London financial markets. Therefore, nonresidents are permitted to buy sterling securities on British stock exchanges. These purchases may be made with the funds of the country of the nonresident; by purchase from other residents of the same country or monetary area with sterling from an appropriate sterling account; by purchase with funds from a blocked account of the nonresident; or by switching from one sterling security to another not maturing within ten years. Nonresidents may buy any security quoted on the British stock exchanges except a prescribed security, provided payment is made in one of the four ways outlined above.[31]

Thus, a Belgian buyer on the London exchange would probably use Belgian account sterling or sterling in a blocked account of the owner. An American buying securities on the London exchange will use either American account sterling (which is unlikely, because the proceeds from the sale of a sterling security would not be convertible into dollars) or sterling from a blocked account in his own name. He could also buy the security from another American against payment in dollars in the New York market. (See Chapter 9.) An American could not buy a British security directly from a Frenchman, however, since the British authorities would not permit the transfer of ownership of a security from a resident of France to a resident of the dollar area.

Nonresident owners of sterling securities can sell them for sterling in the London market, but the sterling must be credited to a blocked account available only for purchasing other sterling securities with a maturity of at least ten years or for sale to another nonresident in the same monetary area. Nonresident owners of sterling securities may also sell them in a foreign market to a resident of the same country or currency area. An important exception to these British regulations is that of the 1950 agreement with the three Scandinavian countries. Residents of Denmark, Sweden and Norway may sell

31. Prescribed securities can be bought by nonresidents if payment is made from a sterling account appropriate to the currency in which the security is payable. Thus a Brazilian could buy U.S. securities only with American account sterling; or a Belgian could buy a security payable in Belgian francs with Belgian account sterling.

any security payable in sterling and quoted on a sterling area market, and freely repatriate the proceeds of the sale.

CONTROLS OF OTHER STERLING AREA TERRITORIES

The control over nonresident accounts in other sterling area territories in general follows the pattern of British regulations. Outside the United Kingdom sterling owned by banks and other residents of the sterling area is held in British authorized banks in the form of resident accounts. Transfers between these accounts and those of nonresidents of the sterling area are under the supervision of the authorized banks and the Bank of England. Hence the regulations of the exchange control authorities of all sterling area countries must conform to the British pattern insofar as they involve transfers of sterling balances. Some members of the sterling area have dollar and other currencies of their own and can finance trade in terms of their own and nonsterling currencies. However, their usual practice is to transact their business with other countries in sterling or in foreign currencies and to sell their excess holdings of nonsterling currencies (above normal working balances) to London banks for sterling. Thus Australian banks ordinarily sell their excess dollars or Belgian francs for sterling and acquire dollars (or Belgian francs) against sterling whenever they need them.

This pooling of foreign currency reserves is perhaps the most significant single characteristic of the sterling area.

Controls over Trade

What and how much residents of each sterling area country may buy from other countries and where they may sell their goods and services are determined by the local exchange and trade control authorities. From the standpoint of the balance of payments, two types of consideration, in general, are involved in controlling imports.[32]

---

32. Commercial and even political interests of particular sterling area countries are reflected in their import policies. For example, certain imports may be prohibited from any country on grounds of protection although this would appear to be a clear violation of the General Agreement on Tariffs and Trade to which most sterling area countries are signatories. An example of special restrictions dictated largely by political factors is provided by India's prohibition against imports from South Africa during 1950 and 1951. The controversy over the exchange rate between the Indian and Pakistani rupees led to severe trade restrictions between these two countries during 1950 and 1951.

First, there is the over-all balance of payments position of the individual sterling area country which governs the degree of its liberality in granting import licenses and exchange permits. The second type of consideration relates to the balance of payments position of the sterling area as a whole vis-à-vis other currency areas. This is the primary responsibility of Britain, as custodian of the reserves of the sterling area; but a high degree of cooperation among all members is required since Britain does not, as a rule, place definite limits on the hard-currency expenditures of other sterling area countries.

Members of the sterling area usually follow Britain's lead in regard to the licensing of payments to hard-currency countries and the degree of hardness of a nonsterling currency during any particular period. For example, before the establishment of the EPU Belgium was treated as a relatively hard-currency country by all members of the sterling area, but after June 1950 Belgium was treated as a soft-currency country, on a par with all other EPU countries. From time to time Argentina is treated as a hard-currency country, depending upon the status of the sterling area's balance of payments position with her. The general import policies of the sterling area countries are determined at the annual Commonwealth Conference of Finance Ministers and through informal agreements from time to time. For example, at the Commonwealth Conference in the fall of 1949 all sterling area members agreed to cut dollar imports by 25 per cent.

Although other sterling area countries were under no obligations to free their trade with OEEC countries in accordance with the rules of the trade liberalization program, most of them followed Britain in expanding the list of commodities for which open general licenses were issued to include all the OEEC countries plus a number of other soft-currency countries from which quota-free imports would be permitted. The degree of liberalization, of course, reflected to some extent the over-all import policy of each sterling area member. Members producing raw materials such as Australia, Ceylon, New Zealand, South Africa and Southern Rhodesia, which had favorable over-all trade positions in 1950 and 1951 tended to adopt relatively liberal policies for imports from soft-currency areas.[33] During 1952,

33. Some sterling area countries have even followed Britain's lead with respect to capital transactions outside the sterling area. For example, India permits the repatriation of capital owned by residents of Scandinavia and has issued a regulation permitting

however, these countries reimposed quotas on a large number of imports from all soft-currency countries, including other members of the sterling area.

Differences in Exchange Control Practices

While the regulations which relate to the acquisition and use of sterling accounts by nonresidents are similar for all sterling area countries, there are marked differences in those governing the acquisition and use of foreign currencies, including sterling itself, by individual sterling area members. We have seen, for example, that Britain imposes no restrictions on payments by her own residents to residents of other sterling area members. A British citizen can write a check on his local bank and send it to anyone in the sterling area to whom he wishes to make payment. This is not true of most other sterling area countries where a license is required to make payments in any currency including sterling, and sterling receipts from some or all transactions must be surrendered to the exchange control authorities.

All sterling area countries require licenses for imports even within the area. However, during 1950 and 1951 most of them permitted a large number of imports from the sterling area and other soft-currency countries under open general license. Foreign exchange is usually granted automatically upon presentation to an authorized bank of an import license and other documents evidencing orders for imports. Payments for invisibles and capital transfers usually require licenses even within the sterling area. Licenses for payments for invisibles within the area are in general granted on a fairly liberal basis by most sterling area members.

Sterling area countries as a rule, require their own residents to surrender the proceeds of all exports, including those to sterling area countries. The United Kingdom, New Zealand, Iraq and South Africa, however, do not require the surrender of sterling currencies. Some sterling area countries permit their citizens to retain sterling receipts from invisibles and capital imports, but their use is usually subject to license.

Most individuals and firms in the independent sterling area are not

the repatriation of capital owned by residents of any currency area which has been brought in after January 1, 1950.

permitted to have their own sterling accounts; instead, they purchase sterling from their local banks and sell sterling receipts to their local banks as in the case of nonsterling exchange. This is no special hardship since it was the usual practice before exchange control was introduced. In general, however, exchange controls over transfers within the sterling area tend to be rather mild and the private trader or investor suffers little interference with his operations. This, of course, is not true with respect to controls over payments outside the sterling area, especially hard-currency areas.

Most sterling area countries have unitary rate systems. However, Iceland has multiple exchange rates and retention quotas. Hong Kong and Jordan also have multiple rates.

Finally, it should be made clear that the sterling area is not a single monetary area without internal exchange controls in the sense that the United States and its possessions or the Belgium-Luxembourg Economic Union is a monetary area. Each independent country has its own exchange control and is responsible for its own balance of payments with the rest of the sterling area. Except for Hong Kong,[34] the United Kingdom together with its colonies, territories and mandates do form a true monetary area even though there are separate local currencies within this group. But there are no exchange controls affecting payments within the area under the sovereignty of the British government.[35] The sterling area is a currency area in the sense that Britain does not restrict sterling transfers within the area, that transfers of sterling to and from nonresidents are regulated in accordance with common rules established by the British authorities, and that there is a pooling of external reserves.[36]

34. Because of the existence of free hard-currency markets in Hong Kong transactions between the residents of Hong Kong and the rest of the sterling area are subject to control.

35. It is recognized, of course, that some of the British territories enjoy a considerable degree of self-government and operate their own import controls but there are no controls on sterling transfers to other parts of the sterling area.

36. The pooling of gold and foreign exchange resources is by no means complete since most independent sterling area countries have reserves of their own.

Chapter 11

AGREEMENTS OF THE UNITED KINGDOM

THE STERLING EXCHANGE system which provides the means of financing a substantial portion of the world's trade is based on many financial agreements and informal understandings between the United Kingdom and other countries. These have grown from economic developments affecting Britain's financial and trade relations with other countries during the war and postwar periods. They have had two principal objectives: (1) to enable Britain to obtain the imports required to maintain her domestic economy; (2) to preserve and extend the use of sterling as an international currency.

This study will divide these agreements into two main categories: (1) financial agreements with sterling area countries; (2) payments agreements with nonsterling countries.[1]

AGREEMENTS WITH STERLING AREA COUNTRIES [2]

The sterling area was not established by formal agreements between Britain and the other independent nations of the area but was the outgrowth of informal understandings and acquiescence in United Kingdom regulations affecting the transferability of sterling balances. In recent years the sterling area has become a somewhat more democratic organization. The meetings of the Commonwealth Finance Ministers have become important in determining the broad policies of the sterling area. In 1947 and 1948 two committees were created to serve as a permanent secretariat for the conferences of the Commonwealth Finance Ministers.

The Sterling Area Statistical Committee, representing the different

---

1. Excellent reviews of Britain's postwar economic relations are given by A. R. Conan, *The Sterling Area*, Macmillan, New York, 1952; and in *The Sterling Area: An American Analysis*, Economic Cooperation Administration, Special Mission to the United Kingdom, London, 1951, and Washington, 1952.

2. British agreements with other sterling area countries which deal with the conditions governing the use of their sterling balances are termed "financial" agreements.

sterling area countries, provides factual information and analyses upon which policy decisions may be based.

The Commonwealth Liaison Committee operates on a policy level and provides a vehicle for the continual exchange of views between member governments. One of its important functions is to deal with issues arising out of the sterling area's relations with the EPU and the OEEC.[3]

Membership in the sterling area has advantages and disadvantages for Britain and for the other independent nation members. All members share in the advantages of a system of multilateral payments based on sterling transfers. This system was maintained throughout the war and early postwar period when most other soft-currency countries financed their trade with one another on a strictly bilateral basis. The relative freedom of capital transfers, particularly from Britain to the rest of the sterling area, also provides certain advantages, but these transfers have resulted in a serious drain on Britain's resources in recent years.

Britain's ability to purchase goods and services from other sterling area members during the war and the first years after its end worked to her advantage, but this was a drain on the other members. The subsequent depreciation of sterling has reduced the real value of the balances accumulated by other sterling members during and following the war. On the other hand, Britain's willingness to free most of these wartime accumulated balances and to convert a considerable portion of them into foreign exchange has hampered her progress toward financial stability.

Finally, the practice of pooling the foreign exchange reserves of the sterling area in London has tended to cut both ways. At times, Britain has had to use part of her own gold and dollar receipts to meet the deficits of the outer sterling area, while some members of this group have cut back their own dollar imports in order to contribute dollars to the London pool.

There are, of course, certain intangible economic and political benefits from the sterling currency ties which help bind together the members of the British Commonwealth. These are difficult to assess but are nevertheless kept in mind by Commonwealth statesmen in making major decisions affecting the sterling area.

3. See *The Sterling Area: An American Analysis*, p. 29.

Bilateral agreements between the United Kingdom and other sterling countries have dealt with the availability of accumulated sterling balances, the availability of dollars from the London pool, and, in the case of South Africa, the sale of gold to the United Kingdom. Before considering these agreements, it is necessary to review briefly the problem of the sterling balances.

THE STERLING BALANCES

The large sterling balances accumulated during the war period created difficulties for the United Kingdom already discussed briefly in this study. The terms "sterling balances" and "sterling liabilities" have been used interchangeably and have been variously defined even by official British publications.[4] Sterling liabilities—what are usually spoken of as sterling balances [5]—are not limited to deposits in British banks. The "sterling liabilities" reported in official British government statistics include long- and short-term U.K. Treasury securities, and certain other British government obligations such as the capital value of annuity payments due India and Pakistan under the pension plan for civil servants, and the liabilities of British banks to overseas banks, governments and private persons.[6] The sterling balances (or liabilities) are owned by foreign private banks, currency boards, treasuries and other foreign governmental organizations as well as

4. For an excellent discussion of sterling balances see H. A. Shannon, "Sterling Balances of the Sterling Area," *Economic Journal,* September 1950, pp. 531–51.

5. *The Economic Survey for 1950* (Cmd. 7915), uses the term "sterling balances" (p. 12) while *The United Kingdom Balance of Payments, 1946 to 1949* (Cmd. 7928) refers to the identical figures as "sterling liabilities" (p. 14).

6. The official definition of British sterling liabilities is as follows: "Sterling liabilities comprise the net liabilities in sterling of banks (including accepting houses and discount houses) in the United Kingdom to their overseas offices and to other account holders abroad, including any British Government securities held for account of banks and funds held as cover for overseas currencies; funds held by the Currency Boards and the Crown Agents for the Colonies; overseas loans to H. M. Government expressed in sterling or sterling area currencies, including the capital value of payments due to India and Pakistan under the Pensions Annuities Schemes of 1948 (£157 million on 30th June, 1951); and, so far as known, U. K. sterling securities held by official bodies but not those held by private individuals or firms. Holdings of Dominion and Colonial sterling securities are excluded." *United Kingdom Balance of Payments, 1948 to 1951,* Cmd. 8379, H.M.S.O., London, October 1951, p. 36.

This definition differs from that given in the 1950 U. K. Balance of Payments White Paper (Cmd. 7928) by the inclusion in the former of funds and investments of the Colonial Marketing Boards. This accounts for a difference of £73 million in the figures for sterling liabilities at the end of 1949 given in the 1950 and 1951 White Papers.

by private persons and nongovernmental institutions holding accounts with British banks. While most of the sterling liabilities are short-term, many take the form of long-term investments in British government securities.[7]

There have been substantial changes in the total volume of sterling balances and in their ownership during the postwar period. At the end of 1947 sterling balances totaled £3,603 million, of which £2,297 million were owned by sterling area countries and £1,306 million by nonsterling area countries. Total balances rose after 1947 to £4,168 million in June 1951, but fell to £3,397 million a year later. Holdings of nonsterling area countries have fallen, however, to £754 million as of December 1952, while those of the dependent overseas territories have doubled since December 1947. (See Table 10.)

TABLE 10

U.K. STERLING LIABILITIES (STERLING BALANCES) TO ALL COUNTRIES, 1947–1952

(*Millions*)

Item	Dec. 31, 1947	June 30, 1951	Dec. 31, 1951	June 30, 1952	Dec. 31, 1952
Total sterling liabilities to all countries	£3,603	£4,168	£3,807	£3,397	£3,422
To nonsterling area countries					
Total	1,306	1,070	1,018	842	754
Dollar area	18	73	38	19	34
Other Western Hemisphere....	235	55	57	8	6
OEEC countries	480	422	409	349	321
Other nonsterling countries...	573	520	514	466	393
To sterling area countries					
Total	2,297	3,098	2,789	2,555	2,668
Dependent overseas territories..	510	908	964	1,024	1,065
Other sterling area countries...	1,787	2,190	1,825	1,531	1,603

Source: United Kingdom Balance of Payments, Cmd. 8379, Cmd. 8505, Cmd. 8666 and Cmd. 8808, H.M.S.O., London.

The Blocked Accounts

During 1946 and 1947, as a part of the preparation for the restoration of sterling convertibility, Britain negotiated agreements with a

7. In 1951 the balances held in the form of time deposits and Treasury bills yielded about 0.5 per cent while those invested in long-term securities provided a higher rate of return. The average cost of the sterling liabilities in 1951 was probably no higher than one per cent. The recent rise in interest rates in Britain will increase the carrying charge of the overseas indebtedness.

number of sterling area and nonsterling area countries to block a portion of their sterling balances accumulated during the war. All future acquisitions of sterling plus releases from blocked accounts were available for current payments. Blocked accounts are designated as No. 2 accounts with the Bank of England, and only No. 1 accounts may be used for current payments. Balances in No. 2 accounts are restricted to investments in certain approved British securities.[8] At the end of 1948 about £1,600 million out of total external sterling holdings of £3,359 million were blocked or restricted.[9]

Most of the blocked balances were held by India, Egypt, Iraq, Pakistan, Argentina and Ceylon. During 1949 the volume of blocked and restricted accounts was reduced to £1,350 million, largely as a result of releases to Argentina, Egypt and India, and the unrestricted accounts rose from £1,750 million to nearly £2,000 million, with about two thirds owned by members of the sterling area (outside Britain) and the remainder by nonsterling area members.

Since 1949 the volume of blocked accounts has been substantially reduced by their transfer to No. 1 accounts. Thus in the fall of 1951 Britain agreed to transfer £310 million of India's No. 2 account to a No. 1 account, these balances to be held as a currency reserve and not to be drawn on except in an emergency. Of the remainder of India's balances, £90 million were already in a No. 1 account and £210 million will be released over a six-year period for the importation of capital goods under the Colombo Plan.[10] A similar agreement was made with Pakistan under which £30 million was released from the No. 2 account for her currency reserve, and another £24 million to be released over the next six years.[11]

Britain's second largest sterling holder, Egypt, had about £290 million as of April 1951. Of this, £230 million was in a No. 2 account. In 1951 Britain reached an agreement with Egypt whereby £150 million of the No. 2 account balances would be released over the next ten to thirteen years. Agreements for periodic releases of the

8. Portions of the No. 1 accounts of some countries have been restricted by special agreements to the effect that they will not be utilized without consultation.

9. *Economic Survey for 1950,* Cmd. 7915, H.M.S.O., London, 1950, p. 12.

10. *The Banker,* November 1951, p. 386. India's sterling balances were reported to have fallen to £540 million by July 1952. *The Financial Times,* July 17, 1952.

11. *The Banker,* September 1951, p. 193. Pakistan was also permitted to purchase £4 million in gold for her currency reserve. Ceylon's remaining blocked sterling balances were released in October 1952. (*The Statist,* November 1, 1952, pp. 526–27.)

No. 2 accounts of Iraq and Ceylon have also been reached. Except for balances held by Iran, blocked as a result of the oil controversy, most of the other blocked balances have been released.

Under the terms of these agreements the volume of the No. 2 accounts will decline rapidly and it is expected that in the next five years they will virtually be eliminated. This does not indicate a rapid solution of Britain's sterling balance problem. Sterling liabilities to other countries were only £181 million lower in December 1952 than they were at the end of 1947.[12] Most of the £3,422 million in sterling balances are in No. 1 accounts and therefore to a large degree available for current payments to any countries except those in the dollar area.[13] The large holdings of Australia, Ireland, New Zealand and the colonial territories and dependencies have never been blocked, and it is these which have had the greatest growth in the past few years. These large demand liabilities constitute a continual threat to Britain's balance of payments position, and a major barrier to any attempt to restore sterling convertibility into dollars. (See Part IV of this book.)

Members of the sterling area are free to use their No. 1 balances for any purpose anywhere in the area. They may also be used for making current payments to all the countries with which Britain has payments arrangements, including the EPU countries. The use of sterling balances by sterling area members to make purchases in the dollar area is not formally restricted by the British Treasury; the only limitations are those of the exchange control authorities of the individual sterling area countries. Until 1949 certain members including Ireland, India, Iraq, Pakistan and Egypt (which left the sterling area in 1947) were given fixed targets for their net hard-currency expenditures in any given year. Since 1949 dollar expenditures of the sterling area countries have been restricted by informal understandings.

Effects of the Use of Sterling Balances

The British monetary authorities are responsible for maintaining the exchange value of sterling in the official foreign exchange mar-

12. *United Kingdom Balance of Payments, 1949 to 1951,* Cmd. 8808, H.M.S.O., London, 1953.

13. According to *The Financial Times* (July 17, 1952) Australia's holdings were £300 million; New Zealand's, £85 million; South Africa's, £60 million, as of July 1952.

kets and for meeting Britain's obligations under her bilateral payments agreements with nonsterling countries and her membership in the EPU. Thus Britain must consider not only her own balance of payments but also the balance of payments of the sterling area as a whole, in relation to the rest of the world. When other sterling area countries run deficits with the dollar area or with the EPU there is a loss of British gold and dollar reserves, even though Britain herself is in balance with the nonsterling world. Thus during 1952 the United Kingdom experienced a total gold and dollar deficit of $488 million of which $383 million was due to the transactions of the United Kingdom with the dollar area. The other independent sterling area countries had a deficit with the dollar area of $284 million, but this was offset by a dollar surplus of $376 million earned by the dependent overseas territories and by sales of gold to the United Kingdom by the rest of the sterling area amounting to $201 million. Finally, the net gold and dollar payments of the entire sterling area to the nondollar area (including payments to the EPU) reached $399 million, most of which cannot be allocated among sterling area members. (See Table 11).

Since Britain is responsible for maintaining the external position of sterling, the sterling area members tend to pool their gold and foreign exchange reserves in London by selling their receipts of foreign exchange and a portion of their gold output to the Bank of England in exchange for sterling balances. (South Africa has a special relationship to the sterling area discussed later.) The other sterling area countries, however, maintain some gold and dollar reserves of their own; therefore not all the reserves of the sterling area are pooled in London. The gold and dollar reserves of the sterling area as of June 30, 1952 totaled $3,129 million of which $911 million were held outside the United Kingdom. (See Table 12).

Members of the sterling area create a drain on Britain's net foreign exchange and gold reserves when they use their sterling balances to make payments to nonresidents or, alternatively, when they buy nonresident currencies from the Bank of England for making payments outside the area. They make a contribution to Britain's net foreign exchange and gold position when they sell gold or foreign currencies to the Bank of England and when they receive payments

TABLE 11

ANALYSIS OF NET GOLD AND DOLLAR SURPLUS OR DEFICIT OF THE UNITED KINGDOM, 1948–1952

(*Millions of Dollars*)

Item	1948	1949	1950	1951	1952 (Provisional)
Total net gold and dollar surplus or deficit [a]	−1,710	−1,531	805	−1,164	−488
Transactions with the dollar area					
1. United Kingdom:					
Current account					
Imports of goods	1,629	1,604	1,203	2,051	1,667
Imports of services	359	344	255	496	494
Total	1,988	1,948	1,458	2,547	2,161
Exports of goods	761	692	865	1,092	1,138
Services, other credits (net) [b]	161	118	293	250	232
Total	922	810	1,158	1,342	1,370
Balance of current transactions [a]	−1,066	−1,138	−300	−1,205	−791
Other transactions (defense aid, investment, etc.) [a]	−237	17	393	−281	408
Total U.K. surplus or deficit (net)	−1,303	−1,121	93	−1,486	−383
2. Rest of sterling area (R.S.A.) [a] with dollar area:					
a. Dependent overseas territories	164	149	371	462	376
b. Other sterling area countries	−474	−530	62	−197	−284
Gold sales to U.K.	222	234	281	218	201
Total R.S.A. surplus or deficit (net)	−88	−147	714	483	293
Transactions with nondollar areas					
Net gold and dollar receipts from or payments to [a]:					
Other Western Hemisphere	−36	−7	27	−1	58
OEEC countries	−178	−151	−1	−97	−471
Other nonsterling countries	−73	−99	−15	−59	23
Nonterritorial organizations	−32	−6	−13	−4	−9
Total gold and dollar transfers (net) of which:	−319	−263	−2	−161	−399
On U.K. account	31	64	81	c	c
On R.S.A. account	−21	7	−7	c	c
On whole sterling area account	−329	−334	−76	c	c

Sources: United Kingdom Balance of Payments 1948 to 1951, Cmd. 8505; and *United Kingdom Balance of Payments 1949 to 1952*, Cmd. 8666 and Cmd. 8808, H.M.S.O., London.
a. Minus sign (−) indicates debit.
b. Includes overseas transactions of oil companies.
c. Not available.

TABLE 12

GOLD AND SHORT-TERM DOLLAR ASSETS OF STERLING AREA COUNTRIES,
JUNE 30, 1952

(*Millions of Dollars*)

Country	Amount
Iceland	$ 5
India	304
Iraq	13
Ireland	33
New Zealand	38
Pakistan	51
Union of South Africa...	159
United Kingdom	2,218
United Kingdom dependencies..................................	102
Other	206
Total sterling area..	3,129
Sterling area other than United Kingdom.......................	911

Source: *Semiannual Report to the President and to the Congress for the Period April 1–September 30, 1952*, National Advisory Council on International Monetary and Financial Problems, Washington, 1953, Appendix A.

from nonresidents in sterling.[14] Thus in the second half of 1951 the overseas sterling area had a current account deficit with the dollar area of £69 million and a current account deficit with the rest of the world (outside the sterling area and the dollar area) of £162 million. Since a considerable portion of the latter deficit was with the EPU countries, this deficit had to be covered in part with gold and dollars from the British Treasury. These gold and dollar deficits were partly offset, however, by gold sales by sterling area members to Britain amounting to £39 million. On the other hand, during 1950 and the first half of 1951, the overseas sterling area had substantial current account surpluses with both the dollar area and the rest of the world.

The other sterling area members can also create a drain on Britain's resources by running deficits with the United Kingdom, thereby drawing down their sterling balances. For example, in the second half of 1951 the overseas sterling area had a current account deficit of £171 million with the United Kingdom. While this reduced Britain's liabilities to the rest of the sterling area, it meant that Britain had to supply a large volume of exports of goods and services with-

14. The receipt of sterling from a nonresident account reduces the sterling area's liabilities to nonresidents, thereby improving the sterling area's *net* foreign exchange position.

out obtaining an equivalent amount of imports in return.[15] In this sense the deficit of the rest of the sterling area with Britain represented a drain on Britain's resources. Thus the total net drain of the overseas sterling area on Britain's resources was £363 million in the second half of 1951. These various drains on and contributions to the United Kingdom arising from the trade and payments of the overseas sterling area are summarized in Table 13. Britain must finance these

TABLE 13

DRAIN ON UNITED KINGDOM BY OVERSEAS STERLING AREA, 1948–1951

(*Millions of Pounds*)

Item	1948	1949	1950	Jan.–June 1951	July–Dec. 1951	Total 1951
Overseas sterling area's current balance with:						
United Kingdom	−232	−266	−234	− 68	−171	−239
Dollar area	− 77	− 89	+155	+155	− 69	+ 86
Rest of world	+ 76	− 14	+192	+156	−162	− 6
Total	−233	−369	+113	+243	−402	−159
Gold sales to U.K., etc.[a]	+152	+101	+117	+ 47	+ 39	+ 86
Contribution to (+) or drain (−) on U.K.	− 81	−268	+230	+290	−363	− 73

Sources: *The Economist*, April 12, 1952, p. 116, and *United Kingdom Balance of Payments 1948 to 1951*, Cmd. 8505.
a. Includes ERP receipts by Ireland, South African gold loan and sterling area drawings on IMF.

drains by goods and services, by a loss of gold and dollar reserves, or by an increase in sterling liabilities to countries outside the sterling area.

Special Arrangements with the Union of South Africa [16]

The Union of South Africa is frequently spoken of as a country half in and half out of the sterling area. The reason for this situation is the fact that South Africa's principal export, gold, as well as other mineral exports have a ready market in the dollar area. Were it not for South Africa's traditional relations with Britain and the sterling area, she would probably be a hard-currency country. Throughout

15. Such exports are frequently called "unrequited" exports.
16. For a more complete discussion of South Africa's relations with the sterling area see N. N. Franklin, "South Africa's Balance of Payments and the Sterling Area," *The Economic Journal*, June 1951, pp. 290–309.

the war South Africa continued her traditional practice of selling gold to the United Kingdom in exchange for sterling balances. South Africa obtained the dollars and other hard currencies she needed from the London pool but until 1946 her drawings were small compared with her gold exports to Britain. After the war South Africa began to sell a portion of her gold output directly for dollars and at the same time to draw heavily upon the London dollar pool so that in 1946–1947 she became a net user of the sterling area's gold and dollar resources.

Early in 1948 Britain and South Africa reached an agreement whereby South Africa loaned Britain £80 million in gold repayable in three years in gold to the extent necessary to prevent the gold holdings of South Africa from falling below £100 million, and the remainder in sterling. In addition, South Africa agreed to sell gold to the Bank of England against sterling in amounts equal to South Africa's net sterling payments to residents outside the sterling area. This arrangement worked out quite well for Britain since from January 1, 1948 to March 31, 1950 Britain was able to repay the entire loan in sterling.[17] In addition, South African gold sales to Britain during the period totaled £278 million. Not all this represented a net contribution to Britain's gold and dollar reserves, however, since South Africa's purchases outside the sterling area resulted in some drain on British reserves.

In January 1950 a new arrangement was announced whereby South Africa would pay in gold for all imports of essential goods whether from the sterling or the dollar area, while other imports from soft-currency countries would be purchased with sterling or other soft currencies obtained through London. The agreement also provided that South Africa would sell to Britain at least 25 per cent of her gold exports, the total amount of gold sales to Britain depending upon South Africa's imports of essential commodities from soft-currency countries. This arrangement involved the issuance of universal licenses by South Africa for imports listed as essential, but import licenses for nonessentials have been issued on a basis which discriminated heavily against the dollar area.[18]

Since South Africa has been able to sell her exports at good prices

17. N. N. Franklin, *loc. cit.*, pp. 306–08.
18. See "Agreement with South Africa," *The Banker*, March 1950, pp. 182–88.

in the dollar area, what are the advantages of this "half in and half out" of the sterling area? The main one appears to be that South Africa has been heavily dependent upon Britain for capital imports. If South Africa were not in the sterling area, Britain might be inclined to shut off capital exports from the sterling area to South Africa since they would cost her gold. In addition, South Africans undoubtedly consider the soft-currency markets more reliable in time of a U.S. depression. On the other hand, it might be argued that if South Africa were to become a dollar area country and to trade entirely on a dollar basis her bargaining position for nonessentials as well as essentials might be considerably greater.

There also are two sides to this question from the standpoint of what Britain gains from this arrangement with South Africa. On the one hand, Britain receives gold for essential goods sold to South Africa coming from any soft-currency country including the EPU countries. On the other hand, the large capital exports to South Africa represent a drain on the British economy which she may not be able to afford. There are, of course, larger issues including the political and economic advantages of having a strong-currency country like South Africa in the sterling area.

BRITISH PAYMENTS AGREEMENTS WITH NONSTERLING COUNTRIES

In general, sterling area members do not conclude separate payments agreements with nonsterling countries, but conduct their trade in accordance with British payments agreements negotiated on behalf of the sterling area as a whole. There are, however, two important exceptions to this rule, namely, the India–Egypt and the Pakistan–France payments agreements of 1953. These agreements provide for payments arrangements outside of the British payments agreements with Egypt and France. British bilateral payments agreements and arrangements, which establish the conditions for financing transactions between the sterling area and practically every country in the world outside the dollar area, may be divided into five types:

1. *Sterling payments agreements* which provide for payments to and from the sterling area to be made in sterling only, with no automatic transferability between the accounts of residents of the agreement country and third countries.[19]

19. Britain, of course, is always willing to accept dollars or American account sterling

2. *Sterling payments agreements* which provide for payments in sterling only, but which permit transfers to and from transferable sterling accounts for financing direct current transactions between the agreement country and certain other nonsterling countries which are permitted to maintain transferable accounts.

3. *Monetary agreements* which provide for payments to be made in either sterling or the currency of the agreement country, with no provision for automatic transferability between the accounts of residents of the agreement country and third countries.

4. *Monetary agreements* which provide for payments in either sterling or the currency of the agreement country, and permit transfers to and from the transferable sterling accounts held by certain other countries to finance direct current transactions.

5. Special arrangements with a group of *unclassified countries* which provide for payments to and from the sterling area to be made solely in sterling and, in addition, permit automatic transfers between the sterling accounts of members of the unclassified group to finance direct current transactions. Automatic transfers from transferable accounts to the accounts of residents of unclassified countries are also allowed.[20]

Where automatic transferability is permitted, transfers are effected by authorized banks in the United Kingdom on request of the owners of the accounts, under the regulations governing the transaction. In other cases, requests for transfers for each category must be referred to the Bank of England. Unlike some bilateral agreements, transactions under British agreements are not limited to a specific list of items for which payments may be made. Transfers from resident to nonresident accounts require licenses and certain types of transactions such as capital transfers are not ordinarily licensed.

Gold Clauses

Some of the early postwar bilateral agreements included a provision whereby Britain would be required to pay in gold or acceptable

---

from any country and will credit transfers of American account sterling from residents of the dollar area to the residents of any nonsterling country.

20. For a more complete description of the conditions governing the use of different types of sterling accounts see *Digest of the United Kingdom Exchange Regulations,* 10th edition, District Bank Limited, London, April 1953. The texts of a typical *sterling payments agreement* and of a typical *monetary agreement* are given in Appendixes 1 and 2.

third currencies whenever the sterling holdings of the partner country reached a certain amount. Conversely, in the case of two-currency agreements, Britain would receive gold whenever her holdings of the partner country's currency reached the maximum swing credit established by the agreement. Since the inauguration of the EPU, British bilateral agreements providing for a gold conversion clause—for example, the agreements with Belgium, Portugal and Switzerland—were revised to eliminate the gold clause since monthly clearings are made through the EPU.

Under Britain's agreement with Iran (September 1947) the Bank of England approved transfers of sterling to American accounts for current payments for essential goods which could not be obtained on equivalent terms with sterling. This special treatment stemmed from the fact that Britain paid oil royalties to Iran in sterling, but petroleum is a commodity which can be sold readily on world markets for dollars.[21] This arrangement has not been in operation since Iran nationalized the properties of the Anglo-Iranian Oil Company in 1951.

Britain's two-currency (monetary) agreements contain a fixed rate between sterling and the currency of the partner country, usually based on the gold parities established with the Monetary Fund. Sterling payments agreements, calling for payments only in sterling, require no special provisions as to the rate of exchange, except that the agreements require that the rates on sterling in the partner country reflect the official sterling-dollar cross-rates. As was pointed out in Chapter 9, however, this provision is frequently violated by the partner countries. In general, Britain has sought to avoid giving other countries a guarantee against depreciation of sterling in terms of gold. Of the published agreements only four—those with Argentina, Brazil, Iran and Peru—bear a gold-value guarantee.[22]

Most of Britain's bilateral payments agreements specify payments between the partner country and the sterling area solely in sterling. Dual currency or monetary agreements exist only with Belgium,

21. While most of British-produced oil is sold for sterling, a portion of it is sold for dollars. Moreover, since oil has tended to be in short supply from time to time in the postwar period, oil is a dollar-saving as well as a dollar-earning item for the sterling area.

22. All member countries are required to maintain the gold value of their currencies held by the Monetary Fund.

France, Portugal, Switzerland, Western Germany, the Netherlands, Norway, Sweden and Denmark. All these countries are members of the EPU and the last five are also members of the transferable account system. Of the remaining countries with which Britain has bilateral payments agreements, about half are members of the transferable account system and the remainder are bilateral account countries.

The Transferability of Sterling

British bilateral payments agreements generally state that Britain will not restrict the availability of sterling accounts owned by the partner country for making payments to other residents of the same currency area, to residents of the Scheduled Territories or for payments in respect of *direct current* transactions to residents outside the partner country and the Scheduled Territories "as may be agreed between the contracting governments." (See Appendixes 1 and 2.) There is a similar undertaking on the part of the government of the partner country not to restrict the acceptance by residents of that country of sterling from residents of the sterling area and of residents of such countries outside the partner country and the sterling area as may be agreed between the two countries.[23] While these clauses have been included in agreements with both bilateral and transferable account countries, in the case of the second group, *automatic* transferability of sterling for payments arising out of direct current transactions is accorded by Britain between that country and all other countries with transferable accounts. Transfers of sterling between the bilateral accounts of two different countries or between bilateral account and transferable account countries are frequently permitted by agreement between Britain and the two countries concerned, but the transferability in this case is *administrative* and not *automatic*. It may be noted that some agreements specifically exclude the use of sterling in payment for certain exports. For example, there are exceptions to the undertaking to accept sterling payments in Britain's bilateral agreement with Chile because that country requires dollars in payment for copper and some other exports.[24]

23. See H. A. Shannon, "The British Payments and Exchange Control System," *Quarterly Journal of Economics,* May 1949, pp. 212–37.

24. See the Annexes to the *Payments Agreement between the Governments of the United Kingdom and of the Republic of Chile,* June 1948, Cmd. 7497, H.M.S.O., London.

British exchange regulations provide for the opening of transferable accounts only in the name of banks resident in the transferable account countries. The sterling accounts of individuals and non-banking organizations must be held in bilateral accounts. However, bilateral and transferable accounts of residents of the same country are automatically transferable. The reason lies in the obligations of a country which is granted transferable account status. The exchange control authorities of such country must agree to supervise its transferable accounts so that payments will be limited to the financing of direct current transactions between the countries whose sterling accounts are involved. The purpose is to prevent the use of transferable accounts to finance trade with third countries outside the transferable account group. For example, the sterling area would lose dollars if the Netherlands used sterling to finance the shipment of Australian wool to the United States. Further, the British do not want transferable account countries to sell their excess sterling to another transferable account country for gold or dollars, perhaps at a discount. Countries having a deficit in sterling are expected to buy sterling with gold or dollars from the Bank of England at the official rate.[25]

Acceptance of Sterling

Transferable account countries undertake to accept sterling without limit from the sterling area and from other transferable account countries.[26] Before the EPU, this meant that transferable account countries had to be fairly in balance with the sterling area and the rest of the transferable account group; at least, they should not have a large continual sterling surplus. When the transferable account system was established early in 1947, Britain had arranged for the resumption of the convertibility of sterling acquired in current trans-

25. Egypt is reported to have sold sterling to the USSR, another transferable account country, for gold, when the latter was short of sterling. It should be pointed out that violations of these agreements are widespread and countries short of sterling frequently acquire sterling from other countries by purchase with gold or dollars at a discount.

26. While the officials of the Bank of England claim that the acceptance of sterling from other transferable accounts is a firm obligation of members of the system, this obligation is frequently superseded by special agreements between individual transferable account countries and in fact such transfers appear to be subject to administrative decision by the countries concerned.

actions. When convertibility had to be abandoned, some of the original members of the system, e.g., Belgium, dropped out because they did not want to undertake an indefinite accumulation of sterling. After the organization of the EPU, Britain offered transferable account status to all members not already in the system, but only Austria, Denmark, Greece and Western Germany have accepted the invitation. Presumably other countries—Belgium among them—refused to join because they did not want to incur an unlimited obligation to accept sterling.

Under an agreement of May 18, 1953, three EPU members of the bilateral account group—France, Belgium and Switzerland—were permitted to transfer sterling without restriction among themselves and to the Netherlands, Denmark, Germany and Sweden. In practice, there are virtually no restrictions on sterling transfers for financing current account transactions within the EPU area. Even non-members find little difficulty in getting rid of their surplus sterling by using it to buy imports from other transferable account members of the EPU.

According to the EPU rules, a member can hold in sterling that part of its EPU surplus which corresponds to its surplus with the sterling area. Also, holders of sterling balances that have a deficit with the EPU may settle it with sterling.[27] The EPU therefore preserves the workings of the transferable account system so far as its members are concerned.

There is considerable evidence that Britain wants to expand the transferable account system and encourage a greater use of sterling as the means of settlement between nondollar countries. Britain has also permitted administrative transferability to and from bilateral accounts and other nonresident accounts when these would not lead to a drain on British gold and dollar reserves. Britain's sterling payments agreement with Japan[28] provides for a wide measure of administrative transferability including a blanket authorization to pay sterling to transferable account countries and to the "unclassified group." However, Japan has not obligated herself to accept sterling

27. See Albert O. Hirschman, "The European Payments Union," *Review of Economics and Statistics,* February 1951, pp. 51–52.

28. Cmd. 8376, H.M.S.O., London, August 31, 1951 (see Appendix 1); see also "Payments Agreement with Japan," *The Economist,* September 8, 1951, p. 577.

from countries outside the sterling area, nor have the transferable account countries undertaken to accept sterling from Japan.

So long as sterling is not freely convertible into dollars, bilateral agreement countries will be reluctant to accept it in payment from countries outside the sterling area unless they are in approximate balance in sterling or have a deficit with the sterling area. Britain's ability to expand the use of sterling as a world trading medium will therefore depend upon the strength of the pound and the maintenance of a position of balance or of surplus for the sterling area.

MULTILATERAL SETTLEMENTS THROUGH STERLING

The network of British payments agreements and the provisions for sterling transferability afford an opportunity for multilateral settlements over a large area. Commerce among the sterling area countries alone constitutes over 12 per cent of the world's total. Trade among the EPU countries and their associated currency areas accounts for about 40 per cent of the world's merchandise trade. In addition, sterling is automatically transferable between non-EPU countries which are members of the transferable account system. While by no means all the trade between transferable account countries is conducted through sterling, substantial use is made of these facilities by Egypt, the Netherlands monetary area, the Italian monetary area, the Scandinavian countries and Thailand.

Finally, Britain has encouraged administrative transferability to and from bilateral accounts wherever these will not lead directly or indirectly to a drain on her reserves. Together, the sterling system and the EPU provide an opportunity for multilateral settlements covering well over half the world's trade. These facilities are not, however, fully utilized. In 1951 automatic sterling transfers totaled £241 million while £222 million were transferred on an administrative basis. Sterling transfers between nonsterling countries totaled £379 million in 1952. (See Table 14.)

TRADE AGREEMENTS

As a rule, British payments agreements do not deal with the composition of trade, including import and export quotas. Britain and the other independent sterling area countries tend to negotiate sepa-

TABLE 14

STERLING TRANSFERS BETWEEN NONSTERLING AREA COUNTRIES, 1950–1952

(*Millions of Pounds Sterling*)

Item	1950	1951	1952
Total	£298	£463	£379
Automatic facilities	143	241	209
Administrative facilities	155	222	170
Between OEEC countries......................	78	112	78
OEEC countries to other countries outside the sterling area	59	82	63
By other countries outside the sterling area to OEEC countries	99	179	168

Source: *Bank of England Report for the Year Ended February 28, 1953.*

rate bilateral trade quota agreements.[29] Britain, generally speaking, does not negotiate trade quota agreements with members of the sterling area but there are several such agreements between other sterling area members. For example, India has trade agreements with Australia, Ceylon, Iraq and Pakistan. Most of these agreements emphasize the supplying of essential foodstuffs and other materials rather than the granting of licenses for imports.

During 1950 and 1951 most imports of sterling area countries from the rest of the area were on open general license either with respect to the sterling area alone, or a larger group of soft-currency countries. The tendency for all sterling area countries to place a major part of their imports from OEEC countries on open general license reduced the scope of bilateral trade-quota agreements with members of the soft-currency group. The heavy trade deficits of Britain, Australia, South Africa and certain other sterling area countries in 1951–1952 led them to place quota restrictions on a number of imports from all countries, including the sterling area.[30] In general, these cuts were nondiscriminatory as between other soft-currency countries, that is, global quotas for the soft-currency group rather than bilateral quotas were employed.

A number of British trade agreements with OEEC and other non-dollar countries deal with commitments of both parties to export goods in scarce supply rather than with the granting of individual

29. The over-all sterling area trade quota agreement with Japan is an exception to this rule.
30. Britain does not impose restrictions on imports from the sterling area.

country import licenses. For example the Sweden-United Kingdom trade agreement of December 1951 provides for the deliveries of iron ore and other essential commodities to Britain and deliveries of coal, coke and steel to Sweden.[31] The United Kingdom-Spain agreement, also negotiated at the end of 1951, provides for the delivery of Spanish pyrites, iron ore and wolfram against British coal, steel and other essential materials.[32] These agreements to supply scarce materials usually are in the form of firm commitments based on the allocating authority of the governments over essential materials. Britain also has a number of bulk purchase agreements covering imports of butter and bacon and many other foodstuffs and raw materials. Finally, British and other sterling area trade with the Eastern European countries tends to be governed by barter agreements covering both quantities and prices of goods and providing for an approximate balance of trade.

31. *Board of Trade Journal*, November 29, 1951.
32. *Ibid.* The improvement in world supplies of materials has resulted in a reduction in agreements of this type.

Chapter 12

FOREIGN EXCHANGE PRACTICES AND
POLICIES IN WESTERN EUROPE

THE EXCHANGE CONTROL systems of Western (continental) Europe are far from uniform either in degree of restrictiveness or administrative arrangements. It is nevertheless convenient to study them together because of the wide area of similarity and also the special payments arrangements which link these systems together. All these countries except Spain are members of the EPU and they include all the EPU nations except the two sterling area countries (the United Kingdom and Iceland).[1]

All Western European countries maintain exchange controls and, except Switzerland, all have restrictions on dollar payments. However, the degree of restrictiveness varies considerably depending on each country's foreign exchange position. For example, restrictions against dollar imports in Belgium tend to be somewhat less severe than those maintained by most other Western European countries. The degree of restriction against imports from soft-currency countries generally changes with shifts in each country's position with the EPU. Thus during 1951 and 1952 Italy liberalized almost 100 per cent of her private imports from the EPU area while maintaining severe restrictions on dollar imports. Britain and France greatly liberalized their imports from the EPU area in 1951 but the next year they placed restrictions on a number of imports from EPU countries.

All the Western European countries except Switzerland have had large dollar deficits during the postwar period and most of them have received substantial U.S. financial assistance. Generally speaking, the dollar deficits of the countries directly engaged in World War II have been larger than those of neutrals. But even countries whose economies did not suffer wartime destruction have had severe balance-of-payments maladjustments.

1. Although Turkey is in Asia Minor it will be included here.

Before the war the tendency in Western Europe was to have deficits with the United States which were covered by surpluses with Britain and the underdeveloped countries of Asia and Africa. Following World War II, Western European countries found it necessary to increase imports from the Western Hemisphere (partly because goods from Eastern Europe and from the underdeveloped areas were unavailable) while at the same time they were unable to convert their sterling and other soft-currency surpluses into dollars. Western Europe has made substantial progress in expanding production even above prewar levels, but has not succeeded in eliminating the structural maladjustments in trade between these countries and the dollar area.

In 1947 the continental OEEC countries (excluding Switzerland) had a current account deficit with the United States and Canada of $4,264 million. As economic recovery progressed the dollar deficits decreased rapidly until by 1950 the current account deficit of these countries with the entire dollar area had declined to $1,427 million. Although all these countries had current account deficits with the dollar area for the period 1950 to mid-1952, several have been able to accumulate gold and dollar balances as a result of receipts of U.S. aid and settlements.

During the early postwar years the over-all current account deficits of the continental OEEC countries tended to be larger than their dollar deficits. Thus in 1947 their combined over-all current account deficits were $5,441 million as against a dollar deficit of $4,264 million. In 1951, however, the over-all deficit was only half the dollar deficit. In that year Belgium-Luxembourg, Western Germany, Norway and Sweden had over-all surpluses on current account and in the first half of 1952 the Netherlands achieved an over-all surplus. (See Table 15.) However these over-all surpluses often are at the expense of deficits of other Western European countries or of the sterling area, rather than with the dollar area or other non-EPU trading areas. Thus the over-all deficits of some Western European countries tend to drain off exports of others which ought to be directed toward the dollar area. High prices, liberal importing policies and protected markets for the exports of EPU countries in Western Europe and in other soft-currency countries have undoubtedly contributed to Western Europe's deficit with the dollar area.

TABLE 15

CURRENT ACCOUNT BALANCES a OF CONTINENTAL OEEC COUNTRIES, b OVER-ALL AND WITH THE DOLLAR AREA, 1947–1952

(Millions of Dollars)

Country	1947 Over-all Balance	1947 U.S. and Canada	1948 Over-all Balance	1948 U.S. and Canada	1949 Over-all Balance	1949 U.S. and Canada	1950 Over-all Balance	1950 Dollar Balance	1951 Over-all Balance	1951 Dollar Balance	First Half, 1952 Over-all Balance	First Half, 1952 Dollar Balance
Total, continental OEEC	−5,441	−4,264	−4,258	−3,522	−2,355	−2,918	−1,872	−1,427	−922	−1,829	−99	−709
Austria	−224	−176	−256	−217	−285	−164	−128	−91 d	−174	−107 d	−63	−33 d
Belgium-Luxembourg	−373	−493	−111	−246	98	−273	−242	−219	226	−283	151	−125
Denmark	−63	−88	−69	−54	−46	−91	−100	−41	−13	−50	−5	−26
France c	[−1,833]	−1,191	[−1,680]	−1,067	[−269]	−724	10	−303	−733	−395	−290	−63
Western Germany	[−527]	−620	[−875]	−787	−1,030	−745	618	−266	161	−375	238	−147
Greece	−276	−24	−186	−110	−257	−91	−321	−143	−269	−129	−96	−45
Italy	−770	−626	−238	−427	−176	−450	−10	−203	−160	−303	[−162]e	−135
Netherlands	−627	−388	−363	−415	−98	−196	−278	−113	−32	−172	125	−83
Norway	−229	−155	−183	−76	−240	−63	−121	−6	−7	−4	35	−6
Portugal	−67	−102	[−100]	−70	[−93]	−42	−36	−12	17	4	−35	−1
Sweden	−430	−371	−115	−122	118	−38	34	2	176	−28	15	−42
Turkey	−22	−30	−82	−31	−77	−41	−62	−32	−114	13	−12	−3
Rest of French franc area							−248	−100 f	−325	−129 f	−216	−104 f

Sources: Economic Progress and Problems of Western Europe (Third Annual Report of the OEEC), Organisation for European Economic Co-operation, Paris, June 1951, pp. 119 and 124; *Europe, the Way Ahead* (Fourth Annual Report of the OEEC), Organisation for European Economic Co-operation, Paris, December 1952, pp. 44 and 55.

a. Includes goods and services and current transfers. Figures in brackets estimated.
b. Excludes Switzerland.
c. Data for France include an estimate of the balance of payments of France with her overseas territories.
d. Calculated on the basis of foreign exchange statistics for all gold and dollar payments.
e. Provisional: based on foreign exchange control figures not strictly comparable with totals for earlier years.
f. Net balance in gold and dollars on current and capital items settled by France on account of associated areas.

Major Policies

In spite of differences in their economic and financial positions the Western European countries have certain trade and exchange control policies in common. The most important single policy is that of discriminating against dollar imports and against imports from certain countries with which trade deficits above a fixed amount must be settled in dollars. This discrimination is motivated not only by the relative scarcity of dollars as against other currencies, but also by the desire on the part of countries with large surpluses with the EPU— e.g., Belgium—to reduce those surpluses by importing as much as possible from the other EPU countries.[2] Countries with large EPU surpluses have sought to increase their imports from other EPU countries; they have gone further and tried to discourage exports to these countries by special taxes, by blocking export proceeds and by prohibiting the re-export of hard-currency goods.

Western European countries have relied mainly on quantitative controls for adjusting their balance of payments, but during the past two years there has been an increasing tendency to employ indirect measures to reduce the demand for imports. Thus a number of these countries, reversing their cheap money policies of the early postwar period, have raised central bank discount rates, increased bank reserve requirements or applied other measures to restrict credit. While taxation has been quite heavy in most Western European countries and the rearmament effort has complicated any attempt to reduce governmental expenditures, some countries have been able to lessen inflationary pressures through fiscal measures, with a view to improving their balance of payments position.

With the exception of Spain, none of the Western European countries employs explicit multiple exchange rates for current transactions nor have any of the EPU countries sought to achieve balance of payments equilibrium through the use of a floating exchange rate system. During the past three years, however, many Western European countries have adopted special measures to expand their exports to the dollar area. The most important of these devices is the retention quota system, employed by the Netherlands, France, Germany,

2. There is considerable evidence that in the fall of 1951 other OEEC countries put pressure on Belgium to tighten up her restrictions against dollar goods.

Greece, Turkey, Spain, Austria and Denmark.[3] These arrangements give rise to implicit discriminatory exchange rates and their widespread use in Western Europe has undermined somewhat the official exchange parities of the currencies. Export subsidies, government-sponsored commercial switch deals, and secret multiple export rates often concealed in barter deals are also employed to expand dollar earnings.

Administrative Practices

The administration of the exchange controls and the methods of making and receiving payment in Western European countries conform in general to the practices outlined in Chapters 4 and 5. In considerable measure the administration of exchange regulations is delegated to the authorized banks. Banks make foreign exchange available or make transfers from resident to nonresident accounts under regulations established by the exchange control authorities. In most Western European countries, buying and selling rates for dollars are set by the central bank or other governmental authority. In France and Italy there are controlled free markets for dollars but the exchange rates are usually maintained within narrow limits by stabilization operations of the central banks. In Belgium and the Netherlands authorized banks are permitted to trade in dollars at rates determined by demand and supply, within a narrow range above and below the official parities. However, only authorized banks are permitted to engage in such transactions. As was pointed out in Chapter 8, the major EPU countries have instituted a system whereby authorized banks may buy and sell the currencies of other members and may operate in the markets of the other members as well as their own.

The currencies which may be used in financing international trade are determined by the bilateral payments agreements and each Western European country has a payments agreement with nearly every country or currency area in the world outside the dollar area. From the standpoint of the currencies employed, the countries of Western Europe may be divided into three groups: (1) countries whose agreements almost always provide that the home currency shall be one of

3. Several of these countries have recently announced their intention to eliminate retention quotas.

the units of account or the sole unit—Belgium, France, the Netherlands, Portugal, Switzerland and the three Scandinavian countries; (2) countries whose payments agreements almost never provide for payments in the home currency—Austria, Greece, Turkey and Spain; (3) Italy and Western Germany, which have both types of agreements.

The currencies most widely used in international settlements are the Belgian and French francs, the Dutch guilder, the Portuguese escudo and the Swiss franc. The first four named are employed as the means of payments within a currency area which includes other countries and dependencies as well as in trade between the currency area and other countries with which payments agreements exist. None of the Western European currencies is widely used as a medium of multilateral settlements between currency areas outside the EPU group. Unlike Britain, these countries have not developed a system of transferable accounts between which balances can be transferred automatically (except between EPU countries) nor have they encouraged transferability on an administrative basis.

Trade with the dollar area is conducted chiefly in dollars. Although some Western European countries—including France, Belgium, the Netherlands and Sweden—have American accounts similar to American account sterling, these are not used to any large extent in trade with the dollar area. Swiss francs outside the accounts established under bilateral payments agreements are, however, freely convertible into dollars and Swiss exports to the dollar area are frequently invoiced in this currency. Both gold and dollars are used as a medium of multilateral settlements through the EPU and between Western European countries and other countries with whom they have payments agreements.

The nonsterling area OEEC members, as was pointed out in Chapter 11, finance a portion of their current trade among themselves and with countries outside the sterling area in sterling. A substantial proportion of Western Europe's direct trade with the sterling area is also financed with sterling. Even though half the OEEC countries (Belgium, France, the Netherlands, Portugal, Switzerland and Scandinavia) have two-currency payments agreements with Britain, traditional trade practices rather favor the use of sterling in trade between sterling area and nondollar countries.[4]

A certain amount of Western European trade is conducted under state barter or private compensation arrangements. Since the EPU was established this type of trade within the OEEC countries has virtually disappeared. However, official barter trade is conducted with Eastern Europe, and certain countries—notably Greece, Turkey and Austria, among others—permit private compensation with countries with whom there are no payments agreements.

INDIVIDUAL WESTERN EUROPEAN COUNTRIES

The discussion of individual Western European countries will not attempt to provide a comprehensive review of the exchange system of each. Rather, these will be brief case studies of selected exchange practices and policies and the conditions leading to their adoption.

THE BELGIUM-LUXEMBOURG ECONOMIC UNION (B.L.E.U.)[5]

The special characteristics of the B.L.E.U. exchange and trade control system have been largely a response to the problems created by Belgium's strong creditor position in the EPU. During the period 1949–1952 as a whole, Belgium-Luxembourg was in approximate balance on current account. In 1949 Belgium-Luxembourg had a current account surplus of $98 million, followed by a deficit of $242 million in 1950, a surplus of $226 million in 1951 and of $172 million in 1952.[6] While the Union has had sizable trade deficits with the United States and Canada during the postwar period, these have been covered by gold payments from soft-currency countries including the EPU, by U.S. loans and conditional aid, and by credits from the International Bank and the Monetary Fund. The Union's ability to cover its trade deficits with the dollar area is indicated by the fact that in June 1947 its gold and short-term dollar holdings were $831

---

4. In 1948 continental OEEC countries used sterling to the extent of £1,200 million in their trade with the sterling area. ("Sterling and European Payments," *The Economist,* March 18, 1950, p. 607.)

5. The B.L.E.U. constitutes a single exchange control territory with a customs union and a coordinated system of import and export controls.

6. The surplus for 1952 from *International Financial News Survey,* October 1953. Unless otherwise noted balance of payments estimates for the Western European countries are taken from OEEC estimates summarized in Table 15.

million while by June 1952 they had risen to $969 million.[7] Moreover, until the fall of 1951 the Union maintained relatively few restrictions on dollar imports.

The B.L.E.U.'s strong position among the countries of Western Europe and her comparatively favorable dollar position during the postwar period resulted from a combination of circumstances, among them:

1. The comparatively mild war damage and the consequent rapid recovery of the Union's industry.

2. A large capacity for the output of steel and other capital goods together with raw materials produced in the colonies, for which there have been sellers' markets during the postwar period.

3. The relatively low demand for imports, to a considerable degree the result of the strict monetary and credit control measures imposed by the Belgium-Luxembourg monetary authorities.

4. The relatively favorable terms of trade, largely a consequence of the strong bargaining power of the Union in her trade with other countries.

In the prewar period the B.L.E.U. normally had a deficit with the dollar area and a surplus with Europe. Since the war both the surplus with Western Europe and the deficit with the dollar area have been enlarged by (1) the inability of the Union to satisfy her import requirements from the EPU countries; (2) a combination of factors which have stimulated the Union's exports to the EPU countries. Among these factors have been the higher prices in soft-currency markets; the high level of demand for imports by, and the liberalization of trade among, the EPU countries; and the large volume of grants and credits made available to the OEEC countries by B.L.E.U., which were matched in part by U.S. grants and credits to the B.L.E.U.

Until September 1951 Belgium maintained relatively mild restrictions against dollar imports and in 1950 and 1951 the Belgian franc was practically a hard currency, on a par with the free Swiss franc and the dollar. In fact between November 1949 and September 1951 there were free exchange dealings between Belgium and Switzerland, so that it was relatively easy for Western Europeans who had acquired

7. *Semiannual Report to the President and to the Congress for the Period April 1– September 30, 1952,* National Advisory Council on International Monetary and Financial Problems, Washington, 1953, p. 38, Appendix A.

Belgian francs to convert them into Swiss francs and thence into dollars.[8] Between September 1944 and October 1951 the B.L.E.U. received grants and credits from other countries and international institutions totaling 43.6 billion Belgian francs and during the same period B.L.E.U. extended grants and credits to other countries totaling 47 billion francs.[9] Most of the grants and credits extended to Belgium which included ECA conditional grants and loans and Export-Import Bank credits were in dollars, while Belgium extended most of her grants and credits to Western European countries for settling the surplus of the B.L.E.U. with Western Europe and the sterling area. To September 1951 the B.L.E.U. was able to satisfy the demands of her residents for dollar goods with relatively few restrictions.

During 1951 the Union's surplus with the EPU area continued to rise while her dollar deficit increased. The growing dollar deficit was due in part to the inflationary pressures generated by the soft-currency surplus and the rise in the prices of dollar imports. Further, ECA grants and credits were reduced so sharply in 1951 that the Union was unable to cover her surpluses in this manner. In 1951 the B.L.E.U. reversed its liberal exchange policies and adopted a number of measures designed to reduce both the dollar deficit and the EPU surplus.

Measures for Reducing the EPU Surplus

The cumulative net surplus of the B.L.E.U. with the EPU reached $789 million by June 30, 1952. While $365 million of this had been covered by gold payments to the B.L.E.U., $424 million represented credits granted by Belgium.[10] Because of its inflationary impact on the Belgian and Luxembourg economies and because further surpluses threaten the existence of the EPU, the Union has been anxious to reduce this surplus. About 90 per cent of the imports on private

8. Belgian banknotes imported into Belgium by residents of other countries, including the United States, could be credited to a banknote account in the name of the foreign resident. These accounts were available for current or capital transactions with Belgium and were convertible into dollars or Swiss francs. Residents of the Union could take with them up to Bfr. 10,000 when leaving the country and sell them for dollars or Swiss francs at little or no discount on free markets. This system was abolished in May 1951.

9. *Information Bulletin*, National Bank of Belgium, Brussels, December 1951.

10. There were certain other adjustments of a smaller magnitude including the use of special resources and an initial debit position of $29 million. See *Second Annual Report of the Managing Board of the EPU*, 1952, Annexes, Table II.

account into the Union from the EPU have been liberalized. The remaining imports, most of them agricultural, are subject to restrictions imposed for the protection of domestic producers.

Export taxes and the blocking of a portion of the export proceeds to EPU countries for a period of six months have been the principal measures introduced to discourage exports to EPU countries. Export taxes have ranged from 1 to 3 per cent on exports to nondollar countries.[11] The proportion of proceeds blocked varies from 4 to 20 per cent for exports; similarly 32 per cent of the proceeds of capital or income from investments in EPU countries have been blocked.[12] Exporters are, however, permitted to borrow against the blocked proceeds at rates ranging from 4 to 6.5 per cent. Controls on the re-export of hard-currency imports to soft-currency countries is another measure used to reduce Belgian exports to EPU countries.

Capital imports into the Union from residents of other EPU countries have increased the B.L.E.U.'s surplus with the EPU. The Belgian or Luxembourg francs thus acquired by nonresidents have been used to finance exports from the Union or to obtain Swiss francs. (The possibility of getting Swiss francs through Belgium was greatly reduced in November 1951 by the introduction of restrictions on transfers of Belgian or Luxembourg nonresident accounts to Switzerland.) The existence in the B.L.E.U. of a free market for EPU currencies including banknotes, makes it possible for other countries to secure nonresident accounts in Belgian or Luxembourg francs with relative ease, although in most cases such transactions contravene the exchange regulations of the country of the foreign resident.

The use of the free market for financing B.L.E.U. exports served to increase the Union's accounting surplus with the EPU. One method of dealing with this problem would have been to suppress the free market in EPU currencies. The B.L.E.U., however, chose the alternative of reducing the value of EPU currencies acquired in the free market by requiring all importers to purchase their foreign exchange through an authorized bank or to arrange for the transfer of a nonresident account in Belgian or Luxembourg francs only through an

11. Only Belgium has introduced export taxes on certain exports to all nondollar countries except Luxembourg. The tax on goods exported to the Netherlands was reduced to one per cent in June 1952.

12. As of July 29, 1952. See *International Financial News Survey*, August 8, 1952, p. 43.

authorized bank. Thus after October 1951 EPU currencies obtained in the free market in the B.L.E.U. were valid only for foreign travel, outward capital movements, donations and emigrant remittances. The Union also discouraged capital imports by discontinuing the practice of permitting foreigners to acquire nonresident accounts in francs through the importation of Belgian or Luxembourg banknotes.

Measures to Reduce the Deficit with the Dollar Area

In September 1951, at a time when the Union's gold and dollar reserves were not declining, the B.L.E.U. substantially intensified restrictions on dollar imports. In fact, the Union's gold and dollar reserves rose during the second half of 1951 and the first half of 1952. It is possible that the B.L.E.U. might have experienced a drain on reserves without additional restrictions, but there is reason to believe that the restrictions on dollar imports were employed, in part, to reduce the surplus with the EPU countries.[13] Restrictions on the re-export of dollar goods, the taxation of exports to EPU countries and the blocking of export proceeds have also tended to lower the dollar deficit. Finally, the B.L.E.U.'s hard currency payments have probably been reduced by the elimination of the system whereby residents from dollar countries could import Belgian or Luxembourg bank-notes and exchange them for a resident account available for making purchases in B.L.E.U., and the reintroduction of restrictions on capital transfers to Switzerland.

The B.L.E.U. is perhaps in a better position than any other country with an inconvertible currency to restore full convertibility with the dollar. She is not likely to do so, however, in the absence of the convertibility of sterling and other important currencies. If the B.L.E.U. were to become a part of the dollar area, the Union's exports would be subject to the same discrimination as are American exports. This would entail business losses and increased unemployment pending a readjustment, with emphasis on exports to the dollar area. Such a

13. Dollar imports are divided into three classifications for purposes of import licensing: (1) A list of raw materials and other commodities which cannot be obtained outside the dollar area except at substantially higher prices. (These commodities, which constituted over half the value of dollar imports in the first half of 1951, are not restricted.) (2) A list of prohibited dollar imports which constituted less than 10 per cent of the total in the first six months of 1951. (3) A list of imports for which licenses are granted only after scrutiny by the authorities.

step might require some reduction in the exchange value of her currency. All these moves, though necessary for equilibrium, are politically painful and there are very potent vested interests in the Union who want to maintain the protected soft-currency markets. Yet if the strong countries will not break with the system of discrimination and inconvertibility, how can the rest of the soft-currency countries which are tied directly or indirectly to the EPU move in this direction? The answer may be that the problem of convertibility must be attacked regionally and not country by country. (See Part IV.)

FRANCE [14]

In contrast to the B.L.E.U., France has been in a position of serious disequilibrium with the dollar area and on over-all account during the postwar years and has maintained severe restrictions against dollar imports. France's current account deficit was reduced from $1,833 million in 1947 to a condition of approximate balance in 1950, but rose again to $733 million in 1951. In addition, France has had to cover the foreign exchange deficits of the overseas franc area, so that the current account deficits of the French franc area have been from $100 to $200 million larger than those of continental France alone. France's dollar deficits on current account have ranged from $1,191 million in 1947 to $303 million in 1950, and $395 million in 1951.[15] Unlike the B.L.E.U., in most years the French franc area has not had a surplus with nondollar countries. Moreover, French overseas territories have been a dollar drain rather than a dollar earner as is the case with most British and Belgian colonial possessions. In 1950 the French franc area had a surplus of $160 million with the EPU area. However, this was reversed in the spring of 1951 and by 1952 France had become one of the largest debtors in the EPU.[16]

France lacked most of the favorable factors of Belgium's postwar

14. The French franc area includes in addition to Metropolitan France all of the French territories and dependencies except French Somaliland (which has a convertible currency and no exchange controls). The Associated States of Cambodia, Laos and Vietnam (Indochina) are also members of the French franc area. Local currencies are pegged to the French franc, and foreign exchange reserves centrally managed. While transactions within the area are formally subject to exchange controls, restrictions either are not applied or are applied only to minor parts of the area.

15. In addition France had to cover a dollar deficit of $203 million for the account of her overseas territories in 1949, $100 million in 1950 and $129 million in 1951.

16. See Figure 2, p. 126.

experience. French industry suffered enormous direct war damage; France failed to take vigorous deflationary measures in dealing with her swollen currency immediately after liberation; and for the most part French exports did not have a strong competitive position in world markets. In addition, France has had to deal with serious political disturbances in her colonies and to fight a costly war in Indochina. The heavy French deficits were covered by sizable U.S. grants and by loans from the United States and international agencies, including the EPU. Production recovered fairly rapidly and in 1949 and 1950 France not only made considerable progress in reducing her dollar deficit but also achieved a surplus with the nondollar area. This improvement in the country's external position was made possible in large measure by internal wage and price stabilization and by the increase in French exports following the 1948 devaluation of the franc.

After June 1950, however, French prices rose so rapidly in response to both internal and external inflationary pressures that by December 1951, wholesale prices were 46 per cent above the June 1950 level. In the second half of 1951 exports began to decline while imports continued to rise. The over-all deficit of the French franc area climbed from $255 million in the first half of 1951 to $803 million in the second half, and gold and dollar holdings dropped sharply in 1951 as contrasted with an increase in 1950.

Clearly, France's balance of payments difficulties, especially since 1950, have been due in large measure to internal monetary instability. France has sought to deal with her growing deficits by imposing new trade and foreign exchange restrictions and by introducing special measures for subsidizing exports. In February 1952 France reestablished quotas on a number of imports after having liberalized private imports from the EPU area by 75 per cent in 1951. In the latter part of that year, imports of dollar goods were also cut back. In addition, France introduced a number of restrictions on exchange payments which represented a reversal of the earlier trend toward liberalization of her exchange controls. Throughout 1952, in spite of the tightening of restrictions, France continued to have substantial current account deficits with the dollar area and over-all.

The Foreign Exchange Market

After establishing a fixed parity with the Monetary Fund of 119.3 francs to the dollar in 1946, France abandoned her par value in January 1948. She then adopted a floating rate for the dollar and certain other hard currencies, and fixed rates for sterling and other soft currencies. This made it possible for France to devalue with respect to hard currencies, while maintaining a higher value of the franc in terms of sterling and other soft currencies.

In October 1948 France eliminated her system of disparate cross-rates and with the general devaluation of September 1949 she stabilized the franc within a narrow range of 350 francs to the dollar.[17] France was therefore left with a controlled free market for U.S. and Canadian dollars, Portuguese escudos, Swiss francs, Belgian francs and Djibouti francs, in which significant rate fluctuations have not been permitted to take place since September 1949. Since May 18, 1953, authorized banks have been permitted to buy and sell the major EPU currencies in a controlled free market and to conduct arbitrage transactions in EPU currencies. The rate for the French franc is maintained within 0.75 per cent on either side of the basic dollar rate. Outside France free markets exist for capital francs. These represent the blocked capital assets of nonresidents. Capital francs are freely transferable within the monetary area of the nonresident owner and are available for making investments in France and more recently for tourist expenditures of nonresidents in France. The rates for capital francs have been about 10 per cent cheaper than francs available for all current transactions.

As with the British system, only those holding import licenses or exchange permits may purchase foreign exchange and all purchases and sales must be made through the authorized banks. The authorized banks, in effect, function as intermediaries between the buyers and sellers of foreign exchange and operations on their own account are strictly limited. The proceeds of exports of goods and services supply foreign exchange for the free market while the demand comes from authorized payments for imports and other payments in free market currencies. Within the system of controls the prices of currencies traded in the free market are responsive to the forces of demand

17. Both the Monetary Fund and the British government protested against the French system of broken cross-rates.

and supply, though they are supported within narrow limits by the French Exchange Stabilization Fund.

Outside the controlled free markets a number of other specified currencies are dealt in by authorized banks and the French Exchange Stabilization Fund [18] in what is called the official exchange market. The rates on these currencies (except the Italian lira) are based on the relationship between their official dollar parities and the average value of the dollar in the free market. The rate on the Italian lira is determined by the dollar quotations in the "free" French and the "free" Italian markets for dollars. Dealings with countries whose currencies are not on the specified list are almost entirely in nonresident franc accounts or in third (specified) currencies.

Developments after 1948

Following the establishment of the "free" market for dollars and certain other currencies in 1948, France adopted a number of measures tending to liberalize foreign exchange dealings. Nonresident accounts derived from the sale of foreign-owned assets in France could be freely transferred between nonresidents of the same currency area; after March 1951 nonresident capital accounts could be converted into ordinary nonresident accounts available for current transactions. In November 1950 nonresident accounts were made freely transferable between residents of any of the EPU countries.

Authorized banks were granted considerable liberty in foreign exchange dealings, including trading in forward exchange. Banknotes other than Belgian francs, U.S. and Canadian dollars, Djibouti francs, Italian lire, Portuguese escudos and Swiss francs could be traded between authorized banks at any rate. French residents were no longer required to surrender capital receipts in any currency, even dollars and Swiss francs. French banknotes could be brought into France without limit and French tourists could take a maximum of 50,000 francs out of the country. Finally, there was free convertibility into the currency of the nonresident investor for all foreign investments made after August 31, 1949.

With the deterioration of France's foreign exchange position in 1951 a number of these measures were suspended. When a country's

18. These currencies include the Norwegian and Czech crowns, the Yugoslavian dinar, the Mexican peso, the Italian lira and the Egyptian pound.

foreign exchange position is improving, liberalization of the foreign exchange market serves to strengthen the currency by increasing confidence in it. But when a country is incurring large deficits and its reserves are falling, the greater the freedom of the market the more opportunities there are for capital flight. For example, so long as it was possible for a resident of Italy to transfer his French franc account to a Swiss resident in exchange for Swiss francs or dollars, the Italian might prefer to sell his francs for a hard currency rather than to use them to buy something in France. Moreover, the Italian resident may have acquired his French francs, not by exporting goods to France, but by liquidating a capital asset in France, since capital accounts had been made transferable into ordinary nonresident accounts. When the position of the franc began to weaken, therefore, the French authorities announced that after April 15, 1951 capital accounts could no longer be freely transferred to ordinary nonresident accounts of the same country. In June 1951 transfers between nonresident accounts of different EPU nationalities again became subject to license. Authorized banks were permitted to effect such transfers in payment of current transactions, provided the transfer did not involve the crediting of a Belgian, Swiss or Portuguese account. The purpose of these three exceptions was to prevent capital movements through French francs to countries with relatively hard currencies. This regulation was modified in May 1953 when France joined with several other EPU countries in permitting arbitrage operations in EPU currencies by authorized banks.

Measures for Encouraging Exports

France has sought to overcome the disadvantages of an overvalued exchange rate by various devices for stimulating exports, most of which involve an implicit multiple exchange rate. One of these devices is the export retention quota system. Under this system French exporters are permitted to retain part of their export proceeds in special EFAC [19] accounts in the authorized banks, either in foreign currency or in French francs, according to the method of settlement. Fifteen per cent of the proceeds from exports payable in U.S. or Canadian dollars and 10 per cent of the proceeds of exports settled

19. EFAC stands for *Exportations, Frais Accessoires.*

in other ways may be kept in the EFAC accounts. These accounts may be used for a variety of purposes incidental to the exporter's business. Three per cent of the export proceeds in U.S. or Canadian dollars, however, may be utilized for any purpose, except for imports which are absolutely prohibited.

The French export retention system may be regarded, in part, as a device to simplify the exchange control procedure and to make it easier for exporters to import raw materials and equipment and to cover selling and other foreign exchange expenses incidental to their export business. But it must also be regarded as a multiple export rate device, insofar as it permits exporters to import commodities for sale in French markets more readily than can residents who do not have EFAC accounts. This is particularly true of that portion of the dollar proceeds which can be used for any purpose.

Another important device employed by the French government to stimulate exports has been the rebating of social security and other taxes on exported commodities.[20]

THE NETHERLANDS [21]

As in the case of France, postwar disequilibrium in the Netherlands can be accounted for in large measure by the wartime destruction of her productive facilities, the severe burden of reconstruction and the heavy demand for imports due to internal monetary instability. In addition, the Netherlands has had to make major readjustments in the pattern of her trade and payments, especially in her trade relations with Germany.

Before the war the Netherlands tended to have a deficit with the dollar area which was covered by a surplus in sterling and by dollar earnings from her overseas possessions, particularly Indonesia. Since the war sterling has not been convertible and after Indonesia gained independence dollars were not regularly available from that source. The Netherlands' strong prewar creditor position was also weakened by a loss of overseas investments and the accumulation of a heavy dollar indebtedness.

20. See *The Statist*, April 4, 1952, pp. 467–68.
21. The Netherlands and her overseas territories constitute the Netherlands monetary area. In the operation of payments agreements negotiated jointly with Indonesia, that country is considered part of the Netherlands monetary area.

After incurring a large EPU deficit in 1950, the Netherlands reverted in 1951 to her prewar pattern by achieving a substantial surplus with the EPU area and other soft-currency countries. Her over-all deficit on current account was reduced to about $32 million as compared with $278 million in 1950. In 1952 the Netherlands developed an over-all surplus on current account estimated to be about $250 million.[22] The Netherlands' deficit on current account with the dollar area, however, was $172 million in 1951 and an estimated $166 million in 1952, and her surplus with the rest of the world was only partially available for meeting this deficit. Thanks to U.S. aid, however, the Netherlands was able to meet her dollar deficit and to increase her gold and dollar reserves during 1951 and 1952.

In 1950 the Netherlands lifted many of the restrictions on her imports from the EPU area.[23] The Netherlands has had an obligation to achieve complete liberalization of imports from the B.L.E.U. in accordance with the agreement to form an economic union with Belgium and Luxembourg (Benelux). These measures, plus strong inflationary pressures within the Netherlands, were responsible for that country's large deficit with the EPU during 1950. (See Figure 2, page 126.)

In order to reverse her EPU position the Netherlands embarked on two lines of action: (1) the restoration of quotas on a number of imports from the EPU area; [24] (2) the introduction of internal deflationary measures. The second was by far the most important in achieving the objective. This program included (1) a decrease in food subsidies; (2) heavier taxation and reduced governmental expenditures; (3) an increase in the central bank discount rate from 2.5 to 4 per cent; (4) direct control of investment and a contraction of the building program; (5) the negotiation of an agreement with labor and industry to limit wage increases. These measures halted the rise in prices and wages and reduced the demand for imports.

22. Balance of payments estimates for 1952 taken from *Europe, the Way Ahead* (Fourth Annual Report of the OEEC), Organisation for European Economic Co-operation, Paris, 1952, pp. 299–300.
23. In 1950, 65 per cent of the Netherlands' imports on private account from the OEEC area were liberalized and 95 per cent of her imports from B.L.E.U. were without restriction.
24. With the improvement of her balance of payments position in 1951 and 1952 the Netherlands liberalized imports to the 75 per cent level.

Measures to Increase Dollar Earnings

During 1951 and 1952 the Netherlands ran surpluses with the EPU area. Such surpluses with soft-currency countries have aggravated the Netherlands dollar problem since they are only partially convertible into gold. Further, they require an extension of credits which drain off Dutch resources and generate internal inflationary pressures. The Netherlands has maintained strict licensing controls on dollar imports while liberalizing imports from the EPU area. A continuation of this policy is likely to interfere with the plans to form an economic union with the B.L.E.U. since in spite of increased restrictions against them, dollar goods are relatively more plentiful in the B.L.E.U. than in the Netherlands.

However, the Netherlands has tried to encourage exports to the dollar area by permitting exporters to all countries from which the Netherlands receives U.S. and Canadian dollars in payment for exports to retain 10 per cent of their dollar proceeds in export bonus dollar accounts (E.B. accounts). E.B. account dollars may be used by exporters to pay for merchandise bought in the dollar area, for business expenses and travel or for the purchase of other currencies for similar purposes. While the E.B. dollars are not legally transferable,[25] exporters can use them to buy luxury goods which can then be sold at a substantial markup in the Netherlands. In effect, this amounts to a multiple exchange arrangement and a partial depreciation of the guilder against the dollar. The device serves the purpose of increasing dollar earnings by diverting exports from soft-currency countries to the dollar area.

Entrepôt trade has always been important to the Netherlands and it is encouraged by the exchange control authorities so long as it does not increase the dollar drain. The general rule is that transit transactions are permitted if they result in currency earnings as *hard* as, or *harder* than, the currencies which are spent. There is considerable evidence that the Dutch authorities have facilitated cheap sterling deals through the use of Dutch transferable sterling to purchase goods in soft-currency countries for re-export to the dollar area.

The Dutch authorities also are reported to permit their traders to engage in "commercial switch" transactions, which are a means of

25. According to press reports there is a gray market for the E.B. dollars.

earning both dollars and soft currencies. Dutch traders purchase commodities in soft-currency countries with guilders or other soft currencies and sell them (perhaps at a loss) to dollar countries. A portion of the dollar receipts must be surrendered to the Dutch authorities for guilders, but the remainder may be used to buy dollar goods for sale for soft currencies in a third country. The high prices of dollar goods in soft-currency countries make possible a substantial profit to the trader, even after deducting the loss on the first portion of the transaction.

The second part of the transaction may be conducted by another trader who buys the "switch rights" to the dollars obtained from the sale of soft-currency goods to the dollar area. Sales of switch rights are made through authorized banks which act as brokers in the markets for them. Presumably each part of the transaction requires a license so that the buyer of a switch right must obtain a special license to complete the second portion of the transaction, that is, to use the switch dollars to buy dollar goods for sale in a soft-currency area. In commercial switch transactions the purchases and sales of dollars and other currencies are presumably conducted at the official rate. It is the transaction in switch rights which is subject to fluctuation and of course gives rise to implicit multiple exchange rates.[26]

Import Payments Certificates

During 1951 the Netherlands ran a substantial surplus with Argentina under her bilateral payments agreement with that country. In order to reduce her surplus without entirely stopping exports the Netherlands government introduced a system of "negotiable import payment certificates" which Dutch exporters to Argentina were obliged to acquire after May 15, 1951. These certificates must be pur-

26. See J. F. Haccou, "Structural Changes in Trade and Marketing Conditions," *Quarterly Review,* Amsterdamsche Bank, Amsterdam, Second Quarter, 1952 pp. 1–11; see also "Swiss Switch Deals," *The New York Times,* March 10, 1952; *International Financial News Survey,* November 21, 1952, p. 167; and *Europe, the Way Ahead, op. cit.,* p. 301. Official information on Dutch commercial switch transactions is not available and the author has had to rely on press reports and conversations with dealers. Apparently a modification in the Dutch system occurred in March 1953, when a system of general licenses was introduced in place of individual transit licenses. Under the new system the transit trader receives a certain allocation of foreign exchange with which he can deal freely in conducting switch transactions, without obtaining specific approval for each transaction from the central bank. (See *De Maasbode,* Rotterdam, March 11, 1953.)

chased from Dutch importers of Argentine products who acquire them from the governmental authorities when they import, under an import license, from Argentina. Exporters must acquire certificates equal to one and two-thirds the value of their shipment before they are granted a license to export to Argentina.[27]

While this system reduces exports to Argentina and hence redirects exports to other countries, it may also subsidize imports from Argentina unless the importers transship that country's exports to third countries. To the extent that Argentine products are resold to the dollar area the device serves a dual purpose of reducing exports to Argentina and expanding dollar earnings.

DENMARK

While the Danish economy did not endure wartime destruction, its export industries (mainly animal products) suffered severely during the war; the shortage of consumers' goods and a swollen currency created a serious problem of latent inflation. By 1949, however, Denmark had achieved a fair degree of internal monetary stability and her current account deficit was reduced from $63 million in 1947 to $46 million in 1949. During 1950, however, higher import prices and the liberalization of Danish imports from the EPU area resulted in a large deficit with the continental OEEC countries and a sharp reduction in her traditional sterling area surplus. An additional factor in the increase in Denmark's current deficit from $46 million in 1949 to $100 million in 1950 was the sharp deterioration in her terms of trade. After the devaluations of September 1949 prices of imports mounted steeply but the prices received for Danish exports rose relatively little. Denmark herself was thus a victim of her practice of entering into long-term contracts with Britain for the sale of her dairy and meat products.

Denmark's over-all deficit was reduced to $13 million in 1951 and a current account surplus of $12 million was attained in 1952.[28] The rapid improvement over 1950 was due in part to the government's anti-inflationary measures, including an increase in the discount rate from 3.5 to 5 per cent. More important, however, was the increase in

27. *De Maasbode,* Rotterdam, May 14, 1952.
28. *International Financial News Survey,* February 6, 1953, p. 238.

the prices of Danish exports.[29] But even with a nondollar surplus Denmark was still left with a structural imbalance since only a portion of her nondollar surplus can be used to discharge her dollar deficit. The problem of eliminating the dollar deficit has been rendered more difficult by Denmark's large dollar indebtedness, the service payments on which in 1951 were equal to about half of her exports to the United States.[30] Denmark's efforts to expand her dollar exports have been hampered by the U.S. embargo on butter and the restrictions on cheese imports imposed by the Defense Production Act. At the same time Denmark has had to shift a portion of her imports of coal, grain and fodder to the dollar area as a result of restrictions on exports to Eastern Europe imposed for security reasons and unavailability of supplies from the Soviet orbit.

Liberalization of Imports

As in the case of the other OEEC countries, Denmark has liberalized imports from the OEEC countries—up to 75 per cent of the value of private imports in 1948—while maintaining strict licensing controls on most imports from the dollar area. (Imports of coarse grain and feed stuffs are under government monopoly.) Denmark also has taken steps to avoid running a deficit with the EPU. To discourage imports from the soft-currency countries the Danish exchange control authorities have required advance deposits of from 150 to 180 per cent of the value of the imports for certain consumers' goods imported from the EPU area and from some other countries. These advance deposits must be made with an authorized bank which in turn must transfer them to the central bank. Restriction on imports from soft-currency countries may indirectly reduce exports to these countries. This is particularly true in trade with nations outside the EPU with which Denmark has bilateral trade and payments agreements, including Finland, Spain and Yugoslavia. Denmark also main-

29. Readjustment of prices under long-term export contracts permitted a rise in the prices of animal exports to a level consistent with world prices. By the same token, however, British terms of trade with Denmark deteriorated, and this was a factor in transforming Britain's EPU surplus in 1950 to a large deficit in 1951.

30. Denmark's exports to the United States in 1951 were $19.2 million, whereas interest and amortization on her dollar indebtedness was $9.1 million. As of March 1951 Denmark's foreign-held dollar debt was $169 million.

tains export licensing controls on a number of her leading exports and these can be used to channel trade.[31]

In August 1952 Denmark joined the growing list of countries which employ retention quotas to encourage exports to the dollar area. Ten per cent of the dollar proceeds from commodity exports and invisibles may be converted into EPU currencies for the importation of goods from the OEEC countries, Spain, Finland or Yugoslavia, otherwise subject to restriction. Exporters who earn dollars are given import rights transferable to importers if the original recipient does not choose to use them himself. The rights may not be used for the agricultural products which may be restricted for commercial policy reasons, or for certain other imports subject to control. During 1952, 75 per cent of the rights were used to purchase automobiles in France, Italy, Britain and Germany. Prices paid by importers for the rights during 1952 varied between 80 per cent and 150 per cent of the value of the import.[32]

It may be noted that the Danish system differs from the other retention schemes in that the dollar earner is not permitted to retain a portion of the dollars for his own use. While this has the advantage of preventing a dollar drain for luxury imports, the system greatly reduces the value of the rights and hence the incentive to export to the dollar area.

SWEDEN

Unlike most Western European countries, Sweden suffered no wartime destruction and has enjoyed real prosperity during the postwar period, with high levels of consumption and investment.[33] Yet Sweden experienced substantial balance of payments deficits during the early postwar years which led her to adopt severe restrictions against dollar imports and to conduct most of her trade under bilateral arrangements. Sweden had substantial over-all deficits on current account during 1946–1948, largely the consequence of her deficits with the United States and Canada. During this time these deficits

31. Denmark uses export controls as a means of enabling the authorities to meet their commitments under long-term purchase contracts and trade-quota agreements.

32. *Foreign Commerce Weekly,* March 2, 1953, p. 5.

33. In the fourth quarter of 1951 industrial production in Sweden was 81 per cent above the level of 1938. The FAO index of agricultural production was 113 in 1950 as compared with 92 for 1937 (1948 = 100).

were financed chiefly by drawing down her gold and dollar reserves,[34] but since 1948 Sweden's dollar deficits in the main have been covered by ECA grants and loans and by gold earned through the EPU. In the years 1949–1951 Sweden maintained an over-all surplus on current account financed in part by long-term credits to other European countries and by credits to the EPU.

Perhaps it is more true of Sweden than of any other Western European country, that her postwar balance of payments difficulties have been brought about by her own domestic policies. Until recently Sweden had inflationary monetary and fiscal policies, and after incurring large deficits in 1946 and 1947 the nation turned to import restrictions rather than to general anti-inflationary measures to redress her balance. In 1946 Sweden appreciated her currency from the prewar rate of 4.2 kronor to the dollar to 3.6 to the dollar. This was maintained until September 1949 when it was changed to 5.2 kronor. This appreciation undoubtedly hampered the expansion of Sweden's exports to the dollar area.

In the early 1930s Sweden was in approximate balance with the United States and Canada but in the late thirties Sweden had a deficit with these countries which was balanced by a sterling surplus. During the war the structure of the wood pulp market shifted so that Sweden lost most of her wood pulp market in the United States to U.S. and Canadian producers. Apparently part of this loss was due to the price policies of Swedish exporters and to the appreciation of the kronor in 1946.[35] Instead of taking vigorous measures to expand her exports to the dollar area, the Swedish government—seemingly convinced that the United States was headed for a depression—made substantial long-term loans to other European countries, including a $278 million loan to the USSR, in order to enlarge her markets in soft-currency countries.

Sweden's Exchange Practices

Sweden's exchange control system is somewhat more liberal than are most European systems. Surrender requirements are limited to

34. Gold and dollar holdings of the central bank declined by about a half billion dollars in 1946 and 1947.

35. Sweden has good prospects of expanding her exports of iron ore and metals to the dollar area.

U.S. and Canadian dollars, Swiss francs, Portuguese escudos and Argentine pesos.[36] Other currencies may be held in a currency account with a Swedish authorized bank but all transactions in foreign exchange must take place through authorized banks. For most currencies rates are established by the central bank but authorized banks are permitted to trade in spot and forward sterling within a specified range above and below parity.

In May 1953 Sweden joined a number of other EPU countries in permitting its authorized banks to engage in arbitrage transactions in the major EPU currencies. Sweden has liberalized private imports from the EPU area to the extent of 91 per cent of the value of her imports in 1948 [37] and also most invisible payments to the EPU area. Capital transactions between Sweden and the other Scandinavian countries and the sterling area have been liberalized substantially under a special agreement.[38] Imports from the dollar area, on the other hand, are strictly limited in accordance with Sweden's annual import plan.

Sweden is reported to employ retention quotas to encourage dollar exports and also to utilize her bilateral surpluses with certain countries. In 1952 Swedish exporters of specified perishable dairy products were permitted to retain their dollar proceeds for the importation of certain commodities considered important to the Swedish economy. Swedish traders are also permitted to retain the dollar proceeds from the sale of goods purchased in countries with which Sweden has accumulated large bilateral surpluses, and re-exported to the dollar area. These dollars, known as "gray" or "transit" dollars, may be sold at premium rates to Swedish importers through an authorized bank.

NORWAY

Norway's postwar experience differs from Sweden's in several important respects. First, Norway suffered severe war damage, espe-

---

36. *Foreign Exchange Regulations in Sweden,* Skandinaviska Banken, Stockholm, November 1951, p. 16.

37. About 7 per cent of Sweden's imports from the OEEC countries were under government monopoly in 1948. Commodities imported by government monopolies include cereals and fodder, sugars, fats and oils, meat, wine and spirits, and tobacco.

38. The UNISCAN (United Kingdom-Scandinavian) agreement of January 1950. Under this agreement there are no restrictions on the repatriation of capital owned by residents of the other members. Sweden also provides foreign exchange for travel in those countries in any "reasonable amount."

cially in industries which earned foreign exchange. Norway lost half her merchant tonnage, which before the war earned foreign exchange equal to a third of the country's imports. In addition, her richest iron ore mines were destroyed and other export industries severely damaged. Second, during the war the German occupation forces had so flooded the country with money that its volume had increased fourfold. This large purchasing power in a country with depleted stocks and impaired equipment presented a serious problem of latent inflation. In order to reconstruct her economy, Norway, during the postwar period, has devoted a high percentage of her national income to investment; the ratio of net investment to national income averaging 23 per cent over the years 1946–1950. About two thirds of this investment was financed out of domestic saving, the remainder by Norway's import surplus.

Considering the strong inflationary pressures generated by the combination of latent inflation and the heavy investment program, Norway's ability to limit increases in wholesale prices and the cost of living to 60 per cent and 34 per cent, respectively,[39] above 1946 levels is quite remarkable. By 1951 prices had been stabilized and a fair degree of internal monetary stability achieved. Between 1946 and 1951 Norway increased industrial production by 38 per cent, the volume of exports was about 25 per cent above the prewar level, and her shipping had been restored to the point where current earnings from this source were again covering about one third of the country's imports.

Before the war Norway was in approximate current account balance with the dollar area and her over-all trade deficit was covered by earnings from shipping. Immediately after the war Norway had substantial current account deficits covered in part by grants and credits from the United States. In the latter half of 1951 and the first half of 1952 Norway achieved an over-all surplus and her current account deficit with the dollar area had declined to $4 million in 1951 as compared with a deficit with the United States and Canada of $155 million in 1947.[40] The reduction in Norway's dollar deficit has been attained largely by an increase in her earnings from shipping

39. As of January 1953.

40. Dollar amortization payments on Norway's postwar indebtedness represent a substantial portion of her total dollar income. These payments were $34 million in 1951.

and other services which rose from $11 million in 1950 to $64 million in 1952.

If Norway were able to purchase a larger proportion of her coal and grain in the nondollar area, as she did before the war, the country would be in a position to eliminate her entire dollar deficit. In 1938 Norway purchased only 20 per cent of her imports from the United States and Canada; in 1951, 43 per cent of her imports—largely fuel and grain—came from these countries. It may also be noted that in 1950 and 1951, 10 per cent and 7 per cent, respectively, of Norway's exports went to the United States as compared with 10 per cent in 1937. Sweden on the other hand sent 11 per cent of her exports to the United States in 1937, and only 6 per cent and 5 per cent in 1950 and 1951, respectively.

Norway's progress in restoring external equilibrium in the face of highly unfavorable conditions inherited by the liberation government may be attributed in large measure to certain monetary and fiscal measures. These included blocking a portion of her notes and deposits in 1945, a capital levy, budgetary surpluses since 1949, credit and investment controls, and extremely tight rationing and price controls which were maintained until the excessive liquidity had been worked off. By 1952 most consumers' goods had been decontrolled.

Norway's trade and exchange controls follow the usual Western European pattern. Imports from the dollar area have been restricted to essential requirements and in May 1952 Norway had liberalized private imports from the EPU area to the extent of 75 per cent (1948 base). Norway has maintained relatively liberal policies with respect to invisible payments to the EPU and the sterling area. A number of Norway's imports—including coffee, sugar, dried fruit, coal, grains and alcoholic beverages—have been subject to state trading.

Norway has not tried to increase her exports to the dollar area by means of retention quotas. Before November 1952 exporters of goods paid for with dollars were permitted to use 10 per cent of the dollar proceeds for imports needed for their own production. This device was not employed as a subsidy to dollar exports and has now been abandoned in favor of a fairly liberal policy on import licenses for firms producing exports for the dollar area.[41]

41. *International Financial News Survey,* November 14, 1952, p. 160.

WESTERN GERMANY

The rapid recovery of Western Germany since the monetary reform of June 1948 and the general lifting of internal controls has been one of the most remarkable economic developments of the postwar period. Between 1948 and the end of 1951 industrial production in Germany much more than doubled, and was 10 per cent larger than in 1938. Exports rose by an even greater percentage, from 25 per cent of the prewar (1936) volume in 1948 to 134 per cent in 1951.[42] Germany's over-all current deficit of over a billion dollars in 1949 was converted to a surplus of $161 million in 1951. Germany's current account deficit with the dollar area was $375 million in 1951 but this represented only about half of what it was in 1949. Germany's exports to the United States and Canada were only $27 million in 1948, but by 1951 exports to these two countries totaled $261 million and exports to the entire dollar area $380 million. In 1951 Germany's dollar deficit was more than covered by U.S. government grants ($416 million) and by dollars earned through the EPU and from other sources, so that German dollar holdings were increased. In spite of reduced U.S. economic assistance, Germany's gold and dollar holdings rose by $247 million in 1952 to $612 million as of December 31, 1952.[43]

During 1950 Germany had so large a deficit with the EPU that it resulted in the exhaustion of her quota. This was due in part to speculative purchases by German merchants following the liberalization of German imports from the EPU area. This was converted to a substantial surplus in 1951 and the first half of 1952, in part because of restrictive monetary and credit measures and a tightening of import restrictions.[44] More important in the reversal of her EPU position, however, was the substantial increase in 1951 in German exports to the EPU area. Now that Western Germany has achieved an over-all balance on current account, her principal problem will be to eliminate her dollar deficit by increasing exports to the dollar area, or to find alternative sources of essential imports. Germany's trade deficit with

---

42. The value of German exports was $357 million in 1947, $733.5 million in 1948 and $3,472.4 million in 1951.

43. *Foreign Commerce Weekly*, February 16, 1953, p. 5.

44. Germany liberalized her imports from the EPU area up to 81 per cent (1949 base) in March 1953.

the dollar area actually increased during 1951 while in that year her global position developed favorably. During the first half of 1952 Germany's over-all current account surplus rose to $238 million and her dollar area deficit was $147 million.

Trade and Exchange Controls

Western Germany has been extremely active in concluding trade and payments agreements not only with the countries of Western Europe, but with Latin America and the Middle and Far East. Most of Germany's bilateral payments agreements with Western Europe include the Deutsche mark as one of the two currencies of account, the exceptions being the agreements with Turkey and Spain which employ the dollar and agreements with Austria and Greece under which the Deutsche mark is the sole unit of account. Germany's accounts with OEEC countries are cleared through the EPU but most of her other agreements provide for reciprocal swing credits.

Imports into Germany require both a "purchase authorization" and an "import-and-payment" license. Purchase authorizations may be obtained in one of several ways depending upon the type of import and other conditions. For some imports authorizations are obtained from a federal government agency. Under another procedure applications for a purchase authorization may be submitted through an authorized bank to a land central bank which issues licenses on the basis of quotas fixed by the Bank Deutscher Länder. Once the purchase authorization is approved, importers must apply to a land central bank for an import and payments license through an authorized bank. The appropriate exchange is granted automatically on the presentation of the license to the authorized bank.

With certain exceptions, all foreign exchange earnings must be surrendered to authorized banks.[45] Like her neighbors, France and the Netherlands, Germany maintains a retention quota system as a means of fostering exports for dollars and free Swiss francs. Effective April 1, 1952, 40 per cent of the dollars and Swiss francs earned by Germans from export of goods, processing or repair transactions,

---

45. One exception is the case of exporters who have obtained imports of raw materials on credit against the delivery of commodities produced from the imported materials. In such cases the exporters may retain that part of their export proceeds needed to repay the foreign credits. Shipowners and other firms doing business abroad may also retain foreign exchange required for their operations.

freight and charter contracts, shipping and warehousing services, and deliveries to the Allied occupation authorities may be deposited in DM accounts with authorized banks. The DM accounts may be used for importing certain commodities from hard-currency countries. The retained accounts or import rights may be used by the exporter himself or sold to an importer. During 1952 the premium paid for the import rights varied from 4.5 to 20 per cent of their face value, thus yielding a bonus of from 1.8 to 8 per cent of the proceeds of exports to the dollar area.[46]

German authorities have stated that they were forced to adopt a retention quota in order to prevent a continued loss of dollar earnings from commercial switch transactions and the re-exporting of German goods to the dollar area by Dutch, French, Swedish and Belgian traders. Estimates of the dollars thus lost during 1951 and 1952 range from $4 million to $6 million per month.[47] These estimates are based on the difference between German exports paid for by EPU countries and those consumed by those countries. It is also assumed that German goods re-exported to dollar countries would otherwise have been sold directly to the dollar area by German merchants.[48]

In addition to the argument that Germany needs a retention quota system to protect herself against the re-export of German goods by other countries, it is also alleged that only if they are placed on an equal footing can German exporters compete with other European exporters who benefit from retention systems. Thus retention quotas have become a kind of competitive currency device which spread rapidly among Western European countries during 1951 and 1952.[49]

46. See *Foreign Commerce Weekly,* February 23, 1953, p. 10. In addition to the retention quota or import rights system described above, firms which produce for export (as distinct from export merchants) are credited with a portion (up to 4 per cent) of their export proceeds in all currencies in a "foreign exchange working fund" held in special accounts in their own name. These accounts are not transferable but they are available for purchasing certain imports to be used directly in export production.

47. *Monthly Report of the Bank Deutscher Länder,* April 1952, p. 41; see also, *Wall Street Journal,* May 5, 1952.

48. It is reported that German exporters sometimes receive a portion of the dollars obtained from the goods which are re-exported to the dollar area, and that these dollars are not surrendered to the German central bank.

49. On June 22, 1953, the German government announced that it would abolish its system of import rights. This step was taken after consultation with the Monetary Fund and in the expectation that similar steps would be taken by other countries. *International Financial News Survey,* July 17, 1953, p. 17.

ITALY

Italy (along with Greece and Turkey) is one of the "underdeveloped" countries of Western Europe in the sense that her basic problem is a deficiency of capital required to give her population employment which will provide a level of real income consistent with Western European living standards. Italy suffered great destruction during World War II and much of her savings had already gone into armaments and a costly war with Ethiopia. Such countries as France, Belgium and the Netherlands have experienced disequilibrium as a result of structural maladjustments in their trade, wartime destruction and internal monetary instability. But these countries possess the fundamental human and material resources to attain reasonably high living standards and to go on improving them without further external assistance and without trade and exchange restrictions. Italy's problem, however, is the fact that her population is far too large for her resources and that the capital needed for economic development can only come from the outside.

During the postwar period Italy's balance of payments has been characterized by sizable over-all deficits on current account, but with even larger dollar deficits, partially offset by surpluses with other areas. Since 1947 Italy has usually had a surplus with the sterling area and with the continental OEEC countries. Italy's current account deficits with the dollar area, which were $203 million and $303 million, respectively, in 1950 and 1951, have been more than offset by U.S. grants and loans and by gold receipts of her EPU surplus. Italy's gold and dollar reserves therefore rose from $247 million in June 1947 to $635 million in December 1951.

Italy's trade and foreign exchange policies have reflected the pattern of her regional balance. In 1951 and 1952 Italy liberalized to 99 per cent her imports on private account from the EPU area, but kept severe restrictions on dollar goods. Internal inflationary pressures have certainly contributed to her over-all deficit, but the ability to adopt more restrictive internal monetary and fiscal measures was hampered by large-scale unemployment.[50] Severe unemployment accompanied by rising prices reflects a structural maladjustment which

---

50. Unemployment in 1949–1950 ranged between 4 and 5 per cent of the total population, perhaps 10 per cent or more of the working population.

can only be cured by a carefully planned program of investment and land reform.

The Foreign Exchange Market

In the immediate postwar period Italy sought to encourage exports to hard-currency areas by the establishment of a "floating" rate for the lira vis-à-vis the dollar, the Swiss franc and sterling.[51] Exporters were required to surrender half their proceeds in these currencies to the exchange control at the official rate while the remainder could be used for authorized imports or sold in the "free market." Thus the export rate for these currencies was the average of the fluctuating free market rate and the official rate. The private import rate was the free market rate, and the official rate was applied to government imports.[52] After the suspension of convertibility of sterling in August 1947 the lira-pound rate fell to a discount against the rate corresponding to the official cross-rate with the dollar. In addition, the effective dollar rates broke the official cross-rates between the dollar and other currencies traded at pegged rates in Italy. This system served to encourage exports for dollars and Swiss francs as against exports for soft currencies; at the same time it provided a discriminatory cost restriction against hard-currency imports.

Beginning in November 1947 the Italian system was modified by the elimination of the fixed official rate and the establishment of an official monthly rate based on the average of free rates during the previous month. This helped eliminate the spread between the export and the import rates for each currency for which a "free" market had been established. In September 1949 the official rate was fixed daily with reference to the "free" rate and the free market rate has been virtually pegged at 625 lire to the dollar since that time. Thus, like France, Italy has abandoned her floating rate, although neither has a par value. The rate cannot fluctuate more than a fraction of a percentage because of government stabilization operations and controls over the demand for foreign exchange achieved through the licensing system.

In November 1948 as a result of pressure from Britain, Italy also

---

51. This system was established in March 1946.

52. The official rate was 225 lire to the dollar; the free rate rose to around 625 lire soon after the system was put into operation.

abandoned her system of broken cross-rates. Since then the lira-sterling rate has been adjusted to reflect changes in the lira-dollar rate and thus to maintain the official dollar-sterling cross-rate.[53] With the elimination of the discriminatory rate system it became necessary to impose new discriminatory controls against dollar goods in favor of soft-currency imports. In order to limit the accumulation of sterling balances after November 1948, Italy reduced the number of items on the list of goods payable in hard currencies for which no import license is required (List A), and established a new and larger List S of goods payable in sterling for which import licenses are not required. With the establishment of the EPU, Italy placed most of the imports from the OEEC countries and the sterling area under open general license, while restricting her List A to a small number of items available only in hard-currency areas. The elimination of disparate cross-rates removed the special incentive to export for hard currencies and undoubtedly contributed to Italy's dollar deficit.[54]

At the time of writing, the Italian practice of permitting exporters to sell half their U.S. and Canadian dollar proceeds in the "free" market while surrendering the remainder is little more than a complicated administrative technique. Exporters either must sell the retained portion of their proceeds in the free market (where the rate is kept stable and equal to the official rate) or use the proceeds themselves within 60 days. But the right to purchase or use dollars for imports or nontrade payments is closely controlled and only a few items may be imported for dollars without a license.

GREECE

All the elements unfavorable to external balance are present in the Greek economy: a basic poverty of resources, severe destruction during the German occupation and the postwar civil conflict, hyperinflation, lack of confidence in the local currency, and an overvalued exchange rate. Without substantial foreign aid in the postwar period there would have been starvation and general economic and political collapse. Up to mid-1952 Greece had received $1,600 million in for-

---

53. The official rates for other currencies are also adjusted to changes in the dollar rate in order to reflect official cross-rates.

54. The head of the Banca di Roma has stated publicly that British insistence that Italy maintain the official dollar-sterling cross-rate has been harmful to Italy. (See *The New York Times,* December 3, 1951.)

eign assistance, equal to about 25 per cent of the Greek national income during the postwar years. While production in many industries has been restored well above prewar levels, Greece is far from achieving an external balance at a scale of imports consistent with her existing low standard of living. Foreign exchange earnings from exports covered about a fourth of Greece's imports of goods and services in 1950 and about a third in 1951. Greece's over-all deficit on current account was $321 million in 1950 and $269 million in 1951. Deficits with the dollar area were $143 million and $129 million in 1950 and 1951, respectively. The major part of the deficits have been covered by U.S. aid made available either directly in dollars or indirectly through grants of special resources through the EPU.[55]

Retail prices in Greece are more than 500 times the prewar level and the cost of living in Athens rose from 283 in December 1949 to 370 by March 1952 (1938=1). Between December 1948 and December 1951 the supply of money increased two and a half times. Anti-inflation measures introduced in the winter of 1951–1952 seem to have stemmed the tide of inflation, and by 1953 Greece had achieved a degree of internal monetary stability. Lack of confidence in the drachma led to a widespread use of gold as a store of value and the Greek government has sold several million dollars worth of gold sovereigns internally in order to stabilize the currency.[56]

Hyperinflation during and following the war resulted in the almost complete depreciation of the old drachma. In 1944 a new drachma was introduced at a ratio of one new to 50 billion old drachmas, and the new drachma has depreciated rapidly since that time. Lack of confidence in the currency has also led to capital flight through leaks in the exchange controls.[57]

The Exchange Control System

Prior to the devaluation of the drachma from 15,000 to 30,000 to the dollar in April 1953, the Greek exchange system involved a

55. Greece has deficits with both dollar and nondollar countries so that part of the American aid has financed Greece's deficit with the EPU.

56. The Greek government spent $18.7 million for gold sovereigns in 1950–1951. See K. Varvaressos, *Report to the Greek Government on the Greek Economic Problem* (mimeograph), Washington, February 1952, p. 156.

57. Principally through overvaluation of imports and undervaluation of exports. See Varvaressos, *op. cit.*, p. 154.

hodgepodge of special devices designed to overcome the disadvantages of a highly overvalued currency. Until October 1952 Greece sought to encourage the exportation of a number of commodities by means of a complicated system of retention quotas and negotiable import rights. Exporters of certain commodities were granted import rights to use a portion of their export proceeds to bring in luxury and less essential commodities. The import rights were freely negotiable by the exporter and their prices reflected the nature of the commodities which could be purchased with them. In October 1952 this system was displaced by subsidies ranging from 15 to 50 per cent on designated exports, and by taxes on designated imports ranging from 25 to 200 per cent.

Following the April 1953 devaluation of the drachma, Greece was reported to have abolished all multiple currency practices and to have removed quantitative restrictions on a large percentage of her imports.

AUSTRIA

The postwar economic and financial history of Austria reveals some similarities to the Greek experience. Before 1950 exports covered less than half of Austria's import requirements. Since 1948 the cost of living has more than doubled and the level of wholesale prices in March 1953 was 236 (1948 = 100). While the political division of Austria into Allied and Soviet zones has retarded Austrian recovery, her self-support has exceeded that of Greece, and between 1948 and mid-1952 Austria's industrial production increased by more than 80 per cent. This recovery was reflected in Austria's commodity exports which rose from $207 million in 1948 to $454 million in 1951, and in her current account deficit which fell from $256 million in 1948 to $174 million in 1951 and to an annual rate of about $126 million in the first half of 1952. Austria has had deficits with both the dollar area and the EPU and other nondollar areas. These have been covered by U.S. dollar grants and credits and by indirect U.S. aid through the OEEC and EPU machinery. However, Austria has been in closer balance with the EPU area than with the dollar area and in the second half of 1952 she ran a small surplus with the EPU.

The Exchange Control System

The general structure of Austria's system of exchange and trade controls resembles that of the Western European countries. Most merchandise imports and invisible payments require licenses. Some imports from EPU countries are under open general license but Austria has not liberalized her imports so fully as have most other EPU countries. Foreign exchange income from all sources must be surrendered. Austrian bilateral payments agreements do not provide for the schilling as a currency of account so nonresident accounts in schillings have little significance in international trade.

The special features of Austria's postwar exchange system grew from the efforts of the government to deal with a highly distorted internal price structure, a product of rigid controls and latent inflation during the war. The government sought to remove these disparities by a series of controlled wage and price adjustments, but this process was complicated by continued inflationary pressures generated by the expansion of commercial credit and budgetary deficits. In an effort to hold down prices of essential imports Austria maintained the highly overvalued rate of 10.1 schillings to the dollar from 1946 to November 1949. This rate was in fact a subsidy to consumers and tended to increase inflationary pressures. It was also necessary to subsidize exports by a variety of devices which involved a complicated structure of *de facto* multiple exchange rates.

In November 1949 the Austrian system was simplified by the adoption of three selling rates of 14.57, 21.53, and 26.17 schillings per dollar; and two buying rates of 21.19 and 25.83 schillings per dollar. Under this system the volume of exports increased in 1950 by 51 per cent. In October 1950 the system was further simplified by the elimination of the 14.57 import rate, leaving a single rate of 21.23 schillings for all exports and commercial invisible earnings, a selling rate of 21.49 schillings for all imports and commercial invisible payments, and buying and selling rates for capital and noncommercial invisibles of 25.87 and 26.13 schillings respectively. The premium rates for invisibles encouraged tourists and also capital imports into Austria, while discouraging invisible payments not related to trade.

Even though the devaluation of November 1949 resulted in an expansion of Austrian exports, there were still certain exports which were not competitive at the 21.23 schilling rate. The Austrian authorities therefore employed a retention quota arrangement for several groups of exports including textiles, hats, iron and steel, aluminum and chemicals, with retention quotas from 20 to 60 per cent. This was abolished in December 1951 in favor of a system of "tied" or "linked" transactions. Under this, the exporter was permitted to retain a portion of his export proceeds, varying from 25 to 90 per cent, to purchase luxury or less essential commodities prescribed in a list of commodities eligible for linked transactions; or he may sell the retained exchange at rates approved by the national bank of Austria to other importers for the purchase of eligible commodities.

The Austrian authorities have also permitted barter transactions between Austrian exporters and exporters in countries with which Austria has no payments agreement. Since the exports require licenses, these transactions must be approved by the Austrian authorities who may require the exporter to collect a portion of the value in free exchange. Both the linked and the barter transactions involve an implicit multiple exchange rate, subject to regulation by the Austrian authorities.

On May 4, 1953 Austria established a par value with the International Monetary Fund of 26 schillings per U.S. dollar and is reported to have discontinued all multiple currency practices.

TURKEY

Government participation in industry and in economic development have been greater in Turkey than in any of the OEEC countries.[58] The Turkish government has employed rigid exchange and trade controls to mobilize her foreign exchange resources. In addition, Turkey has tried to direct her purchases toward soft-currency countries in order to utilize her inconvertible currency earnings. However, by increasing the proportion of her exports going to the dollar area and by reducing the percentage of her total imports coming from the dollar area, Turkey shifted her regional balance in 1951 so that she had a small surplus with the dollar area ($13 million) and a large deficit ($127 million) with the rest of the world. Since 1947 Turkey has had substantial over-all deficits on current account and

58. Recently Turkey has begun to return some of the state-owned industries to private ownership.

the substantial reduction of her deficit to $12 million in the first half of 1952 was offset by a deterioration of her position in the second half of 1952.[59] Turkey had an EPU deficit of about $100 million in 1951 and in 1952 of $118 million.

Turkey's exchange controls usually follow the Western European pattern, although as with Greece and Austria the domestic currency is ordinarily not employed as a unit of account in payments agreements. Imports are licensed and are divided into three categories: (1) goods of primary necessity and those which have been "liberalized" for importation from other OEEC countries; [60] (2) imports which may be purchased with the proceeds of specified exports or exchanged directly against specified exports; (3) other imports classified in order of their necessity or importance for which individual applications must be made to the central bank.

Permits are granted automatically by the central bank for imports included in the first group. The second group may be purchased with the proceeds of certain exports to the dollar area as well as to soft-currency countries. These exports, constituting only about one per cent of the total, are difficult to sell and the retention system is a means of subsidizing their exportation. Exporters may sell the right to use the retained proceeds to importers who want to import the commodities on the prescribed list. The price of the rights varies with the currency, and in 1951 rights to use U.S. dollars were sold under this arrangement at a premium of more than 70 per cent.

Except for returns from exports under the retention scheme all foreign exchange proceeds must be surrendered at the official rate. Most exports do not require a license, but documents relating to exports must be delivered to an authorized bank within ten days of the time of export. Export prices are checked against price lists issued by the Ministry of Commerce to determine whether or not there has been any undervaluation. The export proceeds must be appropriate for the country of destination as determined by Turkey's payments agreements. Where there is no agreement, payments must be made in U.S. dollars, "free" Swiss francs, or in sterling credited to the account of the central bank of Turkey. Certain goods may be ex-

---

59. *Europe the Way Ahead, op. cit.,* p. 325.

60. In 1951 Turkey had placed 60 per cent of her private imports from OEEC countries under open general license (1948 base). However, trade liberalization was abolished in 1952.

ported only under license to prevent their re-export for hard currencies. Thus Turkey seeks to prevent Dutch importers of Turkish tobacco from re-exporting the tobacco to the United States, thereby reducing Turkey's dollar market for her products.

OTHER WESTERN EUROPEAN COUNTRIES

Switzerland maintains no exchange restrictions on dollar payments but is a member of the EPU and in addition has negotiated payments agreements with twelve countries outside the EPU area. Switzerland's exchange and trade controls are designed to implement her bilateral agreements, including her agreements with the EPU countries. Her fundamental objective is to provide a market for her exports of goods and services (including tourism) to soft-currency countries and to obtain from these countries the imports they can supply. Switzerland, with a strong gold and dollar position, has no foreign exchange problems with respect to the dollar area. However, the country's tendency toward a surplus with the EPU area creates a problem. Her controls are designed to prevent an increase in her accounting surplus with the EPU area through capital imports from EPU countries and through the re-export of certain commodities by EPU countries to the dollar area.

Portugal also tends to run large surpluses with the EPU, but, unlike Switzerland, she has maintained restrictions on dollar imports similar to those imposed by other Western European countries. Early in 1952 Portugal blocked 30 per cent of the export proceeds of certain items to the EPU area and placed additional restrictions on a number of exports to the sterling area. During 1952 these measures reversed Portugal's position with the EPU.

Spain is not a member of the EPU and is the only country in Western Europe which has a system of explicit multiple exchange rates applying to current trade. Spain has a complicated system of effective exchange rates varying from eleven pesetas to the dollar to forty pesetas to the dollar. The large number of effective buying and selling rates is derived from the practice of requiring varying percentages of the export proceeds to be surrendered at the official buying rate, the remainder to be sold on the official "free" market. Foreign exchange for different classes of imports is purchased in varying percentages on the "free" market and the remainder at the official rate. In addition to cost restrictions achieved through multiple selling rates, all imports require import licenses granted in accordance with the need for the commodity. Unlike most Western European systems the issuance of an import license by no means assures the holder that he will be able to obtain the foreign exchange and frequently payments for imports are subject to long delays. In general the Spanish system closely resembles the systems prevailing among South American countries, to be described in the following chapter.

Chapter 13

EXCHANGE CONTROLS IN LATIN AMERICA

THE INDEPENDENT COUNTRIES of Latin America may be divided into three main groups from the standpoint of their exchange control systems. The first group, consisting of Cuba,[1] the Dominican Republic,[2] El Salvador, Guatemala, Haiti, Honduras, Mexico [3] and Panama are virtually free of foreign exchange controls.

A second group of countries—Colombia, Costa Rica, Ecuador, Nicaragua, Peru and Venezuela—maintain few quantitative restrictions or none at all, but use multiple exchange rates to control trade and payments.

The third group, comprising Argentina, Bolivia, Brazil, Chile, Paraguay and Uruguay, maintain more or less severe quantitative restrictions in combination with multiple exchange rates. In some of these countries the reliance upon quantitative controls as opposed to cost restrictions through multiple exchange rates is greater than in others. The degree of restriction achieved through denying import licenses for various categories of goods varies from time to time with the availability of foreign exchange. Quantitative restrictions usually discriminate between imports from different countries or currency areas in accordance with the availability of the currencies in which payment is made.

The Dollar Countries

It will be noted that the countries in the first group finance their trade with the rest of the world almost exclusively in dollars and

1. Cuba places a 2 per cent exchange tax on sales of foreign exchange for payments abroad. Her payments agreement with Spain provides for the financing of transactions between the two countries through a dollar account, and she has a franc-account agreement with France.

2. The Dominican Republic maintains a formal exchange control system but does not restrict payments. Import licenses are required for a few commodities and export licenses are required for sugar.

3. Mexico has no foreign exchange restrictions on dollar transactions. There are payments agreements with Argentina (for books and periodicals) and with France and Czechoslovakia.

maintain a high percentage of gold and dollar reserves behind their local currencies. Generally speaking, they do not have a balance of payments problem as such.[4] Some of these countries, including Cuba,[5] Mexico, El Salvador[6] and Haiti[7] have negotiated bilateral agreements with nondollar countries, but thus far these arrangements have accounted for only a small proportion of their trade.

Of the second group of countries, those relying principally on multiple exchange rates as a means of restricting payments, all but Peru are regarded as dollar account countries by British exchange regulations and the bulk of their trade with nondollar countries is conducted in dollars. However, Colombia, Ecuador and Peru do have several payments agreements with nondollar countries. Venezuela has had no balance of payments problems during the postwar period but uses a multiple rate device to tax the foreign oil companies and to subsidize certain exports. The other members of the group have been faced with serious balance of payments deficits from time to time but with improved positions since 1950 they have been able to relax their import restrictions.

The Nondollar Countries

All in the third group of countries, except Bolivia, are considered nondollar countries and most of their trade with the nondollar area is financed through bilateral payments agreements.[8] Balances in local

4. Mexico has been assisted from time to time by stabilization credits from the U.S. Exchange Stabilization Fund and in 1948 borrowed from the International Monetary Fund. All such credits had been repaid as of 1952.

5. In addition to a payments agreement with Spain in 1952, Cuba has entered into bilateral agreements with the United Kingdom, Western Germany, France and Chile. These agreements involve the sale of Cuban sugar against commitments to purchase certain commodities in the other countries. Payments to Spain require a license and must be effected through a special clearing account. A recent agreement with France involved the sale of sugar against payment one third in dollars and two thirds in French francs.

6. In 1952 El Salvador concluded an agreement with Western Germany whereby the latter will make available 75 per cent of the dollar proceeds from exports to El Salvador for imports from that country.

7. In 1952 Haiti concluded an agreement with France under which France is committed to an annual purchase of coffee from Haiti in exchange for a Haitian commitment to reduce tariffs on principal French exports.

8. Nondollar Latin American countries receive some gold and dollar payments through transactions with nondollar countries from the following sources: (1) offshore purchases for Western Europe with U.S. aid; (2) gold and dollar payments resulting from the exhaustion of credits in bilateral payments agreements; (3) dollar payments for certain commodities, e.g., Chilean copper, not covered by the payments agreements; (4) capital investments made with dollars.

currencies of Latin American countries are not generally used for international payment. Payments agreements with European countries usually employ a European currency or the dollar as the unit of account. If a Latin American currency is used, as with certain Brazilian and Argentine agreements, the accounts are usually single accounts maintained with the central bank, as distinct from the decentralized accounts employed in trade between Western European countries.

Reasons for Payments Difficulties

Postwar payments difficulties of Latin American countries have stemmed from four general sources:

1. Most Latin American economies have been under inflationary pressures generated by currency expansion for financing governmental deficits, increased borrowing for financing industrial and agricultural development, and export surpluses financed with credits to soft-currency countries.

2. Sharp fluctuations in the prices of raw materials and rising prices of imports have made for domestic instability and have complicated the problem of exchange stability and the provision of adequate supplies of exchange for essential needs.

3. Economic development programs have added to the foreign exchange requirements of these countries.

4. The nondollar countries have been unable to convert the proceeds of their export surpluses with soft-currency countries into dollars to meet their hard-currency deficits.

Raw material exporting countries have difficulty in insulating their domestic price structures from the sharp fluctuations in the prices of their exports. This has been a major reason why the Latin American countries have adopted multiple rate systems, which help insulate their economies from fluctuations in world demand. Many of these countries have meager gold and dollar reserves so they have lacked an adequate cushion against fluctuations in their export receipts. On the other hand, those Latin American countries whose currencies are backed largely or wholly by gold and dollars and whose exports have gone principally to the United States, have experienced less payments difficulties.[9]

9. This experience may reflect the monetary policies of these countries rather than the backing of their currencies or the direction of their trade.

TABLE 16

TRADE OF LATIN AMERICAN REPUBLICS WITH EUROPE, BY TYPE OF SETTLEMENT,
1948 AND 1949

(*Millions of Current Dollars, F.O.B.*)

Country Group	Year	Dollar Trade [a]	Bilateral Trade [a]	Total	Dollar Trade Turnover as Per Cent of Total
Total Latin American republics (excluding Venezuela)	1948	$1,176	$2,214	$3,390	35
	1949	902	1,802	2,704	33
Argentina, Uruguay and Paraguay	1948	186	1,747	1,933	10
	1949	91	1,258	1,349	7
Brazil, Chile, Peru and Bolivia	1948	442	458	900	49
	1949	368	525	893	41
Other Latin American republics [b] (excluding Venezuela)	1948	548	9	557	98
	1949	443	19	462	96

Source: Economic Bulletin for Europe, January 1951 (Economic Commission for Europe, Geneva),
p. 40.
a. Trade figures represent sum of merchandise exports and imports. "Bilateral trade" refers to
trade carried on under payments agreements which provide for either (1) extension of unilateral or
reciprocal credits before a settlement of clearing account balances is required, or (2) settlements of
clearing balances in currencies other than the dollar. "Dollar trade" refers to all other trade and
involves the assumption that payment must be made in freely disposable dollars when no provision
is made for other types of settlement. Approximate f.o.b. values for imports have been obtained by
a uniform deduction of 12.5 per cent from the recorded c.i.f. figures.
b. Colombia, Costa Rica, Cuba, Dominican Republic, Ecuador, Guatemala, Haiti, Honduras,
Mexico, Nicaragua, Panama, El Salvador.

Latin American Bilateral Agreements

Bilateral trade and payments agreements negotiated by the Latin
American republics are largely confined to countries in the central
and southern part of South America, including Argentina, Brazil,
Bolivia,[10] Chile, Paraguay, Peru and Uruguay, most of whose trade
with nondollar countries is on a bilateral basis. Most of the trade
and payments agreements of the Latin American countries are with
Western Europe. In 1949, 96 per cent of the European trade of the
Latin American republics in the dollar area (excluding Venezuela
whose trade is entirely on a dollar basis) was financed on a dollar
basis. On the other hand, in that year only 7 per cent of the European trade of Argentina, Uruguay and Paraguay was financed on a
dollar basis, the remainder being financed under bilateral payments
agreements. Brazil, Chile, Peru and Bolivia also have a number of
bilateral payments agreements with Europe, but 41 per cent of their
trade with Europe was financed with dollars and the remainder
under bilateral arrangements. (See Table 16.)

10. While Bolivia is a dollar account country under British exchange regulations,
she has bilateral payments agreements with Belgium, France, Spain and Argentina.

Second in importance are the bilateral agreements between the Latin American countries themselves, which link together most of the countries of central and southern South America.[11] Argentina and Brazil have several agreements with the countries of Eastern Europe and several Latin American countries have open dollar account arrangements with Japan.

Agreements with Western Europe

The early postwar agreements between Latin America and Western Europe enabled Western Europe to finance a substantial portion of its import surplus with Latin America without gold or dollar payments. This surplus was financed in part by swing credits and increased holdings of sterling, and in part by the sale of European investments in Latin America or the repayment of European loans. As European production and exports expanded under the Marshall Plan, several Latin American countries had deficits with Europe, thus tending to reduce their holdings of European currencies. Marshall Plan dollars have also financed a portion of Europe's purchases in Latin America.

The countries of Western Europe having the largest number of payments agreements with Latin American countries are the United Kingdom, France, Western Germany, Italy, the Netherlands, Sweden and Spain. The United Kingdom has bilateral payments agreements with all the Latin American countries except those listed in the dollar area. Only Chile is a member of the transferable account system, but sterling is frequently used to finance trade between Latin American countries. All the British agreements provide for the use of sterling as the unit of account, with accounts kept in London. Agreements with other Western European countries provide for a variety of arrangements, the most frequent involving single accounts with the European currency or the dollar as the unit of account. In a few instances, as for example the Brazil-Netherlands payments agreement, the unit of account is the Latin American country's currency.

The Latin American agreements with Western Europe are frequently complicated by special provisions for debt settlements and

11. The only payments agreements between the northern Latin American countries are between Colombia and Ecuador and between El Salvador and Nicaragua.

the unblocking of old balances arising from earlier commercial transactions or from interest, dividend and amortization payments. For example, some sterling balances accumulated during or prior to the last war were blocked and the postwar agreements provided for their gradual release. Some sterling balances held by Argentina and Brazil have been used to purchase British-owned railroads and other public utilities in these countries.[12] The agreements generally provide for swing credits with provisions for settlement in gold, dollars and occasionally sterling, when the credit limits are exceeded.[13] While Western Europe has paid a substantial sum of dollars in settlements with Latin American countries, these nations have been reluctant to use dollars for payments outside the dollar area.

Purpose of Agreements to Save Dollars

Both the Latin American countries and their European payments agreement partners have sought to save dollars by obtaining essential goods under the payments agreement arrangements. There has been little effort to liberalize trade in nonessentials and hence to balance trade at a high level. Latin American countries have tried to import commodities which contribute to economic development— machinery, steel, tin, heavy chemicals, petroleum and coal. They have been less interested in the admission of perfumes, wines, fine textiles and automobiles and have restricted payments for invisibles.[14] Latin American export prices have frequently been noncompetitive as a result of domestic inflation and overvalued exchange rates. Exports to Europe have also been curtailed by the desire to direct exports to dollar markets. Some Latin American commodities are not sold for soft currencies. For example, Chilean copper is ordinarily sold only against dollars and at times Chilean nitrates, Uruguayan wool and Brazilian coffee have been sold only against dollar payment.

12. British net disinvestment in Argentina, Brazil, Chile, Paraguay, Peru and Uruguay over the period 1946–1950 amounted to £210 million. *United Kingdom Balance of Payments 1946 to 1950,* Cmd. 8201, H.M.S.O., London, 1951.

13. With the notable exception of the April 1951 U. K.–Argentine agreement, the British agreements with Latin American countries do not provide for gold payments by Britain.

14. For example, the British have complained that Argentina's multiple rate system tends to keep out British exports of less essential goods.

Effects of the Agreements on Trade

An analysis of Latin American trade statistics reveals that their bilateral trade agreements with Europe have not achieved for the Latin American countries either stability of markets or a high level of exports, as compared with their trade with the United States. Latin American exports to Europe in 1951 were only 74 per cent by volume of the 1938 level while exports to the United States in 1951 were 178 per cent of the 1938 volume. Moreover, Latin American exports to the United States seem to have been somewhat more stable during 1948–1951 than Latin America's exports to Europe. Further, the European bilateral partners have not been able to achieve a high volume of postwar exports to Latin America relative to that of United States exporters. United States exports to Latin America in 1951 were 380 per cent of the 1938 level as compared with 155 per cent for European exports. (See Table 17.) British exports to the nondollar countries of Latin America were lower by volume in 1951 than they were in 1938.[15]

TABLE 17

INDEXES OF VOLUME OF LATIN AMERICAN MERCHANDISE TRADE WITH THE UNITED STATES AND EUROPE, 1938–1951

(Per Cent)

Direction of Trade	1938	1948	1949	1950	1951
Latin American exports to:					
Europe	100	81	65	73	74
United States	100	179	175	189	178
Latin American imports from:					
Europe	100	91	100	129	155
United States	100	329	301	314	380

Source: A Study of Trade Between Latin America and Europe, Economic Commission for Europe, Geneva, January 1953, p. 3.

Altogether the bilateral trade and payments arrangements between Latin America and Western Europe have not worked very smoothly nor have they provided either stability or a high volume

15. An important factor in Latin American trade with Western Europe, 1948–1951, has been the volume of offshore purchases with dollars under the ECA programs. In 1948 these amounted to $142 million but rose to $326 million in 1949, dropping to $193 million in 1950, and still lower in 1951. The high level of exports in 1948 can be explained in part by the extension of Latin American credits and the sales of capital assets owned by Europeans in Latin America. By 1949 most of these sources had disappeared. (See *World Economic Report, 1949–50,* U. N. Economic and Social Council, New York, 1951, p. 119.)

of postwar trade. The relatively small amount of transferability of balances, the restrictive Latin American import regulations and administrative delays and red tape have contributed to this result. In many Latin American countries, exporting firms and banks are unable to provide letter of credit facilities, and remittances from these countries are subject to such long delays and frequent changes in exchange regulations as to make the granting of credit a considerable risk. It is quite possible that both the Latin American countries and their European partners would have been better off if they had traded on a dollar basis.

Intra-Latin American Arrangements

Most of the nondollar Latin American countries are linked together with payments agreements. While credits have been extended by the creditor countries, principally Argentina and Brazil, trade under these agreements has not proceeded smoothly. Although trade among the nondollar countries is substantially higher than before the war, both the bilateral and the over-all trade figures reveal an exceedingly erratic pattern from year to year. Bilateral balancing is especially difficult among countries whose economies are not diversified and whose export commodities are few. Although sterling and dollars have been used to some extent for multilateral settlements, bilateral balancing has been the rule. Moreover, rigid controls over trade and administrative delays have kept trade balanced at minimum levels. As with trade with Western Europe, there has been a reluctance to use dollars for settling bilateral deficits within the area.[16]

16. In June 1948 the Economic Commission for Latin America requested the International Monetary Fund to study the desirability of establishing an arrangement for multilateral compensation within Latin America, presumably patterned along the lines of the intra-European payments arrangements. The Fund's study concluded that owing to the character of Latin American trade the possibilities for intraregional multilateral compensation were limited and that an expanded regional payments system could not materially assist Latin American countries in dealing with their fundamental balances of payments problems with the dollar area and with Europe. The Fund's report also pointed to the technical difficulties presented by multiple exchange rates and the lack of close cooperation between the central banks in the area. Another serious barrier to the establishment of an intra-Latin American clearing union is the existence of both dollar and soft-currency countries in the area. See *Multilateral Compensation of International Payments in Latin America,* U.N. Economic and Social Council, New York, May 1949.

Nearly all types of trade and payments arrangements are to be found in Latin America. However, there are relatively few two-account payments agreements and most of the agreements provide for a centralized clearing account as distinct from the decentralized agreements among Western European countries. Presumably this reflects the general lack of banking facilities for financing in terms of Latin American currencies along traditional lines. Also, the wide use of multiple exchange rates complicates two-currency arrangements, as well as arrangements involving transfers of commercial bank accounts to nonresidents. Most agreements designate the unit of account as the currency of one of the partners, predominantly Argentine pesos or Brazilian cruzeiros, or the U.S. dollar.

Other Bilateral Agreements

Latin American countries have a number of payments agreements with Eastern European countries including Yugoslavia, Finland, Czechoslovakia, Hungary, Bulgaria, Romania and Poland. Most of these provide for payments to be recorded on clearing accounts denominated in dollars. Swing credits are small or nonexistent and trade is rigidly controlled or conducted by state enterprises. Much of this trade is barter. As regards the East, several Latin American countries have dollar account clearing arrangements with Japan. Argentina has a payments agreement with Israel, and there have been a few barter arrangements with Asiatic countries.

COUNTRIES WHICH RELY MAINLY ON MULTIPLE EXCHANGE RATES

In 1952 Costa Rica, Nicaragua, Peru and Venezuela maintained virtually no quantitative restrictions on exchange payments, but relied exclusively upon cost restrictions achieved through multiple exchange rates. Ecuador and Colombia prohibit certain imports, but rely on multiple exchange rates to control the bulk of their trade. With some exceptions, the essential elements of the exchange restriction systems of these six countries consist of (1) requiring exporters to surrender all or a portion of their exchange proceeds at the official buying rate or rates; (2) permitting importers to obtain foreign exchange for certain categories of imports or for certain invisible payments at more favorable selling rates; (3) permitting most other transactions to take place without restriction at less favorable rates.

Postwar Foreign Exchange Problems

The postwar foreign exchange problems of these six countries may be traced in large measure to the fluctuations in prices of their principal raw materials exports. Coffee is an important export of all but one of these countries (Peru) and in the case of Colombia this single export constitutes 75 per cent of the foreign exchange income. The price of coffee approximately doubled between June 1949 and January 1950. The price of cacao, a leading export of Ecuador and Venezuela, and the price of cotton, a leading export of Nicaragua and Peru, have also behaved erratically in the postwar period.[17]

These countries have had difficulty in maintaining internal economic stability in the face of rapid changes in their foreign exchange income from basic exports. An increase in the prices of their exports brings about an expansion of the money supply and a general increase in demand for imports. Higher foreign exchange and gold holdings of the banking system frequently result in a multiple expansion of bank credit. By the time imports have expanded in response to the inflationary forces generated by the export surpluses, the demand for their exports may have fallen so they are left with the problem of curtailing imports by quantitative restrictions.

Inflationary pressures in these countries have also resulted from the export surpluses during the war and from government-sponsored economic development projects. There has been a general increase in the propensity to import brought about by the requirements for economic development and by changes in the spending habits of the populations.

The inability of these countries in the postwar period to adopt adequate fiscal and monetary measures to safeguard their internal economies against rapid shifts in external conditions has led them to employ a number of trade and exchange control expedients. Before 1950 most of them—with the notable exception of Venezuela—employed quantitative restrictions along with a complicated system of multiple exchange rates. Following the improvement in their terms of trade in 1950, these countries got rid of most of their quantitative restrictions and in some cases simplified their multiple exchange rate systems. For example, Costa Rica reduced the number of her selling

17. In 1950, 35 per cent of Peru's foreign exchange income was derived from cotton.

rates from six to two and abolished quantitative restrictions. Colombia and Ecuador also simplified their rate structures and eliminated quantitative restrictions on imports except for certain prohibited commodities. Similarly, Peru and Nicaragua have largely abandoned quantitative restrictions on imports.

Purposes Served by Multiple Rates

The multiple exchange rate systems of these countries are designed to serve one or more of the following purposes: (1) to hold down the prices of essential imports; (2) to keep the demand for less essential and luxury imports from reducing official exchange reserves without the use of quota restrictions; (3) to provide revenue for the state; (4) to foster economic development and protect local industry; (5) to permit certain invisible payments and capital exports at penalty rates but without quantitative restrictions. Not all these purposes apply to every country. For example, Colombia and Nicaragua control capital movements while Venezuela permits capital transactions without restriction at the basic rate.[18]

Four of these countries—Ecuador, Colombia, Nicaragua and Venezuela—depend for a portion of their governmental revenues on the spread between the rates at which the central banks buy and sell foreign exchange.[19] Governmental revenues may be derived from the application of surrender rates for exports below the average rate at which foreign exchange sales are made, or by the use of highly unfavorable rates or exchange surcharges for imports. The net governmental revenue derived from the exchange system depends of course upon the excess of the value of total foreign exchange receipts (in terms of the local currency) over the value of foreign exchange sales, after allowance for the operations of government import and export monopolies. Such profits are frequently used to finance economic development.

In countries where important exports are under the control of foreign companies, as in the case of Venezuela's petroleum, the multiple export rate is a means of taxing the foreign companies, which are

18. The multiple rate structures of all countries with multiple rate systems are outlined in Appendix 6.
19. Relatively small amounts of exchange profits have also been earned by the government of Peru.

required to purchase local currency at a penalty rate. While the multiple rate could be abolished in favor of other taxes, this would require a change in the concession contracts with the foreign concerns.

All these countries, except Colombia and Nicaragua, permit capital exports and the transfer of earnings without restriction. While in some cases transfers of earnings and the repatriation of registered capital may take place at more favorable rates, the existence of an unrestricted market undoubtedly tends to encourage foreign investment. Capital movements through unrestricted markets cannot affect official reserves so long as no attempt is made to stabilize the market rate with earnings derived from basic exports, the proceeds of which are subject to surrender. However, several of these countries from time to time stabilize the rates applying to capital movements with exchange from their official reserves.

Bilateral Payments Agreements

While none of the six countries in this group employs import quotas to balance payments, three of them—Colombia, Ecuador and Peru—finance an appreciable volume of their trade with the nondollar area through bilateral payments arrangements. Colombia has centralized or clearing account types of agreements with several European countries including Spain, Denmark, Western Germany, Sweden, the Netherlands and Italy. Some of these are limited to an agreement for the use of the proceeds of Colombian coffee exports, while Colombia's agreement with Western Germany provides that all current payments for commodities and invisibles are to be financed by crediting or debiting special clearing accounts denominated in dollars. Ecuador also has payments agreements with Western Germany, France, Italy and Chile, all of which employ a dollar clearing account as the means of settlement. Since neither Colombia nor Ecuador use import quotas, balance must be achieved by the import and export controls of the partner country, by government purchases undertaken by the Colombian or Ecuadorian authorities, or by permitting imports of commodities which are on a generally prohibited list. Thus Colombia allows imports of commodities on the generally prohibited list from France up to $1.5 million in exchange for an agreement by France to purchase $5 million worth of Colombian coffee. Colombia also permits imports of commodities which are on the generally prohibited list, in order to balance trade with countries with whom she has payments agreements. These same commodities may also be imported from other countries with which Colombia is maintaining a balanced trade.

Peru

Peru is the only member of the group outside the dollar area. Peru finances a considerable portion of her trade with soft-currency countries with sterling and in addition has bilateral payments agreements with several other countries including France and Italy. As with the other members of this group, Peru does not employ discriminatory import restrictions or quotas. Bilateral balance with payments agreements countries is achieved through a fluctuating multiple rate system with disparate cross-rates.

THE MULTIPLE RATE SYSTEMS

Each of these countries except Venezuela requires exporters to surrender all or part of their export proceeds to the central bank at the appropriate official rate. In Venezuela, only the petroleum-producing companies are subject to controls: they must obtain the local currency they require by selling foreign exchange to the central bank at the unfavorable rate of 3.09 bolivares to the dollar.[20] When world prices of coffee and cocoa fall below certain levels exporters of these products are permitted to sell their export proceeds at favorable rates ranging from one to 1.5 bolivares above the free market rate for dollars.

In Costa Rica the proceeds from merchandise exports and certain invisibles must be sold at a single official buying rate of 5.6 colones to the dollar.[21] Nicaragua also demands the surrender of proceeds from exports and invisibles at a fixed rate (6.6 cordobas per dollar)

20. A rate of Bs 3.046 to the dollar is applied to exchange sold by the oil companies in excess of the central bank's sales of exchange to domestic buyers during the year. In 1950 the spread between the petroleum rates and the basic selling rate of 3.35 bolivares produced a gross revenue of 136 million bolivares. Most of this was available for general governmental revenues and only a small proportion has been used to subsidize imports or exports.

21. Foreign-owned banana companies must surrender a portion of their export proceeds at the 5.6 colones rate. Domestic growers must surrender banana export proceeds at the official rate up to $1.00 per 100 pounds.

but surrender requirements of foreign-owned companies at this rate are limited to their local currency needs. In Ecuador the proceeds from most commodities must be surrendered at the official rate of 15 sucres per dollar but there are exemptions for the proceeds from exports of balsa wood, bananas,[22] ivory, petroleum, gold and certain minor items. Since the returns which need not be surrendered at the official rate may be sold at the free rate which ranged from 17.35 to 17.55 sucres per dollar in 1952, a multiple export rate is in effect.

Peru's multiple export rate is based on varying surrender requirements for different currencies which are exchanged for exchange certificates negotiable in the certificate market. In January 1953, 100 per cent of all dollar, French franc and sterling proceeds and 10 per cent of the proceeds of Argentine pesos had to be surrendered against certificates.[23] While the spread between rates in the certificate and draft markets was quite narrow during 1952 (ranging from 0 to 0.5 soles) official cross-rates between dollars and sterling in both the certificate and the draft markets were not maintained.[24] Thus Peru has employed a broken cross-rate system to balance her trade with the sterling area and with Argentina.[25]

Colombia maintained a special export rate for coffee during 1952. This was derived from the requirement that coffee exporters surrender a portion of their proceeds at 1.95 pesos to the dollar and the remainder at the basic buying rate of 2.50 pesos. However, Colombia is planning to eliminate the multiple export rate for coffee by progressively increasing the percentage of foreign exchange to be surrendered at the 2.50 peso rate by 1.5 per cent per month. As of June 15, 1953, the percentage of coffee receipts to be surrendered at the 2.50 peso rate was 70, and the remainder at the less favorable 1.95 peso rate. A differential between the 2.50 peso buying rate and the basic selling rate is maintained by a 3 per cent stamp tax on

22. As of April 1953 the proceeds from banana exports must be surrendered to the extent of $1 per stem.

23. Surrender requirements for dollars ranged from 50 to 100 per cent during 1951, and surrender requirements for sterling have ranged from 10 to 100 per cent.

24. In August 1952 the rate for dollar drafts was 15.39 soles and that for sterling drafts was 41.80 soles, reflecting a cross-rate of $2.72, as compared with the official dollar-pound rate of $2.80. In December 1951 the dollar-sterling cross-rate in the Peruvian market was $2.39.

25. Peru maintains official cross-rates between the dollar and the French franc. Francs acquired by the Bank of Peru may be converted into dollars by the Bank of France in accordance with the terms of the Franco-Peruvian payments agreement.

exchange sales, payable at the time of the issuance of the import license. Colombia gives special encouragement to certain minor exports [26] by permitting the export proceeds to be used to import some commodities, including automobiles and canned meats, which are otherwise prohibited. Exporters receive "export certificates" upon the surrender of their proceeds from minor exports, which they may sell to other residents if they do not use them to import the otherwise prohibited items themselves.

Import Licensing

Since the countries in this group rely largely upon cost restrictions rather than quantitative restrictions to limit imports, the purpose of import and exchange licenses, where they exist, is to make sure that the appropriate exchange rate is applied to the imported commodity or invisible payment. Licensing regulations differ among these six countries. Peru has no licensing requirement and Venezuela employs licenses and import quotas only for a few locally produced commodities primarily for protection. Costa Rica requires exchange licenses only for commodities for which exchange is granted at the more favorable official selling rate. Nicaragua requires licenses for imports but they are freely granted if the importer deposits 100 per cent of the local currency value. Ecuador also licenses imports but the permission is readily granted unless the items are on the prohibited list. Colombia requires a prior registration and an advance cash deposit of 10 per cent of the value of the import, but imports are permitted freely except for certain luxury items and goods of a type produced locally. These may be imported from certain countries. Most of these countries allow invisible payments without restriction.[27]

Multiple Import Rates

The systems of import rates range all the way from the free unitary rate of 3.35 bolivares to the dollar, which applies to all foreign exchange payments in Venezuela, to Nicaragua's system involving sev-

26. The list includes certain agricultural exports, salt, hides, leather manufactures, textiles, cement, beer, sugar, sulphur, tobacco, gold manufactures, nonprecious metals and nonmetallic minerals.

27. Colombia and Nicaragua limit expenditures for foreign travel and student remittances.

eral effective import rates. Costa Rica and Ecuador maintain an official selling rate for essential imports and a free rate for nonessential imports. In August 1952 the free market rate in Ecuador was 14 per cent higher than the official selling rate; in Costa Rica the corresponding spread was about 17 per cent.

Colombia does not have a regular free market although rights to import certain commodities which are otherwise prohibited may be purchased from exporters of minor exports. Except for government imports, student remittances and aircraft imports, most commodity imports and commercial invisibles are subject to a 3 per cent stamp tax (on 2.50 pesos per dollar) which is added to the basic selling rate of 2.51 pesos per dollar. For certain nontrade payments the stamp tax is only 2 per cent while in the case of other invisible payments, including foreign travel, there is a resident tax of 3 per cent in addition to the regular 3 per cent stamp tax. Except for the multiple export rate on coffee (gradually being abolished), Colombia's multiple rate system is derived from these special taxes, and from the sale by exporters of minor products of negotiable rights to foreign exchange to import commodities on the prohibited list.

In Peru, designated imports and certain invisibles may be paid for with exchange certificates acquired in a free market. These certificates are obtained from exporters who receive them when they surrender their export proceeds to the banks and are designated in dollars, sterling or other currencies. Since the certificates are normally slightly cheaper than the price of drafts in the same currency, imports which may be bought with certificates are paid for at a lower rate of exchange than other imports of goods and services which must be financed at the draft rate. Changes in the demand and supply for dollar certificates and drafts and in the demand and supply for sterling certificates and drafts frequently result in relative changes in the values of dollars and sterling in terms of soles. In 1951 the dollar-sterling cross-rate as represented by the prices of the two currencies in terms of soles averaged around $2.40, but in the spring of 1952 there was a shortage of sterling which caused a rise in the rate for sterling drafts and certificates to approximate parity with the official dollar-sterling cross-rate.[28]

28. When the sterling rate falls sharply relative to the dollar rate, there is a tendency for the Peruvians to sell Peruvian bilateral account sterling in the unofficial market in New York. (See Chapter 9.)

Nicaragua does not have a legal free foreign exchange market, except for notes and coins. There is a basic rate of 5 cordobas to the dollar which applies to government transactions and to 20 per cent of the proceeds of all exports and of receipts from invisibles; the remaining 80 per cent is surrendered at 7 cordobas to the dollar. The basic selling rate of 7.05 cordobas applies to most imports and non-trade remittances; the basic selling rate plus a surcharge of one cordoba applies to semiessential imports and designated invisible payments; and a surcharge of 3 cordobas is added to the basic selling rate for luxury imports and other invisible payments. Import licenses are freely granted if the importer deposits in cordobas 100 per cent of the value of the imports, including the surcharge. The advance deposit requirements help deter imports.

Transfers of Capital and Earnings

All these countries permit transfers of earnings on foreign capital although in some cases the capital must be registered with the exchange authorities. Colombia requires approval for transfers of capital and earnings but this is generally given if the capital is registered. In Peru and Venezuela all such transactions are made without restriction, while in Costa Rica and Ecuador registered capital and the earnings on registered capital may be transferred at the more favorable official rate.[29] Nonregistered capital and dividends may be transferred at the free rate in Costa Rica and Ecuador. In Nicaragua transfers of capital abroad require approval, but foreign-owned companies may transfer capital and earnings in accordance with their contracts. Transfers of registered capital may be effected freely up to 10 per cent annually of the value of the investment at the rate of 7.05 cordobas per dollar as against 10.05 cordobas for unregistered capital.

In countries where transfers of earnings and principal of registered capital are permitted at more favorable rates, the proceeds from capital imports must be surrendered, usually at rates corresponding to the transfer rates, before they will be registered. Registration of capi-

29. In Costa Rica transfers of registered capital at the official rate and transfers of earnings on registered capital are limited to 10 per cent respectively of the value of the capital. In Ecuador transfers of profits and amortization on registered capital may be made up to 12 per cent per year at the official rate of 15.15 sucres. All other transfers may be made at the free rate.

tal helps protect investors from fluctuations in the free market rates which tend to be less stable than the fixed official rates.

COUNTRIES WHICH RELY HEAVILY ON QUANTITATIVE RESTRICTIONS

Latin American countries which rely heavily on quantitative restrictions include Argentina, Bolivia, Brazil, Chile, Paraguay and Uruguay. While these countries benefited from the increased demand for raw materials in 1950, they have not achieved either internal stability or external balance in the postwar years. In contrast with their northern Latin American neighbors, who have made considerable progress in eliminating quantitative restrictions and in simplifying their exchange structures, most of these countries have had substantial reductions in their gold and dollar reserves and have had to increase their import restrictions.

The basic causes of their exchange difficulties have been (1) the expansion of bank credit and governmental deficits; (2) exchange rate structures which discourage exports and set subsidy rates for imports; (3) a complex of governmental regulations, including exchange controls, which reduce productivity and discourage foreign investment. All these countries use multiple exchange rate systems in addition to quantitative import controls. All of them have bilateral payments agreements with nondollar countries,[30] and most of their trade with nondollar countries is financed with soft currencies or through clearing accounts.

Import Licensing

All six members of this group use import licensing for balance of payments reasons and in some cases for the protection of home industry. Import licensing promotes balance of payments objectives by controlling the quantity and source of particular imports and by making sure that the appropriate rate of exchange and type of foreign exchange is employed in each transaction. The import licensing and quota systems tend to discriminate between sources of supply, particularly between hard- and soft-currency countries. Exchange

30. Bolivia is a dollar account country from the standpoint of British regulations but she trades on a bilateral basis with other countries including Belgium, France, Spain and Argentina.

budgets are drawn up on the basis of expected supplies of the various currencies and of the quotas established in their trade agreements.

The procedure for allocating exchange as between commodities and sources of imports differs widely from country to country. Several categories of goods on the basis of their essentiality are usually established. Licensing is generally fairly liberal for the "most essential" category, while licenses may be denied altogether for items at the bottom of the list. In Brazil, Chile and Uruguay certain necessary commodities are free of license, while in the other three countries all imports are subject to license.

Different exchange rates are usually assigned to different categories of imports so that there is a combination of cost restrictions and quantitative restrictions for the less essential items. Quotas for imports with particular currencies may be announced for six months or a year in advance, and in some countries "calls" may be issued from time to time for applications for certain classes of goods. Imports from hard-currency countries are frequently prohibited if the goods are available from soft-currency countries.

The volume of imports permitted from certain countries is usually determined by the bilateral payments position with the individual country. The existence of payments agreements and the necessity for maintaining a bilateral balance with partner countries or currency areas greatly influence the allocation of exchange and the issuing of import licenses. Bilateral payments positions also influence the determination of the commodities included in the exchange rate categories in the operation of the multiple rate systems. Thus there frequently is a form of implicit discrimination between sources of supply in the multiple rate systems.

Delays in Making Foreign Exchange Available

While in most countries an import license assures the importer of his ability to acquire the appropriate foreign exchange (practically, if not legally), the exchange control authorities of the countries in this group frequently fail to provide the exchange against valid import licenses. This means that foreign exporters must wait—sometimes for months—before they can collect drafts drawn on importers in these countries. Thus in the summer of 1952 the waiting period for the release of dollar exchange covering imports into Brazil averaged about four months. From time to time, Argentina and Chile have had a similar situation.[31]

Certain of these countries, notably Argentina and Bolivia, permit importers to purchase imports more freely if they furnish their own exchange. While this practice is designed to encourage residents with capital assets abroad to import their capital in the form of commodities of their own choosing, it is also a way to import commodities with exchange purchased in the black markets which flourish in most of these countries.

Exchange Surrender Requirements

As in all countries with multiple exchange rate systems, exporters have to surrender the appropriate type of foreign exchange at the designated rate of exchange. Where a "free" market rate applies to certain exports, as in Argentina, Bolivia, Brazil, Chile and Paraguay, exporters may be permitted to sell all or a portion of their proceeds from certain exports in the "free" market. But in most cases the "free" market is in fact a controlled market and simply provides a mechanism for subsidizing certain exports. Foreign-owned mining companies are sometimes exempt from the requirement to surrender exchange proceeds, but special (unfavorable) rates are applied to the companies' purchase of local currencies against foreign exchange.

Control over the export proceeds is exercised by requiring an export license before the goods can be passed through customs. Applications are generally approved by authorized banks on condition that the proper exchange payments are called for and that the proceeds will be sold to the bank within a given time. Licenses must show the value, destination and physical character of the exports and the licenses are checked against the commodities by the customs officials. Exporters are sometimes permitted to retain part of their proceeds to cover expenses in connection with exporting. In Paraguay exports are given *aforo* values which determine the amount of exchange to be surrendered. The remainder can be used by the exporter to meet expenses or sold in the free exchange market.

31. In 1950 the U.S. Export-Import Bank made a loan of $125 million to a group of Argentine banks to assist Argentina in liquidating past-due obligations to American commercial creditors. In February 1953 the Export-Import Bank made a loan of $300 million to Brazil to enable her to pay off similar obligations.

Control over foreign exchange receipts from nontrade items is usually less rigid in Latin America than in Europe. In Argentina and Uruguay all nontrade receipts may be sold in the "free" markets, but even where the regulations provide that all exchange receipts must be surrendered, black markets flourish openly and tourist dollars and other payments not subject to customs control rarely pass through official channels. Incoming capital must be surrendered in most of these countries in order to be registered and hence eligible for repatriation or dividend transfers at one of the more favorable rates. However, transfers of dividends at the preferential rates are frequently held up for long periods because exchange is not available. For example, before the establishment of the free exchange market in Brazil in February 1953, no transfers of profits from most American investments there had been permitted for well over a year.

THE MULTIPLE EXCHANGE RATE SYSTEMS

The multiple exchange rate systems of Argentina, Chile, Paraguay and Uruguay are rather complex, involving a number of buying and selling rates with wide spreads between them. Moreover, the rate structures and the commodities and services in each rate category are shifted from time to time in response to economic conditions. Unlike their northern neighbors, these countries have made relatively little progress in simplifying or stabilizing their rate structures. The complexity of the rate structures is perhaps surprising in view of the fact that these countries rely heavily on quantitative restrictions to control their trade. The free market rates for various currencies in Brazil, Chile and Uruguay break the official cross-rates, but the controlled free rate in Argentina does not.

In most of these countries the rate which applies to basic exports is less favorable than the free market rate or the rate on other exports. When world prices of their basic exports decline substantially, these countries usually change their rate structures in order to give exporters more favorable rates. Thus when wool prices fell in 1952 both Argentina and Uruguay so adjusted their rate structures as to offset the declining receipts of wool producers. Such changes in favor of exporters are often financed by increasing surcharges on luxury commodities imported by means of exchange purchased in the free market, without increasing the rates applying to essential commodities. Surcharges and exchange taxes on less essential imports also provide a way to mop up excess purchasing power in periods of high foreign exchange income. The following paragraphs will summarize the rate structures (as of June 1953) of each of the six countries in this group.

Argentina

Argentina has two fixed buying and selling rates of 5 and 7.5 pesos to the dollar and a controlled free market rate which in 1952 fluctuated around 14 pesos to the dollar. The 5 peso rate applies to certain basic exports including grains, fresh meats, hides and mineral products and to a few preferential imports including coal and petroleum. Before July 1952 the 5 peso export rate applied to all wool exports but with a declining wool market the effective export rate was changed to 6.25 pesos to the dollar.[32] While this more favorable rate applied to sales of wool against dollars and Argentine account sterling, it did not apply to wool exported for other soft currencies or to countries with which Argentina had payments agreements. In May 1953 the 5 peso rate again became applicable to exports of wool sold for sterling, leaving only wool exports for dollars at the more favorable rate. Thus the new wool rate tends to break official cross-rates by discriminating in favor of exports for dollars.

The 7.5 peso rate applies to exports of some processed meats, tanned leather and certain manufactures, and to a number of essential imports. In September 1952 Argentina devalued the effective export rate for salted and cured beef by permitting exporters of these products to sell half their proceeds at the controlled free market rate (14 pesos per dollar in February 1953) and to surrender the remainder at the 7.5 peso rate. During the same month Argentina shifted all canned meats from the 7.5 peso rate to the free market export rate. The export rate for quebracho extract was also devalued in October 1952 by permitting exporters to sell 40 per cent of their proceeds on the free market and to surrender the remainder at the 7.5 peso rate. All these changes were made without altering the two basic export rates or the effective rates for imports.

The "free" market rate in Argentina applies to a number of minor exports and to nonessential imports and invisibles.

32. In addition, wool exports for dollars and sterling were exempted from the 8 per cent export tax.

Chile

Compared with Chile's system, Argentina's multiple rate structure is a model of simplicity. Chile has at least eleven buying rates and eight selling rates, as far as the author has been able to determine. The excessive number of buying rates arises in part from the use of mixing rates (varying percentages of basic and free market rates) for certain animal products and agricultural commodities, and from a highly unfavorable rate applied to the foreign copper and iron mining companies for their purchases of local currency. The second rate of 19.37 pesos per dollar is in reality a tax on these foreign companies. While about a third of the purchases of foreign exchange by the central bank are from the foreign companies at the 19.37 peso rate, no sales are conducted at that rate. In fact, the bulk of the transactions in 1952 were at the 50 and 60 peso rates and at the "free" banking rate which fluctuated around 118 pesos per dollar in the summer of 1952. A few essential and government imports are at the subsidy rate of 31 pesos, but most of the essential imports which affect the cost of living pay either the 50 or the 60 peso rate per dollar.

Chile maintains four fluctuating rates: (1) a "free" market banking rate which applies to small mining, agricultural and industrial exports and to private capital inflow, on the buying side; and on the selling side to certain textile products, capital equipment and the transfer of profits on foreign capital; (2) a nonbanking free market rate [33] which applies only to invisibles; (3) a fluctuating wine rate which applies to wine exports and to a list of semiessentials including clothing, higher-grade textiles and tableware; [34] (4) a gold rate which applies to gold exports and to imports of designated nonessentials.[35] Disorderly cross-rates exist in the free markets since there is no attempt to support the markets for sterling and other soft currencies at levels corresponding to the rates for the dollar.

33. In June 1953 the free banking rate was 110 pesos to the dollar and the non-banking free market rate about 180 pesos per dollar.
34. The wine rate is set at the free banking rate plus 20 pesos.
35. The gold rate is usually higher than the nonbanking free rate. Permitted imports at the gold rate included a list of automobile accessories, motorcycles, watches and liquors.

Brazil

Brazil has relied less on cost restrictions achieved through multiple rates than have the other five members of this group. The official buying and selling rates of 18.36 and 18.82 cruzeiros per dollar, respectively, have been in effect since 1946. Before February 1953 these rates applied to all exports and to designated essential imports and certain nontrade payments including transfers of earnings on registered capital. All other remittances were subject to an 8 per cent tax, making the effective rate for such transactions 20.22 cruzeiros per dollar. An increase in wholesale prices of 150 per cent (as of December 1952) since 1946 resulted in a substantial overvaluation of the cruzeiro. The overvaluation was responsible for Brazil's substantial balance of payments deficits in 1951 and 1952. Although Brazilian imports are subject to license, import licenses have been issued in excess of the foreign exchange available to pay for them. Consequently a backlog of unpaid commercial drafts, estimated at over $400 million, had accumulated by the end of 1952.

The free exchange market introduced in February 1953 applies to only a portion of Brazil's foreign exchange transactions. On the demand side the free rate applies to financial remittances, and to licensed merchandise imports for which exchange is not made available at the official rate. On the supply side, the free market is fed by capital imports and by partial sales of commodity exports provided the commodity exported represents less than 4 per cent of the value of Brazil's total exports.[36] Proceeds of coffee and cotton exports, which account for nearly 75 per cent of Brazil's total exports, must be surrendered at the official rate.

In February 1953 the free market rate ranged from 38 to 40 cruzeiros per dollar (as compared with the official selling rate of 18.72 cruzeiros) and from 100 to 107 cruzeiros per pound. These rates indicate a breaking of the official dollar-sterling cross-rate. By June 10, 1953 the value of the cruzeiro on the free market had declined to 49 cruzeiros to the dollar. (See Addendum for new auction system.)

Bolivia

As with most other members of this group, Bolivia's economy has been highly inflated during the postwar period. The money supply

36. The percentage of export proceeds which may be sold in the free market ranges from 15 per cent in the case of menthol to 50 per cent in the case of raw wool.

has increased by two and a half times since 1946 and the cost of living more than doubled. Bolivia changed her par value from 42 bolivianos per dollar in 1950 to 60 bolivianos. While this rate was maintained for tin exports,[37] other rates ranging up to 130 bolivianos were applied to nontin exports. Thus the retention of the unfavorable rates for tin exports must be regarded as a tax on the foreign companies. Tin exporters were, however, permitted to retain from 40 to 42 per cent (depending upon the price of tin) of their export proceeds to cover their foreign currency costs. A selling rate of 60.6 bolivianos to the dollar was used for certain government payments, student remittances, and earnings on registered capital up to 15 per cent. The rate for essential imports was 63.6 bolivianos while a number of other authorized import and invisible payments were made at 104 bolivianos per dollar. Certain luxury imports and nontrade payments were permitted at 190 bolivianos per dollar and other invisibles and nonregistered capital exports were authorized at 247 bolivianos per dollar. Varying percentages of the proceeds of nontin exports had to be surrendered at the 60 boliviano and the 100 boliviano rates. In addition, small mining companies were given a special export rate of 130 bolivianos for designated transactions with European countries.

In May 1953 Bolivia eliminated her complicated rate structure and established a new par value of 190 bolivianos to the dollar. The 190 rate applies to all trade transactions, government payments, registered capital and certain specified invisibles. However, an ad valorem tax of 50 per cent is levied on less essential imports and one of 100 per cent on certain other imports. All other transactions take place at a fluctuating free market rate.

Bolivia's experience, together with that of other countries which have adopted complicated rate structures to avoid devaluing their basic rate, indicates that such rate structures create greater and greater price disparities which in turn require further complications in the rate structure until the system becomes virtually unmanageable. Bolivia's recent action may indicate a general trend toward the simplification of Latin American multiple rate systems.

37. In October 1952 the Bolivian government nationalized the three large tin mining organizations, the Patino, Hochschild and Aramayo companies.

Paraguay

In Paraguay the cost of living has increased more than tenfold since 1946. Since the war Paraguay has employed a number of expedients to adjust her effective exchange rates to changing internal and external conditions, sometimes involving the use of literally hundreds of effective rates.

In January 1953 the Paraguayan government undertook to reform its exchange system with monetary and fiscal changes designed to stem the tide of inflation. In the field of foreign exchange and trade, the policy objectives and measures of the new system are (1) stimulation of exports by higher effective rates of exchange; (2) the allocation of exchange for imports and other payments through strict adherence to the 1953 exchange budget; (3) gradual reduction and eventual elimination of import subsidies; (4) limitation of preferential import rates to goods "absolutely essential" to the national economy; (5) reintroduction of the exchange auction system for the payment of nonessential imports; (6) normal operation of the free exchange market, with rates fluctuating in response to market forces; (7) encouragement of the inflow of foreign capital and the repatriation of Paraguayan capital by the normal operation of the free market, by the authorization to import capital goods without exchange restrictions if paid for with funds held abroad, and by the guarantee of free withdrawal of, and remittance of investment income earned by, foreign capital.[38]

The new system provides for a basic export rate of 15 guaranis per dollar, which also applies to essential imports and designated nontrade payments.[39] There are, however, export taxes ranging up to 33 per cent of the value of the exports, which result in effective multiple export rates; subsidies are paid on certain exports up to 80 per cent of their value. The difference between the official valuation of exports (*aforo* values) and the actual export proceeds may be sold on the free exchange market or retained in deposits abroad.

Four import rates apply to different categories based on essentiality. A "free" market rate applies to nontrade transactions, to a portion of the export proceeds (the difference between *aforo* values

38. *International Financial News Survey,* January 23, 1953, pp. 227–28.
39. The par value of the guarani is 6 to the dollar. This rate applies only to government transactions.

and actual export proceeds), to the proceeds of certain minor exports, and to limited quantities of specified imports.[40] Of the four import categories, Group I is composed of merchandise "absolutely essential" for livestock raising, farming, manufacturing industries and public health, and also to imports of merchandise by the government and government corporations. Group I is subject to the rate of 15 guaranis per dollar or its equivalent in other currencies. Group II covers essential imports and is subject to the rate of 15 guaranis plus a 40 per cent surcharge, with an effective rate of 21 guaranis per dollar. Group III covers semiessentials and is subject to the 15-guarani rate plus a 100 per cent surcharge, with an effective rate of 30 guaranis per dollar.

Group IV consists of nonessentials and luxuries at the 15-guarani rate plus an exchange surcharge of 100 per cent and an additional auction surcharge. The auction system, provided for in the basic exchange legislation of 1945 but discontinued in 1949, has thus been reintroduced for merchandise classified in Group IV. Under this system, the central bank is to grant the available exchange for these imports to the highest bidders. Trade with Argentina is subject to special exchange treatment in which the basic rate of 2.5 guaranis per peso is applied to all exports and Group I imports but with lower surcharges on the other categories of imports.[41]

Uruguay

Uruguay has had less postwar inflation than any other member of this group. Like other raw material producing countries, however, Uruguay's economy has suffered severe strains because of fluctuations in world prices for her exports. While Uruguay maintains quantitative controls over import and export transactions and a complex system of multiple exchange rates, nontrade transactions in the free market are unrestricted. The free market has undoubtedly encouraged the substantial private capital movements into the country which have taken place from time to time. The buying rate for basic exports including wool, meat, linseed and wheat has been maintained at approximately 1.5 pesos per dollar since before the war, but buying

40. The free market rate averaged 49 guaranis per dollar in December 1952.
41. *International Financial News Survey*, February 6, 1953, p. 243; see also *Foreign Commerce Weekly*, February 23, 1953, p. 9.

rates for other exports, among them wool tops and canned meats, range up to 2.35 pesos per dollar.[42] Selling rates for imports vary from 1.5 pesos for newsprint to 2.45 pesos for luxuries, but the bulk of the sales have been at the rate of 1.9 pesos per dollar, which applies to essential imports. The free rate, subject to stabilization by the central bank, fluctuated between 2.40 and 2.76 pesos per dollar during the first nine months of 1952.[43]

When the wool market is strong, Uruguay has limited exports of certain grades of wool for sale against dollars, but in periods of declining wool sales they may be sold against inconvertible currencies. In the summer of 1952 the Uruguayan authorities permitted sales of wool to American importers against sterling and other soft currencies.[44] This in effect represents a depreciation of the wool export rate since Americans can arrange to pay for the wool in cheap sterling or other soft currencies purchased in the unofficial markets.

THE MEANS OF PAYMENT

Owing to the nature and direction of their principal exports most exports of Bolivia and Chile are financed with dollars while the bulk of the exports of Argentina and Paraguay are paid for in sterling and other soft currencies. In Uruguay the percentage of dollar proceeds from exports depends upon her wool sales to the United States, which have fluctuated substantially in the postwar period, and the extent to which Uruguay demands dollars for her wool. When wool is in short supply over half of Uruguay's exports are paid for with dollars.

Bolivia's tin and Chile's copper, which account for over half the exports of these two countries, are generally sold for dollars regardless of their destination. Bolivia is regarded as a dollar account country and has only a few payments agreements. However, a num-

---

42. During the first nine months of 1952, $120 million out of a total of $147 million in foreign exchange was purchased by the central bank at the basic buying rate of 1.519 pesos per dollar. About $9 million of exchange was bought at the 1.78 peso rate and about $17 million at mixed rates of 2.15 and 2.35 pesos per dollar.

43. In addition to the free market, subject to stabilization operations by the central bank, there is a parallel free market which is not. While speculative capital movements are understood to be restricted in the official free market, there are no controls over the parallel market. There is also a free gold market in Uruguay with no restrictions on imports and exports of gold.

44. See *International Financial News Survey*, June 6, 1952.

ber of her minor exports are traded under barter or compensation arrangements with European countries. Chile is a transferable account country and in addition has separate payments agreements with Argentina, Brazil, Ecuador, France, Spain and Western Germany. Chile also has limited payments and trade agreements with certain Western European countries covering her exports of nitrates and iodine. According to the special agreements with Sweden, Denmark, Portugal, the Netherlands and Italy, these products may be paid for in the currency of the purchasing country.

Argentina and Brazil (in that order) lead all other Western Hemisphere countries in the number of trade and payments agreements in operation. These countries have payments agreements with nearly all Western European countries and with most Latin American nations outside the dollar area. Both countries have bilateral account agreements with Britain, but sterling is frequently accepted for exports to nonsterling countries. French francs may also be accepted from third countries for certain commodity exports. Although most bilateral agreements provide for the liquidation of deficits beyond swing margins in gold or dollars, such payments are rarely made.

When one country reaches the limit of its credit facilities, exports to it usually cease unless additional credits can be arranged, or payment made in another soft currency. The exchange authorities frequently prescribe the currencies which may be accepted for exports according to the nature of the commodity as well as its destination. For example, in the spring of 1952 Brazil accepted dollars or sterling for exports other than coffee or cotton to Colombia, Denmark, Ecuador, Finland, Greece, Paraguay, Peru and Turkey; but required exports of coffee and cotton to these countries to be paid in dollars. On the other hand, cotton exports to Germany, Italy, Japan and the sterling area could be paid for in sterling. Argentina will accept soft currencies or clearing account credits for certain grades of wool when the wool market is depressed, but at other times she may require dollars.

Argentina's Trade and Payments Agreements

Argentine trade and payments agreements with certain countries are complicated affairs. Her agreement of January 1953 with Britain includes bulk purchase agreements for exports of meat and grain and for imports of petroleum, coal and tin plate; a provision covering overdue transfers of profits and other remittances due British residents; the provision of sterling swing credits to Argentina and the right of Argentina to convert sterling balances in excess of 20 million pounds into dollars; and an interchange of commodities valued at £167 million in both directions during the year.[45]

Argentina's five-year agreement with Italy, made in June 1952, provides in addition to a reciprocal swing credit of $100 million, a $75 million credit from Italy for the sale of capital goods to Argentina. Argentina is committed to supply grain, meat, oil seeds, hides and other raw materials to Italy. Under this arrangement Argentina also agrees to facilitate the immigration of a half million Italians into Argentina, the colonization costs to be financed in part out of peso balances held in Argentina by Italy. The detailed nature of Argentina's agreements and the absence of flexibility in their operation from the standpoint of freeing private trade arises from the tight administrative controls over foreign trade imposed by the Argentine government.

Paraguay

Only a small proportion of Paraguay's exports go directly to the dollar area but in 1948 and 1949 over half her exports were shipped in transit and a portion of these probably went to the dollar area. About 35 per cent of Paraguay's exports go to Argentina with whom she has a payments agreement using the Argentine peso as the unit of account. However, settlements may be made in sterling through a special arrangement with Britain. Although some exports to non-dollar countries are paid for in dollars, Paraguay (as of March 1952) required specific portions of certain exports including castor oil and tung oil (75 per cent), quebracho extract (60 per cent) and hides, cotton and coconut oil (50 per cent), to be paid for in dollars. However, other payments arrangements have been provided for in bilateral trade agreements involving an exchange of hard-currency commodities. Presumably Paraguay alters her requirements for dollar payments with changes in world market conditions for her exports.

45. *International Financial News Survey,* January 16, 1953.

Chapter 14

EXCHANGE ARRANGEMENTS IN THE FAR EAST [1]

FROM THE STANDPOINT of payments arrangements the countries of the Far East are a heterogeneous group. Exchange control systems range all the way from mild restrictions in Thailand and Hong Kong to quite stringent controls in Japan and India. Most of this group are regarded as soft-currency countries but the Philippine peso is a dollar currency and Japan, while a bilateral account country from the standpoint of the sterling area, is sometimes considered a hard-currency country. A majority of these countries, including Burma, Ceylon, Hong Kong, India, Malaya and Singapore and Pakistan in the sterling area, and the Associated States of Indochina in the French franc area are members of European currency areas. Until 1950 Indonesia was formally included in the Dutch guilder area and her currency continues to be closely associated with the guilder by virtue of her participation in the operation of Dutch payments agreements with third countries. Some of these countries, including Thailand, Ceylon and Malaya, have had favorable balances of payments during most postwar years, while others, like India, have had serious balance of payments problems.

Intraregional Relationships

In spite of their differences there are significant reasons, other than geographical proximity, for considering these countries as a group. A relatively large proportion of the trade of the Far East is among the countries of that region. In 1951 imports from other Far Eastern countries accounted for about 25 per cent of the region's total imports.[2] By way of comparison, trade between the continental OEEC

1. For purposes of this discussion the Far East will include Burma, Ceylon, Taiwan (Formosa), Hong Kong, India, Indochina, the Republic of Indonesia, Japan, Korea, Malaya and Singapore, the Republic of the Philippines, Pakistan and Thailand.
2. Source of data: *Economic Survey of Asia and the Far East, 1951*, United Nations, New York, 1952, p. 123 and Appendix Tables VI and VII.

countries represented 42 per cent of the total trade of that region during the same period, while trade among Latin American countries represented only 10 per cent of their total trade. As Japanese trade in the Far East recovers and industrial development proceeds throughout the area, intraregional trade is likely to grow.[3]

The currency links among these countries—their membership in the sterling area or their payments relations with the sterling area—and their relationship to the EPU because of membership in European currency areas provide a mechanism for multilateral settlements throughout much of the Far East. Only the Philippine Republic lies completely outside this network of payments arrangements; her only payments agreement is a dollar account arrangement with Japan.[4] A further common element in this region is the fact that most of the members are producers of raw materials, actively seeking foreign capital and other assistance for agricultural, industrial and general economic development. Most of them have ambitious development programs which make heavy drains on both internal and external resources, and which probably will influence their balance of payments positions and foreign exchange and trade policies for many years to come. Finally, political independence is so recent an achievement in most of these countries that they tend to be extremely nationalistic in their approach to both economic and political questions.

The Balance of Payments

In general, the balance of payments positions of the Far Eastern countries have been characterized by substantial current account deficits, especially during the early postwar years, and by sharp fluctuations in export proceeds reflecting the movements of raw material prices. In 1938 the exports of these countries—excluding China, Korea and Japan—were 16 per cent higher than their imports; in 1946 exports of these countries were 17 per cent below imports. This

3. Over half of Japan's exports went to Far Eastern countries during 1951, and about a third of her imports came from that region.

4. The system is by no means complete even without the Philippines. For example, Japan has been reluctant to accept sterling from nonsterling area countries. For a discussion of trade and payments arrangements of Far Eastern countries see *Country Reports on the Working of Trade Agreements*, August and November 1951, and *Working of Trade Agreements in the ECAFE Region*, November 1951, both prepared by the UN Economic Commission for Asia and the Far East, Bangkok, Thailand.

import surplus continued to rise until 1948 when it reached a maximum of about $800 million, but two years later nearly all these countries had developed export surpluses.[5] However, the volume of exports remained below prewar levels. Of the principal commodity exports, rice, fats and oils, jute and tin were all below their prewar level and only tea and rubber were above.[6]

In the postwar period exports of the Far East to Western Europe have been substantially less than before the war. In 1950 and 1951 the indexes of the volume of imports from the Far Eastern countries (excluding Japan) into seventeen Western European countries (including Finland) were 109 and 132 respectively (1948=100) as against a volume index of 162 in 1938.[7] Latin American exports to Europe have followed much the same pattern, a factor in the greater dependence of Western Europe upon imports from the United States. Imports of Far Eastern countries from Western Europe have been considerably higher than before the war; in 1951 the volume was approximately 65 per cent larger than in 1938.

The large import surpluses of the early postwar years were financed by drawing down sterling balances accumulated during the war in the sterling area countries and by American aid to Japan, China, Taiwan, the Philippines and Korea. The 1950–1951 export surpluses achieved by most of these countries could not have been realized without the highly restrictive import policies which have characterized the area. In general, the current account positions of these countries are less favorable than their trade balances since they normally have a substantial deficit on investment income and services account.

During 1950 and 1951 several Far Eastern countries, including Ceylon, Malaya, Pakistan, Indonesia and Thailand, restored their prewar surplus positions with the United States. To some extent these dollar surpluses were used to settle deficits with Europe but it is by

---

5. In the latter half of 1950 all of the Far Eastern countries except Indochina and Korea had export surpluses. In 1951 India developed a large deficit on current account and the Philippine current account shifted from a surplus in 1950 to a deficit in 1951. On the other hand Pakistan's current account position shifted from a deficit in 1950 to a large surplus in 1951. However, the fall in raw materials prices resulted in deficits for most Far Eastern countries in 1952.

6. *Economic Survey of Asia and the Far East, 1950,* United Nations, New York, 1951, p. 318.

7. *Preliminary Report on Trade Between the ECAFE Region and Europe,* UN Economic Commission for Asia and the Far East, Bangkok, Thailand, December 1952, p. 15.

no means clear that Europe can count on large dollar receipts from this area as was the case before the war. The competitive advantage of dollar goods, the desire to build up their own gold and dollar reserves and their greater political and financial independence have made these countries less willing to turn over their dollars to European financial centers. In addition, Western Europe has found it more difficult to maintain a current account surplus with the area because of the reduction of investment income from these countries.

During the latter half of 1951 the favorable current account positions of several countries in the Far East were reversed and the surpluses of most of the others reduced.[8] This change occurred largely as a result of the decrease in the prices of such major exports as rubber, tea and jute. But the demand for imports remained high due to the inflationary impact of the export surpluses of the previous years, and the accompanying expansion of bank credit. Fiscal deficits arising partly from the large developmental expenditures of the governments have also contributed to the unfavorable trade balances. With the sharp increase in foreign exchange earnings, import restrictions were relaxed in 1951 but they were tightened again following the deterioration of the balance of payments of the Far Eastern countries in the second half of that year.

TRADE AND PAYMENTS MECHANISMS

All members of the Far East area have exchange control systems and all but two—Thailand and Hong Kong—maintain fairly severe quantitative import controls for balance of payments reasons. All these countries require exporters to surrender export proceeds to the control authorities though in Thailand surrender requirements are generally limited to a portion of the proceeds from rice, tin and rubber, the principal exports. Multiple exchange rates are employed in Hong Kong, Indonesia, Korea, the Philippines, Taiwan (Formosa) and Thailand and cross-rates apparently are broken in all these countries except the Philippines.

8. Total export earnings of ten principal raw material countries of the Far East (excluding China and Japan) were $4,400 million in the first half of 1951—more than double that of the corresponding period of 1950. Earnings fell to $3,400 million in the second half of 1951. *Economic Survey of Asia and the Far East, 1951*, United Nations, New York, 1952, p. 79.

Currencies Employed in Trade

The major countries in this area, except Japan and the Philippines, use European currencies, principally sterling and French francs, to make international payments among themselves and with other non-dollar currency areas. Apart from Japan, the Far Eastern countries have entered into only a few payments agreements but they participate in the payments agreements of the Western European countries to whose currency areas they are attached. Thus so long as there is a multilateral payments system in Western Europe the problem of multilateral settlements among most of the countries in the Far East is automatically solved. The vast bulk of the intraregional trade of the area is financed with sterling.

The Philippines trade on a straight dollar basis except with Japan; in 1951 over two thirds of the trade of this country was with the United States. Japan, on the other hand, sells more than half of her exports to Far Eastern countries and less than a fourth to the dollar area. Her trade with the sterling area is conducted in sterling under a bilateral agreement (with no provision for gold settlements) and with other nondollar countries and the Philippines through clearing accounts denominated in dollars with modest swing credits.

Trade Agreements

The independent countries of the Far East have entered into a number of trade agreements which to a considerable degree govern their trade among themselves and with other nondollar countries. Except in the case of countries with dollar clearing account arrangements with Japan, the objective of most of these trade agreements is not primarily to establish a bilateral balance of trade. The multilateral trading facilities offered by the payments arrangements make bilateral balancing unnecessary. The major objectives of the trade agreements have been (1) to insure a source of supplies of essential foodstuffs, industrial raw materials and capital equipment; (2) to develop markets for exports; (3) to conserve hard-currency exchange.[9]

The trade agreements of the Far East are of various types. Some involve bulk purchase contracts for rice, wheat or other essential

9. *Economic Survey of Asia and the Far East, 1950*, p. 293.

foodstuffs or raw materials. For example, Thailand makes annual contracts to supply certain quantities of rice. There are also barter arrangements such as the 1951 agreement between India and the USSR for the exchange of raw jute against 50,000 tons of wheat.[10] Other trade agreements are little more than an exchange of letters including lists of commodities which each country is interested in importing from the other, or general arrangements to ease import controls on specific commodities. Still other agreements provide minimum quotas for the issuance of import and export licenses covering a long list of commodities and an estimate of the value of trade each way. Some of the more detailed of these agreements are called "trade plans" covering import and export quotas for a number of commodities. They frequently provide for joint commissions to supervise the operation of the plans and to recommend changes from time to time.

Except for the bulk purchase contracts and some of the export commitments, the trade agreements, as a rule, are permissive rather than binding. Where specific quantities of imports are listed each country agrees to issue licenses at least up to the amount indicated but actual imports may be larger or smaller and trade may take place in items not listed if the governments decide to issue the appropriate licenses. During 1950 and 1951 there was a tendency for countries to issue open general licenses for a number of commodities, authorizing importation from any soft-currency country. This usually included all the countries of the Far East except the Philippines and Japan.[11]

While much of the trade of the Far Eastern countries is subject to import and export licensing, most of it is conducted through private channels. In Burma the state has a monopoly over the exports of rice and timber while in Thailand rice exports are handled by the government. State import monopolies over basic foodstuffs are maintained in Ceylon, India, Malaya and the Philippines, all of which tend to be food-deficit countries. In India the government handles certain other essential imports as well.

10. See *Economic Bulletin for Asia and the Far East,* Vol. II, No. 1, UN Economic Commission for Asia and the Far East, Bangkok, Thailand, August 1951, pp. 17–19, for summaries of trade agreements.

11. In November 1951 India included Japan in the list of soft-currency countries.

The Exchange Control Systems of Individual Countries
THE STERLING AREA COUNTRIES

The independent countries of the sterling area—Burma, Ceylon, India and Pakistan—have exchange controls over all foreign currencies including sterling. In the British dependencies of Malaya, Singapore and British Borneo there are no controls with respect to payments within the sterling area, but controls over payments to and from nonsterling countries follow the British pattern.

In all sterling area countries the regulations of the manner of payments and receipts in transactions with nonsterling area countries are practically identical with British regulations. Payments and receipts are credited or debited to the appropriate sterling accounts held in British banks or, where payments agreements or other arrangements provide for the use of foreign currencies, payments and receipts are made through the appropriate foreign accounts. In India and to some extent in Pakistan some transactions are financed through Indian or Pakistan rupee accounts but these are generally convertible into the appropriate sterling account of the nonresident owners. However, the vast majority of the international transactions of these countries are financed in sterling.

All the independent sterling area countries in the region require the proceeds of exports to be surrendered at a single official rate. Thus even sterling and sterling area currencies are treated as foreign currencies from the standpoint of exchange control. Before the sterling devaluation of 1949 there were virtually no exchange restrictions between India and Pakistan. However, following Pakistan's refusal to devalue her currency, trade between the two was brought to a temporary standstill. Under the terms of an agreement of February 1951, all remittances between India and Pakistan are subject to the same restrictions which apply to any other sterling area country. Remittances for trade and service payments are made on a rupee basis through authorized dealers. Trade transactions require licenses except for goods under open general license, and other nontrade payments are subject to certain restrictions imposed by each country. India agreed to the exchange parity established by Pakistan with the Monetary Fund,[12] and balances of each country's currency with the central

12. In India the official selling rate for Pakistan rupees is 69.4 Pakistan rupees to 100 Indian rupees.

bank of the other country are freely convertible into unblocked sterling.

All the sterling area countries of the Far East discriminate against dollar imports and in most cases against imports from Japan as well. Imports from the sterling area and other soft-currency countries are liberalized or restricted according to the over-all balance of payments position of each country. However, liberalization of imports of particular commodities may be governed by trade agreements.

The mechanism for the control over foreign exchange payments and receipts is similar for all four countries but the degree of restriction differs from country to country. All foreign exchange receipts must be surrendered and foreign exchange dealings are conducted through authorized banks; both merchandise and invisible payments are licensed. Usually certain imports are prohibited while others are under open general license either from all countries or from all soft-currency countries. Other commodities require specific import licenses which are allocated to importers on the basis of past imports (with an allowance for new firms) or to actual users on the basis of their current requirements.[13] Holders of valid licenses may purchase the appropriate exchange from authorized banks but the exchange and customs authorities maintain a check on actual imports to see that they conform to the terms of the license.

Import control authorities usually give priority to essential consumers' goods and capital goods needed for economic development. In 1950 and 1951 Ceylon and Pakistan granted import licenses quite liberally, particularly for imports from soft-currency areas; it is estimated that 70 per cent of Pakistan's imports were free from restriction in 1950.[14] However, in July 1952 Pakistan substantially reduced the number of items which could be imported freely. Pakistan exports declined rather sharply in 1952, partly because she maintained an overvalued rupee.[15]

India's policy has been to permit the maximum volume of imports allowed by her current exchange earnings plus the release of sterling balances previously blocked by Britain. Nevertheless, India has had

13. For a discussion of India's import policy see "Import-Licensing Policy for January-June, 1952," *Foreign Commerce Weekly*, March 3, 1952, p. 15.

14. *Economic Survey of Asia and the Far East, 1950*, p. 289.

15. See "Pakistan's Interest in Barter," *The Statist*, September 27, 1952, p. 375.

to adopt a more restrictive import policy than have Pakistan and Ceylon, both of which attained substantial trade surpluses in 1951. India is also influenced in her exchange control policies by the desire to protect local industries. One of the conditions for putting a commodity on open general license in India is that there is no significant local production of it.[16]

In India, Pakistan and Ceylon exchange is freely granted under license for invisible payments in connection with trade transactions and for the remittance of earnings due to nonresidents. Foreign exchange for business or educational travel abroad is permitted up to certain amounts depending upon the country to be visited, but exchange for pleasure travel in hard-currency areas is usually denied.

Trade-Quota Agreements

Although the independent sterling area countries do not as a rule negotiate payments agreements, all of them have trade-quota and barter agreements with other countries, including other sterling area members. India has the largest number of trade-quota agreements, including agreements with Austria, Burma, Ceylon, Czechoslovakia, Egypt, Finland, Western Germany, Hungary, Indonesia, Iraq, Norway, Pakistan, Poland, Spain, Switzerland, Yugoslavia and Japan (as a participant in the wider sterling area trade agreement). In addition, India has barter agreements with the USSR, Argentina, China and Egypt calling for the exchange of specific quantities of commodities. The purposes allegedly served by these trade agreements include: (1) helping to achieve balance of payments equilibrium; (2) obtaining needed imports; (3) providing a market for India's exports. About one sixth of India's trade in 1950 was with trade-agreement countries.

Pakistan has entered into fewer trade-quota agreements than India and, until December 1952, a smaller proportion of Pakistan's imports were controlled by single country licensing.[17] Ceylon has relatively

16. *Ibid.*, p. 287. Other conditions in India are (1) that the commodity is essential for industrial or agricultural production or for living or health; (2) that the volume of imports will not seriously affect India's balance of payments position.

17. In December 1952 Pakistan canceled all open general licenses. (See *International Financial News Survey*, December 5, 1952, p. 184.) In February 1953 the Pakistan government announced a policy of permitting barter transactions in cotton exports. (See *The New York Times*, February 5, 1953.)

few trade-quota agreements and most private imports from countries outside the dollar area (plus Japan and Western Germany) are under open general license.[18] Ceylon's basic food imports are under government monopoly.

Reasons for the Existence of Restrictions

The restrictive systems of the Far Eastern sterling area countries have a variety of purposes. As cooperative members of the sterling area these systems all maintain discriminatory restrictions against dollar imports and against imports from any country with which a sterling area deficit must be settled in gold. However, these countries have generally followed Britain's lead with respect to imports from the EPU area. India, Pakistan and Burma maintain restrictions on current transactions to protect their over-all balance of payments positions. India and Pakistan have had current account deficits in most postwar years, financed chiefly by drawing down their sterling balances.[19] Burma, on the other hand, had current account surpluses during the period 1948–1952, but these were accompanied by restrictions on payments for imports.[20]

India and Pakistan have been in a condition of disequilibrium throughout the postwar period. The reasons are similar in the case of both: (1) latent inflation resulting from the large internal expenditures during the war, accompanied by a sharp reduction in imports due to wartime shortages; (2) large capital expenditures financed by a rise in commercial bank loans and increased governmental indebtedness, which gave rise to a further expansion of the money supply in the postwar period; (3) an increase in the propensity to import resulting from the capital development programs and changes in the spending habits of the population; (4) fluctuations in the prices of exports which gave rise to an expansion of incomes and money supply in years of high prices not offset by internal deflation in years of lower prices; (5) food shortages resulting from occasional crop failures but more generally from the failure of the food supply to expand with the needs of the rapidly growing populations.

18. Imports from Germany and Japan are licensed to insure that they will be used by Ceylonese residents only.

19. India had a current account surplus of $128 million in 1950 and Pakistan a surplus of $166 million in 1951. In 1952 both countries had current account deficits.

20. In 1952 Burma's trade surplus was $72 million.

While some of these factors making for disequilibrium are amenable to better monetary and fiscal management, others are less tractable. The economies of all of these countries, including Ceylon, are highly vulnerable to sudden shifts in the terms of trade and to changes in the demand for their exports. The economic impact of the current social revolution in these countries is enormous. Widespread famine with thousands of deaths due to starvation is no longer regarded as the normal means of adjustment to the food shortages which have characterized those lands for generations. The urge for economic development at a rate far exceeding local savings available for investment is also a powerful force making for external and internal disequilibrium.

Ceylon: a Special Case

Ceylon is an exception to the general rule. That country had a current account surplus in every year except one (1947) during the period 1946–1951, and yet has maintained few restrictions on imports except those from the dollar area. In 1951 there were practically no restrictions on nondollar commodity imports or upon imports of essential goods from the dollar area, including capital goods, food grains, typewriters, refrigerators and even toothpaste. Restrictions on imports of luxury items from the dollar area were maintained largely as a means of enabling the country to make a maximum contribution to the dollar reserves of the sterling area. Ceylon's dollar surplus has tended to be even larger than her over-all surplus.

Ceylon's external position, however, is very vulnerable to changes in the prices of her major exports, 90 per cent of which are tea, rubber and coconut oil. On the other hand, two thirds of Ceylon's requirements of staple food, 90 per cent of her cotton textiles, and all her fuel must be imported. Between March 1951 and July 1952 the world price of tea declined by 38 per cent, the price of rubber by 49 per cent, and the price of coconut oil by 65 per cent. In addition the United States sharply reduced customary purchases of natural rubber from Ceylon. These changes in the world market were largely responsible for the shift in Ceylon's current account position from a surplus of $35 million in 1951 to a deficit of $83 million in 1952. As a consequence, Ceylon tightened her restrictions on dollar imports in August 1952.

Hong Kong

Although the British crown colony of Hong Kong officially belongs to the sterling area, its exchange system differs markedly from the usual pattern because there is a free market for dollars in the colony. Traditionally a large part of Hong Kong's international transactions have served to finance entrepôt trade with the mainland of China and between other areas of the Far East both within the area and with the outside world. The elimination of a free exchange market for U.S. dollars would have crippled this trade. Therefore the British government permitted the free market to continue after 1939 when the rest of the sterling area adopted controls. However, Hong Kong has both trade and exchange controls, including a multiple rate system. The combination of controls and a fluctuating free market for U.S. dollars makes for a fairly complicated arrangement.

The U.S. dollar proceeds of most Hong Kong exports which originate in the colony itself, in China, Macao, or Korea are freely disposable. However, portions of the dollar proceeds from exports of cotton yarn, lead, silver, tin, copper and wood oil must be surrendered; the remainder may be sold in the free dollar market. This requirement gives rise to several export rates since the percentage of export proceeds to be surrendered at the official buying rate of 5.7 Hong Kong dollars to one U.S. dollar varies from 15 per cent for wood oil to 50 per cent for cotton yarn. All U.S. dollar proceeds from exports originating in other countries must be surrendered.

Finally, exchange proceeds in other currencies from exports to any country except China, Korea, Macao and the sterling area must be received in the appropriate form and surrendered. While sterling received from exports to the sterling area (and to China, Korea and Macao) need not be surrendered, sterling transfers to Hong Kong from other members of the sterling area are carefully controlled in order to prevent dollar exchange leaks through the free dollar market in Hong Kong.

Capital and invisible transactions through the free U.S. dollar market in Hong Kong are not restricted in either direction.[21] Transactions involving sterling payments require permission, however,

21. On July 9, 1953 the free U.S. dollar rate was 6.05 Hong Kong dollars to one U.S. dollar.

although Hong Kong has unofficial markets for sterling and other nondollar banknotes.

Except for a few specified items most imports from China, Indochina, Indonesia, Macao, the Philippines, Thailand, the sterling area and the United States are free of license. Imports from other countries, however, require both import and exchange licenses. The purpose of the licensing is largely to implement British trade and payments agreements with the countries other than those mentioned above. On the other hand, imports from these specified countries are not ordinarily licensed since this would interfere with Hong Kong's entrepôt trade. Since June 1951 Hong Kong has required a license for the export or import of strategic materials. Partly as a result of controls over exports of such materials to China, Hong Kong's exports to that country fell sharply in 1952.

Payments for authorized imports and invisibles may be made at the official selling rate of HK $5.8 to the U.S. dollar, when payment is made in sterling or other soft currencies covered by British exchange regulations. Except for a few essential imports and certain authorized invisible and capital items which are permitted at the official rate under license, all payments for imports and nontrade payments in dollars must be made by purchasing the dollars at the free market rate. Since this rate frequently is above the official rate which applies to all sterling imports, Hong Kong's multiple rate system involves a broken cross-rate.

Decline in Trade

Partly as a result of the restrictions imposed by the Korean war on trade with China, Hong Kong's total trade in 1952 showed substantial decline over the first half of 1951.[22] There is also evidence that Hong Kong is employing import restrictions to protect local industry and to help reduce the deficit of the sterling area with nonsterling countries. For example, it was announced in May 1952 that Hong Kong had restricted her imports of Japanese goods to about half the 1951 volume. The purposes were (1) to protect local industries, particularly the textile industry; (2) to reduce Japan's rate of accumula-

22. In the first eleven months of 1952 Hong Kong's exports were U.S. $507 million as compared with U.S. $650 million for the same period in 1951. *International Financial News Survey,* February 6, 1953, p. 240.

tion of sterling; (3) to prevent the "dumping" of cheap Japanese goods in southeast Asia through re-exports from Hong Kong.[23] Before October 1951 trade with Japan was conducted under a special dollar account payments agreement. Since that time Hong Kong has financed her Japanese trade with sterling in accordance with the terms of the Anglo-Japanese payments agreement.

THE REPUBLIC OF INDONESIA

Before 1949 Indonesia was under the sovereignty of the Netherlands and until 1951 was a member of the Dutch guilder area. Since 1949 Indonesian trade and exchange controls have been completely independent of Dutch control, but certain economic and financial links with the Netherlands remain. While Indonesia does not pool her hard-currency reserves with those of the Netherlands and has not undertaken an indefinite obligation to hold guilders, the rupiah and the guilder are closely related through joint payments agreements with third countries.

Payments and receipts between the Netherlands and Indonesia and those arising out of transactions with third countries with which the Netherlands maintains a payments agreement are cleared through special accounts known as "A" accounts.[24] The central "A" accounts are kept in the Nederlandsche Bank in the Netherlands and in the Javasche Bank in Jakarta, with subaccounts in authorized commercial banks in the two countries. All payments between the two countries are made by debits and credits to the "A" accounts and there is a swing credit of 25 million guilders.[25] Whenever the swing credit is exceeded the creditor may demand coverage in foreign exchange acceptable to him.[26]

The Dutch-Indonesian Agreement

The unique feature of the Dutch-Indonesian agreement lies in the fact that all payments between Indonesia and third countries with

23. *International Financial News Survey*, May 23, 1952, p. 362.

24. See "Text of the Payments Agreement between the Netherlands and Indonesia" (translation), *Handelingen der Staten-General, Annexes 1949–50*, April 1, 1950.

25. The swing credit may be exceeded by Indonesia so long as the excess is not more than 80 per cent of the estimated value of the tin and tin ore shipped to the Netherlands for the account of Indonesia and not yet sold or otherwise financed. Under a separate loan agreement, the Netherlands made a long-term loan of 280 million guilders to Indonesia.

26. The debtor is charged interest on any debit balance exceeding 5 million guilders at a rate equal to the rate on six-month Netherlands Treasury notes.

whom Indonesia and the Netherlands have joint payments agreements are made through the "A" accounts. The Javasche Bank may sell the currencies of countries with which there are joint payments agreements to the Nederlandsche Bank and credit the amount to the "A" account; and it may buy foreign currencies from payments agreement countries by debiting the "A" account. In such cases the Nederlandsche Bank would presumably credit the guilder account of the foreign country. Alternatively, the Javasche Bank might order the Nederlandsche Bank to debit its account with the Bank of France, for example, to which the Javasche Bank wanted to make a payment, and to debit the "A" account by the same amount.

Under the terms of the agreement Indonesia's positions vis-à-vis third countries are recorded in subsidiary "A" accounts for each third country, and Indonesia's position with the Netherlands is recorded in the central "A" account for direct transactions between the two countries. Indonesia can offset surpluses with third currencies against her account with the Netherlands, but in the case of a deficit with third countries, coverage must be made in acceptable foreign exchange. Indonesia also has the right to sell one third currency against another by debiting and crediting the subsidiary "A" accounts, but these transfers are limited according to the trade and payments position of the Netherlands with these countries. However, so long as balances in EPU currencies are transferable through the EPU, this part of the arrangement is significant only for the non-EPU countries with which the Netherlands has payments agreements.

Before she gained independence, Indonesia shared in all of the trade agreements concluded by the Netherlands with other countries. After the severance of sovereignty Indonesia continued to be a party to the agreements with twenty-six countries, but as these trade agreements expired the Republic began to make separate trade agreements with other countries while for the most part maintaining her payments agreements on a joint basis with the Netherlands.

Two Special Payments Arrangements

Two agreements concluded by Indonesia with Far Eastern countries deserve special mention because they depart from the usual type of payments arrangement entered into jointly with the Netherlands. On May 27, 1950 Indonesia concluded a separate payments agreement with Japan which provided for clearing through an open account on a dollar basis, with a swing credit of $15 million. Indonesia's other separate agreement is with the Federation of Malaya and Singapore through which a considerable volume of Indonesia's exports destined for the dollar area are shipped.[27] In essence this agreement provides for the payment of U.S. dollars against sterling or Straits dollars equal in amount to the cost of goods of Indonesian origin exported to the dollar area, less the dollar cost of goods of dollar-area origin purchased by the Indonesians through Singapore and Malaya.

Balance of Payments

In the immediate postwar period and until 1950 Indonesia had large balance of payments deficits resulting from a low volume of production and exports on the one hand and on the other, heavy imports of both consumers' and capital goods for rehabilitation and reconstruction. Deficits were financed by large grants and loans by the Dutch government, ECA grants and credits and other external sources. In 1950 and 1951 Indonesia achieved a substantial current account surplus as a result of expanding raw materials exports and the high prices for raw materials. Because a large portion of Indonesia's exports have been sold to soft-currency countries in exchange for inconvertible currencies she has had to apply discriminatory as well as over-all balance of payments controls.[28]

With favorable dollar markets for Indonesia's principal exports (rubber, tin and petroleum), her exports have not required the artificial support of bilateral bargaining. However, Indonesia inherited a system of bilateral arrangements from her political and economic ties with the Netherlands, a system she has continued after her independence. Bilateralism has also been employed by Indonesia as a means of obtaining imports in scarce supply. While a number of Indonesia's trade-quota agreements have aimed at a balanced trade, Indonesia has tended to have substantial surpluses with trade agreement countries.

27. See *Country Reports on the Working of Trade Agreements,* UN Economic Commission for Asia and the Far East, Bangkok, Thailand, August 1951, pp. 35–37.

28. During the period 1949–1951 about half of Indonesia's exports went to trade agreement countries.

Purposes of Exchange Restrictions

Indonesia's exchange restrictions have had three major purposes: (1) to conserve exchange earnings for promoting economic development and for building up her hard-currency reserves;[29] (2) to implement her bilateral trade and payments agreements; (3) to expand her exports to the dollar area by means of discriminatory exchange arrangements. To achieve these goals Indonesia employs a combination of quantitative restrictions and multiple exchange rates. All imports and invisible payments require licenses and all incoming exchange must be surrendered, though there are special arrangements for the exports of foreign-owned petroleum companies. As of June 1953, two export rates were in effect: a rate of 11.36 rupiahs per dollar for all nondollar exports and nontrade proceeds; and a rate of 11.53 rupiahs (the official rate plus the value of dollar export certificates equal to 70 per cent of the value of the dollar proceeds). In June 1953 the price of dollar export certificates was 0.25 rupiah.[30]

On the selling side there are a number of rates which discriminate between dollar and nondollar imports and also between different classes of imports and nontrade payments. There are four selling rates of 11.45, 15.26, 22.89 and 34.34 rupiahs per dollar which apply to essential, two categories of semiessential, and permitted nonessential imports respectively, from the nondollar area. In addition, the price of the dollar export certificates must be added to these rates for imports payable in dollars. After May 1952 the dollar certificates were no longer permitted to fluctuate in response to market demand and supply. Instead, the rate is fixed from time to time by the Javasche Bank.[31]

JAPAN

The postwar problems of Japan are more nearly akin to those of Britain and of certain Western European countries than to those of

29. Indonesia's gold and dollar holdings increased from $218 million at the end of 1948 to $420 million at the end of 1951. They declined to $296 million by the end of 1952, however.

30. Dollar proceeds include U.S. and Canadian dollars and payments received from Japan, which are credited to the dollar clearing account maintained under Indonesia's payments agreement with that country. Authorized banks pay to the exporter the value of the dollar export certificates to which he is entitled, at fixed rates established by the central bank.

31. During 1952 the value of the certificates fluctuated from 1.20 rupiahs per dollar to 0.25 rupiah per dollar.

the predominantly raw material producing countries of the Far East. Japan is highly industrialized and heavily dependent upon overseas markets and supplies of raw materials. Her postwar problems have been concerned with the restoration of war-damaged productive facilities, the rebuilding of export markets and the gaining of access to sources of raw materials. Before the war 33 per cent of Japan's import trade and 43 per cent of her export trade were with China, Manchuria, Taiwan and Korea. Japan was heavily dependent upon Manchuria for food and raw materials. Largely as a consequence of political developments, including the loss of Japanese political control on the mainland and the Communist conquest of China, during 1951 trade with these four countries accounted for less than 5 per cent of Japan's total trade.[32]

In 1947 Japan received over 90 per cent of her imports from the United States. Her total exports covered less than a third of her imports and her exports to the dollar area were almost negligible. By 1951 Japan had reduced her 1948 over-all current account deficit of over $500 million, to $61 million, and was able to cover the bulk of her half billion dollar trade deficit with the United States by large invisible earnings ($475 million, net) from American military expenditures in connection with the Korean war. Thus Japan was able to use most of her U.S. grant aid in 1951 ($226 million) to increase her dollar balances.[33] During 1952 Japan had a current account surplus of $232 million, but merchandise imports exceeded exports by $759 million. Japanese commodity exports declined in 1952, probably because of increased restrictions in soft-currency countries.

Dependence on U.S. Military Expenditures

The rapid improvement in Japan's external position has depended heavily on the large volume of U.S. military disbursements, a sudden termination of which would reveal some fundamental weaknesses in the structure of Japan's postwar trade relations. Japan not only has a large over-all trade deficit but until recently she has had a surplus with soft-currency countries who are unwilling to pay in dollars. In

---

32. See "Economic Problems Facing Japan," *Federal Reserve Bulletin,* January 1952, p. 15. See also J. B. Cohen, *Economic Problems of Free Japan,* Center of International Studies, Princeton University, Princeton, 1952, p. 63.

33. Japan's gold and dollar assets rose from $587 million at the end of 1950 to $929 million at the end of 1952. U.S. grant assistance to Japan was terminated in June 1951.

1951 Japan had a trade surplus of $133 million with the sterling area and a surplus of $116 million with the countries with whom she has payments agreements of the clearing account type, while her trade deficit with the dollar area was $677 million.[34] During the year ending June 30, 1953, however, Japan had trade deficits with both the sterling and the dollar areas.

On a volume basis Japan's exports in 1951 were only 31 per cent of the 1934–1936 level and her imports only 56 per cent of the 1934–1936 level. Meanwhile Japan's population is 20 per cent above the prewar figure and her ability to feed and clothe her people will depend upon her ability to expand export industries and to exchange industrial products for food and raw materials. The natural markets for Japan's exports are in the Far East, but she must be able to trade these exports either for the raw materials she needs or for convertible currencies with which to buy her requirements elsewhere. Japan's imports from the Far Eastern countries have been hampered by three principal factors. First, Japan finds the price of cotton and other commodities available in the sterling area considerably higher than the prices of comparable U.S. grades. Second, some of the foodstuffs like rice are in short supply in the Far East. Third, there are transportation and other technical difficulties in obtaining certain mineral raw materials.[35] Japan's exports to these countries have been limited by severe import restrictions.

Japan's problem of achieving a balance in her trade with the dollar area has been hampered by the loss of her principal prewar export— silk [36]—and by the difficulty of shifting her imports of dollar goods to comparable commodities from the soft-currency area. Exports of Japanese industrial commodities are also likely to be hindered by United States tariffs.

Trade and Payments Arrangements

Japan's postwar trade and payments arrangements have been shaped by that country's principal postwar problems: (1) a shortage

34. See Cohen, *op. cit.*, p. 70. During the first half of 1953 Japan had an over-all balance of payments deficit, but had a dollar surplus.
35. See Cohen, *op. cit.*, pp. 72–74. Japanese exports to sterling area countries fell sharply in the first half of 1953, but shipments to the dollar area have increased.
36. In 1951 Japan's silk exports to the United States were one tenth the prewar volume, largely because of competition with nylon.

of means of payment in both dollars and sterling and other soft currencies; (2) the restoration of her export markets in countries unable or unwilling to pay dollars. Dealing with both these problems involved the negotiation of bilateral trade and payments arrangements with the countries of Asia, Europe and Latin America. It is worth noting that both Japan and Western Germany have employed bilateral arrangements quite extensively in their trade with nondollar countries, at a time when both countries were under the control of allied commissions more or less dominated by the United States.

Japan's external trade is financed by three types of arrangements: (1) trade with the sterling area is conducted in accordance with the terms of the sterling payments agreement of 1951, which (with certain exceptions) follows the general pattern of sterling bilateral payments agreements; (2) trade with Argentina, Brazil, Finland, the French Union, Indonesia, Italy, Korea, the Netherlands, the Philippines, Sweden, Taiwan, Thailand and Western Germany is conducted under payments agreements calling for settlements through open accounts in terms of dollars; (3) trade with all other countries is settled in U.S. dollars through normal banking channels.

The Sterling Agreements

Beginning in 1947, the Supreme Commander for the Allied Powers (SCAP) began to enter into trade and payments agreements on behalf of Japan with other countries. Since the bulk of Japan's normal trade was with nondollar countries, it would have been difficult to restore Japanese trade with them on a strictly dollar basis. An interim agreement covering trade with the sterling area, announced in November 1947, provided for the acceptance of sterling in private trade in payment for Japanese goods and the payment in sterling by SCAP for goods imported from the sterling area. A more liberal agreement known as the "Over-All Sterling Payments Agreement," was concluded between SCAP and the United Kingdom on May 31, 1948.[37] Under this agreement (as amended July 25, 1948) all trade between Japan and the United Kingdom and its colonies, and such other portions of the sterling area as may desire to participate, was to be con-

---

37. *Payments Arrangement for Trade Between Occupied Japan and the Sterling Area Effective May 31, 1948, As Amended as of July 25, 1948*, General Headquarters, SCAP, Tokyo.

ducted on a sterling basis. SCAP reserved the right, however, to convert into dollars at six-month intervals any sterling which there appeared to be no reasonable prospect of utilizing within a reasonable period.

On the basis of the May 1948 agreement there was negotiated a sterling area trade plan of November 8, 1948 between SCAP on the one hand, and Australia, India, New Zealand, South Africa and the United Kingdom and colonies (except Hong Kong) on the other.[38] The trade plan, renewed in amended form in succeeding years, provided for target values of total trade between Japan and the participating sterling area countries and lists of commodity imports and exports which the countries would facilitate by granting the necessary licenses. Each sterling area country in the trade plan was allotted a share in the total exports to and imports from Japan.[39] Other sterling area countries, including Burma and Pakistan, have made separate trade-quota agreements with Japan calling for a balanced exchange of goods to be facilitated by granting licenses. During 1951 total trade between Japan and the sterling area amounted to about $1 billion, with a surplus of $133 million in favor of Japan.[40]

On August 31, 1951, a new payments agreement was concluded between SCAP on behalf of Japan, and the sterling area, which abolished the "dollar conversion clause" of the old agreement. Hong Kong, with which Japanese trade had been conducted on the basis of a dollar account clearing arrangement, was included in the new sterling agreement. In addition to using sterling for payments to the sterling area, under the new agreement Japan may make settlements in sterling with any transferable account country and with certain bilateral account and "unclassified" countries, if British administrative approval is given. This agreement greatly expands the possibilities for multilateral trade between Japan and the other countries of the Far East and the rest of the world. The question of preventing unduly large accumulations of sterling by Japan is left somewhat vague.

The new payments arrangement, if liberally administered by the

38. *Foreign Commerce Weekly,* March 21, 1949, pp. 20–21.

39. The 1948–1949 sterling area–Japan trade plan provided for total trade of £55 million; the 1949–1950 trade plan for £100 million; and the 1950–1951 trade plan for £186 million. For information on trade and payments agreements in the Far East see the (quarterly) *Economic Bulletin for Asia and the Far East,* UN Economic Commission for Asia and the Far East, Bangkok.

40. See *Foreign Exchange Statistics,* published monthly by the Bank of Japan, Tokyo.

British, was expected to give Japan a wide area in which to spend her sterling. But the actual course of trade between Japan and the soft-currency countries is likely to be determined by commercial interest, including the growing fear of Japanese competition in the sterling area, and the willingness of other countries to grant export licenses for the shipment of scarce raw materials to Japan.[41] Until the middle of 1952 Japan had been accumulating a substantial sterling surplus which kept her from accepting sterling in payment for exports to nonsterling countries.[42] In fact, the Japanese Ministry of Trade and Industry put a ceiling of $650 million on exports to the sterling area for the year March 1952–February 1953 in an effort to limit Japan's sterling surplus.[43] By mid-1953, however, this problem no longer existed since Japan had drawn down her sterling holdings to a relatively low level.[44]

Prior to 1953 Japan also had a surplus with most of the other countries with whom she has bilateral payments (open account) agreements,[45] but in 1953 Japan developed a deficit position with these countries.

Japan's Open Dollar Account Agreements

Japanese trade with nonsterling countries outside the dollar area has been conducted largely under bilateral payments agreements which provide for clearing accounts kept in dollars. The Japanese–Philippine agreement of May 18, 1950 is representative of Japanese trade and payments arrangements with nonsterling countries. Under the financial part of the agreement, the Philippine Central Bank maintains a special dollar account in which export and import transactions between the two countries are recorded, while parallel accounts are kept in the Bank of Japan. According to the agreement these accounts are balanced monthly and any balance exceeding the swing credit of $2.5 million must be settled in dollars.

41. For discussions of the August 31, 1951 payments agreement see *Foreign Commerce Weekly*, October 15, 1951, p. 12, and *The Economist*, September 8, 1951, pp. 577–79.

42. As of June 30, 1952, Japan's sterling holdings were £127 million as compared with £90 million at the end of 1951. *The Banker*, August 1952.

43. *International Financial News Survey*, March 1952, p. 291.

44. By April 1953 Japan's sterling balances had fallen to £25 million. *Foreign Commerce Weekly*, June 29, 1953, p. 4.

45. As of June 30, 1952, Japan's net credit position with open account countries was $135 million. *The Banker*, August 1952.

Trade between the two countries is financed by letters of credit through authorized banks. In the case of exports from Japan, Japanese banks will receive letters of authority (or letters of credit) from the importer's bank against which drafts may be drawn by the exporter. The Japanese banks which purchase these drafts thereupon notify the Bank of Japan so that the proper credits will be made to the account. Japanese banks issuing letters of authority or letters of credit in favor of foreign importers also advise the Bank of Japan so that the appropriate debit can be made when the transaction is completed. Both trade and service transactions are settled through these accounts.

Trade Agreement with the Philippine Republic

The trade agreement between Japan and the Philippines lists commodities and quantities to be licensed for export and import over the period of the arrangement. The items and quantities are based on what is known as the "trade plan" which is drawn up by representatives of the two countries. This plan may be altered from time to time as need arises. The trade plan is not a commitment on the part of either country to ship the quantities provided for but only an agreement to license private trade. The total values of trade stated represent expectations of probable trade based on export availabilities and import requirements known to the contracting parties at the time of the negotiation. In addition to the aim of a balanced position in commodities and invisibles, the determination of the items and quantities in the trade plan appears to rest on the following principles:

Exports. (a) The inclusion of exports produced in excess of dollar area demand and of essential home needs. (b) The exclusion of exports of raw materials needed for local industries.

Imports. (a) The inclusion of imports essential to economic welfare and development. (b) The exclusion of products competing with local industry or which may prevent the development of desired local industry.[46]

Other Trade and Payments Agreements

Japan has similar trade and payments agreements with Thailand, Indonesia, Indochina, Korea and Taiwan in the Far East; with Swe-

46. See *Country Reports on the Working of Trade Agreements,* UN Economic Commission for Asia and the Far East, Rangoon, Burma, August 1951.

den, Belgium, France, Western Germany, Italy, the Netherlands and Finland in Europe; and with Argentina and Brazil in Latin America. Swing credits range from $500,000 in the case of Finland to $15 million for the Indonesian agreement.

In practice, credit balances are frequently permitted to exceed the stipulated swing margins. One recent means employed to settle excessive balances has been for the debtor country to purchase commodities in third countries and sell them to Japan. Sweden is reported to have agreed to sell Cuban sugar, German potash and Thailand rice to Japan in order to reduce Sweden's clearing debt of $11.6 million (as of July 1952) to Japan. Indonesia has employed a similar "switch" arrangement under which that country agreed to re-export $15 million worth of dollar goods to Japan at a premium of 8 to 10 per cent over their prices in the country of origin. The remainder of Indonesia's clearing debt to Japan (reported to total $60 million in July 1952) will be repaid in dollars over a five-year period.

Exchange Restrictions

Foreign exchange transactions in Japan are handled through authorized banks acting as agents for, and under the direction of, the Ministry of Finance and its agent, the Bank of Japan. Exchange receipts must be surrendered and exporters must secure a bank certificate of export declaration, the purpose of which is to make sure that payment is received in the proper form and surrendered. The yen is not used as an international currency.[47] With a few minor exceptions, such as personal effects, all imports into Japan require a license which must be applied for through an authorized bank and submitted to the Bank of Japan for approval. The policy for the approval of licenses is determined within the framework of the "foreign exchange budget" which is prepared on a semiannual basis. The budget sets forth estimates of exchange income and exchange schedules for merchandise imports and invisible payments.

Three types of allocations for imports are the subject of periodic announcements by the government: (1) the "first-come-first-served allocation" system; (2) the "semi-automatic approval allocation" system; (3) the "prior allocation" system. In the first system the im-

47. Certain firms may open U.S. dollar and sterling accounts. These accounts replaced the earlier system of convertible yen accounts in December 1951.

port allocation announcement specifies both the total amount of each commodity and the share to be imported from each currency area. These shares are determined with reference to the trade agreements with the source countries and the expected exchange availabilities. In the semi-automatic system, lists of commodities which can be imported from any currency area are announced, so long as there is exchange of the appropriate type available. In the case of the prior allocation system, a lump sum of exchange is allotted to each importer for certain commodities, largely food and raw materials.

All invisible payments and capital exports require approval. Foreign exchange is freely granted for expenses incidental to trade transactions and for the remittances of profits and amortization of foreign investments in accordance with the terms specified and approved by the Japanese government in the investment contract.

Dollar Export Bonus System

In July 1952 Japan adopted a "dollar export bonus system" designed to encourage exports to the dollar area. Under this, exporters who receive payments in dollars are given retention credits ranging from 5 to 15 per cent of their export proceeds, depending upon the nature of the exported commodity.[48] The dollar retention credits may be used by the exporter to purchase under license certain goods and services (including foreign travel) required for his business. There is no evidence that these credits are being sold for a premium to importers since their use and transfer is closely controlled by the Japanese authorities.[49] The purpose of the arrangement is simply to facilitate the acquisition of imports required by firms exporting to the dollar market.

THAILAND

Thailand has had a favorable balance of payments position in recent years, and during 1950 and 1951 a current account surplus with

48. Category 1 exports, including certain metals, textiles, timber products, etc., entitle the exporter to a retention credit of 5 per cent; category 2 exports, including certain chemicals, machinery and transport equipment entitle the exporter to a retention credit of 10 per cent; and category 3, including farm and marine products, entitle the exporter to a retention credit of 15 per cent.

49. In May 1953 Japan's retention system was reported to have been revised to cover both dollar and nondollar exports and the percentage of retained foreign exchange fixed at 10. *International Financial News Survey,* May 29, 1953, p. 371.

both the dollar area and the rest of the world. Except for controls on capital exports, which were introduced in April 1952, and the prohibition of a few imports, Thailand relies upon cost restrictions achieved through a multiple rate system, rather than on quantitative restrictions on current transactions.

Thailand's multiple rate system consists of a fixed official rate for the surrender of export proceeds of rice, and for the partial surrender of proceeds from the sale of rubber and tin, with the remainder to be sold at a freely fluctuating rate which applies to all other exports except those to Japan; fixed selling rates which apply to government imports, sales of exchange to U.S. oil companies, and payments for certain imports paid for with sterling; a freely fluctuating selling rate for all other imports, invisibles and capital, except for imports from Japan; and a rate for transactions with Japan financed through the Thailand-Japanese clearing account which is fixed from time to time with reference to the free market rate for dollars.[50] All export proceeds not surrendered at the official rate must either be deposited with an authorized bank or sold to an authorized bank at the free market rate.

Like Peru, Thailand has dealt with the problem of balancing her sterling receipts and expenditures by a broken cross-rate which results from the operation of the free markets in both dollars and sterling.[51] As a member of the transferable account system Thailand uses sterling and sterling currencies in her trade with the sterling area and with the transferable account countries. In addition Thailand has been granted administrative transferability privileges in trade with certain bilateral account countries. Thailand's only other payments agreement is her open dollar account agreement with Japan, supplemented by a trade-quota agreement with that country aimed at bilateral balancing. Unlike most imports from other countries, imports from Japan require licenses.

There are fewer trade and exchange restrictions in Thailand than in any other independent country in the Far East.[52] Thailand had a

50. Exports of rice are largely handled by a government agency. However, private exports are permitted provided the exporters sell to the government Rice Bureau 4.5 tons of rice for every ton exported.

51. It is reported that some of Thailand's dollar imports are obtained through Hong Kong, payment being made in sterling or Hong Kong dollars.

52. Until March 1952 there were no controls on capital exports and invisible pay-

current account surplus every year during the period 1948–1951 and official gold and dollar holdings had increased from $89 million at the end of 1946 to $294 million in December 1952.[53] The free market value of the baht has fluctuated between 16.7 and 23.5 to the dollar since 1947 and in December 1952 attained the relatively appreciated value of 16.7 to the dollar. In May 1953 the central bank began selling dollars for essential imports at prices below the free market rate. The cross-rate between the dollar and sterling in the Bangkok market has fluctuated between $2.71 [54] and $2.31 [55] per pound.

Thailand's relatively strong foreign exchange position has been due to the large demand and favorable prices for her principal exports—rice, rubber and tin. In 1951 about 40 per cent of Thailand's exports went to the United States but only 22 per cent of her imports came from the United States.

Purpose of Multiple Rates

Thailand's multiple rate structure serves several purposes. The existence of a broken cross-rate between the dollar and sterling encourages exports to the dollar area and imports from the soft-currency countries without resort to quantitative restrictions. The penalty rates on rubber, tin and rice, resulting from the full or partial surrender of the proceeds at a fixed rate, have tended to absorb some of the profits of the exporters which they would have earned from the increases in world prices, had they been able to sell their entire proceeds at the more favorable free market rate. Rice is collected from the farmers at local currency prices which reflect world prices in sterling converted at the official rate rather than at the more favorable free market rate. This practice may have affected production but the output of rice and rubber has risen while production of tin has declined during the postwar period. The subsidy rate for government imports which include capital goods and certain essentials has encouraged the use of exchange resources for these purposes. The operation of the multiple rate system also provides a substantial portion of total government revenues.

ments in Thailand. Import licenses are required for motor cars, sugar and a few minor commodities, and for all imports from Japan.

53. Thailand had a current account deficit of $18 million during 1952.

54. Average, December 1952. In May 1953 the average rates were 21.5 baht to the dollar and 54 baht to the pound, giving a cross-rate of $2.51 per pound sterling.

55. Average, October 1951.

THE PHILIPPINE REPUBLIC

Postwar Balance of Payments

During the early postwar period, 1945–1949, the Philippines had a large current account deficit balanced by U.S. assistance and a liberal use of foreign exchange reserves. It was not until January 1949 that import restrictions were imposed while exchange controls were not introduced until December 1949.[56] In May 1950 an over-all import control system was established, subjecting all imports to licensing. In 1950 and 1951 the inflationary trend, which with the large reconstruction needs was responsible for the exchange deficits, was brought under control. This, coupled with the new restrictions and the increased foreign exchange earnings following the outbreak of war in Korea, resulted in a current account surplus in 1950. In 1951 there was a current account deficit of $53 million, financed largely by a decrease in dollar reserves.[57]

The Exchange Control System

The exchange control system of the Philippines involves both quantitative restrictions on trade and nontrade payments and a cost restriction in the form of a 17 per cent tax on sales of exchange. The sale of exchange for certain purposes is exempt from the tax, including the importation of machinery and raw materials to be used by new and necessary industries, medical supplies, books and magazines, government imports and payments, and certain private nontrade payments, among them insurance premiums and transportation costs of imported foods.[58] Thus the multiple rate tends to limit the demand for foreign exchange and serves as a source of government revenue, while at the same time it provides an artificial stimulus to industrial development.

The quantitative exchange restriction system follows the usual

56. For a discussion of postwar economic conditions in the Philippines, see *Report to the President of the United States by the Economic Survey Mission to the Philippines,* Department of State, Washington, October 1950.

57. Official gold and dollar holdings declined from $489 million at the end of 1948 to $331 million at the end of June 1952.

58. It is worth noting that the adoption of the multiple rate device was recommended by the U.S. Economic Survey (Bell) Mission to the Philippines. However, this device was considered by the Bell Mission as the least desirable of three alternative recommendations. *Ibid.,* p. 87.

pattern: all exchange proceeds must be surrendered to the central bank or to an authorized bank; all imports (except those of a noncommercial character) require import licenses which are issued by the central bank; all foreign exchange transactions must be with authorized banks acting as agents for the central bank; all nontrade foreign exchange transactions are controlled in accordance with regulations issued by the central bank.

There are a few import items for which licenses are freely granted and a somewhat larger list which are prohibited altogether. Certain items, including government imports, capital equipment, raw materials, and items needed for the economic development of the country, are given a high priority over other imports. The balance of the available foreign exchange is distributed among business firms and bona fide importers in proportion to their average importations in 1949, with an allowance for new firms. Licenses are not granted unless the foreign exchange is available.

Unlike most Far Eastern countries the Philippines follow a relatively nondiscriminatory import licensing policy. The vast bulk of Philippine trade is with the United States and she trades with all areas except Japan on a straight dollar basis. Trade with the latter is governed by a trade plan covering a number of items [59] and is financed through an open dollar account. The only other nondollar transactions engaged in by the Philippines are under barter agreements.

While strict controls are maintained over nontrade payments, the treatment of invisible payments is fairly liberal. Licenses are freely granted for a large number of invisible payments. Exchange for foreign travel is granted for reasons of health, education, and even for cultural pursuits and to visit families abroad. Net profits on investments by nonresidents may be transferred up to 10 per cent of the capital stock outstanding, and approved capital investments may be repatriated in installments as determined by the exchange control authorities.

The Need for Restrictions

The Philippine Republic suffered severe destruction and economic disorganization during the war. The question may be raised, how-

59. The trade plan with Japan for 1951–1952 called for a balanced trade of $50 million.

ever, as to why a country with exports largely directed toward the United States and which has received nearly $800 million in grants and credits from the United States in addition to substantial U.S. military and other disbursements, should require severe exchange restrictions seven years after V-J Day. The answer is to be found largely in the expansion of bank credit and in the inflationary policies of the Philippine government since the war and in the civil disturbances and economic policies which prevented a more rapid recovery of production and exports.

A considerable measure of economic stability was achieved in 1952, accompanied by an improvement in the balance of payments position. The special tax on exchange sales accounts for about 25 per cent of the government's revenue and this tax could not be eliminated without a revision of the tax system. The Philippines' foreign exchange position is highly vulnerable to changes in world prices of her principal exports—copra, sugar and abacá. These three commodities accounted for 83 per cent of Philippine exports in 1951. Moreover, the Philippines will have to face stiffer competition in United States markets when the duties on United States imports from the Philippines begin to rise in 1954.[60]

TAIWAN (FORMOSA)

As a result of political developments since the Nationalist government of China was established in Taiwan, balance of payments and foreign exchange conditions have been quite abnormal. In 1951 exports were only $102 million (50 per cent of this represented sugar) as against imports of $144 million, the balance being covered by MSA aid. Taiwan's exchange control system is complicated by the fact that many of its residents who have come from the mainland of China possess substantial amounts of gold and foreign exchange, which have not been taken over by the government although their disposition is controlled. Private dealings in gold and foreign currencies were prohibited in April 1951, but holders may sell their assets to the Bank of Taiwan at official rates.[61]

60. According to the Philippine Trade Agreement Act, Philippine commodities will be admitted free of duty until 1954 after which duties on them will increase gradually to the level of those applying to products from other countries in 1974.

61. Foreign currencies are purchased by the Bank of Taiwan at the exchange certificate rate and gold at rates which reflect prevailing dollar prices for gold in other Far Eastern countries converted into local currency at the prevailing certificate rate.

The exchange restriction system involves both cost and quantitative restrictions including the prohibition of certain imports. The proceeds from most private exports must be surrendered at 15.55 New Taiwan dollars per U.S. dollar while a less favorable rate applies to government exports. Exporters surrender a portion of their proceeds at the official rate of 10.25 NT dollars per U.S. dollar and the remainder at the foreign exchange certificate rate. Certificates are issued in terms of dollars, sterling, Hong Kong dollars and Straits dollars. The rates are controlled by the government but they involve broken cross-rates between the dollar and the other currencies, thus providing a means of balancing receipts and expenditures in different currencies. Sugar and rice are sold under government monopoly at a rate of 14.49 NT dollars per U.S. dollar.

Importers must obtain a license for all imports by applying to the government's "screening committee," and must at the same time deposit a portion of the value of the imported goods in local currency with the Bank of Taiwan.[62] Imports are paid for at the certificate rate of 15.65 NT dollars per U.S. dollar.

Taiwan trades with Japan under an open dollar account arrangement and is treated as a bilateral account country by British exchange regulations.

THE REPUBLIC OF SOUTH KOREA [63]

Current conditions in South Korea have rendered extremely difficult the establishment of an orderly foreign exchange system. The presence of a large foreign military population, most of whom use dollars or military payments certificates (MPCs), which are also valid in Japan, in their transactions with one another and for buying hwan in the unofficial markets, has resulted in the establishment of two effective currency systems. Korean exporters are required to surrender their foreign exchange proceeds in exchange for private exchange accounts designated by the type of exchange. Relative freedom is granted to the holders to use the exchange so deposited to import goods on an approved list under license or for other approved expenditures, or to transfer the exchange to other residents at "trans-

62. The advance deposit requirement was suspended in September 1953.
63. Some of the material in this section was derived from Arthur I. Bloomfield, *Report and Recommendations on Banking in South Korea*, The Bank of Korea, Pusan, 1952, pp. 44–51.

fer rates" mutually agreed upon. However, receipts from invisibles including transactions with UN personnel are almost impossible to control. This is due to the wide disparity between the open market rates for dollar currency, dollar checks and military payment certificates, on the one hand, and the UN military conversion rate of 180 hwan to the dollar, on the other. There is thus a constant incentive for foreign personnel to acquire their local currency (or to buy local merchandise) with dollar instruments or MPCs in the unofficial market. This, of course, reduces the amount of foreign exchange available to the Korean government and provides a medium for capital export and the smuggling of luxury goods into the economy.

The official rate structure also involves a multiple rate system, with a fixed official rate, several import rates applying to different commodities, and a fluctuating "transfer rate" for private exchange accounts in the Bank of Korea. Since the transfer rates apply to different currencies, the effective rates undoubtedly break the cross-rates between the dollar and sterling and other currencies.[64]

64. On February 15, 1953 the South Korean government replaced the old won currency by a new currency, the hwan, at the rate of 100 units of the old currency for one of the new. The official rate of 6,000 won per U.S. dollar thus became 60 hwan per dollar. In June 1953 the UN conversion rate was changed to 180 hwan to the dollar. During the fall of 1953 the MPC rate was approximately equal to the UN conversion rate while the U.S. currency note was about 250 hwan to the dollar.

Chapter 15

TRADE AND EXCHANGE PRACTICES OF EASTERN EUROPE [1]

WHEN A GOVERNMENT pledged to the immediate socialization of economic activities comes into power, one of its first acts is to create a state foreign trade monopoly.[2] This is to be expected since without state control over trade and foreign exchange a comprehensive control over internal production, trade and money would be impossible. In fact for most countries even a partial socialization of the economy has usually required a fairly tight control over external economic relations. Except in Finland, there is very little strictly private international trade in Eastern Europe.[3] In Yugoslavia, however, trade and exchange practices differ substantially from those of the members of the Soviet bloc.

THE SOVIET COUNTRIES

While the details of foreign trade organization differ from country to country, the essential pattern is the same among all members of the Soviet bloc. Each government draws up an annual foreign trade program which is an integral part of the over-all economic plan of the country. Trade with most nondollar countries is planned in accordance with trade agreements with fixed quotas and over-all trade totals, although these arrangements are frequently subject to

1. Eastern European countries include Albania, Bulgaria, Czechoslovakia, Eastern Germany, Finland, Hungary, Poland, Romania, the USSR and Yugoslavia. All of these except Finland and Yugoslavia are members of the Soviet group.
2. The Soviet government promulgated a decree making foreign trade a complete state monopoly in April 1918. It was not until 1926, however, that imports and exports of Soviet currency were forbidden and all operations in foreign exchange and gold concentrated in the state bank (Gosbank) and certain other state banking institutions. See M. V. Condoide, *The Soviet Financial System*, Ohio State University Press, Columbus, 1951, p. 113.
3. The only Communist country where private foreign trade has been permitted is China, but this trade is being taken over to an increasing degree by government enterprises.

interim modifications. Trade transactions in the Soviet bloc are carried on by the ministries of foreign trade rather than by the state enterprises which actually produce or consume or distribute the commodities. The usual practice is for the ministry of foreign trade to organize a number of export-import corporations each specializing in a category of commercial transactions. The foreign exchange transactions are generally handled exclusively by the state bank which maintains all foreign exchange or clearing accounts with correspondents abroad.

The Influence of Soviet Political Controls

The trading relations and trade programs of the Soviet countries are greatly influenced by political controls exercised by the Soviet Union. An important objective of the USSR has been to expand its own trade with the satellites and perhaps to a lesser extent, to expand trade among the satellites themselves. To a considerable degree the expansion of trade with Russia in the postwar period has reflected the export of goods to the USSR in payment of reparations, the taking over of alleged Nazi assets, and levies for the maintenance of Russian occupying armies. But two-way trade between Russia and the other countries of Eastern Europe has expanded very rapidly in recent years.[4]

Russian trade statistics indicate that 75 per cent of the foreign commerce of the USSR was with Eastern Europe and China in 1951,[5] whereas before World War II Russia's trade with central and southeastern Europe was negligible. While Czechoslovakia's trade was largely with Western Europe and overseas countries during the early

4. According to Soviet sources the relative share of the trade of the Soviet bloc countries of Eastern Europe with other Soviet countries increased from 12 per cent of the total trade of these countries in 1937 to 65 per cent in 1951. The following table shows the percentage of total trade represented by trade with Soviet countries for selected Soviet-orbit countries in 1937 and in the postwar years:

	1937	1948	1949	1950	1951
Albania	5	38	100	100	100
Bulgaria	12	74	82	88	92
Hungary	13	34	46	61	67
Poland	7	34	43	59	58
Romania	18	71	82	83	79
Czechoslovakia	11	30	45	52	60

Source: N. Ivanov, "The Foreign Trade of the European Countries of Popular Democracy," Vneshnyaya Torgovlya, Moscow, October 1952, p. 21.

5. Harry Schwartz, "Soviet Solidifying Own Trading Bloc," The New York Times, April 14, 1952, p. 41.

postwar period, by 1951 60 per cent of her trade was with the Soviet bloc.[6] This shift away from the West cannot be explained entirely by the restrictions growing out of the cold war. The Soviet government has embarked upon a deliberate policy of reorienting the entire trade and production of its satellites.

In January 1949 the Soviets organized a Council for Mutual Economic Assistance on which the USSR, Poland, Czechoslovakia, Romania, Bulgaria and Albania are represented. According to press reports the Council serves to coordinate economic relations among the six members of the Council, to standardize industrial production, and to provide material aid through trade, exchange of experience, and loans and investments. The Council, whose headquarters are in Moscow, apparently provides a channel through which the decisions of the Soviet government on trade relations within the Soviet orbit are communicated to the satellites.[7]

Prices and commodities to be traded appear to be dictated by Soviet missions, and satellite leaders who have pressed the interests of their own country too eagerly have been purged.[8] Before the split with Tito, Russia took the bulk of Yugoslavia's production of copper, zinc, iron ore and lead, promising in payment to deliver plants and machinery for Yugoslavia's industrialization program. Because of the break in diplomatic relations with the USSR, most of the promised items were never delivered, and those which had been delivered before the break were sold at high prices. In some cases important industries in the satellite countries have been taken over by joint corporations dominated by Russian officials.[9] It is obvious, therefore, that in considering trade among the countries of the Soviet bloc we are not dealing with negotiations between independent state trading monopolies but rather with an area of centralized planning in which

6. See *Problems of Economics* (a monthly journal published by the USSR Institute of Economics, Moscow), March 1952, pp. 23–24.

7. See C. L. Sulzberger, "Moscow Satellites Bound in 20-Year Economic Pact," *The New York Times,* June 4, 1949.

8. This was one of the principal reasons for the trial and conviction of the Bulgarian Communist leader Tricho Kostov. Kostov was accused of showing an unfriendly attitude toward the Soviet Union by arguing with the Russian negotiators on the exchange rate of the ruble, prices, and the question of German assets. See Margaret Dewar, *Soviet Trade with Eastern Europe, 1945–1949,* Royal Institute of International Affairs, London, 1951, p. 8n.

9. See Michael L. Hoffman, "Problems of Trade between Planned Economies," *American Economic Review, Supplement,* May 1951, pp. 445–55. See also Harry Schwartz, *Russia's Soviet Economy,* Prentice-Hall, New York, 1950, pp. 514–25.

the conditions under which trade takes place are more or less dictated by Moscow.

Means of Financing Trade

A considerable portion of the Soviet Union's imports from Austria, Bulgaria, Eastern Germany, Finland, Hungary and Romania has represented reparations payments, capital items claimed by Russia as having belonged to the Nazis, and levies for the support of the Russian army. A certain amount of trade is also accounted for by the transactions of Russian dominated enterprises within the satellite countries themselves. Two-way commercial trade between satellite countries is conducted in accordance with trade agreements which provide for the exchange of specific quantities of commodities.

The early postwar agreements as a rule were limited to one year but more recently longer-term agreements covering periods of four to six years have been negotiated.[10] These longer-term agreements provide a framework for continued negotiations by joint commissions established for this purpose. The means of financing current trade are generally provided for in the basic trade agreement.[11] Before 1949 the agreements usually provided for the establishment of clearing accounts maintained in the central banks of the trading partners, with the dollar as the unit of account. Definite swing credits were established and any excessive balances had to be settled at the end of each six-month period in goods, gold or convertible currencies at the choice of the creditor. The ruble was first introduced as the unit of account in 1949 and has been used in agreements published since that time. Articles 5 and 6 of the 1949 trade and payments agreement between the USSR and Romania are typical of settlement provisions of Soviet agreements with its satellites.[12]

Article 5. Payment for goods delivered under the contracts provided for in Article 3, as well as payments for expenditure incurred in connection with trade, shall be made in the USSR through the State Bank of the USSR and in the Roumanian Republic through the Roumanian State Bank.

10. See *Problems of Economics, loc cit.*, pp. 25–27.

11. As of 1951 the network of trade agreements among the Soviet group was complete except for China which had agreements with the USSR, Czechoslovakia, Hungary and Poland but none with the remaining members.

12. The text of this agreement together with those of several other Soviet agreements is given in Dewar, *op. cit.*, pp. 100–16.

For this purpose the State banks shall open for each other special non-interest bearing accounts in roubles and shall immediately report to each other all deposits made.

On the receipt of such information the respective bank shall immediately make payment to the corresponding institutions or persons irrespective of whether the means of such payments are available in the said accounts.

Article 6. The total of all payments by each of the parties should balance each other, and the balance should be drawn at half-yearly intervals while this Agreement is in operation.

In this connection, however, the balance of the said payments shall not be regarded as disturbed if, at the end of any half-yearly period, the value of the goods delivered by one party shall exceed the value of the goods delivered by the other party by a sum not exceeding 11 million roubles.

Article 10 of this agreement provides for the liquidation of any excess balances within three months of the termination of the agreement either in deliveries of goods, or by freely convertible currency "at the choice of the creditor party," or by gold.

Recent Operations under the Agreements

While provisions for monetary settlements of balances may still be included as a part of the standard terminology of these agreements, there is little evidence that such payments are in fact made. In a recent discussion of the operations of trade agreements between the USSR and her satellites the following statement is made by an official USSR publication:

The trade agreements between the USSR and the People's Democracies are based on the principle of balanced deliveries for each six-month period throughout the term of the agreement. If in the course of a six-month span one of the contracting parties ships goods to a greater value than the other, the difference must be balanced at the end of the period. In case one of the parties does not equalize by the end of the year, it is given another three months in which to make good the lag.[13]

There is no mention in this discussion of payments in gold or third currencies. Unbalanced trade takes place, however, through the provision of credits, reparation payments and transfers of profits accumulated by Soviet enterprises in the satellite countries. Long-term credits were made available by the USSR to Poland in 1948 and to China in 1950. So far as is known, multilateral settlements through

13. *Problems of Economics, loc. cit.,* p. 25.

transfers of rubles or balances in other currencies are not employed in trade among the Soviet countries. However, several trilateral barter contracts covering trade between the USSR, Finland and a third (Soviet) country are known to have been negotiated.[14]

The prices of commodities traded under the agreements must be determined by subsequent negotiations. Since internal production costs and local market prices bear little or no relation to world market prices when converted at official exchange rates, the foreign trade values which are established in rubles usually do not reflect internal prices in the exporting country. Official exchange rates therefore do not have the same significance for Soviet trade which they have in other countries.[15]

The "Gold" Ruble

There is nothing so closely associated with orthodox capitalist doctrine as the gold standard. Yet the Soviet Union loudly advertised the "pegging" of the ruble to gold in March 1950 and has claimed that the ruble is the only currency in the world with a hard, gold content.[16] The significance of this declaration was largely political and psychological. Not only was it calculated to increase confidence in the ruble at home and abroad but homage to the gold standard is quite consistent with the teachings of Karl Marx.[17] In practice, however, the ruble is not a gold standard currency in any sense of the term, since it is not convertible into gold internally nor are ruble balances held by foreigners freely convertible into gold. In fact it is not even an international currency in spite of the efforts on the part

14. See Dewar, *op. cit.*, p. 6. For example, a tripartite trade agreement between China, Finland and the USSR was announced in September 1952 under which Finland will supply China with goods valued at 34 million rubles, in exchange for Russian wheat, cars and scrap iron of a corresponding value. *The Journal of Commerce,* September 23, 1952.

15. The ruble was appreciated from 5.3 to 4.0 rubles per dollar in February 1950. It is quite possible that this upward valuation enabled the USSR to obtain better terms of trade with her satellites.

16. For a discussion of the Soviet literature on the subject of gold see Alfred Zauberman, "Gold in Soviet Economic Theory and Policies," *American Economic Review,* December 1951, pp. 879–90; see also Condoide, *op. cit.,* Chapter 3.

17. Karl Marx followed the classical position with respect to the gold standard as a safeguard against inflation. Although the triumph of pure Communism will eliminate the need for bourgeois trappings such as money, present-day Communist doctrine accepts the position that the Marxian laws of value hold during the stage of socialism. See Marx, *Capital* (1930 ed.), J. M. Dent, London, pp. 108–09.

of the Soviet Union to develop a "ruble bloc" among the members of the Soviet orbit. Balances in ruble accounts arising out of trade transactions are not transferable to third countries and can be settled only by the delivery of goods to the partner country holding the balances. They represent little more than an accounting device for measuring the progress of barter transactions.

For a country to have an international currency two conditions must exist. First, its currency or drafts payable in its currency must be used in making payments to and receiving payments from other countries for financing international transactions. Second, prices of goods and services moving in international trade, which are expressed in terms of that country's currency, must be related to internal prices expressed in the same currency, and prices expressed in terms of foreign currencies must also be related to internal prices through the established exchange rates. Thus a country which claimed to have an international currency could not maintain two systems of accounting and two units of account, one for internal transactions and another for external transactions.[18]

While bank drafts payable in ruble credits to clearing accounts are actually drawn on importing organizations in Soviet countries, these accounts are not freely available for financing trade transactions in the sense that a country can use its Belgian franc or its sterling balance to pay for an import from Belgium or from the sterling area. But even if the Soviet Union should adopt a system of nonresident ruble accounts freely available for making payments to the Soviet Union or to third countries, the ruble would still not be an international currency since the prices of international goods, when they are expressed in rubles, bear no relation to the accounting system within Russia. In other words, the official ruble exchange rate of 4 rubles to the dollar has no practical meaning except for travelers and the foreign diplomatic corps. Since the exchange rate for the ruble does not even approximately reflect the relationship of prices and costs of production in the Soviet Union to world prices and costs, internal USSR prices cannot be used as a basis for calculating export prices in terms of rubles or of foreign currencies, nor can import prices in terms of foreign currencies be converted into rubles as a

18. See Marcin R. Wyczalkowski, "The Soviet Price System and the Ruble Exchange Rate," *Staff Papers*, September 1950, pp. 203–23.

basis for internal prices of imports.[19] Internal transactions take place at domestic prices and the ministries of foreign trade absorb the difference between domestic buying or selling prices and the foreign exchange prices translated into rubles at the official rate. Thus there may be a balance of imports and exports valued in terms of foreign exchange, while at the same time there may exist a surplus or deficit in terms of the domestic prices paid and received by the trading organizations.[20]

Trade with the Non-Soviet World

So far as Soviet trade with the non-Soviet world is concerned, the ruble is not even used as a unit of account. Russia has no payments agreements outside of Eastern Europe and China in which the ruble is a unit of account.[21] Since there is little relationship between inter-

19. Wyczalkowski points out that the existence of consumers' taxes of from 60 to 90 per cent of the retail price makes for a very wide spread between wholesale and retail prices in the Soviet Union. Moreover, the calculation of wholesale or producers' prices differs substantially from the calculations of cost plus profits in capitalist countries since certain items like interest and a return for the use of natural resources are omitted, while certain other arbitrary additions may be made. Wyczalkowski suggests that in 1950 on the basis of retail prices a proper value of the ruble might have been 20 to 25 rubles per dollar while on the basis of wholesale prices a proper value might be 10 rubles per dollar. (Wyczalkowski, op. cit., pp. 212–20.)

In March 1950 a kilogram (2.2 lbs.) of butter which cost $1.52 in Washington, D. C., would have cost between $8.58 and $11.03 in Moscow at the official exchange rate. White bread costing 26 cents a kilogram in Washington cost $1.40 in Moscow; and beef costing $1.39 per kilogram in Washington was $6.07 in Moscow. The New York Times, March 28, 1950.

20. Dr. Edward Ames has pointed out in a forthcoming article that even though the exchange rate in a Soviet-type economy does not directly affect foreign trade or internal prices and production, a change in the exchange rate may nevertheless have an effect upon the domestic money supply. This is true because the exchange rate determines the amount of local currency proceeds which the foreign trade ministry receives from the central bank when it transfers clearing account rubles or other foreign exchange. The exchange rate also determines the amount of local currency which the ministry of foreign trade must pay in local currency for foreign exchange or for clearing account rubles. While a change in the official exchange rate may not bring about a direct change in internal prices of imports and exports, it will affect the profits or losses of the ministry of foreign trade and in turn the volume of its monetary expenditures and those of the budgetary authorities.

21. At the Bretton Woods Conference in 1944 the Soviet delegation argued that since the ruble was not used in international trade, the USSR should not be subject to the Fund's rules on the maintenance of exchange rate parities. The conference agreed to the following provision in the Articles of Agreement of the International Monetary Fund (Article IV, Section 5e): "A member may change the par value of its currency without the concurrence of the Fund if the change does not affect the international transactions of members of the Fund." See R. F. Mikesell, "Negotiating at Bretton Woods," in Negotiating with the Russians, World Peace Foundation, 1951, pp. 100–16.

nal and external prices and since all trade is conducted on the basis of the national economic plan, agreements with respect to tariffs, exchange rates or even exchange restrictions between the Soviet Union or its satellites and Western countries seemingly can have little significance. This is not to say of course that codes of fair trading between state-trading and free-enterprise economies could not be formulated. But such a code would have to be predicated upon a system in which internal and external prices and costs could be compared, and would require an obligation on the part of state-trading enterprises to buy and sell on the basis of commercial decisions with respect to world market prices and other economic conditions. Under these conditions the exchange values of the Soviet-bloc currencies would have significance for trade even though they were not employed as a means of international payments.

EAST-WEST TRADE

Except for a small amount of trade with the dollar area, trade between Soviet-dominated areas and the rest of the world is based on bilateral trade-quota and barter agreements. The general form of the trade and payments arrangements is similar to that applying to those between non-Soviet countries, but in practice they operate somewhat differently. Western European countries and members of European currency areas as a rule place a large number of commodities from other soft-currency countries outside the Soviet bloc on general open license. If they apply restrictions, the restrictions are usually on a nondiscriminatory basis with respect to nondollar countries outside the Soviet orbit. The licensing of imports and exports in trade with Soviet countries, however, tends to be on an individual license basis. This is partly due to controls over trade for reasons of security. There is also a need to maintain a stricter bilateral balancing of trade with the Soviet group since there are not the same opportunities for multilateral settlements as in the case of trade among Western countries. Still another reason for the greater degree of control over trade with the Soviet countries is the fact that Western private traders are dealing with foreign trade monopolies on the Soviet side rather than with other private traders. In other words, Western countries may desire to achieve a greater degree of control over their trade with Eastern

Europe in order to offset the bargaining advantage of their state-trading partners.

While much of East–West trade is conducted by private traders on the side of the West and is financed through the usual payments agreement facilities, a substantial portion is handled under barter arrangements, many of them participated in by the governments of the Western countries.

Early in the postwar period Sweden, Italy, the United Kingdom and certain other Western countries made available long-term credits to the USSR and other Soviet countries which provided for shipments of steel, machinery, transport equipment and other capital goods in exchange for future deliveries of coal, metals and grain. More recently, however, trade agreements have been limited to one year, with swing credits established under the payments agreements limited to modest amounts. When deliveries by one party or the other lag behind schedule, trade tends to decline since neither party is ordinarily willing to make gold or hard-currency payments.

East–West Payments Agreements

With the exception of the sterling agreements, the payments agreements between Soviet countries and other nondollar countries usually are of the clearing account variety with highly centralized administration. Except for the Czech koruna, none of the Soviet-country currencies is used as the unit of account in these agreements.[22] The unit of account is either the dollar or the currency of the Western European country. The agreements usually provide for periodic settlements of excessive balances in goods within a specified period, or in gold or an agreed third currency. In the case of certain commodities, e.g., Polish coal, part payment is frequently required in dollars or in transferable account sterling. Czechoslovakia, Poland and the USSR are members of the transferable account system, but sterling is seldom used as a means of settlement between these Soviet countries and Western members of the transferable account group.[23]

Foreign exchange transactions in Soviet countries, including those which involve clearing accounts with Western countries, appear to be

22. In 1950 OEEC countries had 93 bilateral agreements with Eastern European countries out of a possible 160 combinations.

23. The USSR has been known to buy sterling with dollars or gold in the unofficial markets of the world when she has been short of sterling.

handled entirely by the state banks of the USSR and her satellites. Except for barter trade with no foreign exchange transaction, trade is usually financed by letters of credit opened up by the importer's bank. On the Soviet side, trade is handled almost exclusively by foreign trade monopolies rather than by the producers, distributors, or users of the commodities to be traded. Since the prices in terms of foreign exchange bear little or no relation to the prices at which the commodities are bought and sold by the foreign trading monopolies in the Soviet countries, the trading monopolies absorb the gains or losses on such transactions in their own currencies.

NON-SOVIET COUNTRIES OF EASTERN EUROPE

Finland

Of the two non-Soviet countries of Eastern Europe only Finland maintains any degree of private enterprise in foreign trade. Finland has had a serious balance of payments problem since the war as a consequence of severe postwar inflation and the necessity of making large reparations payments to Russia.[24] All foreign payments are subject to license and foreign exchange proceeds must be surrendered. Finland is a member of the sterling transferable account group and finances much of her trade with Western Europe in sterling. Finland also has bilateral payments agreements with a number of Western European countries and clearing account agreements with Eastern European countries.[25]

Wholesale prices in Finland have risen about fourfold since the end of the war while the official value of her currency has been depreciated from 136 markkaa to the dollar in 1945 to 231 markkaa to the dollar as of September 1952. To offset the effects of the highly overvalued rate for her currency, Finland employs a fluctuating preferential rate for tourists. Finnish commercial banks are permitted to purchase foreign banknotes, travelers checks and letters of credit from tourists at rates determined on the basis of free market quotations abroad for Finnish banknotes as well as the prospective supply

24. The total burden of Finland's reparations has been estimated at $949 million in 1944 dollars. See *International Financial News Survey,* October 3, 1952, pp. 111–12.

25. In December 1951 Finland signed an agreement with Poland and the USSR whereby a Polish surplus with Finland would be compensated by deliveries from the USSR to Poland, the USSR in turn being compensated by exports from Finland. *Foreign Commerce Weekly,* February 18, 1952, p. 12.

and demand for foreign banknotes in Finland. The rates vary with the nationality of the foreign currencies and in December 1952 the travel exchange rate for dollars exceeded the official parity rate by more than 50 per cent.

Yugoslavia

Before 1952 Yugoslavia's foreign trade was conducted more or less along the same lines as that of the countries of the Soviet orbit. While Yugoslavia's industrial and commercial activities are carried on largely by state-owned enterprises and cooperatives, the government has introduced a new pattern of administration. Under this, individual state-owned enterprises have a large measure of autonomy with respect to business decisions including those related to imports and exports.[26] Formerly such enterprises were not permitted to obtain foreign exchange and did not deal directly with foreign exporters and importers.

Since July 1952 certain individual state-owned enterprises and cooperatives have been licensed to buy and sell in foreign markets. Up to 20 per cent of the foreign exchange proceeds from exports may be retained for use by the exporting firm or sold on a controlled free market. Import licenses are not required for imports paid for with retained exchange.[27] However, only authorized state enterprises and cooperatives can engage in foreign trade and acquire foreign exchange. Since particular enterprises are permitted to set their own prices for both exports and domestically marketed goods in relation to their costs, there is established a link between internal and external prices which does not exist in the other Communist countries.

In line with this objective, Yugoslavia devalued her currency in January 1952 from 50 dinars to the dollar to the more realistic rate of 300 dinars to the dollar. However, since there are substantial disparities between domestic prices and world prices, a complex system of subsidies and surcharges has been applied to some exports and

26. See J. V. Mladek, E. Sturc, and M. R. Wyczalkowski, "The Change in the Yugoslav Economic System," *Staff Papers,* November 1952, pp. 407–38.

27. In October 1952 the percentage of export proceeds which could be retained was reduced from 45 to 20. *Foreign Commerce Weekly,* November 24, 1952, p. 5. In February 1953 the free market rate for retained exchange was approximately 1,800 dinars to the dollar as compared with the official rate of 300 dinars to the dollar. This rate declined to 1,000 dinars in the summer of 1953.

imports. World prices paid for imports are adjusted to domestic prices by a system of coefficients. Thus in some cases an importing firm may pay four times the official rate, or 1,200 dinars, for a commodity whose foreign exchange cost is one dollar. Similarly, there are several coefficients for exports, so that a firm exporting certain commodities may receive 900 dinars for a commodity which it exports at the foreign exchange price of one dollar. As disparities in the existing price and cost structure are gradually eliminated, Yugoslavia expects to remove these subsidies and surcharges.

Chapter 16

THE MIDDLE EAST, AFRICA AND OCEANIA

THE MIDDLE EAST [1]

BEFORE WORLD WAR II practically all the currencies of the Middle East were closely tied to European currencies (the pound sterling and the French franc) and their currency reserves were largely in the form of European currency balances. Since the war all the Middle dle Eastern currencies have become independent of European currency areas except the sterling area countries of Jordan, Iraq and the British protectorates and territories of the Arabian peninsula. However, Egypt, the Sudan, and until very recently Iran,[2] are in the transferable account group; Saudi Arabia is in the unclassified group; Lebanon and Syria are bilateral account countries which have enjoyed considerable latitude in using sterling for financing transactions with countries outside the dollar area. Egypt, Israel and the Sudan left the sterling area during the postwar period; Syria left the French franc area in 1948 and Lebanon officially withdrew from it in 1950. Except for the sterling area countries, most of the Middle Eastern countries have sought to build up independent gold and dollar reserves and to reduce their holdings of the currencies with which their monetary systems were formerly associated. Nevertheless, a large portion of the currency reserves of Egypt and the Sudan [3] consist of

1. For purposes of this discussion, the independent countries of the Middle East include Egypt, Iran, Iraq, Israel, Jordan, Lebanon, Saudi Arabia, and Syria. In addition, there are several British protectorates, the British crown colony of Aden off the Arabian Peninsula and the condominium of the Sudan.

2. As a result of the controversy over the expropriation of the British oil properties, Iran was taken off the transferable account list in 1951 and all her sterling payments, including those to the sterling area, were subject to British administrative approval. No sterling payments can be made to Iran for oil exports. *Journal of Commerce,* September 11, 1951, p. 90.

3. The Sudan employs the notes of the National Bank of Egypt as its banknote currency. Prior to February 1953 there were no exchange restrictions between the two countries.

sterling while Lebanon holds about $11 million of its reserves in French francs.

Except for Egyptian pounds, Middle East currencies are not generally used as media of international payments. The bulk of the trade of these countries is conducted in sterling, French francs and dollars, and trade within the area is financed largely with sterling. The countries of the Middle East other than Egypt, Iran and Israel have entered into few payments agreements with other countries. Lebanon and Syria have close economic and financial ties with France and have payments agreements with that country. Egypt has entered into a large number of payments agreements with other countries; some of these employ the Egyptian pound as a unit of account. In addition to their bilateral agreements with Britain, Iran and Israel have a number of clearing account type payments agreements with other countries.

Nature of Exchange Restrictions

Exchange arrangements among Middle East countries involve both cost and quantitative restrictions. Except for the sterling area countries most of these—including Egypt, Iran, Israel, Jordan, Lebanon and Syria—employ multiple exchange rate systems. The multiple rate systems (except in the case of Israel) involve broken cross-rates between the dollar and nondollar currencies. Quantitative restrictions in the sterling area countries are fairly severe against hard-currency goods except in Kuwait and the other British protectorates where there are no exchange controls. Until the summer of 1952 imports into Egypt from most soft-currency countries were largely unrestricted. Syria, Lebanon and Saudi Arabia are relatively free of quantitative controls. On the other hand, Israel and more recently, Iran have had to maintain very tight controls. While the exchange control systems differ substantially among countries of this area nearly all of them have been loosely administered and smuggling and black market transactions are quite extensive.

Exchange control systems are complicated by the free gold and foreign currency markets of the area and while most countries prohibit gold exports, such movements are known to be quite large. In the desert areas of the Middle East most monetary transactions are on a hard-money basis, with the British gold sovereign the standard monetary unit of the Bedouin. Saudi Arabia, for example, has no paper money of its own, and conducts its internal trade and a portion of its external trade in gold sovereigns and Saudi Arabian riyals.[4]

Balance of Payments

The Middle Eastern countries have tended to have current account deficits since the war. However, in the case of Egypt, Iraq, Syria and Lebanon these deficits have been offset in considerable measure by reductions in the large sterling and franc holdings accumulated during the war. Except for Israel and Iran the foreign exchange earnings of the Middle Eastern countries improved in 1950 and 1951. Egypt benefited from the rise in cotton prices while Iraq and Saudi Arabia experienced a substantial increase in oil royalties, partly at the expense of Iran whose petroleum production was shut down in 1951 as a result of her conflict with the Anglo-Iranian Oil Company.[5]

Syria and Lebanon have benefited from the new pipelines and other petroleum installations as well as from the higher prices of their agricultural exports. Much of Lebanon's foreign exchange income is derived from transit trade in both commodities and gold. This trade was adversely affected by the termination of the Syro-Lebanese customs union in March 1950 and by the decision of Syria to channel a large part of her foreign trade through the Syrian port of Latakia rather than through Beirut. The importance of transit trade for Lebanon was largely responsible for the abandonment of import licensing controls in 1948 in favor of a free exchange market and a multiple rate system. In addition, the Lebanese authorities found it virtually impossible to administer exchange controls.

The Desirability of Abandoning Controls

Exchange control administration presents special problems in the Middle East because of (1) the importance of entrepôt trade; (2) the long borders across desert areas; (3) the tendency in the rural areas to distrust paper and deposit money. Hence, a strong argument

4. The Saudi riyal is a silver coin containing about 25 cents worth of silver. In Saudi Arabia it is illegal to export riyals or gold, but large amounts of both are known to be exported.

5. Egypt experienced a current account deficit and a loss of foreign exchange reserves during 1952.

can be made for the abandonment of exchange controls in these countries in favor of a fluctuating exchange rate system. An additional advantage of fluctuating rates is that they provide a means of balancing receipts and expenditures of hard and soft currencies without the use of discriminatory import controls.

THE STERLING AREA COUNTRIES

Of the sterling area countries of the Middle East only Iraq and Jordan have an organized system of exchange and trade controls.[6] Iraq's principal source of foreign exchange income is the royalties from her growing petroleum production, a considerable portion of which that country is devoting to economic development. Her import restrictions are therefore designed in part to conserve her foreign exchange for this purpose. Licenses are required for all imports into Iraq from hard-currency countries, but since August 1952 most imports from soft-currency countries have been free of licensing requirements. Certain goods from soft-currency countries are subject to an over-all quota fixed for each commodity but the usual purpose of the limitation is the protection of local industry. Imports designated as luxury goods can only be imported if the importer provides his own foreign exchange. Since there is a free unofficial market for foreign exchange in Iraq, foreign exchange can be obtained fairly readily for such imports. Dollars sell at a premium over official parities in the free or tolerated black maket, but because sterling is readily obtainable for most imports through official channels, since the latter half of 1952 it has no longer sold at a premium. The fact that luxury imports are permitted with the importer's own exchange undoubtedly encourages dealings in the unofficial market.

Import licenses for goods from hard-currency countries are granted in accordance with an annual import program covering categories and quantities of imports. In general, dollar exchange is provided only for items which are not available in soft-currency countries. As a member of the sterling area Iraq would discriminate against dollar goods regardless of her own dollar earnings.[7]

---

6. Exchange controls in the crown colony of Aden are administered in accordance with British regulations.

7. Since most of Iraq's oil royalties are paid in sterling, Iraq tends to be a net drain on the London dollar pool. However, British firms sell a portion of Iraq's oil for dollars which accrue to the British Treasury.

Iraq follows British regulations with regard to the type of currency that must be paid and received in trade with other countries. With certain exceptions, foreign exchange proceeds from exports and invisible transactions must be surrendered,[8] but existing foreign balances in currencies other than U.S. and Canadian dollars need not be surrendered.

Jordan

Jordan [9] is a very poor country with meager exchange reserves and little capacity for exports. The bulk of Jordan's imports are paid for by British military subsidies and UN payments to the Palestine refugees. All payments with official exchange are subject to license and registered importers are granted quotas for essential imports, based on annual import allocations. There is a 2 per cent exchange-license fee for soft-currency imports and a 6 per cent fee for hard-currency imports, with corresponding exchange taxes on authorized invisible payments. Export proceeds from certain commodities sold to neighboring countries, which constitute about 75 per cent of total exports, need not be surrendered but may be retained or sold in the unofficial free market. All other export proceeds must be surrendered at the official rate. Receipts from invisibles also need not be surrendered. Imports from Syria and Lebanon purchased with free market exchange do not require exchange licenses but do require import licenses which are freely granted. However, only about 10 per cent of Jordan's imports are paid for with exchange from the unofficial market.

The Persian Gulf Sheikdoms

Responsibility for exchange control in the Persian Gulf sheikdoms [10] is in the hands of the British political residents and the British banks. The official currency of this area is the Indian rupee which

8. The petroleum companies are not subject to the surrender requirement. The proceeds of certain exports to neighboring countries are also exempt from surrender.

9. Jordan formerly had a common currency with Palestine while both countries were British mandates. It rejoined the sterling area in 1950.

10. The British protectorates include Bahrein, Kuwait, Dubai, Adu Dhabi, Shargah, Ajman, Ras al-Kahimah, Umm-ul Qaiwain, Kalba, Qatar, Muscat and Oman. Local affairs are administered by the local authorities but Britain controls their foreign relations under the terms of her treaties with the local governments.

is freely convertible into sterling through the banks. However, much of the internal and external trade of these countries is financed with gold sovereigns. Individuals seeking to make payments outside the sterling area by exchanging rupees or sterling against official foreign exchange must make application to the banks supported by a letter of recommendation from the political resident. There is no system of import licensing nor local exchange control in this area. There are free local markets for gold, foreign bank notes and drafts. Kuwait is an important gold-trading center forming a link between the markets of the Middle East and India and Pakistan.

EGYPT

Until Egypt left the sterling area in 1947 Egypt's exchange control was in the hands of the British-managed National Bank of Egypt.[11] Since then Egypt has sought to become independent of the sterling area in two important ways. First, Egypt has substantially reduced her sterling holdings and has at the same time increased her gold and dollar reserves.[12] Second, Egypt has negotiated payments agreements with other countries providing for the use of Egyptian pounds and other nonsterling currencies to finance her trade. In 1946 practically all of Egypt's foreign trade was conducted in terms of sterling; four years later 66 per cent of her total foreign financial transactions were in sterling, 20 per cent in Egyptian pounds and the remainder in other currencies, mostly dollars.[13] The relative importance of the Egyptian pound in Egypt's trade has probably increased substantially since 1950.

The Egyptian Pound in Foreign Trade

Egypt has sought to develop the use of the Egyptian pound as an international payments medium in several different ways. First, her recent bilateral payments agreements with Lebanon, Western Germany, Saudi Arabia, Belgium, Italy, France and Switzerland provide for the use of Egyptian pounds as a unit of account. In addition to the usual type of nonresident Egyptian pound accounts, at the end of

11. The management of the Bank is now in Egyptian hands.
12. At the end of 1948 Egypt's sterling holdings were £346 million; by May 1953 they had been reduced to about £190 million.
13. *International Financial News Survey*, October 12, 1951, p. 120.

1949 Egypt introduced a transferable account known as the Egyptian export pound, the purpose of which was to provide a substitute for transferable account sterling in financing triangular deals. Before the British exchange control decided to limit transferable account facilities to *direct* current transactions between transferable account and sterling area countries, Egypt, as well as other transferable account countries, frequently financed the importation of hard currency goods through other transferable account countries by paying transferable account sterling.[14]

Following the issuance of the new British regulations late in 1949, Egypt began to issue import licenses for the importation of hard-currency goods, the imports being paid for in Egyptian export pounds. These export pounds could be used to pay for Egyptian exports to soft-currency countries with whom Egypt did not have a payments agreement.[15] These funds could be transferred to other export accounts of soft-currency countries in the same or different monetary areas or they could be used for payments to residents of Egypt.[16] During 1952 the export pound sold at a discount of from 10 to 30 per cent as compared with the official rate for the Egyptian pound.[17] There is a fluctuating rate both for export pounds and for bilateral agreement Egyptian pounds wherever they are traded in free markets. The system also involves a breaking of cross-rates since the discounts from the official rate vary as between currencies.

Early in 1953 the Egyptian government broadened the use of the export pound to permit Egyptian exports of cotton and other goods not subject to export restriction, to the dollar area and to the sterling area, to be paid for up to 75 per cent in export pounds or in goods for which export pound credits may be given, and the remainder in dollars or sterling.[18] Egyptian importers pay for imports from the

14. It has been reported that Egypt also financed the importation of gold in this way.
15. *Economic Bulletin,* National Bank of Egypt, Vol. IV, No. 4, 1951, p. 265.
16. According to the *Annual Report of the National Bank of Egypt for 1952* Egypt had a $60 million surplus in dollars during 1951 and a trade deficit with the United States of $21.5 million. The *Report* attributes the dollar surplus to the wide use of export pounds in 1951. *International Financial News Survey,* April 11, 1952, p. 309.
17. It is quite likely that export pounds or the dollar goods obtained in exchange for export pounds are sold for dollars or other currencies. *The Annual Report of the National Bank of Egypt for 1952* suggested that an increased rate of capital outflow was a contributing factor to the 12 per cent decline in the market value of the export pound during 1951. In the summer of 1953 quotations for the export pound ranged from $2.57 to $2.62.
18. *International Financial News Survey,* February 20, 1953, p. 256; see also *ibid.,* March 27, 1953, p. 296, and *Foreign Commerce Weekly,* April 6, 1953, p. 5.

dollar and sterling areas by crediting the transferable export pound accounts of the nonresident exporters.

In addition to the use of the export pound accounts, Egypt has sought to expand her exports by a retention quota scheme introduced in February 1953. Egyptian exporters of cloth or yarn are permitted to retain 100 per cent of their dollar or sterling proceeds in "import entitlement accounts" which may be used to import certain commodities. Exporters of other commodities may exchange 75 per cent of their dollar or sterling proceeds for "import entitlement accounts" and the remainder must be surrendered against Egyptian pounds at the official rate. The balances in these accounts are transferable and entitle the holder to receive import licenses and to purchase exchange to pay for the designated imports. The purpose of the retention quota scheme is to encourage exports by providing a premium to Egyptian exporters, which is derived from the sale of goods imported with the accounts or from the sale of the right to use the accounts. In the summer of 1953 the premia for entitlement accounts were about 7 per cent for sterling and 12 per cent for dollars. In August 1953 import entitlement accounts were established for trade with Western Germany.

Barter Agreements

Another way in which Egypt has departed from her pre-1947 trading practices has been the liberal use of barter arrangements by means of which cotton and to a lesser extent rice are exchanged for wheat, sugar, industrial raw materials and other commodities. Egypt has recently concluded barter arrangements with the USSR, Hungary, Romania, Czechoslovakia and Chile.

Import Policies

Until recently licenses were not required for imports from the sterling area, the French franc area, transferable account countries and other countries to which sterling transfers can be made, and from countries with which Egypt has payments agreements, including Switzerland. As a consequence of a large unfavorable trade balance in 1952, the Egyptian government decreed on October 6, 1952, that all imports would require a prior permit.[19] Licenses for imports from

19. In the first eight months of 1952 Egypt had a trade deficit of 38 million Egyptian

countries with which Egypt has payments agreements (other than Britain) are granted liberally. Imports from the dollar and sterling areas are limited to essentials and semiessentials, which may be imported by payment of export pounds or under the import entitlement account system. Nontrade payments require licenses and remittances for travel abroad are subject to a 10 per cent tax.[20]

Egypt's exchange control policy reflects her objective of reducing her sterling balances and accumulating gold and dollars. The country has maintained a current account deficit in every postwar year (1946–1952) except 1949, and the deficits have been financed largely by the liquidation of her sterling balances which decreased by £185 million sterling between July 1947 and September 1952.[21] At the same time Egypt was accumulating gold and dollars, her official gold and dollar reserves having risen from $56 million in June 1947 to $292 million in June 1952. What in effect Egypt has done is to keep her direct purchases in the dollar area low while liberalizing her imports from sources which will accept sterling and even to use sterling balances indirectly for the acquisition of dollar goods and gold and dollars. During the latter part of 1952, however, a shortage of sterling necessitated a reversal of this policy and Egypt had to use some of her dollars to acquire sterling.

SYRIA AND LEBANON

The Levantine states have had the double problem of adjusting their currency and exchange systems to the severance (1948) of relations with the French franc area and to the dissolution (1950) of the currency and customs union between themselves. After attempting unsuccessfully to impose tight trade and exchange restrictions, they introduced multiple rate systems in 1948 and in May 1952 Lebanon removed all restrictions on exchange transactions.[22] Syria

---

pounds. At the same time Egypt received an emergency release of £5 million sterling from her blocked sterling account.

20. In January 1953 the Egyptian government announced that exporters of textiles and yarn would be permitted to use their sterling and dollar proceeds without limitation. *International Financial News Survey,* January 30, 1953, p. 232.

21. *Economic Bulletin,* National Bank of Egypt, Vol. V, No. 3, p. 203.

22. Certain government transactions take place at the official rate in Lebanon, but all private transactions are at the free rates in the uncontrolled foreign exchange market. Before January 1952, 10 per cent of all foreign exchange receipts from invisibles had to be surrendered at the official rate. The requirement that certain foreign com-

still maintains mild exchange controls in the form of a surrender requirement for export proceeds. Both countries have free exchange markets. These are more or less uncontrolled and there is no attempt to maintain official cross-rates between foreign currencies.

Before Syria and Lebanon became independent of France, the cover for the Syrian and Lebanese pounds was largely French francs.[23] Since the break with France, both countries have reduced their holdings of francs and have achieved a modest accumulation of gold and dollars.[24] Following the termination of the customs union between the two countries in 1950, Syrian and Lebanese pounds were no longer interchangeable at parity.[25]

Syria and Lebanon have had serious problems over their trade relations since the dissolution of the customs union. Prior to 1950 the bulk of Syria's imports and exports to the outside world was channeled through the port of Beirut. Late in 1951 Syria decreed that merchandise had to be exported directly to foreign countries through the Syrian port of Latakia and all imports had to be purchased directly from the country of origin and imported through Latakia. A new commercial agreement between the two countries in February 1952 provided for the free exchange of locally produced agricultural and industrial goods between the two countries and the importation of some commodities into Syria through Beirut.[26] Most of Syria's imports from outside the two countries now come through Latakia.

Both Syria and Lebanon require import licenses but with the exception of a few commodities, imports are unrestricted and there are no restrictions on nontrade payments. In Lebanon certain government transactions are conducted at the official buying and selling rates. In Syria some foreign enterprises (mainly petroleum companies) must

---

panies (mainly petroleum) must purchase 80 per cent of their local currency needs at the official rate was abolished in May 1952, thereby eliminating all surrender requirements.

23. Banknotes are issued in both countries by the Bank of Syria and Lebanon, a French private bank.

24. In June 1947 the combined official gold and short-term dollar holdings of Syria and Lebanon were only $7 million. In June 1952 official gold and official and private short-term dollar holdings were $17 million and $44 million for Syria and Lebanon, respectively. (*Semiannual Report to the President for the Period April 1, 1952—September 30, 1952*, National Advisory Council, Washington, 1953.)

25. In January 1953 the Lebanese pound sold at a 4 per cent premium over the Syrian pound.

26. *International Financial News Survey*, February 22, 1952, p. 256.

acquire their local currencies at the official buying rate of 2.19 Syrian pounds per dollar. The purpose is to tax these companies.

Sellers of Syria's major exports [27] to all countries except Iraq, Jordan, Kuwait, Bahrein and Saudi Arabia [28] must sell them for specified currencies (according to destination) and deliver the proceeds to authorized banks as "exportation exchange." The exporter has the option of retaining the foreign exchange in an "exportation exchange" account with the authorized bank, selling it to the bank at the "exportation exchange" rate, or using it to buy goods and services. So long as the "exportation exchange" rate is equal to the free rate, the surrender requirement makes little real difference to the exporter.[29] This may not always be the case—particularly, if with a sharp drop in the volume of foreign exchange receipts the exchange authorities should decide to limit the sales of "exportation exchange."

The Free Markets and Broken Cross-Rates

The free exchange markets in Syria and Lebanon give rise to cross-rates which break official cross-rates between dollars, sterling, French francs, Egyptian pounds and other currencies traded in the markets.[30] It is unnecessary therefore for these countries to maintain discriminatory trade controls or trade controls of any kind, in order to keep a bilateral balance with other countries. The opportunities for arbitrage among the various currencies makes possible multilateral settlements as between trading partners.[31] Syrian and Lebanese traders usually convert their surpluses of soft currencies into dollars in the free market, or into gold, since there are no restrictions on gold sales. Despite the termination of the monetary union between Syria and Lebanon, the free market values of their currencies have fluctuated within a relatively narrow range of parity. In mid-July 1953

27. The surrender requirement applies to live animals and a number of animal products, vegetables, grain, cotton, cottonseed, textiles, licorice, wool, hemp, olive oil, fruit, tobacco, soap, apricot paste, leather and footwear. These commodities constitute 80 per cent of Syria's exports.

28. The probable reason for excepting exports to these countries is that the existence of long desert borders would make adequate supervision impossible.

29. In March 1953 the "exporation exchange rate" and the free rate were unified.

30. The rates for "exportation exchange" denominated in different currencies in Syria also break official cross-rates.

31. Without the possibility of arbitrage, bilateral balancing would be achieved automatically through exchange rate fluctuations and broken cross-rates.

the Syrian pound was 3.57 pounds per dollar and the Lebanese, 3.37 pounds per dollar in the free market. The official parity of both countries is 2.19 pounds per dollar, but this rate is used only in a few transactions.

ISRAEL

As a British mandate Palestine was a member of the sterling area until February 1948, and her currency was backed 100 per cent by sterling. With the formation of the new state of Israel and the setting up of an independent currency and exchange control system, the link with sterling was broken. Israel has expended practically all of her sterling balances—over £100 million—to meet current deficits. Israel has had a severe balance of payments problem throughout her brief history, largely caused by mass immigration and economic development programs.

In 1951 current receipts covered only about 15 per cent of Israel's expenditures on current account, with the deficit financed by gifts, capital imports and a reduction of sterling balances. The failure to control inflationary forces within the country, coupled with a high propensity to import, has necessitated rigid exchange and import controls. In 1953 foreign exchange was granted only for the most essential needs, mostly foods, fuel and fertilizer, plus such capital goods as could be financed by foreign loans and direct investments. However, a substantial volume of imports is permitted with the use of the importer's own exchange. While licenses for such imports are considered necessary in order to encourage residents to repatriate their foreign capital assets and to permit friends, relatives and charitable institutions abroad to send gifts in kind to Israel, the system has certain disadvantages. It tends to encourage black market currency operations and the evasion of exchange controls, and in addition results in a dissipation of the foreign exchange assets of Israeli citizens in luxury imports. During 1953 the exchange control authorities have maintained a closer supervision over imports paid for with the importer's own foreign exchange.

Trade Pattern

Since the war with the Arab countries, which accompanied Israel's stormy entrance into statehood, legal trade with the neighboring states of the Middle East (except Cyprus and Turkey) has been very small. The bulk of Israel's exports go to the United States, Western Europe, Britain and other sterling area countries. Israel is a bilateral sterling account country and most of her nondollar trade is financed in sterling. Israel also has payments agreements with Turkey, Argentina, Denmark, the Netherlands, Finland, Norway, Hungary, Poland and Yugoslavia, all of which involve the use of a clearing account, usually denominated in dollars.

Multiple Rate System

Israel devalued her currency in September 1949 in order to maintain the official parity of her currency with the pound sterling but it was generally recognized that the official rate of $2.80 was grossly overvalued.[32] In February 1952 Israel adopted a multiple rate system with the following legal rates: (1) a rate of $2.80 per Israeli pound was applied to imports of essential foodstuffs; (2) a rate of $1.40 per pound was applied to imports of other foodstuffs and drugs, and to exports of citrus fruits, potash, phosphates, and to certain other exports and invisible transactions; (3) a rate of $1.00 per Israeli pound was applied to all other exports and imports, and to foreign capital imports, private gifts and income on, or repatriation of, investments abroad. Continued inflation in Israel made necessary certain adjustments in these rates, and in the fall of 1952 the $1.00 per pound rate was applied to exports of citrus fruits and to tourist expenditures in Israel. In April 1953 the tourist rate was changed to 56 cents per pound and in July 1953 most exports and the less essential imports were shifted to this rate. Most essential imports were shifted to a one pound per dollar rate.

Should Israel Have Exchange Controls?

There is controversy within Israel and among her friends abroad regarding the desirability of abandoning exchange controls. Those who favor this move argue that the absence of controls would stimulate foreign private investment and the immigration of Jewish people with capital and skills needed to develop the young nation's econ-

32. In the summer of 1953 the black market rate for the Israeli pound was about 35 cents. There is a large black market in operation in Israel, and much of Israel's income from her tourist trade is not surrendered to the exchange control.

omy. Undoubtedly the removal of controls of all kinds in Israel would stimulate private initiative and contribute to Israel's economic progress. On the other hand, it is difficult to see how an economy which depends so heavily upon foreign gifts and loans to the government could be organized on the basis of complete economic freedom.

The problem would be to regulate the volume of purchasing power within the country so that it would be consistent with maximum production without creating a demand for foreign goods which would exceed the fluctuating and uncertain volume of foreign assistance in the form of grants and loans plus the small amount of foreign exchange income from exports. As the Israeli economy achieves a larger measure of self-support, and as her export capacity expands, a larger amount of economic freedom should be possible. But at the present time it is questionable whether Israel, whose very existence depends upon a substantial volume of international charity, should dispense with balance of payments controls.

IRAN

Before the denouncement of the Anglo-Iranian Oil Company's concession agreement and the termination of oil revenues, the control over foreign exchange payments in Iran was exercised mainly by a multiple exchange rate system and a requirement to surrender export proceeds. Import quotas for some goods were imposed during 1950 but quota limitations were suspended in December 1950. In addition to a list of prohibited imports, certain commodities including sugar and tobacco are under the control of government import monopolies. However, in the spring of 1951 the principal control over imports into Iran arose from the multiple rate system and the supervision of exchange payments and receipts by the central bank. As a result of the loss of revenues from petroleum production, Iran restricted the items which could be imported without a license to a limited number of essential commodities. Requests for licenses to import commodities not on the permissible list were not being granted in the fall of 1952. Permissible imports were divided into two groups: Category 1 for the most essential imports and Category 2 for the less essential. No restrictions were imposed on Category 1 imports other than those involved in the multiple exchange rate system.

Multiple Exchange Rates

The multiple rate structure in Iran arises from the use of exchange certificates. Prior to June 28, 1953 exporters surrendered their foreign exchange at the official buying rate of 32 rials to the dollar, and in addition they received an exchange certificate for the face value of 95 per cent of the surrendered exchange. The certificates could then be sold by the exporters to importers at the market rate for certificates. Importers obtained a certificate equal in value to the amount of foreign exchange which they purchased at the Bank's official selling rate of 32.50 rials per dollar. There were two types of exchange certificates which were traded in the market at different prices. Exporters of Category 1 exports received exchange certificates salable to importers of Category 1 imports. Exporters of Category 2 commodities, those which are harder to sell abroad, received exchange certificates salable to importers of Category 2 commodities, those which are less essential. The market price of Category 2 certificates was normally higher than that of Category 1 certificates, but during 1953 the spread was usually under 3 per cent.

Exchange certificates were denominated in either sterling or dollars, depending upon the exchange which was surrendered by the exporter. Since the prices of the certificates was determined by market demand and supply, the effective import and export rates broke the official cross-rates between the dollar and sterling.

On June 28, 1953 the free market in exchange certificates was abolished and the central bank was authorized to purchase all dollar proceeds at 100 rials per dollar (the official rate of 32 rials plus the certificate rate of 68). The selling rate was set at 100.5 rials per dollar (the official selling rate of 32.5 rials plus the certificate rate). Other currencies were bought and sold at rates corresponding to the certificate rates for such currencies in the certificate market on June 24, 1953.[33] Thus while the new system abolished the separate categories for essential and less-essential commodity imports, the effective rates for dollars and sterling break the official cross-rates between the two currencies.

Special rates apply to tourists, profits on registered capital and cer-

---

33. *International Financial News Survey,* July 17, 1953, p. 21. Cross-rates with the dollar for other currencies later based on cross-rates ruling in world free markets on June 24, 1953. See *ibid.,* August 7, 1953, p. 45.

tain other invisibles. Most tourists, however, obtain their rials in the unofficial market where the rates are higher than the official rates. The buying rate of 32 rials to the dollar applied to local currency purchases by the Anglo-Iranian Oil Company before the nationalization edict. Since this was an overvalued rate for the rial, it operated as a form of tax on the oil company.

The Means of Payment

The conflict over oil resulted in a suspension of the Anglo-Iranian payments agreement whereby Iran was permitted to convert her sterling into dollars to the extent necessary to meet Iran's purchases in the dollar area.[34] In addition Iran was dropped from the list of transferable account countries and her use of sterling has been closely controlled by the British authorities. With Britain's permission sterling is still used in trade with the sterling area and with certain other countries. Transactions with Western Germany, France, Turkey and Poland are financed through clearing accounts. Exporters must obtain and surrender dollars for exports to the dollar area and Swiss francs for exports to Switzerland. Exporters who sell to certain other countries for currencies which are not purchased by the authorized banks, may use the proceeds for their own imports provided they produce evidence of having imported an equivalent value of goods. Such a system would appear to give rise to practices which dissipate the foreign exchange earnings of the country. In the spring of 1952 Iran adopted a policy permitting barter transactions, and barter agreements were made with the Netherlands, Belgium and Sweden.

AFRICA

With few exceptions the countries and territories of Africa are members of European currency areas. Of the independent countries of Africa, the Union of South Africa and Libya are members of the sterling area; Liberia[35] uses the U.S. dollar as its currency and has no exchange control; Ethiopia[36] has an exchange control system and is a member of neither the dollar area nor of any European currency

---

34. The agreement provided that Iran would limit her dollar purchases to goods not obtainable on equivalent terms outside the dollar area.

35. Liberia was transferred from an "unclassified country" status to a dollar account country status under British exchange control regulations in 1952.

36. Egypt and the Sudan are discussed in the section on the Middle East.

area. Some of the British, French, Belgian, Italian, Spanish and Portuguese territories and protectorates have more or less autonomous exchange control systems but their local currencies are usually interchangeable with the currency of the metropolitan country and their exchange and trade policies tend to follow those of the European power. Significant exceptions are French Somaliland which has its own freely convertible currency, the Djibouti franc, and Tangier, which does not have a currency of its own but has no exchange or trade controls.[37] In this section special consideration will be given only to Ethiopia and the Union of South Africa.

ETHIOPIA

Ethiopia had no paper currency of its own until after its liberation from Italian control following the war.[38] Exchange restrictions were not introduced until September 1949, when all export proceeds had to be surrendered in the appropriate currencies and exchange licenses were required for all remittances. The purpose of Ethiopia's exchange control system is to conserve the limited foreign exchange income for imports of essential commodities such as sugar and cotton cloth and for the purchase of capital goods and the servicing of development loans. Since certain commodities such as Cuban sugar must be paid for in dollars, the Ethiopian authorities have sought to compel exporters of coffee and goatskins to surrender 80 to 100 per cent of their proceeds in U.S. dollars.

As a rule exchange licenses are granted only for essential goods, and licenses for the payment of dollars are generally confined to commodities not available from soft-currency countries. Import licenses are not required for imports purchased with the importer's own exchange. Since Ethiopia is a transferable account country and has only one other payments agreement,[39] most of her trade with nondollar countries is financed with sterling. Exporters must obtain dollars for exports whose final destination is the dollar area.

37. Tangier has a gold certificate which is used widely in Europe and elsewhere as a hoarding medium since it is freely convertible into gold.
38. Formerly the principal exchange medium was the Maria Theresa dollar. The Ethiopian paper dollar was introduced in July 1946 to replace the Maria Theresa dollar and the East African shilling.
39. Ethiopia has a payments agreement with Norway.

Desirability of Controls in a Primitive Economy

The question may be raised as to whether a primitive country like Ethiopia should have exchange controls. It is quite likely that in the absence of restrictions a considerable portion of Ethiopia's exchange income would not be used to buy essential consumers' goods for the masses, but would be employed by traders and the large landowners for luxury commodities.[40] Whether or not the elimination of controls would contribute to the economic progress of the country depends upon the social and economic structure. If it is the desire of the government to give every inhabitant a ration of sugar and cotton cloth and to leave something over for economic development, exchange controls would seem to be the only alternative when exchange income is only 3 or 4 dollars per capita. On the other hand the existence of exchange controls undoubtedly acts as a deterrent to both domestic and foreign investment in the country.

THE UNION OF SOUTH AFRICA

South Africa is rich in mineral and agricultural resources and her major products are in heavy world demand. The country is self-sufficient in a number of essential commodities and in 1951 South Africa's exports represented about 40 per cent of her gross national product. Gold accounts for about 35 per cent of South Africa's exports and most of her other major exports, including diamonds and nonferrous metals, have enjoyed a ready market in the dollar area during the postwar period. It is hard to imagine conditions more conducive to balance of payments equilibrium and freedom from exchange restrictions, yet South Africa has maintained both over-all restrictions on current trade and discriminatory restrictions against dollar imports.

Nature of Restrictions

Restrictions on imports are implemented through a list of prohibited imports and quota limits for the issuance of general and restricted licenses which may be used for different categories of imports. General licenses entitle the holder to import certain commodi-

40. In 1952 Ethiopia's exports were valued at $46 million and her imports at $38 million.

ties from any country, while restricted licenses may be used for imports only from soft-currency countries. There is also a list of commodities which may be imported without license from any soft-currency country. Except for sterling area currencies, exchange receipts must be surrendered in the appropriate form as determined by sterling area regulations.[41] There are no restrictions on remittances to other parts of the sterling area but nontrade payments to countries outside the sterling area are licensed and in some cases subject to quota limitations.

During the postwar period South Africa has usually had a current account deficit balanced largely by capital imports and a reduction in her monetary gold holdings.[42] In 1951 the current account deficit exceeded capital imports so that South Africa's gold and foreign exchange holdings declined by over $100 million.[43] Moreover, in spite of over-all restrictions, South Africa's foreign exchange assets continued to decline during 1952, although at a much lower rate than in 1951.

Reasons for Restrictions

The reason for South Africa's balance of payments deficits and the continuing need for import controls is to be found in the inflationary pressures generated by budgetary deficits and a high level of investment expenditures.[44] Wholesale prices rose by 52 per cent between 1948 and November 1952. These inflationary pressures and the accompanying balance of payments disequilibrium appear to have diminished during 1953 and South Africa has relaxed her import restrictions.

South Africa's discriminatory restrictions arise from her relations with the sterling area, rather than from the nature of her regional trade balance. In 1951 South Africa's gold exports plus her dollar receipts from exports of other goods and services totaled about $590 million while her imports of goods and services from the dollar area

41. South Africa's special relationship to the sterling area was described in Chapter 10.

42. South Africa's gold holdings declined from $757 million in June 1947 to $159 million in June 1952. Exports of current gold production, amounting to about $400 million annually in the postwar period, are included in South Africa's current account.

43. Most of the fall in reserves represented a reduction in South Africa's sterling balances.

44. In 1950 net domestic capital formation was 15 per cent of gross national product.

totaled only $420 million. However, South Africa sells a portion of her gold exports to Britain in exchange for sterling,[45] thereby contributing to the gold reserves of the United Kingdom. The advantage of membership in the sterling area is that private capital imports from Britain provide an important source of financing South Africa's economic development. So long as South Africa remains in the sterling area Britain will permit her own residents to export capital to South Africa. But membership in the sterling area requires that South Africa obtain a large portion of her imports from countries which accept inconvertible sterling, and that South Africa restrict her dollar purchases by means of discriminatory controls.

OCEANIA

Both of the independent countries of the Oceania region—Australia and New Zealand—are members of the sterling area, and their economies and exchange control systems are similar in many respects. Wool, meat and dairy products [46] are the major exports of both countries and the bulk of their trade has been with Britain and the sterling area. While both countries are predominantly agricultural, they have had a sharp increase in industrial production during the postwar period. Today more workers are engaged in manufacturing and trade than in agriculture.[47] To a considerable degree this shift from agriculture to secondary industries has been the result of governmental monetary, price, wage and investment policies.[48]

During most postwar years both countries have had over-all balance of payments surpluses with a consequent increase in their sterling assets. Except during 1950 and 1951, however, they have tended to run deficits with the dollar area.[49] Until 1952 these countries main-

45. The Union agreed to sell a minimum of $140 million of her gold exports to the United Kingdom during 1952 and a like amount in 1953.

46. Wheat is a major export of Australia but New Zealand is an importer of wheat. In 1951 wool represented 65 per cent and 52 per cent of the exports of Australia and New Zealand respectively.

47. Before the war the distribution between agricultural and nonagricultural employment was about half and half. In 1950 the proportion was about 3 workers in industry to 2 in agriculture. The emphasis on wool growing is partly responsible for the low number of agricultural workers.

48. For a discussion of economic conditions and trade policies in Australia and New Zealand see *The Sterling Area* (Economic Cooperation Administration, Special Mission to the United Kingdom, London, 1951), Mutual Security Agency, Washington, 1952, Chapter 6.

49. In 1952 New Zealand had a surplus with the dollar area and a deficit with the sterling area. *International Financial News Survey,* February 6, 1953, p. 244.

tained few restrictions against imports from soft-currency countries, but limited their imports from the dollar area by means of discriminatory restrictions. During the latter half of 1951 and in 1952 both countries ran over-all deficits and as a consequence introduced severe restrictions on imports from all countries. These deficits were due in large measure to domestic inflationary pressures generated by budgetary deficits (in the case of Australia), and by a high level of capital expenditures for industrial development.

Australia's Import Restrictions

Before March 1952 most Australian imports from soft-currency countries were under open general license, while imports from the dollar area, Argentina, Japan, the Russian zone of Germany and the USSR were restricted and in most cases subject to individual license. The large over-all deficits and the sharp decline in Australia's foreign exchange reserves from $1.9 billion in May 1951 to less than half that amount a year later, led to the introduction of import quotas for imports from all sources. In the case of soft-currency imports the method of restriction was to assign import quotas for Category A goods to 60 per cent of the individual importers' purchases during the financial year 1950–1951. In the case of Category B goods—imports of a less essential character—imports were limited to 20 per cent of individual importations during the base period.[50] A third category of goods was subject to administrative decision. It was expected that the effect of these restrictions would be to reduce imports from nondollar countries by about 50 per cent for the year beginning April 1952. The import restrictions were largely responsible for an export surplus of over a half billion dollars in the five-month period ended November 30, 1952.[51]

Australia also controls nontrade payments, even to sterling area countries. Her controls over receipts from exports of goods and services are similar to those employed in Britain except that all foreign exchange, including sterling, must be surrendered.

50. These limitations were announced for the first quarter of the financial year beginning in April 1952. See *The Economist*, May 17, 1952, p. 473. Australia relaxed her import restrictions substantially during 1953. *The Economist*, February 21, 1953, p. 504. See also *International Financial News Survey*, October 9, 1953, p. 124.
51. *The Economist*, February 7, 1953, p. 372.

Restrictions in New Zealand

In New Zealand a number of commodities which could be imported from soft-currency countries were taken off the free list in 1951.[52] New Zealand also established quotas for individual importers in 1952 equal to 80 per cent of their 1950 foreign exchange expenditures, and announced further cuts for 1953.[53] However, applications for exchange in excess of the quotas may be made to the central bank.

Agriculture and World Disequilibrium

Both Australia and New Zealand have adopted policies tending to expand the industrial sector of their economies at the expense of agriculture. Inflation, high wages and heavy investments in consumers' goods industries, together with price controls on agricultural commodities and import restrictions on industrial goods have been largely responsible for these shifts in production. This tendency has had unfortunate results both for the countries themselves and for other nations depending on them for primary commodities. A very similar pattern has been followed in Argentina, South Africa and a number of other less developed countries during the postwar period. Instead of placing primary emphasis upon increasing agricultural productivity, so that agricultural output could expand while employing a smaller number of workers, productivity and output in the primary industries have been neglected in favor of uneconomical industry supported by artificial controls. This development, one of the fruits of widespread trade and exchange controls during the postwar period, has contributed in no small measure to world disequilibrium. Food deficits and shortages of other primary commodities in the non-dollar world have resulted in a continued heavy dependence for these commodities upon the dollar area.[54]

52. At the beginning of 1951 about 1,000 commodity imports from soft-currency countries were on open general license, but by the end of the year the list had been reduced to some 260 items.

53. *The Economist,* August 23, 1952, p. 469. In 1953 importers were allowed only 40 per cent of what they spent in 1950. *International Financial News Survey,* July 31, 1953, p. 40.

54. In 1952 the Australian authorities adopted measures to encourage agricultural production including the elimination of the wheat export tax, more liberal depreciation allowances for farm investments and a revision of the import program to take account of farming needs.

Chapter 17

THE UNITED STATES AND THE WORLD'S
PAYMENTS MECHANISM

BEFORE 1914, 70 per cent of United States foreign trade was financed in sterling and only a small proportion by dollar bills of exchange. The dollar emerged from World War I as a major international currency and a large part of the world's trade came to be financed through New York. The predominant position of the United States in world trade and international finance, together with the stability of the dollar in relation to gold, led to a substitution of the dollar for sterling as the principal standard of international payments in the interwar years.[1] The importance of the dollar in world trade has been further enhanced by the huge demand for the exports of the United States and the other members of the dollar area since World War II. With the exception of the Canadian dollar and the Swiss franc, no major currency is freely convertible into dollars and the potential demand for dollars in terms of other foreign currencies is substantially greater than the supply of dollars available to meet it.

The total exports of the United States and other members of the dollar area plus the exports of the rest of the world to the dollar area represented about 40 per cent of world exports in 1951; the vast bulk of this trade was financed with dollars. In addition, there were in 1951 about $1.5 billion net in multilateral dollar transfers among nondollar countries.[2] Most of the world's currency reserves which

1. Except for the period March 1933 to February 1934, during which the price of gold was raised from $20.67 to $35.00 per ounce, the price of gold in terms of dollars has been stable since 1879.

2. Rough estimate based on U.S. balance of payments statistics. Quarterly interarea payments to other areas plus errors and omissions totaled $1,991 million for 1951, and the total (net) errors and omissions items for the year was $511 million. Difference between these totals should give a rough value of net interarea transfers assuming $511 million represented hidden capital movements to the United States. However, gross interarea transfers may be substantially larger. See *Survey of Current Business*, March 1952, pp. 16–17.

are held in the form of convertible foreign exchange are represented by dollars. Short-term dollar balances held by foreign banks, treasuries and private individuals and firms residing in other countries, totaled about $9.0 billion at the end of 1952. Most of these funds represent working balances and international reserves of foreign countries.

World Trade and the Supply of Dollars

These observations, however, do not reveal the full significance of the dollar in the international economy. Sterling accounts for the financing of about as much of the world's trade as does the dollar, and sterling balances available for international transfers exceed the foreign holdings of U.S. dollars. Moreover, most of the countries of the world use dollars in their trade only with the dollar area. The major international significance of the dollar is to be found in the relationship of the world's supply of dollars to world production and trade. World recovery and economic progress have depended heavily upon the resources of the dollar area. To a considerable degree these resources have represented a net contribution from the United States and Canada in the form of large grants and loans. Resources paid for with earned dollars have been extremely important but trade alone never could have met the requirements of Europe in the early postwar period; nor can trade alone provide the capital for the economic development of Asia, Africa and Latin America.

But a flow of dollars with which to buy the goods and services of the dollar area is by no means the only reason why the world's supply of dollars is important. The supply of dollars influences weightily the volume and character of trade among the nondollar countries of the world. The trend to bilateralism in the 1930s was due chiefly to the sharp reduction in the current volume of dollar payments to the rest of the world. The postwar restoration of currency convertibility will also depend in considerable part upon the volume and stability of the supply of dollars available to the rest of the world.

Of course a large volume of trade can be financed with inconvertible currencies. But trade financed with currencies or clearing account credits not convertible into the world's leading currency will be less economical than multilateral trade. Moreover, without some provision for multilateral settlements through dollars or gold, all devices for financing trade on an inconvertible basis tend either to break down or to restrict trade to a relatively low volume. Even the EPU and the sterling area, the most successful of the arrangements for the financing of trade on an inconvertible basis, depend upon a pool of gold and dollar reserves and a partial settlement of balances in gold and dollars.

The successful operation of the world's payments mechanism rests upon the existence of adequate reserves of gold and dollars outside the United States and upon a large and stable flow of dollars to the rest of the world equal to the demand for them by the holders of other currencies. Theoretically, of course, the world's payments system could adjust itself to any level of dollar outflow, but in practice these adjustments are sluggish and difficult in a world of managed economies. It is quite possible, therefore, that a world system of multilateral payments may require a continually expanding flow of dollars to the rest of the world.

THE UNITED STATES BALANCE OF PAYMENTS PROBLEM

Over the three years 1950–1952 the United States had a surplus on goods and services account (excluding exports furnished under military aid) of $7,804 million or about $2.6 billion per year. A portion of this surplus was covered by what might be regarded as "normal" means of financing, including $2,962 million (net) in private long-term capital investments abroad, private donations and immigrant remittances of $1,308 million,[3] and $373 million (net) in loans by the Export-Import Bank over the three-year period, largely for long-term development projects. After deducting "normal"[4] financing amounting to $4,643 million the U.S. balance of payments surplus becomes $3,161 million for the 1950–1952 period or about a billion dollars per year. This surplus was more than compensated by U.S. government grants (other than military aid) and extraordinary loans, and by private short-term loans, so that the nondollar world gained

3. Prior to 1944 the U.S. Department of Commerce included private remittances and donations in the current account. There is considerable justification for including it as a normal means of financing.

4. The concept of normal financing includes long-term loans by public lending institutions which are made for capital development and not to meet an emergency balance of payments problem. A few of the Export-Import Bank loans made during the 1950–1952 period do not meet this criterion for normal financing.

substantial gold and dollar assets in their transactions with the United States over the three year period. (See Table 18.)

Does the United States Have a Balance of Payments Problem?

A balance of payments problem is popularly regarded as one which involves a deficit or a tendency toward a deficit in a country's balance of payments, either over-all or with respect to certain currency areas. While the United States does not have a balance of payments problem in this sense of the term, this country has had a serious postwar balance of payments problem. The nature of this difficulty

TABLE 18

U.S. EXPORT SURPLUS AND MEANS OF FINANCING, 1950–1952

(*Millions*)

Item	1950	1951	1952	1950–1952
Goods and services account				
Exports of goods and services.....	$14,425	$20,218	$20,701	$55,344
Exports furnished under military aid	574	1,462	2,594	4,630
Imports of goods and services.....	12,128	15,054	15,728	42,910
Balance on goods and services (excluding military aid)..........	1,723	3,702	2,379	7,804
Normal means of financing export surplus [a]				
U.S. private long-term capital outflow (net)	− 1,168	− 963	− 831	− 2,962
Private donations	− 481	− 412	− 415	− 1,308
Export-Import Bank loans, less repayments	− 74	− 92	− 207	− 373
Total	− 1,723	− 1,467	− 1,453	− 4,643
Export surplus less normal means of financing	0	2,235	926	3,161
Other means of financing [a]				
U.S. government grants (net) (exclusive of military aid).........	− 3,546	− 3,039	− 2,034	− 8,619
U.S. government long-term loans (other than Export-Import Bank), less repayments	− 53	− 48	− 202	− 303
Private and U.S. government short-term loans (net)..............	− 186	− 126	− 110	− 422
Gold and net change in foreign dollar assets	3,629	442	1,182	5,253
Errors and omissions............	156	536	238	930
Total	0	− 2,235	− 926	− 3,161

Sources: Balance of Payments of the United States, 1949–1951, U.S. Department of Commerce, Washington, 1952, and *Survey of Current Business*, March 1953, pp. 8–9.

a. Minus (−) sign indicates debit item in U.S. balance of payments.

is not to be explained simply by the existence of a large surplus on current account. In 1950 the current account surplus was covered almost entirely by private long-term investments and private remittances to other countries; during the 1950–1952 period the bulk of the current account surplus was covered by normal means of financing. Moreover a considerable portion of the remaining surplus in 1950–1952 was made possible by U.S. government grants and extraordinary credits.

One aspect of the U.S. balance of payments problem lies in the fact that the supply of dollars from U.S. imports and other normal sources was not sufficient to finance the volume of U.S. exports required to realize certain foreign policy objectives of the United States. This deficiency of resources other countries needed for their economic recovery and rearmament was made up in part by extraordinary assistance in the form of grants and loans.[5]

A second aspect of the U.S. balance of payments problem arises from the unwillingness or inability of most of the countries of the world to adjust their economies to the postwar supply of dollars so as to restore world trade on a nondiscriminatory basis. The fact that other countries have over-all deficits is not peculiarly a U.S. balance of payments problem, but the fact that the world's deficits are virtually concentrated on the United States is the essence of the so-called "dollar shortage."

The idea that a creditor country can have a balance of payments problem in the sense that the creditor country is in some respects responsible for a persistent balance of payments surplus has been the subject of considerable debate during the postwar period.[6] An analysis of the factors responsible for world disequilibrium is presented in Part IV. It may be said at this point, however, that America's persistent surplus represents a balance of payments problem for government policy makers in two respects. First, U.S. foreign economic policies to a degree, at least, have been responsible for this surplus and much can be done by the United States to restore equilibrium in its international accounts. Second, the disequilibrium between

5. During 1946–1948 many of the foreign loans made by the U.S. government and the International Bank were of an emergency character and could not be classed as normal long-term investments.

6. For an excellent analysis of the causes of the U.S. balance of payments surplus, see C. P. Kindleberger, *The Dollar Shortage*, Wiley and Sons, New York, 1950.

the dollar and nondollar areas has made it impossible to realize certain international commercial policy objectives of the United States, including the restoration of world trade on a nondiscriminatory basis.

Two Aspects of the U.S. Balance of Payments Problem

The aspect of America's postwar balance of payments problem concerned with the need for additional resources to implement certain U. S. foreign political objectives is closely related to the reestablishment of world equilibrium and the elimination of the so-called "dollar shortage." Increased U.S. imports and a larger flow of long-term capital from the United States could undoubtedly have reduced the need for extraordinary postwar assistance. Moreover, if foreign countries had adopted different internal financial and exchange policies in the postwar period the volume of U.S. aid required to achieve her foreign policy objectives would probably have been smaller. Nevertheless, extraordinary U.S. assistance would have been necessary to further the rapid recovery of Western Europe and Japan even if the major countries of the world had restored currency convertibility immediately after the war.

It is also true that currency convertibility and nondiscriminatory trade could have been restored in the absence of any extraordinary assistance from the United States in the immediate postwar period. However, this would have required drastic internal economic measures on the part of most foreign countries, so drastic, in fact, as to make them politically unwise and even dangerous from the standpoint of promoting economic recovery. Large amounts of extraordinary U.S. aid were therefore a necessary, but obviously not a sufficient, condition for the restoration of U.S. balance of payments equilibrium within a reasonable time after World War II.[7]

The remainder of this chapter will deal with the postwar foreign exchange practices and policies of the United States government and of U.S. residents which have a bearing on the U.S. balance of payments position and the system of international payments.

---

7. The $3,750 million U.S. loan to the United Kingdom in 1946 had two closely related objectives—the promotion of economic recovery in Britain and the restoration of sterling convertibility. The loan proved insufficient for the realization of either objective.

Grants and Loans

The major effort of the United States government in dealing with the U.S. balance of payments has been the provision of grants and loans for the restoration and expansion of the productive capacities of other countries. Much of the U.S. economic assistance has been "tied" to the purchase of American commodities so that a great deal of this assistance has not meant a direct addition to the world's supply of dollars.[8] On the other hand, "tied" assistance from this country has released other dollars for purchases in the United States and elsewhere by the aid recipients. U.S. assistance has enabled most of the countries of Western Europe to achieve self-support at prewar living standards without further economic aid (excluding military assistance) from the United States. This does not mean the restoration of equilibrium for the United States, however, since most foreign countries maintain tight exchange and trade controls over dollar purchases.

Recent Emphasis on Foreign Military Aid

Since 1950 the major emphasis of the U.S. grant programs has been on military assistance. Military aid in the form of goods produced in the United States makes no direct contribution to the world's supply of dollars or to the world's capacity to earn dollars. Such assistance, of course, eases the defense burden of other countries. "Tied" grants for civilian commodities made available as economic support for defense production in other countries do little more than offset the additional dollar drain caused by foreign defense programs. However, offshore purchases and dollar expenditures by U.S. military establishments abroad may be significant in increasing the world's supply of dollars, but the total U.S. military assistance program has probably not been large enough to offset the direct and indirect dollar drain traceable to the expanded defense programs of the North Atlantic Treaty nations.[9]

8. During the years 1947–1950 about 70 per cent of U.S. government grants and loans were "tied" to U.S. exports. See H. K. Zassenhaus and F. C. Dirks, "Recent Developments in the U.S. Balance of Payments," *Staff Papers,* April 1952, p. 248.

9. Offshore contracts for the procurement of military equipment in European countries totaled $1.5 billion in the fiscal year 1953. *Report to Congress on the Mutual Security Program for the Six Months Ending June 30, 1953,* Mutual Security Administration, Washington, August 1953.

Public Foreign Investment

In addition to extraordinary grant and loan assistance, the United States government has sought to increase "normal" long-term foreign investment through both public lending agencies and private firms.[10] The outflow of U.S. capital for productive purposes in other countries not only increases the world's supply of dollars in the short run, but helps reduce the world's heavy dependence upon U.S. goods while expanding export capacities abroad. Whether or not U.S. long-term investment makes a net contribution toward U.S. balance of payments equilibrium in the future will depend upon the rate of our capital outflow. An erratic pattern of lending with periods of large net capital outflow followed by periods of net repayment is likely to have a disequilibrating influence, especially if the periods of net repayment correspond with periods of low U.S. imports.

There is the danger that the large net capital outflow of the early postwar period will be followed by a relatively small outflow or even by an inflow of capital in the next few years. In the fiscal year 1952-1953 repayments on U.S. government loans abroad reached $530 million as against new loans of $748 million. In this same year the Export-Import Bank made long-term loans totaling $516 million but received payments on principal and interest on old loans amounting to $358 million and $76 million respectively. Unless gross foreign lending expands at an increasing rate, service payments on old loans will shortly exceed new foreign lending.

Private Foreign Investments

Much the same problem exists in the case of direct private investments abroad. While it is true that a portion of the profits from direct foreign investments is reinvested, the rates of return are much higher than in the case of public loans. In 1952 income received

10. "Normal" foreign loans are to be distinguished from extraordinary loan assistance to meet emergency conditions. The principal sources of public loans of a long-term character are the U.S. Export-Import Bank and the International Bank for Reconstruction and Development. In addition, the Mutual Security Agency guarantees private U.S. investments in certain areas against the inability to transfer profits and against loss by expropriation. Private investment is also encouraged by the negotiation of investment treaties. For a discussion of U.S. government measures to promote foreign investment, see R. F. Mikesell, *United States Economic Policy and International Relations*, McGraw-Hill, New York, 1952, Chapters 12 and 13.

from U.S. private foreign investment exceeded the net outflow of private capital by about $700 million. Gross private capital outflow will need to expand at an increasing rate if private investment is to make a contribution to the world's dollar supply.

Except for the purchase of Canadian securities the vast bulk of the U.S. private foreign investment has been direct investment. Much of this takes the form of shipping American capital equipment and other commodities to other countries, so that such investment makes only a small initial contribution to the world's supply of free dollars. The ultimate contribution of U.S. direct foreign investment to the world's supply of dollars depends upon (1) the extent to which the investment is dollar-saving or dollar-earning for the rest of the world as a whole; (2) the rate of earnings on the investment and the proportion transferred to American residents.[11]

Measures Affecting Imports

Measures taken by the United States government in dealing with the U.S. balance of payments problem have been largely concerned with the making of grants and loans to reduce foreign dependence upon U.S. exports and to increase export capacities abroad. Relatively little has been done to increase the supply of dollars by encouraging U.S. imports. Some benefits have been derived from the reciprocal tariff negotiations, but the total expansion of U.S. imports traceable to postwar tariff reductions probably does not exceed $200 million per year.[12]

Offsetting these benefits to imports have been the imposition of import quotas on agricultural commodities required by the Agricultural Adjustment Act of 1934, as amended, and the Defense Production Acts of 1950 and 1951. Perhaps of even greater significance in keeping out imports have been the tariff administration and other customs regulations written into U.S. customs legislation in the prewar period with the full knowledge and intent of Congress that these

11. For a more complete discussion see *The Balance of International Payments of the United States, 1946–1948,* U.S. Department of Commerce, Washington, 1950, pp. 140–41.

12. The immediate effect on U.S. imports gained from the tariff concessions granted at the Torquay conference during 1950–1951 has been estimated at between $20 and $30 million. See J. H. Adler, E. R. Schlesinger and E. V. Westerborg, *The Pattern of United States Import Trade Since 1923,* The Federal Reserve Bank of New York, May 1952, pp. 54–56.

regulations would deter imports.[13] An Administration bill known as the "Customs Simplification Act of 1950" was introduced in Congress to remove many of these cumbersome and uncertain regulations, but the bill was permitted to die in the Senate.[14] A modified version of this bill was enacted by Congress in 1953.

The federal and state "Buy American" legislation stands as a significant barrier to U.S. imports.[15] With total governmental expenditures for goods and services equal to one fourth of the gross national product of the United States, government discrimination against foreign goods has become an important factor affecting our trade relations with other countries. Another departure from the principle of free and nondiscriminatory trade is to be found in the action of the Reconstruction Finance Corporation in nationalizing imports of tin and rubber in 1951. Other countries looked upon U.S. bulk buying activities as an attempt to deprive them of higher prices for their raw materials exports, of which the United States is the chief consumer.

The recent imposition of a countervailing duty on wool tops imported from Uruguay represents another form of U.S. import restriction which, although provided for by law in cases of imports found to be "subsidized" by foreign governments, had not been used since before the war. The application of an export rate of 2.15 pesos per dollar to Uruguayan wool tops, as compared with a rate of 1.9 pesos for essential imports, a free rate for invisibles of 2.87 pesos per dollar and other rates ranging from 1.52 to 2.45 pesos, was declared by the U.S. Treasury Department to represent a "bounty" to Uruguayan wool exporters. Such findings are likely to be arbitrary and largely a result of pressure from American producers. This revival of the countervailing duty may, however, portend a general use of this

13. For postwar case studies on the restrictive effects of U.S. customs administrative procedures, see *Report of the ECA-Commerce Mission,* Economic Cooperation Administration, Washington, February 1950.

14. The operation of U.S. controls over meat from countries in which cattle have been infected by the hoof and mouth disease has tended to restrict imports to a greater degree than is warranted by the objective of preventing the spread of the disease to American cattle.

15. In addition to the federal "Buy American" Act of March 3, 1933, there have been a number of special acts of Congress limiting U.S. government procurement to domestic products. For example, the Department of Defense Appropriation Act for fiscal 1953 provides that funds appropriated under the act shall be used for the procurement of domestic food and clothing, and cotton and wool in all forms. This provision relates to procurement for use abroad as well as for use in the United States. A number of states also have "Buy American" laws.

restrictive device for products coming from countries employing multiple exchange rates.

United States Export Controls

Except for the blocking of dollar funds of residents of North Korea and the Chinese mainland, the United States maintains no controls over foreign payments.[16] U.S. export controls do have an effect upon the U.S. balance of payments, directly and indirectly. Export controls over strategic commodities to Soviet countries and the embargo on shipments to the mainland of China have virtually reduced to zero U.S. exports to the members of the Soviet bloc.[17]

Of greater significance for the U.S. balance of payments, however, are the indirect effects of the U.S. export control program. Under the terms of the Battle Act,[18] countries receiving U.S. economic assistance are required to place an embargo on the shipment of certain items to the Soviet zone. In addition, Title II of the Battle Act requires the U.S. government to negotiate, with other countries receiving U.S. aid, agreements to control shipments of items not subject to embargo under Title I of the Act. The operation of the U.S. security export controls has not only narrowed the markets for the products of the Western European and other free-world nations, but it has been a factor in reducing the supplies of grain, coal, timber, metals and other commodities available to the free nations from nondollar sources. The effect of these controls has been to increase the dependence of Western Europe upon dollar imports. However, an even more important factor in reducing East-West trade has been the policies of the Soviet countries themselves.

The United States also maintains quantitative controls over exports of certain commodities in short supply in the United States or in the free world. These controls, together with U.S. domestic allocation and price controls, probably benefit the payments position of

16. For a description of the U.S. foreign assets control program see *Annual Report of the Secretary of the Treasury for the Fiscal Year Ended June 30, 1951,* 1952, pp. 56–57. The U.S. government also regulates the importation or exportation of gold.

17. In 1948 U.S. exports to the Soviet bloc totaled $397 million but in 1951 they were only $3 million and in the first half of 1952 they were negligible. For descriptions of U.S. export controls see *First Report to Congress Covering the Operations Under the Mutual Defense Assistance Control Act of 1951 (Battle Act),* 1952; and *Export Control* (quarterly reports by the Secretary of Commerce).

18. Public Law 213, 82d Congress, 1951.

the industrial countries of Western Europe by assuring a more equitable distribution of raw materials and by keeping down their prices. However, to the extent that international allocations hold down the prices of commodities of which the United States is a net importer, the world's dollar supply is probably reduced.

INTERNATIONAL PAYMENTS PRACTICES IN THE UNITED STATES

Foreign payments practices in the United States during the postwar period have been affected by the developments in the world's payments mechanism even though exchange controls do not exist in the United States. We may list the following major factors making for changes in the methods of financing U.S. trade as compared with the prewar period: [19]

1. A large proportion of U.S. exports has been financed by U.S. government grants and loans (approximately one third of total U.S. merchandise exports in 1950 and 1951).

2. The inconvertibility of most of the world's currencies has reduced the importance of the New York foreign exchange market.

3. The existence of comprehensive import and exchange controls in most countries of the world has probably resulted in a greater use of letter of credit financing in order to avoid exchange risks.

4. The existence of exchange controls abroad has brought about the development of a number of nontraditional practices including financing by means of cheap currency deals.

Means of Financing U.S. Exports

The bulk of the U.S. private exports are financed by the traditional methods of dollar export letters of credit, dollar drafts drawn on the foreign buyer, cash in advance, and open book account.[20] Letter of credit financing is especially popular in the handling of shipments to Western Europe and to the sterling area. In spite of frequent delays in receiving dollar payments, a substantial proportion of U.S.

19. For an excellent discussion of U.S. payments practices see A. H. von Klemperer, "Present Foreign Payments Practices in the United States," *Staff Papers*, April 1952, pp. 199–212.

20. For a description of the traditional methods of financing exports and imports see *A Review of Export and Import Procedure*, Guaranty Trust Company of New York, 1950; see also M. S. Rosenthal, *Techniques of International Trade*, McGraw-Hill, New York, 1950.

exports to Latin America are financed by drawing drafts directly on the buyer or on open book account. From October 1950 through February 1951 approximately 38 per cent of U.S. exports to Latin America were financed by drafts drawn under letters of credit, 25 per cent by commercial drafts drawn on buyers, and the remaining [21] 37 percent by open book account and other means of financing. The large proportion of open book account financing may be explained in part by the fact that most shipments from American firms to their Latin American subsidiaries are handled by that method.

Importance of Letter of Credit Financing

The proportion of U.S. exports to Latin America financed under letters of credit tends to rise and fall with the relative bargaining power of American exporters. Given a sellers' market for commodities essential to Latin American economies, U.S. exporters are in a position to demand letters of credit or even cash in advance. Many Latin American countries refuse to authorize dollar letter of credit facilities unless the imports are highly essential and are not available on a commercial draft basis. Thus during the third quarter of 1948, when there was a sellers' market for many commodities, about half the U.S. exports to Latin America were financed by letters of credit. With the change to a buyers' market in the fourth quarter of 1948 and the first quarter of 1949 the percentage of letter of credit financing fell to less than 40 per cent.[22]

Delays in Collecting Drafts

United States exporters to Latin America are frequently required to wait for payment on commercial drafts drawn on Latin American buyers for periods ranging from a few weeks to several months in the case of Brazil. Latin American importers usually make local currency payments promptly upon presentation of the drafts; the delays arise from a shortage of dollars available for transferring the

21. This is a residual item which includes in addition to open book account and consignment financing, goods shipped for cash. Much of the goods shipped for cash may have involved the circumvention of Latin American exchange controls.

22. The author is indebted to Dr. H. J. Dernburg of the Federal Reserve Bank of New York for the estimates of the relative importance of various means of financing U.S. exports to Latin America.

local currency balances into dollars. This situation rarely arises in the case of trade with Western European countries since foreign exchange is ordinarily made available upon presentation of the documents by the importer, provided, of course, he has a valid import license. Moreover, European and sterling area exchange control authorities are usually willing to authorize letter of credit facilities to importers holding valid import licenses. Letter of credit financing generally means cheaper prices for imports since the importer does not need to find a firm willing to export on a commercial draft basis. Undoubtedly exporters who are required to export to certain Latin American countries on a commercial draft basis add a sufficient margin to their selling prices to more than compensate for the delay and risk of collecting payment.

The Use of Foreign Currencies in U.S. Trade

While most U.S. exports are financed with dollars,[23] a substantial volume of imports appear to be financed in sterling, Canadian dollars and Swiss francs. Most U.S. imports of staple commodities such as rubber, jute, burlap, tea, wool and tin are traditionally financed in American account sterling.[24] Since the freeing of the Canadian dollar from all exchange controls in 1951, a large volume of Canadian exports to the United States has been invoiced in Canadian dollars. The only other currency which is employed to a considerable extent in U.S. trade is the Swiss franc. A substantial proportion of the U.S. imports of Swiss watches is invoiced in Swiss francs.

The predominant means of financing U.S. imports is the irrevocable letter of credit.[25] In addition to the preference of foreign exporters for this method over commercial drafts or open book account, the exchange control authorities of foreign countries frequently demand the presentation of a letter of credit or cash payment in advance as a condition for granting an export license. In

23. Some grain and petroleum exports to the sterling area have been financed in sterling during the postwar period, and more recently a few cotton shipments have been financed with sterling.

24. At times as much as 25 per cent of the imports of sterling area raw materials have been financed with "cheap sterling." However, the narrowing of the margin between the rates for American account and "cheap sterling" has substantially reduced such financing.

25. See Max J. Wasserman, "United States Import Financing Methods," *The Journal of Finance,* September 1951, pp. 325–28.

some instances the requirement of a letter of credit may deter American imports since most domestic trade is conducted on an open book account basis.

FINANCING EXPORTS UNDER ECONOMIC ASSISTANCE PROGRAMS

During the fiscal year 1952 the United States government made available to foreign countries approximately $5 billion in grants and loans, and in addition over $300 million was disbursed by the International Monetary Fund and the International Bank. The bulk of the U.S. government grants and loans were made by the Mutual Security Agency (MSA) and the Export-Import Bank. Most of the U.S. economic assistance is tied to specific U.S. commodity exports.[26] While the recipients of International Bank loans are not required to use the proceeds of the loans in the United States, the loans are tied in the sense that the funds must be employed for specific purposes authorized by the Bank. However, dollars made available through the International Monetary Fund are not tied in any way.[27]

Exports Financed by MSA

The various methods of payment employed by the MSA, the Export-Import Bank and the International Bank are outlined in Appendix 4. With few exceptions [28] these agencies do not make available free dollars to the recipients of grants or loans. Ordinarily the MSA provides dollars to foreign countries against procurement authorizations for specific items, after the authorizations have been approved by MSA. The most common method of financing is the issuance by the MSA of a letter of commitment to a U.S. bank, against which letters of credit for the approved purchases may be issued to the American suppliers. Under another method the foreign government receives reimbursement after it has financed the approved purchases out of its own funds.

26. A portion of MSA funds are used for offshore purchases; in addition MSA has made dollar contributions to the European Payments Union which are not tied to U.S. exports. In June 1953 the MSA became the Foreign Operations Administration.

27. Dollars made available by the U.S. Exchange Stabilization Fund are also untied.

28. The principal exception is the MSA contributions to the EPU. Both the Export-Import Bank and the International Bank, in special circumstances, will finance local currency expenditures in the borrowing countries, with free dollars, but this has rarely been employed.

Most of the MSA-financed shipments to Western Europe involve the use of private channels, with the foreign importer making his arrangements as to deliveries and prices with a private U.S. exporter. The foreign importer is granted a license by his government to import certain commodities, the procurement of which has been authorized by MSA. The issuance of the letter of credit is arranged by the importer's bank in accordance with procedures agreed to by the foreign government and the MSA. In the case of shipments financed by MSA grants (as opposed to MSA loans) the local currency funds paid to the bank by the importer are deposited in a counterpart fund, under the joint control of the MSA and the foreign government. Counterpart funds cannot be released for use by the foreign government without the consent of the MSA.

Financing of Exports under Loan Agreements

The Export-Import Bank and the International Bank use a variety of methods in financing purchases by the borrower. Loans, in general, are made only for approved projects and the loan agreements include lists of items to be financed. In many cases the borrower is reimbursed for authorized purchases only after the purchases have been made with his own funds or under credits arranged by him. In other cases the Export-Import Bank or the International Bank may guarantee a letter of credit issued by a commercial bank to the supplier for the account of the importer. The two banks may also establish revolving funds in a commercial bank for the borrower's use in making approved purchases.

Most U.S. exports financed by public foreign assistance involve the use of the export letter of credit. Where the foreign importers use their own funds to make purchases and are simply reimbursed by the agency making the grant or loan, other methods of financing, including the commercial draft and open book account, may be employed.

THE AMERICAN FOREIGN EXCHANGE MARKET

The vast bulk of all foreign exchange dealings in the New York foreign exchange market are in American account sterling, Canadian dollars and Swiss francs. There are both spot and forward markets in sterling and Canadian dollars but the forward market in Swiss francs is not significant. In fact, dealings in Swiss francs are relatively small as compared with transactions in sterling and Canadian dollars.

Since most U.S. exports to Canada and the sterling area are financed in U.S. dollars, the U.S. demand for foreign exchange to finance sterling and Canadian dollar imports greatly exceeds the supply derived from exports. In the case of the Canadian dollar, however, there has been an active demand arising out of the purchases of Canadian securities. Since September 1950 the Canadian government has made no effort to peg the Canadian dollar and it sold at a premium over the U.S. dollar during 1952. (The Bank of Canada has however intervened in the market to level off fluctuations.) The Bank of England maintains the rate on the pound sterling between $2.78 and $2.82.[29] Sterling tended to remain below $2.80 in the U.S. market during most of 1952, partly because of sales of sterling by British banks in order to furnish spot dollars for their customers, and to provide cover against forward contracts to deliver dollars to British importers. Toward the end of 1952 sterling rose above par and sold at the maximum level of $2.82 in February 1953.

The Forward Sterling Market

Since December 1951 when Britain restored free dealings in foreign exchange for British banks, the New York market in forward sterling has become much more important than at any time since 1939. Before December 1951 arbitrage dealings between London and New York were not permitted but there was an indirect relation between the free New York market for forward sterling and the pegged London price for forward dollars. The demand for forward sterling comes, in part, from American buyers of sterling commodities, about 50 per cent of whose purchases are covered by contracts to purchase sterling against dollars in the future. When the price of forward sterling is well below the spot price, U.S. importers are able to buy their sterling commodities somewhat more cheaply through the forward market. There also is a demand for forward sterling from British banks which operate in the American market, but they must cover

29. The Federal Reserve Bank of New York, as agent for the Bank of England, operates in the New York market at the same rates.

their forward purchases of sterling with short-term dollar funds.[30] British banks also sell forward dollars to their customers. These contracts must be covered by dollars held in U.S. banks or in the form of short-term securities.

The supply of sterling for future delivery comes from U.S. exporters selling for sterling, from U.S. traders holding large inventories of sterling goods who want to hedge against a fall in the dollar prices of sterling commodities which would accompany a devaluation of sterling, and from other Americans expecting sterling payments in the future. There is occasionally a supply of forward sterling from speculators who anticipate a devaluation of sterling. Forward sterling fluctuates with changes in expectations regarding the future price of sterling, and these in turn are affected by movements of British gold and dollar reserves and other indexes of Britain's international economic position.[31] In October 1950 when many people believed that sterling might be appreciated, three-month sterling futures rose to $2.83 in the New York market, but forward sterling began to fall rapidly after September 1951 with the sharp decline in British reserves.

U.S. Holdings of Foreign Balances

Movements in the spot rate for sterling are largely influenced by short-term capital movements rather than by shifts in the trade balance, since the demand for spot sterling for imports is always considerably heavier than the supply from U.S. exports. When the likelihood of sterling depreciation is considered to be greater than the likelihood of appreciation, American importers and others having payments to make in sterling tend to delay them and to borrow sterling in Britain and in other sterling area countries for their operations.[32]

30. After interest rates rose sharply in the United Kingdom in March 1952, British banks reduced their forward sterling purchases in the U.S. market and withdrew a portion of their dollar cover. Thus the profitability of forward exchange operations is affected by the spread between money rates in London and New York.

31. In October 1951, when British reserves were declining rapidly, three-month forward sterling in the New York market fell to $2.71¼ per pound. During 1952 three-month forward sterling fluctuated between $2.75 and $2.80 per pound.

32. The sharp rise in both the spot and the forward sterling rates which occurred at the time of the increase in the Bank of England's discount rate from 2.5 to 4 per cent (March 11, 1952) can be explained in part by the increase in the cost of borrowing in the British money market and the restriction of sterling credit to foreign borrowers.

American banks normally do not hold large amounts of sterling since the cost of covering their position in sterling becomes fairly heavy when the price of forward sterling is well below the spot market price. Following the outbreak of the war in Korea, holdings of short-term sterling balances by American banks rose from a low of $17 million to $112 million in October 1950. This increase was prompted by the necessity of covering their forward sales of sterling to American importers and speculators who anticipated an appreciation of sterling. Thereafter sterling holdings of American banks fell rapidly and under the impact of devaluation rumors in the winter of 1951–1952 fell to $13.5 million at the end of January 1952. During 1952 sterling liabilities of American banks and their customers were substantially in excess of sterling deposits of American banks and their customers.[33] In February 1952 sterling liabilities of U.S. banks and their customers to United Kingdom residents amounted to $112 million, but these liabilities subsequently declined, partly as a result of the decision of the British authorities to limit drafts under letters of credit to 90 days and to restrict refinancing facilities in London.[34]

Holdings of Canadian dollar balances by American banks and their customers have tended to be substantially higher than short-term Canadian dollar liabilities, while the opposite was true in the case of sterling.[35] In June 1953 total deposits of American banks and their customers in all foreign currencies amounted to only $61 million as against foreign holdings of dollar deposits in U.S. banks of $5,857 million. To meet a seasonal demand for a foreign currency U.S. banks may borrow in the foreign money market by drawing finance bills on their foreign correspondents. Some banks have an arrangement with their foreign correspondents whereby they may sell drafts in foreign currency and immediately credit the account of the foreign correspondent in dollars at the official rate.

33. At the end of June 1952 deposits of U.S. banks and their domestic customers with British banks amounted to $24.4 million while short-term sterling liabilities of American banks and their customers amounted to $63.7 million. Figures on short-term liabilities to and from foreigners are to be found in the *Treasury Bulletin,* published monthly by the U.S. Treasury Department, Washington.

34. The author is indebted to Dr. Fred Klopstock of the Federal Reserve Bank of New York for portions of this analysis.

35. As of the end of June 1952 American deposits in Canadian banks totaled $23.8 million while short-term Canadian dollar liabilities to Canadian banks amounted to $12.7 million.

PART IV

INTERNATIONAL CURRENCY PROBLEMS

Chapter 18

THE PROBLEM OF BALANCE OF PAYMENTS
EQUILIBRIUM

THERE IS A CERTAIN artificiality in speaking of the world's "foreign exchange" problems, the world's "trade" problems or even the world's "economic" problems, since these traditional categories cannot be analyzed except in the context of the totality of the political, social, economic and physical environment in which we live. When we pass from the description of the world's payments system to an analysis of the world's foreign exchange problems, we must broaden the discussion to include economic relationships and objectives which go beyond the mechanism of financing world trade. In identifying the world's payments problems we shall not be guided simply by the departure of postwar practices and policies from the traditional practices of the past. To do so would be to ignore or to condemn the enormous changes in the economic, social and political environment since 1939. Since this study is not concerned with the development of a blueprint for a new world order, we shall approach the solution of international monetary problems largely in terms of the world as it exists today.

The Significance of Equilibrium

Trade and exchange controls are sometimes viewed as necessary concomitants of the trend toward a greater degree of social control over economic affairs. This may be true in the sense that increased governmental controls have interfered with the automatic forces which in earlier years could be counted on to maintain balance of payments equilibrium. It is not true, however, in the sense that most governments or their citizens have regarded exchange and trade controls as such as a desirable extension of governmental participation in economic activities. On the other hand, nations have not regarded the existence of balance of payments disequilibrium which has necessitated this form of governmental interference as a desirable state of affairs. While socialist-minded governments have sometimes "nationalized" domestic and foreign trade in certain commodities and services, the introduction of over-all trade and exchange controls has been viewed by all non-Communist governments as a necessary evil.[1] This does not mean, of course, that some governments do not deliberately adopt economic policies which make balance of payments disequilibrium and exchange restrictions inevitable.

Disequilibrium gives rise to unwanted and economically harmful restrictions on the economic activities of residents of the deficit countries and frequently causes inflation and economic dislocation in the surplus countries. The isolation of internal from external markets creates price distortions which cause an uneconomical distribution of productive resources. Whether or not this distribution of resources is desirable as a means of encouraging economic development along certain lines will be considered in Chapter 19. It is sometimes argued that the rationing of foreign exchange is desirable on welfare grounds since it conserves exchange for essential imports, thereby keeping down the prices of commodities consumed by the masses; or that controls conserve foreign exchange for imports required for economic development. While this argument may have merit for temporary periods, as a permanent policy it means the substitution of rationing for the operation of the price system. Whatever the objectives of the welfare state, they should not be achieved by creating price and cost distortions which reduce the total value of the social product. The same objectives can generally be achieved by methods of taxation which do not have this undesirable result.

Disequilibrium and World Income

Disequilibrium and trade restrictions reduce real income for the world as a whole. Surplus countries must either finance their export surpluses by making grants and loans or they must reduce their exports. The *real* loss to the rest of the world in policies which lead to disequilibrium is not in the reduction of exports to the countries

1. The United States government as well as the governments of other capitalist countries have from time to time nationalized foreign trade in certain commodities such as rubber and other scarce materials as a temporary measure.

employing restrictions, but rather the reduction of imports from these countries. The distortion of prices and production in raw material countries is in part responsible for the failure of the world's supplies of foodstuffs and industrial raw materials to expand with growing world requirements. The failure of certain industrial countries to increase their output of capital equipment has deprived the less advanced countries of imports needed for their development programs. World disequilibrium has been a factor in keeping U.S. imports lower than would otherwise have been the case and it has substantially increased the burden on the American taxpayer for supporting the U.S. foreign aid program. A larger measure of world equilibrium would, in the absence of foreign aid, probably be accompanied by a smaller volume of U.S. exports, but the character of U.S. trade would be altered. A larger volume of U.S. private foreign investment is also likely to take place under conditions of world equilibrium.

Equilibrium and the Defense of the Free World

International equilibrium also has significance for the defense of the free world. The vast resources of the Soviet-controlled area are being mobilized to create the most powerful war machine the world has ever known. A large portion of the world is being developed and the activities of its residents coordinated by a centralized economic and political dictatorship. If total war can somehow be avoided for a generation, the final decision as to whether the world of the future will be governed according to the principles of dictatorship or the principles of democracy and free private enterprise, may very well be determined by the relative economic progress achieved under these two systems.

The coordinating principle of the free world must be the flow of trade and investment among its members as determined by the voluntary decisions of private individuals and friendly governments. These voluntary forces cannot operate effectively in a world of disequilibrium and uneconomic restraints on trade and investment. The twin objectives of the free world—adequate defense and rising living standards—require the mobilization of the human and material resources of the non-Soviet countries. The successful realization of these objectives in the next generation will depend in considerable measure upon the restoration of international equilibrium and the creation of an efficient payments mechanism.

INTERREGIONAL DISEQUILIBRIUM

We shall divide our analysis of balance of payments equilibrium and disequilibrium into a discussion of interregional disequilibrium and of disequilibrium for the individual country. Interregional disequilibrium is a condition in which a group of countries (not necessarily in the same geographical area) finance their trade with one another by arrangements which discriminate against imports from another region or regions with which the group as a whole has a persistent deficit.[2] Thus before 1950 the sterling area countries discriminated against and tended to have deficits with both the dollar area and certain other hard-currency countries such as Belgium and Switzerland. The persistent deficit of the nondollar countries of the world with the dollar area and their almost universal tendency to discriminate against dollar area imports may also be considered a form of interregional disequilibrium.

Over-all disequilibrium of an individual country is a condition in which, in the absence of controls, imports of goods and services from all countries would exceed exports of goods and services plus net long-term capital imports.

Reasons for Bilateralism

Following World War II most nations turned to bilateralism and the financing of trade with inconvertible currencies for two basic reasons. First, it was difficult to restore export trade with nondollar countries on a convertible currency basis since the marginal utility of the dollar was so much higher when spent in the dollar area than it was when used for purchases in nondollar countries. Second, bilateral payments agreements provided a means of financing trade with short-term credits, which would not have been available for trade conducted on a convertible currency basis.

This second reason for bilateralism arose from a shortage of international reserves of gold and convertible currencies. Had this been

2. By a balance of payments deficit we mean a condition in which imports of goods and services exceed (or would exceed in the absence of import and exchange controls) exports of goods and services plus net long-term capital imports. If this condition exists for a period of time sufficient to allow for seasonal and other temporary factors a country is said to be in disequilibrium.

the only reason why most nations turned to bilateralism and discrimination in order to maintain a satisfactory level of trade among themselves, the remedy could have been found in the short-term credits available from the Monetary Fund and the untied dollars provided by the $3,750 million loan to Britain in 1946. There is considerable doubt as to whether the dollar assets of the Fund were in fact sufficient to provide the additional international liquidity required to maintain a satisfactory level of world trade on a convertible currency basis, but there is reason to believe that these assets would have been supplemented by the United States government, had a shortage of international liquidity for meeting short-term fluctuations in the balance of payments of individual countries been the principal barrier to the restoration of multilateral trade.

Relative Prices vs. the Structure of Production

The primary reason for bilateralism in the early postwar period was the overwhelming demand for dollar goods in most nations, in relation to their capacity to earn dollars. This disequilibrium between the dollar area and the rest of the world, which has come to be called "the dollar shortage," was in part a matter of relative prices. In one sense the problem could have been "solved" by severe deflationary measures in the nondollar area, or by an adjustment in exchange rates. But equilibrium secured entirely by exchange rate adjustments or deflation would probably have resulted in hyperinflation in the one case, or in severe unemployment and very low rate of recovery in the other.

The basic causes of the disequilibrium were to be found in the low levels of production in many nondollar countries and the high level of demand for goods and services of all kinds. As recovery progressed, levels of production were restored and some countries at least were able to bring the over-all level of demand more or less into line with the volume of goods available to be purchased. In fact the expansion of production in Western Europe and in a large number of other nondollar countries has been quite impressive.[3] The reason for the persistence of the dollar problem in the world eight years after V-J Day is not to be found in the over-all levels of production, but rather in the structure of production in the nondollar world in relation to the pattern of world demand.

3. In 1951 industrial production in continental Western Europe was about 32 per cent above the 1938 volume; in Britain about 55 per cent above the 1938 level.

It is frequently argued that if every country were to take measures to reduce its demand for imports from all countries to the level of its foreign exchange earnings, there would be no dollar problem. But if every nondollar country in the world today reduced the level of its over-all demand for foreign goods and services to an amount equal in value to its exports in the *previous period*,[4] the aggregate demand for goods and services from the dollar area would be greater than the nondollar world's ability to purchase them with current dollar earnings. This is true because if countries reduced their total demand for imports on a nondiscriminatory basis they would tend to reduce their demand for dollar goods to a lesser degree than for nondollar goods. This means that for equilibrium to be restored without a drastic cut in world trade, the nondollar world must either produce more of certain basic commodities for its own use,[5] or produce more commodities which it can sell at competitive prices for dollars.

The magnitude of this structural deficit is difficult to determine since it cannot be separated from that part of the world's dollar deficit attributable to the over-all deficits of individual countries caused by improper monetary policies. As was pointed out in Chapter 17 (see Table 18) the average annual export surplus of the United States during the period 1950–1952 (excluding military aid exports) was only $2.6 billion and all but a billion dollars of this surplus was covered by normal means of financing, that is, long-term capital exports of a nonemergency character and private remittances. Moreover, in the first half of 1953, the U.S. export surplus was only $156 million, an amount which was more than covered by private capital outflow. However, a condition of disequilibrium with the rest of the world continued to exist since nearly every nondollar country maintained discriminatory import restrictions. Also, Western Europe's favorable dollar position during this period depended heavily upon the large U.S. military expenditures in that area.

4. If all countries were in over-all equilibrium in the sense that *current* foreign exchange earnings from all sources were equal to the total demand for foreign goods and services from all sources, there could be no dollar shortage. However, over-all equilibrium for all countries could only be achieved at the present time by a sharp reduction in total trade, assuming the complete abandonment of all discrimination and the financing of trade on a convertible currency basis.

5. Three fourths of the imports of the OEEC countries from the dollar area in 1951 consisted of grains, cotton and textile fibers, metals and ores, timber products, animal and vegetable oils, petroleum, machinery, chemicals and coal.

Considering the vast resources made available by the United States, it does not seem unreasonable to believe that a somewhat different pattern of world economic recovery during the postwar period could have eliminated this disequilibrium between the dollar and nondollar areas. If, in addition, internal monetary policies had been directed toward achieving over-all balance of payments equilibrium, most countries would have been able to dispense with trade and exchange restrictions eight years after the close of World War II.

Reasons for the Failure of Structural Adjustments

Why haven't the necessary changes in the structure of world production and trade taken place more rapidly? Some students have sought to lay the blame on United States import policies, or, alternatively, on the failure of nondollar countries to exploit the dollar market. Undoubtedly a reduction in U.S. barriers to imports, improved marketing methods and more competitive prices for foreign goods would expand sales to the dollar area. But there is a serious question whether the gap between the demand for dollar goods and the supply of means of payment can be closed entirely by larger exports to the dollar area. In other words, a fundamental cause of world disequilibrium is to be found in the failure of the nondollar countries to expand the production of a number of basic commodities for which they have been so heavily dependent upon the United States during the postwar years.

One of the most important categories of commodities for which the rest of the free world has increased its dependence upon the dollar area is foodstuffs. United States exports of crude foodstuffs in 1951–1952 were 400 per cent above the volume exported in the period 1936–1938, and manufactured foodstuffs were more than 150 per cent over the prewar volume. It is estimated that the volume of world grain exports (exclusive of rice) was 40 million tons for 1951–1952 of which 25 million tons was supplied by the United States and Canada. Before the war these two countries supplied only 7 million tons out of total world exports of grains of 32 million tons. This growing reliance by the rest of the world on U.S. and Canadian grain accounted for about $2 billion of the world's dollar deficit.

The increased dependence of the rest of the world on foodstuffs produced in the dollar area reflects in considerable part, at least, a shift in the structure of production in the nondollar world. In 1951 world industrial production (exclusive of the United States and the USSR) was about 34 per cent above the 1937–1938 level,[6] while industrial production in the OEEC countries was 40 per cent above prewar totals. On the other hand, food production in Asia in 1950–1951 was only slightly above the prewar level while population had increased by 20 per cent; in Latin America food production had increased 22 per cent above prewar by 1951–1952 but population had increased 36 per cent.

These figures indicate why Western Europe has had to shift purchases of grain and other foodstuffs from nondollar to dollar sources. Of course a part of this shift may be attributed to the decline in East–West trade, but Western Europe's imports of foodstuffs from nondollar countries of the free world have also declined. Mention has been made in the preceding chapters of the effects of economic policies in a number of the primary producing countries on the expansion of agricultural production. It seems reasonable to believe that had a larger portion of the capital investment in the underdeveloped countries been devoted to agriculture and had agricultural prices been higher relative to those of protected industrial products, the world's dollar problem would have been closer to a solution than it is today.

Western Europe's Imports from Nondollar Area

Evidence of the structural maladjustment in world trade and production is provided by a comparison of the real values of European imports from the dollar and nondollar areas in 1938 with the real values of imports from these areas in 1951. In that year imports of the OEEC countries from the nondollar area (excluding the OEEC countries) were only 83 per cent of the volume of imports in 1938. In 1951 the continental OEEC countries imported 86 per cent more from the dollar area and 18 per cent less from the nondollar area, than they did in 1938. The United Kingdom's imports from the dollar and the nondollar areas were 78 per cent and 86 per cent respectively, of the 1938 volume. (See Table 19.)

Another indication of structural disequilibrium is the increased dependence of the underdeveloped areas upon United States ex-

6. *United Nations Monthly Bulletin of Statistics*, October 1952, p. xiv.

TABLE 19

INDEXES OF REAL VALUE OF IMPORTS OF THE OEEC COUNTRIES FROM THE
DOLLAR [a] AND NONDOLLAR [b] AREAS IN 1951

(*1938 = 100*)

| | 1951 | |
Area	Dollar Area	Nondollar Area
United Kingdom	78	86
Continental OEEC [c]	186	82
Total OEEC	128	83

Sources: Calculated from trade statistics taken from *United Nations Monthly Bulletin of Statistics,* August 1952. Price deflators used in preparation of indexes are based on incomplete export price indexes of the countries in the nondollar area weighted in proportion to the value of trade with the area concerned. In the case of the dollar area, the export indexes of the United States and Canada are used, weighted in the same manner. Export price indexes were obtained from *International Financial Statistics,* December 1952.

a. Includes the United States, Canada, the Central American republics (including the Caribbean republics), Bolivia, Colombia, Ecuador, Mexico and Venezuela.
b. Excludes intra-OEEC trade but includes imports from overseas possessions of the U.K. and the continental OEEC countries.
c. Includes Austria, Belgium–Luxembourg, Denmark, France, Western Germany, Greece, Italy, the Netherlands, Norway, Portugal, Sweden, Switzerland and Turkey.

ports. Out of thirty-four non-European countries, thirty had increased the percentage of their imports from the United States in 1950 and 1951 over the corresponding percentage in 1937. (See Table 20.) These shifts in imports were almost invariably at the expense of Western European countries, and occurred in spite of the universal discrimination of nondollar countries against imports from the United States. In general this change has taken the form of a shift from consumers' goods, including textiles, formerly obtained in Britain and Western Europe, to machinery, vehicles and other capital goods, now imported in large quantities from the United States.

The sharp decrease in Western Europe's imports from Eastern Europe has been an important factor in increasing the dollar deficit of Western Europe. Including the United Kingdom, Western Europe's imports from Eastern European countries totaled $2,530 million in 1938 (in 1950 prices) but in 1951 imports from Eastern Europe had declined to $619 million (in 1950 prices) and in 1952 they dropped even further.[7] These imports from Eastern Europe consisted largely of coal, grain, timber and other raw materials, and their reduction has meant increased dependence of Western Europe on dollar sources.

7. *Economic Bulletin for Europe,* United Nations Economic Commission for Europe, New York, November 1952, p. 37.

TABLE 20

IMPORTS FROM THE UNITED STATES AS A PERCENTAGE OF TOTAL IMPORTS, FOR
SELECTED NON-EUROPEAN COUNTRIES, 1937–1951

Country	1937	1950	1951
Argentina	11	15	16
Australia	15	10	8
Bolivia	28	42	55
Brazil	24	34	42
Burma	4	4	2
Ceylon	3	3	5
Chile	29	48	55
Colombia	47	70	89
Costa Rica	42	67	66
Cuba	69	79	77
Dominican Republic	52	73	71 [b]
Ecuador	39	67	65
Egypt	6	6	15
El Salvador	40	72	67
Guatemala	45	68	67
Honduras	58	78	73
Iceland	1	19	13
India	7	9	30
Indonesia	10	21	20
Iran [a]	9	26	22 [b]
Iraq	8	8	14
Japan	25 (1935–37)	44	35
Lebanon	6	13	16
Mexico	62	88	81
New Zealand	12	7	9
Nicaragua	54	82	72
Panama	52	66	69
Paraguay	8	25	28 [b]
Peru	36	53	56
Philippines	58	75	71
Thailand	7 (1938)	16 (1949)	20 [b]
Turkey	15	25	12
Union of South Africa	21	16	19
Uruguay	14	20	38

Source: International Financial Statistics.

a. Percentage of dutiable imports only.
b. 1952, from the United States and Canada.

The Reduction in Earnings from Gold Production

Another factor in the structural change in world trade which should be noted is the decrease in gold production outside the United States and the USSR, available for sale to the United States or for increasing the official monetary reserves of nondollar countries. In 1938 the value of the world's gold output outside the United States and the USSR was $969 million, practically all of which was either sold to the United States or was added to official gold reserves of other countries. In 1951 the value of gold production in these countries was only $761 million,[8] more than three fourths of which "disappeared" into private hoards and industrial uses. If the value of gold production outside the United States and the USSR had borne the same relation to the value of world trade in 1950–1952 as it did in the late 1930s, and if all newly mined gold were available for monetary uses, the free world would have had an additional $2.6 billion annually available for dollar purchases or for increasing monetary reserves. This is equivalent to the average annual current account surplus of the United States during 1950–1952.

Structural Changes in U.S. Imports

Important structural changes in U.S. imports help explain the persistence of the postwar disequilibrium. In 1950 U.S. real gross national product (GNP) was about 81 per cent higher than it was during the period 1935–1939.[9] During the same years, however, the quantity of U.S. imports rose by about 52 per cent.[10] U.S. imports from the OEEC countries were only 30 per cent higher by volume than they were in the 1935–1939 period. On the other hand, U.S. imports from North American countries (all of which are members of the dollar area) rose by 161 per cent above the 1935–1939 level.

The sharp decrease in the ratio of total U.S. imports to real GNP was accompanied by an even greater decrease in the ratio of U.S. imports of foodstuffs and finished manufactures to real GNP. Only in the category of crude and semimanufactured materials was the ratio of total U.S. imports to real GNP even approximately maintained in 1950 as compared with prewar.[11] It is worth noting that the sharp decrease in the ratio of imports of finished manufactures to

8. Production figures taken from *International Financial Statistics*, published monthly by the International Monetary Fund. For a further discussion of the role of gold in international disequilibrium see R. F. Harrod, "Imbalance in International Payments," *Staff Papers*, April 1953, pp. 1–46.

9. *National Income, A Supplement to the Survey of Current Business*, U.S. Department of Commerce, Washington, 1951, p. 146.

10. Quantity indexes of U.S. imports have been taken from *The Pattern of United States Import Trade Since 1923*, The Federal Reserve Bank of New York, May 1952. In 1951 U.S. imports were about 50 per cent larger by volume than they were in the 1935–1939 period.

11. In 1950 U.S. imports of finished manufactures were 47 per cent higher than in 1935–1939 and imports of crude and semimanufactured materials were 72 per cent higher than prewar. However, imports of finished manufactures from the OEEC countries increased by 89 per cent over prewar, but total imports from these countries by only 30 per cent.

real GNP was accompanied by a substantial reduction in U.S. tariffs on dutiable imports.

The reasons for these changes in the structure of U.S. imports are exceedingly complex. The relative decrease in the importation of finished manufactures and manufactured foodstuffs can be explained partly by the failure of foreign suppliers to compete with sufficient vigor to maintain their share of the American market. The development of synthetic substitutes for a number of imported materials— nylon and rayon for silk, for example—has also been responsible for the decrease in the ratio of raw materials imports to total production in the United States. Whatever the causes, it is significant that had the prewar ratio of U.S. imports to real GNP been maintained in 1950, the value of U.S. imports would have been about $3 billion higher in 1950 than was actually the case. This calculated level of U.S. imports would have resulted in a current account deficit of about $800 million in 1950 instead of a surplus of approximately $2.2 billion, assuming the level of U.S. exports did not change.

Changes in Price and Financial Relationships

Taken together, the quantitative effect of all these structural changes in production and trade which have affected the demand for dollars and the supply of them add up to more than three times the U.S. current account surplus in 1950. In addition to these structural changes, there have been important developments since 1939 in international price and financial relationships. The United Kingdom and the countries of Western Europe have lost a substantial portion of their foreign investments in both the dollar area and in the raw materials producing countries. These same countries have accumulated heavy dollar debts on which they must make service payments and Britain also has incurred a large sterling indebtedness.

Of even greater significance for some of these countries has been the deterioration of their terms of trade, which means that they must export a larger volume of their own goods to buy the same volume of imports. The ratio of the index of British export prices to British import prices stood at 108 (1950 base) in 1938, while in 1951 it was only 85. Except for the Scandinavian countries, the terms of trade of the continental OEEC countries also deteriorated as compared with prewar ratios. The beneficiary of this development was not the United States, whose terms of trade have also deteriorated since before the war, but rather the raw materials producing countries of Latin America, Asia and Africa.[12]

The Means of Solution

Clearly, some of these structural developments which have helped to bring about the increase in the demand for dollar area goods and services relative to the supply of dollars are a consequence of the economic policies of the nondollar countries themselves; others were independent of these policies. Regardless of their origin, however, the pattern of world production and demand must be brought into line with the changed conditions if equilibrium is to be restored. In considering the means of solving the problem of world equilibrium we must assume that countries are willing to adopt standard of living goals consistent with the value of home production less the value of domestic and foreign investment which cannot be covered by long-term capital imports.[13]

The problem for the nondollar world thus becomes one of so adjusting its production and the pattern of its foreign trade as to meet its consumption and investment goals without balance of payments restrictions. Changes in the structure of production, however, require investment and in a free enterprise economy investment follows the market. To a considerable degree the trading arrangements and internal financial policies of Western Europe have not produced the proper incentives for a pattern of investment which would correct the elements of disequilibrium outlined above. It is also true that the economic policies of the underdeveloped areas have not promoted the changes in the structure of production required to restore world equilibrium.

In part, the solution to the problem of world equilibrium lies in the economic policies of the nondollar countries. This is largely a matter of over-all balance and the means of attaining that balance for the individual nation. But a full solution lies beyond the control of any one country. Each country must operate within the con-

---

12. Indexes of import and export prices may be found in the monthly issues of *International Financial Statistics*. Europe's terms of trade improved substantially in 1952 and 1953.

13. We have ignored for the time being foreign military assistance.

text of the world's trade and payments system which is, in turn, a product of the cooperative actions of all nations.

THE OVER-ALL BALANCE OF INDIVIDUAL NATIONS

Most nondollar countries are in a condition of over-all balance of payments disequilibrium in the sense that if they were to remove all their restrictions (except tariffs) on current trade with other countries, they would experience a net loss of gold and foreign exchange at their present exchange rates. There are a few nondollar countries which in the absence of controls might be in over-all balance in the sense that their net earnings of inconvertible currencies and credits would equal their current loss of gold and hard currencies. These countries might not be in over-all equilibrium, however, if they demanded gold or convertible currencies in settlement of all current balances, since their exports might fall as a consequence of demanding hard-currency settlements. Moreover, there is a tendency for these countries to maintain a balance with the dollar area by means of controls and to expand imports from soft-currency countries by shifting their trade to soft-currency countries. The export surpluses with the soft-currency countries, which cannot be balanced by an import surplus with the dollar area, create inflationary pressures with a consequent increase in the demand for imports. At this point, of course, the country is in over-all disequilibrium since the total demand for imports exceeds its current foreign exchange earnings.

When a Soft-Currency Country Seeks Over-all Equilibrium

Thus we see that many soft-currency countries are faced with a dilemma. If they adopt monetary and fiscal policies consistent with over-all balance they are likely to have a surplus with nondollar countries which must be settled wholly or partially in credits. With few exceptions, therefore, they adopt internal financial policies inconsistent with over-all equilibrium. A few countries have dealt with this dilemma by applying export controls on soft-currency exports or by breaking cross-rates between the soft currencies and the dollar. But both these practices are frowned upon by other members of the soft-currency group.[14]

14. Belgium, Portugal and Switzerland have sought to limit exports to soft-currency

Many countries employ controls to avoid deficits with both soft-currency and hard-currency nations. In some cases balances with soft-currency countries are subject to wide swings between deficit and surplus positions. This has been true, for example, in the case of Britain, France, the Netherlands and Germany in Western Europe, as well as with Australia, Pakistan and several other less-developed countries in the nondollar area. These swings are usually accompanied by alternate liberalizing and restricting policies toward imports from other soft-currency countries. While these fluctuations are to be expected, they tend to aggravate the world's dollar problem by diverting exports from the dollar area, and by increasing dollar expenditures by the amount of the dollar content of the excessive exports. The net soft-currency deficits of the majority of the nondollar countries have been concentrated on a few soft-currency countries, thereby tending to divert the exports of these countries from the dollar area, or alternatively, reducing their incentive to produce dollar-saving commodities.

Factors Making for Over-all Deficits

It is clear from this analysis that there is a reciprocal relationship between over-all deficits and interregional disequilibrium. On the one hand, interregional disequilibrium and the financing of trade with inconvertible currencies encourages over-all deficits; on the other hand, over-all deficits tend to accentuate the dollar problem by diverting resources from the production of dollar-earning or dollar-saving commodities. Aside from the existence of interregional disequilibrium, however, there are other important factors making for over-all disequilibrium in the postwar period: [15] (1) the employment, wage and social policies of postwar governments; (2) changes in the structure of internal and external demand and supply; (3) the efforts on the part of governments to push investment beyond

countries. Peru, Lebanon, Syria and Thailand achieve a balance with both hard- and soft-currency countries by breaking cross-rates.

15. In the immediate postwar period excessive liquidity and a shortage of stocks of goods of all kinds made over-all disequilibrium inevitable for most countries whose economies were severely affected by the war. However this situation can scarcely be regarded as a "cause" of disequilibrium in 1953.

the level which can be financed by domestic saving and long-term capital imports.[16]

It should be said at the outset that full employment policies, increased social services and a redistribution of income in favor of the working classes, are not necessarily incompatible with internal and external equilibrium, provided three conditions are observed. First, there must be sufficient mobility of labor and the other factors of production to permit adjustments in output required by the balance of payments. Second, over-all demand must not exceed the total value of goods and services available for purchase. Third, the relation between the prices of imported goods and services and those of home-produced goods and services must be such as to avoid a demand for imports in excess of current foreign exchange receipts. Unfortunately, these conditions are seldom easy to achieve.

A monetary demand consistent with stable prices may not be compatible with full employment at a given level of wages without increased investment and a change in the structure of production. Shifts in the structure of production cannot take place without either forcing the temporary unemployment of some factors of production or bidding them away by higher rewards. The volume of investment required to change the structure of production as required by the new demand and supply relationships may be greater than current savings. Current saving and the willingness to invest may be dampened by the heavier taxes needed to provide a greater measure of social services.

Adjustment to External Disequilibrium

Even if the problem of internal stability is successfully solved, the change in the propensity to import brought about by the redistribution of income may require further adjustments. In the absence of additional changes in the structure of production, deflationary pressures sufficient to bring the demand for imports into line with foreign exchange earnings may cause unemployment. Adjustment of the balance of payments by means of devaluation may lead to an increase in wages and prices and, if the demand for exports is inelastic,

16. The relationship of balance of payments equilibrium to economic development will be considered in Chapter 19.

a reduction in foreign exchange receipts. In time, devaluation will help to bring about the structural changes in the economy necessary to achieve equilibrium, but in the interim additional disequilibrating forces may be generated.

The problems of adjustment arise in large measure from the rigidities of modern price structures, the imperfections of world markets and the time and capital required for changes in the character of production in a highly mechanized world. The heavy risks and uncertainties coupled with high taxes also impede the mobility of capital. While internal adjustments to world supply-and-demand conditions are necessarily slow, changes in world demand have been exceedingly rapid during the postwar period. For example, the balances of payments of both industrial nations and raw-material countries have been greatly affected by the movements in raw material prices. World political conditions have required the Western industrial nations to expand substantially their outlays for defense. These changes have been superimposed upon the vastly altered structure of the world economy to which nations were just beginning to make a satisfactory adjustment by mid-1950.

Measures Required for Over-all Equilibrium

The purpose of these comments is not to support the conclusion that over-all equilibrium is impossible of attainment by most countries. Rather, it is to indicate some of the difficulties encountered in achieving and maintaining equilibrium under present-day conditions. These difficulties can be overcome provided countries are given time to make the necessary adjustments in the structure of their production required by sudden changes in external conditions. If nations are to avoid a continual or frequent use of exchange and trade restrictions, they must have access to a larger amount of international reserves than most of them now possess.

In summary, over-all equilibrium for the nations of the world requires (1) a world-wide system of multilateral settlements and the elimination of trade discrimination; (2) a determination on the part of governments to apply deflationary pressures by monetary and fiscal measures to the extent necessary to achieve mobility of labor and other factors of production; [17] (3) a willingness to adjust exchange rates whenever costs and prices are out of line with those prevailing abroad; (4) the availability of sufficient international reserves to permit nations to make the appropriate structural adjustments without resorting to exchange and trade restrictions. In cases of severe structural maladjustment nations may require long-term foreign loans to finance additional investments needed to develop new export industries or industries designed to save foreign exchange.

17. This does not mean that deflation should be pushed to the point of large unemployment. However, unemployment of from 5 to 7 per cent of total employables may be necessary for short periods in order to make the desired adjustments.

Chapter 19

FOREIGN EXCHANGE PROBLEMS OF UNDER-
DEVELOPED AREAS

BALANCE OF PAYMENTS problems of primary producing countries have been more acute than those of industrial nations for three reasons: (1) concentration of production on a few basic commodities leaves the economies of these countries more vulnerable to fluctuations in the demand for their exports; (2) the degree of fluctuation in world prices of raw materials is substantially greater than in the prices of industrial commodities; (3) the far-reaching social revolutions in the underdeveloped countries in recent years coupled with a determination on the part of their governments to speed up the process of economic development have produced severe strains upon the balance of payments. This chapter will analyze the foreign exchange problems peculiar to the primary producing countries in an effort to reach conclusions regarding their practices and policies in this field.

FLUCTUATIONS IN FOREIGN EXCHANGE EARNINGS

A United Nations study of the annual fluctuations in prices and foreign exchange proceeds of major primary commodities during the first half of the twentieth century shows that the average year-to-year fluctuation in the prices of twenty-five primary commodities was 14 per cent for the period 1901 to 1951; the average year-to-year fluctuation in foreign exchange receipts from the sale of eighteen of these commodities was 23 per cent in the same period.[1]

1. The twenty-five commodities covered by the United Nations study are bananas, *cocoa, coffee, copper,* copra, *cotton, hemp,* hides and skins, *jute, linseed,* manganese, nickel, *petroleum, rice, rubber,* shellac, *silk,* sisal, *sodium nitrate, sugar, tea, tin, tobacco, wheat* and *wool.* The italicized items are the eighteen commodities included in the calculation of the average (year-to-year) percentage fluctuation in export receipts. For the eighteen commodities the average year-to-year fluctuation in export receipts was 22.6 per cent in money terms and 22 per cent in real terms. The average percentage

One half or more of the national income of many countries is derived from raw materials exports. Sharp fluctuations in foreign exchange income make for instability of domestic income and employment and create even greater disturbances in the external balance. Such fluctuations also discourage investment in the raw materials industries. Internal stability could be maintained by compensatory fiscal and monetary operations or by schemes for stabilizing domestic raw materials prices and subsidizing the raw materials exporters (or taxing their excessive profits). But unless the country has substantial foreign exchange reserves, the maintenance of domestic income in the face of a sharp decline in foreign exchange earnings requires the imposition of import restrictions.

The adoption of a freely fluctuating exchange rate or a policy of changing the exchange rate with changes in foreign exchange income tends to stabilize the local currency receipts of the exporters, but has little effect on foreign exchange earnings, at least in the short run. The disadvantage of a shifting rate for primary producing countries is that local currency prices of essential imports become subject to fluctuations, possibly of the same magnitude as the movements in world raw materials prices. Such fluctuations in major cost-of-living commodities would work a hardship on certain economic classes and if wages also were flexible, might generate a wage-price spiral.[2]

Use of Multiple Exchange Rates

Many primary producing countries have sought to deal with the problem by means of multiple exchange rates, restrictions on unessential imports or a combination of both. By manipulating a system of multiple exchange rates it is theoretically possible to stabilize both local currency receipts from exports and the prices of essential commodities while at the same time balancing the total demand for, and supply of, foreign exchange.

---

fluctuation of export receipts in money terms for the period 1901 to 1950 ranged from 15 per cent in the case of wool to 36 percent in the case of rubber. The eighteen primary commodities chosen for study represent the major exports of forty-seven underdeveloped countries and territories. See *Instability in Export Markets of Under-Developed Countries*, United Nations, New York, 1952, pp. 3–7.

2. For an analysis of this problem, see Henry C. Wallich, "Underdeveloped Countries and the Monetary Mechanism," in *Money, Trade, and Economic Growth* (Essays in Honor of John H. Williams), Macmillan, New York 1951, pp. 15–32.

In actual practice, multiple rate schemes do not operate on such a highly rational basis. Instead of being employed to offset the price and income distortions caused by temporary fluctuations in foreign exchange income, multiple rate systems are frequently products of *ad hoc* decisions which inhibit adjustments to fundamental balance of payments conditions by creating permanent distortions in the price system. For example, to maintain low prices to consumers through subsidy import rates tends to create inflationary pressures which result in a misdirection of resources; to have subsidy rates for some exports and penalty rates for others may in the longer run weaken the more efficient industries at the expense of the less efficient. While it may seem expedient to tax windfall profits of the exporters of certain commodities in a time of high world prices, these same windfall profits may provide the incentive and the financial means to expand and increase the efficiency of an important foreign exchange earner.

Seeking Stability through Bilateral Agreements

Many underdeveloped countries have tried to secure a more stable level of demand for their products through bilateral payments and barter arrangements. As was pointed out in Chapter 13, postwar experience reveals that exports to bilateral agreement countries have certainly been no more stable than exports to dollar countries—if as stable.

It will be readily admitted that some countries whose traditional markets have been largely in soft-currency countries and which have been in competition with other soft-currency suppliers, have found it necessary to export for inconvertible currencies in order to sell their products. However, there are real disadvantages in bilateral trading. Prices of some raw materials in soft-currency markets are little if any higher than prices in dollar markets, while the exporting country is at a distinct disadvantage in buying its imports with soft currencies. Prices of imports are higher, deliveries are frequently slow and many commodities are not obtainable except with dollars. Yet a number of underdeveloped countries with exports readily salable in dollar markets have entered into bilateral arrangements in order to expand or stabilize the demand for their exports. Brazil and Colombia, for example, have entered into agreements with a number of European countries for the sale of their coffee on a bilateral basis.[3]

The most desirable solutions to the problem of insulating the economies of the primary producing countries against fluctuations in foreign exchange earnings are those which do not rest on the use of exchange restrictions. So long as the industrial countries of the world avoid major depressions, swings in the demand for raw materials are likely to be of relatively short duration and the long-run outlook is for an expanded world demand for most raw materials.[4] Provided primary producing countries adopt appropriate internal measures for avoiding both inflation and deflation, the impact on their international reserves originating in fluctuating raw material prices could probably be handled by drawings from the Monetary Fund.[5] A further contribution to stability might be provided by international buffer stocks which could be used to iron out temporary fluctuations in world prices of raw materials.[6]

ECONOMIC DEVELOPMENT AND THE BALANCE OF PAYMENTS

In addition to the strains put on the balance of payments by rapidly fluctuating foreign exchange receipts, national programs for economic development have been important disequilibrating factors in many primary producing countries. The problems of financing the local currency and foreign exchange requirements of economic development have been dealt with extensively in the literature and need not concern us here.[7] The fact that in recent years economic development has generally been accompanied by inflation and balance of payments disequilibrium, is largely responsible for the employment of exchange restrictions by most underdeveloped countries. Underdeveloped countries have also sought to influence the direction of

3. The International Bank's economic mission to Colombia questioned the need for Colombia's bilateral agreements. See *The Basis of a Development Program for Colombia,* International Bank for Reconstruction and Development, Washington, 1950, p. 581.

4. For a discussion of the long-run demand for raw materials, see *Resources for Freedom,* Vol. I, President's Materials Policy Commission, 1952, pp. 23–25.

5. The adequacy of the Monetary Fund's resources will be discussed in Chapter 22.

6. For a discussion of buffer stocks see *Resources for Freedom,* Vol. I, pp. 88–90.

7. See *Formulation and Economic Appraisal of Development Projects,* United Nations, New York, 1951, Vol. I, Part V; see also *Methods of Financing Economic Development in Underdeveloped Areas,* United Nations, New York, 1949; and Paul T. Ellsworth, *The International Economy,* Macmillan, New York, 1950, Chapters 28 and 29.

economic development by using trade and foreign exchange controls. However, the desire to influence the character of development is usually not the primary reason for introducing a system of exchange controls. But once a system of controls is established as a means of dealing with disequilibrium, measures are introduced to implement a variety of special objectives.

Exchange Restrictions as a Means of Fostering Development

Four basic arguments have been put forth in favor of exchange controls on current transactions for countries seeking to achieve a rapid rate of economic development. The first argument is based on the assumption that domestic investment in underdeveloped countries must be financed to a considerable degree by forced saving which results from inflation.[8] Inflationary financing of investment reduces the real incomes of wage and salaried workers and others whose incomes do not keep pace with rising prices. Imports must be restricted in order to avoid the impact of the inflation upon monetary reserves.

While it is generally admitted that some increase in investment can be achieved through forced saving, there is a real question as to whether such investment contributes to the productive capacity of a country. It has been pointed out, for example, that inflation encourages investment in construction and inventories rather than in industry and agriculture.[9] Inflation may initially shift some resources from consumption to investment, but continuous inflation will create distortions in the income and price structure which tend to reduce the country's productive capacity. A more basic solution to the problem of financing development programs lies in the field of taxation and in the establishment of savings institutions to channel savings into productive investment.

A second argument in favor of import restrictions in underdeveloped countries is that they can be used to conserve foreign exchange for imports necessary for development programs at the expense of luxury imports.[10] To test the validity of this argument we

8. The argument in favor of forced saving is based on the fact that most underdeveloped countries lack money markets and savings institutions and that the few wealthy landlords and merchants who are able to do any substantial saving prefer to invest in land, buildings, gold or foreign securities.

9. See E. M. Bernstein and I. G. Patel, "Inflation in Relation to Economic Development," *Staff Papers*, November 1952, pp. 377–78.

10. Professor Ragnar Nurkse has given an excellent analysis of this problem in *Some*

must consider what happens to income which is diverted away from luxury imports. If it is all spent on domestic consumers' goods, the investment goods imported with the diverted foreign exchange will in fact be financed either by forced savings or by a reduction of other types of investment in the economy. In either case the pattern of domestic investment will probably change in favor of less productive investments. To the extent that some of the income formerly used to buy luxury imports is saved, investment will increase without inflation and forced saving. However, it is unlikely that the propensity to consume can be reduced for more than short periods of time by restrictions on imports.

Systems of import and exchange controls designed to conserve foreign exchange for essential uses, including capital equipment and materials for economic development, seem not to have been generally successful in achieving their objectives. The cumbersome systems of import licensing and the inefficiency and corruption of their administration have discouraged imports for long-term capital investment in industry and agriculture, in favor of consumers' goods and materials for luxury houses and office buildings. A comparison of Colombia's imports in the 1930s (before exchange controls) with imports in the postwar period reveals little change in favor of capital goods.[11] In the view of the IBRD mission, "It is very doubtful whether in practice the operation of exchange control in Colombia has actually resulted in a better use of foreign exchange resources than would have occurred in its absence."[12] This conclusion probably applies to other underdeveloped countries in the postwar period.

It has been suggested that raw materials producing countries can improve their terms of trade by adopting overvalued exchange rates and exchange restrictions. Since in the short run, at least, the world demand for raw materials is fairly inelastic, output restriction through an overvalued export rate will, according to this argument, increase foreign exchange receipts.[13]

This argument is fallacious for several reasons. First, few underdeveloped countries control a sufficiently large proportion of the

---

Aspects of Capital Accumulation in Underdeveloped Countries (Fiftieth Anniversary Commemoration Lectures), National Bank of Egypt, Cairo, 1952, pp. 53–60.

11. *The Basis of a Development Program for Colombia*, p. 330.
12. *Ibid.*
13. See Wallich, *loc. cit.*, pp. 30–32.

world's total supply of a commodity to improve their own terms of trade by output reduction and it is unlikely that they could band together for this purpose. Second, in the longer run, demand is responsive to price and the failure of raw materials production to rise with expanding world requirements seems certain to encourage the use of substitutes, including synthetic materials. The principal long-run effect of overvalued export rates is likely to be the discouragement of investment in the primary industries. This will not only reduce foreign exchange receipts but also prevent increased productivity in agriculture and mining. The best way to increase living standards in the underdeveloped areas is not to seek a short-run improvement in terms of trade by output restriction, but rather to promote an increase in productivity per man-hour through the mechanization of mines and plantations, use of scientific farming methods, and so on.

The Use of Restrictions to Shift Production

This brings us to the fourth argument for exchange restrictions for underdeveloped countries, namely that they are desirable as a means of encouraging industrial production, for home use or for export, at the expense of agriculture and mining. A basic fallacy lies in the syllogism: "Countries with a high proportion of secondary to primary industries have high living standards; therefore by increasing the proportion of secondary production, living standards can be raised." Countries with high per capita incomes like the United States reached this happy state of affairs not by less primary production but through a larger volume of agricultural and minerals production with a smaller number of workers. Workers required for industrialization should be released from primary production by expanding output per man-hour, not by reducing primary production. This path to increased living standards and industrialization has been emphasized frequently by economic survey missions to underdeveloped countries. The following passage from the report of the International Bank's mission to Colombia illustrates this point:

In order to achieve industrial development and a concomitant increase in productivity, imports of equipment are needed. In order to obtain these imports, the country must export agricultural products. Yet the agricultural sector lags in economic development and thus an inordinately large fraction of the country's labor force is tied up in providing for a relatively small volume of capital imports.

The answer to the problem cannot be found in early development of heavy industries at home. Among many other difficulties that would arise, it is evident that the domestic market for most products is still too small to warrant such development. Nor can the answer be found in reduced emphasis on capital imports. On the contrary, modernization of agriculture, as well as industry, is essential for a rising standard of living in Colombia . . . By increasing the efficiency of agriculture, it will be possible to release manpower from the agricultural sector for industry and it will then be possible to increase industrial output by the reduced real cost of manpower, as well as equipment.[14]

In Argentina the combination of an unfavorable rate for exports of basic agricultural products and the use of profits from the export of agricultural commodities by the government selling monopoly to promote industrialization has reduced agricultural output and discouraged investment in agriculture. Many of Argentina's current economic troubles can be traced to her foreign trade and exchange policies which discriminate against agriculture.

Unfavorable export rates for minerals in Bolivia and Chile have affected investment in these industries—the principal source of foreign exchange and the chief means of financing economic development in both countries. In Bolivia, for example, no new tin mine of any importance has been opened up for over twenty years and the available reserves of high grade ore are being rapidly depleted. A recent report of a United Nations mission to Bolivia describes that country's system of foreign exchange regulations as having "developed through a series of *ad hoc* measures and is complex, intricate and inconsistent; it includes import prohibitions, multiple and 'mixed' rates of exchange, exchange and import licensing and retention of exchange by importers, all in accordance with a set of changing and ill-defined rules." [15]

Import Restrictions and Protection of Local Industry

Import policies of underdeveloped countries have also been directed toward stimulating economic progress. Local industry is protected by shutting out competitive products and by giving favorable

14. *The Basis of a Development Program for Colombia*, p. 47.
15. *Report of the United Nations Mission of Technical Assistance to Bolivia*, United Nations, New York, 1951.

treatment to wage-goods and capital equipment for industrialization programs. Since favorable import rates must be subsidized by less favorable export rates if the exchange budget is to balance in terms of local currency, the promotion of industrialization is at the expense of the raw materials exporters. In some cases the subsidy rates for essential agricultural imports have discouraged the local production of these products. For example, the preferential exchange rate for sugar imports into Chile has probably delayed development of the beet sugar industry in that country.[16] The introduction of a multiple rate system in Peru, establishing a favorable import rate for meat, so reduced the domestic price that the production of domestic meat was cut in half.[17]

THE TREATMENT OF FOREIGN INVESTMENTS

The foreign exchange practices of underdeveloped countries undoubtedly constitute a major obstacle to the flow of private foreign investment into these areas. A recent National Industrial Conference Board report,[18] based on replies to a questionnaire from companies representing at least 54 per cent of American direct investments abroad, showed that 37 per cent of these companies mentioned limitations on the remittances of profits as a hindrance in their foreign investments. Out of twenty-two obstacles to direct foreign investment mentioned in the questionnaire replies, the most frequently cited were, in order of their ranking: (1) the existence of import or export quotas; (2) limitations on the remittance of profits; (3) the control of capital movements. Multiple exchange rates ranked seventh in importance among the twenty-two obstacles mentioned.[19] It is clear

16. The import rate for sugar in Chile was 31.1 pesos to the dollar in 1952, as compared with rates ranging from 50 to 130 pesos for most other imports. At the same time the country is reported to be capable of producing its own sugar from sugar beets. See *Economic Survey of Latin America in 1949*, United Nations Economic Commission for Latin America, New York, 1951, Chapter 9.

17. E. M. Bernstein, "Some Economic Aspects of Multiple Exchange Rates," *Staff Papers*, September 1950, International Monetary Fund, p. 230.

18. *Obstacles to Direct Foreign Investment*, National Industrial Conference Board, New York, April 1951. (This report was prepared for The President's Committee for Financing Foreign Trade.)

19. In the order of the frequency of mention the twenty-two obstacles to investment were: export or import quotas; limitation on remittance of profits; control of capital movements; burden of social security legislation; lack of trained native personnel; lack of adequate roads, railroads, harbors or storage facilities; multiple exchange rates; inadequacy of housing, recreational and shopping facilities for employees; inadequate

therefore that American foreign investors consider foreign exchange practices serious deterrents to an expansion of their foreign operations.

It would be wrong, however, to conclude that restrictions on the transfer of capital and earnings have proved a significant barrier to investment in all countries or for all types of investment, since more than half the replies to the Board's questionnaire indicated no difficulties in this field. Most American companies engaged in mining or producing petroleum abroad are not required to surrender the proceeds of their exports except to pay local expenses, taxes and royalties. However, they are frequently subject to unfavorable exchange rates for the purchase of local currency with foreign exchange.[20] It would also be wrong to conclude that the removal of exchange controls alone would open up a flood of American private capital into the underdeveloped areas. The instability of governments, the threat of expropriation or nationalization, restrictions on ownership and management, unfavorable labor laws and trade union practices, demands for changes in concession contracts, changes in tax laws and arbitrary treatment of various kinds, taken together represent a far greater deterrent to private foreign investment than do foreign exchange controls. Recent events in Bolivia and Iran have undoubtedly increased the importance of the fear of nationalization in preventing foreign investment. Even where foreign exchange regulations are a

---

power facilities; foreign restriction on importation of personnel from home country; instability of government; lack of health and sanitary facilities; nationalization and expropriation; special taxation of foreign enterprises; undeveloped banking system or other credit facilities; inability to recruit personnel in the United States; restriction of foreign investment to certain fields; inability to deal with responsible government officials; required local participation; discriminatory enforcement of tax laws; unequal treatment before the law with respect to property holding and conveying, contract enforcement, right to use local courts for redress, etc.; requirement for reinvestment of earnings. (*Obstacles to Direct Foreign Investment*, p. 8.)

The results of this survey must be carefully interpreted. In some instances limitations on the remittance of profits or multiple exchange rates were listed as obstacles for countries in which exchange restrictions did not in fact exist, or where other firms reported that no restrictions existed. In many cases it is the fear of unfair or arbitrary treatment rather than the actual existence of such treatment which is significant.

20. An investigation of obstacles to American direct investment in foreign mining and petroleum was made during the summer of 1951 by the Harvard Law School for the President's Materials Policy Commission. Most concerns interviewed during the course of the investigation did not rate the inability to transfer earnings into dollars as the most important obstacle although some firms operating in countries using multiple exchange rates were subjected to unfavorable conversion rates for the purchase of local currencies. See *Resources for Freedom*, Vol. I, pp. 64–67.

significant influence it is frequently the fear in the mind of the investor that treatment may become less favorable in the future rather than the existing situation which keeps the investment from taking place.

Private Foreign Lending

Private foreign lending to underdeveloped countries largely came to an end at the beginning of the 1930s after the wholesale defaults in Latin America and elsewhere. Most non-Communist countries have resumed their external debt service though this has frequently been accompanied by a scaling down of interest and principal. Although loan funds are available on favorable terms from public lending institutions, e.g., the International Bank and the Export-Import Bank, private loan financing for development has not become available on reasonable terms. The field of public utilities is no longer an outlet for direct private investment since most underdeveloped countries have already nationalized these industries or are anxious to do so. This leaves trade, manufacturing and raw materials and their processing as the major fields for foreign private investment; of these only investment in manufacturing and the production and processing of raw materials are significant sources of capital for economic development.

Obstacles to private foreign investment arising out of foreign exchange practices and policies may be divided into three main categories: (1) limitations on the ability to transfer earnings or to repatriate invested capital; (2) unfavorable exchange rates either for remittances or for the purchase of currency for local expenditures; (3) limitations on the ability to acquire imports of goods and services needed for business operations.[21] The third obstacle listed is the one most frequently mentioned in the NICB survey and probably applies in some degree to all countries employing exchange and quantitative import controls. It is a limitation which in most countries is equally burdensome to domestically owned industries; indeed, foreign-owned enterprises are frequently better off since they can make their original

21. Limitations on the ability to export has also been cited as an obstacle to foreign investment but such measures are usually not related to exchange policies. Sometimes limitations on imports may be for protection or for other purposes not related to the balance of payments.

investment in the form of equipment and materials purchased abroad. Where the foreign investment is important as a dollar-earner, the companies seldom have difficulty in obtaining foreign exchange for imports. Even so, the fact that in most exchange control countries exporters must turn over their foreign exchange proceeds to the exchange control authorities or sell them to authorized banks means that the enterprise can never be sure of obtaining all its foreign currency requirements. This difficulty has been almost universally avoided in the petroleum industry since concession contracts generally permit the retention of export proceeds by the foreign producer. Some of the mining and fruit companies in Latin America also have concession contracts which permit them to retain their foreign exchange proceeds.

Multiple Exchange Rates as a Deterrent to Foreign Investment

Multiple exchange rates are not always harmful to foreign investors. If a concern is selling in the local market a commodity produced by local labor from local materials and if the rate applying to imports of foreign capital is the same as the rate for remitting earnings, the enterprise is likely to experience little disadvantage from the system. However, a serious disadvantage to the foreign investor can result from the existence of a relatively overvalued rate for capital imports and the conversion of foreign exchange proceeds into local currency, and a relatively undervalued rate for exports and the remittance of earnings. Profits may also be affected by a relatively overvalued rate for exports and a relatively undervalued rate for imports. In some countries the unfavorable export rate or the rate for converting foreign exchange into local currency is deliberately designed as a tax and if the tax were removed, some other means of collecting an equivalent amount of taxes would no doubt be devised. The conversion of a multiple rate designed to produce revenue into an income tax would however have certain tax advantages for American firms operating abroad.[22]

Perhaps the greatest obstacle to foreign investment arising from

22. United States firms operating abroad can deduct income taxes paid abroad from the U.S. tax applicable to their net income under U.S. tax laws. While the existence of the multiple rate reduces net profits, the tax advantage is not as great as in the case of a deduction of an equivalent amount of foreign income tax from the U.S. income tax.

the existence of multiple exchange rates is the fear that the remittance rate will be changed unfavorably after the initial investment has been made. While most countries maintain the same rate for new capital imports and for remittances on old investments, the investor never knows when the rate structure will be altered. This same fear is present in a country maintaining an overvalued unitary rate. This is not simply a matter of exchange rate instability since under a free but fluctuating rate the investor might have some expectation of preserving the real value of the investment through price changes. But in countries with unstable domestic conditions and an overvalued rate, there is little protection for the investor.

Restrictions on Transfers of Earnings and Capital

The most widely discussed barrier to foreign investment is that of limitations on the transfer of earnings and capital. Many firms have not only been unable to repatriate their capital but their earnings have been blocked in the foreign country for several years. Nearly all exchange control countries put limitations upon the repatriation of capital although several have introduced liberal provisions for remittances of both capital and earnings for investments made after a certain date in the postwar period.

A substantial number of countries permit the transfer of earnings either without limit or up to a certain percentage of invested capital each year. Where the transfer of earnings is limited to 10 per cent or less, the return is often too small relative to earnings of similar enterprises in the United States to warrant the foreign investment, especially in view of the generally higher risks. Frequently the privilege of transferring earnings and capital is limited to registered capital and only approved investments can be registered. Even where exchange laws and regulations provide for the transfer of earnings or the repatriation of capital, such transfers are usually contingent upon the exchange availabilities of the country. In some countries, particularly in Latin America, periods of exchange shortage are accompanied by heavy arrears in meeting foreign exchange claims for authorized purposes. The threat of such shortages in the future may be sufficient to deter investments in exchange control countries even though current conditions are satisfactory.

Existence of Exchange Controls Creates Uncertainties

The basic obstacle to foreign investment arising out of exchange practices is the very existence of foreign exchange and other governmental controls and the uncertainty as to the future uses of these measures. Even if exchange controls were removed, exchange instability or the threat of the reimposition of controls would remain for a long time as deterrents to foreign investment. Only a long history of political and economic stability, such as Canada's, can banish these fears. Barring the removal of exchange controls, what can be done to make them less of an obstacle to foreign investment? Complete freedom for the foreign investor is probably incompatible with a system of exchange controls. Unlimited freedom for the foreign investor to transfer capital and earnings and to obtain foreign exchange for imports of goods and services would be extremely unpopular in countries having balance of payments difficulties; it would also create serious leaks and avenues for abuse in the exchange control system.

One possible solution is for governments with exchange controls to enact laws setting forth the basic rules for the treatment of foreign capital and the transfer of earnings, and to establish a foreign investment commission to administer the regulations. It would be even more desirable if the fundamental regulations could be embodied in national constitutions to give investors greater confidence in their permanency.

The conditions governing the treatment of new foreign investment ought to be regarded as contract obligations between the foreign investor and the government and specific written agreements might be negotiated with each foreign investor by the foreign investment commission of the country concerned. These arrangements ought to include the transfer of all net profits after taxes payable to the local government, and specific provisions for the withdrawal of capital over a reasonable period of time. Inevitably the country making such agreements would insist that transfers could be limited during a severe exchange shortage, but the priority to be given to investment service in such periods and the provisions for working off arrears ought to be stated definitely in the contracts. These specific arrangements also ought to deal with the problem of exchange rates. While no country is likely to be willing to give an exchange rate guarantee to foreign investors, countries ought to agree not to change their multiple exchange rate systems in a manner prejudicial to the investor. This is admittedly a difficult criterion to apply in practice.

Another approach is for exchange control countries to adopt a free market for all invisibles including imports and exports of capital and the transfer of earnings. While investors run the risk of having to withdraw their capital and earnings at less favorable rates than existed at the time the investment was made, they would be assured of the ability to make transfers without restriction. Such an arrangement would also protect the country in which the investment was made from a foreign exchange drain resulting from transfers of capital and earnings, provided of course the exchange authorities made no attempt to support the free exchange market.

Investment Treaties

Investment treaties between the governments of the borrowing and the lending countries can be of value in setting forth the general policies of borrowing countries and providing machinery for negotiation in cases of disputes between the private investors and the government of the country in which the investments are made. Such a treaty, however, cannot deal with administrative details and is not a substitute for the kind of specific contractual arrangements described above.[23] The following provisions on the withdrawal of capital and earnings included in the Treaty of Friendship, Commerce and Economic Development between the United States and Uruguay are considered to be the best which have been obtained in any agreement up to the present time:

4. Nationals and companies of either Party shall be permitted freely to introduce capital funds into the territory of the other Party and, by means of obtaining exchange in the currency of their own country to withdraw therefrom capital funds and earnings, whether in the form of salaries, inter-

23. Multilateral investment agreements such as are provided for in the proposed Havana Charter for an international trade organization have been unpopular with business. Underdeveloped countries have insisted upon the inclusion of statements in both the Havana Charter and the economic agreement of the International Conference of the American States at Bogotá, setting forth in broad terms the rights of the host countries with respect to the control of existing and future foreign investments. (See Henry Chalmers, "The Economic Agreement of Bogota: an Inter-American Milestone," *Foreign Commerce Weekly*, June 12, 1948. See also "Comment on Investment Provisions of the Havana Charter" by the International Chamber of Commerce in *Methods of Financing Economic Development in Underdeveloped Areas*, United Nations, New York, 1949, pp. 161–63.)

est, dividends, commissions, royalties or otherwise, and funds for the amortization of loans, for transfers of compensation for property referred to in paragraph 2 of Article VIII, and funds for capital transfers. If more than one rate of exchange is in force, such withdrawals shall be at an effective rate of exchange, inclusive of any taxes or surcharges on exchange transfers, that is just and reasonable. However, a Party shall retain the right in periods of exchange stringency to apply exchange restrictions to assure the availability of foreign exchange for payments for goods and services essential to the health and welfare of its people. In the event that either Party applies such restrictions it shall within a period of three months make reasonable and specific provision for the withdrawals referred to, giving consideration to special needs for other transactions, and shall afford the other Party adequate opportunity for consultation at any time regarding such provision and other matters affecting withdrawals. Such provision shall be reviewed in consultation with the other Party at intervals of not more than twelve months.

Government Guarantees

U.S. government guarantees against the inability of American foreign investors to transfer earnings and capital have been proposed as a means of substantially expanding private foreign investment. Legislation providing for such guarantees, which formed a part of President Truman's Point Four Program, was introduced in both houses of Congress in 1949.[24] While this legislation was not voted upon by Congress, a limited program of foreign investment insurance was provided for in both the Economic Cooperation Act of 1948 and the Mutual Security Act of 1951. Foreign investors have not found the terms especially attractive and between 1948 when the program went into operation and September 1953, only $41.2 million in guarantees were issued by ECA and MSA. The experience with government guarantees to date seems to indicate that the removal of the transfer risk is not sufficient to stimulate a large flow of foreign investment.[25]

24. See *Hearings before the House Committee on Banking and Currency on H. R. 5594*, 81st Congress, 1st Sess., August 17 to 27, 1949; see also *Hearings before the Senate Committee on Banking and Currency on S. 2197*, August 9 and 10, 1949.

25. The Mutual Security Acts of 1951 and 1952 also provide for guarantees against loss from expropriation or confiscation. See *First Report to Congress on the Mutual Security Program, December 31, 1951*, Mutual Security Agency, Washington, March, 1952, p. 41.

Chapter 20

DEVELOPING A CODE OF FOREIGN EXCHANGE
PRACTICES

BALANCE OF PAYMENTS disequilibria are inevitable in a dynamic world economy. Their automatic correction by severe deflation leading to large-scale unemployment and widespread hardship is no longer tolerated by modern governments. Balance of payments adjustments require deliberate action on the part of the monetary, fiscal and other governmental authorities, and frequently the objective of restoring equilibrium is in sharp conflict with other goals of public policy.

The ideal system of maintaining equilibrium, as envisaged by the Articles of Agreement of the Monetary Fund was that countries would maintain the parities of their currencies and seek financial help from the Fund while at the same time taking appropriate internal action to restore international balance. If the disequilibrium required an exchange adjustment, that is, if it were of a "fundamental" character, countries would change their parities with the Fund's approval. In special circumstances the Fund might give the country permission to place temporary restrictions on current transactions. Because of the conditions immediately after the war the Fund's Articles gave a more or less blanket permission to its members to retain their wartime restrictions for a period of five years after the Fund began operations. After this date—March 1952—any member which still employed restrictions would be required to consult with the Fund regarding their continued use.

The Scope of Agreements in the Foreign Exchange Field

One of the lessons of the postwar period is that it is impossible by means of international agreements to outlaw the use of restrictions for the protection of a country's balance of payments. This follows from the right of every sovereign nation to control its own monetary and fiscal systems without outside interference. If disequilibrium results in a loss of foreign exchange beyond what can prudently be covered by a country's own reserves plus what international lending institutions such as the Monetary Fund are prepared to provide, the country must introduce controls to halt the drain. However, no nation is likely to surrender to an international institution the right to change its exchange rate.[1] International institutions can so influence the policies of countries as to reduce or avoid the need for restrictions and they can affect the character of the restrictions employed; but they cannot legislate against foreign exchange and trade restrictions which may be required as a consequence of improper policies.[2]

It is suggested that the scope of international agreements and institutions in the foreign exchange field be confined to (1) exerting an influence on national policies which affect the balance of payments; (2) providing financial assistance to enable countries to avoid exchange restrictions during periods of temporary disequilibrium; (3) determining the conditions under which restrictions are permissible and the kinds of restrictions appropriate to those conditions; (4) outlawing certain types of practices which are deemed unfair or especially harmful to other countries, and which are not necessary for the protection of the foreign exchange reserves of a country in disequilibrium. This chapter will deal with the development of criteria for the exercise of functions (3) and (4) by the Monetary Fund and the GATT, dividing this broad problem into five components: (1) competitive exchange depreciation; (2) nondiscriminatory exchange restrictions; (3) discriminatory restrictions; (4) the treatment of foreign investment; (5) miscellaneous.

COMPETITIVE EXCHANGE DEPRECIATION

Competitive exchange depreciation was considered the major exchange problem of the 1930s. It is usually thought of as an act of depreciation not required to correct a fundamental balance of payments disequilibrium.[3] In practice this is a very difficult criterion to

1. The Monetary Fund Agreement provides that changes in par values must be initiated by the member country concerned.
2. In the words of Lord Keynes, you can legislate against sin but not against stupidity!
3. See W. R. Gardner and S. C. Tsiang, "Competitive Depreciation," *Staff Papers,*

apply. For example, is a country which permits its rate to depreciate in response to a temporary fluctuation in its balance of payments engaging in competitive exchange depreciation? If the reason for the depreciation were a speculative movement of capital or a seasonal decline in exports, the argument could be made that the country has an undervalued rate. On the other hand, the undervalued rate might be followed by an overvalued rate a few months later when the temporary movements are reversed, so that the average rate might be a correct one. The problem then becomes one of deciding on the merits of a fluctuating versus a fixed rate. The answer to this question may turn on another: Is it easier for a country to maintain balance of payments equilibrium with a fluctuating rate or with a fixed rate? Where countries have established a bona fide free market for their currency and where there is no evidence of deliberate undervaluation by the monetary authorities, there is little basis for opposition to a fluctuating exchange rate on the grounds that the fluctuations involve competitive depreciation.

Certainly a case against depreciation can be made for a country which has a balance of payments surplus and deliberately devalues in order to expand its exports and reduce its imports.[4] It has been argued, however, that a country with prices and income depressed by falling prices abroad might properly devalue even though it does not have a current account deficit.[5] Devaluation under these conditions might be justified provided the country in question took immediate steps to expand income and employment to a point where it no longer had a surplus not covered by foreign investments. The question has also been raised as to whether a country with a balance of payments deficit clearly due to internal inflationary policies should employ devaluation to improve its position.[6] While it may be argued that the proper course for such a country is disinflation rather than devaluation, the case against devaluation on grounds of unfair competition seems weak.

November 1952, pp. 399–408, for an excellent analysis of competitive depreciation under a system of unitary rates.

4. This assumes that the additional surplus will be financed by gold or foreign exchange and not by long-term capital exports.

5. A. Hansen, "Fundamental Disequilibrium," in *Foreign Economic Policy for the United States* (S. E. Harris, ed.), Harvard University Press, Cambridge, 1948, pp. 379–83.

6. See Gardner and Tsiang, *loc. cit.*, pp. 404–05. Devaluation under such conditions would probably be useless unless the country took steps to halt the inflation.

It is quite possible that a country with an over-all surplus may have a deficit with the dollar area and decide to devalue in order to improve its position with that area. The net effect might be a larger surplus with soft-currency countries. Under these circumstances, devaluation by the surplus country might force other soft-currency countries to devalue. It would seem quite improper to deny any country the right to redress a deficit with the dollar area by devaluation. Devaluation by the whole soft-currency group with varying percentages of devaluation for each member might make possible a better structure of rates than unilateral devaluation, but to wait for concerted action is likely to prolong indefinitely the restoration of equilibrium.

Devaluation with Broken Cross-Rates

Several countries, as earlier chapters have noted, employ broken cross-rates to balance their trade with both hard-currency and soft-currency countries, without the use of discriminatory trade restrictions. This practice usually results in a devaluation of the dollar rate relative to the rates on soft currencies. In certain cases, the Monetary Fund has regarded this as an unfair competitive practice. While it is true that broken cross-rates distort trade, trade is already distorted from its normal pattern by the existence of inconvertible currencies and trade discrimination. If Britain does not want the value of her currency to fall below the value corresponding to the official dollar-sterling cross-rate, she has the alternative of supporting the pound in the free foreign market just as she supports the market for sterling in New York. A country might of course be subject to censure if it deliberately devalued against the dollar when it had a substantial dollar surplus which it did not use to discharge deficits with third countries. In this case the real purpose is not to establish an equilibrium with the dollar area but rather to build up dollar reserves.

The question of the propriety of a broken cross-rate must be considered in the context of the country following the practice. A country which desires to avoid discriminatory trade controls has a choice either of becoming a hard-currency country or of permitting a free market with broken cross-rates. A country whose principal markets are in the dollar area may have little justification for entering into bilateral payments agreements which provide for the acceptance of inconvertible currencies. This might also apply to any country with a strong dollar position. In such cases the practice to be condemned is not the broken cross-rate device but the bilateral payments agreement which gives rise to the acceptance of inconvertible currencies.

The conclusion of this study as to the broken cross-rate issue is that if a country is justified in entering into bilateral payments agreements involving the use of inconvertible currencies, broken cross-rates are certainly no more objectionable than are discriminatory trade controls. There are, however, other practices which involve implicit broken cross-rates to which special consideration must be given.

Retention Quotas

The practice of permitting exporters to retain a portion of their hard-currency proceeds for imports not otherwise permitted has been regarded as an unfair competitive exchange practice. In the absence of exchange controls on current transactions, exporters are free to use their exchange proceeds to purchase goods and services in any currency area. The fact that import restrictions are generally applied means that a retention quota discriminates in favor of exporters and presumably gives them an advantage over exporters in countries which have exchange restrictions but do not have exporters' retention quotas. This argument assumes, however, that the degree of restriction in all exchange control countries is roughly the same. Exporters in countries with mild restrictions might be better off than exporters in countries maintaining severe restrictions but which have a retention quota. Retention quota schemes undoubtedly tend to undermine the official exchange rate parities, but they cannot be considered to involve competitive exchange depreciation as here defined.

On the other hand, retention quotas have little to recommend them as devices for freeing trade or for reestablishing world-wide multilateral trade. They are not a substitute for exchange rate devaluation or deflation, either or both of which may be necessary to bring internal costs and prices into line with world prices. In fact, to use retention quotas may delay these fundamental adjustments. Moreover as an implicit multiple exchange rate device which is constantly being changed without consultation with the Monetary Fund, retention quotas create uncertainties for competitors in other countries. A particularly vicious form of retention quota is that of permitting traders to retain part of the dollars earned from buying goods in other soft-currency markets and selling them in dollar markets. By undercutting the dollar prices of the producers (which the transit traders can afford to do because of their privilege of retaining a portion of the dollar proceeds) the country maintaining the retention quota can "capture" dollars which would otherwise have been earned by the country producing the commodity.

In May 1953 the Monetary Fund's Board reached the following decisions on retention quotas:

1. Retention quotas and similar practices may constitute, in certain cases, exchange restrictions or multiple currency practices.

2. Members should remove retention quotas and similar practices particularly where they lead to abnormal shifts in trade which cause unnecessary damage to other countries.

3. The Fund will enter into consultation with each of the members concerned, with a view to agreeing on a program for the removal of harmful retention quota practices.

4. "The Fund does not object to those practices which, by their nature, can be regarded as devices designed solely to simplify the administration of official exchange allocations." [7]

It is clear that the Fund regards retention quotas as a type of exchange practice, subject to the same procedures of consultation and review as other exchange practices. This appears to be a sound position. While each case should be considered on its own merits, it would seem desirable for the Fund to encourage countries employing retention quotas to abolish them in favor of more orthodox measures for expanding their exports.

Commercial Switch Transactions and Cheap Currency Deals

Commercial switch transactions may take place with or without the knowledge of the exchange control authorities of the countries where those responsible for the transactions reside. Where explicit permission for such transactions is given by the authorities in one country, but where one leg of the deal violates the exchange control regulations of another country, the practice is regarded as an unfair competitive device. Let us assume that a resident of Country A pur-

7. *Press Release No. 205,* International Monetary Fund, Washington, May 13, 1953.

chases commodities in Country B and that the commodities are then transshipped to the dollar area and sold for dollars at a discount from the purchase price. It may be argued that Country B has lost dollars which it would otherwise have gained by selling the commodities directly to the dollar area.[8] Such transactions represent a kind of arbitrage in commodities involving the dollar market and one or more soft-currency markets. Much the same result is achieved by cheap currency transactions in which inconvertible currencies are purchased with dollars in order to buy goods in soft-currency markets for importation into dollar markets. The dollars are then used to purchase dollar goods for sale in soft-currency markets.

Some exchange control countries seek to eliminate commercial switch transactions and those financed by cheap currency deals by means of bilateral agreements. Countries may also police their own transactions by requiring exporters to obtain certificates of final destination from the customs authorities of other nations. But are such practices undesirable from the standpoint of the world trading community as a whole? Should they be outlawed by multilateral agreement or by the decision of an international organization? One possible approach is that any action by one country which is in violation of the exchange control regulations of any other, provided those regulations are not inconsistent with an international undertaking, should be outlawed as an unfair practice. To implement this policy would require all countries to adopt such controls over their own residents that they could not become parties to violations of the regulations of other countries.[9] Aside from the fact that such a requirement would give rise to enormous legal difficulties,[10] the basic princi-

8. The other leg of the transaction involves the purchase of dollar commodities for sale at a premium against soft currencies in soft-currency markets.

9. While the Monetary Fund Agreement does not go so far as to require members to police the transactions of their own residents which are in violation of the exchange controls of other countries, Article VIII, Sec. 2(b) provides that "Exchange contracts which involve the currency of any member and which are contrary to the exchange control regulations of that member maintained or imposed consistently with this Agreement shall be unenforceable in the territories of any member. In addition, members may, by mutual accord, co-operate in measures for the purpose of making the exchange control regulations of either member more effective, provided that such measures and regulations are consistent with this Agreement."

10. Governments would be required to pass new legislation or issue new regulations whenever other countries changed their exchange control regulations. A law which stated that a transaction was illegal if it contravened the regulations of a foreign country would certainly be vigorously opposed in most countries.

ple that all countries should assist in the enforcement of regulations of other nations for which they have no responsibility is of doubtful validity. At the very least such a policy would require that the exchange control regulations of every country be subjected to international sanction in the most minute detail. But this would still leave other countries powerless to deal with the policies of nations which led to the employment of exchange restrictions.

Outlawing by International Agreement

This leads to the conclusion that the criteria for outlawing any foreign exchange or trade practice by international (multilateral) agreement must be related to the general aims of the international community as a whole and not to the special interests or problems of individual countries. One broad objective, of course, is to maximize the economic gains from world trade. But an exchange or trade practice leads to a misallocation of world resources if it encourages the expanded production of a commodity or service in an area where its cost is comparatively high at the expense of an area where that commodity can be produced at lower relative cost. There may be special reasons for permitting countries to employ temporary restrictions which lead to a misallocation of world resources, but such practices should never be required by international agreement. Arbitrage transactions between hard- and soft-currency areas cannot be restricted by international agreement on the grounds that they lead to a misallocation of world resources. In fact, on balance they may contribute to a more efficient use of resources.

The final conclusion is that commercial switch transactions and cheap currency dealings should not be outlawed by international action. Countries which maintain exchange restrictions should bear the full responsibility for preventing violations of those restrictions by their own residents.

Multiple Export Rates

A multiple export rate which involves an export subsidy for one or more commodities generally leads to a misallocation of resources in the sense that production is expanded beyond the point dictated by the relative productive efficiency of the country employing the subsidy rate. However, not all multiple export-rate systems involve an export subsidy rate. A subsidy rate must be regarded as one which is more favorable to the exporter than the equilibrium rate for that country. Differential export rates may also lead to a misdirection of resources if one or more of them are penalty rates in the sense that they are less favorable to the exporter than the equilibrium rate for that country. The penalty rate may of course be employed as an export tax, and the revenues from it used either for general governmental expenditures or to subsidize imports or other exports.

Subsidy export rates are clearly a matter of international concern both because of their effects upon the structure of world production and because of their effects on other countries producing competing products for export. This is true even where the country has an over-all balance of payments deficit since an export rate which provides a subsidy for a particular commodity or group of commodities affects the competitive position of the country in regard to these items. The effects of a penalty export rate upon the rest of the world are less direct and are usually felt only in the longer run. For example, a penalty rate on raw material exports may reduce the volume of investment in the industry and thus over a period of time reduce the world's supply.

NONDISCRIMINATORY IMPORT RESTRICTIONS

The reasons usually given for the imposition of nondiscriminatory restrictions on imports are (1) to prevent or limit a foreign exchange drain; (2) to promote economic development; (3) to protect certain industries. The second purpose often becomes merged with the first since the promotion of economic development frequently leads to a balance of payments deficit which must be checked by import restrictions.

Because sovereign nations will not ordinarily submit internal policy measures to international review, it is impossible to forbid the use of import restrictions as such, when countries have balance-of-payments deficits. International agreements are therefore limited to (1) the determination of the conditions under which restrictions for the protection of the balance of payments may be employed; (2) the outlawing or the review of a particular type of restriction.

Within this context, it seems clear that balance of payments restrictions are harmful to international trade when they are used to prevent temporary drains on the foreign exchange reserves of countries during short periods of deficit which may reasonably be expected to be followed by periods of surplus. An argument could be made for an exception to this rule in cases where the country in question has a low level of reserves. But this argument should not apply when the country is in a position to borrow adequate foreign exchange from an international institution. In other words, countries should not use restrictions on current account to increase the level of their reserves. They might, however, be permitted to adopt an exchange rate which would make possible an increase in their reserves.

A blanket permission to employ exchange and quantitative trade restrictions to promote economic development, regardless of a country's balance of payments position, is likely to destroy any system of orderly exchange practices. The means of furthering economic development should be confined to tariffs on specific commodity imports. This same rule should also apply to agricultural imports when their restriction is directed by farm price support programs. Restrictions required by the operation of international commodity agreements in which the interests of both consuming and producing nations are represented might be permitted, however.

Restrictions Should Not Be Designed to Provide Protection

What type of balance of payments restrictions should be permitted or outlawed, should be determined by a consideration of the effects of the restrictions on the structure of world trade and production. The type of restriction which would have the least effect upon the structure of world trade is probably a multiple rate system with a single export rate and a single import rate involving a uniform percentage increase in the prices of all imports. Most countries, however, prefer to maintain domestic currency prices of certain imports while restricting imports of other commodities and services.

If the purpose of the restrictions is to provide temporary protection of the balance of payments, the system of restrictions should not be employed specifically to protect certain industries which the national authorities are seeking to develop. This means that the same degree of restrictions—whether quantitative or cost—ought to be applied to broad categories of items which are not selected on the basis of protection. Unless the means adopted to protect the balance of payments are separated from those designed to protect particular industries, tariff negotiations become a mockery and the development of a code of fair trade and exchange practices is made impossible.

Multiple import rates have certain definite advantages over quantitative restrictions employed for balance of payments purposes. First, they are relatively easy to administer since they do not require quotas and licensing systems. When the number of import rates is confined to no more than two or three, each of which covers a large number of items classified according to essentiality or on some other basis, there is less danger that the system will involve elements of industrial or agricultural protection.

DISCRIMINATORY RESTRICTIONS

The need for over-all balance of payments restrictions is generally a product of the internal policies of individual countries, but the need for restrictions which discriminate in their application between countries and currency areas is frequently the result of the international economic environment in which a country finds itself. This is obviously true of small countries whose markets may be chiefly in nations with inconvertible currencies. It may also be true of a whole group of countries, large and small, whose trade among themselves would decline sharply unless they traded on a discriminatory basis.

The Scarce Currency Principle

The scarce currency principle was recognized by the Monetary Fund Agreement in Article VII, but the Agreement did not provide adequate procedures for dealing with the problem and its solution. The authors of the Agreement did not intend the scarce currency clause to apply during the transition period. Under Article VII each country would be permitted to continue to discriminate against the scarce currency country so long as it had a deficit or a tendency to be in deficit with the scarce currency country. But no mechanism by which the countries other than the scarce currency country could trade with one another on a multilateral basis was provided for in the Fund Agreement.

Discriminatory restrictions have been defended as less harmful to world trade than nondiscriminatory restrictions since countries can expand their imports beyond what they could afford to pay for with convertible currencies. But if all countries traded only on a bilateral basis, trade would not be maximized, nor would the maximum gains from it be realized. Hence it is argued that trade discrimination should be confined to countries whose currencies are relatively scarce, while trade among other countries should be liberalized and conducted on a nondiscriminatory basis.[11] While under certain conditions it may be possible to increase the volume of world trade by means of discrimination, the quality as well as the quantity of trade is of concern. So long as the marginal utility of the export proceeds earned by selling to one country differs from the marginal utility of export proceeds from exports to another, the gains from trade are not being maximized. It must be admitted, however, that adjustments to shifts in world demand and supply conditions may be sluggish and that a sudden reduction in the supply of an important international currency like the dollar is capable of causing a sharp reduction in world trade.

Discriminatory restrictions may therefore be justified as temporary measures when (1) the initial cause of the interregional disequilibrium is believed to be of short-term duration, or (2) if the initial cause or causes are permanent but time is needed for adjustments to the new conditions without substantially reducing the total trade and national incomes of the countries concerned. An example of the first case might be a sharp depression in the United States of sufficient duration so that a large number of countries would find it necessary to adopt or intensify their import restrictions. The situation in Western Europe at the end of World War II is an example of the case where many of the factors responsible for the disequilibrium are permanent, and time was needed for adjustment. In both these cases a continuation of nondiscriminatory trade would lead to a sharp fall in trade and production for the countries concerned.

Once the desirability of discrimination under certain circumstances is admitted, three problems arise in the development of a code of

11. It has also been argued that trade would be maximized by permitting each country to discriminate against every other country in accordance with a formula determined by the analysis of the trade matrix. See R. Frisch, "On the Need for Forecasting a Multilateral Balance of Payments," *American Economic Review*, September 1947, p. 540. For a discussion of this problem see R. F. Mikesell, "Discrimination and International Trade Policy," *Review of Economics and Statistics*, August 1950, pp. 227–34.

orderly trade and exchange arrangements: (1) It is necessary to determine whether or not there is a justification for discrimination and to define the area or scope of that discrimination. (2) The types of discriminatory measures to be permitted or outlawed must be determined. (3) A mechanism must be provided to promote adjustments which will eliminate the continued need for discrimination. Unless this third problem is dealt with the discriminatory arrangements are likely to become permanent since they are inherently self-perpetuating.

Conditions under Which Discrimination May Be Sanctioned

In what situations should discrimination be sanctioned? First, it should be evident that the disequilibrium is of such duration that it cannot be dealt with without the general use of restrictions by a group of countries which have been affected by the forces responsible for the disequilibrium. Temporary recessions like that in the United States in 1949 should be handled by drawing on exchange reserves including those of international institutions. Second, discrimination is justified only when a substantial reduction of trade among a group of countries is threatened by a shift in world demand-and-supply relationships, *not* brought about by the improper monetary and fiscal policies of members of the group. This requirement would sanction discrimination in the case of a severe U.S. depression, for example, but not in the case of disequilibrium resulting from a tendency to over-all disequilibrium brought about by inflation in a group of countries. Where disequilibrium results from inflationary policies in a group of countries, discrimination tends to perpetuate the inflationary forces and to divert exports from countries outside the group.

The Area of Discrimination

The area of discrimination to be sanctioned presents a difficult problem. Discrimination by members of a relatively small group in favor of one another affects adversely the trade of certain countries other than the scarce currency country itself. If all countries are permitted to discriminate against the scarce currency country, the discriminating group may include countries which have no need of restrictions on balance of payments grounds, but which may choose to join the discriminatory group on purely commercial grounds. There may also be countries not affected appreciably by the forces which brought about interregional disequilibrium but which had previously employed nondiscriminatory restrictions on imports. To put the problem concretely, should Canada and Switzerland be permitted to discriminate against the United States under present-day conditions, when these countries have no balance of payments problems? Should Colombia, which is a dollar currency country, be permitted to join a soft-currency group, when that country requires balance of payments restrictions but does not have a dollar problem as such? [12]

The larger the group of countries liberalizing trade among themselves but discriminating against the scarce currency country, the higher total trade is likely to be. On the other hand, it will become increasingly difficult for any country to earn the scarce currency in trade with third countries. Moreover, there will be a tendency to shift exports away from the scarce currency country and hence to perpetuate the disequilibrium. This problem will be discussed in greater detail in the following chapter. Meanwhile, here is a tentative rule: Membership in a discriminatory group should be confined to countries which would experience a substantial decrease in their exports and would therefore be required to adopt balance of payments restrictions if they remained outside the group. If a country has employed balance of payments restrictions before the scarce currency situation developed, membership in a discriminatory group is justified only in case that country's situation is materially worsened by the scarce currency condition, and its balance of payments position would be materially strengthened by joining the group.

Discrimination against Third Countries

Except under special circumstances discrimination should be permitted only in the case of a general scarcity of a leading currency, and the discrimination should be limited to the scarce currency country. Bilateral trade and payments agreements should not be sanctioned. However, this means that there must be a multilateral trading mechanism for all countries which are members of the discriminating

12. Certain countries may have an over-all foreign exchange problem but if their exports are sold in dollar markets their foreign exchange problem is not specifically a dollar problem.

group. Moreover, there should be no discrimination within the group. (A possible exception to these general rules is in the case of countries which are in the process of forming bona fide customs unions.)

There remains, however, the problem of trade with countries other than scarce currency countries, which have not joined the discriminating group. For example, if the U.S. dollar is declared a scarce currency and Canada does not discriminate in its trade, should the discriminating countries discriminate against Canada? If they do, Canada might be forced to employ import restrictions because of a loss of trade. On the other hand, if trade between Canada and the discriminating countries remains free, residents of the group might import U.S. goods through Canada. A suggested solution is that restrictions against imports from Canada be limited to those necessary to prevent the transshipment from Canada of goods originating in the United States. This rule would limit discrimination to the scarce currency country since discriminatory restrictions against any other would be outlawed. Countries with over-all balance of payments deficits would of course be permitted to maintain import restrictions against all other countries but any discriminatory aspects would be limited to imports from the scarce currency country.

Administration of Discriminatory Restrictions

The types of discriminatory restrictions to be sanctioned depend in part upon the kind of regional multilateral trading mechanism adopted by the discriminating group. If hard-currency earnings are pooled, as in the case of the sterling area, the degree of discrimination against dollar imports will tend to be more or less uniform. Under the EPU type of mechanism the degree of discrimination will differ with the dollar position of each member. Certain general principles may be suggested, however: (1) Discriminatory restrictions should be regarded as temporary devices and should not stimulate production and trade unlikely to be maintained under conditions of multilateral trade. (2) The import items discriminated against should not be selected to give special commercial preference to another discriminating country on a reciprocal basis.

Ideally, the discriminatory restrictions should take the form of a uniform percentage decrease in imports from the scarce currency country. Departures from this ideal pattern may be necessary for countries heavily dependent upon that nation for essential commodities. The degree of restriction may therefore differ between two or three broad classes of commodities and services from the scarce currency country. However, the element of individual industry protection or bilateral commercial preference should be eliminated so far as possible. The purpose and the effects of the discriminating restrictions should be to protect the balance of payments of the discriminating group and to maintain trade among members of the group.

Discrimination may take the form of cost restrictions or of quantitative restrictions. The author regards discriminatory cost restrictions achieved through broken cross-rates as preferable to quantitative restrictions. Nevertheless the same conditions for the use of discriminatory quantitative restrictions should apply to discriminatory cost restrictions achieved through import or export rates which break cross-rates. However, there are exceptions to the rule which the author would like to emphasize. Whenever a country maintains a bona fide free market in both hard and soft currencies the resulting broken cross-rates system should be permitted. The country whose inconvertible currency is involved should be solely responsible for the discriminatory arrangement. This follows from the principle established earlier in the discussion of competitive exchange depreciation.

THE TREATMENT OF FOREIGN INVESTMENTS

Governmental actions (political and economic) which tend to impede the flow of international capital are probably more harmful to world production and trade than are restrictions which affect trade between residents of different countries. The failure of capital to move from countries with abundant savings to regions which possess little capital but large populations and underdeveloped natural resources has meant a level of world output and consumption far lower than the world's physical potential. Exchange restrictions are of course not the only impediments to private foreign investment and the effect of their removal on investors cannot be determined in advance. Nevertheless, they form an important part of the "climate" for international investment, and measures to reduce their impact should be included in any plan for expanding private foreign investment.

In today's context, a program to abolish all exchange controls affecting foreign investment is highly unrealistic. Even nations which are able to abolish restrictions on current transactions are likely to impose—or will want to leave themselves free to impose—controls over capital movements. The best that can be hoped for through international agreements is that countries will permit transfers of interest and profits on foreign investments plus a reasonable amount of capital repatriation. Most nations are likely to insist that the right to transfer interest, profits and capital be limited to registered capital, and that incoming capital must be devoted to purposes which meet certain standards as a condition for registration. These standards usually relate to the contribution of the investment to the economy and to its effects on the balance of payments.

Agreements regarding transfers of capital and earnings by foreign investors are not likely to be made unconditionally. Countries will reserve the right to impose restrictions when they encounter balance-of-payments difficulties. The protection of the foreign investor, however, requires that limitations on transfers of earnings and the repatriation of capital should be temporary and that such transfers should have a definite place in the scale of priorities when foreign exchange is rationed. Many countries limit the earnings which may be transferred in any one year to a certain percentage of the capital investment. This is a serious impediment since many investments yield little or nothing for several years after they are made, and many are quite speculative in character. Considering the risks involved in foreign investments, they will not be attractive unless there is at least a possibility of exceptional profits.

Some nations consider that limitations on the repatriation of foreign capital are necessary to prevent speculative withdrawals during periods when the international position of the host country is weak. While there is a measure of justification for such restrictions, they undoubtedly impair the confidence of prospective foreign investors. Some countries have established a legal free market for capital transactions, through which transfers may always take place though the rate may be less favorable than the controlled official rate. If the free capital market is not available for merchandise transactions and no attempt is made to stabilize the market, these capital transfers can have little effect upon the economy. The existence of such a market, however, gives foreign investors assurance that they will always be able to withdraw their capital.

OTHER FOREIGN EXCHANGE PRACTICES

Countries employing exchange restrictions usually limit payments for services of various kinds such as foreign travel, shipping, banking, insurance, etc. Tourism is a luxury item which should probably bear a heavy share of any program of import restriction. However, services rendered in connection with imports and exports of merchandise should not be restricted as to source. Shipping restrictions are usually imposed to protect domestic industry rather than the balance of payments. Moreover, they are likely to result in a misdirection of investment in shipping and to have harmful effects upon this industry which is so very important to the defense of the free world.[13] A highly desirable step would be to request countries employing exchange controls to abolish all controls over services except those on tourism.

The Administration of Exchange and Trade Controls

The administration of trade and exchange controls frequently results in uncertainties and injustices which are harmful to trade and which are unnecessary and unjustifiable on balance of payments grounds. One such practice, common to certain Latin American countries, is the issuing of import licenses in excess of the amount of foreign exchange made available to pay for the imports when payment is due. This practice increases the cost of imports to the buyer and imposes special burdens and risks on the seller. Some countries interfere with normal trading practices by requiring importers to make advance payments or by forbidding banks to afford letter of credit facilities. Another harmful trade practice is to revoke licenses after goods have been ordered or to impose restrictions on commodities in transit.

The field of exchange and trade control administration is exceedingly complex and can only be touched upon in this study. At the fifth session of the contracting parties to the GATT at Geneva in 1950 a code of standard practices was adopted for recommendation to the governments of the contracting parties.[14]

13. The United States requires that 50 per cent of exports paid for with U.S. foreign aid must be carried in U.S. ships. In addition, foreign companies cannot engage in coastwise shipping or in transporting goods between the United States and its possessions. Such restrictions are harmful on balance of payments grounds because they interfere with the allocation of the shipping resources of the free world.

14. The text of this code is reproduced as Appendix 3.

A SUGGESTED CODE OF FAIR EXCHANGE PRACTICES

It is not the purpose of the author to set forth a detailed code of fair trade and exchange practices. Such a code must be developed out of the experience of institutions like the Monetary Fund and the GATT. However, the following general conclusions of this chapter may be suggested as tentative guide lines for the development of a code.

1. While nations should not be permitted to engage in competitive exchange depreciation, they should be permitted to adopt a bona fide free foreign exchange market.

2. Nations should not be permitted to employ exchange restrictions affecting current transactions [15] except to halt a substantial drain of foreign exchange reserves which is not the result of temporary and reversible factors. (The term, "exchange restrictions," includes both cost and quantitative restrictions. If the rules regarding exchange restrictions are to be effective, there must be parallel regulations covering quantitative trade restrictions including import and export licensing, quotas and embargoes.) There should be, however, certain exceptions to this general principle.

a. A country which maintains controls on capital movements should be permitted to employ a free market rate for capital transactions.

b. A raw materials exporting country might be permitted to employ multiple exchange rates for a temporary period provided the system is designed for purposes of economic stabilization and is not directed specifically to protect local industry or to subsidize exports.

c. Import and export controls for reasons of security or to implement international commodity control arrangements should be exempted from the general rules respecting restrictions on current transactions.

3. Countries which are eligible to employ exchange restrictions affecting current transactions stated in (2) above should be encouraged to substitute cost restrictions, including multiple exchange rates, for quantitative restrictions. There should be no export (buying) rate which has the effect of subsidizing any export. (That is,

15. The definition of current transactions is the same as that given in Article XIX of the Monetary Fund Agreement. The definition includes amortization and depreciation payments as well as goods and services.

no export rate should be more favorable to exporters than the long-run equilibrium rate.) Retention quotas and similar devices which result in implicit multiple rates should be subject to review by the Monetary Fund and should be discouraged where their effects on trade are considered harmful.

4. Exchange restrictions employed for the purpose of providing temporary protection of the balance of payments should be reviewed to determine whether they have been designed to encourage industries which could not be expected to survive in the absence of controls and at an equilibrium exchange rate.

5. Permitted trade and exchange restrictions should normally be nondiscriminatory in their application to trade with different countries and currency areas. However, realism not only requires recognition of the scarce currency problem, but orderly procedures should be devised for dealing with it. The following approach to this problem is suggested:

a. When there occurs a shift in the demand for, and supply of, a leading international currency which threatens to reduce substantially the trade among a group of countries by requiring them to introduce restrictions on current transactions, and when the scarcity of the key currency is not due to temporary causes or where the deficits cannot be handled by drawing on available reserves, those countries forced by the existence of the interregional disequilibrium to adopt exchange restrictions on current transactions or to intensify existing restrictions may be permitted to discriminate against the country whose currency is scarce. There should be no discriminatory restrictions against any country other than the scarce currency country except that the nations eligible to discriminate should be permitted to limit imports of goods originating in the scarce currency country from third countries. Discriminatory restrictions should be regarded as temporary arrangements for assuring the maintenance of trade among the members of the discriminating group. Discrimination should not be employed specifically to encourage trade within the discriminating group which could not be maintained in the absence of discrimination under equilibrium conditions. Finally, countries should not be permitted to discriminate if the cause of the disequilibrium with the scarce currency country is to be found in inflationary policies leading to a general tendency toward over-all deficits among the members of a group of countries seeking the right to discriminate.

b. Any country should be permitted to establish a bona fide free market in both hard and soft currencies even though the operation of the free market results in broken cross-rates, provided no quantitative discriminatory restrictions are employed.

c. The same rules should apply to controlled broken cross-rates as apply to quantitative discriminatory arrangements. Cross-rates on currencies other than the scarce currency must be maintained consonant with one another except under conditions in 5b.

6. A scarce currency condition should not have an indefinite duration, but should be regarded as a period which may be required for adjustments in production and trade to a new equilibrium position. Consequently, the Monetary Fund and the GATT should establish a definite schedule for the elimination of discriminatory restrictions within a reasonable period of time after the scarce currency declaration. (Alternative procedures for dealing with the present dollar scarcity condition will be discussed in Chapter 22.)

7. The Monetary Fund should develop regulations regarding transfers of earnings and capital on foreign investments, which would apply when countries introduce exchange restrictions.

8. Countries employing exchange restrictions should not restrict payments for transportation and other services related to the importation of commodities for which exchange or trade licenses have been granted. Standard administrative practices for trade and exchange controls along the lines of the GATT code of December 1950 [16] should be adopted.

The Conditions for the Operation of a Code

The Monetary Fund and the GATT have made little progress in removing restrictive exchange and trade practices. They have been hampered by the prolonged world disequilibrium and the concentration of deficits against the United States. In addition, they are not equipped to deal with a scarce currency situation even though the principle is recognized in their charters. Consequently the problem of limited multilateralism has been handled by other organizations.

16. See Appendix 3.

Moreover, the Monetary Fund and the GATT have not been in a position to take the initiative for moving out of the present condition of world disequilibrium and discrimination against the dollar.

Let us begin by admitting the existence of a scarce currency condition and consequently the justification for discrimination against the United States in accordance with our suggested code. We are then faced with a twofold problem: (1) How can we move toward the reestablishment of a free world multilateral payments system within the existing institutional framework of the world's payments arrangements? (2) What should be the roles of the Monetary Fund and the GATT (or a successor organization) in the creation of the fundamental conditions within which they can administer a code of fair trade and exchange practices?

Chapter 21

THE STERLING AREA, THE EPU AND CURRENCY CONVERTIBILITY

WHAT KIND OF CONVERTIBILITY?

THE GENERAL CONCEPT of currency convertibility may be defined as the availability of a currency or means of international payment for making payments in international transactions with any country or currency area. Convertibility may be restricted to balances held by nonresidents or it may apply to both resident and nonresident holdings. It may be limited to current international transactions (as defined in Article XIX of the Monetary Fund Agreement) or it may apply to both current and capital transactions. There are, however, a number of types of convertibility or arrangements which meet the essential conditions of convertibility. Eight principal types of convertibility are: [1]

1. General convertibility into gold. Under the gold coin or gold bullion standard, domestic currencies were freely interchangeable with gold at a fixed ratio and there were no restrictions on exports and imports of gold or upon transactions in foreign currencies. This type of convertibility virtually disappeared in the 1930s and is not likely to be revived.

2. General convertibility into foreign currencies with limited convertibility into gold. This is the type which characterizes the monetary system of the United States. There is general convertibility into foreign currencies through the free exchange markets but convertibility into gold for monetary purposes is limited to the sale of gold against balances of U.S. currency held by foreign central banks and treasuries.

3. General convertibility through free exchange markets without official convertibility into gold for any purpose. The existence of completely free foreign exchange markets gives every resident of a coun-

---

1. For a further discussion of this subject, see A. O. Hirschman, "Types of Convertibility," *Review of Economics and Statistics,* February 1951, pp. 60–62.

try the right to exchange his own currency for the currency of any other country for any pupose he chooses. Free exchange markets also imply complete freedom of transfer of the domestic currency among nonresidents in foreign markets. Exchange rates in the market may be stabilized by the intervention of the monetary authorities, or the rates may be permitted to fluctuate freely. Free gold markets may exist or they may be outlawed, as in the case of the United States. Under this system there is no automatic convertibility into gold by the monetary authorities for any purpose.

4. *Convertibility for residents limited to the financing of current transactions, and complete freedom of transfers for domestic balances held by nonresidents.* Countries employing controls on capital transactions may limit the acquisition of foreign currencies by their own residents to the financing of current transactions. The control over the withdrawal of foreign capital investments (as opposed to international currency balances held by foreigners) is achieved by treating foreign-owned balances derived from the liquidation of capital assets as resident balances and hence not available for capital transactions. This type would meet the tests of convertibility outlined in Article VIII of the Monetary Fund Agreement.[2]

5. *Convertibility of foreign-held balances.* A country may limit convertibility of its currency to balances owned by nonresidents. In such cases it may restrict the convertibility of balances held by its own citizens but freely convert balances held by foreigners into gold or gold-convertible currencies, or permit nonresidents to sell such balances in free markets abroad.

6. *Convertibility of balances owned by foreign central banks and treasuries.* Under this type only balances owned by foreign central banks and treasuries are convertible into gold or gold-convertible currencies. In practice this type of convertibility differs little from that described in (5). If the foreign country maintains exchange controls, the private individual or firm receiving payments would in any case be required to surrender the foreign exchange proceeds to the central bank. On the other hand, if the country of the foreign resident receiving payment did not have exchange controls he could sell the foreign currency in the exchange market and buy whatever currency he de-

2. Transfers of amortization and depreciation on foreign-owned capital must be permitted in accordance with Articles VIII and XIX of the Fund Agreement.

sired. The central bank of the foreign country could support the market for the foreign currency and demand gold from the foreign central bank for its surplus holdings of that currency.

7. *Convertibility of balances owned by foreign central banks and treasuries for payments arising out of current transactions with any currency area.* This type is a modification of (6) since it limits the availability of means of payment to financing current transactions. This was the type of convertibility established by the United Kingdom in 1947 in accordance with provisions of the Anglo-American Loan Agreement of 1946.

8. *Convertibility of balances owned by foreign central banks through a multilateral clearing union.* Under this type foreign-owned balances would be exchanged for credits in a clearing union which would be generally available for making payments to any country. Lord Keynes's proposal for an international clearing union envisaged this type of universal convertibility.[3] The EPU provides for this type of convertibility among its own members, but only partial convertibility into gold. Hence the EPU system does not satisfy the conditions for convertibility as here defined. Convertibility through a multilateral clearing union may also be limited to the use of credits for making payments arising out of current transactions with any currency area.

Finally, mention should be made of the possibility of a combination of currency convertibility for residents and inconvertibility for nonresidents. This type of arrangement exists in Switzerland, which maintains a free market for dollars and other free currencies and places no restrictions on their use, but restricts the convertibility of Swiss francs acquired by residents of countries with which Switzerland has bilateral payments agreements, in payment for exports of goods and services to Switzerland. This system gives rise to two types of Swiss francs: a freely convertible franc and a number of bilateral account francs whose convertibility is strictly limited.

All Can Provide Systems of Multilateral Settlements

Under the first four types of convertibility there are no restrictions on current transactions imposed by the monetary authorities and no

3. J. M. Keynes, "Proposals for an International Clearing Union," in *Proceedings and Documents of the United Nations Monetary and Financial Conference,* Vol. II. pp. 1548–73.

exchange discrimination. If this type of convertibility is to be meaningful, however, there can be no general imposition of import licensing and quota restrictions. Under types (5), (6), (7) and (8) governments may impose restrictions on the current transactions of their own residents but other countries are free to use the proceeds of their exports for purchases in any currency area. These last four systems of convertibility may be accompanied by discriminatory import restrictions on residents, but no discrimination arises through restrictions on the use of balances held by nonresidents. Under all eight systems the traditional means of financing foreign trade such as the letter of credit and the commercial draft can be used. Since many countries will undoubtedly be faced with the necessity of imposing restrictions on their own residents from time to time and since the greatest need of world commerce is a system of world-wide multilateral settlements, it seems desirable to establish the type of convertibility which will meet the needs of the majority of the free nations and which can be adopted in the shortest time. To be fully effective, however, a system of multilateral payments must be accompanied by the elimination of all discriminatory trade restrictions.

It is quite possible that Britain would find it easier to restore convertibility of the pound under type (7) or perhaps a combination of types (6) and (7). For example, the sterling area countries and perhaps the members of the transferable account system might agree to limit convertibility of their sterling, or the sale of their sterling in dollar markets, to the amounts required to settle their current deficits with nonsterling countries. It might also be possible to retain the structure of the EPU, but to make EPU credits representing the net position of an EPU member with all other members freely convertible into dollars when dollars were needed to settle a current deficit with the dollar area. We shall examine these possibilities in the course of discussion of the sterling area and the EPU.

Convertibility through Commodities

It has been suggested that if Britain were to establish free markets in a number of dollar commodities and permit unlimited purchases by British traders for resale in other markets, a kind of sterling convertibility could be created and British merchants could earn commissions on the sale of dollar goods. While such a scheme would be an important step toward convertibility and would have many of the same consequences for the British balance of payments and the demand for pounds as the types of convertibility listed above, it does not seem appropriate to include such an arrangement in our categories of convertibility.

THE CONDITIONS OF STERLING CONVERTIBILITY

Since sterling convertibility is a primary condition for the restoration of a system of multilateral settlements for the countries of the free world, we shall begin with a discussion of the conditions under which Britain might make her currency convertible, at least for nonresident holders, *i.e.*, types (5), (6), (7) and (8). Many of these same conditions, however, apply equally to other countries.

Let us assume Britain suddenly announced that from now on all sterling paid by British residents to residents of other countries would be freely available for use in any currency area including the dollar area. What would happen to the structure of Britain's balance of payments if in addition Britain restricted her total imports of goods and services to her total exports of goods and services less net capital exports? If other countries immediately shifted a substantial portion of their imports from Britain to the dollar area, Britain would find it necessary to reduce her total imports by an equivalent amount. The British economy might suffer severely until Britain was able to restore her exports in competition with those of the dollar area. The resulting unemployment of the factors of production and the sharp fall in British prices would eventually bring about a shift in the structure of British production and a sufficient lowering of British export prices to restore her export trade. But this process might be prolonged by a lack of capital to develop new industries, including the inability to finance the purchase of raw materials and capital equipment from other countries. Unless Britain possessed a large volume of foreign exchange reserves the price she would have to pay for this "dash for convertibility," in terms of widespread unemployment and reduced living standards might be greater than the British public would tolerate. Hence the shift in the structure of production and trade would have to take place gradually. But this shift is not likely to take place at all without the proper incentives.

Structural Changes in Britain's Trade

The structural changes in Britain's balance of payments since the war have been enormous. In 1951 the volume of British imports was slightly less than in 1937–1938, while the volume of exports was over 70 per cent higher than in 1937–1938. But in spite of this rise in exports Britain in 1951 had a deficit on current account of £389 million. The principal reasons for this shift in Britain's over-all balance of payments position are well known: the large reduction in net invisible income and the deterioration of Britain's terms of trade. Britain's current account deficit was turned to a £270 million surplus in 1952 partly through tighter import restrictions and partly as a result of some improvement in her terms of trade. Britain also had a current account surplus of £221 million in 1950 and a current account surplus of £21 million in 1949, but these also depended upon the maintenance of trade and exchange restrictions, particularly upon imports from the dollar area.

The Regional Structure of Exports and Imports

The regional structure of British exports has not changed substantially since the prewar period but such changes as occurred were significant. In 1937 the United States and Canada took about 12 per cent of British exports and about the same percentage in 1952. British exports to the sterling area, on the other hand, increased from 39 per cent of total exports in 1937 to 46 per cent in 1952. The percentage of British exports to Latin America declined slightly from the prewar figures. The percentage of Britain's total imports from the United States and Canada fell from 20 per cent in 1937 to 18 per cent in 1952 while the percentage of imports from the sterling area rose from 31 per cent in 1937 to 41 per cent in 1952. Britain's current account deficit with the dollar area was somewhat smaller in real terms in 1951 and 1952 than in the prewar period, but Britain's gold and dollar income from other sources (not counting U.S. aid) was vastly reduced. Hence Britain's regional trade and payments structure must undergo a shift in one or both of two directions if she is to achieve a balance on dollar account as well as an over-all account under conditions of sterling convertibility.

First, Britain could shift more of her imports from the dollar area to nondollar sources; second, she could export more to the dollar area and to other countries where she can earn dollars. But where can Britain earn dollars outside the dollar area? The answer is that she can earn dollars from any country which is now spending them by out-competing dollar products. But won't those countries continue to buy goods from Britain with sterling rather than with dollars? The answer is that if sterling is made sufficiently scarce in the world by Britain's import and capital export policies (including her policies with respect to sterling balances), other countries will have to buy their sterling with dollars from Britain just as Americans must buy their American account sterling with dollars from British banks when American account sterling is scarce in the New York market.

Britain's ability to reduce her dependence upon dollar imports and to earn dollars in nondollar markets will require certain shifts in the structure of her own commodity production and trade and also in the structure of production in the countries of the sterling area and other nondollar countries with which Britain trades. In spite of the large increase in British exports between 1937 and 1950, Britain's share of world exports of manufactures declined (excluding the exports of Germany and Japan), particularly in the categories of industrial equipment, heavy transportation equipment, and iron and steel.[4] While Britain's exports of heavy manufactures to the overseas sterling area increased sharply in the postwar period her share of the markets for these commodities in the Western Hemisphere and in other areas was greatly reduced. Britain must recapture a larger share of the markets for her manufactures where she can earn dollars both by shifting the direction of her exports and by increasing her output of commodities for which the rest of the world has become so heavily dependent upon the United States. These shifts are closely related to Britain's internal and external financial policies.

The Rest of the Sterling Area

Britain's prospects for convertibility are bound up with her relations to the rest of the sterling area. Before the war the overseas sterling area contributed greatly to the strength of Britain's interna-

---

4. For an analysis of British exports see *The Sterling Area, an American Analysis* (Economic Cooperation Administration, Special Mission to the United Kingdom), ECA, Washington, 1951, Chapters 12–24.

tional position, largely because Britain's current account surplus with the rest of the sterling area (RSA) was settled by gold transfers, which exceeded the net deficits of the RSA with the rest of the world.[5] In the postwar period the current account deficits of the RSA have been financed to a large extent by the drawing down of accumulated sterling balances and by capital exports from the United Kingdom.[6]

Since Britain's dependent overseas territories have had a substantial surplus with the dollar area and have in addition tended to increase their holdings of sterling, the responsibility for the drain on British resources by the RSA lies with the independent sterling area countries. The surpluses of the United Kingdom with the RSA which have not been compensated by gold and dollar transfers to the British Treasury serve to divert British exports from the dollar area and other places where Britain could earn dollars. In addition, the large dollar deficits of the independent sterling area, which usually exceed the gold sales of the independent sterling countries to the United Kingdom, cause a drain of British gold and dollar reserves.[7]

Sterling Balances and U.K. Capital Exports

The principal cause of the heavy postwar drain of the RSA on British resources has been the capital exports from the United Kingdom, including both capital investments by British residents in the RSA and the drawing down of sterling balances by the RSA. This drain, which has taken the form of both unrequited British exports and the loss of gold and dollars, has been estimated at £876 million from the beginning of 1946 to June 1952, or an average rate of £135 million annually.[8] The amount of this drain has fluctuated sharply

5. In 1938 gold sales of the RSA to the United Kingdom totaled $550 million and their current account deficit with all countries including the United Kingdom was $450 million. *Economic Bulletin for Europe,* 2d Quarter 1949, p. 12.

6. For an analysis of the drain of the overseas sterling area on the United Kingdom see Table 13, page 254.

7. The deficit of the independent sterling area countries with the dollar area during the period 1948–1951 was $1,151 million. In addition, however, these countries were responsible for a considerable share of Britain's gold and dollar payments to nondollar countries which totaled (net) about a billion dollars during this period. Partially offsetting this gold and dollar drain were gold sales to the United Kingdom by the RSA of $955 million, most of which was accounted for by the independent sterling area. *United Kingdom Balance of Payments, 1948 to 1951,* Cmd. 8505, H.M.S.O., London, 1952.

8. E. H. Stern, "The Pattern of Sterling Area Payments," *The Banker* (London), November 1952, pp. 271–77.

from year to year with the net outflow of capital. It is quite likely that Britain will have to take steps to reduce it as a condition for re-establishing convertibility.

But whatever the rate of capital exports Britain can stand, her economy and her balance of payments cannot be subjected to heavy and sudden drains such as have occurred in the past. For example, during the eighteen months ending December 31, 1952, Britain's sterling liabilities to all countries declined by £746 million. This sharp decrease was largely due to a reduction of £587 million in the sterling holdings of the independent sterling area countries, most of which had large current deficits during this period. The sterling holdings of the dependent overseas territories rose by £157 million during this period while the sterling holdings of nonsterling area countries fell by £316 million. (See Table 10.)

A primary condition for sterling convertibility is the immobilizing of the large sterling balances, which totaled £3,422 million as of December 31, 1952. Most of the one billion pounds in balances held by the dependent overseas territories represents currency reserves and their utilization can probably be controlled by Britain. The holdings of the nonsterling countries have been reduced almost to the level of working balances. Even so, Britain ought to fund part of these balances in order to avoid their sudden conversion into dollars. The most vulnerable balances are the £1.5 billion held by the independent sterling area countries, principally Australia, South Africa, India, Pakistan, Ceylon and Ireland. A long-term funding of these balances would present political difficulties for the British. Britain has been anxious to maintain the sterling area ties as a means of preserving close political relations with the Commonwealth and also as a protected market for British exports. But if the independent sterling countries are unwilling to reach a satisfactory settlement with Britain on the issue of their balances, it would be better for Britain, on economic grounds at least, to let the sterling area fall apart.[9]

9. "But the Commonwealth Ministers should recognize now that the sterling area system must no longer be used to subsidize employment in the mills of Lancashire and the mushroom factories of Australia, while the world cries out for capital equipment, raw materials, and food. If they do not recognize this, it might actually be better for Britain if the sterling area system were to fall apart." "A Programme for the Commonwealth," *The Banker,* September 2, 1952.

Contribution of RSA to Sterling Convertibility

There are three ways in which the independent sterling area countries could ease Britain's balance of payments problem. First, they could expand their production of foodstuffs and industrial raw materials. This would enable Britain to reduce her imports of dollar grains and meat, and to the extent that additional industrial raw materials could be sold outside the area for dollars, the sterling area countries could reduce their deficits with the dollar area. The second way that the sterling area dominions could help restore sterling convertibility is to get into over-all balance of payments equilibrium, preferably by reducing inflationary pressures within their borders. Third, the Commonwealth countries should obtain more of their development capital in the form of loans from the International Bank and from private dollar investors, instead of relying so heavily upon capital imports from Britain and the drawing down of sterling balances.[10]

Internal stabilization in both Britain and the RSA might reduce voluntary capital outflows from Britain to a point where they could be tolerated by the British economy. In fact, if Britain's current surplus with the RSA were approximately equal to gold sales and if the RSA eliminated its over-all deficits with the nonsterling countries, transfers of financial capital from Britain to the RSA would have no real impact upon Britain. However, it would probably be in Britain's own interest to permit a modest amount of real capital investment in the RSA, particularly in foodstuffs and industrial raw materials.

Internal Stability in Britain

Conceivably, Britain could restore convertibility of sterling held by foreign residents or central banks, without removing her own restrictions on current transactions. However, unless Britain takes steps to reduce the demand for imports on the part of her own citizens to a point where they can be satisfied by her available current foreign exchange, the process of establishing a structure of production and trade compatible with sterling convertibility will be inhibited. When

10. All these recommendations were contained in the reported conclusions of the Commonwealth Conference of Ministers held in London in December 1952. See *The New York Times,* December 12, 1952, p. 14.

imports are restricted the unsatisfied demand seeks an outlet in the consumption of domestic commodities and services. This diverts current output away from exports and stimulates investment in industries designed to satisfy domestic demand. Moreover, if exports to soft-currency countries were to decline with the restoration of currency convertibility, the slack in demand might be taken up by domestic consumption, giving exporters little incentive to seek markets abroad. This point is illustrated by the experience of British car manufacturers in 1952. The import restrictions of the RSA countries reduced British car exports and while there was a small increase in exports to dollar markets, the domestic market readily mopped up a portion of the unsold cars.[11]

During 1952 Britain took several steps to reduce monetary demand including the raising of the Bank of England's discount rate, limiting installment credit and reducing food subsidies. But Britain still had a substantial budgetary deficit in 1952, wages and the cost of living continued to rise, and there was considerable evidence of "excess liquidity" in the economy. Additional deflationary measures perhaps leading to some unemployment in the consumers' goods industries are probably necessary before Britain will be in a position to undertake convertibility with a chance of success. Success in freeing the pound and in keeping it free depends upon sufficient mobility of the factors of production to permit changes in the pattern of production and trade to take place quickly. Large and prolonged general unemployment, however, is unnecessary and modern governments are well equipped with monetary and fiscal devices to keep unemployment and deflation from getting out of hand.

Exchange Rates and Convertibility

The price and wage rigidities and the lack of mobility of the factors of production, which characterize modern economies, have led some economists to the view that the maintenance of currency convertibility requires a fluctuating exchange rate. While it is true that at any given moment of time there is always some rate at which the demand for, and supply of, foreign exchange will be balanced, these same rigidities may require large adjustments in the exchange rate

11. "The Fall in Car Exports," *The Economist,* November 29, 1952, p. 642.

to compensate for small changes in the level of exports or imports. A large depreciation not required by longer-run demand and supply conditions may be harmful to a country by creating domestic instability and affecting adversely its terms of trade. However, a country with a fluctuating rate could prevent sharp fluctuations in its rate due to temporary causes by stabilization operations.

It would certainly be wrong to say that most countries could not maintain convertibility without a freely fluctuating exchange rate. Not all shifts in the balance of payments should be corrected by rate changes. In some cases adjustment should take place through monetary and fiscal measures. In other cases, an increase in productivity or a change in the direction of investment may be required. Countries should be prepared, however, to change their rates whenever their international competitive position requires such adjustment. There are certain situations in which a fluctuating rate appears to be desirable, at least on a temporary basis:

1. A country may be uncertain as to the proper rate for its currency and rather than establish provisional parity, it may prefer to test its value in the market. This was done by Mexico in 1948–1949.

2. A country may want to discourage one-way speculation. Canada permitted her rate to rise well above the prewar parity with the dollar in 1952 in order to discourage capital imports of a temporary or speculative character. The adoption of a fluctuating rate by a weak currency may also tend to reduce bear speculation. When a country with a weak currency has a fixed parity, e.g., Britain in 1949, speculators know that the currency can only move in a downward direction. But if the currency is permitted to fall to what is believed to be a proper level, bear movements against the currency are discouraged. Thus when Britain devalued the pound to $2.80 in September 1949, there was a substantial inflow of short-term capital.

3. A country may want to adopt a fluctuating rate because changes in a fixed parity which may be necessary from time to time are politically difficult.

4. A country may adopt a fluctuating rate because another country with which it has close economic and financial ties has one. This was the situation in the 1930s when the members of the sterling bloc stabilized their currencies in terms of the fluctuating pound.

It is certainly true that if sterling and other key currencies moved freely in terms of the dollar, trade would be more difficult than it would under conditions of rate stability. However, during the period of transition to convertibility, there may be an advantage in letting the pound fluctuate beyond the present range of $2.78 to $2.82. (The September 1953 issue of the British journal, *The Banker,* revealed that a floating rate for sterling was included in the British Commonwealth plan for sterling convertibility of December 1952.) Other European currencies also might be permitted to fluctuate either independently or with the pound sterling.

Productivity and Convertibility

It has been argued that an increase in British productivity is essential if Britain is to be able to compete successfully in world markets without the aid of discriminatory arrangements. Moreover, as we have seen in Chapter 7, there are some who hold that the restoration of world-wide equilibrium and convertibility may be impossible because other countries cannot maintain the same rate of increase in productivity as exists in the United States.

There are real opportunities for increasing productivity in Britain and Western Europe,[12] and they provide an important means of reducing costs of production. In fact the restoration of convertibility and world-wide competition will be a factor in encouraging the adoption of new techniques provided the capital is available for utilizing them. However, different rates of growth in productivity are not barriers to convertibility provided countries are willing to adjust their exchange rates from time to time and provided there is a reasonable amount of flexibility in their internal economies.

The Problem of British Reserves

For two reasons, adequate gold and dollar reserves constitute a necessary (but not a sufficient) condition for the successful restoration of sterling convertibility. First, Britain probably should anticipate a temporary run on sterling immediately after convertibility is established. A temporary loss of British export markets to exporters in the dollar markets, if accompanied by deflationary pressures in Brit-

12. See, for example, *The Sterling Area, an American Analysis* (Economic Cooperation Administration, Special Mission to the United Kingdom), ECA, Washington, 1951, p. 161.

ain, will help bring about the necessary shifts in British production and force British exporters to compete more vigorously against dollar products. There also will be some tendency for holders of sterling to reduce their balances to the lowest possible level until they are convinced that sterling can make the grade. The second reason Britain must have substantial reserves is that even if sterling meets fair weather on its venture into convertibility, subsequent fluctuations in world demand might quickly reduce British reserves to the danger point and bring on a wave of speculative selling of sterling.

Estimates of a "safe" level of British reserves for restoring convertibility range from $5 to $10 billion.[13] The required level of reserves depends somewhat upon whether Britain adopts a floating rate for the pound or continues to stabilize the pound at a fixed level. With a floating rate temporary speculative pressures on the pound could probably be absorbed with little loss of reserves by modest decreases in its market value. This would not be true, however, if the market were convinced that Britain's balance of payments was in fundamental or long-run disequilibrium. The required level of British reserves will also depend upon the extent to which other currencies become convertible, the nature of Britain's trade restrictions and the status of the sterling balances.

Convertibility of Other Currencies

A final question to be considered in discussing the conditions for sterling convertibility is whether or not sterling could "go it alone," without the convertibility of the currencies of the major Western European countries. If the other OEEC countries were to trade on a bilateral basis or continue to finance their trade through the EPU, they would tend to divert imports from Britain and the RSA to one another and to other nondollar countries. If on the other hand the major continental countries were to embrace convertibility with Britain they would all be on an equal footing, although these countries might lose trade to the dollar area until there was a shift in the pattern of their export trade. But no categorical answer to this question can

13. Britain's prewar reserves of $4 billion would be equivalent to $10 billion at present prices. In 1938 the ratio of Britain's reserves to sterling area imports was about 50 per cent. If this same ratio is applied to sterling area imports for the period 1949–1951, a reserve requirement of $9 billion is indicated.

be given in advance. Much depends upon the future of the EPU and Britain's relations to that institution. Clearly, however, there are real advantages in a program of convertibility for the pound which would be closely integrated with a program of multilateral settlements for all the countries of the free world. This subject will be explored after we have considered certain alternative possibilities for the EPU.

How Convertible Is Sterling?

A degree of convertibility for sterling already exists. All American account sterling is fully convertible. Sterling is convertible for the settlement of current transactions within the group of countries constituting the sterling area, the EPU countries and the transferable account countries. Administrative transferability facilities provide an even wider area of convertibility within the soft-currency group.

The principal limitation is convertibility of sterling (other than American account sterling) into dollars. In one sense all No. 1 account sterling held by sterling area countries is automatically convertible into dollars or into American account sterling, since there are no specific limitations imposed on sterling area members on the use of unblocked sterling for purchases in the dollar area. But if formal sterling convertibility were combined with agreements between Britain and the RSA to continue trade discrimination against the dollar area in order to limit the use of sterling balances for dollar area purchases, it would be meaningless. Convertibility must therefore be accompanied by the elimination of discrimination by countries which acquire sterling balances. Conceivably Britain herself could apply discriminatory restrictions against the dollar area and still establish convertibility for nonresidents, but such restrictions would limit the area of multilateral trade and would tend to encourage other countries to retain their discriminatory practices in favor of Britain and RSA.

The Desirability of a Gradual Approach

Assuming that the several conditions for successful convertibility were in process of being established, what type of convertibility should Britain undertake and how might she go about it? As a matter of caution it would appear desirable to begin with the type of convertibility which would involve the least threat to British reserves and to proceed gradually with its adoption. With respect to the sterling area countries Britain might agree that discrimination against dollar area imports be gradually removed so that by the end of a given period all discriminatory restrictions against dollar goods would have disappeared. As to the bilateral and transferable account countries Britain might begin by offering to grant any country the right to convert currently acquired sterling into American account sterling provided that country would not discriminate in its trade against any member of the sterling area. This approach would help avoid a loss of British exports to soft-currency countries. After gradually expanding the number of countries which had the privilege of converting their current sterling receipts into American account sterling, Britain might require that certain sterling area exports be paid for only in American account sterling; in addition she might buy certain imports from all countries with American account sterling. The list of commodities to be traded in American account sterling could then be expanded slowly.

Under a cautious approach to convertibility it is suggested that instead of making sterling convertible on a gross basis, countries with which Britain had established convertibility under the conditions outlined above would be entitled at the end of each month to receive American account sterling in payment for any net surplus with the sterling area. This procedure would have the advantage of preventing countries from using their inconvertible sterling working balances, which they held at the time convertibility was inaugurated, to make purchases in the dollar area.

If sterling were to become convertible, what would be the relationship of the sterling area to the EPU as it is presently constituted? Other EPU countries might very well be led to run up large deficits in the EPU in order to acquire dollars or dollar goods through sterling. This could result in a large dollar drain on Britain, only partially compensated by gold payments from the EPU.

Another possibility would be for Britain to settle in American account sterling all deficits with individual EPU members on a bilateral basis and receive from the EPU gold payments for all surpluses. Such a system would tend to drain the EPU of its gold, however, since it would be paying out gold for British surpluses with EPU members without receiving gold or convertible currencies for British deficits. It seems likely therefore that Britain would have to withdraw from the EPU unless sterling convertibility became part of a general program of convertibility for the EPU countries as a whole.

The Need for United States Assistance

Assuming that Britain is willing to adopt the internal measures necessary for convertibility, there are certain essential conditions which she could not establish by her own efforts. The most important of these is gold or dollar reserves or free access to them, in an amount not less than, say, $5 billion. The highest postwar level of British reserves was $4 billion, and this peak was the result of a number of temporary factors. It seems likely that it would take several years at best for Britain, through ordinary trade, to increase her present level of gold and dollar reserves (about $2.5 billion in mid-March 1953) to $5 billion. Moreover, Britain could not count upon obtaining more than a few hundred million dollars from the Monetary Fund. Since a U.S. grant to Britain for this purpose is probably not politically feasible, the only alternative would be a loan on terms even more generous than the fifty-year loan of $3.75 billion at 2 per cent interest made to Britain in 1946. Unlike the 1946 loan, the new loan should be not for reconstruction but solely for currency stabilization. Such a loan would not be drawn upon except to meet short-term drains—seasonal, cyclical or speculative—and should not be used to finance continuing balance of payments deficits resulting from internal inflation or capital exports. These funds should be available to Britain for a long period, say twenty-five years, or until Britain's own reserves had risen to an adequate level. Drawings on the stabilization loan should be paid back gradually as Britain's temporary deficits were reversed, but no payments should be required for three or four years after the drawings were made.

Britain might also need some assistance in funding her sterling liabilities. Some of the holders of these balances depend upon them to finance their development programs. The United States government together with the International Bank might institute a lending program for the holders of the sterling balances which would make up the difference between the present contribution of British capital exports, including the drawing down of sterling balances, and Britain's payments to the sterling area countries under an arrangement whereby the balances would be funded over a long period.

CONVERTIBILITY AND THE EPU

In Chapter 6 it was noted how the European Payments Union provides for multilateral settlements among its members and enables surplus countries to obtain partial conversion of their net surpluses in gold. Despite the fact that several EPU members had to reestablish quotas on their imports from EPU countries during 1952, the EPU has contributed substantially to the liberalization of trade on a non-discriminatory basis among its members.[14] The removal of import restrictions must await the restoration of over-all balance by the individual members but the existence of the EPU has made trade discrimination between its members unnecessary. The EPU, however, which is based on the principle that the dollar is a scarce currency, is essentially a mechanism of group discrimination against the dollar area. In fact the failure of any member to discriminate against dollar imports or in favor of dollar exports is alleged to "weaken" the system.[15] The system is also designed to promote a balance between each individual member and the EPU as a whole. Deficit countries are "penalized " by having to settle an increasing proportion of their deficits in gold up to 100 per cent after they have exhausted their quota. Surplus countries are "penalized" by having to extend credits to cover a portion of their surpluses with the EPU. Since the normal prewar trade structure of most EPU countries was characterized by either a substantial deficit or surplus with the countries constituting the EPU, the maintenance of an approximate balance with the EPU has required the use of discriminatory restrictions against the dollar area even for countries which are in more or less over-all balance.

14. The United Kingdom reduced the percentage of liberalization of private imports from EPU countries from 90 per cent (1948 base) in 1951 to 46 per cent in 1952. France, which had liberalized 75 per cent of her private imports from EPU countries in 1951, subsequently placed practically all of her imports under quotas. On the other hand, Germany and the Netherlands further liberalized their imports from EPU countries during 1952.

15. EPU members have brought pressure on Belgium to tighten discriminatory controls on dollar imports. Failure of a member to discriminate against dollar imports increases the surplus of the nondiscriminating member with the EPU since many EPU exports are not competitive with dollar goods. Efforts to expand dollar exports through the use of retention quotas are also frowned upon for the same reason.

One of the stated purposes of the EPU is to facilitate a return to "full multilateral trade" and "the general convertibility of currencies."[16] While it may be argued that intra-OEEC-country trade has become more competitive under the EPU than under bilateralism and that there have been certain economic gains from the freeing of trade within Western Europe, there has been little real progress toward the objective of "full multilateral trade."

Termination of the EPU

One approach to this goal would be to terminate the EPU and encourage countries to get rid of their bilateral trade and payments agreements. There is a real danger that this would result in a return to bilateralism in intra-European trade. Moreover, there are important arguments for retaining the EPU, at least for the time being. The EPU has afforded a source of liquidity for the trade of a large area of the world, which the Monetary Fund under its present policies and resources has not been able to provide. There is also a need for some kind of institution for regional multilateral clearings under the type of scarce currency conditions described in Chapter 20. While the Monetary Fund Agreement recognized the scarce currency principle, it did not provide a mechanism for its operation. Such a mechanism might be developed within the Monetary Fund itself, but the Fund has not dealt with this problem nor has it until recently sought to cooperate with the EPU in any concrete way. What is required is a regional multilateral mechanism through which members can move gradually toward universal convertibility but which will remain as an avenue of retreat to regional or limited multilateral settlements in the event of the reappearance of a scarce currency condition.

Substitution of a Sterling Transferable Account System

A possible substitute for the EPU is to broaden the sterling transferable account system. If sterling were to become convertible under the procedure outlined above, some EPU members might accept transferable account status with the privilege of converting current sterling surpluses into dollars or American account sterling on condition that

16. *Agreement for the Establishment of a European Payments Union*, Organisation for European Economic Co-operation, Paris, 1950, p. 4.

they would not enter into bilateral agreements which discriminated against the sterling area. If in addition the members of this "convertible" transferable account group were to agree to conduct their trade with one another solely in sterling or in balances of their own currencies which were convertible into sterling, there might be formed a fairly sizable group of countries trading with one another on a fully convertible basis.

An important feature of such an arrangement, however, would be the agreement that no member would employ any restrictions which discriminated against imports from the sterling area or against other members of the convertible transferable account group. This would mean that while members of this special group might negotiate bilateral payments agreements with nonmembers, such agreements could not be accompanied by commodity trade quotas which in any way discriminated against the sterling area or against other members of the group. When sterling became fully convertible in the sense that every country was treated as an American account country, there would be little reason for discrimination on balance of payments grounds and all cases of discriminations would be subject to the GATT and IMF rules applying to the post-transition period. Such a program, however, would depend upon (1) the gradual convertibility of sterling and (2) the willingness of the major OEEC countries to accept the special transferable account status under the conditions outlined here.

What would happen to the EPU under the suggested arrangement? As members joined the convertible transferable account system they would probably have to drop out of the EPU since their payments positions with one another would be settled in sterling which would be convertible into American account sterling under the suggested plan. As convertible transferable account status was extended to more and more EPU members the justification for the EPU would gradually disappear. However, it might be possible to retain the EPU under a special arrangement for settlements between the sterling area and the EPU itself.

Retention of the EPU and Establishment of Convertibility

Another approach to convertibility would be to retain the EPU structure, with or without the United Kingdom, and to move toward full multilateral trade and settlements with currency areas outside the EPU. Progress toward this goal could only take place by the adoption of a definite schedule for the removal of discriminatory trade controls, and their replacement by open general licenses valid for imports from any source, or by the adoption of global quotas and licenses issued on a nondiscriminatory basis. The success of any program of convertibility for the EPU area would also depend upon the elimination of over-all disequilibrium by each member through domestic monetary and fiscal measures or through currency adjustments. The elimination of discriminatory controls would mean that some countries would develop continuous surpluses with the EPU, which would have to be settled by 100 per cent payments in gold or convertible currencies; other countries would develop more or less continuous deficits, which they would need to discharge in gold or convertible currencies. However, the EPU might require creditors to hold their EPU surpluses in the form of EPU credits until the surplus countries needed gold or convertible currencies to discharge a current deficit with a non-EPU country.[17] The advantage of having EPU creditors retain their EPU credits in the form of balances with the EPU is that it would increase the working capital of that institution.

New System of Quotas

Under a fully multilateral EPU system each country might be given a quota similar to the quotas in the present EPU. In normal circumstances deficits would be settled 100 per cent in gold or convertible currencies at the end of each month and surpluses would be settled in EPU gold credits, fully convertible for settling current deficits with the dollar area or with countries requiring gold payments in settlement of deficits. Countries having over-all deficits with both the EPU and the dollar area would be permitted to discharge their EPU deficits by a credit from the EPU up to the limit of their quota. EPU countries with surpluses would be required to accept inconvertible EPU credits in an amount equal to the uncovered deficits of the debtor

17. During the transitional stage to full convertibility the EPU might accept a certain amount of inconvertible currencies of non-EPU members tendered by EPU members in discharge of their EPU deficits. The inconvertible currency—for example, Argentine pesos—could then be paid to EPU creditor countries having a deficit with Argentina.

countries in any particular month, but the total amount of such inconvertible credits which any one member would be required to accept would not exceed that country's quota. However, EPU gold credits accumulated in the past could always be converted into gold to discharge a current deficit with the dollar area. The EPU would also need a fund of gold or convertible currencies, somewhat larger than its present capital, in order to function during periods when a large volume of deficits was concentrated on a few countries.

Removal of Discriminatory Controls

During the transition to full convertibility under the suggested system, deficit countries would be required to discharge their old deficits with the EPU or to arrange for their funding over a period of time, and to get into over-all balance. As soon as the new payments system was inaugurated members would be obligated to remove their discriminatory controls according to a definite schedule so that within two years or so all trade restrictions would be nondiscriminatory. By common consent the rules regarding nondiscrimination could be relaxed if a sharp recession in the United States or some other circumstance brought about a deterioration of the position of the EPU countries with the dollar area.

There would be several advantages in retaining the EPU structure under these conditions. First, a group of countries could gradually remove discriminatory controls together and hence avoid the serious loss of trade which might occur if only one or two EPU countries were to adopt convertibility. Second, the EPU mechanism would continue to provide liquidity for its members, most of whose gold and dollar reserves are quite inadequate. Third, the discriminatory characteristics of the EPU could be quickly reestablished if a scarce currency condition developed.

It has been objected that the removal of discrimination against dollar imports would interfere with the intra-OEEC trade liberalization program which by the autumn of 1953 had exceeded 80 per cent of private trade for the major trading countries. There is no reason why this program should not be continued in the transition period during which EPU members are gradually eliminating their discriminatory restrictions against imports from all sources. In fact the ultimate success of the convertibility program will depend upon the ability of

EPU members to achieve international balance without relying upon quantitative restrictions, first, on imports from other EPU members, and ultimately, on imports from all countries.

Relations with the Sterling Area

Special problems would arise for the EPU during the process of transition to convertibility if the sterling area were to break away from that institution. If sterling were to remain inconvertible there would be a tendency for EPU members to shift their trade from other EPU countries to the sterling area, since EPU deficits would have to be settled fully in gold. If sterling were to become convertible under the conditions suggested earlier, an arrangement might be devised whereby the whole EPU area might become a part of the "convertible" transferable account group and EPU members might use sterling to discharge deficits with the EPU. Under such an arrangement the EPU might pay out sterling to creditor members to discharge their deficits with the sterling area. In addition the EPU might be permitted to convert its sterling surpluses into American account sterling with the Bank of England to meet its surplus members' current account deficits with the dollar area.

There remains the problem of the relationship between the EPU and other nondollar countries, particularly the Latin American nations and Japan.[18] If sterling became convertible Japan would probably become a dollar country and avoid discrimination. The nondollar countries of Latin America will undoubtedly want to continue to use sterling and Western European currencies in most of their trade with the nondollar world. One approach would be to permit the nondollar Latin American countries to exchange their Western European currencies for EPU credits, which would be available for discharging a current account deficit with any EPU member, or convertible into gold after the credits exceeded a certain level.[19] The EPU members would not be permitted to negotiate discriminatory trade

18. Most other countries of the free world are either in the dollar area, the transferable account group (which would probably maintain close relations with sterling) or are a part of the sterling area or some other Western European currency area.

19. The purpose of restricting convertibility to amounts in excess of the Latin American quotas would be to require these countries to contribute to the working capital of the EPU. EPU currencies tendered for EPU credits would be charged against the account of the EPU member whose currency was tendered.

agreements with these countries (or with any other country) and Latin American currencies would not be employed as the means of payment in trade with EPU members. Another approach would be to make the Latin American countries full members of the EPU; but this would probably not be feasible since Latin American currencies and credits are not generally acceptable to European countries. In periods when the dollar was declared scarce EPU credits would no longer be fully convertible into dollars.

U.S. Government Support

As these pages were being written, early in 1953, the conditions and prospects for the convertibility of sterling and of the other EPU currencies were the subject of high-level diplomatic discussions in Washington and in the Council of the OEEC in Paris. The decision reached by the British Commonwealth Conference of Ministers in December 1952 to make a definite advance toward the restoration of convertibility [20] and the subsequent discussions of concrete proposals for the restoration of convertibility by British officials in Washington [21] and in Paris [22] have given rise—and quite properly—to hopes for the restoration of a multilateral payments system for the free world. The British program, however, lays considerable stress upon the role of the United States in creating the conditions that would make convertibility possible. These include (1) the provision of additional gold and dollar reserves through liberalization of the lending policies of the Monetary Fund and by U.S. stabilization loans; (2) the opening up of U.S. markets for European products; (3) the stabilization of the prices of international raw materials through international commodity agreements; (4) an increased flow of U.S. capital both to Europe and to the underdeveloped areas. It seems clear that unless the United States is willing to meet this challenge the current interest in currency convertibility both in the United Kingdom and on the European continent is likely to recede without any concrete accomplishment.

On the other hand it would be unwise for the United States to

20. "The Commonwealth Decisions," *The Economist*, December 20, 1952, pp. 837–38.
21. *The New York Times*, March 6, 1953.
22. "Convertibility à la Muette," *The Economist*, March 28, 1953, pp. 887–88.

make available any additional funds for stabilization purposes or to agree to underwrite the restoration of currency convertibility by Britain and other EPU countries in the absence of a determined effort on the part of these nations to achieve over-all balance without controls. This would require the restoration of price competition and sufficient deflation to bring about the necessary readjustments in the pattern of Western Europe's production and trade for equilibrium with the dollar area. It is quite possible that neither the United States nor Western Europe is prepared to adopt the necessary measures for the restoration of equilibrium, because of their political unpopularity.[23] It is not the purpose of this study, however, to judge the political feasibility of the measures necessary for the convertibility of the world's leading currencies. Rather, what we are seeking to determine are the minimum conditions for their convertibility.

23. There was growing evidence in mid-1953 that the major barrier to convertibility in Western Europe was not the balance of payments position of these countries but the unwillingness to give up the large degree of commercial protection afforded by discrimination against dollar imports.

Chapter 22

THE ROLES OF THE INTERNATIONAL MONETARY
FUND AND THE GATT

THE STERLING AREA, the OEEC and the EPU are mechanisms for promoting multilateral trade and payments among a limited group of countries. The International Monetary Fund and the General Agreement on Tariffs and Trade (GATT)[1] were organized in the early postwar period to perform this function on a global basis, but their major objective has not been even approximately achieved. Many have come to the conclusion that these institutions were designed to deal with the problems of a bygone era and that it is time for another Bretton Woods monetary conference and a new approach to the whole problem of global or at least free-world trade and finance.[2] This chapter will consider the possible contributions of the Fund and the GATT to meeting the world's payments problems.

THE INTERNATIONAL MONETARY FUND

The Monetary Fund was designed to come into full operation with the restoration of world equilibrium but the authors of the Fund Agreement were extremely vague as to what the Fund was to do in the interim. The problem of the transition was viewed as involving the postwar recovery of production and trade of individual countries, which one by one would become financially strong enough to accept the convertibility obligations of Article VIII of the Fund Agreement.

1. The GATT was to be superseded by the International Trade Organization but the ITO never came into being. For an excellent discussion of the history of the ITO, see William Diebold, Jr., *The End of the I.T.O.*, International Finance Section, Princeton University, Princeton, 1952.
2. On September 24, 1952 the Consultative Assembly of the Council of Europe meeting in Strasbourg adopted a report recommending the calling of a world-wide conference to reconsider the basic assumptions of the postwar trade and payments plans including the Bretton Woods agreements. *International Financial News Survey,* October 3, 1952, p. 109.

The Transition Period

While there certainly has been a problem of expanding production and of restoring over-all balance for individaul countries, the major barrier to the restoration of convertibility for nearly all nondollar countries regardless of their over-all position has been their disequilibrium, as a group, with the dollar area. Moreover, as was pointed out in Chapter 20, the existence of interregional disequilibrium has been to a considerable degree responsible for the over-all disequilibrium of certain individual countries. The policy of the United States government in its administration of Marshall Plan aid clearly recognized the interregional nature of Western Europe's disequilibrium, and sought to deal with it, in part, through regional arrangements. The policy of the Monetary Fund, on the other hand, has been to deal with disequilibrium on an individual country basis.

The unwillingness or the inability of the Fund to consider the problems of postwar trade in terms of interregional disequilibrium lies at the heart of the Fund's failure to make effective use of its pool of gold and currencies or to do anything significant toward restoring multilateral trade. While the Articles of Agreement recognized the principle of interregional disequilibrium in the scarce currency clause (Article VII), the Agreement virtually ruled out a scarce currency declaration during the transition period. Moreover the Articles of Agreement provided no machinery for orderly discrimination against the scarce currency country during periods when the Fund might properly declare the existence of a scarce currency condition.

The Fund Agreement requires that before a currency can be declared scarce, there must be not only a finding of the general scarcity of the currency, but the Fund's own supply must be threatened with exhaustion.[3] Yet if the Fund were to open its doors to large dollar drawings to cover fundamental or long-term deficits, and thus exhaust its own gold and dollar holdings, the Fund would be violating the requirement that financial assistance to a member must be solely for short-term currency stabilization.

The Articles of Agreement are by no means clear regarding the criteria for the use of the Fund's resources during the transition period. The target date for the termination of the transition period

3. Article VII, Sec. 3.

was March 1952, five years after the Fund began operations. However, there is no time limit on the employment of exchange restrictions by members under the general escape clause of Article XIV, the transition-period Article. Members are permitted to retain discriminatory and nondiscriminatory restrictions so long as they can justify their retention to the satisfaction of the Fund. But while the condition of interregional disequilibrium, or dollar scarcity, continues, few nations will be in a position to drop their restrictions without suffering a serious loss of trade, regardless of their internal policies. Meanwhile, the Monetary Fund is limited in lending its dollar resources since for the duration of the dollar shortage, the dollar deficits of most of its members cannot be considered temporary phenomena, reversible by transitory external forces or a change in domestic policies. Thus we are presented with the spectacle of a world which is sorely in need of liquidity to meet balance of payments fluctuations, and an institution designed to meet this need but which has made relatively little use of its large gold and dollar resources for this purpose.

How Can the Fund Help Eliminate Interregional Disequilibrium?

For the Fund to operate effectively within the terms of its charter it must find a way to contribute to the elimination of interregional disequilibrium. Chapter 21 explored the means by which the sterling area and the EPU might move toward full multilateral settlements. If it is admitted that the problem of currency convertibility must be approached through existing regional payments arrangements and not by waiting for individual countries to undertake convertibility by unilateral action, then the Fund must devise ways to promote its objectives through the EPU, or the sterling area or both. Alternatively, the Fund might sponsor a nondollar multilateral settlement system of its own and promote a gradual transformation of this into a fully multilateral system. To create such a system at this late date would raise both political and organizational difficulties, although the Fund might have been able to evolve a nondollar trading system before the EPU was established.[4]

4. In 1948 the late Dr. Harry D. White, author of the original American draft of the Monetary Agreement, proposed a system of special accounts to be held in the Fund, which would be available to purchase imports from countries other than a few, includ-

A Suggested Program of Action

In promoting convertibility for the sterling area and the EPU the Monetary Fund might take the following steps:

1. The Fund might establish a definite time schedule for the gradual elimination of discriminatory controls among the members of the EPU, the members of the sterling area, the members of the proposed convertible transferable account group (discussed in Chapter 21) and other important trading countries. The purpose of the agreed schedule would be to assure each member of the soft-currency group that it would not be penalized if it removed discriminatory controls in advance of other members. This part of the program would require the cooperation of the GATT.

2. The Fund might undertake to provide the additional reserves required by the EPU, the mechanics of which will be discussed in a later section. It might also provide some financial assistance to the sterling area, but the problem of supplementing British reserves is probably too large to be handled by the present resources of the Fund.

3. The Fund might rely heavily on regional associations of countries including the EPU, the sterling area and any other regional grouping which might be formed, in dealing with such questions as exchange rates, the use of exchange restrictions, and the provision of short-term credits.[5] The Fund's own lending activities might be coordinated with those of the regional organizations.

4. Once a program for the gradual elimination of discrimination and the restoration of full multilateral settlements had been agreed upon with the regional organizations, the Fund should use its authority under the Articles of Agreement to request all members to eliminate bilateral agreements which restrict the use of balances arising out of trade between any two countries for making payments in third countries. For example, two Latin American members of the Fund would not be permitted to make agreements under which the resulting balances were not convertible into dollars, sterling or some EPU

ing the United States, which tended to have large export surpluses. (For a discussion of this plan, see J. N. Behrman, "A Suggested Amendment to the International Monetary Fund Charter," *The Economic Journal,* June 1953, pp. 471–77.)

5. See Robert Triffin, "Monetary Reconstruction in Europe," *International Conciliation,* June 1952, pp. 263–308. Dr. Triffin has outlined a proposal for the decentralization of the administrative and other functions of the Fund in an unpublished memorandum.

currency.[6] The GATT should likewise insist that purely bilateral trade-quota agreements be abolished and that discrimination against any currency area be gradually eliminated.

5. The Fund should be represented on the managing boards of all regional multilateral organizations.

The program outlined above envisages the Monetary Fund as taking the initiative in negotiating agreements with regional monetary organizations for the restoration of full multilateral settlements.[7] The Fund would also have a responsibility for making recommendations to the United States and to international institutions such as the International Bank as to measures which would help alleviate the dollar shortage and permit rapid progress toward full multilateral settlements.

The Lending Policies of the Fund

The approach here suggested would require a change in the Fund's lending policies. At present the Fund is severely limited in two important ways in the use of its resources to meet the need for international liquidity. First, the demand for currencies from the Fund has been largely a demand for dollars since members are required to repay the Fund in dollars. If no legal way can be found whereby both drawings and repayments can be made in soft currencies, the Fund cannot serve as a source of nondollar liquidity during periods of dollar shortage. Unless the Articles are amended, the Fund may be unable to set up a system of multilateral settlements among nondollar countries in periods of dollar scarcity, and countries must therefore rely upon special regional multilateral arrangements.[8]

A second limitation on the Fund's lending power is that, according

6. It is conceivable that a regional multilateral settlements group would be formed among certain Latin American countries, in which case balances arising out of bilateral agreements between members of the Latin American group would be automatically convertible into the currencies of other members.

7. The regional—as opposed to the country-by-country approach—was recommended as the basis for the Fund's policies in an address by M. Pierre Mendes-France, Governor of the Fund for France, in an address given at the annual meeting of the International Monetary Fund in September 1952. See *Summary Proceedings of the Seventh Annual Meeting of the Board of Governors,* International Monetary Fund, Washington, 1953, pp. 96–107.

8. Without going into the technical problems involved, the author is of the opinion that the Fund could set up a system of nondollar drawings and repayments without amending its charter.

to a decision by the executive directors of the Fund, "authority to use the resources of the Fund is limited to use in accordance with its purposes to give temporary assistance in financing balance of payments deficits on current account for monetary stabilization operations." [9] Since repayment to the Fund must be made in dollars or gold, members have been reluctant to obtain nondollar credits from the Fund. Hence members have looked to the Fund for assistance in financing their dollar deficits but have rarely obtained credits from the Fund for meeting temporary deficits in other currencies. Since the "dollar deficits" of most members are fundamental or long term under conditions of world dollar shortage, the Fund has made only limited use of its lending powers.[10] On the other hand, a number of the Fund's members have had wide postwar fluctuations in their over-all current account balances ranging from substantial surpluses to heavy deficits. These imbalances have been financed chiefly by bilateral credits, sterling balances, EPU credits, U.S. foreign aid and the gold and foreign currency reserves of the individual countries. Only a small proportion of the liquidity required for financing the temporary deficits and surpluses (that is, those which did not involve net deficits or surpluses for the postwar period as a whole) have been financed by drawings on the Monetary Fund.

Liberalization of the Fund's Lending Policy

In recent months the Monetary Fund has taken steps to liberalize its lending policies. The policy which practically eliminated drawings by Western European members during the European Recovery Program was terminated. The Fund also announced that countries needing assistance over a relatively short period might be permitted to purchase currencies from the Fund under special agreements which provide for the repurchase with gold or dollars of the member's currency within eighteen months. Presumably this arrangement would

9. *Report of the Executive Directors and Summary Proceedings,* First Annual Meeting of the Board of Governors of the International Monetary Fund, September 27 to October 3, 1946, Washington, November 1946, p. 106.

10. Total currency sales by the Fund to September 30, 1953 were $988 million, of which $287 million had been repaid. As of September 30, 1953, the Fund held about $3 billion in gold and dollar balances. In 1950 there were no drawings from the Fund; in 1951 drawings were only $34.6 million and in 1952 they amounted to $85.1 million. During January 1950 to September 1953 repayments were substantially in excess of drawings. Over 90 per cent of the drawings have been in dollars.

apply in cases where the member would not be eligible for drawings without a special agreement to repurchase. Countries whose drawings from the Fund have been less than their gold subscription "can count on receiving the overwhelming benefit of any doubt respecting drawings" up to the limit of their gold subscriptions.[11] Finally, in November 1952, the Fund's Executive Board announced a policy under which members could apply for stand-by drawing accounts, and these could be negotiated in advance of any probable need for drawings. Thus if a member expected to require temporary assistance sometime over the next six months, it could make plans with the knowledge that help from the Fund up to a certain amount would be forthcoming, if it were needed.[12] The Fund's liberalized policies still quite properly require that members should not remain in debt to the Fund for more than three to five years and that there must be a reasonable expectation that their deficits will be reversed within this period.

Even in a world of continued disequilibrium and discriminatory controls the Fund could play a useful role as a short-term dollar lender. The additional dollar liquidity would enable some countries to avoid tightening their discriminatory restrictions against dollar goods in order to deal with a temporary worsening of their conditions. But we should expect much more of the Monetary Fund than this. The Fund and its resources should become the principal instrument through which equilibrium for the free world is restored. If the regional approach to this problem is adopted, the Fund should be ready and able to assist the EPU or other regional monetary organizations in achieving full multilateral settlements.

Assistance to Regional Monetary Organizations

The Monetary Fund has no authority to lend directly to international organizations. However, arrangements might be worked out whereby EPU creditor countries could convert a portion of their credits by drawing dollars from the Monetary Fund, when the EPU itself was not in a position to make full gold or dollar settlements.[13]

11. See *Annual Report of the Executive Directors for the Fiscal Year Ended April 30, 1952*, The International Monetary Fund, Appendix I.

12. *International Financial News Survey*, November 7, 1952, p. 149.

13. As was mentioned in Chapter 6, Belgium was granted special permission to draw

The creditor country could then repay the Fund when the EPU was in a position to settle its obligation to the creditor country or payment would be made to the Fund when the creditor country's position with the EPU was reversed. Since the assistance extended by the EPU to its members would take the form of short-term credits and since EPU members would be required to get into over-all balance within a reasonable time, the inability of the EPU to convert the EPU credits held by its members into gold or dollars would be temporary.[14] The additional reserves supplied indirectly by the Fund would not only assist the EPU in helping its members meet the inevitable pressures on their balance of payments during the period of transition to full multilateral settlements, but the Fund's resources could provide a more or less permanent addition to the working capital of the EPU. Finally, the willingness of the Fund to use its resources in this way should insure it the right to participate in the policy decisions of regional monetary organizations.

The Fund Cannot Restore Convertibility by Itself

It should be emphasized that no alteration in the lending policies of the Fund and no change in the structure and policies of international organizations will by themselves provide the necessary conditions for the restoration of international equilibrium. The special contributions of the Monetary Fund to the restoration of universal multilateral settlements in the program set forth above would be (1) the provision of additional liquidity and (2) the development of an agreed schedule for the ending of discrimination by all its members, which would remove the disadvantage to countries which elected to abandon discriminatory controls and to restore convertibility by themselves. But these conditions are not sufficient to restore currency con-

---

up to $50 million from the Monetary Fund, as part of the settlement of her credit with the EPU in June 1952.

14. An alternative method would be for countries running deficits with the EPU which they were temporarily unable to cover by their current dollar earnings, to draw dollars from the Fund for meeting their obligation to the EPU. However, this would transfer to the Fund the control over the extension of credits to the deficit countries and absolve the regional organization of the important responsibility of getting the deficit country back into balance. Moreover, the Fund would be lending to the weakest members of the EPU rather than to the strongest members as in the proposal outlined above. By having the EPU creditor draw from the Fund in lieu of payment by the EPU, the indebtedness to the Fund would be in effect underwritten by the entire resources of the EPU.

vertibility. There must be a willingness on the part of the major nondollar countries to achieve over-all equilibrium without the use of trade or exchange restrictions. International capital must be available to assist the nondollar world in making the structural adjustments in production necessary to reduce the heavy dependence upon the United States. Further, nations must adopt economic policies and programs which will encourage the movement of resources required for these structural changes. Finally, the United States must help Western Europe earn dollars by reducing its barriers to imports and by an expanded program of offshore procurement of defense items.

It is obvious that the conditions for currency convertibility in the free world are substantially broader than the terms of reference of the Monetary Fund. The creation of these conditions requires the close cooperation of a number of regional and free-world organizations. It also calls for the cooperation of the leading nations of the free world including the United States, Canada and Britain, whose governments would be called upon for special assistance and for far-reaching changes in their policies. The problems of international organization for the restoration of convertibility and multilateralism in the free world are considered in the concluding chapter of this study.

Implementing the Suggested Code of Fair Exchange Practices

The remaining functions of the Monetary Fund would be concerned with the administration of a code of fair exchange practices such as that outlined in Chapter 20. This suggested code, though somewhat less idealistic than the one provided by the Articles of Agreement for the Monetary Fund, seems much better adapted to the realities of postwar conditions. Moreover, it is a code of practices applicable to a scarce currency situation, a condition recognized in principle by the Articles of Agreement though no adequate provision was made for the conduct of the Fund and its members after a currency had been declared scarce.

While the suggested code of fair practices would require certain changes in the present policies of the Fund, it is the view of the author that an amendment to the Fund's charter would be unnecessary for the adoption of this code. The Fund has ample powers for granting exceptions to the fundamental rules of the Articles of

Agreement. The successful application of this code would be a vast improvement over the chaotic foreign exchange conditions of the present, and would provide the basic conditions for realizing the maximum gains from foreign trade.

THE PROBLEM OF INTERNATIONAL RESERVES

One of the important objectives of the Fund is to provide the additional liquidity necessary for a successful multilateral payments system. While we must reject the position that the lack of adequate international reserves is the sole or even the principal cause of disequilibrium and foreign exchange restrictions in most of the free nations, it is readily admitted that a successful system of multilateral payments is impossible with the present distribution of gold and convertible foreign exchange reserves among the countries of the free world. At the time of the Bretton Woods Conference many delegates sincerely believed that the pool of gold and dollars to be subscribed to the Monetary Fund would be inadequate to supplement the reserves of members for meeting seasonal and short-term cyclical deficits in their balances of payments, particularly because they feared these deficits were likely to be concentrated upon the United States. Since 1944 the problem of international liquidity has become confused with the problem of fundamental disequilibrium and dollar scarcity. However, before contemplating the restoration of a system of universal multilateral settlements, provision must be made for reserves adequate for normal or expected balance of payments fluctuations under conditions of long-run equilibrium and currency convertibility.

Gold and dollars are not the only form which international reserves may take. With the present dollar scarcity, sterling balances and EPU quotas are also sources of international liquidity. Under conditions of universal convertibility, sterling balances and the ability to obtain credits from regional monetary organizations would be sources of liquidity usable in any currency area. Given world equilibrium, many of the nondollar assets of the Monetary Fund would undoubtedly be available for loans. But at present the Fund's gold and dollars represent a practical limit to the Fund's supply of international liquidity.

Decrease in Reserves since Prewar Years

Official gold reserves and short-term dollar balances outside the United States were about $15 billion at the end of 1938 as compared with $19 billion on June 30, 1952. In terms of 1938 prices, however, the value of the 1952 gold and dollar holdings was less than half of those of 1938. Moreover, in 1938 the world's gold and dollar holdings outside the United States represented about 70 per cent of total world trade, whereas in 1952 the corresponding percentage was only about 25. For current holdings of gold and dollars outside the United States to represent the same percentage of world trade as in 1938, they would have to be increased by about $30 billion. Nothing like this increase in world gold and dollar reserves or access to them through international institutions, is believed to be essential for universal currency convertibility. The required addition to reserves differs greatly from country to country, since existing reserves are not well distributed from the standpoint of need. For example, the world's gold and dollar reserves are heavily concentrated in Switzerland and in the dollar area countries of the Western Hemisphere. On the other hand Britain, France and the Netherlands had less gold and dollars in 1952 than they had before the war. (See Table 21.)

In spite of the fact that the United States has not had a major postwar depression, the world's leading trading countries have experienced wide swings in their gold and dollar positions. Small changes in business conditions, changes in terms of trade brought about by the movements of raw material prices, and speculative actions against currencies have fallen with enormous impact on the thin shield of foreign exchange reserves. These movements have occurred in spite of fairly comprehensive trade and exchange controls in most countries. Under more liberal exchange and trading conditions we could expect the shock of these movements to be even greater before they could be arrested by the orthodox methods of monetary and fiscal policy and changes in exchange rates. We must conclude, therefore, that even if other conditions were more favorable, the reestablishment and maintenance of currency convertibility is probably impossible without a substantial increase in the foreign exchange reserves of most countries or their availability from other sources.[15]

15. It is estimated that a twelve-month reduction in dollar supply at the same relative severity as that which occurred during the U.S. recession of 1937–1938, even if

TABLE 21

ESTIMATED GOLD AND SHORT-TERM DOLLAR RESOURCES OF FOREIGN COUNTRIES, DECEMBER 31, 1938 AND JUNE 30, 1952

(*Millions*)

Area and Country	December 31, 1938		June 30, 1952	
	Gold [a]	Gold and Short-term Dollar Holdings [b]	Gold [a]	Gold and Short-term Dollar Holdings [b]
Total, all areas [c]	$12,930	$14,972	$10,677	$19,012
Total, Western Europe (excluding the sterling area)	6,459	[d]	4,553	7,091
Belgium, Luxembourg, and Belgian Congo	625	[d]	747	969
France and dependencies.......	2,765	2,956	593	938
Western Germany	29	49	92	545
Italy	192	216	348	615
Netherlands, Netherlands West Indies and Surinam........	998	1,096	368	603
Portugal and dependencies.....	69	[d]	292	340
Sweden	321	[d]	213	281
Switzerland	701	918	1,408	2,009
Other Western Europe........	759	[d]	492	791
Total, other Europe............	[d]	[d]	382 [e]	402
Total, U.K. and other sterling area.	3,211	[d]	2,036	3,129
United Kingdom	2,690	3,129	1,425	2,218
Other sterling area..........	521	[d]	611	911
Total, Canada	192	427	893	2,396
Total, Africa [f]	55 [g]	[d]	178	331
Total, Asia [h]	208	[d]	804	2,364
Total, Latin America [f]..........	708	963	1,831	3,300
Dollar area Latin America.....	195	[d]	947	1,979
Nondollar area Latin America [i].	513	[d]	884	1,321

Sources: National Advisory Council, *Semiannual Report to the President and to the Congress for the Period April 1–September 30, 1952;* Export-Import Bank of Washington, *First Semiannual Report to Congress for the Period July–December 1945.*

a. Official gold holdings: for countries whose current holdings have not been published, available estimates have been used, or the figures previously published or estimated have been carried forward.

b. Short-term dollar holdings as reported by U.S. banking institutions; includes both private and official dollar holdings.

c. 1938 totals estimated, including USSR. 1952 totals exclude holdings of the IMF, the IBRD, the EPU and other international organizations, and those of the USSR.

d. Data not available.

e. Includes gold to be distributed by the Tripartite Commission for the Restitution of Monetary Gold to the claimant countries, including Western European countries, in accordance with the Paris reparations agreement.

f. Excludes sterling area countries and dependencies of European countries.

g. Egypt and Egyptian-Sudan only.

h. Excludes sterling area countries.

i. For 1938, includes Argentina, Brazil, Chile and Peru; for 1952, also includes Uruguay. Uruguayan holdings in 1952 totaled $309 million of which $211 million was in gold.

Amount of Additional Reserves Required

What does this conclusion mean in quantitative terms as to the adequacy of the gold and dollar assets of the Monetary Fund, the United Kingdom as banker for the sterling area, and the EPU if it remains as a monetary organization under conditions of convertibility? Only the most tentative answer can be given to this question. It has already been suggested that Britain might need an additional $2.5 billion above the $2.5 billion which she had in September 1953, before that country can embark on convertibility with safety. The EPU might depend upon the Monetary Fund for temporary assistance but the EPU ought to have reserves of its own of at least a billion dollars [16] and the ability to draw (indirectly) on the Monetary Fund for another billion. The gold and dollar assets of the Monetary Fund will probably need to be doubled, or increased by about $3 billion if that institution is to play a significant role in the restoration and maintenance of currency convertibility. The $6 billion in the hands of the Monetary Fund plus the additional $2.5 billion suggested for Britain would raise the gold and dollar assets of the free world (outside the United States) available for meeting short-term deficits by about $8.5 billion. Moreover, these assets could be mobilized for use by countries whose need is likely to be the greatest under conditions of convertibility.

Where would these additional reserves come from? There are just two possible sources, both of which would depend upon action by the United States. As was suggested in Chapter 21, the United States government might make a loan to Britain on somewhat more liberal terms than the 1946 loan to that country, but unlike the 1946 loan, it would be solely for currency stabilization purposes. The Fund's dollar resources might be increased by raising the United States quota by $3

---

followed by a quick recovery in the following twelve months, might mean a reduction of $10 billion in the supply of dollars over the twenty-four-month period. See *Measures for International Economic Stability* (report by a group of experts appointed by the Secretary-General, and under the chairmanship of James W. Angell), United Nations, New York, 1951, pp. 33–34.

16. The increased working capital of the EPU might be obtained from an assessment on its members, which would be equivalent to a partial pooling of their reserves. Such a move would be consistent with the plans for economic integration under discussion by six of the continental OEEC countries but would probably not be acceptable to Switzerland. Switzerland would probably become a fully convertible country outside the EPU if discrimination against hard-currency countries were abandoned.

billion. By reason of its heavy voting power in the Fund the United States could make certain that these additional resources would be used to promote the restoration of convertibility along the lines suggested above. However, the United States is not likely to consider an increase in its subscription to the Fund until convertibility has been achieved and the Fund has demonstrated that it can operate in accordance with the principles of its charter.

The second way in which the additional reserves required for universal convertibility could be made available would be for the United States to increase the price of gold.[17] This alternative has advantages and disadvantages. To double the price of gold would double the dollar value of the monetary gold holdings of the world, estimated at about $11 billion, exclusive of the USSR and the United States. This could be done without United States loans or grants to foreign countries or to the Monetary Fund. So long as the U.S. monetary authorities followed anti-inflationary policies, the increase in the value of the world's monetary reserves need not be inflationary; at least, no more inflationary than stabilization grants and loans to the Fund and to Britain of an equivalent amount. A further advantage of this approach would be the increase in the annual contribution of gold production to the total value of world reserves. In 1938 the value of gold production outside the United States and the USSR was nearly a billion dollars or about 4.5 per cent of total world trade. In 1952 the value of gold production outside the United States and the USSR was only $784 million or about one per cent of world trade.

Disadvantages of Raising the Price of Gold

To increase free world reserves by raising the dollar price of gold has several serious disadvantages. A doubling of the price of gold, while it would increase the value of free world reserves by $11 billion, would not distribute the increased reserves in a way that would fulfill the conditions necessary for convertibility. The reserves of the Monetary Fund would be increased by less than $2 billion and British reserves by about $2 billion. The largest increases in the value of

17. According to press reports, Britain's Chancellor of the Exchequer, Richard A. Butler, during his visit to Washington in March 1953, urged the U.S. government to increase the price of gold as a means of assisting Britain's plan for restoring sterling convertibility. *The Financial Times* (London), March 27, 1953, p. 7.

reserves would accrue to the countries with the least need. Moreover the United States would not be able to determine by negotiation how the expanded reserves could make their maximum contribution to convertibility. At the same time, to raise the price of gold would mean a drain on U.S. resources to the extent that other countries financed additional purchases in this country with gold.

Doubling the price of gold would mean a sharp increase in gold production to levels which would represent a misallocation of free world resources and hence a detriment to economic welfare and to the defense program. To the extent that a higher price for gold would mean larger gold sales to the United States, this country would be exchanging goods and services for an asset of which its supply was already redundant and which would contribute nothing to its well-being. Gold purchases are a poor substitute for foreign aid. When the United States provides financial assistance in the form of grants and loans, it seeks to accomplish specific objectives in specific areas. This is not true when the United States buys gold.[18] Continual net gold purchases by the United States are not a desirable means of dealing with the problem of dollar shortage nor should its production be encouraged as a commodity for which the United States maintains an unlimited demand. To do so would be to destroy the basic rationale of the international gold standard which the United States has been seeking to maintain.

Nor should we regard an increase in the price of gold to supplement the world's monetary reserves as any less burdensome to the American economy than a stabilization loan. If the increase in the value of the world's gold reserves results in a higher value of gold sales to the United States to finance exports from this country, the immediate burden on the American economy will be the same as that resulting from the spending of a stabilization loan. In the longer run the burden may be greater than in the case of a loan since no interest would be paid on additions to reserves resulting from a revaluation of gold stocks and foreign countries would be under less pressure to avoid dollar deficits.

18. As one of the largest gold producers and gold holders, the USSR would benefit substantially from an increase in the price of gold.

The General Agreement on Tariffs and Trade

A distinction between quantitative trade restrictions and exchange restrictions can only be made on a legalistic or administrative basis. In the formulation and implementation of a code of fair exchange practices they must be considered one and the same. In the development of postwar international institutions, however, jurisdiction in the foreign exchange field was given to the Monetary Fund while the administration of a code of trade practices was made the province of the GATT. Although a good case can be made for combining these functions in one institution, this would require a rewriting of the Articles of Agreement of the Monetary Fund. The GATT, on the other hand, has no charter subject to ratification by member governments and is therefore more flexible. Moreover the GATT has an important function in conducting multilateral tariff negotiations which are closely related to other trade practices, but which would probably not be appropriate for a financial institution like the Fund. The most expedient course would be to redefine the functions of the GATT in relation to those of the Fund and to strengthen the GATT by giving it legislative status and adequate funds for the performance of the tasks assigned to it.[19]

One of the confusing elements in GATT–Fund relations lies in the fact that the General Agreement embodies special balance of payments criteria of its own setting forth the conditions under which a contracting party may employ discriminatory or nondiscriminatory quantitative restrictions on trade. However, the GATT does provide for consultation with the Fund on all problems relating to balance of payments, monetary reserves and foreign exchange practices, and these consultations have resulted in common policies in a number of cases. It would be desirable to establish common rules for the use of discriminatory or nondiscriminatory restrictions, along the lines of those included in the code of fair practices recommended in Chapter 20. The determination of the justification for the use of restrictions for balance of payments reasons should be left to the Monetary Fund or perhaps to a decision arising out of joint consultations between the Fund and the GATT.

19. The U.S. Congress has never given legislative recognition to the GATT nor has it voted funds for its operating expenses. U.S. participation as a contracting party to the GATT is derived from the general authority of the Reciprocal Trade Agreements Act.

The primary function of the GATT should be in the field of commercial policy as opposed to financial policy. If a member were permitted to employ over-all restrictions on balance of payments grounds, but not discriminatory restrictions, it would be the duty of the GATT to see that the restrictions imposed were not designed to give protection to uneconomical domestic industries or to discriminate between countries or currency areas. Or if a member were permitted to employ discriminatory restrictions it would be the duty of the GATT to see that the discrimination was limited to the scarce currency country and that the member did not employ discriminatory controls to encourage production which could not be sustained in their absence.

The GATT or a successor organization will be concerned with various commercial policy problems in addition to those relating to the use of quantitative trade restrictions for balance of payments reasons. There is the problem of import controls undertaken in connection with domestic farm price support programs, of export controls to implement international commodity agreements, of controls to protect the domestic economy in periods of commodity shortages, and of controls for security purposes. While practices in other commercial policy fields, including tariff practices, have important balance of payments implications, they must be subject to principles and regulations which are kept separate and distinct from those applying to temporary restrictions permitted on balance of payments grounds.

Cooperation between the Fund and the GATT

There must be the closest cooperation between the Monetary Fund and the GATT in any program for the restoration of currency convertibility. Progress toward a condition of full multilateral settlements must be measured by the reduction in the degree of discrimination employed by members in their quantitative trade controls. While it would be desirable to obtain an agreement under which every member of the Fund and the GATT would gradually eliminate all quantitative restrictions for the protection of its balance of payments, the effective maintenance of such an agreement is too hazardous, and the success of the convertibility program should not be endangered by the failure of a few countries to achieve continuing over-all balance without the use of controls.

The essential requirements for a convertibility program are that countries maintain over-all balance except for temporary deficits held within the limits of their quotas or drawing rights, and that any restrictions on current transactions be nondiscriminatory. It would be the function of GATT to supervise the gradual elimination of discrimination by the substitution of global quotas for bilateral or regional quotas. Members of the GATT might agree to put an additional percentage of their imports under world open general license or under global quotas each year, so that by the end of, say, three years no discriminatory controls would remain. The removal of discriminatory trade controls would of course have to be accompanied by the gradual establishment of payments facilities for full multilateral settlements. This would be the task of the Monetary Fund and of the regional payments organizations.

The Need for a Strong International Trade Organization

The present GATT, which was intended simply as a temporary organization pending the establishment of the International Trade Organization under the terms of the Havana Charter, must either be strengthened or replaced if it is to perform the functions necessary for the administration of a code of fair trade practices. A code of fair exchange practices without its counterpart in fair trade practices would have limited significance. There are two possible ways of developing an effective international trade organization. First, the United Nations might call another international conference to rewrite the ITO charter in a manner acceptable to the U.S. Congress and the American business community. This procedure would take several years and might easily fail for the same reasons the ITO failed.

The second approach would be for Congress to pass legislation specifically authorizing U.S. membership in the GATT and accepting its obligations. Acceptance of the obligations of the GATT as presently written would require certain changes in U.S. customs laws,[20] and changes in the Agricultural Adjustment Act of 1934, as amended. Substantial amendments to the GATT itself should be made before

20. While the U.S. Congress enacted a Customs Simplification law in July 1953, the act eliminated certain important features of the bill as proposed by the Administration, including the substitution of export value for foreign value as a basis for customs valuation.

the Agreement is presented to the contracting parties for legislative approval. The GATT has been seriously hampered by lack of funds. By giving it legislative status the governments of the members could be asked to appropriate money for its operation.

Just as the Monetary Fund would cooperate with regional monetary organizations so also would the GATT work with regional organizations in the trade field. Such regional organizations include the OEEC which has in operation a code of trade liberalization of its own, and the European Coal and Steel Community.

Chapter 23

THE PAYMENTS SYSTEM AND FREE
WORLD DEFENSE

INTERNATIONAL EQUILIBRIUM and currency convertibility are not ends in themselves and like free markets in strategic raw materials and low taxes, it may be well to sacrifice them to important national and international objectives. It is the conclusion of this study, however, that trade discrimination and exchange restrictions on current transactions are not only economically harmful, but they are responsible for a misallocation of resources which the free world can ill afford if it is to defend itself against internal and external aggression. Paradoxically, however, the defense program is frequently cited as one of the reasons why nations cannot achieve equilibrium and currency convertibility.

In the preceding chapters we have seen that world trade is directed by a monstrously complex network of trade and payments arrangements which has minimized the role of market forces in determining what nations will produce and what they will sell to one another. However inexact and inefficient the control mechanism of the Moscow dictatorship may be, the Soviet economic machine with its rich resources, its vast area and a third of the world's population, is guided and coordinated in accordance with a unified plan of action. Regardless of projected plans for military forces, the outcome of a generation of continued cold war will be determined by the relative rates of economic growth in the free and the Soviet areas of the world. The free world cannot compete with the Soviet sphere in this struggle for world power without some kind of an organizing principle. In the absence of political unification the principal coordinating force available to the free world economy is the operation of unfettered markets for goods and capital. In the broadest sense therefore the defense of the free world and its institutions depends upon the creation of a payments mechanism which will permit the unrestricted operations of these market forces.

The creation of an adequate payments mechanism would also help eliminate recurrent financial crises such as have occurred in Britain, France and other countries during the postwar period. These crises interfere with defense production and cause a disruption of trade and production in other countries. They have been due in part to a lack of sufficient foreign exchange reserves to permit countries to make an orderly adjustment to shifts in their balance of payments positions. They are also the products of haphazard exchange practices and improper internal economic policies of the nations which have been in more or less continuous disequilibrium since the war.

Problems of the Defense of the Free World

In addition to the contribution of free trade and orderly exchange arrangements to the strength of the free world there are certain immediate problems arising out of the defense program, the solution of which involves the system of world payments. We may list these problems as follows:

1. The allocation of defense production in accordance with the principle of comparative cost, except where strategic considerations modify the application of this principle.

2. The problem of sharing the burden of defense among the North Atlantic Treaty Organization (NATO) countries.

3. Minimizing the burden of U.S. foreign aid and maximizing the contribution of U.S. foreign aid to the defense of the free world.

4. The achievement of a greater degree of economic integration among the European members of NATO.

These problems are closely interrelated and the manner in which they are dealt with will have an important bearing upon any program which might be developed for the restoration of currency convertibility in Western Europe and the sterling area. Moreover, any program for the creation of a free world multilateral payments system must include the coordination of military procurement and defense support with foreign trade and exchange.

REARMAMENT AND INTRA-EUROPEAN TRADE AND PAYMENTS [1]

European defense involves far more than the assembling of divisions and the determination of a chain of command. A unified Euro-

1. Some of the ideas in this section have been taken from William Diebold, Jr.,

pean army must be supported by a coordinated system of supply and of defense production. At this writing, the extent to which supplies for the European defense forces will be procured by individual governments or, alternatively, by NATO and the proposed European Defense Community have not been determined.[2] Whatever mechanism is chosen, the defense program requires an efficient system of trade and foreign exchange which will permit a proper allocation of resources for defense production not only within Europe but among all the NATO countries.

Financing Defense Programs in Europe

The production of armaments and the raising of armies places two kinds of burdens on national economies. There is first of all the burden of local currency expenditures which are a charge against domestic budgets. A portion of these expenditures, however, gives rise directly or indirectly to a foreign exchange drain. Under present conditions this may be divided into a hard-currency drain and a soft-currency drain. Two countries which have the same level of defense expenditures may have substantially different foreign exchange drains, while two countries with the same ratio of defense expenditure to their national income may find the relative burdens of the accompanying foreign drains substantially different. This may lead to serious balance of payments disturbances, especially if the countries with the heaviest foreign exchange drain due to rearmament are also the countries with the weakest balance of payments position.

One way in which this problem might be handled is by making available special EPU credits to countries unable to finance the additional foreign exchange drain resulting from their share of the defense program. These credits could be financed either by special grants made available by other NATO countries, as a part of their contribution to the defense program, or by special grants to the EPU from the United States.[3] This plan would enable countries to place orders for military supplies and materials for producing

Trade and Payments in Western Europe (Harper, New York, 1952), especially Chapter 23.

2. The proposed treaty for the establishment of the EDC provides for a common budget.

3. See Albert O. Hirschman, "The European Payments Union: Negotiations and the Issues," *The Review of Economics and Statistics*, February 1951, pp. 49–55.

them throughout the EPU area without regard to the impact of such orders on the balance of payments. If procurement were in the hands of the EDC it could require local currency contributions from its members which would be freely available for use in any EPU country. Defense expenditures, however, should be made on the basis of quality and price, with no attempt to use the common defense fund to correct disparities in the balance of payments positions of member countries arising from nondefense trade. If the EDC so allocated its orders as to reduce the deficits of countries in over-all disequilibrium as a result of inflation or overvalued exchange rates, it might hinder the rearmament effort by encouraging an improper use of resources.

Financing the Dollar Drain with MSA Funds

So long as European currencies are not convertible into dollars we must make a distinction between the dollar and the nondollar drains of the defense expenditures. An immediate dollar drain arises from the employment of raw materials and equipment which must be acquired with dollars. But there may be an indirect dollar drain in the use of local materials and labor, if these resources could have been employed for dollar-earning or dollar-saving production. An indirect dollar drain may also result from the importation from soft-currency countries of commodities needed for defense production since these must be paid for by exports of goods which might otherwise have gone to the dollar area.

In a sense, every expenditure on rearmament is a potential dollar drain since the resources might have been used in a way to earn or save dollars. Morevover, when NATO members increase their purchases from other members of the EPU these purchases will as a rule result in at least a partial loss of gold which can be traced to the defense program. Thus if only the direct dollar cost of the expanded defense program of a NATO nation is covered by U.S. aid, the dollar position of the country will suffer as a consequence of rearmament. If on the other hand the combined direct and *potential* dollar drain is covered by dollar aid, the dollar position of the country is likely to be improved over what it might have been without rearmament. This is true because covering defense expenditures with dollar aid is equivalent to providing a dollar market for defense production. Thus when the United States government purchases defense goods in NATO countries for delivery to Western European armies, it is improving the dollar position of these countries by providing an additional dollar market for their products. The only case where this would not be true is that of a country which could fully utilize for the output of dollar-earning or dollar-saving commodities the resources it directed to defense production.

The Mutual Security Act of 1952 provided for three types of grant assistance for Western Europe. The purpose of all three was to promote European defense. (1) About $3.1 billion was appropriated for military items to be made available either to individual countries or to NATO or to the proposed EDC. (2) A portion of these military items could be purchased with dollars through "offshore procurement" in Europe. (3) About $1.3 billion was made available for raw materials, commodities and equipment needed to support Europe's defense production program.[4] It has been estimated that about a billion and a half dollars in contracts were placed in the fiscal year 1953 to procure military items in Europe and at the time of writing (mid-1953), U.S. government officials were strongly in favor of expanding this form of U.S. military assistance to contribute both to Europe's defense and to the solution of the dollar problem.[5]

Since the offshore purchase technique is likely to become the principal form of U.S. governmental financial assistance to Western Europe over the next few years, it is important to consider how this help can make a maximum contribution to both defense production in Europe and to the solution of international payments problems. At the

4. Appropriations are contained in Public Law 547 (82d Congress), Chapter 11, Title 3. The Department of Defense may also use a portion of its own appropriation for the purchase of equipment in Europe for United States armed forces.

In 1953 Congress appropriated for use in Europe in fiscal 1954, $1.9 billion for military assistance (plus $1.3 billion carried over from fiscal 1953). These funds may be used for military items purchased in the United States for delivery to European countries or for offshore procurement abroad. In addition, $390 million was appropriated for "mutual defense financing" (plus $116 million carried over from fiscal 1953) to be used for the purchase of goods and services needed for the support of Western Europe's defense production.

5. The Director of the Mutual Security Agency, Harold Stassen, has stated that the Administration expects to use about $1.5 billion for offshore procurement in Western Europe during the fiscal year 1954. (*The New York Times,* May 6, 1953, p. 16.) See also *Eighth Quarterly Report to the President,* Director of Defense Mobilization, Washington, January 1, 1953, pp. 48–49; "Text of Ambassador Draper's Report to President Truman on European Situation," *The New York Times,* August 29, 1952, p. 6; and "Secretary Sawyer's Survey of Europe," *Foreign Commerce Weekly,* December 22, 1952, p. 16.

time of writing, there appear to be three principal criteria employed by the U.S. Defense Department in negotiating offshore purchase contracts. First, there is the desire to place orders with firms which can meet the tests of quality, price and delivery. Except as this criterion is modified by strategic considerations, it should be the principal factor governing decisions on procurement throughout the NATO area, including the United States. European firms ought to compete for orders on the basis of price and quality, among themselves and with American and Canadian firms. Offshore procurement should encourage competitive biddings and the lowering of costs, not provide guaranteed and protected markets to be won by political negotiations or determined solely with reference to the balance of payments of the nation in which a firm happens to be located. Strategy may of course require that production facilities for certain defense goods be located in one area rather than another but within these limitations there should be plenty of scope for procurement decisions based on market principles.

The balance of payments criterion has loomed large in the determination of offshore procurement policy. For example, at the Lisbon Conference of NATO in February 1952, the United States agreed to place orders for at least $200 million worth of equipment and materials in France,[6] in order to assist that country in meeting its dollar deficit. The offshore procurement program can and should contribute to the permanent solution of Europe's dollar problem, but without detracting from the fundamental task of expanding Western European defense output. This major objective cannot be realized if offshore procurement is to be determined by the dollar positions of particular European countries.

The National vs. the Regional Approach to the Dollar Problem

The present offshore procurement program applies the dollar-balance criterion to the individual country rather than to the NATO countries as a whole or to a smaller group of continental OEEC countries such as the European Defense Community. This approach has serious limitations from the standpoint of progress toward a broader

6. During the fiscal year ended June 30, 1952, $335 million out of a total of $684 million in offshore procurement contracts were placed in France. See "Text of Ambassador Draper's Report," *The New York Times*, August 29, 1952, p. 6.

solution of Europe's payments problem. By using U.S. aid dollars to procure military items in Western Europe for use by European defense forces, a separate system of payments for financing trade within the area is superimposed upon the EPU system. If European countries are to compete for U.S. aid dollars it will mean a dual pricing system, which in fact exists for a number of European commodities.[7] Dual pricing inhibits progress toward unified world markets and currency convertibility. One way to avoid this practice would be to eliminate all offshore purchases directly with dollars in favor of making all purchases in the currencies of the NATO countries acquired with dollars from the EPU. Under present conditions, however, this system would have the disadvantage of leaving countries no incentive to compete for dollars.

The other way to avoid dual pricing and a dual method of financing intra-European trade would be to establish currency convertibility in Europe, so that it would make little difference to a country whether it sold for dollars or for European currencies. Only under these conditions is it possible to have prices and markets in Western Europe which are fully competitive with dollar goods. This then should be the goal of our offshore procurement program.

Contribution of Offshore Procurement to Currency Convertibility

The approach which the author suggests is a combination of the two alternative methods described above; it would complement the program for convertibility outlined in Chapters 21 and 22. Most offshore purchases, whether by the United States government directly or through NATO or the EDC, would be financed with the currencies of the NATO countries acquired with dollars from the EPU. At the same time, however, the EPU agreement should be altered to provide for 100 per cent convertibility of surpluses into dollars when needed by the creditor countries to meet current deficits payable in gold or dollars.[8] In addition, a definite schedule for the removal of all discriminatory trade controls should be adopted, which would achieve a fully multilateral system within a period of, say, two years. If Britain

7. For a discussion of dual prices in Western Europe, see Diebold, *op. cit.,* Chapter 15.

8. The convertibility of surplus positions into gold or dollars would be modified by the extension of credits and of drawing rights, as suggested in Chapters 21 and 22.

should withdraw from the EPU, offshore purchases in the sterling area and in countries belonging to the "convertible" transferable account system but outside the EPU, might be financed with sterling acquired with dollars from Britain.

The advantage of directing U.S. offshore procurement through the EPU during the period of transition to full multilateral settlements is twofold. First, it would avoid a two-currency and possibly a two-price system for the purchase of military supplies and equipment for the EDC and for other military agencies. Second, it would strengthen the dollar position of the EPU so that it would have less difficulty in achieving 100 per cent convertibility of surpluses into dollars. There may be cases, however, in which the system would need to be modified to enable a country which was in debt to the EPU and extremely short of dollars, to cover the direct dollar costs of filling defense orders. In such cases a partial payment in dollars might be made by the purchasing authorities.[9]

It should be emphasized that the system of offshore procurement suggested above is desirable only in the context of a program for convertibility along the lines suggested in Chapter 22. Offshore procurement through the EPU mechanism under present conditions would make no contribution to convertibility and would remove the incentive for competing for dollars.

Dollars earned through offshore procurement not only provide a means of financing Western Europe's dollar deficit but the offshore purchase program can facilitate the transition to full convertibility. For a permanent solution of Europe's dollar problem, however, the OEEC countries must be able to meet their dollar requirements without offshore procurement. This means that Western Europe must either expand her dollar earnings or reduce her dollar purchases as offshore procurement declines, or both. It is quite possible that the expansion of Europe's capital goods industries made necessary by the defense production program will assist the OEEC countries in making the structural changes required to capture a larger share of the dollars from third countries. The OEEC and NATO should give serious

9. The technique of channeling dollars through the EPU might also be used by the U.S. government in making other defense expenditures in European NATO countries. U.S. government expenditures on goods and services used abroad, including offshore procurement, totaled $2.6 billion in the fiscal year 1953.

consideration to the problems of the transition in making recommendations with respect to the offshore procurement program.

THE PROBLEM OF EUROPEAN ECONOMIC INTEGRATION

One objective of American foreign policy in the postwar period has been the promotion of economic integration among the OEEC countries. U.S. policy has favored the economic and political unification of Western Europe for three principal reasons. First, the policymakers believe that the elimination of barriers to the free flow of goods, capital and manpower in Western Europe will contribute to that region's economic strength as a bulwark against Communism. Second, measures for economic unification help support political unification and solidarity. Closer economic and political ties seem essential not only for presenting a united front against Communism but as a primary condition for the economic and military rearmament of Germany. Unless German sovereignty can be at least partially submerged in a political and economic federation which includes the major Western European countries, her rearmament might constitute a threat to France and other Western European nations. Finally, economic unification is believed to be a necessary counterpart to a European Defense Community, since a common defense force must be supported by a coordinated defense production program.

These reasons have also been the driving force behind concrete European measures and specific proposals for economic integration such as the EPU, the European Coal and Steel Community, the various economic and political recommendations of the Council of Europe, the Benelux Customs Union and other proposed customs unions including the Franco-Italian and the Scandinavian.[10] All these arrangements for breaking down trade barriers involve currency issues and any proposal for dealing with European payments relations inevitably has a bearing on the problem of economic integration. For example, European officials have expressed the fear that the restoration of sterling convertibility in advance of the convertibility of other EPU currencies might destroy the EPU.[11] Belgium, Western

10. For a discussion of various proposals for European economic integration see Diebold, *op. cit.*, Chapters 11, 13, 17–21.

11. See, for example, "Europe Fears Deal for Convertibility by Britain and the United States," *The New York Times*, January 25, 1953, p. 1.

Germany and Switzerland might restore convertibility along with Britain, and the remaining countries would be left to bilateral trading. It is feared that such a development would endanger the Benelux Customs Union, the European Coal and Steel Community and perhaps the European Defense Community. For example, the single market for coal and steel and the proposed single markets for agricultural commodities could scarcely exist without a multilateral payments system among the members of the trading group.

Economic Integration and Trade Discrimination

The term "economic integration" has been used rather loosely in the literature and too often systems of trade discrimination have been justified as being, in fact, a form of economic integration. The economic integration of sovereign states involves the distribution of their total resources in accordance with some economizing principle or rational plan.[12] While the unhindered flow of goods and services across national boundaries may be an essential condition for economic integration based on the coordinating principle of free markets,[13] it is neither a sufficient condition for economic integration as we have defined it, nor is it a condition which can be maintained for long without additional measures of economic coordination or unification. The EPU and the OEEC have for example not been able to create a system of intra-European trade unhampered by quantitative trade restrictions through the establishment of a payments mechanism and the formulation of a code of trade liberalization. The EPU must inevitably fail in seeking to force intra-European trade into an artificial mold in which each EPU member maintains a balance with the EPU area as a whole. Moreover, it is only with a free movement of capital and other mobile factors of production across national boundaries and the coordination of governmental investment programs, fiscal and monetary policies and foreign exchange and trade practices, that true economic integration can exist. Further, to develop a balance of payments pattern consistent with

12. For a discussion of this subject see Raymond F. Mikesell, "Economic Integration of Sovereign States: Some Fundamental Problems," in *Money, Trade, and Economic Growth* (Essays in Honor of John H. Williams), Macmillan, New York, 1951, pp. 76–93.

13. It is also possible to have economic integration along Soviet lines in which the coordinating principle is state planning and operation, dictated by a single authority.

free trade within the EPU area or any part of it requires other measures for economic integration.

Except possibly under a scarce currency condition, progress toward true economic integration is not promoted by discriminatory trade and currency arrangements. An arrangement like EPU is not to be confused with economic integration, and the demise of the EPU in favor of currency convertibility and nondiscriminatory trade would not be a retrogression from economic integration. Of course, if certain Western European countries were to develop a full monetary union with a common monetary, fiscal and foreign exchange control system as well as a common currency, economic integration could be achieved under present conditions of interregional disequilibrium. But in spite of the progress of the Benelux Union there is little hope for the early creation of a larger economic and monetary union in Western Europe.[14] Meanwhile the disciplines required of nations to restore convertibility and nondiscrimination in their trade relations with the world as a whole will provide a wholesome experience for any group of countries contemplating the even harsher disciplines of economic integration, if indeed economic integration can be accomplished without a complete merger of national sovereignties.

Why Western Europe?

It may be appropriate to ask at this point whether Western Europe is the proper subject for economic integration. In view of the need to mobilize the resources of the free world for its defense against Communism, why not work for the economic integration of all the NATO states, or of the entire free world? Economic integration of the free world should indeed be our goal, and one of the surest ways to move toward it is to eliminate the barriers which hamper the flow of goods and capital. To this end, all free world trade should be financed solely in currencies or means of payment which are readily available for use in any currency area, so that the need for discrimination on currency grounds will disappear. Interconvertibility between the dollar, the pound sterling and the major currencies of Europe is particularly important because they finance the vast bulk of the world's trade.

14. See "Lessons for Economic Federation," *The Economist*, November 15, 1952, pp. 434–35, for a review of the progress of the Benelux economic union.

There are, however, other measures of economic integration which at least for the time being will have to be limited to a smaller group of countries. For example, coordinated plans for defense production which are possible among the NATO countries are not politically feasible for the entire free world. Other measures such as the European Coal and Steel Community or perhaps the initiation of a broader economic federation among the EDC countries [15] may be possible for a group of continental countries but could not include Britain, because of her sterling area ties, nor Sweden and Switzerland because they are not members of NATO. But if a small group of countries achieves economic union among themselves will not this result in discrimination against nonmembers unless there are no restrictions of any kind, including tariffs, on trade with the rest of the world? It is true that the formation of a customs union involves discrimination, just as Michigan discriminates against Ontario in favor of Ohio. But a complete customs union or economic union normally has the advantages of the free movement of capital and other factors of production lacked by the typical preferential tariff or trade agreement between two countries. Thus in a customs union there may be a net gain in total trade rather than simply a shift in the pattern of trade at the expense of other countries.

Finally, we may say that while any proposal for the restoration of currency convertibility ought to take into account regional groups of countries which are seeking to develop greater economic integration, universal multilateral settlements as such will not interfere with such efforts. What this conclusion does imply, however, is that it would be far better for Belgium or Britain to achieve convertibility in accordance with some common program embracing all EPU members.

Free World Organization

One of the lessons of postwar experience is that international economic and political problems are not solved by the creation of international organizations. In the economic field international organizations have no sovereign powers and their ability to impose their collective will on individual member states is largely limited to persuasion, the denial of financial assistance, trade discrimination by

15. Belgium, France, Germany, Italy, Luxembourg and the Netherlands are members of the Coal and Steel Community and of the proposed EDC.

other members, or the threat of public rebuke and suspension of membership. The exercise of sanctions cannot be relied upon to achieve the objectives set forth in the charters of international organizations. Regardless of the commitments contained in its charter, an international organization is powerless to carry out measures which are contrary to the policies of even a substantial minority of its members. The primary contribution of international organizations is to provide an instrument for coordinating and implementing the currently agreed policies and programs of the great majority of their members. They also provide a forum for airing complaints against other members and a means of avoiding retaliation. Finally, an organization with a strong secretariat can continually remind members of their obligations and require them to justify actions contrary to international agreements.

The most successful international organizations are those which have well-defined functions and ample powers for discharging them. Organizations charged with the formulation of broad policies, without the power to implement them, have not in general been successful. This helps to explain why the EPU and the International Bank have a significant record of concrete accomplishment while the Monetary Fund and the United Nations Economic and Social Council have not realized the high hopes of their founders. The Monetary Fund might become a highly successful operating institution if its functions were agreed upon by a group representing its largest stockholders. But it cannot proceed effectively on the basis of the broad objectives and obligations of members set forth in its Charter.

Proposals for a New International Monetary Organization

Recently proposals have emanated from a branch of the United States government and from *The Economist* for the establishment of a new international organization with large dollar resources to be used to restore the convertibility of sterling and other "key" currencies into dollars.[16] The principal objection to these suggested plans

16. A proposal for an Atlantic Reserve System by certain officials of the Mutual Security Administration and put forth in a classified document popularly known as the "Green Book" was widely reported in the press in October 1952. The ideas expressed in the "Green Book" did not express the official position of the MSA or of the United States government but simply represented a working document which was circulated among officials in Washington. According to press reports the "Green Book" pro-

is that while they may represent some improvement over the Monetary Fund, they offer little promise of overcoming the fundamental difficulties which have beset the Fund throughout the postwar period. They provide larger resources but, as we have seen, the availability of adequate international reserves is only one of the several requirements for universal convertibility. No voluntary association of sovereign powers can keep its members from engaging in internal monetary and fiscal practices which lead to balance of payments disequilibrium. These practices are the very essence of national sovereignty itself. International control over governmental budgets and central banking policies means, in fact, the merging of national sovereignties in a single federated state. The United States government is unlikely to subscribe $10 or $20 billion to a new international monetary institution with the same inherent weaknesses as the Bretton Woods organization.

Basis for U.S. Assistance

But on what basis then should the United States subscribe additional resources to the Monetary Fund or make available another large line of credit to Britain? Certainly it should be made very clear just what we may hope to achieve by any new effort for monetary reform. General undertakings of currency convertibility with broad escape clauses covering vaguely defined conditions will be of little benefit. For example, we should not seek an agreement that countries will not control their own imports. This would be no more effective than the Monetary Fund agreement. The basic condition for additional U.S. financial assistance to Britain, the Monetary Fund and the EPU should be the removal of all *discriminatory* trade controls in accordance with a definite schedule and the creation of a fully multilateral payments system. This would mean, as a minimum, an agreement on the part of every EPU member, including Britain, to abandon all discriminatory controls within a specified period—say, two years.

---

posed the establishment of an Atlantic Economic Board which would serve as a forum for discussing the coordination of economic policies among its members; an Atlantic Commodity Board which would deal with problems of development and long-term purchase contracts; and an Atlantic Reserve System to which each member would contribute according to its gold holdings. The Atlantic Reserve System would tie together the dollar, the pound sterling and a common international currency of the six EDC countries. (For a review of American press reports on the "Green Book" proposals, see "Is Discrimination Inevitable?" *The Economist*, November 22, 1952, pp. 591–93.)

It would also mean the convertibility of sterling currently acquired by nonresidents and the creation of a fully multilateral EPU or some other arrangement whereby intra-European trade would be financed on a convertible basis.

The United States could not ask for such an agreement without certain undertakings of its own as to its imports and foreign investments. Other countries cannot be required to maintain convertibility in the face of a severe reduction in the supply of dollars. One approach would be to relieve foreign countries of the obligation to maintain the convertibility of their currencies whenever the total amount of dollars currently made available by the United States to the rest of the world fell below an agreed level. During the period 1936–1938 the supply of U.S. dollars arising out of imports of goods and services, private remittances and long-term capital outflow averaged about $4 billion annually. This was the equivalent of about $9 billion in current U.S. export prices. In 1952 U.S. dollars from these same sources plus U.S. government and IBRD loans totaled nearly $18 billion. Even taking into account the structural changes brought about by the war it is difficult to believe that the world's payments mechanism could not adjust to this level of current dollar outflow.

An obvious drawback to making convertibility depend upon the level of U.S. dollar availabilities is that a reduction in U.S. imports or foreign investment might be brought about by improper policies on the part of other countries as well as by a depression here or higher U.S. trade barriers. Moreover, short-term fluctuations in our imports and foreign investments are inevitable, and their impact ought to be dealt with by the use of national and international reserves, not by a return to inconvertibility. However, foreign countries should not be expected to maintain convertibility in the event of a prolonged U.S. depression. Moreover, the United States certainly should be expected to lower its tariff walls, eliminate the "Buy American" Act, and reform its customs administration, as contributions to the success of any convertibility program.[17] In fact, unless

17. The recommendations of the Public Advisory Board for Mutual Security which are set forth in *A Trade and Tariff Policy in the National Interest* (Washington, February 1953) provide an excellent basis for a U.S. trade and tariff policy designed to facilitate world-wide currency convertibility. It is estimated that the adoption of the meas-

the United States is willing to adopt measures which will give foreign producers greater access to American markets, it would be unwise for this country to risk additional funds to promote world-wide currency convertibility.

Maintenance of Over-all Balance

Except for short-term fluctuations in their balance of payments resulting from seasonal, cyclical and other temporary factors, all countries would need to maintain over-all balance. Nations threatening to exhaust their credit lines because of continual deficits would be asked to take appropriate measures to get into balance as a condition for further assistance from the EPU or the Monetary Fund. The same principle would apply to Britain with respect to any special line of credit made available by the United States. Certain countries might find it necessary to restrict imports, but the restrictions could not be discriminatory, nor could these countries enter into bilateral arrangements with other nations.

While many of the raw materials countries might continue to employ quantitative restrictions and multiple exchange rates to balance their foreign exchange receipts and expenditures, the ultimate success of the proposed arrangements would depend upon the willingness and ability of the larger industrial countries of Western Europe to achieve a balance on current account without heavy dependence on direct trade controls. Unless the local demand for both domestic and foreign goods is maintained at a level which can be satisfied without artificial restriction of the demand for foreign goods, Britain and the other EPU countries will not be able to compete successfully in world markets. If domestic producers as a group cannot compete successfully with foreign goods in the home market, how can they compete in world markets? The failure of Western European countries to compete in world markets would necessitate a continual reduction of their imports both from the dollar area and from one another in order to maintain a balance in their international accounts. If import restrictions within Europe were carried very far the various programs for European economic integration would be threatened and the defense program itself would suffer. The end result would

ures recommended in this report would have the effect of increasing U.S. imports by $700–$1,000 million annually (p. 65).

probably be a breakdown of the multilateral system and the reestablishment of a discriminatory system for Western Europe.

It is essential therefore that Britain and the other EPU countries embark upon a program of convertibility and nondiscrimination only if they accept the disciplines such a program entails. Against the risk of failure from this source the United States cannot expect to insure itself, not even by the most solemn covenants. It is a risk which is inherent in the shifting economic policies of modern democratic states. But if an agreement on currency convertibility were reached with Britain and the other EPU countries, these countries would be hazarding their economic destinies upon the future policies of the United States, since the successful operation of a multilateral payments system would depend in large measure upon the domestic and foreign economic policies of this country.

A Program for Convertibility

It is not the purpose of the author to set forth a detailed program for the restoration of convertibility. In fact, many of the specific suggestions which have been made throughout this book may be rendered obsolete within the next few months. There are, however, certain broad conclusions from this study which seem relevant for the development of a program for convertibility. These are summarized in the following paragraphs.

1. Convertibility is more likely to succeed if it is undertaken gradually and through the cooperative action of Britain and the leading Western European countries. Although the creation of a new organization is not recommended, a program of convertibility would require the coordinated efforts of existing institutions, including the EPU, the British Commonwealth Conference, the Monetary Fund, the GATT, the OEEC and NATO (or other organizations which control military procurement in Western Europe). This coordination might be achieved by a committee of high level representatives from the United States, the United Kingdom, the Commonwealth Conference, the OEEC, the GATT, NATO and the Monetary Fund, which would formulate a plan of action for submission to the governments and international bodies which would have to act upon it. Since the plan would call for a revision of the EPU, all the members remaining in

that organization would be required to ratify the program. The GATT would need to be amended in order to carry out its assigned functions. The Monetary Fund Agreement would not need amendment but appropriate changes in policy would have to be made by its executive board.

2. The assistance of the United States would be crucial to the success of any convertibility plan which is likely to succeed. Such assistance would include a liberalization of U.S. trade policies, a substantial stabilization loan to the United Kingdom, and eventually, an additional subscription to the Monetary Fund.

3. The approach to convertibility would consist of (a) a gradual removal of the degree of discrimination achieved by the substitution of global quotas or world open general licenses for existing bilateral or regional quotas and regional open general licenses and (b) a shift to a system of 100 per cent gold settlements in the EPU. The process by which sterling would become convertible would depend upon Britain's relationship to the EPU.

4. The resources of the Monetary Fund should be available for assisting the EPU when that organization was temporarily unable to meet its obligations. It would seem desirable for the Fund to have a representative on the Managing Board of the EPU.

5. While substantial funds should be available from the Monetary Fund, the EPU and other sources for meeting temporary deficits in the balance of payments, all countries must achieve over-all balance within a reasonable period of time. Some countries undoubtedly will find it easier to establish and maintain equilbrium by the adoption of a fluctuating exchange rate.

6. While the convertibility of sterling and of other major currencies does not require the elimination of all quantitative import restrictions, it is not likely to succeed if Britain and other leading countries find it necessary to maintain tight restrictions on imports. The removal of these restrictions will require a reduction of monetary demand achieved through monetary and fiscal measures, increased productivity, and in some cases a readjustment of exchange rates.

7. The establishment of international equilibrium requires an adjustment of the structure of production in the nondollar world, with a view to reducing the dependence on the United States for raw materials, foodstuffs, and capital equipment. While the restoration

of convertibility will help to promote this adjustment, other more direct measures are needed to hasten this process. These measures include international loans and technical assistance for the expansion of primary production in the underdeveloped areas, planning and direction by regional economic development bodies such as the Colombo Plan organization and a large flow of capital to Western Europe for the expansion of the capital goods industries.

8. Even if a system of free world multilateral payments is reestablished, there is always the possibility that it may break down as a result of a major U.S. depression or some other economic or political disturbance. For this reason it may be wise to retain the structure of limited multilateral payments systems such as the EPU and the sterling area, so that world trade will not revert again to bilateralism. The code of fair exchange and trade practices suggested in Chapter 20 sets forth certain rules for the Monetary Fund and the GATT, which would apply in the event of the recurrence of a scarce currency situation.

Conclusions

It should be emphasized that the world's payments problems cannot be dealt with apart from a vast complex of other international economic and political issues. Currency convertibility is not likely to be achieved by pious resolutions that countries "will work toward convertibility and the removal of restrictions as a desirable long-range objective." Nor is a "dash for convertibility" by Britain or by most other major powers outside the Western Hemisphere likely to succeed. It must be achieved by concerted action of the leading countries of the free world to create a system of universal multilateral settlements. Moreover, this coordinated program must include not simply a mechanism for convertibility and the provision of reserves, but must encompass all those aspects of the world economy which are basic to the reestablishment of world equilibrium. Above all, there must be the will among the major nations of the free world—including the United States—to adopt the policies and programs which are essential to the creation of an orderly system of world payments.

Our suggested program for achieving an orderly system of world payments is a marked departure from the pre-1914 gold standard and even a substantial modification of the system envisaged by the postwar planners at the Bretton Woods Conference. We have sought to define the minimum conditions for a workable system of multilateral trade and orderly trading arrangements. Yet in the light of prevailing political attitudes both in the United States and abroad, these proposals may be regarded as highly unrealistic. If they are, we may have to give up for the indefinite future any idea of a return to multilateralism. Although there may continue to be limited multilateral settlements, regional clearing mechanisms such as the EPU are likely to prove unstable. If the EPU and the sterling area were to break down before currency convertibility is restored, much of the world's trade would probably be conducted on a bilateral basis. Without currency convertibility, efforts to establish a code of fair trade and foreign exchange practices are doomed to failure. Under these conditions cooperative action among the free nations in the field of international trade must take the form of intergovernmental deals. Foreign trade policy then turns from the effort to establish the conditions of a free market and passes into the realm of intergovernmental planning.

ADDENDUM

SINCE THE COMPLETION of the text of this book in May 1953, there have been a number of developments in the field of foreign exchange practices and policies, only a few of which could be noted in correcting the galley proof. While no attempt will be made to catalogue the changes in exchange control systems of individual countries, the following paragraphs indicate some of the major events in the foreign exchange field which occurred during the summer and fall of 1953.

The European Payments Union

In June 1953 the Council for the Organisation for European Economic Co-operation agreed to extend the operations of the EPU for another year until June 30, 1954. No significant changes were made in the operation of the clearing union. However, certain alterations were made in the amounts of credits which extreme creditors agreed to extend to the Union above the limits set by their regular quotas. Provision was made also for a rise in interest rates to be paid by debtor countries to the Union and to be paid by the Union to creditor countries.

During the EPU's fiscal year, July 1, 1952 to June 30, 1953, there was a reduction in important extreme creditor positions. The surpluses of the B.L.E.U., Portugal and Sweden were reduced, and Italy—which had been a large creditor country—became a debtor country. Germany, the Netherlands and Switzerland increased their surpluses during 1952–1953, and Britain reduced her deficit position by $371 million during this period, $172 million of which can be attributed to the operation of the dollar commodity arbitrage scheme in August 1952.[1] The volume of intra-EPU-country trade remained approximately the same as the previous year but the value was slightly lower.

Before the agreement to extend the EPU for another year was reached, there was considerable discussion within the OEEC on the question of currency convertibility. The British, in particular, were

---

1. *Third Annual Report of the Managing Board of the European Payments Union,* Organisation for European Economic Co-operation, Paris, 1953, p. 17.

anxious that their membership in the EPU would not prejudice any measures which they might want to take toward convertibility. The EPU managing board was fearful that sterling convertibility might wreck the EPU and argued for a gradual movement of all members toward convertibility. It was argued that sterling convertibility would encourage other EPU members to run up large EPU deficits in order to obtain dollars or dollar goods through sterling.[2]

Trade Restrictions and Convertibility

British and continental spokesmen also differed on the question of lifting trade barriers. The British plan for convertibility formulated at the Commonwealth Conference in December 1952 provided for the lifting of payments restrictions prior to the reduction of trade barriers.[3] Many of the continental countries, however, took the position that the removal of trade restrictions on both dollar and non-dollar goods should come first, or at least *pari passu* with currency convertibility. They were fearful that currency convertibility might result in an increase in trade restrictions and a loss of trade. This same concern was voiced by the Monetary Fund in its *Annual Report* for 1953: "If convertibility were to be achieved only by methods which require at the same time the imposition of types of restrictions and other hindrances which might reduce the volume of trade, the achievement would imply the frustration of the very purposes that convertibility was intended to serve." [4]

It is true that unless a country's competitive position is strong when it makes its currency convertible, a loss of trade to the dollar area might require that country to restrict its imports from all countries. On the other hand, currency convertibility will help make a country's industry more competitive since it can no longer sell in a protected foreign market. Moreover, currency convertibility for the major Western European countries would signal the end of the postwar transition period of dollar shortage, and the blanket provisions of the GATT and the IMF which sanction bilateral trade and payments

2. *Ibid.*, pp. 93–94; see also, "Europe against Convertibility," *The Banker*, March 1953, pp. 130–33; "Europe's Currency Plans," *The Banker*, June 1953, pp. 326–30; and "Clouds over the Plan," *The Banker*, May 1953, pp. 265–70.

3. "Strategy for Sterling," *The Economist*, June 6, 1953, pp. 677–79.

4. *Annual Report, 1953*, International Monetary Fund, Washington, September 1953, p. 41.

arrangements would presumably no longer apply. Finally, currency convertibility would mean that countries must subject the official values of their currencies to the test of free foreign exchange markets. Thus convertibility and the restoration of a fully multilateral payments system would be a major step in integrating world markets and price systems even though initially convertibility may be accompanied by some increase in trade barriers of a nondiscriminatory character.

Douglas Report on Sterling Convertibility

Lewis W. Douglas, in his report of July 14, 1953 to President Eisenhower, stated the case for sterling convertibility as follows:

Because sterling is a world currency, its fuller convertibility is essential to the restoration of economic freedom in large parts of the world. Other currencies may become convertible, but, in the absence of convertibility of sterling, the influence on the international economic environment will be limited. The convertibility of sterling, on the other hand, would have favorable and marked effects on the international economic environment, even in the absence of convertibility of other currencies. Accordingly, as sterling becomes more and more freely transferable into other currencies, particularly into the dollar, the economic choices which individuals enjoy become greater, the dominion of competition and of individual initiative becomes larger and the area of economic freedom expands. It is doubtful whether the world can recover a high degree of economic freedom or whether American exports—so important to large segments of our country—can enter foreign markets without benefit of continued American subventions and subsidies, unless sterling makes further progress toward its own emancipation. If further progress is not made toward the removal of restrictions on trade and a more unfettered exchange of currencies, it is quite likely that, despite any international political institutions that have been erected or that may be erected in the future, the unity of the free world will remain precarious and fragile. On these points American national interests are vitally concerned.[5]

While Mr. Douglas' report recognized that Britain and the other sterling area members must take additional measures to strengthen the competitive position of sterling exports, and to reduce internal inflationary pressures, he placed great emphasis on the removal of U.S. trade barriers and the elimination of violent fluctuations in the prices of internationally traded commodities, as conditions for the successful restoration of sterling convertibility. In this Mr. Douglas is in complete agreement with official British opinion.

5. White House Press Release, August 24, 1953.

At the time of writing it appears unlikely that Britain will embark upon convertibility until there is a clear indication of the course of American foreign economic policy. This will have to await the report of the President's Commission on Foreign Economic Policy (Randall Commission) and the willingness of the Administration and Congress to act upon its recommendations.

European Trade Liberalization

During the year ended June 30, 1953 the percentage of private trade between EPU members freed from quota restrictions was raised from 61 to 70. By July 1, 1953 Italy, Portugal, the Netherlands, Sweden, Switzerland and Western Germany had liberalized their private trade to the extent of 90 per cent or more, Belgium by 87 per cent, and the United Kingdom by 58 per cent.[6] (Government trading accounts for about 9 per cent of the trade between the OEEC countries.) Iceland, Norway and Denmark had liberalized about 75 per cent of their OEEC trade; and Austria 38 per cent. The remaining countries including Greece, France and Turkey had liberalized to a relatively small extent or not at all. Since July 1953, however, Greece has liberalized substantially and in October 1953 Britain announced that she would remove quota restrictions up to 75 per cent of her private imports from the OEEC countries. This leaves France as the only major OEEC country which has not achieved a substantial degree of liberalization.

The Dollar Shortage

During the twelve-month period ended June 30, 1953, there was a marked improvement in the dollar balance of other countries as a group. During this period the United States lost a billion dollars in gold to other countries, and the dollar assets of these countries increased by $1.2 billion. The largest gainers were Western Europe, Britain and Latin America. During the first half of 1953 the United States had an export surplus of only $156 million (excluding military aid items), an amount which was more than covered by private capital outlays and private donations to foreigners.[7] In short, the

6. *European Economic Cooperation,* Organisation for European Economic Co-operation, Paris, September 1953, p. 151.
7. *Survey of Current Business,* October 1953, p. 9.

United States had a balance of payments deficit if we exclude military aid exports.

Especially significant was the improvement of Western Europe's position with the dollar area. In the first quarter of 1953, Western Europe's imports from the dollar area declined by $660 million to $1,190 million as compared with the corresponding quarter in 1952. This represented a reduction in the volume of dollar imports of about one fifth while the total volume of Western Europe's imports from overseas remained about the same,[8] indicating a shift away from dollar sources of supply. At the same time, Western Europe's exports to the dollar area in the first quarter of 1953 increased about 20 per cent by value over the corresponding quarter in 1952. During the first six months of 1953, Western Europe had a surplus on current account with the United States of $265 million (excluding goods and services financed with military aid), as compared with a deficit of $748 million during the corresponding period in 1952.[9]

Does this mean that the dollar shortage is over and that international equilibrium is at hand? There are several reasons why this inference must be rejected. First, and foremost, most countries still retain tight controls over dollar imports and many restrict nondollar imports as well. In fact, some of the improvement in the dollar positions of other countries has been brought about by the tightening of controls in 1952. Second, there are some temporary factors in the current situation. United States government purchases of goods and services for use abroad during the year ended June 30, 1953—including offshore procurement and U.S. army expenditures for construction of airfields and military installations—amounted to about $2.6 billion.[10] The termination of the Korean war undoubtedly will bring sharp reductions in certain of these expenditures. Third, in spite of the recent increases in gold and dollar reserves of other countries, the reserves of many countries are probably inadequate to enable them to maintain convertibility without the use of trade and exchange restrictions in periods of U.S. recession.[11]

8. *Economic Bulletin for Europe,* July 1953, pp. 17–18.
9. *Survey of Current Business,* March and October 1953.
10. *Federal Reserve Bulletin,* October 1953, p. 1042.
11. For a discussion of this problem see "The Adequacy of Monetary Reserves," *Staff Papers,* October 1953, pp. 181–227.

New Trends in Exchange Practices

During 1953 there occurred certain developments in exchange practices which may indicate a trend toward greater freedom and simplification. A number of Western European countries have adopted the British system introduced in December 1951, of granting freedom to authorized banks to deal in foreign currencies at rates determined by the market within a narrow range of parity. The most important advance in restoring prewar exchange operations occurred in May 1953 when eight EPU countries agreed to permit their authorized banks to engage in arbitrage operations in their respective currencies. In October 1953 arbitrage operations among these EPU countries were extended to forward as well as spot transactions.

While these new techniques do not enlarge the freedom of individual foreign traders, they provide the technical setting for a return to genuine freedom of exchange operations including the possible future establishment of a system of fluctuating exchange rates.[12] Moreover, by permitting a wider margin of fluctuation in rates, there is some tendency to discourage speculative operations against currencies.

A special liberalizing action was taken by the Netherlands in August 1953 when she permitted private banks and individuals to hold foreign exchange balances except U.S. and Canadian balances and Swiss francs. The use of the foreign exchange is still controlled, however.

Another move toward exchange freedom is to be seen in the relaxation of the regulations on blocked or capital accounts. In the past, blocked accounts owned by nonresidents usually could not be transferred to other nonresidents and were available only for investment in low-yielding government securities. Britain has gradually relaxed her restrictions on blocked sterling owned by nonresidents so that now it can be sold to residents of the same currency area and can be used for a wide variety of investment in the sterling area. French capital francs can be employed in a similar fashion. Even greater freedom is accorded to the holders of German blocked marks since nonresident holders can sell them in international markets without restriction.

12. See "European Arbitrage Again," *The Economist*, May 23, 1953, pp. 531–33.

Multiple Exchange Rates and Retention Quotas

Considerable progress toward simplifying multiple rate structures also may be discerned. Austria and Greece eliminated their multiple rate and retention quota systems during 1953, and Bolivia and Chile simplified their multiple rate structures. Brazil largely eliminated quantitative import controls by the introduction in October 1953 of an auction system with separate auction markets for each of five categories of imports. (See Appendix 6.)

The latter part of 1953 has also seen a marked reduction in the use of retention quotas by European countries. Germany announced the elimination of her import rights system effective July 1, 1953, and the Netherlands announced the abolition of the "export-bonus" dollar retention quota system in October 1953. During this same month France announced a modification of her "EFAC account" system under which exporters retained 15 per cent of their dollar proceeds and 10 per cent of other proceeds. After November 1, 1953 exporters were no longer permitted to use the 3 per cent retained dollar proceeds freely for any purpose. Retained proceeds may be used only for normal export accessory expenses and to import goods for the direct use of the exporting firm.

It should be said that much of the progress in eliminating objectionable currency practices has been due to the efforts of the Monetary Fund. Through its consultations with members, the Fund has been able to persuade countries that certain practices are not only harmful to the interests of the country itself, but that they invite retaliation from others.

Premium Gold Markets

The value of world gold production (outside the USSR) in 1952 was estimated at $861 million.[13] About $575 million of this was produced outside the dollar area. In spite of greater freedom accorded gold miners for selling in premium gold markets, a larger amount of gold was added to official reserves in 1952 ($310 million) than in 1951 ($130 million). Total gold "disappearance" in 1952 was estimated at $550 million, of which $230 million went for indus-

13. *Twenty-Third Annual Report of the Bank for International Settlements,* Basel, June 1953, p. 149. Production valued at $35 per ounce.

trial purposes and $320 million into hoards. Total disappearance in 1951 was estimated at $710 million.[14]

The explanation for the lower volume of disappearance is to be found in a greater confidence in local currencies in Western Europe and a decrease in absorption in the Far East. The local currency price of premium gold has continued to fall in most markets. In October 1953 the free market price of bar gold in Western Europe was quoted at less than $36 per ounce.[15] A significant factor in the decline in gold prices in the fall of 1953 was the large sales by the Soviet Union.[16]

Developments in the Sterling Area

From March 30, 1953 to the end of October 1953 British gold and dollar reserves rose by over $350 million to $2,520 million, but in October and September the increase was only $50 million.[17] Excluding defense aid Britain had a deficit with the dollar area of only $59 million in the first half of 1953, as against a dollar area deficit of $232 million in the second half of 1952. The deficit was covered by gold purchases from South Africa against sterling, which have been running at an annual rate of nearly $200 million.[18] However, Britain's over-all current account surplus declined from £93 million in the second half of 1952, to £26 million in the first half of 1953. The overseas sterling area had a surplus of £132 million in the first half of 1953 which, combined with Britain's surplus, gave the sterling area as a whole a surplus of £158 million.

The improvement in the balance of payments position of the overseas sterling area has been an important factor in strengthening sterling. Sterling liabilities rose by £172 million during the first half of 1953, representing increased holdings of sterling area members. Holdings of nonsterling countries decreased by £38 million. There was also a reduction of £56 million in the sterling held by the Monetary Fund during 1953, reflecting an increase in the demand for sterling by members of the Fund.

14. *Ibid.*
15. *International Financial News Survey,* November 6, 1953, p. 149.
16. "Gold Slump Laid to Soviet Sellings," *The New York Times,* November 9, 1953.
17. *International Financial News Survey,* November 20, 1953, p. 165.
18. *The Economist,* October 31, 1953, p. 349; and October 24, 1953, p. 261.

The growing strength of sterling has been reflected not only in increased gold and dollar reserves held by London but by an increase in the rates for security sterling—available for purchasing securities in Britain—of from $2.54 in July 1952 to $2.70 in October 1953. During the same period rates for transferable account sterling rose from $2.62 to $2.73, reflecting a growing scarcity of sterling relative to dollars in nonsterling countries.

Greater Freedom of Trade

While the Commonwealth proposals of December 1952 for restoring sterling convertibility appear at the time of writing to be temporarily shelved, Britain has been taking a number of steps toward greater freedom in trade relations. These include the transfer of trade in a number of commodities from the government to private importers and the reestablishment of free markets in internationally traded commodities. In 1947 four fifths of all British imports were being bulk-purchased by the government. By September 1953 only meat, cheese, canned fish, canned and dried fruits, fats and oils, butter, tungsten, magnesium, jute, sulfur and pyrites were under government purchase.[19] Traders operating in commodity markets are not required to have individual licenses to purchase abroad and even the grain traders, whose purchases are largely from dollar sources, may buy where they please. They are prohibited from re-exporting dollar grain without a license, however.[20] The domestic counterpart of this freeing of the international markets in foods and raw materials is the elimination of rationing except for meats, fats and cheese.

The improvement in the balances of payments of the overseas sterling area has resulted in some relaxation of their import restrictions during 1953. Of special significance is the decision of South Africa to remove all discriminatory restrictions against dollar imports, beginning in January 1954. South Africa will still sell a minimum of £50 million in gold per year to Britain, the exact amount depending upon her requirements of sterling.[21]

NOVEMBER 1953

19. "Britain's March Towards Freedom," *The Banker,* October 1953, pp. 215–23.
20. As of September 1953, American cotton and dollar coffee were under individual license.
21. "South Africa and the Sterling Area," *The Economist,* October 24, 1953, pp. 261–63.

APPENDICES

APPENDIX 1

STERLING PAYMENTS AGREEMENT BETWEEN THE GOVERNMENT OF THE
UNITED KINGDOM OF GREAT BRITAIN AND NORTHERN IRELAND
AND THE SUPREME COMMANDER FOR THE ALLIED
POWERS ACTING IN RESPECT OF
OCCUPIED JAPAN

The Government of the United Kingdom of Great Britain and Northern Ireland (hereinafter referred to as "the Government of the United Kingdom") and the Supreme Commander for the Allied Powers acting in respect of Occupied Japan (hereinafter referred to as "SCAP")
Have agreed as follows:

Article 1

All payments between residents of Japan and residents of the Scheduled Territories, other than such as must necessarily be made in yen, shall be settled in sterling.

Article 2

SCAP will ensure that the appropriate Japanese authorities shall buy and sell sterling and that their rates for sterling and for the United States dollar shall be related to one another at the middle rate quoted by the Bank of England for the United States dollar.

Article 3

All sterling payments to residents of Japan which residents of the Scheduled Territories or of countries outside the Scheduled Territories are permitted to make under the Exchange Control Regulations in force in the United Kingdom shall be made to Japanese Accounts.

Article 4

(1) The Government of the United Kingdom shall not restrict the transfer of sterling which is at the disposal of residents of Japan to other residents of Japan or to residents of the Scheduled Territories.

(2) The Government of the United Kingdom shall not restrict the availability of sterling under the control of the Japanese Foreign Exchange Control Board for making payments in respect of direct current transactions to residents of such countries (other than Japan and the Scheduled Territories) as may be agreed between the Bank of England and the Japanese Foreign Exchange Control Board.

Article 5

SCAP will ensure that the Government of Japan shall not restrict the acceptance by residents of Japan of sterling from residents of the Scheduled Territories and, as regards payments in respect of direct current transactions, from residents of such countries (other than Japan and the Scheduled Territories) as may be agreed between the Bank of England and the Japanese Foreign Exchange Control Board.

Article 6

SCAP will ensure that, in so far as the Japanese Exchange Control Regulations from time to time permit, the Government of Japan will facilitate the transfer of yen accruing to residents of the Scheduled Territories from permitted current transactions to other residents of the Scheduled Territories or to residents of Japan, and the transfer of such yen into Sterling.

Article 7

For the purposes of the present Agreement:

(a) the expression "the Scheduled Territories" shall have the meaning from time to time assigned to it under the United Kingdom Exchange Control Act, 1947;

(b) the expression "Japanese Account" shall mean an account of a resident of Japan which is for the time being recognized by the Bank of England as a Japanese Account for the purposes of the present Agreement;

(c) the expression "payments in respect of direct current transactions" means payments in respect of transactions of the type defined in Article XIX (i) of the Articles of Agreement of the International Monetary Fund which are made by a principal resident in the country from which payment is made and which relate exclusively (1) to goods (other than gold bullion, gold coin or gold either in semi-manufactured or fully manufactured form) imported into, and for use or consumption in, that country and originating in the country to which payment is made or (2) to services rendered to residents in the former country by residents of the latter country.

Article 8

For the purposes of the present Agreement the Bank of England shall act as agent of the Government of the United Kingdom and the Japanese Foreign Exchange Control Board as agent of SCAP.

Article 9

The present Agreement shall come into force on 31st August, 1951. At any time thereafter either Contracting Party may give notice to the other of its intention to terminate the Agreement and the Agreement shall cease to have effect three months after the date of such notice. It shall terminate upon the entry into force of a Peace Treaty between the Governments of the United Kingdom and Japan or, unless both Contracting Parties agree to the contrary, on 31st August, 1952, if a Peace Treaty has not entered into force between the two Governments by that date.

In witness whereof the undersigned, being duly authorised by the Government of the United Kingdom of Great Britain and Northern Ireland and by the Supreme Commander for the Allied Powers respectively, have signed the present Agreement and have affixed thereto their seals.

Done at Tokyo this Thirty-first day of August, 1951, in duplicate.

For the Government of the United Kingdom of Great Britain and Northern Ireland:
(L. S.) GEORGE CLUTTON.

For the Supreme Commander for the Allied Powers:
(L. S.) C. C. B. WARDEN,
Colonel, AGC.
Adjutant General.

APPENDIX 2

Monetary Agreement between the Government of the United Kingdom of Great Britain and Northern Ireland and the Government of Sweden

The Government of the United Kingdom of Great Britain and Northern Ireland and the Government of Sweden,

Desiring to modify the arrangements agreed between them for the regulation of payments so as to take account of the establishment of the European Payments Union and to conform with the provisions of the Agreement relating to the establishment of the Union which was signed in Paris on 19th September, 1950, hereinafter referred to as the "European Payments Agreement"

Have agreed as follows:

Article 1

(a) The rate of exchange between the Swedish crown and the pound sterling shall be Swedish kronor 14.48 = £1 and this rate (hereinafter referred to as "the official rate") shall not be varied by either Contracting Government except after giving to the other as much notice as may be practicable.

(b) The Contracting Governments shall enforce the use of the official rate as the basis of all transactions involving a relationship between the pound sterling and the Swedish kronor.

(c) The Bank of England and Sveriges Riksbank, as agents of their respective Governments, shall fix by agreement the maximum spread above or below the official rate which will be authorised on the markets which they control.

Article 2

The Bank of England and Sveriges Riksbank, as agents of their respective Governments, shall make such arrangements as may be necessary to implement Article 8 of the European Payments Agreement as between those Governments.

Article 3

(a)-(i) The Government of the United Kingdom shall not restrict the availability of sterling at the disposal of residents of Sweden for transfer to other residents of Sweden or to residents of the Scheduled Territories.

(ii) The Government of the United Kingdom shall not restrict the availability of sterling under the control of Sveriges Riksbank for making payments in respect of direct current transactions to residents of such countries outside Sweden and the Scheduled Territories as may be agreed between the Bank of

England and Sveriges Riksbank, acting as agents of their respective Governments.

(b)-(i) The Swedish Government shall not restrict the availability of Swedish kronor at the disposal of residents of the Scheduled Territories for transfer to other residents of the Scheduled Territories or to residents of Sweden.

(ii) The Swedish Government shall not restrict the availability of Swedish kronor under the control of the Bank of England for making payments in respect of direct current transactions to residents of such countries outside Sweden and the Scheduled Territories as may be agreed between the Bank of England and Sveriges Riksbank, acting as agents of their respective Governments.

Article 4

(a) The Swedish Government shall not restrict the acceptance by residents of Sweden of sterling from residents of the Scheduled Territories and, as regards payments in respect of direct current transactions, from residents of such countries outside Sweden and the Scheduled Territories as may be agreed between the Bank of England and Sveriges Riksbank, acting as agents of their respective Governments.

(b) The Government of the United Kingdom shall not restrict the acceptance by residents of the Scheduled Territories of Swedish kronor from residents of Sweden and, as regards payments in respect of direct current transactions, from residents of such countries, outside Sweden and the Scheduled Territories as may be agreed between the Bank of England and Sveriges Riksbank, acting as agents of their respective Governments.

Article 5

The Contracting Governments shall co-operate with a view to assisting each other in keeping capital transactions within the scope of their respective policies.

Article 6

For the purposes of the present Agreement:

(a) The expression "the Scheduled Territories" shall have the meaning from time to time assigned to it under the United Kingdom Exchange Control Act, 1947;

(b) The expression "payments in respect of direct current transactions" means payments in respect of transactions of the type defined in Article XIX (i) of the Articles of Agreement of the International Monetary Fund which are made by a principal resident in the country from which payment is made and which relate solely to goods (other than gold bullion, gold coin or gold either in semi-manufactured or in fully manufactured form) imported into, and for use or consumption in, that country and originating in the country to which payment is made or to services rendered to residents in the former country by residents of the latter country.

Article 7

The Monetary Agreement between the Government of the United Kingdom of Great Britain and Northern Ireland and the Government of Sweden, signed in London on 30th December, 1949, is hereby abrogated.

Article 8

The present Agreement shall come into force on this day's date. At any time thereafter, either Contracting Government may give notice to the other of its intention to terminate the Agreement and the Agreement shall cease to have effect three months after the date of such notice. It shall in any case be reviewed before 1st July, 1952.

In witness whereof the undersigned, being duly authorised thereto by their respective Governments, have signed the present Agreement and affixed thereto their seals.

Done in London, in duplicate, this 10th day of November, 1950.

(L. S.) ERNEST BEVIN

(L. S.) GUNNAR HAGGLOF

APPENDIX 3

CODE OF STANDARD PRACTICES FOR IMPORT AND EXPORT RESTRICTIONS AND EXCHANGE CONTROLS *

1. The grant of an import license should imply that the necessary foreign exchange will be obtainable if applied for within a reasonable time. When both import licenses and exchange permits are required, the operation of the two requirements should be coordinated. If more than one rate of exchange applies in payment for imports, the import license or exchange permit should indicate the type of exchange which will apply in the settlement of the particular transaction.

2. Any new or intensified restrictions on importation or exportation should not apply to goods shown to the satisfaction of the control authority to have been en route at the time the change was announced or to have been paid for in substantial part or covered by an irrevocable letter of credit.

3. Goods proven to have been covered by adequate confirmed prior order at the time new or intensified restrictions are announced, and not marketable elsewhere without appreciable loss, should receive special consideration on an individual case basis, provided their delivery can be completed within a specified period. Such goods, as well as those covered under paragraph 2, should be accountable against any import or export quota or exchange allocation that may have been established for that particular class of goods.

4. The administrative formalities in connection with the issuance of import and export licenses or exchange permits should be designed to allow action upon applications within a reasonably short period. A license or permit should be valid for a sufficient period to allow for the production and delivery of the goods, taking into account the character of the goods and the conditions of transport from the country of origin. The control authorities should not withdraw licenses or permits unless they are satisfied that exceptional circumstances necessitate such action, and should give sympathetic consideration to requests for renewal or revalidation of licenses or permits when exceptional circumstances prevent their utilization within the original period.

5. Under a system involving the fixing of quotas for particular classes of goods or of allocations of exchange in payment for them, any period that may be set, within which applications for such quotas or allocations must be made, should be sufficient to allow for the exchange of communications with likely foreign suppliers and the conclusion of purchase contracts.

6. When foreign products subject to quantitative limitations are apportioned among importers largely in the light of their past participation in the

---

* The Contracting Parties to the General Agreement on Tariffs and Trade, *Standard Practices for Import and Export Restrictions and Exchange Controls,* Geneva, December 27, 1950. This code does not constitute an obligation on the part of the contracting parties but only a recommendation.

561

trade, the control authorities, at their discretion and without undue prejudice to the interests of established importers, should give consideration to requests for licenses or permits submitted by qualified and financially responsible newcomers.

7. If an assurance regarding the issue of an import license is required as a condition of consular legalization of shipping documents in the country of exportation, a reliable communication giving the number of the import license should suffice.

8. The authority given to customs officials should be adequate to allow them, at their discretion, to grant reasonable tolerance for variations in the quantity or value of individual shipments as delivered from that specified in the prior import or export authorization, in accordance with the character of the product involved and any extenuating circumstances.

9. Where, owing to exceptional and unforeseen balance-of-payment difficulties, a country is unable to provide foreign exchange for imports immediately payment becomes due to the supplier, transfers of foreign exchange in respect of goods already imported or licensed for importation should have priority over transfers in respect of new orders, or should at least have a definite and equitable share of the total amounts of foreign exchange currently available for imports.

APPENDIX 4 *

METHODS OF FINANCING UNITED STATES EXPORTS UNDER LOANS AND GRANTS OF UNITED STATES AGENCIES AND INTERNATIONAL INSTITUTIONS

DURING THE PERIOD July 1, 1945 to June 30, 1952, the Mutual Security Agency (MSA, and its predecessor the Economic Cooperation Administration), the Export-Import Bank of Washington (EIB), and the International Bank for Reconstruction and Development (IBRD) financed exports of goods and services from the United States valued at over $11 billion.[1] Loans by the Export-Import Bank are made almost entirely for the purchase of U.S. goods and services as stipulated in the loan agreement.[2] The MSA and the IBRD have made loans and grants for procurement in other areas of the world as well as for financing U.S. exports.[3] The IBRD makes loans in various currencies; the MSA makes only dollar grants and loans. The purpose of this discussion is to describe the methods by which dollars are made available by these three agencies to other countries for the purchase of goods and services in the United States.

Each agency employs several methods of financing U.S. exports to the recipients of grants or loans. The particular method of financing any given shipment depends in large part upon the preference of the foreign government concerned, subject of course to the limitation imposed by the general policies of the grantor or lendor agency. The choice of the method of financing by the foreign government is determined by a number of factors, including (1) the level of the dollar exchange holdings of the recipient country; (2) the nature of the purchases made; (3) the nature of the general import licensing and exchange control system of the country concerned; and (4) the preference of the U.S. exporter for certain types of financing. How these factors bear on the decision of choosing the method of financing will be discussed in the description of individual methods.

The means of financing U.S. exports employed by each of the three agencies will be considered in the order of the relative importance of each method.

---

* Written by Merlyn Nelson Trued, a graduate student at the University of Virginia.

1. MSA figures cover the period April 1948 through June 1952; IBRD, May 1947 through August 1952; EIB, July 1945 through June 1952. The figure given in the text is the total amount of paid shipments which have shown the United States as the source of supply. Total paid shipments for the three institutions for all sources of supply totaled $16,444.5 million during the same period. (The MSA was replaced by the Foreign Operations Administration (FOA) in June 1953. FOA export financing techniques are in general the same as those of the MSA.)

2. The EIB has made a limited number of loans for purchases in other countries, and loans for the liquidation of commercial credits owed to American exporters.

3. The MSA employs the Export-Import Bank as the lending agency for loans made with MSA funds.

THE MUTUAL SECURITY AGENCY

The Allocation of MSA Aid

The MSA does not ordinarily put free dollars at the disposal of foreign countries; rather it provides dollars for purchases of authorized goods or services, or reimburses the participating country after dollar payment has been made. The method operates generally in the following manner. First, an allocation of dollars among the countries entitled to receive assistance under the Mutual Security Act is made. Thereupon, the participating governments submit requests to the MSA (usually through the MSA mission located in that country) for "procurement authorizations" (PAs) to be issued against these funds. PAs are given a number which is written upon every document used in the trade, including the sub-PAs, the letter of commitment and the letters of credit (if the procedure utilized calls for those instruments). The PA specifies the source from which the goods are to be purchased, the amount which may be used, the period of validity and the method of financing the procurement. Approved PAs are then issued on broad commodity classifications.

The issuance of the PAs constitutes authority for the participating country to issue sub-PAs, bearing the same number, to importers for the purchase of specific items. In the sub-PA the participating country specifies to the importer the commodity or service, the source, the dollar value, the period in which delivery is to be made and any other details of the PA pertinent to the sub-PA. At this time, the importer may reach an agreement with a U.S. exporter for the shipment of goods. Some purchases are made directly by the foreign government or its purchasing mission or agency, but the preponderance of shipments are through private trade channels. Up to this point the procedure is the same for all shipments, regardless of the method of reimbursement.

Methods of Reimbursement

The MSA utilizes four methods of providing reimbursement for MSA-financed shipments:

1. Direct reimbursement to a foreign government for paid purchases
2. The issuance of a letter of commitment to a United States bank against which letters of credit are drawn
3. The issuance of a letter of commitment directly to a supplier
4. The establishment of a revolving fund account in a Federal Reserve Bank.

The first two methods are the ones most frequently used while the latter two play relatively minor roles.[4] The method of reimbursement is selected at

4. Procurement may also be financed by advances to procurement agencies of the United States government. In the early years of the MSA, a considerable amount of exports were procured through the Departments of Agriculture and the Army. In such

the time the participating government requests the PA. Once the reimbursement procedure has been chosen, the documents used in the trade automatically follow.[5]

Direct Reimbursement to a Participating Country

It is estimated that the method of direct reimbursement to the participating country is utilized for nearly one half the value of MSA-financed shipments. Its relative importance has been declining, however. Under this method of financing, the MSA does not become directly involved with the commercial banking system or with the supplier. Except for the receipt of a supplier's certificate and invoice-and-contract abstract (MSA Form 280) executed in a modified manner directly from the supplier, the MSA is unaware of the exact nature of the original method of financing. The MSA reimburses the dollar account of the participating government upon presentation of the full documentation noted above (together with the usual export shipping documents).

The transaction usually proceeds in one of two ways depending upon the nature of the importer or purchaser. The purchase may be made directly by a foreign government or its purchasing mission from a U.S. supplier. In this event, the participating country concludes a purchase contract with a U.S. supplier, advising the supplier of the PA number. After

---

cases, the procuring agency is reimbursed by accounting transfers on the books of the U.S. Treasury.

5. Whatever the method of reimbursement, the MSA requires the submission of certain documents before any payments can be made.

A. For the cost of any commodity, including ocean freight in c. & f., and ocean freight and insurance in c.i.f. transactions, the following documents must be executed and submitted by the agency noted, and approved by the MSA before final settlement:

1. A voucher stating that payment has not been received from MSA and that the bill is a valid claim. Under a letter of commitment issued to a supplier, this is prepared by the supplier or his bank; under the other methods, it is prepared by the supplier, his bank, the participating country or its designated representative.

2. A supplier's certificate with invoice-and-contract abstract (MSA Form 280). Executed by the supplier, this document contains representations as to price, commissions, etc.

3. An ocean or charter party bill of lading, airway bill or parcel post receipt.

4. A supplier's detailed invoice either marked "Paid" by the supplier or endorsed by, or accompanied by a certificate of, an officer of a bank indicating that payment has been made in the amount shown on the invoice.

B. For the cost of ocean transportation, the following documents must be presented:

1. A voucher stating that the claim is valid and that payment has not been received. This is prepared by the participating country, its designated representative or bank.

2. A supplier's certificate and invoice-and-contract abstract executed by the supplier of the transportation.

3. For cargoes shipped under charter party, one copy or photostat of the charter party.

4. An ocean or charter party bill of lading or airway bill.

5. A detailed invoice of the supplier of transportation.

6. Special tanker documents, in the case of tanker shipments.

Minor exceptions to the presentation of these documents before reimbursement will be noted later in discussing the specific use of the various methods.

preparing and shipping the goods, the supplier presents the shipping documents (the bill of lading, insurance contract, etc.) together with the required MSA documents to the foreign government or its agency and the purchaser pays the supplier with a draft on its own dollar exchange holdings. The supplier, in this case, also presents a supplier's certificate executed in a modified manner directly to MSA, Washington, in order to fulfill his obligation to the MSA. The purchaser then submits the required documents to the Controller, MSA, Washington, whereupon he receives a U.S. Treasury check issued to the foreign government or its designated agency in the United States (the British Supply Office, for example).

The second method which may be used under this procedure involves the utilization of a letter of credit. This method most nearly approaches the normal exporting procedure under an export letter of credit. MSA, as an "extra wheel" simply replenishes the dollar account of the participating country after the entire transaction has been completed and the proper documents are presented. Under this method, the importer secures a sub-PA, an import license and other required documents from his government. Thereupon, he contacts the U.S. supplier, arranges contract terms and delivery, indicates that the shipment is to be financed by MSA and submits the PA number to be used. At the same time, the importer arranges with his bank to issue a letter of credit to be confirmed by a U.S. bank (alternately, the importer may request the U.S. bank through which he does business to issue the letter of credit). The U.S. bank notifies the U.S. supplier of the establishment of the irrevocable letter of credit in his favor. Upon shipment of the goods, the supplier submits the shipping documents, MSA documents, and a sight draft drawn on the bank issuing the letter of credit to the bank for payment. The U.S. bank forwards the documents to its foreign correspondent and is reimbursed by its correspondent for the amount of the draft. The importer pays into his bank the equivalent in local currency ("counterpart funds" [6]) of the dollar value of the shipment and receives the necessary shipping documents in order to claim his goods at the port or station. Meanwhile, the importer's bank forwards the documents to the MSA, Washington, and requests reimbursement. The MSA, after auditing the purchase, reimburses the foreign bank by a dollar deposit to its account in the U.S. bank.

Letter of Commitment Issued to a United States Bank

This method is used to about the same extent as the direct reimbursement procedure. Between April 3, 1948 and June 26, 1952, a total of slightly over $5.4 billion in letters of commitment were issued by MSA to sixty-seven

6. Foreign importers must pay for all purchases in local currency, which funds are called "counterpart funds." The funds are held in this account pending disposal of them at the direction of the MSA and the foreign government for agreed purposes or projects. A small percentage is allowed for the payment of expenses of the MSA mission located abroad.

different U.S. banks at the request of the participating countries.[7] The utilization of this method, as contrasted with the direct reimbursement procedure, depends to a large extent upon the level of the dollar exchange reserves of the participating country. This method is especially attractive when dollar holdings of the participating country are low or when, for any reason, there is a desire not to reduce the level of its dollar reserves. Unlike the direct reimbursement procedure, this method makes it unnecessary for the participating country to tie up its dollar funds for the period of time from payment to reimbursement.

Under the letter of credit procedure, the foreign government requests the MSA to issue a letter of commitment (which represents an obligation of the United States) to a particular bank in the United States for a definite sum and for a stated period of time. The letter of commitment indicates the amount which may be drawn, the documents required for presentation, the nature of the merchandise, and the date up to which shipment may be made and payment collected. In the letter of commitment, the MSA advises the bank that it guarantees the reimbursement of sight drafts upon the bank by an American exporter and paid by that bank for the account of the importer's bank in the participating country. The U.S. bank's security is represented by the foreign bank's assignment to the American bank of the right to receive all monies due or to become due under the MSA's letter of commitment. The foreign importer, after securing a sub-PA, import license, etc., requests the U.S. bank to issue an irrevocable letter of credit against the letter of commitment to a certain-named supplier with whom he has earlier arranged contract terms. The importer will also have furnished the PA number to the supplier indicating MSA-financing at the time he arranges his contract.

The exporter prepares the goods and makes shipment. He then submits the required documents to the U.S. bank. The bank pays the sight draft when it is presented and forwards the originals of the shipping documents and MSA forms to the foreign bank. Copies of the shipping documents and MSA forms are sent to MSA, upon presentation of which, the MSA reimburses the U.S. bank within a maximum period of thirty days. From the time the bank makes payment until it receives payment out of MSA funds, it has a claim on the foreign bank in the participating country. When the foreign banks receives the documents, it collects from the importer the local currency equivalent of the value of the shipment and deposits that amount in the counterpart funds account.

The diagram on page 568 illustrates the movement of goods and documents under this method of financing.

---

7. Of this total, over $4.5 billion were issued to eleven major U.S. banks: Bank of America; National Trust and Savings Association; Bank of Manhattan Company; Bankers Trust Company; Chase National Bank of the City of New York; French-American Banking Corporation; Guaranty Trust Company of New York; Irving Trust Company; Manufacturers Trust Company; J. P. Morgan and Company; and the National City Bank of New York.

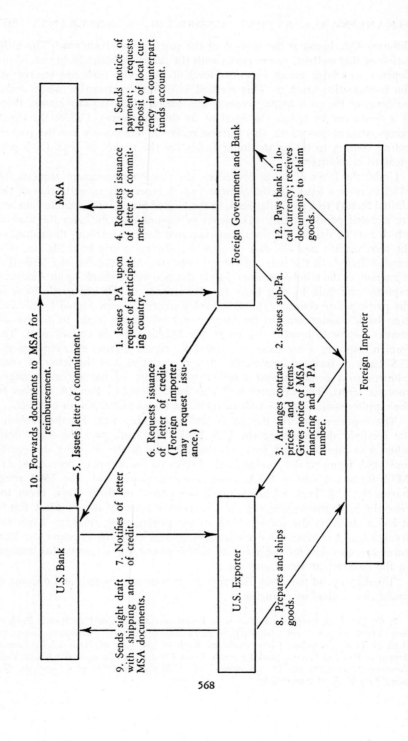

568

The letter of commitment issued to a U.S. bank is popular with traders and banks alike because it follows closely normal export procedures and makes maximum use of private traders and the commercial banking system. Exporters contacted by the author signified that this method has been used exclusively in their shipments of MSA-financed goods from the United States.

Letter of Commitment Issued Directly to a U.S. Supplier

The MSA may issue a letter of commitment directly to the supplier. Under this method, the commercial banking system is bypassed since MSA directly guarantees to pay for the purchases upon presentation of the required documents by the U.S. supplier to MSA, Washington. Therefore, upon shipment of the goods as described in the letter of commitment, the supplier is paid by a Treasury check issued directly to him. The foreign importer may be either a government (or a government agency) or a private importer.

This method is selected primarily for the financing of specific contracts for industrial projects and for equipment involving complicated terms or advance and progress payments. The letter of commitment may provide for progress payments upon the submission by the supplier of a certificate of the progressive fulfillment of the contract. In addition, some U.S. suppliers prefer, for special reasons, to have a letter of commitment issued directly to them by MSA. Payments, including progress payments, are prompt and made with a minimum of delay and trouble by direct contact between the supplier and the MSA, Washington. This method is also used at times for financing engineering and other technical services. In such cases MSA may prefer this method since under this arrangement the MSA may audit the account before any payment is made.

The issuance of a letter of commitment directly to the U.S. supplier avoids bank service charges. These charges are not insignificant and inasmuch as the MSA does not finance such charges, the purchaser takes them into consideration in arranging the method of financing to be followed. Nevertheless, only a very small portion of the total MSA financing is handled in this manner. This is due in part to the fact that the method has been viewed with disfavor by the commercial banking system both in this country and abroad.

Establishment of a Revolving Fund Account

The fourth method of reimbursement has almost gone out of use since its inception in February 1949. The only countries that used this method were Britain and France and though the British account is still open and used to a small extent, the French account has been closed. The procedure is described by the following illustration.

Upon the request of the MSA, the U.S. Treasury established an account in the Federal Reserve Bank of New York for the use of Great Britain. The account is maintained as a subaccount of the U.S. Treasury's General Account and was credited with $10 million.[8] After the MSA issues a PA, the British Supply Office completes a contract with a U.S. supplier. Upon the shipment of the goods and the surrender of the required documents by the supplier, the British Supply Office makes payment by issuing a draft made out to the order of the supplier and drawn against the account in the Federal Reserve Bank. The supplier then endorses the draft and subscribes at the same time to the "Suppliers Certificate" (on the reverse side of the draft form) which contains representations as to price, commissions and the terms of sale. The draft is then deposited with the supplier's bank for collection.

Under this method, Britain may at her discretion issue the draft as an advance payment.[9] This follows from the fact that the participating government is not required to furnish full documentation to the MSA immediately upon the drawing of a draft. The British Supply Office must forward a copy of the draft to the MSA and to the Federal Reserve Bank immediately upon issuance. Upon receipt of this notice the Federal Reserve Bank debits the subaccount and then pays the draft upon presentation by the supplier's bank by debiting the Treasury's General Account and crediting the account of the collecting bank. No later than three months after the issuance of the draft, however, Britain must furnish full documentation to the MSA. Thus MSA dollars may be used by Britain for periods up to three months without documentation. From time to time, as the subaccount becomes depleted, the U.S. Treasury replenishes the subaccount, at the request of MSA, for the amount of the authorized purchases.

Both the revolving fund account and the letter of commitment methods benefit countries which find it impossible, or impracticable, to advance dollars out of their exchange holdings, pending reimbursement by the MSA. These methods are therefore in sharp contrast to the direct reimbursement procedure under which the participating country pays the supplier for purchases and receives reimbursement at a later date upon presentation of the documents to the MSA.

Conclusion

MSA financing has provided for the utilization of the commercial banking system and normal trading channels to a large degree, especially through the use of letters of credit. The relative importance of the several means of MSA financing is indicated by the following estimates of the percentage of total MSA exports:

1. Fifty per cent by MSA letter of commitment to commercial banks
2. Forty-five per cent by direct reimbursement to the participating country
3. Five per cent by MSA letter of commitment to the supplier and by the use of a revolving fund account.

8. The French account was also opened for $10 million in the Federal Reserve Bank of New York.
9. Drafts are issued only to suppliers furnishing goods or services from the U.S. and not for offshore purchases. The drafts are limited in amount to $500,000.

THE INTERNATIONAL BANK FOR RECONSTRUCTION AND DEVELOPMENT

The International Bank is authorized to make loans for purposes of reconstruction or development to member governments, or to nongovernmental borrowers with a guarantee by the government of the country in which the project is to be located. By the end of October 1952, the Bank had made seventy-three loans totaling nearly $1.5 billion to twenty-eight countries. Shipments financed by the Bank through June 30, 1952, totaled $876.5 million of which $622.1 million was paid for commodities and services procured in the United States.

Preliminary Arrangements

Before any individual transactions are entered into, an over-all loan agreement is effected between the borrower and the Bank. This agreement specifies the project, the materials to be procured, the source of procurement and other details pertinent to the loan. Once these arrangements have been completed, there are a number of procedures by which the proceeds of the loan may be utilized. The Bank's Charter does not specify the particular methods of financing which are to be used; thus the procedures which are outlined in the following pages are not the only methods permissible. Generally, however, the procedure follows one of the methods outlined below.

Most borrowing countries maintain a "borrower's representative" in the United States in order to facilitate the orderly progression of transactions. This designated representative deals with the IBRD and, in some cases, with the supplier. The representative may consist of a permanent mission or merely a designated person (usually a member of the embassy of the particular country concerned) authorized to sign the various papers involved. Therefore, whenever the word "borrower" is used in this paper, it may be taken to mean either the borrower itself or the representative acting as an agent in its behalf.

Reimbursement for Completed Purchases

The method of reimbursement for completed purchases may or may not utilize a letter of credit. If a letter of credit is used, it is issued by a U.S. bank upon the request of its correspondent abroad and specifies payment in dollars upon presentation of the usual commercial documents and a sight draft. After the commerical bank has made payment against the documents, it submits to the borrower a special IBRD form, "Bank's Report of Payment." The borrower, in turn, submits to the IBRD an "Application for Reimbursement in Dollars," together with the "Bank's Report of Payment."

The borrower may not use a letter of credit but rather may conclude a contract with a supplier specifying direct payment to the supplier upon presentation of the usual commercial and shipping documents. These transactions are usually handled through a purchasing mission and involve purchases on government account. The borrower then submits to the IBRD an "Application for Reimbursement in Dollars," together with the documents denoting the shipment of, and payment for, the goods. The IBRD then reimburses the dollar account of the borrower.

The method of direct reimbursement by the IBRD closely parallels the procedure used by the MSA in similar transactions and need not, therefore, be explained in greater detail at this point.

The direct reimbursement method is utilized to a great extent but its relative use has been decreasing. In the majority of cases where it is used, a letter of credit is used also. Its decreasing use may be explained in part by the change in the type of loans made. The first loans made by the IBRD were relatively large loans and in many cases government purchases for purposes of reconstruction in well-developed but war-torn countries. As the Bank has shifted from reconstruction to development loans, the methods of financing have altered in favor of the letter of credit guaranteed by the IBRD, or of advance payment procedures. It is estimated, however, that reimbursement for paid purchases is currently used for over one half the value of loans disbursed.

Reimbursement for Advance or Progress Payments

If, for reasons of length of time needed for the completion of the contract or the high value of the contract, advance or progress payments are called for, the borrower follows a procedure in which the Bank finances these payments. Again, letters of credit may or may not be used. In either case, the procedure follows that employed in the first method outlined above except that the documents presented to the IBRD are accompanied by a statement of undertaking by the supplier to furnish the goods for which the advance is made or by a progress report. In any case, the method of final settlement is the same as that employed in reimbursement for completed purchases.

This method is used rather extensively since a large amount of the IBRD loans are utilized for the purchase of heavy machinery, or other goods calling for a long period of contracts covering relatively high values. Furthermore, not only do a number of borrowers find it impracticable or impossible to commit dollar exchange holdings to purchases for the period of time needed to secure reimbursement but the loan agreement stipulates that the borrower must request reimbursement promptly after the down payments are made. This method allows the borrower to use the IBRD dollars for the necessary advance and progress payments.

Requests for Advancement of Funds to the Borrower

In some cases, the borrower may find it difficult either to secure the issuance of a letter of credit by a U.S. bank or to make payment in dollars pending reimbursement. In such cases, the borrower may secure an advance of dollars through the following procedure.

At about the same time that the supplier has the goods ready for shipment, the borrower submits to the IBRD an "Application for Advance in Dollars," together with a statement indicating the nature of the necessity for making payment. The IBRD then puts the dollar funds at the disposal of the borrower. The borrower then makes payment directly to the supplier upon the delivery of the goods and the surrender of the usual export documents. These documents are then presented, together with a "Report Showing Use of Advances," to the IBRD.

Deposit of Collateral for Letter of Credit

In some cases, the commerical bank in the United States may desire collateral before issuing the letter of credit requested. It may request such collateral by sending a "Bank's Advice of Requirement of Deposit of Collateral" to the borrower. The latter in turn submits to the IBRD an "Application for the Deposit of Collateral in [named bank] to Secure Letters of Credit" with the bank's advice attached. The IBRD then deposits the requested collateral directly with the bank in a segregated collateral account for each letter of credit, notifying the borrower of each action. The commercial bank then makes payment to the supplier against the usual export documents and submits a "Bank's Report of Payment" to the borrower. The borrower, in turn, submits a "Report of the Use of Collateral Deposited by the IBRD to Secure Letters of Credit," accompanied by the "Bank's Report of Payment," to the IBRD.

This method of financing is used at the present time to a small extent. When it is used, it is to a large degree the result of the limited ability of the borrower, or his bank, to secure the confirmation or issuance of a letter of credit by a U.S. bank. It was used to a major extent in the early postwar years when U.S. banks hesitated to confirm letters of credit without additional assurances of payment, and before the method of guarantees of letters of credit by the IBRD was put into effect. The deposit-of-collateral method was not popular because when such collateral was deposited by the IBRD with a U.S. bank, interest charges began immediately upon deposit. Under other methods (such as the guaranteed letter of credit) interest charges begin only when disbursement is actually made. This method of payment has, therefore, decreased in importance and is now seldom utilized.

Guarantees of Letters of Credit by the IBRD

The International Bank may issue either a "qualified agreement" or an "irrevocable agreement to reimburse" a United States commerical bank for payments made under a letter of credit. In either case, the U.S. bank commits itself—upon acceptance of the Bank's terms—irrevocably to confirm the letter of credit, to request prompt reimbursement, to notify the IBRD of any cancellation of the letter of credit and to advise the Bank of any unused balance upon the expiration of, or the final payment under, the letter of credit.

Guaranteeing a letter of credit furnishes an alternative approach for a borrower in cases where the U.S. bank desires further security before issuing or confirming a letter of credit. In effect, as one moves downward in the credit rating of the borrower, or his bank, the U.S. bank may feel that credit should not be extended (above that normally extended to its correspondent or the borrower) without some additional assurances. If, for example, the U.S. bank desired some assurance that the IBRD was financing purchases such as those contemplated under the letter of credit, that the proposed letter of credit covered suitable commodities, and that the prices were generally acceptable, and upon this assurance would feel that the issuance of a letter of credit was feasible, the IBRD's qualified agreement to reimburse would be used.

The Qualified Agreement to Reimburse

The correspondent bank upon requesting the U.S. bank to confirm a letter of credit (or the borrower upon requesting the U.S. bank to issue a letter of credit) indicates that the IBRD is to agree to reimburse the bank for payments made. The U.S. bank, after obtaining the appropriate forms from the IBRD, sends two copies of the proposed letter of credit to the borrower with a request ("bank's request for agreement to reimburse") for an agreement by the Bank to reimburse the commercial bank for payments made under the letter of credit. The borrower sends the bank request and copies of the letter of credit with an "application for an agreement to reimburse" to the IBRD irrevocably authorizing the Bank to make payments as requested by the U.S. bank. In the application, the borrower authorizes and requests the IBRD to pay to the U.S. bank from time to time, as withdrawals from the loan account, such amounts as will be required for reimbursing the U.S. bank. The IBRD returns one copy of the proposed letter of credit to the U.S. bank with an original and duplicate agreement to reimburse for the U.S. bank's acceptance. Immediately after each payment under the letter of credit, the U.S. bank notifies the Bank by sending a "bank's report of payment and request for reimbursement" with the shipping documents attached. The IBRD then makes payment directly to the commercial bank within a maximum period of thirty days, forwarding the documents and notifying the borrower of the debit to the loan account. Amendments to the letter of credit may be made upon agreement between the borrower, the IBRD and the U.S. bank.

The Irrevocable Agreement to Reimburse

The U.S. bank may, however, be reluctant to issue or confirm a letter of credit. If, for example, there is a serious political disturbance in the borrower's country, the bank may want not only assurance of the suitability of goods, etc., but a guarantee of payment. In this event, the following method may be used.

The procedure followed is exactly the same as in the case of the qualified agreement. In this case, however, the U.S. bank is fully guaranteed by the IBRD for reimbursement for payments made under the letter of credit. In the case of the qualified agreement, in the event that the right to make withdrawals under the loan agreement were to be suspended or canceled, the IBRD is not bound to reimburse the U.S. bank for any payments made by the bank subsequent to the date of suspension or cancellation. In such an event, the U.S. bank would have recourse for payment to the correspondent bank and/or the purchaser.

Other Methods

Other methods, and combinations of methods, may be and are used by the Bank as circumstances dictate a need for alternative approaches. Occasionally the IBRD establishes a revolving fund account for the use of the borrower. Under that method, a line of credit is established by and in the IBRD for the use of the borrower. Upon presentation of the required documents and acceptance of them by the Bank, the account is replenished for the amount of the authorized purchases. The use of this method is discouraged and it is rarely used. Though the locations of the accounts differ, the method of setting up and utilizing a revolving fund account is the same for the Export-Import Bank, the IBRD and the MSA. This method has been used to a very minor extent by all three institutions.

Reluctance to use the revolving-fund-account method is due in part to the preference of traders for the letter of credit method and for the use of normal export procedures. In addition, its use is discouraged by the Bank since it is preferable for the auditing of purchases to precede the utilization of funds (even though the borrower agrees to reimburse the Bank for unauthorized purchases).

Conclusion

The methods of financing described above cover the vast majority of shipments made under loans by the IBRD. It is to be noted that a high percentage of financing is done under the letter of credit procedure, reimbursement for which may take place in various ways. Naturally, domestic and foreign banks desire to participate as much as possible in the financing of shipments under IBRD loans. However, inasmuch as most of the letters of credit are guaranteed by the IBRD, the U.S. bank looks primarily to the Bank for reimbursement and not to the foreign bank or the borrower requesting the issuance or confirmation of the letters of credit.

THE EXPORT-IMPORT BANK OF WASHINGTON

The Export-Import Bank (EIB) of Washington was created in 1934 primarily to finance foreign exports from the United States. Since its inception, its lending authority has been increased and its operations expanded. It is the principal foreign lending agency of the United States government.

Loans of the EIB for its own account (direct loans) originate in authorizations resulting from approval of credits by the Board of Directors. Agent-bank loans occur when U.S. commercial banks participate in certain loans under agency agreements which specify that at the option of either party, the EIB will reimburse the agent-bank for the unpaid principal amount of the loan with accrued interest. Credits utilized by borrowers of the EIB during the period July 1, 1945 through June 30, 1952, totaled $3,121 million of which only $130.5 million were through agent banks.[10]

Utilization of EIB loan proceeds represent disbursements of United States dollars to, or for the account of, the foreign government or other borrowing entity. The borrower, therefore, may be any approved person, or group of persons, with which the EIB may reach an agreement. Loans are not restricted to governments and need not be guaranteed by the government of the borrower. Credits established by the EIB are normally limited to financing the cost of U.S. equipment, materials and services.

After the Board of Directors approves a credit, the EIB enters into a comprehensive loan agreement with the borrower. The agreement sets forth the terms and conditions under which the dollars are to be made available. Also, as with other institutions, the EIB has sought to utilize normal export financing methods and the commercial banking system.

The Revolving Fund Account

The revolving fund account method is utilized primarily by borrowers who have little, or no, dollar funds. The amount of the fund is usually 10 to 15 per cent of the total line of credit and is established in any U.S. commercial bank of the borrower's choice. The method operates in the same manner as similar accounts set up by the MSA or the IBRD. After the establishment of the account, the borrower makes payment to the supplier from the account. Then, upon presentation of the required documents, and their examination by the EIB, the revolving fund account is replenished for the amount of the

10. All MSA loans, except deficiency material development project loans, which come under the Defense Materials Production Administration (DMPA), are made by the EIB acting as agent for the MSA. Utilization of these loans for the same period totaled $1,480 million; $1,284.6 million of this total was for the European program (under the ECA Act of 1948), $171.8 million under the India loan of June 1951, $23.6 million under the Spanish loan of September 1950. European program loans originate in commitments by the MSA but the loan agreements are executed by the EIB.

The EIB also makes loans under Executive Order 10281, of August 28, 1951, and subject to the provision of Section 302 of the Defense Production Act of 1950, as amended, for the production abroad of strategic materials. These loans are authorized only upon a certificate of essentiality (which may be issued only by the Secretary of Agriculture, the Defense Production Administrator and the Defense Materials Production Administrator) and permit the financing of essential projects with which there are associated risks precluding assistance by the EIB under the Export-Import Bank Act of 1945, as amended. Two credits had been authorized as of June 30, 1952: $202,260 for the production of sisal in Haiti ($60,655 had been disbursed) and $337,500 for zinc production in Mexico (none of which had been disbursed).

authorized purchases. The factors influencing its minor use are the same as those mentioned earlier in the cases of the MSA and the IBRD and need not be repeated here.

In rare cases, a letter of credit may be employed under this method by using the revolving fund account as collateral against the issuance of the credit.

Guarantees of Letters of Credit by the EIB

It is estimated that approximately 70 per cent of the financing by the EIB during the last five years has been done under letters of credit guaranteed by the EIB. Under this method, the borrower selects a U.S. bank which he desires to issue a letter of credit to a named supplier. The borrower then informs the EIB where the letter of credit is to be opened whereupon the EIB completes the arrangements for guaranteeing letters of credit directly with the U.S. bank.

When the supplier requests the letter of credit, the U.S. bank draws up a proposed letter, completes it except for the date and signature and sends three or more copies to the borrower. The borrower presents the proposed letter of credit to the EIB for its guarantee. It is then returned to the U.S. bank for issuance to the exporter. The U.S. bank usually makes a claim upon the EIB for reimbursement once each month or upon the disbursement of a certain amount of funds.

Advance or progress payments are usually handled under the letter of credit method with a guarantee by the EIB. The U.S. bank looks primarily to the EIB for reimbursement and not to the purchaser or his bank.

In transactions financed by loans funds of the EIB, as with other institutions, the borrower usually has a designated representative or purchasing agent in the United States who handles relations with the EIB and the suppliers.

Inasmuch as a high proportion of the purchases made with EIB loans are for equipment requiring a long period to manufacture and costing relatively large amounts, the letter of credit guaranteed by the EIB constitutes the most widely used method of financing these transactions.

Other Letter of Credit Transactions

The borrower may also use a letter of credit without a guarantee by the EIB. In such a case, the normal export procedure is followed. The usual export letter of credit procedure is seldom used in view of the nature of the purchases, the low level of dollar exchange holdings of the borrower, and the reluctance of U.S. banks to issue letters of credit because of the nature of the borrower and the proposed location of the project.

Other Methods of Financing

While U.S. suppliers usually prefer to use the letter of credit method, a small percentage of purchases are made on an open-account basis. In such cases, reimbursement for authorized purchases is not made until the EIB receives the usual export documents including a detailed invoice marked "Paid" by the supplier.

Conclusion

In transactions of the EIB, as with those of the IBRD and the MSA, the use of the letter of credit predominates, with minor use of the open account and the revolving-fund-account methods. Moreover, a high percentage of the letters of credit are issued with a guarantee by the EIB. In most cases, the EIB finances the entire portion of dollar purchases under a loan agreement involving specific shipments for projects. In some cases, however, the EIB may provide credits for only a portion of the purchase price, the remainder being covered by the borrower or by a credit from the supplier.

APPENDIX 5

NONSTERLING BILATERAL PAYMENTS AGREEMENTS

THE TABLES AND NOTES in this appendix are based on a study of the texts or summaries of the texts of over three hundred and sixty bilateral payments agreements between countries and monetary areas outside the sterling area. In addition there are about fifty formal payments agreements and informal arrangements between the United Kingdom and fifty nondollar countries and monetary areas outside the sterling area. The sterling agreements are discussed in Chapters 10 and 11 and the countries with which Britain has bilateral payments agreements or informal arrangements are given in Figure 3. The methods of settlement between Britain and other countries are summarized in Table 9 (page 236). The agreements dealt with in this appendix are therefore confined to the nonsterling bilateral payments agreements. It must be emphasized that the following material is based on the texts of the payments agreements. The actual operation of an agreement may involve practices which deviate from the strict wording of the agreement. Some instances will be noted of these discrepancies and the factors giving rise to them.

The nonsterling payments agreements are summarized in tabular form and arranged for purposes of analysis on the basis of six major geographical areas: continental OEEC; other Western Europe (Spain); Latin America; the Far East; the Middle East; and Eastern Europe. Beginning with the first geographical category the bilateral agreements with partner countries in each of the other geographical categories are summarized in alphabetical order. In order to avoid duplication the agreements are not repeated in the reverse order of partnership. Each of the geographical groupings is accompanied by supplemental notes indicating characteristics of the agreements not included in the tables.

A large number of unpublished agreements were studied in the preparation of this material. In a number of cases important characteristics of agreements have had to be discussed without specific mention of the particular agreements to which these characteristics apply.

The tables summarizing the basic features of the agreements are divided into four columns: Column 1: Partners to the Agreement; Column 2: Date and Termination; Column 3: Nature of Accounts; Column 4: Swing Credits.

Date and Termination

The initial date given in Column 2 usually refers to the date on which the agreement entered into effect. In some cases, however, the date refers to the time of ratification or of signature to the agreement. Insofar as possible, the dates of major changes in the provisions of the agreements are also listed in

Column 2. The designation "a.t.r." means "annual tacit renewal," which signifies that the agreement remains in effect until it is specifically denounced by one or both of the partner countries. The designation "indefinite," means that no definite provision has been made for the termination of the agreement.

Nature of Accounts

Column 3, Nature of Accounts, indicates the currency or currencies used and the number and location of the accounts which are maintained. When a single currency is shown and a location is not noted, the account is maintained in the country whose currency is used as the currency-of-account. Where two currencies are used, one account is maintained in each of the partner countries.

Whenever an agreement provides for the use of multiple accounts, i.e., sub-accounts under one general account, for specified purposes or transactions, this fact is also noted in Column 3. The operation of several of the agreements employing multiple accounts is discussed in the introductory material accompanying the tables.

Swing Credits

The existence of a swing credit, noted in Column 4, indicates that the agreement permits debit or credit balances to occur without the necessity for settlement during the life of the agreement. Swing credits are of two kinds, *unilateral* and *reciprocal*. Where a definite swing credit is not provided, the credit element depends upon the frequency of the settlement period. If the settlement periods are reasonably long, say six months to a year, the amount of actual credit provided by one of the partners may be fairly substantial. If the settlement periods are fairly short and if trade is planned so that each country exports equal values of commodities to the other, trade tends to be financed on a barter basis. In general the larger the swing credits, the greater is the flexibility in trade relations and the farther is trading removed from a rigid equal-valued commodity exchange or from a barter basis. In practice swing credits are often unilateral. In a number of cases, reciprocal swing credits were introduced to offset trade fluctuations but have actually resulted in one-sided credit facilities.

Features of Agreements Not Shown in the Tables

An important feature of bilateral payments agreements not revealed in the tables, relates to the nature of the banking relationships which are permitted. Under agreements between certain countries, neither banks nor individuals may hold balances in foreign commercial banks. This is generally true of agreements which use a third currency (mainly the U.S. dollar) as the currency-of-account but it may also be true for agreements which employ the currency of one or both of the partners. In such cases, only a designated bank (generally the central bank) may hold accounting balances. This method of "centralized administration" of the accounts generally signifies a more rigid control of trade transactions. On the other hand, a "decentralized administration" of the accounts permits normal correspondent relationships between banks. This type of administration of the accounts generally signifies a more liberal and flexible trade policy. The general nature of the administration of the accounts are noted in the introductory notes of each section.

Exchange Rates

Provisions relating to exchange rates are included in all agreements in order to provide for the conversion of other currencies into the currency-of-account (i.e., conversion of invoice values into currency-of-account values) and for the conversion of balances in two-currency accounts into a common denominator for balancing and settlement purposes. Where a single currency-of-account is employed, there is no need for an exchange rate for the conversion of balances into a common denominator, but an exchange rate provision is necessary for purposes of converting the values of exports invoiced in other currencies. In a few agreements, it is stipulated that all invoices must be made out in the currency-of-account. Such a provision, of course, eliminates all need for an exchange rate provision.

The general nature of the exchange rate provisions relevant to the agreements are noted in the introductory notes to each section of this appendix.

Revaluation Guarantees

A revaluation guarantee is included in a large number of bilateral payments agreements. In fact, it is only in agreements using the U.S. dollar as the currency-of-account that the provision is excluded to any significant extent. Some countries, however, take special care to ensure that the revaluation guarantee is included in the agreement regardless of the currency-of-account. This is notably the case in Argentine agreements using the U.S. dollar as the currency-of-account.

There are two types of revaluation guarantees: (1) There may be a guarantee of balances held in the accounts in the event of devaluation of the currency-of-account. In this case the guarantee generally provides that balances will be revalued with changes in the official gold value of the currency-of-account. (2) The guarantee may provide that the value of the swing credit will be increased proportionately with a devaluation of the currency-of-account.

Swing Credits: Settlement of Excess Balances

In a majority of the agreements, partner countries are permitted to exceed the swing credit limit; in other cases, strict provisions are included forbidding any excess balance to arise. In the former case, settlement procedures for excess balances generally provide for the payment of the excess balance in U.S.

dollars, gold or an agreed third currency within a stipulated time period. In fewer cases, the agreement merely provides for consultation between the governments to determine a method of liquidating the excess balance.

In the second case, when no excess is permitted, the agreement usually states that import or export licenses which would create an excess balance will not be issued. This provision generally denotes a more rigid trade relationship although it may denote only that one or both of the partners desire absolute assurance that excess balances will not be "induced."

In practice swing credits tend to exceed the amount stipulated in the agreements by roughly 10 per cent. This occurs because payment for excess balances are usually limited to some figure and multiples of that sum. For example, the swing credit may be $5 million as stated in the agreement, while excess balances are to be paid in dollars but only in minimum sums of $500,000. Thus the actual swing credit balance permitted is an amount just less than $5.5 million.

Although explicit provision is usually made for the settlement of balances in excess of the permitted swings, creditor countries frequently permit partner countries to accummulate large deficits in excess of the swings. For example, at the end of February 1953, Brazil's bilateral indebtedness to Western Germany was over $94 million as compared with an agreed swing margin of $13.5 million. On the same date Yugoslavia's debit balance under her agreement with Western Germany was $17.7 million as against an agreed swing margin of $7.5 million. The attitude of the creditor country depends on three primary considerations: (1) the gold and dollar reserves of the debtor and the debtor's ability to pay an excess balance; (2) the importance of the market of the debtor country and the effect of a decrease in exports on domestic employment and income in the creditor country; (3) the importance of the import items obtained from the debtor for domestic consumption and/or production. Generally if the debtor country makes some effort to increase exports to the creditor, the latter may allow the debtor to exceed considerably the swing margin without dollar payment. Serious difficulties in liquidating the balances sometimes arise.

Swing Credits: Settlement of Final Balances

All agreements provide for the method of settlement in case of the abrogation or expiration of the agreement. Generally the accounts are to be maintained for a specified period of time in order to provide for the completion of pending transactions. After that time, the accounts are closed and settlement may take place in a number of ways. In most cases the payment of dollars, gold or an agreed currency is required within a specified time or in specified installments. In other cases, the balance is to be liquidated by shipments of goods. In fewer cases, provision exists for consultation on the method of liquidating the balance. In either of the two latter cases, however, it is generally provided that if the settlement by shipments of goods or by the method agreed in the consultation is not completed within a certain length of time, any remaining balance will be paid in dollars or gold.

In a very few cases, provision is made for the issuance of Treasury bonds in favor of the creditor. These bonds bear interest and are amortized over a period varying from one to five years. This type of provision was common in the intra-OEEC agreements before the establishment of the European Payments Union.

In those agreements which have no stipulated limit to the swing credit, provision is made for periodic settlement of balances. Settlement is most frequently monthly or semiannual. In other cases, periodic settlement of balances is provided along with a swing credit arrangement. The Japanese "open dollar account" agreements, for example, provide both for swing credits and annual settlement of balances.

Discouraging High Credit Balances

In a number of cases, provision is made for discouraging large balances even within the permitted swing credits. In a few cases (e.g., the French-Brazilian agreement) interest is charged on the entire credit balance. More common, however, is an agreement to consult whenever a certain percentage of the permitted swing credit is reached. In the agreement between Germany and Japan, consultation is required whenever balances reach 80 per cent of the permitted swing.

Some agreements provide for interest charges on balances beyond a certain percentage of the permitted swing. The interest may be payable either in gold or stipulated currencies, or it may be payable through the account. In some cases the creditor may invest any balance in excess of a stated minimum in Treasury bonds which bear interest equal to the current rate in the debtor country.

Permitted Transactions

Payments agreements usually denote the types of transactions for which payment may be made through the account. Payments are generally restricted to those arising out of current transactions. The approved transactions may be listed in the agreement itself or reference may be made to Article XIX of the International Monetary Fund Agreement which defines current transactions.[1] Capital transactions, if allowed at all, are provided for under separate agreements (e.g., the UNISCAN agreement of the Scandinavian countries). Payments on past obligations may be provided for in the payments agreement or by a separate agreement.

Some agreements specifically exclude the making of payments for certain commodities or services through the bilateral agreement accounts, or they may provide that only a portion of the payments for certain items may be

1. See page 27, footnote 11, for the Fund's definition of current transactions.

made through the accounts and the remainder made in dollars or other currencies.

Relation to Trade Agreements

In most cases payments agreements are accompanied by trade agreements which are embodied in separate documents and concluded annually.[2] Because of their close relationship to the operation of payments agreements the general nature of the trade agreements are described in the notes accompanying each of the tables. Bilateral trade agreements may be divided into the four following general categories.

1. Bilateral Quotas for a Target Trade Balance

The most prevalent type of bilateral trading arrangement provides for two lists of commodities with corresponding quotas or values for which the two countries agree to grant the necessary import and export licenses. Although trade in other commodities is not excluded, special permission must generally be obtained before payment may take place through the account. Neither country guarantees that the trade will actually take place; each agrees only to grant the necessary licenses. This type of trading arrangement will be referred to as "bilateral quotas for a target trade balance." Most trade agreements of this type read somewhat as follows: "Both governments pledge themselves to grant within the framework of the valid general provisions, the import and export licenses necessary for the utilization of these quotas," or, "Consistent with import, and exchange laws and regulations which are in effect or may come into effect, each Party agrees to permit the import and export of goods and services . . . at least up to the amounts set forth in the Trade Plan."

Export commitments may also be included in the agreements. They usually cover relatively scarce commodities which the partner countries are anxious to secure. Export quotas usually indicate a firmer commitment than import quotas since goods in short supply are frequently subject to government allocation and their exportation often requires special government action. The general use of export commitments is a relatively new phenomenon introduced to assure supplies of goods after the outbreak of the Korean war. Their use decreased considerably in 1952 and 1953.

2. Bilateral Quotas for an Exact Trade Balance

The designation "bilateral quotas for an exact trade balance" indicates that the trade agreement provides for more rigidly controlled trade with a view to achieving an exact balance over a given period of time. Usually the accom-

---

2. Trade agreements, however, are frequently not accompanied by payments agreements.

panying payments agreements have narrow swing credit limits and low values of contemplated trade. Nevertheless, some flexibility remains in the disposition by the creditor of balances in the account for purchases among items on the quota list even though trade is more or less rigidly controlled.

3. Barter and Compensation Trade

A "barter or compensation transaction" designation indicates that trade consists of shipping goods against goods with prices and quantities determined so as to achieve an exact balance. While the arrangements for financing such trade are usually called "payments agreements," they do not involve foreign exchange transactions as we have defined them in Chapter 4. Some of these agreements are, nevertheless, included in the tables even though the accounts may be considered as mere bookkeeping devices for implementing special equal-value transactions.

4. Nonquota Agreements

The designation "lists of goods but no quotas established" indicates that the partner countries have drawn up lists of goods which each partner desires to import. Each partner pledges to facilitate trade in those commodities but there are no obligations to issue licenses or to take any specific action to implement trade in these commodities.

SOURCES OF DATA

A large number of sources have been employed in the preparation of the tables and the accompanying notes, some of which are noted below. The tables are incomplete because much of the information on payments agreements has not been made public. The texts of many of the agreements have not been published and in some cases even adequate summaries are not available. In addition, there have been numerous modifications of the original agreements, not all of which have been traced and accounted for even in cases where they may be available.

An attempt has been made to include in the tables all nonsterling payments agreements concluded prior to November 1952. A few agreements of a later date have also been cited. It is not possible to know in some instances if agreements have been allowed to lapse or have been denounced. In the following tables, it is assumed that the agreements have remained in effect—even those requiring positive annual renewal—unless public announcement has been made of the termination. Therefore, a limited number of agreements may be listed which in fact have been allowed to lapse.

Much of the data for the tables and the accompanying notes have been taken from the following sources:

Aussen handelsdienst (Cologne) *Commercial Trade News* (London)
Board of Trade Journal (London) *Far East Trader* (San Francisco)

Financial Times (London)

Foreign Commerce Weekly, U.S. Department of Commerce (Washington)

Forex (Zurich)

International Trade News Bulletin, GATT (Geneva)

International Financial News Survey, International Monetary Fund (Washington)

Journal of Commerce (New York)

Le Monde (Paris)

Le Moniteur Officiel (Paris)

Neue Zürcher Zeitung (Zurich)

New York Herald Tribune

New York Times

Oriental Economist (Tokyo)

Press Reports, Bank for International Settlements (Basel)

Wall Street Journal (New York)

INTRACONTINENTAL OEEC PAYMENTS AGREEMENTS

Bilateral payments agreements between continental OEEC countries during the early postwar period provided for relatively small swing credits, usually $1.5 to $3 million.[3] This was due in large measure to the low levels of production and to the unwillingness to extend any appreciable amount of credit. The desire to have balanced trade was further evidenced by the provisions relating to balances in excess of the swing credits. Such balances were usually payable in gold or U.S. dollars immediately upon the demand of the creditor. In addition, penalties were often provided for the use of swing credits above a stipulated percentage of the total permitted swing. In a few cases, penalties were even imposed on any net credit balance which existed over a given period of time. These penalties usually took the form of interest charges on balances in excess of minimum amounts, which charges were frequently payable in gold or U.S. dollars. In some cases, however, the interest charges could be credited to the payments accounts, or balances could be invested in interest-bearing Treasury bonds.

Agreements after the Establishment of the European Payments Union

With the establishment of the EPU, the agreements shown in Table I were altered to make them consistent with the provisions of the EPU Agreement. The swing credit and excess balance clauses, as well as the final settlement and the exchange rate clauses, were suspended. Monthly settlement of bilateral balances take place through the EPU mechanism. The EPU Agreement also provided for the establishment of an exchange rate for each currency vis-à-vis the EPU "accounting unit" and for settlement of balances in accordance with the established rate. Members of the EPU may freely change their rates but the balances arising out of transactions subsequent to the change are settled at the new rate. Final settlement provisions are provided in the EPU Agreement in the event of its termination. Nevertheless, some bilateral agreements make provision for the settlement of balances which have not been cleared through the EPU.

3. Notable exceptions were the Western German-Italian swing credit of $20 million and the Western German-French swing credit of $40 million.

Agreements between the EPU countries usually make special provision for their operation in the event that the EPU is discontinued, or one of the partner countries to an agreement withdraws from the organization. The payments agreements frequently provide for either (1) a reversion to a previously existing agreement, or (2) the automatic application of alternate provisions in the current agreement.

The accounts maintained by the EPU countries tend to be decentralized. Normal bank-to-bank deposits are permitted although the banks are limited in the amounts of foreign currencies they may hold and they must report foreign exchange balances to the central bank. The EPU Agreement provides that members must take the necessary steps to insure that the bilateral balances reported to the EPU for compensation are correctly calculated. French banks, for example, were put under an obligation on November 22, 1951, to transfer to the accounts of the French Stabilization Fund any part of their foreign balances which were in excess of those held on June 6, 1951.

In cases where the U.S. dollar is utilized as the currency-of-account, primarily in agreements between Austria, Turkey and Greece, the accounts are held exclusively in the central banks.

Characteristics of Trade Agreements

Since the establishment of the EPU in July 1950 the vast bulk of the trade between EPU countries has not been subject to quota limitations. The nonliberalized sector of the trade, however, is in part governed by trade-quota agreements. These agreements are not determined with a view to achieving a bilateral balance and do not provide for quotas which discriminate against EPU countries.

Some barter and compensation transactions outside the agreements are permitted by certain of these countries, notably Greece and Austria. These transactions occur under fairly strict government supervision and generally involve trade in luxuries or nonessentials frequently accompanied by an overvalued currency or high domestic prices. In some instances, however, barter trade takes place in scarce raw materials or essential manufactured goods. For the most part, however, compensation or barter transactions are prohibited, or at least discouraged by the other continental OEEC countries. In agreements with Greece, provision is occasionally made for permitting barter or compensation in specified goods which are denoted as "hard-to-sell."

Export commitments are sometimes included in the intra-OEEC agreements. Commodities covered by these provisions include such items as coal, copper, iron and iron ore. (These are included in agreements between Austria–France, B.L.E.U.–Sweden, Denmark–Portugal, Western Germany–Italy, Western Germany–Sweden, Italy–Turkey.)

A few agreements contain no quotas (Austria-Greece) and, in two instances (Austria-Turkey, Denmark-Turkey) there are no lists of goods. A few import commitments (as opposed to agreements to issue import licenses) have been noted. Import commitments represent a firm obligation and are, therefore, usually a matter of intergovernmental sales and purchases. The agreement between Switzerland and Turkey requires that a certain percentage of exports must be paid for in free Swiss francs. No other agreement has been found to require payment in hard currency.

Abbreviations Used in Tables

A.t.r., "annual tacit renewal."
N.a., "not available."
Currencies: Bfr, Belgian franc
Ffr, French franc
Sfr, Swiss franc
Dkr, Danish kroner
Nkr, Norwegian kroner
Skr, Swedish kronor
DM, Western German Deutsche Mark

TABLE I

PAYMENTS AGREEMENTS BETWEEN CONTINENTAL OEEC COUNTRIES

Countries	Date and Termination	Nature of Accounts	Swing Credits
Austria–B.L.E.U.[a]	October 1951; indefinite	Single Bfr account	EPU[b]
Austria–Denmark	November 1948; amended February 1950; a.t.r.	Single Dkr account	EPU
Austria–France [c]	November 1949; indefinite	Single Ffr account	EPU
Austria–Western Germany	May 1950; a.t.r.	Single DM account	EPU
Austria–Greece	May 1950; a.t.r.	Single U.S. dollar account in Austria	EPU
Austria–Italy	June 1950; indefinite	Two accounts in U.S. dollars	EPU
Austria–Netherlands [d]	March 1951; a.t.r.	Single guilder account	EPU
Austria–Norway	November 1948; indefinite	Single Nkr account	EPU
Austria–Portugal [e]	June 1951	Single U.S. dollar account	EPU
Austria–Sweden	April 1948; amended February 1951; a.t.r.	Single Skr account	EPU
Austria–Switzerland	August 1946; amended July 1949; 1951	Single Sfr account	EPU
Austria–Turkey	July 1949; a.t.r.	Single U.S. dollar account in Austria	EPU
B.L.E.U.–Denmark	August 1951; indefinite	Two accounts: Bfr, Dkr	EPU
B.L.E.U.–France	August 1946; amended January 1950; indefinite	Two accounts: Bfr, Ffr	EPU
B.L.E.U.–Western Germany	July 1951	Two accounts: Bfr, DM	EPU

TABLE I—*Continued*

Countries	Date and Termination	Nature of Accounts	Swing Credits
B.L.E.U.–Greece	December 1948; a.t.r.	Single Bfr account	EPU
B.L.E.U.–Italy	March 1951; indefinite	Single Bfr account	EPU
B.L.E.U.–Netherlands	October 1943; amended November 1945, May 1946, 1949, January 1951; indefinite	Two accounts: Bfr, guilder	EPU
B.L.E.U.–Norway	September 1951; indefinite	Two accounts: Bfr, Nkr	EPU
B.L.E.U.–Portugal	February 1949; a.t.r.	Two accounts: Bfr, escudo	EPU
B.L.E.U.–Sweden	December 1950; indefinite	Two accounts: Bfr, Skr	EPU
B.L.E.U.–Switzerland	November 1951; indefinite	Two accounts: Sfr, Bfr	EPU
B.L.E.U.–Turkey	December 1948; amended February 1951	Single Bfr account	EPU
Denmark–France	October 1945; amended June 1949; a.t.r.	Two accounts: Ffr, Dkr	EPU
Denmark–Western Germany	December 1949; amended April 1950; October 1951; indefinite	Two accounts: Dkr, DM	EPU
Denmark–Greece	February 1949; indefinite	Single Dkr account	EPU
Denmark–Italy	October 1950; indefinite	Two accounts: Dkr, lire	EPU
Denmark–Netherlands	January 1946; indefinite	Two accounts: Dkr, guilder	EPU
Denmark–Norway	April 1951; indefinite	Two accounts: Dkr, Nkr	EPU
Denmark–Portugal	April 1949; indefinite	Two accounts: Dkr, escudo	EPU
Denmark–Sweden	February 1951; indefinite	Two accounts: Skr, Dkr	EPU
Denmark–Switzerland	January 1951; indefinite	Two accounts: Sfr, Dkr	EPU
Denmark–Turkey	December 1948; a.t.r.	Single U.S. dollar account in Denmark	EPU
France–Western Germany	February 1950; indefinite	Two accounts: Ffr, DM	EPU
France–Greece	April 1946; amended 1949	Single Ffr account	EPU
France–Italy	January 1951; a.t.r.	Two accounts: Ffr, lire	EPU
France–Netherlands	October 1948; indefinite	Two accounts: Ffr, guilder	EPU
France–Norway	June 1946; a.t.r.	Two accounts: Ffr, Nkr	EPU
France–Portugal	February 1952. (Financial clause in trade agreement of 1952.)	Single Ffr account	EPU
France–Sweden	July 1948; amended March 1949, January 1951	Two accounts: Ffr, Skr	EPU
France–Switzerland	November 1945; amended and extended September 1950	Two accounts: Ffr, Sfr	EPU
France–Turkey	August 1946; annual renewal	Single Ffr account	EPU

TABLE I—*Continued*

Countries	Date and Termination	Nature of Accounts	Swing Credits
Western Germany–Greece	July 1950; indefinite	Single DM account	EPU
Western Germany–Italy	November 1950; amended February 1952	Two accounts: DM, lire	EPU
Western Germany–Netherlands	September 1949	Two accounts: DM, guilder	EPU
Western Germany–Norway	October 1949; amended November 1950; a.t.r.	Two accounts: DM, Nkr	EPU
Western Germany–Portugal	April 1952; indefinite	Two accounts: DM, escudo	EPU
Western Germany–Sweden	September 1950; a.t.r.	Two accounts: DM, Skr	EPU
Western Germany–Switzerland	August 1949; amended September 1950	Two accounts: DM, Sfr	EPU
Western Germany–Turkey	January 1952; a.t.r.	Single U.S. dollar account in Turkey	EPU
Greece–Italy	April 1949; amended July 1950; a.t.r.	Single U.S. dollar account in Italy	EPU
Greece–Netherlands	August 1951; indefinite	Single guilder account	EPU
Greece–Norway	March 1950; amended May 1951	Single Nkr account	EPU
Greece–Portugal	December 1949; amended May 1951	Single U.S. dollar account in Portugal	EPU
Greece–Sweden	June 1948; amended December 1950	Single Skr account	EPU
Greece–Switzerland	April 1947; amended May 1951	Single Sfr account	EPU
Greece–Turkey	April 1949; a.t.r.	Single U.S. dollar account in Turkey	
Italy–Netherlands	August 1946	Single guilder account	EPU
Italy–Norway	February 1951; indefinite	Two accounts: lire, Nkr	EPU
Italy–Portugal	February 1950; extended June 1952	Single U.S. dollar account in Italy	EPU
Italy–Sweden	November 1949; amended February 1950; a.t.r.	Two accounts: lire, Skr	EPU
Italy–Switzerland	October 1950; indefinite	Two accounts: lire, Sfr	EPU
Italy–Turkey	February 1952	Single U.S. dollar account in Italy	EPU
Netherlands–Norway	November 1945; indefinite	Two accounts: guilder, Nkr	EPU
Netherlands–Portugal	March 1946; indefinite	Two accounts: guilder, escudo	EPU
Netherlands–Sweden	November 1945	Two accounts: guilder, Skr	EPU
Netherlands–Switzerland	October 1945	Two accounts: guilder, Sfr	EPU

TABLE I—*Continued*

Countries	Date and Termination	Nature of Accounts	Swing Credits
Netherlands–Turkey	September 1949	Single U.S. dollar account in the Netherlands	EPU
Norway–Portugal	November 1949; a.t.r.	Two accounts: Nkr, escudo	EPU
Norway–Sweden	February 1951	Two accounts: Nkr, Skr	EPU
Norway–Switzerland	July 1947; amended January 1951; indefinite	Two accounts: Nkr, Sfr	EPU
Norway–Turkey	February 1949	Two accounts in U.S. dollars	EPU
Portugal–Sweden	May 1950; amended April 1952	Two accounts: escudo, Skr	EPU
Portugal–Switzerland	1952	Two accounts: escudo, Sfr	EPU
Portugal–Turkey	n.a.	n.a.	EPU
Sweden–Switzerland	June 1951; indefinite	Two accounts: Skr, Sfr	EPU
Sweden–Turkey	July 1948; amended June 1950, July 1951; a.t.r.	Single Skr account	EPU
Switzerland–Turkey	October 1945; a.t.r.	Single Sfr account	EPU

a. Includes Belgium, Luxembourg and the Belgian territories.
b. Monthly settlement through EPU eliminates necessity for bilateral swing credits.
c. Includes French franc area.
d. Includes guilder area.
e. Includes Portuguese overseas territories.

CONTINENTAL OEEC WITH OTHER WESTERN EUROPE (SPAIN)

FEATURES OF PAYMENTS AGREEMENTS

The Accounts

All continental OEEC countries, except Austria, have concluded payments agreements with Spain. These agreements are listed in Table II. The agreements generally provide for a single account denominated in the currency of the continental OEEC partner country or in U.S. dollars. In only one instance is the peseta used as one of two currencies-of-account. In two of these agreements, provision is made for the use of subaccounts, the operation of which will be discussed in a later section.

Exchange Rates and Revaluation Guarantees

In a majority of the agreements, provision is made for invoicing only in the currency-of-account. Revaluation guarantees are provided in all agreements except those which utilize the dollar as the currency-of-account. In the latter case, there is usually no provision pertaining to revaluation of balances or swing credit limits.

Swing Credits

In most continental OEEC-Spanish agreements reciprocal swing credits are very small, ranging from $200,000 to $1 million. In one instance, no swing credit is provided while in two others the swing credit is significantly higher.

Settlement Provisions

Settlement of balances in excess of the permitted swing credit is generally provided by payment in gold, dollars or an agreed currency. In a few instances, there is a provision to consult but, significantly, these agreements also specify that if an agreement is not reached within a short time (two months or so) on a method of eliminating the excess balance, the excess will be paid immediately in a convertible currency. In only one agreement is no excess balance permitted to arise and in this agreement an exact trade balance is presumably contemplated.

The provision for settlement of balances in the event of the termination of the agreement usually takes the form of payment in goods within a stipulated time period (usually about six months) with any balance then remaining payable in a convertible currency. This balance may be payable immediately or, less frequently, in proportionate monthly installments. In one instance, any final balance is to be invested in Treasury bonds with amortization over a one-year period.

Extent and Nature of Trade

Trade between continental OEEC countries and Spain has not reached high levels in the postwar period. Swing credits, though relatively small, have evidently proved to be adequate. Most trade agreements are of the "bilateral quota for a target trade balance" type. In one agreement (Greece-Spain), an exact balance in trade is presumably contemplated. Trade between these two countries has been almost insignificant. In the Norway-Spain agreement, Norway has extended her OEEC free list to imports from Spain. In only one agreement was provision made for the payment of a specified portion of exports in dollars. In all other agreements, payments for all current transactions are permitted through the payments agreement account.

The Use of Multiple Accounts

In the Belgium-Spain and the Switzerland-Spain agreements, provision is made for multiple accounts. The use of multiple accounts, or subaccounts, provides a convenient method for (1) disposing of portions of the export proceeds in a defined manner or (2) implementing trade agreements which require certain exports to be exchanged only against certain imports. In some cases, swing credits are provided for each subaccount. In the agreements between continental OEEC countries and Spain, however, multiple swing credits are not provided. Therefore, the reciprocal swing credits refer to the total balance which may be permitted on all subaccounts combined.

The agreement between Belgium and Spain uses three subaccounts. It provides that 8 per cent of Spanish export proceeds are to be credited to a subaccount, balances in which are to be used for the transfer of profits and the settlement of outstanding financial claims on Spain. A further 15 per cent (but not more than Bfr 90 million) must be used for the purchase of "nonessential goods," as defined in the agreement, including hides, paper, textiles, glassware, etc. The remaining 77 per cent may be used by Spain for the purchase of Belgian goods as enumerated in the regular quota list. The agreement thus ensures that (1) certain invisible payments will be made and (2) certain Belgian exports will receive at least minimum consideration.

The Swiss-Spanish agreement provisions are similar to the Belgian-Spanish provisions in that certain percentages of total Spanish export proceeds are credited to special accounts. In the Swiss-Spanish agreement, however, only two accounts are utilized. To one account is credited $92\frac{1}{2}$ per cent of the value of Spanish exports. Balances in this account are used for purchases of Swiss goods enumerated in the quota list. The remaining $7\frac{1}{2}$ per cent is credited to a second account. Balances in the second account are used for making certain stipulated invisible payments including insurance, pensions, earnings on Swiss investments in Spain and student expenses.

TABLE II

PAYMENTS AGREEMENTS BETWEEN CONTINENTAL OEEC COUNTRIES AND SPAIN

Countries	Date and Termination	Nature of Accounts	Swing Credits
Belgium–Spain[a]	April 1949; effective to July 1952	Single Bfr account	Reciprocal
Denmark–Spain	July 1950	Single Dkr account	Reciprocal
France–Spain	July 1949; a.t.r.	Single Ffr account	No provision
Western Germany–Spain	October 1952; a.t.r.	Single DM account	Reciprocal
Greece–Spain	February 1950; a.t.r.	Single U.S. dollar account in Spain	Reciprocal
Italy–Spain	April 1952; a.t.r.	Single U.S. dollar account in Italy	Reciprocal
Netherlands–Spain	October 1946	Single guilder account	Reciprocal
Norway–Spain	January 1951; amended February 1951	Two accounts: Nkr, peseta	Reciprocal
Portugal–Spain	February 1943; amended 1951	Single U.S. dollar account in Spain	Reciprocal
Sweden–Spain	July 1948; extended April 1951	Single Skr account	Reciprocal
Switzerland–Spain	May 1949	Single Sfr account	Reciprocal
Turkey–Spain	June 1951; amended April 1953	Single U.S. dollar account in Turkey	Reciprocal

a. Spanish monetary area.

CONTINENTAL OEEC WITH LATIN AMERICAN COUNTRIES

Continental OEEC countries have concluded a large number of bilateral agreements with Latin American countries, primarily with the nondollar countries (Argentina, Brazil, Chile, Paraguay, Peru and Uruguay). However, a limited number of agreements exist with Bolivia, Colombia and Ecuador, and Mexico and Cuba have agreements with France. Table III contains a list of these agreements.

The Accounts

Usually only one account is established, employing either the dollar or the currency of the continental OEEC partner country as the currency-of-account. In some instances, two dollar accounts are maintained, one in the central bank of each partner country. The dollar is commonly employed in order to avoid difficulties which arise from multiple exchange rate systems or a lack of confidence in the partner's country's currency.

Exchange Provisions

Where the dollar is the currency of account, there is as a rule no provision in the agreement for either an exchange rate or a revaluation guarantee of the balances against a change in the gold content of the dollar.[4] In agreements employing a continental OEEC currency as the unit of account both an exchange rate and a revaluation guarantee are usually provided.

Swing Credits

Reciprocal swing credits are the general rule in the agreements noted in Table III but in four of these agreements a unilateral credit is provided. Unilateral credits are generally small while reciprocal swing credits vary widely, ranging from $500,000 to $100 million. In a few agreements, no provision for swing credits is included. The absence of a stipulated swing credit may indicate one of four possible conditions. (1) There may be frequent settlement dates so that neither partner would be in a position to run a substantial deficit in the account. (2) The total volume of trade contemplated might be very small and perhaps limited to a relatively few items. (3) Trade under the agreement may take place on a barter basis. (4) There may be a secret swing provision not included in the agreement.

Settlement Provisions: Excess Balances

The general rule on the settlement of balances in excess of the permitted swing credits is that the debtor will make payment, immediately or within a short time, in dollars, gold or an agreed currency. In a few cases, provision is made for consultation, so that the imbalance may be corrected during the

4. Argentina's dollar account agreements usually provide for a revaluation guarantee.

next trade period. In practice swing margins are often exceeded, sometimes by substantial amounts.

In those agreements which provide for frequent settlement of the entire balance, there is usually no provision concerning excess balances since frequent settlement provides some assurance that high balances will not be permitted to accumulate. Nevertheless, in one agreement a swing credit is provided along with monthly settlement of total balances.

In a number of other agreements annual or biannual settlement of balances is provided. A swing credit is also included and presumably may not be exceeded since there is no provision relating to excess balances.

Settlement Provisions: Final Balances

In the agreements concluded in the early postwar period, settlement of final balances was usually very strict, providing for payment in gold or dollars immediately or within a very short time. These provisions have been made more flexible in the later agreements so that current agreements usually provide for liquidation of final balances in goods and services within six to twelve months, with any balance then remaining payable in dollars, gold or an agreed currency. Other agreements provide for payment in gold or dollars within approximately a year or in stipulated installments over a one- to two-year period. In a very few agreements, provision is made only for consultation between the partners for a determination of the method of settlement.

Provisions for Discouraging Large Balances

A high proportion of the continental OEEC–Latin American agreements have a provision relating to the maintenance of large balances within the swing credit limits. Generally, these measures were not included in the early postwar agreements due to the acknowledgment that Western European partners would undoubtedly be maintaining high balances in the accounts for some considerable period. In later agreements, however, provisions discouraging high swing credit balances were included. In a number of agreements, e.g., Western Germany-Argentina, this provision took the form of an agreement to consult on the measures to be taken whenever the balance reached 80 per cent of the permitted swing credit. In other agreements, e.g., Norway-Argentina, this provision took the form of providing for a 2 per cent interest charge on balances in excess of certain percentages of the permitted swing. Charges are usually payable through the account while balances in excess of the permitted swings are usually payable in gold or U.S. dollars within a short period of time.

The Western Germany-Paraguay agreement illustrates the methods used to discourage high swing credit or balances in excess of the swing. Under this agreement provision was made for a reciprocal swing credit of $2.5 million but it was also provided that whenever the balance reached $1.25 million, the two governments would consult in order to take action for preventing any further imbalance. If, however, a balance in excess of $1.5 million evolved and continued to be in excess of that figure for six months, the excess was then payable in U.S. dollars. If at any time the balance exceeded $2.5 million, the excess was payable immediately in dollars.

Exclusion of Commodities from Payment through the Account

Agreements with Latin American countries frequently exclude payments for certain Latin American exports through the payments agreement accounts. This is generally true of payments for Chilean copper, and in certain instances, payments for petroleum and derivatives, tin, coffee and wool are excluded. Trade in these goods usually takes place under the provisions of a separate agreement which generally specifies payment in dollars.

Except for specified items payment for all direct current transactions is usually permitted through the accounts. The acceptable accounting items are generally listed in the payments agreements although reference is occasionally made to the definition of current transactions given in the IMF Agreement. In one agreement, Western Germany-Colombia, payment for invisibles up to approximately 5 per cent of the total contemplated value of trade is permitted.

Transferability

Few evidences of transferability have been noted in these agreements. In certain French agreements provision is made for consultative transferability, and in the French-Peruvian agreement it is provided that Peru may use accrued franc balances for settlement of commitments to specified third countries.

Multiple Lists of Goods

A number of recent agreements have incorporated provisions to encourage trade in "nonessentials" or luxury items. Sometimes these provisions take the form of establishing multiple lists of goods which provide for trade in specified European commodities against specified Latin American goods. For example, the French-Bolivian agreement provides that the export proceeds of Bolivian rubber up to 1,000 tons annually are to be used for the purchase of goods in List A, while proceeds of exports in excess of 1,000 tons are to be used for the purchase of goods in List B. Certain other agreements incorporate similar provisions.

A number of the agreements incorporate provisions establishing more than one account. As a rule, multiple accounts are incorporated in order to provide for the exchange of certain commodities against commodities of equal economic importance. In one of the agreements, multiple swing credits have been noted; their use, therefore, may be conveniently illustrated at this point.

In the five-year trade and payments agreement between Argentina and the Netherlands, the Netherlands obligated itself to import annually specified quantities of bread grains, feed grains and some other agricultural products. Argentina, on the other hand, obligated itself to import vessels up to 50 million guilders, along with specified quantities of rubber and tin. These commitments were subject to subsequent agreements relating to prices, and terms of delivery. Two accounts were established by the agreement. The B Account has a swing credit of 75 million guilders and is used for making payments for Netherlands ships and Argentine wheat. The A Account has a swing of 67.5 million guilders and is used for payments for other commercial transactions.

Assuring Minimum Levels of Trade

The trade and payments agreements between continental OEEC and Latin American countries sometimes contain provisions designed to assure that a minimum level of trade will take place. One method, which is employed in the Western Germany-Argentina agreement, is to require that each country issue import permits up to say 25 per cent of the value of imports contemplated by the agreement, at the time of the effective date of the trade agreement. Another method, which is employed by the France-Mexico agreement is to impose a penalty upon a partner which has failed to import up to a minimum value. This agreement provides for a semiannual clearing of accounts with the entire net balance payable in dollars. However, if during the twelve-month period preceding the date of settlement, it is determined that the debtor has made payments through the accounts for imports from the partner country totaling at least $2.5 million, the debtor is entitled to deduct $2.5 million from the balance that is subject to settlement in dollars at that time. Thus if the partners wish to take advantage of a more desirable settlement provision, each must encourage imports up to at least $2.5 million during the trade period. If the debtor does not import at least $2.5 million in goods, payment of the entire balance in U.S. dollars must be made on the settlement date.

The agreement between Western Germany and Brazil illustrates the use of a combination of both of these methods. This agreement provides for annual settlement of the entire balance on the account. The agreement also provides that each country will issue import licenses up to the quotas fixed by the trade agreement. If, upon the annual settlement of balances, it is determined that the creditor party has not supplied import licenses as required by the agreement, the debtor is entitled to deduct the difference between the value of licenses which the creditor was required to issue and the amount actually issued, from the balance in the account to be settled.

TABLE III

PAYMENTS AGREEMENTS BETWEEN CONTINENTAL OEEC AND LATIN AMERICAN COUNTRIES

Countries	Date and Termination	Nature of Accounts	Swing Credits
Austria–Argentina	March 1950	Single U.S. dollar account in Argentina	Unilateral, favor of Austria
Austria–Brazil	May 1951; a.t.r.	Single U.S. dollar account in Brazil	Reciprocal

TABLE III—*Continued*

Countries	Date and Termination	Nature of Accounts	Swing Credits
Austria–Uruguay	February 1951; annual renewal	Single U.S. dollar account in Uruguay	Reciprocal
Belgium–Bolivia	April 1949; a.t.r.	Single Bfr account	Unilateral, favor of Belgium
Belgium–Colombia	April 1948	Single Bfr account	Reciprocal
Belgium–Uruguay	June 1946	Single Bfr account	Reciprocal
Denmark–Argentina	December 1948; amended August 1951; five years	Single Dkr account	Reciprocal
Denmark–Brazil	May 1951	Single Dkr account	Reciprocal
Denmark–Colombia	January 1951; a.t.r.	Single U.S. dollar account in Denmark	No provision
Denmark–Uruguay	April 1948	Single Dkr account	Reciprocal
France–Argentina	January 1947; amended January 1951; valid to December 1953	Single Ffr account	Reciprocal
France–Bolivia	May 1949; a.t.r.	Two U.S. dollar accounts	No Provision
France–Brazil	March 1946; amended April 1948; valid to July 1953	Single Ffr account	Reciprocal
France–Chile	November 1948; annual renewal	Two U.S. dollar accounts	No provision
France–Cuba	September 1952; three years	Single Ffr account	Unilateral, favor of France
France–Ecuador	October 1949; a.t.r.	Two U.S. dollar accounts	Reciprocal
France–Mexico	June 1950; indefinite	Two accounts: Ffr, peso	Reciprocal
France–Paraguay	December 1949; a.t.r.	Single U.S. dollar account in France	No provision
France–Peru	December 1950; a.t.r.	Single Ffr account	No provision
France–Uruguay	March 1950; annual renewal	Single U.S. dollar account in France	Reciprocal
Western Germany–Argentina	August 1950; amended October 1951; a.t.r.	Single U.S. dollar account in Argentina	Reciprocal
Western Germany–Brazil	September 1950; a.t.r.	Single U.S. dollar account in Germany	Reciprocal
Western Germany–Chile	February 1952; a.t.r.	Single U.S. dollar account in Chile	Reciprocal
Western Germany–Colombia	February 1952; a.t.r.	Single U.S. dollar account in Germany	Reciprocal
Western Germany–Ecuador	March 1950	Single U.S. dollar account in Ecuador	Reciprocal
Western Germany–Paraguay	May 1950	Single U.S. dollar account in Germany	Reciprocal

TABLE III—*Continued*

Countries	Date and Termination	Nature of Accounts	Swing Credits
Western Germany–Uruguay	January 1952; a.t.r.	Single U.S. dollar account in Germany	Reciprocal
Greece–Brazil	July 1952; a.t.r.	Single U.S. dollar account in Brazil	Reciprocal
Greece–Uruguay	June 1951; annual renewal	Two U.S. dollar accounts	Unilateral, favor of Uruguay
Italy–Argentina	June 1952; valid to December 1958	Single "CAI dollar" account (U.S. dollar at the Argentine basic selling rate)	Reciprocal
Italy–Brazil	July 1950; a.t.r.	Single U.S. dollar account in Italy	Reciprocal
Italy–Colombia	July 1952; a.t.r.	Single U.S. dollar account in Colombia	n.a.
Italy–Ecuador	May 1951	Two U.S. dollar accounts	Reciprocal
Italy–Paraguay	April 1952; two years, then a.t.r.	Single U.S. dollar account in Italy	Reciprocal
Italy—Peru	December 1949; extended December 1951	Two accounts in pounds sterling	Reciprocal
Netherlands–Argentina	March 1948; five years	Two guilder accounts in the Netherlands	Reciprocal
Netherlands–Brazil	June 1953	Single U.S. dollar account	n.a.
Netherlands–Colombia	March 1949	Single U.S. dollar account in the Netherlands	No provision
Netherlands–Paraguay	February 1950; two years, then a.t.r.	Single guilder account	Reciprocal
Netherlands–Uruguay	June 1947; extended June 1948; indefinite	Single guilder account	Reciprocal
Norway–Argentina	August 1949; a.t.r. to August 1954	Single Nkr account	Reciprocal
Portugal–Brazil	November 1949; renewed November 1950, 1951, 1952	Two U.S. dollar accounts	No provision
Sweden–Argentina	November 1948; amended January 1951; a.t.r. to December 1953	Single Skr account	Reciprocal
Sweden–Brazil	May 1949; amended May 1950, 1951	Single Skr account	Reciprocal
Sweden–Colombia	November 1948; amended June 1951; a.t.r.	Single U.S. dollar account in Sweden	No provision
Sweden–Uruguay	June 1949; amended August 1952	Single Skr account	Reciprocal
Turkey–Uruguay	August 1950; annual renewal	Single U.S. dollar account in Uruguay	Reciprocal

CONTINENTAL OEEC WITH FAR EASTERN COUNTRIES

Most of the Far Eastern countries are members of European currency areas and therefore do not negotiate separate payments agreements. Six of the seven agreements noted in Table IV are with Japan. The Netherlands-Indonesia agreement not only governs payments between these two countries but makes Indonesia a partner with the Netherlands in a number of the Dutch payments agreements with third countries. Hence Indonesia may be considered as a part of the Netherlands monetary area in the operation of such agreements.[5]

AGREEMENTS WITH JAPAN

Prior to the signing of the peace treaty all payments agreements with Japan were concluded with the Supreme Commander for the Allied Powers (SCAP) acting on behalf of occupied Japan. This fact may, in some degree, account for the uniformity of the agreements and for the settlement of bilateral balances through dollar accounts maintained in private American banks in Japan. In some instances, Japan, looking forward to the eventual signing of a peace treaty, concluded two agreements, one of which was to be effective until the signing of the peace treaty and the other to take effect immediately thereafter (e.g., Western Germany-Japan). Where two agreements were not signed, the original agreements have generally been prolonged by mutual consent until new agreements are concluded (e.g., Netherlands-Japan).

The Accounts

All six of the continental OEEC agreements with Japan have the same basic characteristics: the use of U.S. dollar accounts for recording balances, centralized administration of the accounts and invoicing solely in the currency-of-account. There are no provisions for revaluation guarantees of balances in the accounts.

In the early postwar agreements, the dollar accounts were held in a private American bank located in Japan, or in one case, in a private Dutch bank in Japan. Since the signing of the peace treaty, the main change in the agreements has been the shifting of the dollar accounts to a Japanese bank. The Western Germany-Japan agreement provides for an identical account to be maintained in Germany as well as a dollar account in the Bank of Japan.

Swing Credits

Reciprocal swing credits are provided in all the agreements. The swing credits are for moderate amounts ranging from $1 million to $4 million. In the agreement between Western Germany and Japan, however, the maximum swing credit is established at $9 million. One agreement does not stipulate any swing credit limit.

Settlement of Balances

Provision is generally made for the settlement of balances in excess of the permitted swing credit in gold or U.S. dollars within a short period of time.

5. The operation of the joint Netherlands-Indonesian agreements is described in Chapter 14.

Some of the agreements provide for the periodic settlement of balances within the swing credit limits, in dollars or an agreed currency. In these agreements, balances are usually struck and settled every four to six months.

Settlement of balances at the termination of the agreement is usually required in dollars, gold or an agreed currency. In two recent agreements, however, final balances may be liquidated in goods within six to twelve months after the termination of the agreement, with any remaining balance payable in dollars or an agreed currency.

All the agreements contain provision for the transfer of balances upon mutual agreement between the partner countries.

Features of Trade Agreements

Trade agreements with Japan involve the establishment of a "trade plan," consisting of two lists of goods with stipulated quotas for which the two countries agree to grant import licenses. Prices are established on an individual contract basis by private traders. Mixed commissions are established to facilitate trade between the partner countries.

TABLE IV

PAYMENTS AGREEMENTS BETWEEN CONTINENTAL OEEC AND FAR EASTERN COUNTRIES

Countries	Date and Termination	Nature of Accounts	Swing Credits
B.L.E.U.–Japan	June 1950; amended January 1952; indefinite	Single U.S. dollar account in Japan	Reciprocal
France–Japan	December 1950; indefinite	Single U.S. dollar account in Japan	Reciprocal
Western Germany–Japan	August 1951	Two U.S. dollar accounts	Reciprocal
Italy–Japan	January 1953	Single U.S. dollar account in Japan	Reciprocal
Netherlands–Indonesia	April 1950	Two guilder accounts	Reciprocal
Netherlands–Japan	April 1951; indefinite	Single U.S. dollar account in Japan	Reciprocal
Sweden–Japan	March 1952	Single U.S. dollar account in Japan	Reciprocal

CONTINENTAL OEEC WITH THE NEAR AND MIDDLE EAST

GENERAL FEATURES OF THE PAYMENTS AGREEMENTS

Nearly half the agreements between continental OEEC and Near and Middle Eastern countries involve Egypt as one of the partners. At the end of 1952 Egypt was party to only four agreements with continental OEEC countries. The conclusion of five additional agreements during the first half of 1953 demonstrated Egypt's strong desire to further bilateralize her trade.

Except for Egypt and Israel, countries of the Near and Middle East have few bilateral payments agreements.

The Accounts

Most of the agreements noted in Table V utilize the currency of the continental OEEC partner country as the currency-of-account. The Egyptian pound is used, however, in the two-currency agreements in which Egypt participates, while the U.S. dollar is used as the currency-of-account in Turkish agreements. Multiple accounts are used in the agreement between the Netherlands and Israel and the French agreements with Lebanon and Syria.

Revaluation guarantees are almost always provided in these agreements.

Exchange Rate Provisions

The provisions relating to exchange rates generally establish a rate with reference to the cross-rate on the U.S. dollar. This is almost always true for the two-currency agreements which use the Egyptian pound as one of the two currencies-of-account. Since invoicing is usually permitted in either of the two partner currencies, and sometimes in a third currency as well, an exchange rate provision is included in nearly all the agreements.

Swing Credits

Reciprocal swing credits tend to be of moderate amounts. In the agreement between France and Egypt, a variable swing credit is provided, ranging from one to four million Egyptian pounds or the equivalent in French francs. Presumably adjustments in permissible swing credits are by agreement between the central banks. This unique arrangement was established in recognition of the highly seasonal nature of the trade between the two countries.

Settlement of Balances

Balances in excess of permitted swing credits, as well as final balances, are usually payable in U.S. dollars or an agreed currency. In one agreement, sterling may be used to settle excess balances and, in two other agreements, for settlement of final balances. In some agreements final settlement of balances may be made in goods within a stipulated time period, with any balance remaining at the end of the period payable in dollars, gold or an agreed currency. Two agreements provide for balances to be struck and settled annually.

Transferability

There is provision in the French agreements with Syria and Lebanon for the conversion of balances to certain other European currencies, while the French-Saudi Arabian agreement provides that balances in favor of Saudi Arabia may be used upon mutual agreement for purchases in other areas of the world.

General Features of Trade Agreements

Trade agreements between countries in the group generally provide for bilateral quotas for a target trade balance. Barter and compensation transactions are allowed in a number of instances. In one instance, Denmark-Israel, the OEEC partner country has extended its OEEC free list to imports from the Middle Eastern country.

Some continental OEEC agreements with Israel provide that Israel must pay a certain percentage of the value of her imports in free dollars.

French Agreements with Lebanon and Syria

The French agreements with Syria and with Lebanon are comprehensive long-term agreements which provide (1) a method of payment for current transactions; (2) for agreed transfers of capital; (3) settlement of debts and claims; and (4) for progressive liquidation of franc assets held by Lebanon and Syria. Syria's franc assets form a part of the cover for her currency. France guaranteed the value of these assets in terms of sterling and agreed to liquidate them gradually over a period of years. Both of the agreements established multiple accounts which are used for specified purposes. Syria and Lebanon may use balances in specified accounts for purchases of agreed European currencies from the Bank of France.

TABLE V

PAYMENTS AGREEMENTS BETWEEN CONTINENTAL OEEC AND NEAR AND MIDDLE EASTERN COUNTRIES

Countries	Date and Termination	Nature of Accounts	Swing Credits
Austria– Egypt	April 1953	n.a.	n.a.
Belgium– Egypt	April 1953	Two accounts: Bfr, E. pound	n.a.
Denmark– Israel	November 1952; a.t.r.	Single Dkr account	Reciprocal
France– Egypt	June 1948; a.t.r.	Two accounts: Ffr, E. pound	Reciprocal (See text.)
France– Iran	May 1952	Single Ffr account	Reciprocal
France– Lebanon	January 1948; ten years	Single Ffr account with subaccounts	No provision (See text.)
France– Saudi Arabia	November 1950; two years, then a.t.r.	Single Ffr account in the Bank of Indo- china in Jidda	No provision
France– Syria	October 1949; six years, then tacit renewal for three-year periods	Single Ffr account with subaccounts	No provision (See text.)
Western Ger- many– Egypt	July 1951; extended May 1952	Two accounts: DM, E. pound	Reciprocal
Western Ger- many– Iran	June 1952	Single U.S. dollar ac- count in Iran	Reciprocal

TABLE V—*Continued*

Countries	Date and Termination	Nature of Accounts	Swing Credits
Greece–Egypt	May 1953	Single E. pound account	Unilateral, favor of Greece
Italy–Egypt	November 1952	Two accounts: lire, E. pound	Reciprocal
Netherlands–Egypt	April 1953	n.a.	n.a.
Netherlands–Israel	November 1951; annual renewal	Single guilder account with subaccounts	Reciprocal
Norway–Ethiopia	n.a.	Single pound sterling account	Reciprocal
Norway–Israel	April 1951; amended May 1952; annual renewal	Single Nkr account	Reciprocal
Switzerland–Egypt	April 1950; amended January 1952	Two accounts: Sfr, E. pound	Reciprocal
Turkey–Iran	December 1951; a.t.r.	Single U.S. dollar account in Turkey	Reciprocal
Turkey–Israel	April 1950; renewed to April 1953	Single U.S. dollar account in Turkey	Reciprocal

CONTINENTAL OEEC WITH EASTERN EUROPEAN COUNTRIES

A large number of bilateral payments agreements have been concluded between continental OEEC and Eastern European countries during the postwar period. In recent years, however, the number has declined as a result of the abrogation or expiration of some of the agreements.[5] In addition to trade under payments agreements, an increasing amount of trade is carried on under barter and compensation arrangements.

The Accounts

As a general rule, payments agreements noted in Table VI provide for the use of the currency of the OEEC partner country and the establishment of a single currency account in the central bank of the Western European partner. Sometimes one or more dollar accounts are used, however, and in a few cases, both partner currencies are utilized. The use of Eastern European currencies in two-currency agreements is restricted to the Czech crown, the Finnish markka, and the Yugoslav dinar. In a very few cases, only the Eastern European currency is used under the terms of a single currency agreement, e.g., the crown account under the Czech-Greek agreement. In the Turkish-USSR agreement, which dates from 1937 and which has been renewed annually since that date, two sterling accounts are established.

A number of the agreements utilize multiple, or subaccounts, for payments arising from specified transactions. Usually each account has a stipulated swing

5. Agreements between Eastern Germany, on the one hand, and the Netherlands, Norway and Denmark, on the other, have lapsed and no new agreements have been concluded.

NONSTERLING BILATERAL PAYMENTS AGREEMENTS **605**

credit under these agreements. The agreement between Austria and Poland is typical of these multiple account agreements. Under this agreement, two U.S. dollar accounts are established and in the accompanying trade agreement two lists of goods are provided. One list pertains to transactions in Polish coal and certain Austrian exports, the values of which are debited or credited to an account which is provided with a $2 million reciprocal swing credit. Monthly settlement of balances on this account is provided. In addition only a portion of the values of Polish coal exports may be paid through the account since partial payment in free dollars is required.

Values of trade in opposing lists of goods which appear on the second schedule are debited or credited to a second account which has a reciprocal swing credit of $0.5 million. No periodic settlement of balances in this account is provided. Hence, under this agreement, closer regulation and "offsetting" of goods of an essential nature is required.

Acceptable accounting items usually include only payment for commodities on the quota lists together with expenses which relate directly to that trade. However, certain accounts are used for the progressive liquidation of debts incurred in the past.

Exchange Rates and Revaluation Guarantees

In two-currency agreements specific exchange rates are usually provided. Revaluation guarantees are generally included in all agreements except where the U.S. dollar or the Swiss franc is used as the currency-of-account.

Swing Credits and Settlement of Balances

Reciprocal swing credits are generally provided in the agreements but the swings tend to be small. Excess balances are usually payable in gold, U.S. dollars or an agreed currency. Some agreements provide for the suspension of imports by the debtor country until the excess balance is liquidated. In some few cases, the parties agree to consult as to means of eliminating the excess balance.

Final settlement provisions usually call for settlement in goods within a specified time period (usually four to six months) with any balance then remaining payable in gold or U.S. dollars. Fairly extensive use has been noted of provisions calling for the investment of final balances in Treasury bonds which are amortized over a certain time period, generally five years.

Discouraging High Swing Balances

A number of the agreements contain clauses providing for an interest charge on balances above a stipulated percentage of the permitted swing. Payment of charges is usually through the account. In other cases, balances above a certain percentage of the swing may be invested in Treasury bonds earning the current rate of interest. A few agreements provide for consultation whenever a balance equal to 50 to 75 per cent of the permitted swing is reached, e.g., Italy-USSR.

Trade Arrangements

Trade agreements between continental OEEC countries and Eastern Europe are characterized by detailed lists of commodities for which quotas are established. The quota limits are permissive only, containing no commitment or guarantee of fulfillment. After the trade agreements are concluded, contracts for sales and purchases must be negotiated and contract prices established between private Western European firms and Eastern European representatives operating under a state monopoly of foreign trade. In exceptional cases, a Western European government may sign a contract guaranteeing to export or import certain goods.

Long-Term Trade Agreements under Credit or Investment Agreements

Some Western European countries, including Belgium, Italy and Sweden, have concluded long-term credit or investment agreements with certain Eastern European nations, including Poland, Czechoslovakia, Hungary and the USSR. Separate accounts are established for the operation of these agreements apart from the normal payments agreement accounts. Deliveries of commodities covered by these agreements are usually not included, or counted against, the quotas established in the trade agreements. Thirteen of these investment-type agreements existed in 1951.

Barter and Compensation Agreements

A significant volume of trade is conducted under compensation and barter agreements. Such arrangements are usually permissible under the trade and payments agreements. The movement of goods may take place either inside (Belgium-Czechoslovakia), or outside (Belgium-Romania, Denmark-Hungary) the regularly established quotas.

Payments for Nationalized Properties in Eastern Europe

During the postwar years a large number of agreements have been reached for settling claims of Western Europeans against Eastern European countries which have nationalized foreign-owned properties. These agreements usually operate independently of the regularly established trade and payments agreements. For example, the Denmark-Yugloslavia agreement of October 1950 and the French-Yugoslav agreement of April 1951 provide for the payment of free dollars in regular annual installments.

On the other hand, the progressive liquidation of claims may be handled through the regularly established payments agreement accounts, as for example in the French-Czechoslovakian agreement. The settlement of claims through the regularly established accounts may be illustrated by the arrangements included in the Swiss-Czech payments agreement of January 1950. This agreement provided (1) for the settlement of Swiss financial claims and (2) for current transactions. A total of 71 million Swiss francs was to be paid by Czechoslovakia in twenty semiannual installments. Seven per cent of the value of Czech exports was set aside for the payments of these claims. If the 7 per cent "set aside" did not reach the value of the semiannual payment, the Czech National Bank was required to make up the difference up to 4.3 million francs; if, on the other hand, the "set aside" exceeded one twentieth the total claim, the Czech National Bank received free foreign exchange for the surplus. Thus the agreement served a dual purpose: (1) it encouraged trade by offering Czechoslovakia dollars or gold for exports above a specified minimum, and by imposing a penalty if her exports fell short of that minimum; and (2) it provided for the gradual liquidation of the settlement of Swiss claims. Similar agreements, with some modifications, were made by Western European countries with other countries of Eastern Europe.

TABLE VI

PAYMENTS AGREEMENTS BETWEEN CONTINENTAL OEEC AND EASTERN EUROPEAN COUNTRIES

Countries	Date and Termination	Nature of Accounts	Swing Credits
Austria–Bulgaria	December 1948; amended June 1950	Two U.S. dollar accounts in each central bank	Reciprocal
Austria–Czechoslovakia	October 1948; renewed December 1950	Two U.S. dollar accounts	Reciprocal
Austria–Hungary	March 1947; amended August 1951; a.t.r.	Two U.S. dollar accounts	Reciprocal
Austria–Poland	January 1952	Two U.S. dollar accounts with subaccounts	Reciprocal
Austria–Romania	April 1950	Two U.S. dollar accounts	Reciprocal
Austria–Yugoslavia	October 1949; a.t.r.	Two U.S. dollar accounts with subaccounts	Reciprocal
B.L.E.U.–Bulgaria	April 1947; a.t.r.	Single Bfr account	Reciprocal
B.L.E.U.–Czechoslovakia	April 1946; amended November 1949; effective until May 1954	Two accounts: Bfr, crown	Reciprocal
B.L.E.U.–Finland	November 1945; amended July 1950	Single Bfr account	Reciprocal
B.L.E.U.–Hungary	February 1949; a.t.r.	Single Bfr account	Reciprocal
B.L.E.U.–Poland	April 1950	Single Bfr account	Reciprocal
B.L.E.U.–Romania	September 1948; a.t.r.	Single Bfr account	No provision

TABLE VI—*Continued*

Countries	Date and Termination	Nature of Accounts	Swing Credits
B.L.E.U.–USSR	February 1948; indefinite	Two Bfr accounts	Reciprocal
B.L.E.U.–Yugoslavia	August 1946; amended November 1950; a.t.r.	Single Bfr account	Reciprocal
Denmark–Bulgaria	May 1947; a.t.r.	Two Swiss Franc accounts	Reciprocal
Denmark–Czechoslovakia	December 1949; amended December 1950; a.t.r.	Two accounts: Dkr, crown	Reciprocal
Denmark–Finland	March 1949; amended September 1950; a.t.r.	Two accounts: Dkr, markka	Reciprocal
Denmark–Hungary	January 1948; amended July 1949; March 1951	Single Dkr account	Reciprocal
Denmark–Poland	December 1948	Two Dkr accounts, with subaccounts	Reciprocal
Denmark–USSR	July 1946; amended July 1948; a.t.r.	Single Dkr account	Reciprocal
Denmark–Yugoslavia	June 1947; amended October 1950, November 1951	Single U.S. dollar account in Denmark	Reciprocal
France–Bulgaria	June 1947; annual renewal	Single Ffr account	No provision
France–Czechoslovakia	June 1950; a.t.r.	Two accounts: Ffr, crown	Reciprocal
France–Finland	June 1950; amended January 1952, 1953	Single Ffr account	Reciprocal
France–Hungary	October 1946; amended November 1947, December 1949; a.t.r.	Single Ffr account	No provision
France–Poland	August 1947; amended May 1948; valid to December 1952	Single Ffr account	Reciprocal
France–USSR	July 1953; three years	Two Ffr accounts	n.a.
France–Yugoslavia	May 1949; a.t.r.	Two accounts: Ffr, dinar	Reciprocal
Western Germany–Bulgaria	November 1947; amended November 1950; quarterly tacit renewal	Single U.S. dollar account in Bulgaria	Reciprocal
Western Germany–Czechoslovakia	September 1947; amended October 1949; indefinite	Single crown account	Reciprocal
Western Germany–Finland	February 1952; a.t.r.	Two accounts: U.S. dollar account in Finland, DM account in Germany	Reciprocal
Western Germany–Eastern Germany	September 1951	Two accounts in "units" kept in each central bank. A "unit" is equivalent to the Western German mark	Reciprocal
Western Germany–Hungary	October 1947; amended October 1949, November 1950; a.t.r.	Single U.S. dollar account in Hungary	Reciprocal

TABLE VI—*Continued*

Countries	Date and Termination	Nature of Accounts	Swing Credits
Western Germany– Poland	August 1949; extended August 1950	Single U.S. dollar account in Poland	Reciprocal
Western Germany– Yugoslavia	June 1952; a.t.r.	Two U.S. dollar accounts. (Technically there are two accounts: DM and dinar with the accounts converted to dollars daily at IMF rates.)	Reciprocal
Greece– Czechoslovakia	August 1948; a.t.r.	Single crown account	n.a.
Greece– Finland	March 1949; renewed April 1950; annual renewal	Single U.S. dollar account in Finland	Reciprocal
Greece– Yugoslavia	April 1951	Single U.S. dollar account in Yugoslavia	Reciprocal
Italy– Finland	May 1951	Single U.S. dollar account in Finland	Reciprocal
Italy– Eastern Germany	June 1949; indefinite	Two U.S. dollar accounts	Reciprocal
Italy– Hungary	December 1948; renewed Jan. 1951	Single lire account	Reciprocal
Italy– Poland	July 1949; valid to November 1952	Two U.S. dollar accounts	Reciprocal
Italy– Romania	December 1950	Single lire account	Reciprocal
Italy– USSR	December 1948; three years	Two lire accounts	Reciprocal
Italy– Yugoslavia	April 1947	Single lire account	Reciprocal
Netherlands– Bulgaria	June 1947; amended April 1949; a.t.r.	Single guilder account	Reciprocal
Netherlands– Czechoslovakia	November 1946; amended November 1947, August 1950; a.t.r.	Two accounts: guilder, crown	Reciprocal
Netherlands– Finland	June 1946; amended July 1948; a.t.r.	Single guilder account	Reciprocal
Netherlands– Eastern Germany	June 1949; annual renewal	Single guilder account	Reciprocal
Netherlands– Hungary	December 1947; amended April 1951; annual renewal	Single guilder account	Reciprocal
Netherlands– Poland	December 1946; amended March 1950; annual renewal	Single guilder account	Reciprocal
Netherlands– USSR	June 1948; five years, then a.t.r.	Two guilder accounts	Reciprocal
Netherlands– Yugoslavia	February 1948; amended November 1949; a.t.r.	Single guilder account	Reciprocal
Norway– Bulgaria	September 1951	Two U.S. dollar accounts	n.a.
Norway– Czechoslovakia	December 1945; amended March 1947; November 1950; a.t.r.	Two accounts; Nkr, crown	Reciprocal

TABLE VI—*Continued*

Countries	Date and Termination	Nature of Accounts	Swing Credits
Norway–Finland	November 1945; renewed November 1949	Single Nkr account	Reciprocal
Norway–Hungary	August 1946; amended January 1949, February 1951; indefinite	Single Nkr account	Reciprocal
Norway–Poland	January 1949; amended January 1950	Single Nkr account	Reciprocal
Norway–USSR	January 1947; amended January 1949	Two Nkr accounts	Reciprocal
Norway–Yugoslavia	August 1946; renewed April 1952	Two U.S. dollar accounts	Reciprocal
Portugal–Finland	January 1950	Two accounts: escudo, markka	Reciprocal
Sweden–Bulgaria	October 1947; a.t.r.	Single Skr account	Reciprocal
Sweden–Czechoslovakia	October 1947; amended March 1950; March 1951; a.t.r.	Two accounts: Skr, crown	Reciprocal
Sweden–Hungary	August 1946	Single Skr account	No provision
Sweden–Poland	November 1951; annual renewal	Single Skr account	Unilateral favor of Poland
Sweden–USSR	September 1940; amended October 1946, January 1949, a.t.r.	Single Skr account	Reciprocal
Sweden–Yugoslavia	April 1947; a.t.r.	Single Skr account	Reciprocal
Switzerland–Bulgaria	December 1946; amended January 1949	Single Sfr account with three subaccounts	No provision
Switzerland–Czechoslovakia	January 1951; five years	Single Sfr account	Unilateral favor of Czechoslovakia
Switzerland–Finland	August 1950; annual renewal	Single Sfr account	Reciprocal
Switzerland–Eastern Germany	December 1948	Single Sfr account	No provision
Switzerland–Hungary	July 1950; five years	Single Sfr account	Unilateral favor of Hungary
Switzerland–Poland	July 1949; five years	Single Sfr account	Unilateral favor of Poland
Switzerland–Romania	August 1951	Single Sfr account	n.a.
Switzerland–Yugoslavia	October 1948; five years	Single Sfr account with three subaccounts	No provision
Turkey–Bulgaria	March 1942	Single Turkish pound account	Reciprocal
Turkey–Czechoslovakia	July 1949; amended July 1950; a.t.r.	Single crown account	Reciprocal

TABLE VI—*Continued*

Countries	Date and Termination	Nature of Accounts	Swing Credits
Turkey–Finland	June 1948; amended August 1949	Single U.S. dollar account in Finland	Reciprocal
Turkey–Hungary	June 1949; a.t.r.	Single U.S. dollar account in Turkey	Reciprocal
Turkey–Poland	August 1948; extended August 1950	Two U.S. dollar accounts	Reciprocal
Turkey–USSR	October 1937; renewed 1947; a.t.r.	Two accounts in pound sterling	No provision
Turkey–Yugoslavia	January 1950	Two U.S. dollar accounts	Reciprocal

OTHER WESTERN EUROPE (SPAIN) WITH LATIN AMERICAN COUNTRIES

Spain concluded a number of bilateral payments agreements with Latin American countries during 1950 and 1951. All of the agreements noted in Table VII are similar in nature. In every agreement, the U.S. dollar is used as the currency-of-account and in almost every instance, invoicing in U.S. dollars is stipulated so that exchange rate provisions are unnecessary. In the Spain-Chile agreement, Chile requires that refined copper shipments be paid in free dollars and not through the account.

Swing Credits and Settlement of Balances

Reciprocal swing credits of modest amounts are generally provided. Most of the agreements make no provision for the settlement of balances in excess of the permitted swing credit. Presumably, therefore, excess balances are not permitted to accumulate. One agreement provides for such settlements in U.S. dollars.

Various provisions are made for the settlement of final balances. One agreement stipulates dollar payment within three months, another provides for negotiation, while others indicate settlement in goods within six to twelve months with dollar payment on any remaining balance.

Features of Trade Agreements

Trade agreements almost always provide for bilateral quotas for a target trade balance. In one agreement, the partners merely agree to facilitate trade in specified goods.

The Agreement between Argentina and Spain

The operation and eventual breakdown of Spain's agreement with Argentina is perhaps illustrative of the erratic functioning of the Spanish agreements. An agreement was concluded in October 1946 which provided for Argentine subscription to a Spanish external loan and for a revolving unilateral swing credit of 350 million pesos to finance Spanish purchases of Argentine goods. As trade decreased during 1948 following the exhaustion of the credits, a protocol for an adjustment in trade items was signed. Trade relations further deteriorated until, in April 1949, Spain was granted additional credits of 350 million pesos. These credits were rapidly exhausted by Spain and the maximum swing credit was exceeded. In order to continue trade, Argentina agreed to the establishment of peseta accounts in Spain, balances of which could be used by Argentina for certain goods which Spain was committed to make available. Even after all these efforts, Spanish exports continued to lag. Finally, when Spain failed to fulfill even the adjusted quotas of committed exports, the agreement was denounced by Argentina in September 1951.

The Agreement between Spain and Cuba

The agreement between Spain and Cuba illustrates the functioning of an agreement utilizing multiple accounts combined with measures for encouraging trade. The latest trade and payments agreement was concluded in September 1952. It provided for the use of three accounts:

1. An "EP Account" to which is credited the value of all private remittances, rents and other noncommercial transactions. Balances in this account are at the free disposal of the Spanish Foreign Exchange Institute for the payment of current obligations *in Cuba*.

2. An "A Account" to which is credited from 17 to 50 per cent of the value of Spanish exports depending on the volume of trade. Balances in this account are at the free disposal of Spain and may be used for making purchases in Cuba or in third countries.

3. A "B Account" to which is credited from 50 to 83 per cent of the value of all Spanish exports, and to which is debited the full value of Cuban exports. If the balance of the "B Account" exceeds $7 million, and the specified goods have been purchased, the excess balance may be transferred to the "A Account" which is at the free disposal of Spain for purchases anywhere in the world. Thus, under certain conditions, an element of automatic transferability is introduced into the agreement.

In effect, the working of the agreement means a unilateral credit in favor of Cuba, although no swing credit is specified. Since Spanish exports may reach a balance of $7 million before Spain receives any free dollars, it would appear that Cuba has received a revolving credit to this amount.

TABLE VII

PAYMENTS AGREEMENTS BETWEEN SPAIN AND LATIN AMERICAN COUNTRIES

Countries	Date and Termination	Nature of Accounts	Swing Credits
Spain–Bolivia	February 1948; three years	Single U.S. dollar account	Reciprocal
Spain–Brazil	July 1952; one year	Single U.S. dollar account	Reciprocal

TABLE VII—*Continued*

Countries	Date and Termination	Nature of Accounts	Swing Credits
Spain–Chile	August 1950; three years, then a.t.r.	Two U.S. dollar accounts	n.a.
Spain–Colombia	November 1952; a.t.r.	Single U.S. dollar account in Colombia	Reciprocal
Spain–Cuba	September 1952; two years	Single U.S. dollar account with subaccounts in Cuba	Unilateral (See text.)
Spain–Mexico	March 1951; renewed March 1953 for two years	Two U.S. dollar accounts	Reciprocal
Spain–Paraguay	August 1950; a.t.r.	Single U.S. dollar account in Spain	Reciprocal

LATIN AMERICAN COUNTRIES WITH LATIN AMERICAN COUNTRIES

The agreements noted in Table VIII are primarily agreements between Argentina or Brazil, on the one hand, and some other Latin American country on the other. A number of these agreements include credit or investment provisions. For example, the Argentine-Peruvian agreement of September 1949 provided for an extension of credit by Argentina in favor of Peru so that Peru could install refrigeration plants which would enable Argentina to export meats under the trade and payments agreement.

The Accounts

In agreements which use the dollar as the currency-of-account, there is usually no exchange rate provision. In the two-currency agreements, however, an exchange rate is always specified. Revaluation guarantees are almost always provided for in the agreements.

The Argentine-Uruguayan agreement contains an unusual clause relating to exchange rates. The exchange rate specified is based on a cross-rate on the U.S. dollar with respect to the rate applicable to the specific transaction established by the multiple rate structure. In addition, there is a special provision for an adjustable exchange rate applying to tourists.

Swing Credits and Settlement of Balances

Reciprocal swing credits of moderate amounts are generally provided. Settlement of excess and final balances is usually required in gold or U.S. dollars. In some instances settlement of final balances may be made in goods. In the Brazilian-Chilean agreement, provisions pertaining to excess balances are not included, so presumably excess balances are not permitted. However, a provision is included that requires the entire balance on the account to be settled in dollars if at any time trade is halted for six months or longer.

A number of agreements provide for periodic settlement of entire balances. Settlement may be annual, semiannual or biennial. Balances struck periodically are payable in an agreed currency usually within one to three months.

Discouragement of Constant High Balances

Frequently these agreements incorporate a provision for discouraging constant high swing balances. This provision usually takes the form of an interest charge on balances in excess of a certain percentage of the permitted swing credit. Charges are generally payable through the account.

Acceptable Accounting Items

Payments through the accounts are in most instances limited to current transactions as defined in a clause of the agreement or by reference to the definition contained in the IMF Agreement. The agreement between Argentina and Mexico, however, provides only for the financing of trade in books, periodicals and pamphlets, while the agreement between Colombia and Ecuador covers all trade and invisible payments including capital transfers.

Trade Arrangements

Most trade agreements provide for bilateral quotas for a target trade balance. In a number of agreements, however, no quotas are mentioned. In the latter case, the agreements call for facilitating trade in specified goods.

Barter and compensation trade are usually permitted and, in some instances, are specifically provided for as, for example, in the Argentine-Chilean agreement where prices are established on exports of Argentine beef against Chilean copper and nitrates with actual transactions taking place on a barter basis.

The Colombian-Argentine Agreement

Included in Table VIII is an agreement between the Colombian Coffee Growers Federation (a semiofficial monopoly) and the Argentine government. This agreement operates in the following manner. A coffee export figure was established at $500,000 together with quotas on a limited number of Argentine goods. Argentina credits the value of coffee imports to a dollar account and debits the value of Argentine exports. Balances are struck annually and are payable in U.S. dollars.

Other "Payments Arrangements"

A number of agreements have been concluded between Latin American countries which merely specify the currencies that will be generally accepted in payment for trade items. These agreements are not payments agreements in the sense in which we have defined the term. For example, a Bolivian-Brazilian agreement stipulates that all Bolivian exports except coffee and cotton are payable in cruzeiros or sterling, with coffee and cotton payable in cruzeiros only.

TABLE VIII

PAYMENTS AGREEMENTS BETWEEN LATIN AMERICAN COUNTRIES

Countries	Date and Termination	Nature of Accounts	Swing Credits
Argentina–Bolivia	March 1947; amended August 1951	Single Argentine peso account	Unilateral favor of Bolivia
Argentina–Brazil	October 1948; amended June 1950	Single cruzeiro account	Reciprocal
Argentina–Chile	April 1952	Single Argentine peso account	Reciprocal
Argentina–Colombia	July 1949	Single U.S. dollar account in Argentina	No provision (See text.)
Argentina–Mexico	July 1950; a.t.r.	Single U.S. dollar account in Argentina	Reciprocal
Argentina–Paraguay	December 1949; three years, then a.t.r.	Single Argentine peso account	Reciprocal
Argentina–Uruguay	August 1948; amended September 1950; a.t.r.	Single Argentine peso account	Reciprocal
Brazil–Chile	June 1948; indefinite	Two U.S. dollar accounts	Reciprocal
Brazil–Paraguay	May 1946; five years	Single cruzeiro account	n.a.
Brazil–Uruguay	December 1949; tacit biannual renewal	Two cruzeiro accounts	Reciprocal
Chile–Ecuador	August 1949; a.t.r.	Two U.S. dollar accounts	Reciprocal
Colombia–Ecuador	April 1949; a.t.r.	Two accounts: pesos, sucres	No provision
El Salvador–Nicaragua	Augusts 1951; indefinite	Two accounts: peso, cordoba	Reciprocal
Paraguay–Uruguay	February 1953; 4 years, then a.t.r.	Two U.S. dollar accounts	Reciprocal

LATIN AMERICA WITH FAR EASTERN COUNTRIES

The only agreements between Latin American and Far Eastern countries are those of Argentina and Brazil with Japan. (See Table IX.) Both of the agreements use a single account denominated in U.S. dollars and maintained in the Latin American partner country. Presumably invoicing is done in the currency-of-account since no exchange rate provision is included in the agreements. The Argentine-Japanese agreement contains the usual revaluation guarantee clause and reciprocal swing credits are provided.

Both excess and final balances are payable in gold, U.S. dollars or an agreed currency. In the agreement between Brazil and Japan, no specified limit is stipulated for the reciprocal swing credit. In order to assure that balances will be kept to a reasonable level, therefore, there is a provision under which the creditor country may request an annual settlement of the entire balance in dollars.

Both agreements contain the usual Japanese "trade plan," with bilateral quotas. Both also contain an agreement to consult on the transfer of credits to third countries, thus providing for consultative transferability. Under the agreement with Argentina, Japan must pay a portion of the transportation charges accruing to Argentine shipping companies in free dollars.

TABLE IX

PAYMENTS AGREEMENTS BETWEEN LATIN AMERICAN AND FAR EASTERN COUNTRIES

Countries	Date and Termination	Nature of Accounts	Swing Credits
Argentina–Japan	June 1949; extended indefinitely December 1950	Single U.S. dollar account in Argentina	Reciprocal
Brazil–Japan	July 1952	Single U.S. dollar account in Brazil	Reciprocal

LATIN AMERICA WITH NEAR AND MIDDLE EASTERN COUNTRIES

Only one bilateral payments agreement, the Argentina-Israel agreement, has been concluded between countries of Latin America with those of the Near and Middle East. (See Table X.) The agreement was concluded in June 1950 and provides for a single account denominated in U.S. dollars. No exchange rate provision is included. The agreement provides a revaluation guarantee on balances in favor of Argentina but presumably the guarantee does not apply to balances in favor of Israel. A reciprocal swing credit is provided and excess balances are payable in U.S. dollars. The liquidation of final balances is subject to consultation between the two countries.

Two lists of goods are established without quotas. Israel is required to pay for 70 per cent of her purchases from Argentina with U.S. dollars. Furthermore, Israel must pay 70 per cent of the expenses directly related to the transaction in dollars and 50 per cent of the transportation costs when shipment is made on Argentine vessels. However, these provisions apply only to purchases up to $10 million. For purchases in excess of $10 million, Israel must pay the entire value in dollars.

TABLE X

PAYMENTS AGREEMENTS BETWEEN LATIN AMERICAN AND MIDDLE EASTERN COUNTRIES

Countries	Date and Termination	Nature of Accounts	Swing Credits
Argentina–Israel	June 1950	Single U.S. dollar account in Argentina	Reciprocal

LATIN AMERICA WITH EASTERN EUROPEAN COUNTRIES

General Features of Payments Agreements

The U.S. dollar is used as the currency-of-account in all of the agreements noted in Table XI, except the three agreements which employ the Czech crown. Settlements of final balances, as well as settlements of balances in excess of the permitted swing credit, are usually payable in dollars, gold or an agreed currency. Reciprocal swing credits of moderate amounts are almost always provided.

Provisions for discouraging constant high swing credit balances are generally not included. However, in some of the Argentine agreements, an interest charge is levied on that portion of the balance in excess of 40 per cent of the permitted swing credit. These charges are payable through the account at stipulated times.

Nature of Trade Agreements

Trade with countries in the Soviet orbit has represented only about one per cent of Latin America's total trade in the postwar period. Bilateral quotas for a target trade balance are established by many of the agreements. The Argentine trade agreements generally provide for rigidly controlled trade between state trading monopolies.

Colombia's agreement with Finland provides for exports of coffee to Finland up to $4 million annually. The proceeds are paid into a dollar account against which are charged exports of Finnish paper and certain other specified goods, up to $4 million in value.

Partial Payments in Dollars

Two of Argentina's agreements with Eastern European countries require partial payment for Argentine exports in dollars and the Argentine-Romanian agreement requires full dollar payments for vegetable oils, wool and hides. The Argentine-Yugoslav payments agreements provide an illustration of how changes in Argentina's bargaining position has been reflected in her payments agreements. In the 1948 agreement, Yugoslavia was required to pay for 30 per cent of the value of her imports of Argentine wool and hides in dollars. In addition Yugoslavia was required to pay an interest charge in dollars on any debit balance in the account. The 1950 agreement reduced the percentage of dollar payments for wool and hides to 10 per cent and established a $9 million swing credit free of any interest charges. Interest was charged on balances in excess of the swing, but the interest was payable through the account rather than in dollars.

The Argentine-Bulgarian agreement also provides for partial payment for certain exports in dollars.

The Argentine-Polish Agreement

The Argentine-Polish agreement provides an example of an attempt by trading partners to balance exports of "scarce" or "hard-to-get" exports against imports of comparable economic significance. Under this agreement general lists of the goods to be traded were established but in addition it was specifically provided that Polish exports of coal, railway equipment and iron and steel products were to be balanced against Argentine exports of wool and hides, quebracho extract, vegetable oils and lead and zinc concentrates. In order to implement this provision, the agreement required that whenever contracts for Polish coal were drawn, contracts of equal value for Argentine hides and other "scarce" items had to be negotiated simultaneously. Thus trade in the "scarce" items represented a form of barter.

TABLE XI

PAYMENTS AGREEMENTS BETWEEN LATIN AMERICAN AND EASTERN
EUROPEAN COUNTRIES

Countries	Date and Termination	Nature of Accounts	Swing Credits
Argentina–Bulgaria	May 1949; a.t.r. to May 1953	Single U.S. dollar account in Argentina	Reciprocal
Argentina–Czechoslovakia	July 1947; amended September 1948, August 1949; a.t.r.	Two accounts: crown, peso	Reciprocal
Argentina–Finland	July 1948; amended March 1952; valid to December 1952	Single U.S. dollar account in Argentina	Reciprocal
Argentina–Hungary	July 1948; amended May 1950; August 1951	Single U.S. dollar account in Argentina	Reciprocal
Argentina–Poland	December 1948; indefinite	Single U.S. dollar account in Argentina	Reciprocal
Argentina–Romania	October 1947; amended July 1951; a.t.r.	Single U.S. dollar account in Argentina	No provision
Argentina–USSR	August 1953; a.t.r.	Single U.S. dollar account in Argentina	Reciprocal
Argentina–Yugoslavia	June 1948; amended August 1948, January 1950	Single U.S. dollar account in Argentina	Reciprocal
Brazil–Czechoslovakia	May 1950; two years, then a.t.r.	Single U.S. dollar account in Brazil	No provision
Brazil–Poland	January 1949	Single U.S. dollar account in Brazil	n.a.
Brazil–Yugoslavia	February 1950; a.t.r.	Single U.S. dollar account in Brazil	Reciprocal
Colombia–Finland	March 1951	Two U.S. dollar accounts	No provision
Mexico–Czechoslovakia	October 1950; five years	Two accounts: peso, crown	Reciprocal
Paraguay–Yugoslavia	January 1950; a.t.r.	Single U.S. dollar account in Yugoslavia	Reciprocal
Uruguay–Czechoslovakia	January 1947	Single crown account	Reciprocal
Uruguay–Hungary	n.a.	Single U.S. dollar account	Reciprocal
Uruguay–Yugoslavia	January 1950; a.t.r.	Single U.S. dollar account in Yugoslavia	n.a.

FAR EAST WITH FAR EASTERN COUNTRIES

The bilateral payments agreements noted in Table XII are, with one exception, confined to agreements between Japan and other Far Eastern countries.

All of the agreements involve the use of accounts denominated in U.S. dollars. There are no provisions pertaining to revaluation guarantees or exchange rates. Reciprocal swing credits vary from $2 million to $15 million with settlement of excess balances and final balances in U.S. dollars, gold or an agreed currency. Final balances are to be settled within relatively short periods of time, usually four months.

Trade agreements with Japan are called "trade plans," and provide for bilateral quotas for a target trade balance and the use of a "mixed commission" to supervise trade.

The Agreement between Indochina and Japan

All payments for trade between Indochina and Japan are made through an account established by the Indochina-Japan payments agreement. While this account operates independently of the account set up under the France-Japan payments agreement, the accounts established by the two agreements are merged semiannually and the combined balance is settled in U.S. dollars.

TABLE XII

PAYMENTS AGREEMENTS BETWEEN FAR EASTERN COUNTRIES

Countries	Date and Termination	Nature of Accounts	Swing Credits
Japan–Indochina	May 1948	Single U.S. dollar account in Japan	No provision (See text.)
Japan–Indonesia	August 1952	Two U.S. dollar accounts	Reciprocal
Japan–Korea	April 1951; annual renewal	Single U.S. dollar account in Japan	Reciprocal
Japan–Nationalist China	July 1950	Single U.S. dollar account in Japan	Reciprocal
Japan–Philippines	July 1950; amended March 1951; indefinite	Two U.S. dollar accounts	Reciprocal
Japan–Thailand	September 1952; indefinite	Two U.S. dollar accounts	Reciprocal
Nationalist China–Ryukyus	August 1951	Two U.S. dollar accounts (Taiwan, Japan.)	Reciprocal

FAR EASTERN WITH EASTERN EUROPEAN COUNTRIES

The agreement between Japan and Finland is the only bilateral payments agreement between Far Eastern and Eastern European countries. (See Table XIII.) The agreement establishes one U.S. dollar account and does not contain an exchange rate provision or a revaluation guarantee. It provides a reciprocal swing credit and for consultation when 80 per cent of the permitted swing is reached. If the swing credit limit is exceeded continuously for thirty days, the excess is payable in dollars or an agreed currency. The trade agreement establishes bilateral quotas for a target trade balance.

TABLE XIII

PAYMENTS AGREEMENTS BETWEEN FAR EASTERN AND EASTERN EUROPEAN COUNTRIES

Countries	Date and Termination	Nature of Account	Swing Credits
Japan– Finland	December 1952	Single U.S. dollar account	Reciprocal

NEAR AND MIDDLE EAST WITH NEAR AND MIDDLE EASTERN COUNTRIES

Only three agreements are noted in Table XIV. The Egyptian agreements are less detailed than most other agreements and omit many of the usual provisions, such as reciprocal credits, exchange rates and settlement procedures. There are no quotas established in the trading arrangements.

The Agreement between Egypt and Saudi Arabia

The agreement between Egypt and Saudi Arabia established an Egyptian pound account with final settlement of balances to be made in sterling. The other provisions relate to the items which may be financed through the account. Payments to Saudi Arabia are to be made as follows: (1) Pilgrimage fees and Egyptian banknotes spent by pilgrims in Saudi Arabia are settled by crediting the "Arab nonresident account" in Egyptian pounds; (2) Saudi Arabian exports to Egypt are to be paid in pounds sterling through London; (3) other transactions are to be settled in either sterling or Egyptian pounds. Payments by Saudi Arabia in favor of Egypt are made in the currency stipulated in the export permit. If the permit is denominated in Egyptian pounds, payment is made by debiting the "Arab government account" in the National Bank of Egypt or by debiting "nonresident accounts" held in Egypt in the name of Saudi Arabian bankers.

The Agreement between Israel and Ethiopia

The agreement between Israel and Ethiopia establishes two U.S. dollar accounts and includes a reciprocal swing credit. The balance is struck and settled annually. The trade provision contains no lists of goods or quotas but merely provides that trade up to $2 million each way may be financed through the accounts. Ethiopian exports of goat skins and coffee are excluded from payment through the account and require payment in dollars.

TABLE XIV

PAYMENTS AGREEMENTS BETWEEN NEAR AND MIDDLE EASTERN COUNTRIES

Countries	Date and Termination	Nature of Accounts	Swing Credits
Egypt– Lebanon	September 1951	Single Egyptian pound account	No provision
Egypt– Saudi Arabia	May 1949	Single Egyptian pound account	No provision
Israel– Ethiopia	November 1951	Two U.S. dollar accounts	Reciprocal

NEAR AND MIDDLE EASTERN WITH EASTERN EUROPEAN COUNTRIES

Table XV summarizes the payments agreements of Egypt, Iran and Israel with certain Eastern European countries. A large portion of the trade between Middle Eastern and Eastern European countries takes place under barter and compensation agreements. For example, payments between Egypt, on the one hand, and Bulgaria, Hungary, Czechoslovakia and Yugoslavia, on the other, are made solely in Egyptian pounds through "collector accounts" kept by the National Bank of Egypt. For all practical purposes, these are bookkeeping accounts for implementing barter trade. Trade in Egyptian cotton against USSR wheat has taken place under barter agreements which have been negotiated periodically for the past several years. Similarly the April 1952 agreement between Egypt and Hungary provided for barter trade in cotton against sugar and edible oils.

Israeli agreements use the U.S. dollar as the currency-of-account while Egyptian agreements use either the dollar or the Egyptian pound. Revaluation guarantees are usually not mentioned. Small reciprocal swing credits are the general rule, which indicates that a strict balancing of trade is envisaged. Final settlement usually involves payments in goods within a limited time with remaining balances payable in dollars, sterling or an agreed currency.

Agreements with Israel

Israeli agreements with Eastern European countries tend to be more complicated than most payments agreements since they include provisions for the liquidation of claims of Israeli emigrants against Eastern Euorpean states and for partial dollar payments for Israeli imports.

The agreements establish multiple accounts and stipulate the purposes for which the accounts may be used and the conditions under which transfers between the accounts may be made. Generally there are two accounts used in the following manner: The first account is credited with the value of the claims of persons migrating from Eastern Europe to Israel while the second account is debited and credited for the values of approved current transactions. At the end of a stipulated trading period, a specified portion of the balances in the first account may be used to settle adverse Israeli balances on the second account. However, the transfer between accounts is dependent upon the payment by Israel of a certain percentage of the balance on the second account in dollars. Hence, if Israel wishes to use immigrant holdings in partial payment of its imports, it must make certain dollar payments. Under these agreements, then, Israel pays for imports partly in exports, partly in dollars and partly by the liquidation of claims.

TABLE XV

PAYMENTS AGREEMENTS BETWEEN MIDDLE EASTERN AND EASTERN EUROPEAN
COUNTRIES

Countries	Date and Termination	Nature of Accounts	Swing Credits
Egypt– Czechoslovakia	October 1951; amended February 1952	Single Egyptian pound account	n.a.
Egypt– Poland	June 1949; amended March 1951	Single U.S. dollar account in Egypt	Reciprocal
Egypt– Yugoslavia	August 1950; a.t.r.	Single Egyptian pound account	Reciprocal
Iran– Poland	March 1951; a.t.r.	Single Iranian rial account	Reciprocal
Israel– Finland	August 1949; extended November 1951	Single U.S. dollar account in Israel	Reciprocal
Israel– Hungary	February 1950	Single U.S. dollar account in Israel with subaccounts	n.a.
Israel– Poland	April 1951; a.t.r.	Single U.S. dollar account in Israel with subaccounts	Reciprocal
Israel– Yugoslavia	January 1951; a.t.r.	Single U.S. dollar account in Yugoslavia with subaccounts	Reciprocal
Lebanon– Czechoslovakia	July 1952	Two accounts: Lebanese pounds, crown	Reciprocal

EASTERN EUROPE WITH EASTERN EUROPEAN COUNTRIES (INCLUDING COMMUNIST CHINA)

The line between barter trade and trade involving a foreign exchange payment is sometimes difficult to draw and there is some question as to whether the agreements between Communist countries should be regarded as true payments agreements or simply as a bookkeeping device for recording the progress of barter transactions. Nevertheless all such agreements known to exist have been included in Table XVI.

Information on the bilateral trade and payments agreements between Soviet countries is not readily available, but it is generally believed that the payments network of the Soviet bloc is complete except for Communist China which has only bilateral payments agreements with the USSR, Hungary, Poland and Czechoslovakia. Of the total possible agreements between the eight Soviet countries of Eastern Europe, less than one third are noted in Table XVI. Information on agreements of the non-Soviet countries, Finland and Yugoslavia, is more complete.

It will be noted that the agreements included in Table XVI usually date from the early postwar period. It is not known whether or not certain of these agreements still remain in force. In the absence of information as to their denunciation or replacement, it has been assumed that they are still effective.

Features of Payments Agreements

In the early postwar payments agreements between countries in Eastern Europe, the U.S. dollar was used almost exclusively as the currency-of-account. In revisions of the agreements, or upon the conclusion of new agreements since 1950, there has been a tendency to use the ruble as the currency-of-account. In the agreements between Romania and Yugoslavia, however, the Swiss franc remains as the unit of account. Exchange rates are generally not specified in the agreements, indicating that invoicing is done in the currency-of-account. Where an exchange rate provision is included, it specifies that the official or agreed bank rate is to be used. Revaluation guarantees are not generally provided. Reciprocal swing credits of modest amounts are almost always provided.

In the early postwar agreements, the liquidation of balances in excess of the permitted swing credit and settlement of balances upon the termination of the agreement required payment in gold or dollars. There has been a tendency in recent years for this provision to be replaced by a requirement to consult regarding the disposition of excessive balances and for final settlement of balances to be made by the shipment of goods.

The Finland-USSR Agreement

The Finland-USSR payments agreement of 1950 provided for a limited amount of trade on a trilateral basis. Deliveries of goods between Finland and the USSR and from third countries to Finland were specified in the agreement. Payments for merchandise from third countries to Finland are credited to special accounts denominated in rubles and maintained in the Bank of Finland. Transfers from these special accounts to the accounts regularly maintained under the bilateral payments agreements are made upon agreement among the three central banks. This is the only instance of a specific provision for trilateral trade in a bilateral payments agreement that has been noted.

TABLE XVI

PAYMENTS AGREEMENTS BETWEEN EASTERN EUROPEAN COUNTRIES

Countries	Date and Termination	Nature of Accounts	Swing Credits
Bulgaria–Finland	October 1948	Two U.S. dollar accounts	Reciprocal
Bulgaria–USSR	July 1947; a.t.r.	Two U.S. dollar accounts	Reciprocal
Czechoslovakia–Finland	October 1950	Two U.S. dollar accounts	n.a.
Czechoslovakia–Poland	April 1951	Single Czech crown account	Reciprocal
Czechoslovakia–USSR	January 1948; amended 1950	Two ruble accounts	n.a.
Finland–Eastern Germany	July 1951	Two U.S. dollar accounts	Reciprocal

TABLE XVI—*Continued*

Countries	Date and Termination	Nature of Accounts	Swing Credits
Finland–Hungary	December 1951	Single U.S. dollar account in Finland	Reciprocal
Finland–Poland	March 1947; amended March 1948, 1949	Two U.S. dollar accounts	Reciprocal
Finland–Romania	March 1951; a.t.r.	Single ruble account in Romania	Reciprocal
Finland–USSR	January 1951; five years	Two ruble accounts	Reciprocal
Finland–Yugoslavia	October 1948	Two U.S. dollar accounts	Reciprocal
Eastern Germany–USSR	April 1950	n.a.	n.a.
Hungary–USSR	July 1947; amended July 1949; a.t.r.	Two U.S. dollar accounts	Reciprocal
Hungary–Yugoslavia	December 1946	Single Yugoslav dinar account	Reciprocal
Poland–USSR	December 1946	n.a.	n.a.
Romania–USSR	March 1951; valid to March 1955	Two ruble accounts	Reciprocal
Romania–Yugoslavia	June 1946; amended September 1947; a.t.r.	Two Swiss franc accounts for commercial payments; two U.S. dollar accounts for noncommercial payments	Reciprocal

APPENDIX 6

(As of December 15, 1953)

TABLE XVII summarizes the exchange rate systems and gives the current exchange rates for sixty-two principal countries outside the Soviet orbit. Countries in Category A have virtually no exchange restrictions. Countries in Category B maintain multiple rate structures but either do not employ quantitative restrictions on imports of goods and services or employ only mild restrictions. For countries in Category C the degree of quantitative restrictions is relatively heavy but it varies markedly from county to county. For example, quantitative import restrictions in Colombia are limited to a list of prohibited imports while in Yugoslavia all foreign trade is under the control of state enterprises. No attempt is made to describe the exchange control systems other than by indicating the nature of the exchange market.

The exchange rates quoted in Table XVII are limited to legal or official rates. Unofficial or black market rates are not quoted. Where exchange certificate systems give rise to effective rates these rates are quoted. However, implicit rates arising from the use of retention quota and similar schemes are not quoted.

The terms employed in Table XVII are defined as follows:

Unitary rates. Single buying and selling rates, with less than 2 per cent spread between the buying selling rates.

Multiple rates. More than one buying or selling rate or the existence of a spread of 2 per cent or more between unitary buying and selling rates.

Fixed rates. Rates not subject to market forces.

Fixed and free rates. Rates are fixed or maintained within one per cent of parity but there are no restrictions on buying exchange from authorized banks at the fixed selling rate and all incoming exchange is purchased by the banks at the fixed buying rate.

Fixed and controlled rates. Rates are fixed or maintained within one per cent of parity but transactions are restricted.

Disparate cross-rates. Values of foreign currencies in terms of national currency do not reflect official cross-rates between the foreign currencies.

Freely fluctuating rates. Rates which are not stabilized and for which a bona fide free market exists. In cases where these rates apply only to certain types of transactions such as invisibles and capital movements, that fact is noted.

Controlled free rate. A rate which is subject to market forces but demand and supply for the exchange is closely controlled by the authorities.

Mixing rates. Rates derived from the requirement that portions of export proceeds must be surrendered at different rates, or that portions of foreign exchange purchased by importers must be acquired at different rates.

TABLE XVII

Exchange Rates and Nature of Exchange Markets of Principal Countries

(Currency Units Per U.S. Dollar as of Mid-December 1953)

Country and Currency	IMF Par Value	Nature of Exchange Market	Legal Free Market Selling Rate	Other Official Rates Buying	Other Official Rates Selling
A. Countries with Virtually No Exchange Restrictions					
Canada (dollar)	......	Unitary rates. Freely fluctuating.	.972		
Cuba (peso)	1.00	Multiple rates. Fixed and free, with 2 per cent tax on exchange sales.		1.00	1.02
Dominican Republic (peso)	1.00	Unitary rates. Fixed and free.		1.00	1.00
El Salvador (colon)	2.50	Unitary rates. Fixed and free.		2.49	2.51
Guatemala (quetzal)	1.00	Unitary rates. Fixed and free.		1.00	1.01
Haiti (gourde)	......	Unitary rates. Fixed and free.		5.00	5.00
Honduras (lempira)	2.00	Unitary rates. Fixed and free.		2.00	2.02
Lebanon (pound)	2.191	Multiple rates. Freely fluctuating for all private transactions. Official rate for government transactions. Disparate cross-rates.	3.25 [a]	2.19	2.21

626

Country (currency)		Type of rates			
Liberia (U.S. dollar)	.....	Unitary rates. Free market.			
Mexico (peso)	8.65	Unitary rates. Fixed and free.	.....	8.60	8.65
Panama (balboa)	1.00	Unitary rates. Fixed and free.	1.00	.....	.....
Switzerland (franc)	.....	Unitary rates. Freely fluctuating rate between 4.28 and 4.46. Exchange restrictions employed in trade with payments agreement countries but no restrictions on transactions in free currencies.	4.30 a	.....	.....
United States (dollar)	1.00	Unitary rates. Free market with fixed relation to gold for official international settlements.			

B. Countries with Mild Exchange Restrictions

Country (currency)		Type of rates			
Costa Rica (colon)	5.615	Multiple rates. Fixed and controlled rates and a freely fluctuating rate.	6.65 for portions of proceeds of certain goods and all other transactions not conducted at official rates.	5.60 for most exports. 6.25 for gold and certain other exports.	5.67 for essential imports and specified non-trade transactions.
Ecuador (sucre)	15.00	Multiple rates. Fixed and controlled rates and controlled free rate for invisibles and luxury imports.	17.40 a for invisibles, permitted luxury imports and designated miscellaneous exports.	15.00 for most exports.	15.15 for essential imports.

TABLE XVII—*Continued*

Country and Currency	IMF Par Value	Nature of Exchange Market	Legal Free Market Selling Rate	Other Official Rates	
				Buying	Selling
Nicaragua (cordoba)	5.00	Multiple rates. Fixed and controlled rates and a free market for foreign banknotes and coins.	7.75 [a] for foreign bank notes and coins.	5.00 for 20 per cent of proceeds of exports and invisibles. 7.00 for remaining 80 per cent of proceeds of exports and invisibles.	5.04 for specified government transactions. 7.05 for essential imports and designated invisibles. 8.05 for semiessential imports and designated invisibles. 10.05 for nonessential imports and designated invisibles.
Peru (sole)	......	Multiple rates. Freely fluctuating rates for drafts and negotiable exchange certificates denominated in different currencies. Disparate cross-rates.	19.35 [b] for drafts, 19.25 for certificates. Exporters required to surrender specified portion of proceeds (100 per cent dollar and sterling, 10 per cent Argentine pesos) for exchange certificates. Designated imports and invisibles may be settled with certificates. All other transactions require exchange purchased at the draft rate.		

Syria (pound)	2.191	Multiple rates. Fixed and controlled rates for government transactions and purchases of local currency by concessionaire companies. Other transactions take place at freely fluctuating rates. Disparate cross-rates.	3.575 for most transactions without restriction.	2.19 for local currency purchases by concessionaire companies.	2.21 for specified government payments.
Thailand (baht)	......	Multiple rates. Fixed and controlled rates and freely fluctuating rates for dollars and sterling. Disparate cross-rates.	20.88 e for all transactions not covered by other rates.	12.45 for 20 per cent of officially appraised value of rubber exports, 20 per cent of total value of tin exports and 100 per cent of rice exports.	12.55 for government payments and student remittances. 16.07 for imports of petroleum products. 16.75 for imports of specified essentials.
Venezuela (bolivar)	3.35	Multiple rates. Fixed and free rates for most transactions without restriction. Oil companies must buy local currency needs at less favorable rate and proceeds of coffee and cacao exports are at times purchased at more favorable rates.	......	3.09 for most petroleum proceeds and a few government transactions. 3.05 for petroleum proceeds in excess of amounts of foreign exchange sold by central bank in a given period.	3.35 for all transactions.

TABLE XVII—*Continued*

Country and Currency	IMF Par Value	Nature of Exchange Market	Legal Free Market Selling Rate	Other Official Rates Buying	Other Official Rates Selling
Venezuela—*Continued*				4.25 for proceeds of such exports of cacao and unwashed coffee as are sold at or below specified world prices. 4.80 for proceeds of washed coffee exports sold at or below specified world prices. 3.32 for all other export proceeds.	

C. Countries Which Rely Heavily on Quantitative Restrictions

Country and Currency	IMF Par Value	Nature of Exchange Market	Legal Free Market Selling Rate	Other Official Rates Buying	Other Official Rates Selling
Argentina (peso)	......	Multiple rates. Fixed and controlled rates and controlled free rate.	13.95 for proceeds of minor exports; 60 per cent of cheese exports; 70 per cent tanned cattle hide proceeds; 40 per cent of proceeds of butter, casein, quebracho and uranday extract; also selling rate for nonessential imports and specified financial transactions.	5.00 for total proceeds of most basic exports; for 50 per cent of sheepskin and some processed meat exports and for 50 per cent of wool exports if sold for dollars, 100 per cent if sold for sterling. 7.50 for total proceeds of preferential exports and percentages of certain other exports not sold at legal free market rate and for wool proceeds not sold at 5.00 rate.	5.00 for preferential imports, including coal, coke, fuel oil and crude petroleum. 7.50 for basic imports.

Country (currency unit)				2.2505	2.2365
Australia (pound) U.S. dollars per pound	2.240	Unitary rates. Within specified limits authorized banks quote rates for dollars based on market quotations in London and New York. Fixed and controlled rates on sterling.	2.249 (banks' selling rate)	2.2505	2.2365
Austria (schilling)	26.00	Fixed and controlled rates.	......	25.92	26.08
Belgium-Luxembourg Economic Union (franc)	50.0	Unitary rates. Controlled free rates within limits of 49.50 and 50.50. Freely fluctuating market for EPU currencies but use of exchange limited to capital and a few invisibles.	50.60 [a] (banks' selling rate)	49.77 [d]	49.97 [d]
Bolivia (boliviano)	190.0	Multiple rates. Fixed and controlled rates and a freely fluctuating rate for certain invisibles and nonregistered capital.	634.00 [e]	190.0	190.0
Brazil (cruzeiro) [f]	18.50	Multiple rates. Freely fluctuating rates. Disparate cross-rates.	53.50 [a] for incoming capital and other invisibles; for remittance of profits, for capital transfers and Brazilian tourists' expenditures.	18.36 (basic official rate) 23.36 (official rate plus 5.0 cruzeiros) for proceeds of coffee exports. 28.36 (official rate plus 10.0 cruzeiros) for all other export proceeds.	18.82 (basic official rate) for imports of wheat and newsprint. 18.82 plus one of five rates determined by sale of exchange at auction for different categories of goods classified officially according to "essentiality."

631

TABLE XVII—*Continued*

Country and Currency	IMF Par Value	Nature of Exchange Market	Legal Free Market Selling Rate	Other Official Rates Buying	Selling
Burma (kyat)	4.762	Unitary rates. Fixed and controlled rate on pound sterling. Rates for other currencies determined on basis of official kyat/sterling rate of 13.333 kyats per pound.	......	4.7225	4.770
Ceylon (rupee)	4.762	Unitary rates. A fixed and controlled rate on sterling. Dollar rate based on sterling/dollar rates in London.	......	4.7375	4.7625
Chile (peso)	110.0	Multiple rates. Fixed and controlled rates and freely fluctuating rates.	210.0 brokers' rate for tourist receipts. 238.8ᵍ for specified imports with proceeds of gold exports. Free market rate for wine exports not available.	19.37 tax rate applied to portions of export proceeds of copper, nitrates and iodine, in amounts equal to local costs of production as officially defined. 77.50 for export proceeds of wool and sheepskins. 85.00 for proceeds of seaweed exports. 100.00 for export proceeds of lentils, beans and rice. 110.00 bank rate for other export proceeds.	110.0 basic rate applying to nearly all imports.

Country (currency)	Par or nominal rate	Exchange system		Buying rates	Selling rates
Colombia (peso)	1.95	Multiple rates. Fixed and controlled rates and negotiable exchange certificates which command a premium in free market. Exchange certificate system applies to certain minor export proceeds and specified imports which are otherwise prohibited.	......	1.95 for portion of coffee export proceeds. 2.50 for coffee exports not sold at 1.95 rate; for other exports and nontrade proceeds. 2.50 plus free market premium for certain minor exports.	2.51 for government transactions, certain student remittances and aircraft imports. 2.585 for all imports except aircraft; and most nontrade transactions. 2.51 plus free market premium for nonessential imports.
Denmark (krone)	6.907	Unitary rates. Fixed and controlled rates.	......	6.895	6.920
Egypt (pound) U.S. dollars per pound	2.872	Multiple rates. Fixed and controlled rates with 10 per cent tax on exchange for foreign travel, and certain remittances. Egyptian transferable export pounds freely sold in certain markets abroad at discount of about 9 per cent at end of December 1952.	......	2.8805	2.8619
Ethiopia (dollar)	2.484	Unitary rates. All foreign exchange transactions through State Bank of Ethiopia at fixed and controlled rates.	......	2.48	2.53

TABLE XVII—*Continued*

Country and Currency	IMF Par Value	Nature of Exchange Market	Legal Free Market Selling Rate	Other Official Rates	
				Buying	Selling
Finland (markka)	230.0	Fixed and controlled unitary rates except for travellers' exchange.	350–360 buying and selling rates for travellers' exchange.	229.0	231.0
France (franc)	......	Unitary rates. Controlled free market rate for dollars and certain other hard currencies, stabilized within narrow range of 350. Official rates on other currencies determined with reference to controlled free market dollar rate.	349.95	......	......
Germany (deutsche mark)	4.20	Unitary rates. Fixed and controlled rates.	......	4.195	4.205
Greece (drachma)	......	Unitary rates. Fixed and controlled rates.	......	29,900	30,100
Hong Kong (dollar)	5.714	Multiple rates. Fixed and controlled rates on sterling, fluctuating free market for dollars, and mixing rates. Disparate cross-rates.	5.91375 [h]	5.694 [h] for exports not originating in China, Hong Kong, Macao and Korea, payable in U.S. dollars.	5.776 [h] for specified essential imports payable in U.S. dollars; invisibles and capital; and all nondollar imports.

Four mixing rates applying to various percentages of export proceeds to be surrendered at fixed buying rate and fluctuation free rate. Fluctuating free rate applies to all other exports and receipts from invisibles and capital; and to all other imports payable in U.S. dollars, and to other invisibles and capital exports.

Country	Par value / rate	Monetary system	(market)	Buying rates (exports)	Selling rates (imports)
Iceland (króna)	16.286	Multiple rates. Fixed and controlled rates and exchange premia arising from operation of certificate system. Disparate cross-rates.	......	16.26 for exports not entitled to premia, invisibles and capital. 18.30–21.15 for selected exports entitled to varying premia.	16.32 some imports, invisibles and capital. 20.55 for listed imports from "clearing countries." 26.25 for listed imports from EPU and dollar countries.
India (rupee)	4.762	Unitary rates. Fixed and controlled rates on sterling. Dollar rates based on sterling-dollar rate in London market.	......	4.723	4.765
Indonesia (rupiah)	......	Multiple rates. Fixed and controlled rates and mixing rates derived from varying proportions of official and certificate rates fixed by authorities. Disparate cross-rate.	......	11.355 for all nondollar export and nontrade proceeds. In addition, dollar exports receive premium of .25 rupiah per dollar on 70 per cent of exchange proceeds.	11.445 for all essential imports from nondollar area. 15.260 for specified semiessential imports from nondollar area. 22.890 for designated semiessential imports from nondollar areas. 34.335 for permitted luxury imports from nondollar area. Dollar imports, except rice and wheat, are subject to additional surcharge of 0.25 rupiah per dollar.

TABLE XVII—*Continued*

Country and Currency	IMF Par Value	Nature of Exchange Market	Legal Free Market Selling Rate	Other Official Rates	
				Buying	Selling
Iran (rial)	32.25	Multiple rates. Fixed and controlled exchange certificate rate.	......	32.00 for 5 per cent of all export proceeds. 83.70 for all nontrade exchange proceeds. 96.00 for 95 per cent of most export proceeds. 97.00 for 95 per cent of a few specified export proceeds.	32.50 for government transactions and specially approved student and medical expenses abroad. 41.00 for student expenditures under U.S. Point Four program. 85.00 for general student and medical expenses abroad. 96.50 for most imports and nontrade remittances. 97.50 for a few specified imports.
Iraq (dinar) U.S. dollars per dinar	2.80	Unitary rates. Fixed and controlled rates on sterling; dollar rates based on sterling/dollar rate in London. Legal market for proceeds of certain exports to neighboring countries which do not have to be surrendered.	......	2.8119	2.8106

Country (unit)	Par value	Exchange system	Free/unofficial market	Rate	Rate
Ireland (pound) U.S. dollars per pound	......	Unitary rates, fixed and controlled rates on sterling; dollar rates based on sterling/dollar rate in London market.	......	......	
Israel (pound) U.S. dollars per pound	......	Multiple rates. Fixed and controlled rates.	......	1.00 for capital imports and a few exports. 0.56 one pound per dollar plus exchange premium equal to .80 Israeli pound. Applicable to tourist receipts and most industrial exports.	2.80 for certain government imports. 1.00 for imports of essentials and designated invisibles. 0.56 One pound per dollar plus an exchange surcharge of .80 Israeli pound. Applicable to less essential imports and designated invisibles.
Italy (lire)	......	Unitary rates. Controlled free rate for dollars maintained within narrow range and other rates fixed in relation to the free dollar rate.	625.0		
Japan (yen)	360.0	Unitary rates. Fixed and controlled rates.	......	359.2 for all receipts.	360.8
Jordan (dinar) in U.S. dollars per dinar	2.80	Multiple rates. Fixed and controlled rates with exchange taxes on invisible payments. Certain imports may be paid for with exchange obtained through unofficial market. Disparate cross-rates.	rate in unofficial market not available.	2.82 for all receipts.	2.78 for government imports and imports authorized at the official rate. 2.84 (with 2 per cent tax) for invisible payments to soft-currency countries.

TABLE XVII—*Continued*

Country and Currency	IMF Par Value	Nature of Exchange Market	Legal Free Market Selling Rate	Other Official Rates	
				Buying	Selling
Jordan—*Continued*					2.95 (with 6 per cent tax) for invisible payments to hard-currency countries.
Netherlands (guilder)	3.80	Unitary rates. Controlled free rate for dollars, sterling, Swedish kronor and Swiss, Belgian and French francs, with rates maintained within one per cent of either side of parity. Exchange transactions with banks only.	3.788 (banks' selling rate)	3.7825	3.7875
New Zealand (pound) ...... in U.S. dollars per pound		Unitary rates. Fixed and controlled rates on sterling, and dollar rates based on dollar/sterling rate in London.	......	2.8070	2.7751
Norway (krone)	7.143	Unitary rates. Fixed and controlled rates.	......	7.135	7.150
Pakistan (rupee)	3.309	Fixed and controlled rates on sterling and dollar rates based on dollar/sterling rate in London.	......	3.28	3.315

Paraguay (guarani)	6.00 [1]	Multiple rates. Fixed and controlled rates, a mixing rate which is determined partly by auction rate, and a controlled free rate. Disparate cross-rates.	55.0, buying; 56.0, selling rates;[a] for invisibles, proceeds of major exports sold for dollars in excess of appraised values surrendered at 15.0 rate, for total proceeds of minor exports and specified imports.	15.00 for officially appraised value of major exports sold for dollars and total proceeds of exports sold for other currencies.	6.00 for government nontrade payments. 15.00 for imports of designated essentials and for specified nontrade transactions. 21.00 for imports of specified essentials. 30.00 for imports of semiessentials. 30.00 plus premium in auction rate, for imports of nonessentials and luxuries.
Philippines (peso)	2.00	Multiple rates. Fixed and controlled rates plus 17 per cent tax on most exchange sales.	......	2.004	2.015 for imports of designated essentials and specified nontrade payments. 2.358 (including tax) for all imports and nontrade payments except those made at the 2.015 rate.
Portugal (escudo)	......	Unitary rates. Fixed and controlled rates.	......	28.60	28.95

TABLE XVII—Continued

Country and Currency	IMF Par Value	Nature of Exchange Market	Legal Free Market Selling Rate	Other Official Rates	
				Buying	Selling
Spain (peseta)	......	Multiple rates. Fixed and controlled rates, a controlled free rate and mixing rates determined by partial application of controlled free rate. Disparate cross-rates.	38.95 for 40 and 60 per cent of exchange for imports not supplied at other selling rates and for entire amount of other imports and all nontrade transactions.	21.90 basic rate for most export proceeds. Five other rates dependent on the percentages of receipts that may be sold at the free rate.	11.22 for basic official foodstuffs imports. 16.425 for imports of coal and coke and 60 per cent of designated imports including scrap metals, feeds, etc. 21.90 for 60 and 40 per cent of designated imports including raw materials and semimanufactured goods. 25.00 for liquid fuels and tobacco imports.
Sweden (krona)	5.173	Unitary rates. Fixed and controlled rates.	......	5.17	5.18
Taiwan (Formosa) (New Taiwan dollar)	......	Fixed and controlled certificate rates quoted by Bank of Taiwan.	......	14.49 for export proceeds of sugar and rice. 15.55 certificate rate for all exports, except sugar and rice, and for invisibles.	15.65 certificate rate for all authorized imports and invisibles.

Turkey (lira)	2.800	Unitary rates. Fixed and controlled rates.	......	2.80	2.825
Union of South Africa (pound) U.S. dollars per pound	2.80	Unitary rates. Fixed and controlled rates on sterling; and dollar rates based on sterling/dollar rate in London market.	......	2.81625	2.79875
United Kingdom (pound) U.S. dollars per pound	2.80	Unitary rates. Controlled free rate maintained within 2.78 and 2.82. Only authorized banks operate in "free" market.	2.805	2.8119	2.8106
Uruguay (peso)	......	Multiple rates. Fixed and controlled rates and freely fluctuating rate for capital and invisibles. Disparate cross-rates.	3.10 [1] for capital and invisibles without restriction.	1.519 for 35 per cent of wool top, 90 per cent washed wool, 50 per cent of canned meat export proceeds, 54 per cent of rice and for total proceeds of other basic exports. 1.78 for export proceeds of nonedible oils and packing house products. 2.35 for total export proceeds of woolen, leather and other manufactures, and remainder of wool top, rice, washed wool and canned meat export proceeds.	1.519 for imports of newsprint and printing supplies, and a few government transactions. 1.90 for essential imports. 2.45 for nonessentials and luxury imports.

TABLE XVII—*Continued*

Country and Currency	IMF Par Value	Nature of Exchange Market	Legal Free Market Selling Rate	Other Official Rates	
				Buying	Selling
Yugoslavia (dinar)	300.00	A system of coefficients, varying for different export and import commodities, is applied to the basic exchange rate, together with a system of negotiable retention credits applicable to a percentage of surrendered export proceeds, producing a multiple rate structure. Disparate cross-rates.			

a. End of November 1953.
b. As of December 12, 1953.
c. End of October 1953.
d. As of December 11, 1953.
e. As of July 15, 1953.
f. System effective October 16, 1953. Foreign exchange must be surrendered at the official rate plus 5.0 cruzeiros per dollar for coffee, and 10.0 cruzeiros per dollar for all other exports. Imports require both the purchase of exchange at the official rate and the presentation of exchange certificates which must be purchased at auction sales for the amount of the exchange requested. All import goods are divided into five categories based on "essentiality"; exchange certificates must be purchased for the proper category. At the auction held November 17, 1953, auction rates ranged from 13 cruzeiros for Category I certificates to 132 cruzeiros for Category V import certificates for U.S. dollar exchange for 120-day delivery. The *effective* selling rates, therefore, ranged from 31 to 150 cruzeiros per dollar.
g. End of August 1953.
h. As of December 9, 1953.
i. As of January 1, 1954, par value changed to 15 guarani to the dollar.
j. As of December 5, 1953.

Principal sources: International Financial Statistics, January 1954; and *Fourth Annual Report on Exchange Restrictions,* International Monetary Fund, Washington, 1953.

APPENDIX 7

Countries of the World Classified By Currency Grouping According to United Kingdom Exchange Regulations

A. The Scheduled Territories (Sterling Area)

EUROPE

United Kingdom and Northern Ireland [a]
Republic of Ireland
Isle of Man
Channel Islands
Gilbraltar
Malta
Cyprus

ICELAND [a]

AFRICA

Union of South Africa (including South-West Africa)
Basutoland
Bechuanaland
Swaziland
Kenya
Nyasaland
Tanganyika
Uganda
Mauritius
Morocco Agencies
Northern and Southern Rhodesia
St. Helena and Ascension
Seychelles
Somaliland and Zanzibar Protectorates
Gambia
Gold Coast and Ashanti
Nigeria and Cameroons
Sierra Leone
Togoland
Libia (Cyrenaica, Tripolitania and the Fezzan)

AMERICA

Bahamas
Barbados
Bermuda

British Guiana
British Honduras
Falkland Islands
Jamaica:
  Cayman Islands
  Turks and Caicos Islands
Leeward Islands:
  Anguilla
  Antigua
  Barbuda
  British Virgin Islands
  Montserrat
  Saint Kitts—Nevis
Trinidad and Tobago
Windward Islands:
  Dominica
  Grenada
  St. Lucia
  St. Vincent

ASIA

Aden (colony and protectorate)
Andaman Islands
Burma
Ceylon and Maldive Islands
Hashemite Kingdom of Jordan
Hong Kong
India
Iraq
Labuan Island
Malayan Union
North Borneo and Brunei
Pakistan
Nicobar Islands
Persian Gulf sheikdoms:
  Bahrein
  Kuwait
  Dubai
  Adu Dhabi
  Shargah
  Ajman
  Ras al-Kahimah
  Umm-ul Qaiwain
  Kalba
  Qatar

Muscat
Oman (including Gwadur and Dhofar)
Sarawak
Singapore
Socotra
Perim

PACIFIC OCEAN

Australia
Tasmania
Ashmore and Cartier Islands
New Zealand
Fiji
British Pacific Islands:
  Cook Islands
  Gilbert Islands
  Ellice Islands
  New Hebrides and Pitcairn
  British Samoa
  British Solomon Islands
  Tonga Islands
  Papua
  New Guinea
  Norfolk Island
  Nauru
  Tristan de Cunha
  Kermadec Islands
  Santa Cruz
  Union Islands

B. The American Account Group (Dollar Area)

United States, and dependencies
Bolivia
Canada
Colombia
Costa Rica
Cuba
Dominican Republic
Ecuador
Guatemala
Haiti
Honduras
Pacific Islands formerly under Japanese administration and now under
    United States administration

Liberia
Mexico
Nicaragua
Panama
Philippine Islands
Salvador
Venezuela

C. The Transferable Account Group

Austria [a]
Chile
Czechoslovakia [b]
Denmark, the Faeroes and Greenland [a]
Egypt and that area of the former territory of Palestine at present administered by Egypt. (All payments from Egyptian No. 2 accounts require the specific consent of the Exchange Control.)
Ethiopia (including Eritrea)
Finland
Greece [a]
Italian monetary area [a] (the Italian Republic, the Republic of San Marino, the territory of Somaliland under Italian administration, and Zone "A" of the Free Territory of Trieste)
Netherlands monetary area [a] (the Netherlands, the Republic of Indonesia, Netherlands New Guinea, Surinam, and the Netherlands Antilles)
Norway [a]
Poland [b]
Spanish monetary area (Spain, Canaries, Balearics, Ceuta, Melilla, Spanish colonies and Spanish Zone of Morocco)
Anglo-Egyptian Sudan
Sweden [a]
Thailand
USSR [b]
Western Zones of Germany [a]

D. The "Bilateral" Account Group

Argentina
Belgian monetary area [a] (Belgium, Luxembourg, Belgian Congo and Ruanda-Urundi)
Brazil
Bulgaria [b]
China [b] (including Manchuria)
East Germany [b]
French franc area: [a]
   Metropolitan France, including Corsica

The principality of Monaco

The Saar territory, the French Overseas Departments (Algeria, Guadeloupe, Martinique, French Guiana, Réunion)

The protectorates of Morocco and Tunisia

French West Africa

French Equatorial Africa

The French trust territories of Cameroun and Togo

Madagascar and its dependencies

Comoro Islands

St. Pierre and Miquelon

French Establishments in India

The Associated States of Cambodia, Laos and Vietnam

New Caledonia and its dependencies

French Establishments in Oceania

Condominium of the New Hebrides

French Somali Coast

Hungary [b]

Japan (Hokkaido, Honshu, Kyushu, Shikoku, and the adjacent islands excluding those under U.S. administration)

Lebanon

Iran

Israel

Paraguay

Peru

Portuguese monetary area [a] (Portugal and its colonial empire, Madeira and Azores)

Romania [b]

Switzerland and Liechtenstein [a]

Syria

Tangier

Taiwan

Turkey [a]

Uruguay

Vatican City

Yugoslavia

E. THE UNCLASSIFIED COUNTRIES GROUP

Afghanistan

Albania

Andorra

Korea (South)

Nepal

Saudi Arabia

Yemen

---

a. Member of EPU.
b. Member of Soviet orbit.

INDEX

INDEX

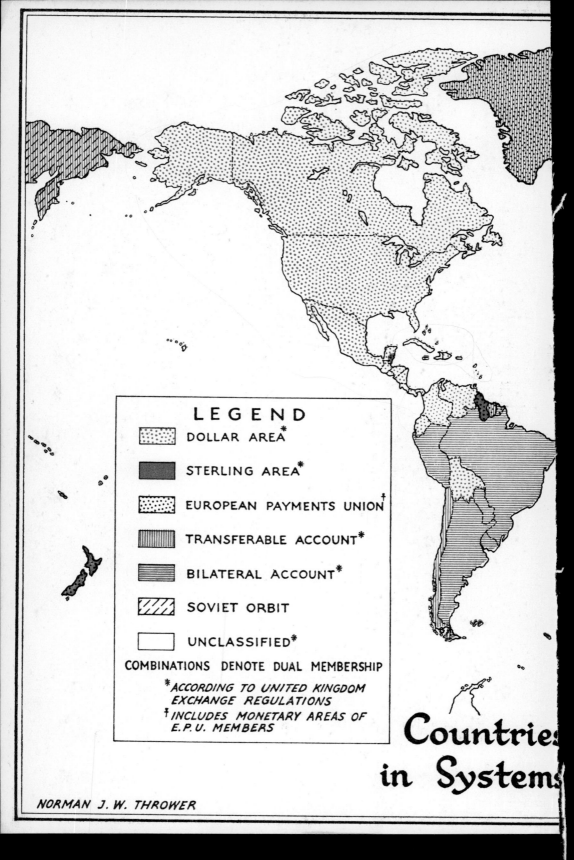

LEGEND

- DOLLAR AREA*
- STERLING AREA*
- EUROPEAN PAYMENTS UNION†
- TRANSFERABLE ACCOUNT*
- BILATERAL ACCOUNT*
- SOVIET ORBIT
- UNCLASSIFIED*

COMBINATIONS DENOTE DUAL MEMBERSHIP

*ACCORDING TO UNITED KINGDOM
EXCHANGE REGULATIONS
†INCLUDES MONETARY AREAS OF
E.P.U. MEMBERS

Countries
in Systems

NORMAN J. W. THROWER